P9-APK-556

"No Legs, No Jokes, No Chance"

"No Legs,

NORTHWESTERN UNIVERSITY PRESS EVANSTON, ILLINOIS

No Jokes, No Chance"

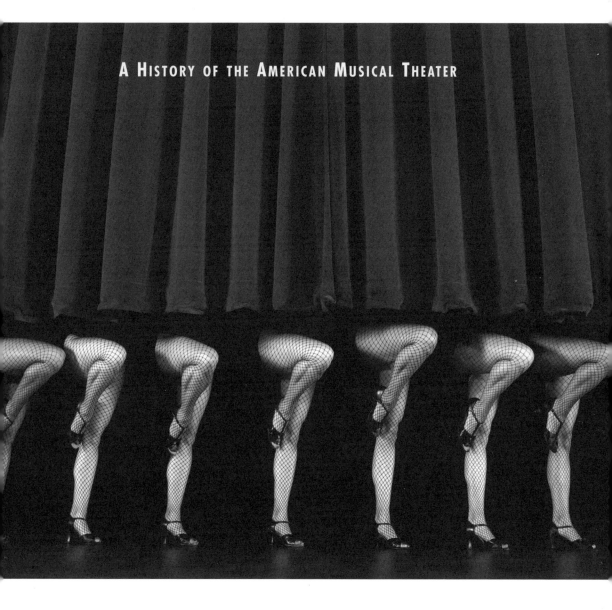

A HISTORY OF THE AMERICAN MUSICAL THEATER

Sheldon Patinkin

Northwestern University Press
www.nupress.northwestern.edu

Copyright © 2008 by Sheldon Patinkin.
Published 2008 by Northwestern University Press. All rights reserved.

Printed in the United States of America

10 9 8 7 6 5 4 3 2

In the face of considerable challenges in locating copyright holders of song lyrics quoted in this book, the publisher has made every reasonable effort to contact those copyright holders and to obtain permission to use the material presented here for educational purposes. Acknowledgments are printed starting on page 533.

All images courtesy of Photofest.

Library of Congress Cataloging-in-Publication Data

Patinkin, Sheldon.
    "No legs, no jokes, no chance" : a history of the American musical theater /
Sheldon Patinkin.
        p. cm.
    "Written in conjunction with a two-semester course taught with Estelle Spector
at Columbia College Chicago . . ."
    Includes bibliographical references and index.
    ISBN-13: 978-0-8101-1994-9 (pbk. : alk. paper)
    ISBN-10: 0-8101-1994-3 (pbk. : alk. paper)
    1. Musical theater—United States—History. I. Title.
ML1711.P37 2007
782.140973—dc22

                                                          2007023777

♾ The paper used in this publication meets the minimum requirements of the American National Standard for Information Sciences—Permanence of Paper for Printed Library Materials, ANSI Z39.48-1992.

Written in conjunction with a two-semester course
taught with Estelle Spector at Columbia College Chicago
and attended by many students,
to all of whom I am deeply grateful.

In essence, theater is poetry, and the musical stage has the spontaneity of poetry. It is the most effective method for creating imaginative drama. . . . Like poetry, it deals in myth. . . . By the richness of its medium, which blends music, dance, verse, costume, scenery, and orchestra, the musical drama makes complete use of the theater. It is the one element of poetry left in a form of literature that was all poetry originally.

—BROOKS ATKINSON

CONTENTS

Part Three: The Golden Age of the Broadway Song, 1925–1939

Part Four: The Transitional Years, 1940–1945

Part Five: The Golden Age of the Broadway Musical, 1946–1964

Part Six: Fade Out—Fade In, 1965–1969

Part Seven: The Splintering of the Form, 1970–2007

PREFACE

This book, developed as a text for college students majoring in musical theater, is a general introduction to how the musical went from European opera, American minstrel shows, and vaudeville to *Oklahoma!* and beyond—so to speak, from *La Bohème* to *Rent.* It contains many generalizations that have countless exceptions, but going into all of them would require far more detail than space permits. Therefore, although the text is meant to be informational, a certain amount of selectivity, analysis, and opinion were unavoidable.

A word of warning: many shows important to the history of the form used minorities in what is now clearly a demeaning way. (Much of what now seems patently racist was considered liberal—and/or funny—at the time.) Such shows aren't revived in their original forms; if they are revived, they're rewritten. There's even one form that can't be revived: the minstrel show, the first musical form created in America and an important antecedent of the first musicals, but performed in blackface and racist even when it was popular.

It's also necessary to understand that the creators of most musicals—by far the majority of them men—were sexists in a sexist society. In most musicals, women—when they weren't there just for display—did not seem able to survive without a man. Even businesswomen were usually looking for a man to take care of them so they wouldn't have to be in business anymore. It's impossible to avoid this in reviving many otherwise excellent shows, since it's invariably a major plot point.

Some materials I've suggested for looking and listening might be hard to find. A significant source of recorded selections from shows, going back to the beginning of the twentieth century, is Paul Gruber's *Original Cast!* series, put out by the Metropolitan Opera Guild. The booklets accompanying each of the eleven double-CD sets are also invaluable sources of information.

One person quoted in the text whom you won't find in the bibliography is Albert "Bill" Williams, my Columbia College Chicago colleague and chief drama critic of Chicago's free weekly newspaper *The Reader.* His comments, additions, corrections, and advice have made him invaluable in the writing of this book. I don't know how to begin to thank him. Similar debts of gratitude are also extended to my co-teacher, Estelle Spector; to composer, lyricist, and author Louis Rosen; to composer-teacher Ed Linderman; and to the unexpected and enormously helpful suggestions of Mary Corsaro.

A Word of Advice to Musical Theater Students

Use this text to help you start *building your repertory* of audition pieces and roles you might be able to play soon, or even not so soon. *Keep lists* of what you already know, what you might work on next, and what you'll want to learn as your instrument matures. Do *further investigation* beyond this book, not only of shows but also of songs that sound interesting. Start trying to *understand the different kinds and styles of musicals* so that you'll know what's expected of you as a performer in any kind of show. And to all of you, good luck finding work; it's not going to be easy.

Note: Words and phrases in boldface in the text are key terms, usually followed by their definitions.

"No Legs, No Jokes, No Chance"

Beginning in the Middle, 1943

Overleaf: (*left*) Aunt Eller (Betty Garde) and Will Parker (Lee Dixon) dancing to "Kansas City" in *Oklahoma!* (1943); (*right*) Ali Hakim (Joseph Buloff) and Ado Annie (Celeste Holm) on the cover of the original souvenir book for *Oklahoma!*

Oklahoma!

> I got to Kansas City on a Frid'y.
> By Sattidy I l'arned a thing or two.
> For up to then I didn't have an idy
> Of whut the modern world was comin' to.
> —"KANSAS CITY," *OKLAHOMA!* LYRICS BY OSCAR HAMMERSTEIN II

Largely a product of the twentieth century, the musical as we now know it is the first major theatrical form developed in the United States. The changes the form has undergone and the crises it has faced are in many ways reflections of the political, social, cultural, and economic changes and crises the nation itself went through over the last century. Much of the history of the musical is, therefore, about a struggle to keep up with or—as often as not—ignore the ever more rapidly changing times.

The musical is the most popular, probably the most difficult, and—outside of grand opera—the most expensive theatrical form. Especially with costs constantly escalating throughout most of the twentieth century, a musical has often needed to do 90 percent or better business over a long run in order to be deemed a **hit.** (A hit is a show that makes enough money on tickets and subsidiary rights to pay off its entire original investment—which is enormous these days—as well as its weekly running costs, which have also become quite large.) In other words, regardless of how good it might be, if a show doesn't turn a profit, it's a flop—aesthetics being irrelevant when discussing the business of show business. More often than not, a good show that flops might have been a hit, though probably a minor one, ten or even five years earlier, but its creators did not keep up with the changing times. There are several reasons a show can fail in this way. A frequent cause is that it's too derivative of earlier shows. Or perhaps it doesn't have the kind of music people want to sing in the shower or dance and romance to anymore. Perhaps it doesn't have the kind of comedy people want to laugh at anymore or doesn't deal with the kind of subject matter people care about now. Sometimes a show isn't strong enough to overcome less-than-rave reviews or is too expensive to produce—both increasingly frequent problems during the Depression and in the last quarter of the twentieth century. Occasionally, shows are ahead of their time or in the wrong venue or have the wrong director or the wrong star or the critics were drunk or it rained on opening night or someone quoted *Macbeth* backstage—whatever. Some shows actually are "discovered" years later and revived in the right time or place or production concept. Several such shows—including Cole Porter's *Out of This World* and Harold Arlen's *St. Louis Woman*—were successfully revived during the 1990s in limited-run concert stagings, a form now being produced by companies in several major U.S. cities.

Occasionally the success of some shows is harder to explain than the failure of others. Some people find it difficult to understand the super-extraordinary success of *Cats* and *The Phantom of the Opera*, for example. Both shows depend on spectacle, sentimentality, lyrics that mercifully don't need to be understood for the most part, and one or maybe two good—though syrupy—tunes repeated endlessly. Obviously, that is what audiences wanted. (The so-called British invasion of the Broadway musical in the 1980s, of which those two pop operas are prime examples, represents probably the most fallow period in the history of the American musical and what looked like the death of the musical comedy.)

It was relatively simple for musical comedies to be successful financially in the carefree Roaring Twenties. Jazz was the new music, and the musical was still a new and rowdy form. It had only recently overtaken the romantic, semi-classical American operetta in popularity and was just beginning to pull ahead of the plotless revue. Costs were low, money was loose, and dozens of shows were produced yearly—many of them hits that were able to make back their investments in a few weeks, then go out on profitable road tours. Most early musicals were loosely structured, empty-headed comedies: girl meets boy, girl loses boy, girl gets boy, or—for variety—boy meets girl, boy loses girl, boy gets girl. Their major purpose was to satisfy the fairly young, largely upper- and middle-class audiences' desires for good songs, dances, and comedy routines surrounded by lots of spectacle and girls—preferably with stars as well.

These shows had little or nothing to say and no particular need to integrate the songs, dances, comedy routines, spectacle, and shapely chorus girls into their often pedestrian scripts. The story would simply stop periodically to accommodate the talents and demands of the stars, the specialty acts, the songwriters, or the producers, usually with little or no relevance to the simple plot or cardboard characters. Credibility was not at a premium. Often, for example, the entire chorus—and there were usually very large ones—would suddenly appear in someone's living room to supply a big finish to a musical number. People wore tap shoes in the most intimate or public of places. There was always a happy ending, and no one ever died, unless it was to leave a fortune to the hero or heroine either to begin or to end the story. The musicals of the twenties were, in fact, so much a product of their free and easy times that hardly any of them had sturdy enough scripts to be revivable today, although many of their songs are still being sung.

Keeping up with the times got more difficult in the thirties. With the Depression, the musical lost much of its audience. Many could no longer afford the tickets to what was, after all, a luxury item. Also, with the advent of sound in 1927, there were now movie musicals—with stars, songs, dances, comedy routines, spectacle, and girls—at a ticket price many could (and did) afford. Furthermore, theater audiences were getting older as well as sparser. Younger people's favorite music was moving from jazz to big band swing (more suitable for dancing than for singing), which was not the kind of music Broadway composers were writing or the older patrons were likely to want to hear. (During most of the twentieth century, younger people's tastes in music often differed considerably from those of their parents—by the end of the century, even from those of their older sisters and brothers.)

Because of the Depression, theater also became more expensive to produce and took longer to pay off its investors. As costs rose, so, of course, did ticket prices. Audiences not only got smaller, they also got choosier, no longer necessarily satisfied with mindlessness and a lack of structure. Some of the more successful shows were more satirical than farcical, and some, though still largely star driven, were beginning to be more organically structured, though with books that were still quite lightweight and characters who were still rather two-dimensional.

Fewer shows opened in the last half of the thirties and into the forties, and producers (and many writers and composers as well) were afraid to take risks, resisting change even when the times had clearly changed. Instead, they rigidified their shows through formulas determined by past successes—their own or someone else's—and, in the process, produced more flops than hits. The musical form began to stagnate, and when stagnation continues for a time, it begins to resemble rigor mortis, and everyone starts saying the musical is on its deathbed.

There have been several such periods in the history of the musical. (There was a long one at the end of the twentieth century, when spectacle sometimes seemed to have overtaken talent, let alone risk-taking.) What has, so far, eventually happened at times when the death knell is being sounded is that some adventurous producers and theater artists have begun to think

Richard Rodgers (1902–79, born in New York) had parents who were operetta enthusiasts, and his love of music began with the romantic scores of Victor Herbert and Franz Lehar. In 1916, he saw Jerome Kern's musical *Very Good Eddie,* which inspired him to begin writing songs himself. There were three distinct periods to his career: from 1919 to 1943, with lyrics to his songs by Lorenz Hart and books by various people; from 1943 to 1960, with lyrics and most books by Oscar Hammerstein II; and from 1960 to 1979, with lyrics and books by different people for almost each new show. Rodgers was disciplined and hardworking, with a great melodic gift. He wrote over nine hundred songs and thirty-nine musicals.

about the present instead of taking comfort and refuge in the past. Realizing that the form isn't building new audiences to take the place of the existing ones who are, literally, dying out, they begin taking risks with new sounds, new forms, new subject matter, new something. Some risks work, some do not, but sooner or later someone takes the right one—often a big one—and ushers in a new period of success and growth for musical theater. The death-rattle phases therefore turn out to be transitional periods, needed while the musical catches up to the tastes of the times. The new path is usually opened up by a hit that recognizes how the times have changed. Two examples of this kind of benchmark show are the 1924 *Lady, Be Good!* (by George and Ira Gershwin, Guy Bolton, and Fred Thompson, starring the brother and sister team of Fred and Adele Astaire), which was the first musical to sound as if it belonged to the Jazz Age, and the 1970 Vietnam- and Watergate-era *Company* (by Stephen Sondheim and George Furth, directed by Harold Prince), which, along with understanding the angst-ridden tenor of the times, began the enduring popularity of the form known as the **concept musical.** A concept musical, rather than telling the kind of linear story found in musical comedies and plays, is made up of a connected series of events centered around and illustrating an idea or concept. The form can, too simplistically, be defined as a revue with a theme and continuing characters. *Hair, Company, A Chorus Line,* and *Cats* are examples.

At the beginning of the twenty-first century, it's hard to see another, so badly needed benchmark. Perhaps it's *Rent,* Jonathan Larson's 1996 rock opera about the young, disaffected, and diseased; perhaps it's *Ragtime,* Stephen Flaherty, Lynn Ahrens, and Terrence McNally's 1998 kaleidoscopic look at the beginning of this century of turmoil; or perhaps it's *The Lion King,* Elton John, Tim Rice, Julie Taymor, and a slew of others' 1997 Disney animated children's movie, live and overamplified. None of them have produced worthy heirs so far, although more Disney shows are already here or on the way. There's also new hope for the revivification of the musical comedy at the beginning of the twenty-first century with the success of such shows as David Yazbek and McNally's *The Full Monty;* Mark Hollmann and Greg Kotis's *Urinetown;* Marc Shaiman, Scott Wittman, Mark O'Donnell, and Thomas Meehan's *Hairspray;* and, most especially, Mel Brooks and Meehan's *The Producers.* All are traditional musical comedies in form, though not in story or tone, and all speak to (or offend) young and old alike, each with a different kind of musical sound that appeals to contemporary audiences.

Possibly the single most influential benchmark show in the history of the musical had its premiere on March 31, 1943, in the middle of World War II. It was *Oklahoma!*—the first collaboration of Richard Rodgers, who composed the music, and Oscar Hammerstein II, who wrote the lyrics and the book. (When speaking of musicals, we will use the term **lyrics** when discussing the words of songs and the term **book** when referring to dialogue scenes or the script. In the early part of the twentieth century, the script was called the **libretto,** a term from opera. Sometimes even now the dialogue scenes plus the lyrics of a musical are called the libretto. However, to avoid confusion, we'll use the term only when discussing operas and operettas.)

Although *Oklahoma!* may seem trivial, dated, or just plain uninteresting to some people today, its importance to the history of the musical can't be underestimated. It almost single-handedly changed everyone's understanding of what a musical should be. It's the show that ushered in what many musical theater scholars refer to as the golden age of the Broadway musical—from the mid-1940s to the mid-1960s, more or less from the end of World War II to the assassination of President Kennedy. Whether or not it was, as many people contend, a golden age for America as well, it was certainly an optimistic time, as were most of its musicals.

Rodgers and Hammerstein called *Oklahoma!* a "musical play." They adapted it from Lynn Riggs's 1931 folk play *Green Grow the Lilacs,* set in the early twentieth century in the part of the Indian Territory that was trying to become the state of Oklahoma. Except for the last scene, the whole musical takes place on the day and evening of a box social. The Theatre Guild, which had produced *Green Grow the Lilacs,* offered the project of musicalizing it to Rodgers and his writing partner, Lorenz Hart, but the witty, sophisticated, and city-oriented Hart didn't think he was right for a romantic period piece set in the wide-open American West. (He was also, by then, an almost nonfunctioning alcoholic.) Rodgers turned to Hammerstein, who had earlier expressed interest in the show to the Guild and who had known both Rodgers and Hart since college. Rodgers and Hammerstein had even worked together on one campus show.

Oscar Hammerstein II

(1895–1960, born in New York) was the third generation of a theater family. He attended Columbia Law School because his father, a theater manager, didn't want him to go into show business. While at Columbia, he began writing scripts and lyrics for campus shows. His first Broadway lyrics were for the song "Make Yourself at Home," with music by Silvio Hein, heard in the 1917 musical *Furs and Frills.* From then until his death, he wrote books and lyrics for operettas, musicals, movies, and even the original TV musical *Cinderella.* Before teaming with Rodgers, Hammerstein wrote thirty-one shows with over a dozen collaborators. Hammerstein was probably the single greatest influence on the development of the musical during the first half of the twentieth century.

Oklahoma!'s most important influence was its structure. Hammerstein had realized early in his career that the book must be the spine from which all the other elements of a show grow organically. He had, for the most part, been writing **American operettas,** romantic musical forms with larger-than-life characters, exotic locales, high-flown language, and music based on the lighter, European, classical models. Since the libretto always came first, operettas were much better integrated than the early musicals; it was with this understanding of the book as the main structure that Hammerstein approached *Oklahoma!* In frequent conference with Rodgers, he worked out the script first.

Because he started this way, the events of the story and the needs of the characters became the determining factors in the placement of musical numbers, dance sequences, and comedy scenes, thereby integrating all the elements of the show into a coherent whole. Furthermore, *Oklahoma!* was more than just the usual frivolous entertainment; it had something to say about the world and the people in it, another major development in how to write a musical (though not considered a necessary one). And it was acted more naturalistically than had been the case beforehand on the musical stage. The show also raised the standards of choral arrangements by breaking them into four or more parts; before *Oklahoma!* they were usually in unison.

Equally important to the development of the form were Agnes de Mille's dances. With *Oklahoma!* dance became an equal partner. In this, the first of her musicals, de Mille established that choreography has to be consistent with character, time, and place. Her dances helped tell the story, define character psychology, and/or create tone and atmosphere. By using ballet and mime more than traditional show choreography, de Mille proved that dance could be more than display, whether of talent or of legs, as it had almost always been till then. Her difficult choreography (influenced by Martha Graham, folk and ethnic dances, ballet, and modern dance) required far more skill of chorus dancers than did the simple dance steps of most earlier shows, setting a new level of performance that soon became the standard. Her dancers also had to be able to act.

Oklahoma! didn't come from nowhere, of course. Rodgers and Hammerstein had, in shows with other collaborators, made important contributions to developing the form. Along with the 1927 landmark, fully integrated, dramatic musical *Show Boat*

Agnes de Mille (1905–93, born in New York) was a dancer and ballet choreographer. After *Oklahoma!* she choreographed fourteen more musicals for Broadway, including *Carousel, One Touch of Venus, Brigadoon,* and *Gentlemen Prefer Blondes.* She occasionally directed as well, though never as successfully as she choreographed.

(which Hammerstein and composer Jerome Kern also called a musical play), Hammerstein had written the integrated scripts and lyrics for the 1920s operettas *Rose-Marie, The Desert Song,* and *The New Moon,* none of which, however, used their few dances structurally. Rodgers, Hart, and George Abbott's 1936 *On Your Toes* told some of its story through ballets created by George Balanchine. Rodgers, Hart, John O'Hara, and Abbott's 1940 *Pal Joey* had a strong story with a far more realistic and cynical view of the world than musical audiences were used to. It also had a **dream ballet** (a long dance sequence showing a character's hopes and/or fears) choreographed by Robert Alton, as did Rodgers and Hart's 1937 *Babes in Arms,* choreographed by Balanchine. There had also been shows by others that had contributed to the gradual integration of the many elements that went into creating a golden age musical. But from the beginning of their partnership, Rodgers and Hammerstein, aided by de Mille and the director Rouben Mamoulian (1898–1987, born in Tiflis, Russia), permanently redefined the form.

Along with making the script the solid spine of the show, Hammerstein retained several other structural attributes of the operetta. Perhaps most important and influential was his use of a romantic main plot paralleling and contrasting with a comic subplot, each with lovers who bicker their way into romance. The main plot of *Oklahoma!* is a love triangle centering on whether independent-minded farm girl Laurey Williams will go to the social with independent-minded cowboy Curly McClain (whom she loves but is constantly squabbling with because she doesn't want to be taken for granted) or with deeply disturbed farmhand Jud (whom she fears). The parallel comic subplot, also a love triangle, centers on whether naive cowpoke Will Parker (a character invented by Hammerstein in order to complete the parallel) will get together the fifty dollars he needs so he can marry Ado Annie Carnes, who "cain't say no" to any man who comes on to her, before her farmer father forces her into a shotgun wedding with lascivious traveling salesman Ali Hakim, who has no intention of getting married to anyone. Hammerstein even added a second subplot—what the territory has to do to become a state—which parallels and informs the other two.

Also as in operetta, after getting the exposition out of the way, *Oklahoma!* spends much of its first half on music and character development and much of its second half tying up the plots. Since *Oklahoma!* this has become a pattern in most musicals: second acts have noticeably less music and more plot and dialogue than first acts. *Oklahoma!*'s second act, for example, has only three new songs. Second acts are also usually shorter, *Oklahoma!*'s by half an hour.

In addition, as in operetta, many of the tunes in *Oklahoma!* recur as **dance music** (music written or arranged for dance sequences), as **reprises** (repeats of part or all of a song, often with different lyrics), or as **underscoring** (music played under dialogue or nonverbal action). This repetition helps give the show a unified feeling and is one of the reasons early audiences left the theater able to hum several of the tunes, helping make the songs popular, which then helped sell more recordings of the songs, in turn helping sell more tickets to the show the songs were from.

However, despite the similarities, *Oklahoma!* is not an operetta in sound, characters, language, or dramatic tension. Rodgers's music is romantic but, unlike operetta, reflects American pop idioms of the day, including folk and country, which fit well in the show's Western setting. (Americana was already in vogue with such classical composers as Aaron Copland and Virgil Thomson and in such contemporary country-and-western pop hits as "You Are My Sunshine" and "Deep in the Heart of Texas.")

Hammerstein's book also has more believable situations than one finds in operettas, and it deals with ordinary people who use ordinary language. Its characters are more complex than those in operettas or earlier musicals, including the near-psychopath Jud, who turns murderous when he loses Laurey. Jud even gets a dramatic musical monologue instead of a pop song as his only solo in the show. The piece, "Lonely Room," gives Jud more psychological depth than the villains of operettas and earlier musicals had, allowing the audience to feel some sympathy for him even though we still don't want him to get the girl. ("Lonely Room" is clearly a warm-up for Billy Bigelow's "Soliloquy" in *Carousel*, Rodgers and Hammerstein's next show.) Unlike the high-flown poetry standard in operetta lyrics, Hammerstein's lyrics are as simple and unsophisticated as the characters singing them. "People Will Say We're in Love," the first-act duet between Laurey and Curly, is a good example of Hammerstein's so-called poetry of the ordinary. The **chorus,** or main body of the song, is sung first by Laurey:

> Don't throw bouquets at me,
> Don't please my folks too much,
> Don't laugh at my jokes too much—
> People will say we're in love!
> Don't sigh and gaze at me
> (Your sighs are so like mine),
> Your eyes mustn't glow like mine—
> People will say we're in love!
> Don't start collecting things
> (Give me my rose and my glove);
> Sweetheart, they're suspecting things—
> People will say we're in love!

My colleague Albert "Bill" Williams notes:

The song uses colloquialisms ("my folks") and **subtext** [what is felt or thought but not spoken; literally, what is beneath the text]. It is a love song that insists the singer is not in love, but with a lilting, romantic melody contradicting the words. The song also helps define character and offers subtle suggestions of her true feelings: "Your sighs are so like mine," and the fact that she calls him "sweetheart." (Albert Williams, personal communication)

Curly sings a second chorus, with different but matching lyrics, and the song ends with both of them singing together in harmony.

Though Rodgers's music for the song is flowingly melodious and romantic (and quite different from most of his work with Hart), it has a narrower vocal range than most operetta music, making it easier to sing. It's composed in his distinctively American sound, which sang directly to the heart of the entire nation. It's also the only song in the show for which Rodgers wrote the music before Hammerstein wrote the lyrics, one reason it's actually slightly less specifically characterized than most of the other songs in the show and therefore why it became the biggest of several pop hits from *Oklahoma!* Many Rodgers and Hammerstein songs understandably became hits for the following reasons: the words are contemporary and idiomatic, the melodies tuneful and memorable, the feelings universal. It's usually the context that makes them specific to their shows. "People Will Say We're in Love," for instance, is a song that many people have identified with at various times in their lives, but Laurey and Curly are basically the only characters in a Rodgers and Hammerstein musical who could sing it to each other. The same kind of specificity is true of such other hits as de Becque's "Some Enchanted Evening" from *South Pacific* and Anna's "Hello, Young Lovers" from *The King and I.*

Two of the other hit songs from *Oklahoma!* are "Oh, What a Beautiful Mornin'" and "The Surrey with the Fringe on Top," both used in ways that were then unusual. "Oh, What a Beautiful Mornin'," written in a simple folk-song form, opens the show quietly, with Curly beginning the song offstage while Aunt Eller sits on stage churning butter, a huge contrast to the usual high-energy number with lots of leggy chorus girls that opened most musicals.

"The Surrey with the Fringe on Top" is actually a complex interweaving of several elements: three choruses, underscored dialogue, and the **recitative,** or sung dialogue, here mostly in the form of the verse. In this case, the **verse**—which is a less tuneful, introductory section that precedes the chorus of a musical number—is sung before each of the first two choruses and played under dialogue before the third chorus. This moving in and out of song is another operetta technique rare in earlier musicals, *Show Boat* being a notable exception. Moreover, not just "The Surrey with the Fringe on Top" is done this way; several of *Oklahoma!*'s songs are intertwined with dialogue, underscoring, and recitative (dropped on the original-cast recording, or when the songs were recorded out of context by pop singers—called **cover recordings**). The technique became a hallmark of Rodgers and Hammerstein's shows, fully developed in the bench scene in *Carousel*.

All these differences helped make the story more believable, the characters more real, and the emotional stakes higher than in most operettas and musicals of the time. And, finally, dance was part of why that was so, particularly at the end of act 1 in de Mille's very influential dream ballet, which not only examines Laurey's psychology but also raises the emotional stakes of the entire show. Laurey, in a fit of anger with Curly, has agreed to go to the box social with Jud, although she now wishes she hadn't. While trying to make up her mind about what to do, she sniffs an elixir, sold to her by Ali Hakim, that is supposed to help her see into the future. She dozes off while singing "Out of My Dreams." In her dream, her romantic love for Curly is pitted against her fear of and fascination with Jud and the carnality and danger he represents. The music for the ballet was constructed by arranger/orchestrator Robert Russell Bennett from several melodies already heard in the show and used in contrast to each other as Laurey moves between Curly's world and Jud's. At the end of the nearly twenty-minute, wordless ballet, Laurey dreams that Jud kills Curly. She's awakened by Jud, who has come to take her to the social, and, fearful that what she dreamed could really happen, she leaves with him—an unusually quiet and suspenseful act-closer for the times. This stylized dream raises Laurey's dilemma to a level far beyond that of a simple musical-comedy plot, presenting us, as it does, with an almost mythic view of the three central characters. (The number was so successful that for years after, a musical could barely hold up its head unless it had a dream ballet.)

This semimythic quality extends to much of the show. In fact, the parallel love stories, which carry forward the action, serve as reflections of the second subplot, showing us that the peace, harmony, and compromise needed to achieve a successful relationship are also needed for the territory to achieve statehood. This was the same need for community the country was feeling during World War II. This necessity is the theme of the show, and the two love stories particularize the constant squabbling and escalating violence between farmers and cowboys in the Oklahoma territory. Laurey and Jud are farmers, while Curly's a cowboy; Ado Annie's a farmer's daughter, and Will Parker's a cowboy. (In "All er Nothin'," a second-act, comic duet for Annie and Will, both set down ground rules for their impending marriage that are no more likely to succeed than the ones Laurey and Curly set down in "People Will Say We're in Love.") All four must give a little before their stories can end happily, just as the farmers and cowboys must compromise before the territory can become a state.

An example of the show's theme as applied to the second subplot is the lively opening number of act 2 at the social. "The Farmer and the Cowman" is about how becoming a state means that "the farmer and the cowman should be friends" and that "territory folks should stick together." It's a traditional second-act, high-energy opener, a comic song and balletic hoedown led by Aunt Eller and Ado Annie's father, Judge Carnes, but with a fight between the farmers and the cowboys threatening to break out any minute. The fourth major dance sequence in the show, it's the only one in the second act. (Michael Kidd got ideas for the barn-raising sequence in the 1954 movie musical *Seven Brides for Seven Brothers* from this number, although his work is more athletic than balletic.)

Even the show's title helped emphasize the theme. It was originally called *Away We Go!* from the "do-si-do and away we go" square-dance call but was changed during out-of-town tryouts when the song "Oklahoma!" was added to Laurey and Curly's wedding scene near the end of act 2. When the show opened out of town, "People Will Say We're in Love" was reprised at that point with the lyrics changed to "Let people say we're in love," but during a rehearsal, director Mamoulian requested a rousing choral number instead. He wanted to lift the show's energy as high as possible before going into the final dramatic scene, which includes Jud's attempted murder of Laurey and Curly and his accidental death. Rodgers and Hammerstein returned with the new song in a half hour, and it was put into the show that evening, fully staged and orchestrated. (Some people question the veracity of this story, but it's certainly possible.)

The song's lyrics draw an explicit parallel between personal relationships and the dream of statehood. Sung by Curly and the ensemble, it's a tribute to the future in more of Hammerstein's poetry of the ordinary. The verse begins:

> They couldn't pick a better time to start in life,
> It ain't too early and it ain't too late.
> Startin' as a farmer with a brand-new wife—
> Soon be livin' in a brand-new state!
> Brand-new state
> Gonna treat you great!

This is the chorus, hardly a traditional wedding song:

> Oklahoma,
> Where the wind comes sweepin' down the plain,
> And the wavin' wheat
> Can sure smell sweet
> When the wind comes right behind the rain.
> Oklahoma!
> Every night my honey lamb and I
> Sit alone and talk
> And watch a hawk
> Makin' lazy circles in the sky.
> We know we belong to the land,
> And the land we belong to is grand.
> And when we say:
> Ee-eeow! A-yip-i-o-ee-ay!
> We're only sayin',
> You're doin' fine, Oklahoma!
> Oklahoma, OK!

Along with the concept of progress as defined by the need for communal cooperation, *Oklahoma!* is about progress in general and about adjusting to it so it too can be lived through in peace and harmony—a recurring theme in Hammerstein's work. Will Parker sings about it to his fellow cowboys in his entrance number, having just returned from the big town, where he won the steer-roping contest:

> Ev'rythin's up to date in Kansas City.
> They've gone about as fur as they c'n go!
> They went and built a skyscraper seven stories high—
> About as high as a buildin' orta grow.
> Ev'rythin's like a dream in Kansas City.
> It's better than a magic-lantern show.
> Y' c'n turn the radiator on whenever you want some heat,
> With ev'ry kind o' comfort ev'ry house is all complete,
> You c'n walk to privies in the rain an' never wet yer feet—
> They've gone about as fur as they c'n go!
> Yes, sir!
> They've gone about as fur as they c'n go!

Although the cowboys are interested in Will's information, life in the big city is in no way the kind of life they want to live. The long dance sequence that follows is a comic Western ballet with progress represented by the new dances Will has brought back from Kansas City. The other men, resisting change, prefer the older dances; only Will, Aunt Eller, and two tomboys prefer the newer ones. As Albert Williams notes:

> This theme—the promise and challenge of change—resonated deeply with American audiences; the war drastically reshaped the American social landscape. Young people from all walks of life were thrust together by military service, women were moving into the industrial workplace, people from small towns were migrating to cities to find work, etc. (Albert Williams, personal communication)

Here's how that same message, having already been demonstrated in song and dance several times in the show, is expressed in dialogue near the end of the second act. Curly has chosen to give up the free and easy life of a cowboy out on the range in order to wed Laurey. Despite their bickering, they truly love each other. She accepts his marriage proposal, and he says:

> "I'll be the happiest man alive soon as we're married. Oh, I got to learn to be a farmer, I see that! Quit a-thinkin' about th'owin' the rope, and start in to git my hands blistered a new way! Oh, things is changin' right and left! . . . They gonna make a state out of this, they gonna put it in the Union! Country a-changin', got to change with it! Bring up a pair of boys, new stock, to keep up 'th the way things is goin' in this here crazy country. Now I got you to he'p me—I'll mount to sumpin yit!"

The project initially didn't look promising. *Green Grow the Lilacs* had been a flop. Although Hammerstein had had success with movie scores over the preceding eleven years—including winning an Academy Award with Jerome Kern for their 1941 song "The Last Time I Saw Paris"—he'd had a long string of failures on Broadway over the same period of time. (After *Oklahoma!* became a huge hit, Hammerstein took out an ad in *Variety,* the show business weekly, listing his string of stage flops and their short runs. Underneath the list it read, "I've done it before and I can do it again.") Although some of Rodgers and Hart's shows experimented with the form, Rodgers had rarely trafficked in nonurban, noncontemporary subject matter or styles, and he hadn't written songs with anyone but Hart in the twenty-plus years of their partnership. De Mille had just created and starred in Aaron Copland's comic, Western-Americana ballet *Rodeo,* but she'd never successfully choreographed a Broadway musical, having been fired from her first two jobs: *Flying Colors* in 1932 and *Hooray for What?* in 1937. Director and Academy

Award–winning moviemaker Rouben Mamoulian had only one previous musical credit: in 1935 for George and Ira Gershwin and DuBose Heyward's *Porgy and Bess,* which not only had been a financial failure but also was really an opera, not a musical. He'd directed movie musicals, though, including the 1932 *Love Me Tonight,* with a Rodgers and Hart score, and the 1937 *High, Wide, and Handsome,* with a Kern and Hammerstein score. The Theatre Guild, which was in serious financial trouble, hadn't produced a musical since *Porgy and Bess* eight years earlier and was best known for producing serious drama, including the plays of O'Neill and Shaw. Furthermore, the cast (including Alfred Drake, Joan Roberts, Celeste Holm, Lee Dixon, Howard da Silva, Joseph Buloff, and Betty Garde) were basically unknowns, all of whom were chosen because they looked and sounded like their roles and because they could act. (Unknowns Howard Keel and Shelley Winters were among the cast replacements during the show's run, and unknowns John Raitt, Barbara Cook, and Florence Henderson were among those who played in it on the road.) At least the show was designed by Lemuel Ayers and Miles White and orchestrated by Robert Russell Bennett, all Broadway veterans.

It was difficult to raise the money needed to produce *Oklahoma!* especially after word got around that it was a complete departure from Broadway musical comedy traditions. (One potential backer refused to invest because he didn't like plays about farmhands.) Walter Winchell, the powerful New York gossip columnist, heard that Broadway producer Mike Todd, in the lobby during intermission while the show was trying out in New Haven, had said, "No jokes, no tits, no chance." Winchell verified the comment with Todd, then cleaned it up for his column to read, "No jokes, no legs, no chance." It's true *Oklahoma!* didn't have chorus girls showing off their legs or whatever. It did not even have chorus girls until a third of the way through the first act, and they were dressed demurely in long skirts—correct for the time and place of the show but potentially disappointing to the men in the audience who'd paid for the tickets. And it's true the show had no jokes; it had laughs that came out of character and situation instead. Nevertheless, audiences loved it out of town and critics adored it in New York. It played to nearly five million people during its original run and to over ten million in its first national road tour, which lasted from 1943 to 1954, with many cast replacements, of course. The original production ran 2,248 performances, including over forty special matinees for people in the armed forces. (Although there is general agreement on 2,248 performances, sources often differ on the number of performances of other shows discussed in this text. The same is true of some birth dates, though not of death dates.) *Oklahoma!* became the longest-running musical on Broadway, a title it held until 1961, when its record was surpassed by

My Fair Lady. Still revived regularly all over the world, *Oklahoma!* has eventually returned millions on its initial $100,000 investment.

The score of *Oklahoma!* was so popular (several of its songs sold millions of copies of sheet music and cover recordings) that it was the first musical to get a relatively complete, major-label, original-cast recording, even with its cast of unknowns. Released in two volumes of 78 rpm records, it sold over a million copies, beginning the trend of recording original-cast albums. (This practice escalated after the war with the advent of the $33\frac{1}{3}$ rpm LP, with its ability to hold nearly an hour of music, and has continued with few interruptions to the present day.) The original-cast album of *Oklahoma!* has almost never been out of print and was one of the first recordings of a show to be rereleased on CD.

There was a successful and quite faithful 1955 movie version of the show as well; its sound track has also almost never been out of print. Directed by Fred Zinnemann and presented in a very wide-screen format by Rodgers and Hammerstein, the cast includes Gordon MacRae, Shirley Jones, Gloria Grahame, Gene Nelson, Rod Steiger, Eddie Albert, and Charlotte Greenwood. De Mille re-created her original choreography for the film. There were Broadway revivals in 1951, 1980, and 2002.

What was so special about *Oklahoma!*? Why did it change forever the very nature of the American musical? Certainly not because of its simple story. It did, of course, get rave reviews and had several hit tunes, which helped draw in audiences. Also, it struck a nostalgic chord with audiences just out of the Depression and then into a world war. (It was a favorite date for servicemen on leave.) But what had the most profound effect on its audiences, and on the future of the musical, was that it had the structure, cohesion, characterization, thematic thrust, and a sense of dramatic build that till then had been expected only of a play. Audiences at *Oklahoma!* actually found themselves caring about what happened next to the characters. (Things like Jud's murderous potential and his death contributed to this effect; before this, villains didn't have psychological problems or die in musicals.)

Since the characters take the situations seriously, the show's style required more of an imagined fourth wall than was usual between the stage and the audience, another reason the show felt like a play; until 1943, musical theater performers were more likely to play to the audience than to the other performers. Furthermore, the few musicals with a message—most of them produced in the thirties—had been satiric and loosely structured, requiring none of the sense of involvement one feels with a play.

Now, suddenly, everyone on Broadway seemed to realize that the musical had found a new form suited to a radically changing world. They hadn't been ready for it when the even more serious musical play *Show Boat* premiered in still roaring 1927. However, from 1943 on, even far less serious musicals than *Oklahoma!* were not likely to succeed unless all the other aspects of the show were more or less firmly attached to the book; in fact, such works are often referred to as **book shows.** *Oklahoma!* was a coalescence of all the best ideas that had been developing over the preceding forty years for how to write a musical. It was the true beginning of contemporary American musical theater. It even has its own U.S. postage stamp (as does *Show Boat*). From 1943 on, the musical began to take itself seriously as an art form. Now let's go back in time to see how it got there.

Suggested Watching and Listening

I strongly recommend the letter-boxed, wide-screen versions of movies, so that you can see all the choreography.

Oklahoma!
There are at least three possible versions to consider:
1) The original-cast recording, available in a recently remastered and reissued CD version from Decca U.S.
2) The 20th Century Fox wide-screen movie version, produced by Richard Rodgers and Oscar Hammerstein and directed by Fred Zinnemann, available on 20th Century Fox DVD.
3) The Royal National Theatre Production of the hit British revival, directed by Trevor Nunn and choreographed by Susan Stroman, which is available as a two-disc Image Entertainment DVD. Since it's a taped stage production of the cast that opened in London, and since it feels more contemporary than the earlier movie, I recommend using samples from it. It transferred to Broadway in 2002 with a largely different cast for an unsuccessful run of almost a year.
   - "Oh, What a Beautiful Mornin'" (performed by Hugh Jackman): It's the opening song, which Curly starts offstage while Aunt Eller sits onstage churning butter. The song helps establish place, time, and character. The tune, in folk-song form, has an eight-bar verse and an eight-bar chorus. Each of its three verses has different lyrics with the same chorus repeated after each verse. The scene continues straight through to Laurey's entrance followed by dialogue establishing the bickering relationship between her and Curly.
   - "The Surrey with the Fringe on Top" (performed by Hugh Jackman, Josefina Gabriella, and Maureen Lipman): This is the beginning of Rodgers and Hammerstein's practice of including dialogue and underscoring within a number. It is, by the way, clear to Aunt Eller from the beginning of the show that Laurey and Curly belong together.
   - "Kansas City" (performed by Jimmy Johnston, Maureen Lipman, and some of the ensemble)
   - "I Cain't Say No" (performed by Vicki Simon): Ado Annie's introduction, it's one of the better comic numbers written for a woman.

- "People Will Say We're in Love" (performed by Josefina Gabriella and Hugh Jackman): Its flowingly romantic music and simple language are a hallmark of Rodgers and Hammerstein's best love songs.
- "Lonely Room" (performed by Shuler Hensley): Jud's dramatic monologue, which was cut from the earlier film, is available on the original-cast CD, as is Ali Hakim's "It's a Scandal! It's a Outrage!" also cut from the earlier film, which means that the only solo numbers of the third points of both love triangles aren't in the movie. However, they are in the National Theatre version.
- "Out of My Dreams" and "Laurey Makes Up Her Mind" (performed by Josefina Gabriella, Hugh Jackman, Shuler Hensley, and the ensemble): In de Mille's original dream ballet, reproduced in the earlier film, dancers played the "Dream Laurey" and the "Dream Curly" on stage and in the film. Onstage there was also a "Dream Jud"; in the movie, through overly simplified choreography and clever camera cuts, Rod Steiger as Jud did it himself. The National Theatre Production cast actor-singer-dancers in all the principal roles, and Gabriella, Jackman, and Hensley did their own dancing.
- "The Farmer and the Cowman" (performed by Maureen Lipman and the company): The thematic content of the show is done as a dance that nearly turns into a fight.
- "All er Nothin'" (performed by Jimmie Johnston and Vicki Simon): Will and Annie's comic duet, paralleling "People Will Say We're in Love."
- "Oklahoma!" (performed by Hugh Jackman and the company): On Laurey and Curly's wedding day, this song ties the union of the young couple to the eventual ratification of Oklahoma as one of the United States.

You might also want to watch scene 2 of the second act, which has some excellent acting from all three principals. Jud comes on very strongly to Laurey. She fires him. He leaves vowing revenge. Laurey, hysterical, calls for Curly, who comforts her, proposes to her, and builds in excitement till he has no choice left but to burst into song with a reprise of "People Will Say We're in Love," only with the lyrics changed to "Let People Say We're in Love."

Of course, you could just watch the whole show.

Some Enchanted Evening: Celebrating Oscar Hammerstein II

This is a 1995 PBS TV concert and retrospective of Hammerstein's career, produced by John Walker and Joann Young, with such performers as Audra McDonald, Bernadette Peters, Mandy Patinkin, Julie Andrews, and Patti LaBelle.

PART ONE

Ancestors and Antecedents, 1791–1900

Overleaf: (*left*) Tamino and The Queen of the Night (Gianna d'Angelo) in *The Magic Flute* (1963); (*right*) Howell Glynne, Marion Studholme, Andrew Downie, and Joan Ryan in *H.M.S. Pinafore*

Opera and French and Viennese Operetta

I like a prizefight that isn't a fake.
I love the rowing on Central Park Lake.
I go to opera and stay wide awake.
That's why the lady is a tramp.
— "THE LADY IS A TRAMP,"
BABES IN ARMS, LYRICS BY LORENZ HART

Music has always been a part of theatrical presentation. The ancient Greeks used choral interludes in their plays, usually as commentary on the action or as prayers and supplications; it's even possible that the dialogue was sung. Music was used in medieval mystery and miracle plays and in early court theatricals. In many of Shakespeare's plays, songs serve as breaks in the action or help to set moods. His plays also have occasional instrumental music—fanfares and dances especially—and it was probably customary to underscore some dialogue with music.

Opera, however, is the earliest true ancestor of the musical. Granted, the music is classical and requires voices with large ranges that can be heard over a symphony orchestra. Nevertheless, opera was the first modern form to use music as a major means of telling a story and shaping character, and the first to integrate story, music, words, and spectacle into a unified whole, with the libretto always written first. (Dance usually remained unintegrated.) The form began in Italy and France in the late sixteenth and early seventeenth centuries. By the nineteenth century, it was one of the most popular kinds of entertainment in the Western world, enjoyed by rich and poor, educated and illiterate alike. Its most famous tunes were even played by organ grinders. Successful new works usually crossed the Atlantic within months and played at houses all across America. Opera wasn't quite as elitist as it is now; it was just one of several kinds of musical entertainments available. In fact, in America there weren't any performance spaces that presented opera exclusively, even the ones called opera houses.

The **singspiel** (German for "a play with singing") is a German/Austrian opera form, usually a comedy or a fantasy. (There are not many comic operas in the standard repertory.) Singspiels usually have romantic main plots and comic subplots. Most of the comic plot scenes are handled in dialogue placed between the arias, duets, ensembles, and other musical numbers, with the recitative often used as a bridge. They are structurally, therefore, the antecedent of operettas and the ancestor of Rodgers and Hammerstein's musical plays. The most enduring ones are Wolfgang Amadeus Mozart's *The Magic Flute* and *The Abduction from the Seraglio*, and Carl Maria von Weber's *Der Freischütz* (one of the sources of what is traditionally accepted as the first musical, *The Black Crook*). The European aristocracy and intelligentsia considered operas with spoken dialogue to be a lesser form. In France, if any opera, comic or serious, had spoken dialogue rather than recitative, it was relegated to Paris's second-ranked house, the Opéra-Comique, including the original versions of *Carmen* and *Faust*.

Mozart's 1791 *The Magic Flute* (*Die Zauberflöte*) was his last opera; he died soon after its premiere. Its libretto was by Emanuel Schikaneder, who commissioned it for his Viennese company and wrote the role of Papageno, the hero of the comic subplot, for himself. He adapted it from various sources, including thinly disguised Masonic religious rituals. (He and Mozart were both Masons.) At a time when Europe was in turmoil because of the American and French revolutions, Mozart and Schikaneder wrote about how peace and harmony are achieved through love and faith, and how even evil can be changed to good in the right hands. Like most singspiels, the opera has several plot elements later used in many operettas, including ones by Hammerstein. It has parallel plots, the main one romantic, the subplot comic; it's set in an exotic locale (ancient Egypt in *The Magic Flute*); and it has characters who fall in love at first sight, characters in disguises, and happy endings achieved only after the heroes of both plots go through great difficulties in order to win the heroines. Some sung sections help carry plot and character development, but most are intended simply to show off the beautiful music and singing, sometimes with much repetition of lyrics.

Most operas are **through-composed,** which means the whole show is set to music, and have larger-than-life characters involved in highly romantic and melodramatic plots, usually ending in the death of one or more of the principals while the others sob. They almost always employ spectacle, a ballet corps, and a larger chorus and orchestra than most comic operas. Although they were hardly the inspiration for the original musicals, some claim that such contemporary through-composed romantic works as Andrew Lloyd Webber, Charles Hart, and Richard Stilgoe's 1988 *The Phantom of the Opera* and Claude-Michel Schönberg, Alain Boublil, and Herbert Kretzmer's 1987 *Les Misérables* have moved very close to their spirit and, especially, to the spirit of Giacomo Puccini. Lloyd Webber says Puccini was as much an influence on his work as were Rodgers and Hammerstein; Schönberg, Boublil, and Richard Maltby Jr.'s hit 1991 through-composed pop opera *Miss Saigon* is a reworking of Puccini's *Madame Butterfly;* and Jonathan Larson's hit 1996 through-composed rock opera *Rent* is a reworking of Puccini's *La Bohème*. So, in a twisted sort of way, Puccini is the ancestor of some of the most successful musicals in the last two decades of the twentieth century.

La Bohème (The Bohemians) has music by Puccini and libretto by Giuseppe Giacosa and Luigi Illica, adapted from Henri Murger's 1848–49 French novel *Scènes de la vie de bohème*. The opera premiered in Turin, Italy, in 1896 and opened in Los Angeles the following year, a time of relative peace and security throughout the Western world when romanticism was in its last full flowering. One of the most popular and romantic operas of all time, *La Bohème* is set in the Latin Quarter of Paris in the 1830s. It's about the lives and loves of poor, struggling young artists and other bohemians. Four of them share an attic: the poet Rodolfo (hero of the romantic main plot), the painter Marcello (hero of the comic subplot), the philosopher Colline, and the musician Schaunard. It is a simple story: two poor young couples love, quarrel, separate, and come back together, and the heroine dies of tuberculosis.

Rent is a reworking of *La Bohème* set on the Lower East Side of Manhattan, with tuberculosis replaced by AIDS, some gender switching, and several added subplots. Puccini's romanticism is toughened up with rock music and contemporary attitudes toward love, sex, and death, except that in *Rent* the heroine (named Mimi, as in *La Bohème*) dies, has an out-of-body experience, and then rather unbelievably returns to life as everyone sings there's "no day but today." Baz Luhrmann's updated production of *La Bohème* ran on Broadway in 2003 with alternating casts, a cut-down orchestra, amplification, and supertitles for those who didn't understand Italian. (Most opera companies now also use supertitles, even for operas in English.) Luhrmann reset the period of *La Bohème* to the late 1950s, and the cast, a group of young, relatively unknown singers, looked their roles—not always the case in opera, where two-hundred-pound sopranos have been known to die of tuberculosis. When you add the appropriate casting to the modern clothing, Luhrmann's *La Bohème* starts looking a lot like *Rent*.

Most of Puccini's operas still play to sold-out houses. Just as with the long-running, through-composed, romantic pop operas *The Phantom of the Opera, Les Misérables,* and *Miss Saigon,* they were usually scorned by serious-minded critics and audiences for their sentimentality and easy romanticism—the same qualities that made them hits with the general public. They were the pop operas of their time.

As opera got more grand in the middle of the nineteenth century, European composers and librettists developed the comic opera into a lighter form known at different points in its history and places of origin as: operetta, opéra bouffe, comic opera, comic operetta, or light opera. (For the most part, we'll stick with *operetta.*) Lighter than opera musically, with a smaller orchestra and, invariably, a happy or at least sentimentally satisfying ending, operetta is somewhat easier to sing than opera, uses both classical and semi-pop musical forms, and has both spoken dialogue and occasional recitative, following the lead of the singspiel. As in opera, the libretto was written first.

In mid-nineteenth-century France, where operettas first flourished, the form was known as **opéra bouffe.** These shows were clever, racy, and light-weight. Socially and politically satiric, they usually took mild jabs at the behavior of the upper classes, particularly at their sexual escapades. First only in one act but soon expanded to two and sometimes three, opéras bouffes were well-constructed farces that often disguised their satiric targets by making them characters in mythology or by placing them in exotic or historic settings but with clearly local and contemporary references. The music combined opera with song and dance forms of the time. Opéra bouffe required performers with operatic or near-operatic voices and lots of style and charm.

Jacques Offenbach (1819–80, born Jacob Eberst in Cologne, Germany) is the most famous composer of opéras bouffes; he wrote over ninety in all. His shows not only established the form but also influenced the creation of similar forms in Vienna and England. Among his best-known opéras bouffes are *La belle Hélène* (*The Beautiful Helen* [*of Troy*]), *Barbe-bleue* (*Bluebeard*), and *La vie parisienne* (*Parisian Life*), all with librettos by Henri Meilhac and Ludovic Halévy. (The very prolific Meilhac and Halévy had a great deal to do with the development of the operetta form, both separately and together. They wrote many successful librettos, including the one for Bizet's opera *Carmen,* as well as plays that were adapted by others.)

Offenbach's first full-length opéra bouffe was produced in 1858, the year Puccini was born and Monet began discovering the tenets of impressionism. *Orpheus in the Underworld* (libretto in two acts by Hector Crémieux and Halévy), had thinly disguised, mythological characters used to satirize contemporary French society. The show created a scandal and made Offenbach's career. (It didn't play New York in English until 1882.) The score includes the most familiar music ever written to accompany the can-can, the shocking nightclub dance of the day in which women not only showed their legs but flipped up their skirts to show their underclothes back and front.

Viennese operettas were more romantic and farcical and less satiric than their French counterparts. (French writers after Offenbach also tended to write more romantic and less satiric works than he did.) Like opéra bouffe, they combined classical music with song and dance forms of the time, particularly the waltz and the polka. They required performers with operatic or near-operatic voices and some skill at comedy. Many also contained nonsinging roles for comic actors. Unlike opéra bouffe, Viennese operettas were almost always set in times and places contemporary with their audiences. Most of them had a secondary love story, usually comic since the main love story was usually romantic (the tradition, along with spoken dialogue, stemming back at least to *The Magic Flute* and continuing on to the extremely influential British operettas of Gilbert and Sullivan, American operettas, and *Oklahoma!*). The two most popular Viennese operettas, *Die Fledermaus* and *The Merry Widow,* are still frequently revived by companies around the world. In fact, *Die Fledermaus* is done annually in many cities as part of their New Year's celebrations.

Die Fledermaus (*The Bat*) premiered in Vienna in 1874—the year the term *impressionism* was first used to describe Monet's paintings and the year Mussorgsky's opera *Boris Gudonov* premiered. *Die Fledermaus* has music by Johann Strauss Jr. (1825–99, born in Vienna and known as the Waltz King) and a libretto in three acts by Carl Haffner and Richard Genée, adapted from the play *Le Réveillon,* by the ubiquitous Meilhac and Halévy. As in most farces and operettas, it has much complexity of plot and little complexity of character. Unusual for Viennese operettas, both the main plot and the subplot are comic. *Die Fledermaus* opened in New York in 1879. It wasn't a success there. It's a sex farce, which is probably why it didn't catch on quickly with American operetta audiences, who were quite prudish. In fact, most of Strauss's best (and most frequently revived) operettas tended to be his least successful when first seen in America.

Until the late 1870s and the arrival on American shores of the British operettas of Gilbert and Sullivan—which they called comic operas—the French and Viennese operettas were usually performed in America in their original languages and therefore had limited appeal. Once Gilbert and Sullivan had enraptured the United States, however, French and Viennese shows were translated, and European operettas became for a while the most popular musical form in the country. By the 1890s, public interest in the form had begun to wane and soon went into semiretirement in America, though not in Europe. Then, in 1907, *The Merry Widow* premiered in New York.

From its 1905 Viennese premiere on, *The Merry Widow* (*Die Lustige Witwe*)—music by Franz Lehár (1870–1948, born in Komárom, Hungary) and libretto by Viktor Léon and Leo Stein, adapted from *The Attaché* by Meilhac (without Halévy)—was one of the most popular and influential European operettas. It was almost a last gasp of romanticism in a Europe where the roots of World War I were beginning to spread and in a United States coming awake as a major player in international politics. The show's romantic main plot centers around who is going to marry the merry—and very rich—widow; the subplot is about an affair between a married woman and her lover.

> Using the new libretto Basil Hood had written for the London production, the New York staging was an enormous success, affecting more than just the theatrical scene: there were "Merry Widow" hats, cigarettes, gowns, and corsets. Other popular operettas from Vienna followed . . . , but more significantly [it] . . . helped launch an American style that was popular for years, particularly with the works of Victor Herbert, Rudolf Friml, and Sigmund Romberg. (Paul Gruber, *Original Cast! Visitors from Abroad*, 5)

There have been three Hollywood versions of *The Merry Widow:* 1925 (silent); 1934 (English lyrics by Lorenz Hart), starring Jeanette MacDonald and Maurice Chevalier; and 1952, starring a nonsinging Lana Turner and costarring Fernando Lamas.

Another, almost equally popular Viennese operetta was the 1908 *The Chocolate Soldier,* by Oscar Straus (no relation to Johann Strauss) and Stanislaus Stange, adapted from George Bernard Shaw's *Arms and the Man.* The operetta premiered in New York in 1909, ran 296 performances, and was revived almost as frequently as *The Merry Widow* throughout the first half of the twentieth century, though its popularity has faded considerably since then. There's a 1941 MGM movie called *The Chocolate Soldier,* starring Metropolitan opera star Risë Stevens and Nelson Eddy. However, MGM couldn't get the rights to Shaw's play (he hated the operetta), so the studio used the title of the operetta (which it owned), turned it into a musical adaptation of Molnár's *The Guardsman* (which it also owned), and used a few of the operetta's numbers, including its most successful song, "My Hero (Come, Come, I Love You Only)," which was famous for years. Hollywood almost always made extensive changes when adapting operettas and musicals into movies but rarely switched to a completely different plot.

Suggested Watching and Listening

La Bohème

The live performance, taped in 1994 in Sydney and available on Image Entertainment DVD (2002), isn't the best sung performance of the opera, but it is the best one visually and holds its own musically. Conducted by Julian Smith with the Australian Opera and the Ballet Orchestra and directed by Baz Luhrmann, it's the version Luhrmann adapted for Broadway. I suggest watching the second half of act 1, starting with the landlord asking for the rent.

Act 1 takes place on a cold Christmas Eve. Schaunard, the musician, has just made the first money any of the four roommates have seen in a while. They've decided to go to the Café Momus to celebrate when they're interrupted by their landlord, Benoit, asking for the rent. The last half of the act starts with a quintet in which the four bohemians get rid of Benoit without paying the rent, followed by a tuneful series of recitative sections. Rodolfo, the poet-hero of the romantic main plot, stays behind to finish a writing assignment before joining the others at the café. He is interrupted by Mimi, a seamstress in the first stages of tuberculosis, who lives above him among the eaves; the two have never met. Her candle has gone out, so he lights it for her. She faints. He revives her with some wine. She loses her key. Both their candles go out. He helps her search for the key in the dark. Their hands touch.

- "Che gelida manina! (How cold your tiny hand is!)" (performed by David Hobson, tenor): This is Rodolfo's famous aria introducing himself.
- "Mi chiamano Mimi (I'm called Mimi)" (performed by Cheryl Barker, soprano): Mimi responds with this famous aria introducing herself.
- "O soave fanciulla (O lovely girl)" (performed by David Hobson and Cheryl Barker): Rodolfo and Mimi sing this famous duet as they leave for the café, having fallen in love in about eighteen minutes.

The Magic Flute (*Die Zauberflöte*)

This 1991 performance, conducted by James Levine with the Metropolitan Opera Orchestra and Chorus, is available on Deutsche Grammophon DVD. It's live and has good subtitles. Any other will also do, including director Ingmar Bergman's 1975 film version available on a special edition Criterion Collection DVD. I recommend watching the first scene of the first act.

The story begins near the castle of the Queen of the Night. Prince Tamino, the romantic lead, enters, pursued by a dragon. He faints. Three ladies of the queen's court appear, slay the dragon, and sing a long and difficult trio during which—after much repetition—they decide to tell the queen of the arrival of the handsome stranger still lying in a faint at their feet. The ladies exit. Tamino revives as Papageno enters.

- "Der Vogelfänger bin ich ja (I am the birdcatcher)" (performed by Manfred Hemm, baritone): Papageno's aria, a simple tune to match the character's simple pleasures and to accommodate the original singer's not quite operatic voice, is done as a direct address to the audience; in it we learn about his character and history. There is then a long, spoken, expositional comedy scene between Tamino, Papageno, and the three ladies during which the ladies punish Papageno for lying about who killed the dragon and give Tamino a portrait of the Queen's daughter, Pamina.
- "Dies Bildnis ist (This portrait is)" (performed by Francisco Araiza, tenor): This is Tamino's aria in which he tells us that he has fallen in love with the woman in the portrait. Tamino's aria is followed by the Queen of the Night's entrance aria.

- "O zitt're nicht (Oh, do not tremble)" (performed by Luciana Serra, high soprano): The aria begins with a recitative in which the Queen calms Tamino, followed by the aria itself, which is constructed as a slow section in which she tells Tamino about Sarastro's kidnapping of Pamina, and a fast section in which—with much repetition—she sends Tamino to rescue her daughter. (If you think this aria is difficult, listen to "Der Hölle Rache" [The Pangs of Hell]," which she sings in the second act.) The scene ends with a quintet for Tamino, Papageno, and the ladies, who give Tamino a magic flute and Papageno a set of magic bells to protect them on their journey. They also send three spirits (sung by boy sopranos) to guide them. The men set off to rescue Pamina, Papageno unwillingly.

French and Viennese Operettas

There's no need to spend much time on French and Viennese operettas. The can-can finale of *Orpheus in the Underworld*, the overture to *Die Fledermaus*, and "Lippen Schweiger," *The Merry Widow*'s most famous waltz will do to get a good enough sense of the music. Any recording will do. The librettos are much better and certainly much funnier in Gilbert and Sullivan's operettas (chapter 4).

The Minstrel Show, Variety/Vaudeville, and *The Black Crook*

Hey, folks! Say, folks!

Come on and hear a minstrel band!

Young folks! Old folks!

You'll want to cheer that minstrel band!

Come and hear 'em play

Songs you used to know;

Taking you away—

Back to long ago.

—"FOLLOW THE MINSTREL BAND,"

SHOW GIRL, LYRICS BY IRA GERSHWIN

Stephen Foster wrote the first popular American songs to break ties with European musical traditions. Many of his songs are simplified versions of traditional forms, but many others have the rhythm and structure of African American music, particularly plantation-slave music. Written in what was known as Negro dialect ("am" for *is,* "de" for *the,* and "massa" for *master,* for example), they often celebrated slave life.

Such longtime favorites as "Oh! Susanna (I Come from Alabama wid My Banjo on My Knee)," "Old Folks at Home (Way Down upon de Swanee River)," "Camptown Races," "My Old Kentucky Home," and "Jeanie with the Light Brown Hair" are only a few of Foster's many once-famous traditional ballads and African American–based songs, most of them written for minstrelsy.

His last song, "Beautiful Dreamer," written a few days before his death, is

Stephen Foster (1826–64, born in Lawrenceville, Pennsylvania) was the best known of the first uniquely American songwriters. He performed and composed both music and lyrics for many minstrel show songs. At a time when the printing and distributing of sheet music was getting easier in the United States, dozens of Foster's songs became best sellers, played on parlor pianos all over the nation. It was, however, his publishers who made the money, not Foster. They would buy songs outright from composers, who were rarely able to arrange royalties. Because of this, many songwriters eventually became their own publishers, but that was long after Foster's death. He died broke and alcoholic in the charity ward of Bellevue Hospital in New York.

a simple American ballad still sung by occasional concert recitalists. A love song, its sentimental message of hope and peace hit a responsive chord among people on both sides of the war-torn America of the 1860s—similar to the effect *Oklahoma!* had on Americans during World War II—and the song became enormously popular.

As with most pop ballads of the day, the chorus is in sixteen bars divided into four sections of equal length in what is called an AABA pattern (a very shortened and simplified variation of the classical sonata form). The first four bars, the **A,** present the principal melody. The second four bars repeat the A, in some songs note for note, but more typically with a variation at the end in order to modulate into the next section. When notes are changed in the second A, it's called the **A′** (A-prime). The first half of "Beautiful Dreamer" is an AA′. (The last note goes up in the A, down in the A′.)

> A: Beautiful dreamer, wake unto me.
>   Starlight and dewdrops are waiting for thee.
> A′: Sounds of the rude world, heard in the day,
>   Lulled by the moonlight have all passed away.

The third four-bar section, the **B** or **the bridge,** introduces a second melody:

> B: Beautiful dreamer, queen of my song,
>   List while I woo thee with soft melody.

The end of the B modulates back to the last four bars, which can be an A or A′ or even an **A″** (A double-prime) with yet a different variation at the end from the one in the A′, usually to accommodate a high note or two. In "Beautiful Dreamer" it is another A′. So the song is an AA′BA′, still following the general AABA pattern:

> A′: Gone are the cares of life's busy throng:
>   Beautiful dreamer, awake unto me.

However, the second chorus, which has a new set of lyrics, changes to an AA′BA, with the last A leading into a **tag,** or **coda,** added at the end of a song to give it a stronger ending.

A: Beautiful dreamer, out on the sea,
     Mermaids are chanting the wild Lorelei.
A': Over the streamlet vapors are born,
     Waiting to fade at the bright coming morn.
B: Beautiful dreamer, beam on my heart
     E'en as the morn on the streamlet and sea.
A: Then will all clouds of sorrow depart.
     Beautiful dreamer, awake unto me.
TAG: Beautiful dreamer, awake unto me.

Early in the twentieth century, instead of sixteen bars, thirty-two bars became the standard length for the chorus of a pop song. Even so, the AABA pattern, with each section having eight bars instead of four, remained one of the two most frequent structures of songs, including those in musicals and revues. Johnny Marks's "Rudolph the Red-Nosed Reindeer" is a familiar example of a thirty-two-bar AABA song (actually AA'BA').

The other standard thirty-two-bar structure is an **ABAC** pattern; the principal melody—the A—reappears once in the middle of the song, followed by a melody completely different from the A or the B: the **C.** (If the second A ends differently from the first in order to modulate into the C, it becomes an A'.) Irving Berlin's "White Christmas" is an ABAC song; both A's are identical musically, and both begin with the words "I'm dreaming of a white Christmas."

Performers have to understand how the chorus of a song breaks down into its separate sections because it's one of the ways of understanding how to build a song correctly in performance. (There is a more detailed discussion of song forms in chapter 11.)

The Minstrel Show

There were no American operas (or operettas) of importance until the twentieth century, but European operas were frequently produced in America throughout the nineteenth century, usually performed by touring companies led by a European star. Even smaller cities and towns had opera houses, which were considered a sign of being truly civilized, despite the fact that few (if any) operas were booked into them. The majority of the bookings were usually less highbrow entertainments, including what was, for all intents and purposes, the first American musical form: the **minstrel show,** which became very popular during the two decades before the Civil War. Though historically important, the form was totally racist, as were the period and place of its creation. Minstrel shows patronized blacks when they weren't making fun of them. They cemented into place many stereotypes of African American life, language, and character that lasted well into the twentieth century.

In 1843, the *Virginia Minstrels,* directed by Daniel Decatur Emmett, composer of "Dixie," was the first minstrel show to play New York. (Among the new songs of that year was American composer Thomas à Becket's "Columbia, the Gem of the Ocean.") All-male, white companies, led by such men as Emmett, E. P. Christy, and Lew Dockstader, toured the country for years. (Women, usually needed for dance numbers, were men in drag.) The cast blackened their faces with burnt cork—eventually black greasepaint—leaving enough space around their mouths to enable the audience to see that they were really white and to accentuate and mock Negroid features. (Even black minstrel-show companies had to put on blackface, at least when playing for white audiences.)

> To its credit, [the minstrel show] promoted a presentational performance style, a direct performer-to-audience relationship that remains an important aspect of our musical theater. . . . Moreover, minstrelsy's colloquial music and lyrics . . . emerged as the first American commercial songs to be something other than imitations of Old World culture. (Dwight Blocker Bowers, *American Musical Theater: Shows, Songs, and Stars,* 2)

The songs and dances were often imitations of African American culture, beginning with Thomas Dartmouth "Daddy" Rice's "Jump Jim Crow," a blackface, song-and-dance routine he first performed in variety shows in 1832. It was built around the movements of a crippled black stableman he'd once observed in Louisville; the music was from work songs he'd heard sung by slaves or by the stableman himself. Many African American dances were popularized by minstrelsy, including the shuffle, the cakewalk, the soft shoe, the buck and wing, and the clog dance (which became the tap dance when around 1903, Broadway choreographer Ned Wayburn, unhappy with the heavy wooden clogs, is usually credited with replacing them with lighter shoes with metal plates attached; at least he was the choreographer who popularized tap versus clog dancing on Broadway).

Minstrel shows, meant as family entertainment, had no plot. They were instead a collection of songs, dances, jokes, topical gags, and skits, all performed within a fairly tight framing structure in three sections. After a full-company walk-around, the first section of the show had the entire ensemble seated in a semicircular row or rows. In the middle was the master of ceremonies, **Mr. Interlocutor,** usually also the producer, and the only one on-stage not in blackface. After the up-tempo ensemble number, he'd begin the show with "Gentlemen, be seated." On either end of the semicircle sat the chief comics—the **end men**—called **Mr. Tambo** and **Mr. Bones** from the tambourine and bone clackers they used to punctuate and underscore their jokes and to show approval of the jokes and songs of others.

> The interlocutor was the quintessential **straight man,** or foil, for the comic end men, feeding Tambo and Bones the setup lines, yet always maintaining the dignity of a man too full of himself to realize that the half-wits around him are getting the best of him. The give-and-take, "crossfire" banter between the interlocutor and the end men was the pretext for introducing the set numbers: tenors singing sentimental ballads and love songs, satiric lectures on topics like women's rights, hit songs, . . . dances [and occasional ensemble numbers]. . . . The first part ended with another up-tempo song and dance by the ensemble—the cakewalk. (Armond Fields and L. Marc Fields, *From the Bowery to Broadway,* 60)

The relationship between the interlocutor and the end men was a rare example, at the time, of a black man getting the better of a white man in front of a white audience. It was acceptable in the minstrel show because it was funny but also because the audience knew the men were really white.

The second section of the minstrel show was a series of variety acts, differing from the first part in that it was shorter, no one appeared twice, and the interlocutor, the end men, and the ensemble were not onstage as bridges between the acts. This section could be anything from dog acts to stump speeches (monologists who parodied politicians and preachers) to musicians to female impersonators to whatever other specialty acts were in the company at the time. It took place on the front apron of the stage before a curtain while the set for the third section of the show was being prepared behind it. This curtain, on which space was sold to local advertisers, was called the olio, also used as the term for the series of acts done in front of it. (Originally, olio was a heavily spiced stew of meat, vegetables, and chickpeas. It then came to mean any kind of hodgepodge, which is certainly what the minstrel show olio was.) After the curtain with advertising went out of fashion, there were still acts which performed on the apron of the stage in front of a curtain or drop while the set for the next act was being changed behind it. Doing your act in front of this curtain was called **playing in 1.** The practice of playing in 1 while sets were being changed moved from minstrel shows to vaudeville to revues and musicals.

Section three of the minstrel show was a long, loosely organized sketch—the **afterpiece**—using the entire company; it's the first glimmerings of what eventually became the musical comedy. At first it was a thinly-held-together series of jokes, routines, songs, and dances meant to illustrate "happy" plantation

Al Jolson (1886–1950, born Asa Yoelson in Lithuania) was probably the most popular American entertainer in the first quarter of the twentieth century. Starting in vaudeville, he moved to minstrel shows during their last days, touring with Dockstader's company. He then starred in Broadway revues and musical comedies, and made many hit recordings and movies. His was the first voice heard in the first sound movie, *The Jazz Singer*, in 1927. His career faded in the mid-1930s and was rejuvenated in 1946 with the enormous success of *The Jolson Story*, which, like most Hollywood musical biographies, is a highly fictionalized movie about Jolson's early life and career. For the movie, Jolson dubbed in the singing for Larry Parks, who played the title role.

life. After the Civil War, it changed to parodies of current events, popular novels, or, most frequently, hit plays but remained a thinly-held-together series of basically racist jokes, songs, and routines.

The minstrel show began fading soon after the Civil War. Although many of its elements and performers transferred directly and successfully to vaudeville, which had just begun its ascendancy as popular family entertainment, minstrelsy itself refused to change with the changing status of African Americans or with the changing tastes in music, comedy, and dance. By 1884, not a single New York theater ran minstrel shows year-round, and by the early twentieth century, the form was dead. Even so, performers like Al Jolson continued working in blackface for years, and there were blackface numbers in many Hollywood musicals all the way through the 1950s.

Variety/Vaudeville

Pre–Civil War American **variety shows** were entertainments for working-class men in working-class neighborhoods, although they were also frequented by wealthy male customers. The bill consisted of an assortment of acts performed one after the other in a sequence that built to the star attraction, known eventually as the **headliner.** As with minstrel shows, the music was contemporary and popular, not classical. The shows were usually performed in rowdy and decidedly unrefined saloons, and the entertainment reflected the atmosphere. The income in these places was dependent on the sale of large quantities of cheap beer and booze served by waitresses who were also available for far more than just serving drinks. In fact, the waitresses were often the main attraction.

Tony Pastor (1837–1908, born in Brooklyn) opened his first variety music hall in New York's Bowery in 1865, just after the American Civil War—also the year of Tolstoy's *War and Peace*, Carroll's *Alice in Wonderland*, and Wagner's *Tristan and Isolde*. Pastor eventually decided to clean up variety. In 1881, he moved uptown to Fourteenth Street and managed to keep the drinking and the waitresses out of the showroom. He hired the best acts around and began advertising his shows as suitable for the family trade. He was soon attracting middle-class families and even more fashionable folks, known as the **carriage trade** because they arrived in their own horse-drawn, coachman-driven carriages. Other producers soon followed Pastor's lead. As part of the campaign to clean up their image, most of them began calling the shows **vaudeville** instead of variety. (Pastor continued calling it variety.) *Vaudeville* was the French term for what was basically the same form, but the word made it seem classier. So did the talent the best of the producers hired and the production values they added.

Vaudeville shows developed into a two-part form of twelve or more separate acts, ranging from dancers to comedians to animal acts to singers to ventriloquists to female impersonators to acrobats to whistlers to jugglers to dramatic sketches to people who played the spoons, and so on. Eventually troupes would tour in **vaudeville circuits**—chains of theaters around the country—and were booked by the season. By then, every performer's dream was to play the Palace, New York's prime vaudeville house, which opened in 1913.

The running order of the first half built to the second biggest headliner. The second half usually opened with a comedy act to get the audience back after intermission in the most active way possible: laughter. It then built to the headliner in the next-to-closing spot. In the early days of the form, the shows closed with a short sketch featuring performers from the various acts on the bill who would improvise a parody of some current play, book, or event, adding songs, dances, comedy routines, and whatever else they felt like. This was, of course, the minstrel show's afterpiece, picked up at the same time that the popularity of minstrelsy was fading and its performers were moving into vaudeville. The afterpiece was eventually expanded into two-act direct forerunners of the musical comedy, just as vaudeville itself was the forerunner of American burlesque and revue.

Most vaudeville and variety theaters soon had two or three curtains at varying depths of the stage that could be closed or dropped to cover the width of the stage, masking what was behind them so that sets could be changed. Playing in 1 was, of course, another tradition adopted from minstrel shows. **Playing in 2** was for performers who needed more room, but not the full stage; they played in front of a drop farther upstage than the olio but still with room behind for set changes. The evening's running order was constructed so that acts that could work in 1 or in 2 were placed between those needing the full stage. Musicals and revues took this structural concept from vaudeville in order to avoid having breaks within an act, until modern technology made it possible to change sets in full view of the audience.

During the 1880s, as European operettas were becoming popular, the carriage trade's interest in vaudeville lessened, and a large part of the audience was soon made up of poorer people, many of them immigrants. Immigrant and minority comic sketches became a variety/vaudeville staple. The laughs tended to come from cheap jokes and violent (knockabout) slapstick. Besides blackface comics, there were also acts—many of them created by immigrants or first-generation Americans living in poor, tough neighborhoods—doing Jewish, German, and Irish dialects, often several dialects each. This kind of humor allowed audiences to laugh not only at themselves but also at others in the same boat, which was important in that difficult transitional time when more and more immigrants (particularly Irish, German, and Jewish) were entering the country and more and more blacks were moving from the rural South to the urban North.

> It is in the variety acts and sketches of the 1880s . . . that we can detect the first stirrings of an indigenous theatrical form. . . . The brutal knockabout was the physical corollary of the crude ethnic caricatures. Variety's shifting gallery of stereotypes—the loutish Irishman, the slow-thinking German, the lazy black, the conniving Jew—all shared their audience's interest in the pursuit of material success, and, implicitly, assimilation. . . . No matter what your background was, variety gave you a target to laugh at. (Fields and Fields, 449–50)

Bill "Bojangles" Robinson (1878–1949, born in Richmond, Virginia) was one of the greatest, most famous, and highest-paid dancers in vaudeville, known best for his tap dances up and down staircases. However, most white audiences knew him best for his dances with little Shirley Temple in some 1930s movies.

Variety/vaudeville began dying with the arrival of all-talking, all-singing movies in the late 1920s. By then, the afterpiece was long gone, having been developed into farce comedies, burlesque-extravaganzas, and early musical comedies. Soon there was a movie playing along with five or so vaudeville acts, which would close with the headliner, if there even was one. The form was completely killed by the arrival of national television in the 1950s. Ed Sullivan's long-running, Sunday-night show, for example, was a star-studded variety show, so why go out and pay to see one?

Many stage, screen, radio, and early TV stars started in vaudeville, including Charlie Chaplin, Buster Keaton, W. C. Fields, the Marx Brothers, Ethel Waters, Bob Hope, Jack Benny, Burns and Allen, Jolson (before switching to minstrel shows), Eddie Cantor, George Jessel, Sophie Tucker, the Astaires, and Bill "Bojangles" Robinson.

The Black Crook

In 1866, *The Black Crook*, which musical theater historians have dubbed the first musical, had its premiere. It was an accident. A large French ballet company, booked into a New York theater, was burned out before the opening. They went to William Wheatley, managing producer of Niblo's Garden and Theatre, to see if he had space available. Wheatley was about to do *The Black Crook*, by Charles M. Barras, a nonmusical and very melodramatic variation on Carl Maria von Weber's singspiel *Der Freischütz*, itself a variation on the Faust legend. Knowing the play was less than perfect, he decided to improve his chances by adding the French ballet company, with its classy dances and its one hundred women in flesh-colored tights. He also tricked out the show with comics, specialty acts, singers, some interpolated songs, and very costly and spectacular stage effects, hardly any of which ended up having anything to do with the plot. Some of the big painted sets—it was years before sets were built architecturally—even transformed into other big painted sets in full view of the audience. (The unsuccessful 1954 Sigmund Romberg musical *The Girl in Pink Tights* is a retelling of the story of how the show got produced.)

The Black Crook was the most expensive theatrical production of that time, costing around $40,000 to produce. Tickets cost from a nickel to $1.50. Opening night the show ran five and a half hours, and the critics hated it. For audiences, however, still recovering from the Civil War and Lincoln's assassination, the escape into spectacle, music, comics, and legs made up for the sagging script—a situation that has happened many times since, though rarely at such length. The show appealed both to the audiences who went to opera and other cultural diversions and to the less-discriminating audiences of variety and other more popular entertainments. The original production ran 475 performances in a time when hit shows seldom ran more than 75. There were successful road companies and revivals throughout the rest of the century (eight in New York alone), which randomly added, dropped, and changed songs, dances, jokes, and spectacle to keep up with changing tastes and changing casts. It had many imitators.

Technically, the show isn't a musical. It's what's called an **extravaganza**: music, lots of dance, comedy, and women dressed in as little as the law allowed, with spectacle as one of its most important selling points. Extravaganzas had become a very popular form by the middle of the nineteenth century. In fact, there have been several periods in the history of the musical theater—including the Ziegfeld and Hippodrome era during much of the teens and twenties and the Lloyd Webber and Schönberg/Boublil era during the last two decades of the twentieth century—when audiences have made extravaganzas and their expensive production values the most popular of all musical forms, often with little or no concern for the merits of their scripts, scores, or both.

British Burlesque

In 1868, Lydia Thompson and Her British Blondes, an almost all-female, almost all-bleached-blonde company, arrived in New York from London and toured successfully for several seasons. (Within a year of Thompson's arrival, touring in the United States became easier when the Central Pacific and Union Pacific railroads were linked, forming the first transcontinental railway and shortening travel time from New York to San Francisco by months.) Thompson's shows were **British burlesques** (not to be confused with American burlesque, which came later). Most of them were full length, providing songs, dances, specialty numbers, laughs, and legs, all grafted onto a silly burlesque (i.e., parody) of an existing story or play. The dialogue was in rhyming couplets and filled with bad puns. Thompson's first show was *Ixion, or The Man at the Wheel*. Some of the others were *Sinbad, The 40 Thieves*, and *Pippin*.

In British burlesques, the principal young male role and most of the other male roles were played by women, since they were able to show their figures off best when dressed as men or in the tights they wore in some dance numbers. All the women in the company, Thompson included, were famous—some said infamous—for their voluptuous beauty. Their success was not totally based on talent or wit—or not at all, according to many of the critics and all the moralists of the time. Thompson was also a notorious publicity hound who once made national news by publicly horsewhipping *Chicago Times* editor Wilbur S. Story for regularly calling her immoral in print.

American vaudeville afterpieces were partly taken from minstrel shows, but they were also copies of Lydia Thompson's parody form, though not at full length and not even as well structured as her shows were. Also, afterpieces didn't have rhyming dialogue or drag as requirements, just as options. In British burlesques, women played men to show themselves off; in American vaudeville, men played women for laughs, a tradition going back at least to the ancient Greeks and continuing on to Milton Berle, Flip Wilson, Divine, Charles Ludlam, Ru Paul, Eddie Izzard, and any number of others on stages and screens up to the present. British burlesques are still performed in England at Christmastime; they're now raucous, loosely structured parodies of children's stories, with the young male lead still usually played by a woman. No longer called burlesques, and no longer with rhyming dialogue, they're known as *pantos,* short for *pantomimes,* although they're not done in mime.

The difficult, post–Civil War economy forced the American theater industry to begin searching for ways to build audiences. When both *The Black Crook* and Lydia Thompson opened so successfully in New York, producers and writers examined them carefully for hints. What both shows had in common—along with the music, dancing, jokes, comedy routines, at least some spectacle, and lots of girls—was some semblance of a plot or parody plot, so they used combinations of exactly those ingredients as they began imitating and experimenting with form, structure, and content. Meanwhile, a new and very influential form of the operetta was developing in England and beginning to travel to the United States.

Suggested Watching and Listening

American Dreamer: Songs of Stephen Foster
Thomas Hampson's 1992 CD *American Dreamer: Songs of Stephen Foster,* available on Angel Records CD, contains the following popular Foster song.
- "Beautiful Dreamer" (performed by Thomas Hampson, baritone)

Broadway: The American Musical
In this PBS series (available in a wide-screen box set on PBS Paramount DVD), "Episode 1: Give My Regards to Broadway (1893–1927)" is a good overview of the beginnings of the musical.

For Me and My Gal
Directed by Busby Berkeley, *For Me and My Gal* is a 1942 MGM movie musical set in 1916, the heyday of vaudeville. It's available on Warner Brothers Home Video DVD. During the film, Judy Garland and Gene Kelly become a vaudeville team. This was Kelly's first movie. He'd just become a Broadway star in Rodgers and Hart's *Pal Joey,* playing an unredeemable heel. In *For Me and My Gal,* he played a redeemable one.
- "Ballin' the Jack" (performed by Judy Garland and Gene Kelly, music by Chris Smith, and lyrics by James Henry Burris): This 1913 song and dance number is done in 1. Other examples of the many movies set in the days of vaudeville are the 1944 *Show Business,* with Eddie Cantor and George Murphy, and the 1954 *There's No Business Like Show Business,* with an Irving Berlin score and an all-star cast including Ethel Merman, Donald O'Connor, and Marilyn Monroe.

The Jolson Story
This is a 1946 hit musical biography of Al Jolson, available on Columbia TriStar Home Entertainment DVD.
- "Rosie, You Are My Posie" (performed by Larry Parks dubbed by Al Jolson, with music by John Stromberg, and lyrics by Edgar Smith): This song was first written in 1900. In an early sequence of the movie, Jolson is helping a drunk, blackface vaudeville performer by blacking up and going on in his spot, the assumption perhaps being that in blackface they all looked alike. Watching from a box in the audience are New York

producer Oscar Hammerstein I (grandfather of Oscar Hammerstein II) and minstrel-show entrepreneur Lew Dockstader, who hires Jolson.

- "I Want a Girl (Just Like the Girl That Married Dear Old Dad)" (performed by Larry Parks dubbed by Al Jolson, and the chorus, with music by Harry von Tilzer, and lyrics by Will Dillon): This song was first written in 1911. For Hollywood, this brief sequence showing the Dockstader troupe in performance isn't far from what the first act of a minstrel show looked like. The formation onstage is correct, the chorus girls are men in drag, and the interlocutor isn't in blackface. This sequence makes it abundantly clear that the minstrel show was doomed not only by its racism but also by its refusal (or inability) to change with the changing times. Other examples of minstrel shows in movies can be found in Jolson's 1930 *Mammy,* the 1939 Stephen Foster pseudo-biography *Swanee River,* and the 1953 *The Eddie Cantor Story,* to name a few.

The Naughty Nineties

This is the 1945 movie *The Naughty Nineties,* available as part of *The Best of Abbott & Costello,* vol. 2, Universal Studios DVD. It includes the following famous vaudeville routine.

- "Who's on First?" (performed by Bud Abbott and Lou Costello): Costello was the comic, Abbott the straight man. The routine was also seen in the TV documentary *Abbott and Costello Live.*

Stormy Weather

A very fictional movie from 1943 (available on 20th Century Fox Cinema Classics Collection DVD), *Stormy Weather* stars Bill "Bojangles" Robinson, who plays himself. The plot, a romance between Robinson and Lena Horne (who doesn't play herself), is mainly an excuse for numbers by some of the best black performers of the time.

- "The Cakewalk" (performed by Bill "Bojangles" Robinson, Lena Horne, and the company): A cakewalk was originally a dance contest held for the entertainment of plantation owners, their friends, and their families. Slave couples danced with cakes on their heads, and the last one to keep the cake in place got to eat it. Another version is that it began as a dance competition slaves did to mimic their masters, and the winner got a cake. Whatever the truth is, it was eventually formalized into a dance (without the cakes). In the film, the cakewalk is performed in a nightclub to music traditional for the dance, including Stephen Foster's "Camptown Races."

Vaudeville: An American Masters Production (1997)

This is an excellent PBS documentary on vaudeville, which has been released on Winstar DVD. It's produced by Rosemary Garner, written by Greg Palmer, and narrated by Ben Vereen.

Gilbert and Sullivan

I can tell undoubted Raphaels
from Gerard Dows and Zoffanies,
I know the croaking chorus
from *The Frogs* of Aristophanes,
Then I can hum a fugue
of which I've heard the music's din afore,
And whistle all the airs
from that infernal nonsense *Pinafore*.

—"I AM THE VERY MODEL OF A MODERN MAJOR-GENERAL,"

THE PIRATES OF PENZANCE, LYRICS BY W. S. GILBERT

The first successful English operettas, usually comedies or satires, were called **ballad operas**; they became popular in colonial America as well. Their music was not original: the songs were familiar tunes of the day with new lyrics written to fit the characters and situations. The most famous and enduring ballad opera is John Gay's 1728 *The Beggar's Opera*, with the music arranged by Johann Pepusch, which had its New York premiere in 1750. Clearly meant as an attack on Robert Walpole, the prime minister of England in 1728, and on court politics, it also makes fun of Italian opera conventions and other targets. Gay's excellent script and well-integrated lyrics still work, even if the satiric references are no longer obvious. The show is revived frequently. There's a 1953 film version directed by Peter Brook that features Laurence Olivier as Macheath, the antihero highwayman. The show was redone by Bertolt Brecht (with music by Kurt Weill) in 1928 as *The Threepenny Opera*, and by Duke Ellington and John LaTouche in a 1946 jazz version called *Beggar's Holiday*. Ballad operas were eventually replaced in popularity by operettas with original music.

Sir William Schwenck Gilbert (1836–1911, born in London) and Sir Arthur Seymour Sullivan (1842–1900, also born in London) first worked together in 1871, the same year Sullivan wrote the famous hymn "Onward, Christian Soldiers." By then, Sullivan was famous as a composer of serious music and Gilbert as a writer of humorous and satiric verse that he illustrated himself. Together they became international superstars. Still frequently revived a century and more later, their **English operettas,** or comic operas, as they called them, are witty, silly, satiric, frivolous, and tuneful. They're tightly constructed out of dialogue, parody recitatives, and musical numbers, all carefully integrated into the complex and usually farcical plots. As with all operettas, the books and lyrics were written first.

The shows are often referred to as the **Savoy operas** because they were eventually housed in the Savoy Theatre. The first theater in the world lit by electricity, it was built in 1881 by producer Richard D'Oyly Carte (1844–1901) and designed expressly to house Gilbert and Sullivan's operettas. These operettas were almost always written in two acts. Their intentionally complicated and absurd plots serve as thinly disguised satires—no matter when or where the show is set—on British politics, class structure, manners, fads, and mores of the time, usually by carrying things to their logically silliest extensions. As with Viennese operetta, the shows have at least two love stories, one romantic and one comic, but even the romantic ones are comic because of the absurd situations the lovers find themselves in.

Among the characters, there are usually people from the nobility, who take themselves far too seriously and bureaucrats who are totally inept; sometimes these two types are embodied in a single character. There are usually couples from different classes who love each other but can't buck society without a convenient plot twist. Unmarried (and usually overweight) middle-aged women frequently appear on the character lists of the shows. Gilbert was uncommonly cruel to them, but he also gave them some of the best songs.

D'Oyly Carte assembled the D'Oyly Carte Opera Company, for which the operettas were written. Gilbert and Sullivan therefore knew the skills and limitations of the performers they were writing for and tailored the roles accordingly. The character types and vocal ranges are almost identical from show to show. The lead comic baritone usually plays a small, middle-aged man and the lead character mezzo a large, middle-aged woman; the lead soprano is always the young love interest, and so is the lead tenor. Most of the performers need light opera voices, though the music isn't as difficult to sing as it is in French and Viennese operettas. The singer/actors also need excellent diction and real comic agility, often physically as well as verbally.

As was also true in other European operettas, Sullivan's music combined classical forms with contemporary song and dance forms. In style, the music ranges from opera parody to ballads to what was then pop. The team excelled at writing **patter songs,** comic songs with several verses (each with many words) and limited vocal requirements in order to amuse with their tongue-twisting verbosity. (Stephen Sondheim's "(I'm Not) Getting Married Today," from *Company,* and Mel Brooks's "The King of Broadway," from *The Producers,* are two more recent examples.) *Iolanthe* has what may be the most difficult of all Gilbert and Sullivan patter songs, "When You're Lying Awake (The Nightmare)." It has an abundance of clever rhymes and gets faster and faster toward the end. (Try saying the lyrics below out loud.) It's often found in poetry anthologies and is clearly a direct ancestor of Broadway lyrics by such masters as Lorenz Hart, Cole Porter, and Stephen Sondheim. The opening recitative is very melodramatically operatic, sung by the Lord Chancellor, who is "very miserable":

> Love, unrequited, robs me of my rest:
> Love, hopeless love, my ardent soul encumbers:
> Love, nightmare-like, lies heavy on my chest,
> And weaves itself into my midnight slumbers!

> When you're lying awake with a dismal headache, and repose is
>   taboo'd by anxiety,
> I conceive you may use any language you choose to indulge in,
>   without impropriety;
> For your brain is on fire—the bedclothes conspire of usual slumber
>   to plunder you:
> First your counterpane goes, and uncovers your toes, and your sheet
>   slips demurely from under you;

> Then the blanketing tickles—you feel like mixed pickles—so terribly
>   sharp is the pricking,
> And you're hot, and you're cross, and you tumble and toss till there's
>   nothing 'twixt you and the ticking.
> Then the bedclothes all creep to the ground in a heap, and you pick
>   them all up in a tangle;
> Next your pillow resigns and politely declines to remain at its usual
>   angle!

> Well, you get some repose in the form of a doze, with hot eyeballs and
>   head ever aching,
> But your slumbering teems with such horrible dreams that you'd very
>   much better be waking;

For you dream you are crossing the Channel, and tossing about in a
  steamer from Harwich—
Which is something between a large bathing machine and a very small
  second-class carriage—
And you're giving a treat (penny ice and cold meat) to a party of
  friends and relations—
They're a ravenous horde—and they all came on board at Sloane
  Square and South Kensington Stations.

And bound on that journey you find your attorney (who started that
  morning from Devon);
He's a bit undersized, and you don't feel surprised when he tells you
  he's only eleven.
Well, you're driving like mad with this singular lad (by the by, the
  ship's now a four-wheeler),
And you're playing round games, and he calls you bad names when
  you tell him that "ties pay the dealer";

But this you can't stand, so you throw up your hand, and you find
  you're as cold as an icicle,
In your shirt and your socks (the black silk with gold clocks), crossing
  Salisbury Plain on a bicycle:

And he and the crew are on bicycles too—which they've somehow or
  other invested in—
And he's telling the stars all the particu*lars* of a company he's
  interested in—
It's a scheme of devices, to get at low prices all goods from cough
  mixtures to cables
(Which tickled the sailors), by treating retailers as though they were
  all vegetables—

You get a good spade man to plant a small tradesman (first take off his
  boots with a boot tree),
And his legs will take root, and his fingers will shoot, and they'll
  blossom and bud like a fruit tree—
From the greengrocer tree you get grapes and green pea, cauliflower,
  pineapple, and cranberries,
While the pastry-cook plant cherry brandy will grant, apple puffs, and
  three-corners, and Banburys—

The shares are a penny, and ever so many are taken by Rothschild and
  Baring,

✦

And just as a few are allotted to you, you awake with a shudder
despairing—

You're a regular wreck, with a crick in your neck, and no wonder you
snore, for your head's on the floor, and you've needles and pins
from your soles to your shins, and your flesh is a-creep, for your left
leg's asleep, and you've cramp in your toes, and a fly on your nose,
and some fluff in your lung, and a feverish tongue, and a thirst
that's intense, and a general sense that you haven't been sleeping
in clover;

But the darkness has passed, and it's daylight at last, and the night has
been long—ditto ditto my song—and thank goodness they're both
of them over!

Sullivan frequently contrasted Gilbert's comic lyrics with lovely melodies,
as in the heroine Yum-Yum's ballad in *The Mikado,* in which she compares herself favorably to the beauties of the sun and the moon. Both men were guilty of
an occasional overdose of sentimentality, common in the Victorian era.

Gilbert's librettos and lyrics were as important to the success of the operettas as was Sullivan's music. Like *The Beggar's Opera,* Gilbert and Sullivan
works still hold up as models of wit, economy, and integration of all elements. (Gilbert was the first writer/lyricist whose name helped sell tickets.)
The shows have maintained their worldwide popularity to the present time,
despite being very Victorian in language and topical references.

Although Gilbert and Sullivan's early shows were successful in England, it
wasn't until their fourth collaboration, *H.M.S. Pinafore, or The Lass That Loved
a Sailor,* in 1878, that they made their first hit in the United States. Productions were immediately done all over the country. Because there were no re-
ciprocal copyright agreements between England and the United States,
several pirated versions were playing before the official D'Oyly Carte production opened in New York in 1879. Furthermore, within five months of the
official U.S. opening, the show had played in almost a dozen theaters in New
York alone. (Gilbert's next libretto featured pirates in the title.) *Pinafore* may
be the single most influential European show in the history of the American
musical, just as *The Merry Widow* was in the history of the American operetta.
It was not just a hit, it was a national craze, as were many of the rest of Gilbert
and Sullivan's works.

Three elements accounted for the universal popularity of *Pinafore*—its wit, its
workmanship, and its accessibility. . . . Words and music alike were written

from the point of view of the audience; they were catchy and easy to learn, and fun to sing at home around a square piano in the evening. From *HMS Pinafore* the American audience began to learn . . . the difference between hack work and first-class professional skill and integrity. (Cecil Smith and Glenn Litton, *Musical Comedy in America*, 41–42)

After *Pinafore*'s huge success, the number of musical evenings on Broadway doubled, and Viennese and French operettas were finally produced in English, further increasing the popularity of the form both in England and in the United States.

Gilbert and Sullivan's repertory includes *Trial by Jury*, their second show and first London hit, which made its debut there in 1875—also the year of its unsuccessful New York debut. It is the team's only one-act, running about thirty minutes, and it's also the only one of their shows with no spoken dialogue, just recitatives and numbers. First performed as a curtain-raiser to Offenbach's *La Périchole*, Gilbert directed it himself, as was the case with all their operettas. A silly satire on the British judicial system and on opera conventions, it's the first of Gilbert and Sullivan's operettas commissioned by D'Oyly Carte, who became both their producer and their partner from then on. With the success of the team's next three shows, D'Oyly Carte was able to build the Savoy.

Their next show, *The Sorcerer*, in two acts, opened in 1877. It satirizes the clergy and the contemporary fad for fortune-tellers and mystics. Gilbert and Sullivan were still not quite up to form, but they were getting there. The original production ran six months, a very long run in those days.

HMS Pinafore, or The Lass That Loved a Sailor, their first huge hit, opened in London in 1878. It had its official (as opposed to pirated) and equally successful New York debut the next year. The tunes from "that infernal nonsense *Pinafore*" (as Gilbert referred to it in a patter song in their next show) were hummed, whistled, played, and sung all over the world. The show is a satire on the British admiralty and its bureaucracy, as well as on the British class system with its concern about who can marry whom. Like many of the other Gilbert and Sullivan operettas, it also satirizes the melodramatic plot twists found in so many Victorian dramas and novels.

The Pirates of Penzance, or The Slave of Duty had its world premiere in the United States on New Year's Eve, 1879, before opening in London immediately afterward. This was done to prevent the copyright infringements and pirated productions so common with *Pinafore*, which had cost Gilbert, Sullivan, and D'Oyly Carte a great deal of lost royalties. Another huge hit, *The Pirates of Penzance* satirizes the police, the army, the House of Lords, and the slightly ridiculous sense of duty so many were claiming to live by in those rather stuffy, hypocritical, imperialistic Victorian days. The score contains what is probably Sullivan's most famous melody, called "Come, Friends, Who Plow the Sea," but known in the United States as the tune to "Hail, Hail, the Gang's All Here." Among many other productions, there was a successful and cleverly camped-up 1981 Broadway revival of the show (772 performances), which had played at Joseph Papp's New York Shakespeare Festival's outdoor theater in Central Park the summer before. Adapted and directed by Wilford Leach, choreographed by Graciela Daniele, and starring Kevin Kline, Linda Ronstadt, George Rose, Rex Smith, and Estelle Parsons, it toured extensively and was filmed in 1983 with Angela Lansbury substituting for Parsons.

Patience, or Bunthorne's Bride, another hit, opened in 1881 and then transferred to the Savoy as the first attraction of the new theater; it premiered in New York the same year. The show is a satire on the extreme romanticism of the day, taking particularly funny pokes at Oscar Wilde and other such aesthetes.

Their next hit, *Iolanthe, or The Peer and the Peri* (1882), was the first of Gilbert and Sullivan's comic operas to premiere at the Savoy. Again, it satirizes the House of Lords, whose members enter singing

> Bow, bow, ye lower middle classes!
> Bow, bow, ye tradesmen, bow, ye masses!

Most of the female characters are fairies. The show pokes fun at class consciousness by having them in love with mortals, which is forbidden in the fairy kingdom. That these mortals are members of the House of Lords, who are in love with the fairies, makes the situation ridiculous.

Princess Ida, or Castle Adamant (1884) is Gilbert and Sullivan's only show in three acts rather than two, and the only one that has dialogue in blank verse (unrhymed lines in iambic pentameter) rather than in prose. Both men felt they were beginning to repeat themselves, and their shows certainly had begun to follow a very set pattern, which they tried to break with this show. A more sensitive issue was that Sullivan wanted to be remembered as a writer of serious compositions and resented being famous only for the comic operas. Gilbert, too, wanted to do more serious work. But the main problem was that the two men did not really like each other and it was starting to affect their working relationship. When *Princess Ida* did not work out for them—it is not one of their better efforts—they returned to their tried-and-true structure.

The Mikado, or The Town of Titipu opened in London in 1885 and in New York the same year, where it ran 250 performances. Although relations between the writing partners were more strained than ever, *The Mikado* is one of their best and most successful shows, probably performed more than any of the others. It's been revived in many forms, including swing and jazz versions. Any resemblance between its characters and real Japanese people is purely makeup and costumes; they're as Victorian English as they could be. The show satirizes both the contemporary British fad for all things Japanese and the exotic locales of most British (and American) musical theater pieces of the time, but, like all Gilbert and Sullivan operettas, it's also an attack on prudery, bureaucracy, pomposity, and self-importance wherever they may be. The D'Oyly Carte production of *The Mikado* was filmed in 1939, when it was still based on Gilbert's fifty-four-year-old staging. With the exception of Kenny Baker as the romantic hero, all the performers were members of the D'Oyly Carte Company at the time. Though it is not very good, the movie serves as a good illustration of the original performance style. Mike Leigh's excellent 1999 film *Topsy-Turvy* is a recounting of the creation of *The Mikado*.

The Yeomen of the Guard, or The Merryman and His Maid (1888, London and New York) is the most serious and operatic of Gilbert and Sullivan's works; it even ends sadly for the central character, a jester.

The Gondoliers, or The King of Barataria (London, 1889; New York, 1890) is Gilbert and Sullivan's last hit, a satire on the then-current rage for turning England into a republic where everyone would be equal. Although barely speaking to each other while working on it—Gilbert was reportedly a very difficult man—they managed to create one of their wittiest, most tuneful, and most ensemble-oriented works. Soon after the opening, the partners broke up for four years, largely because of a fight over the price of a carpet for the Savoy. D'Oyly Carte finally got them back together, and they wrote two more shows, *Utopia, Limited, or The Flower of Progress* in 1893 and *The Grand Duke, or The Statutory Duel* in 1896, both unsuccessful and almost never revived. The partners then broke up for good.

Suggested Watching and Listening

Iolanthe

This Gilbert and Sullivan operetta is available in a two-disc CD format from Angel Records, as well as in several other CD versions. This particular version is conducted by Sir Malcolm Sargent and The Pro Arte Orchestra.
- Recitative, "When You're Lying Awake (The Nightmare)" (performed by George Baker, baritone)

The Pirates of Penzance

The 1983 film of the hit Broadway revival is available on video from Universal Pictures, MCA VHS. There's also a Kultur DVD version of a 1981 live performance of the production in Central Park's Delacorte Theater. Whatever version, I recommend watching the first half of act 1, through "Poor Wandering One," Mabel's parody of a coloratura soprano opera aria.

American Burlesque
and the 1890s

You can pull all the stops out
Till they call the cops out,
Grind your behind till you're banned,
But you gotta get a gimmick
If you wanna get a hand.
—"YOU GOTTA HAVE A GIMMICK,"
GYPSY, LYRICS BY STEPHEN SONDHEIM

In 1840, the United States had fewer than twenty millionaires; by 1880 that figure had grown to well over one hundred. The gulf between rich and poor, educated and uneducated, was widening. Tastes in entertainment were beginning to fragment accordingly. In the 1880s, the popularity of minstrelsy faded, the appeal of spectacle began to wear thin, and the more vaudeville began to depend on raucous immigrant humor, the less it attracted richer, better-educated patrons. They went to opera regularly, to revivals of hit shows like *The Black Crook,* and to more and more British, Viennese, and French operettas. Most Broadway shows were therefore either revivals or imports. (A parallel situation began in the 1980s, when ticket prices had gotten very expensive. Revivals of such earlier Broadway successes as *Guys and Dolls* and *Chicago* and of imported, through-composed, operetta-like extravaganzas like *Cats, The Phantom of the Opera, Les Misérables,* and other long-running, pop-opera, tourist-attraction, and expense-account hits are contemporary and more technically sophisticated versions of the kinds of shows the wealthier audiences of the 1880s would have attended. Of course by 1980, TV, movies, and rock concerts had long since become the entertainments of choice for most Americans, regardless of economic situation or education.)

However, other than vaudeville, the U.S. immigrant population and other poor, less-sophisticated audiences of the 1880s weren't able to find much in the way of entertainment, nor were they able to afford much of what there was. New forms were needed to get them back into theaters.

In 1874, the Women's Christian Temperance Union was formed, Massachusetts made it illegal for women to work more than ten hours a day, and *Die Fledermaus* premiered in Vienna. That same year, American burlesque began with *Evangeline*, music by Edward E. Rice and lyrics and a none-too-coherent book by J. Cheever Goodwin. The two were inspired to write the show, a burlesque of the Longfellow poem, after seeing one of Lydia Thompson's shows, which they found too British in tone and humor. They sold their show as an extravaganza rather than as a burlesque in order to attract the family trade, which was never one of Thompson's goals. *Evangeline* was the first American musical theater work intended as such, unlike the accident that created *The Black Crook* in 1866. It's also the first book for a full-length musical evening written by an American professional and the first original score by a single American composer. As in British burlesque, women played the lead male and most of the other young male characters, and the chorus was dressed in as little as the times allowed. One of the older women was played by an actor in drag, and the heroine was chased by a lovesick whale and danced with a cow, among other plot developments. *Evangeline* was a big hit and, like *The Black Crook,* had tours and updated revivals throughout the rest of that century.

In 1884—the year of Twain's *Huckleberry Finn*—the next successful American musical theater piece was *Adonis,* with music again by Edward E. Rice, lyrics by William Gill, and a book by Gill and Henry E. Dixey, the star of the show. It ran 603 performances in its original New York run, beating *The Black Crook*'s record. It was another Americanized British burlesque; the parody story used the myth of Pygmalion and Galatea to satirize the current New York theater scene. This time, the hero was played by a man. *Adonis* too played around the country for years in tours and revivals, updating the songs and topical jokes to keep up with the times and the performers.

In 1885, Gilbert and Sullivan opened *The Mikado;* Buffalo Bill's Wild West Show signed up Annie Oakley, the first professional woman sharpshooter (heroine of Irving Berlin and Dorothy and Herbert Fields's 1946 musical *Annie Get Your Gun*); and Adah Richmond's Burlesque Combination toured in a show not that different from Lydia Thompson's but different enough to be called the beginning of what we now think of as **American burlesque.** As in *Evangeline* and *Adonis,* there was a parody structure, but Richmond loosened it more and heightened the sexiness of the costumes and dances.

Soon, as other producers imitated the form, the parody story (the burlesque) disappeared, leaving no connecting framework between the acts. The form, as it was first developed by such men as Michael B. Leavitt, emulated the three-act minstrelsy format, this time with girls in a semicircle in the first act. American burlesque soon came to resemble vaudeville, but geared to a working-class male audience looking for something closer to the shows that existed before Tony Pastor cleaned vaudeville up. The new form was a collection of girls, comic sketches based on working-class and immigrant humor, girls, a couple of singers and dancers, girls, inexpensive production numbers, and, by the 1920s, strippers. Early burlesque shows also sometimes included boxing demonstrations.

Unlike vaudeville, where no act returned (except when there was an afterpiece), burlesque used a small company of comedians to do all the comedy scenes, often with characters and scenarios descended straight from commedia dell'arte, with each comic playing his established persona from sketch to sketch. The tenor and the girls also frequently participated in sketches as well as in the musical numbers. (The plotless Broadway revues, most popular in the 1910s and 1920s, though more clearly descended from vaudeville, adopted American burlesque's concept of having performers work together as well as doing their own spots.) There was a standard hierarchy among burlesque comics: **top banana** (usually dressed in baggy pants, as were some of his cohorts), **second banana, third banana,** and straight man. (*Banana* is from a sketch about a man who tries to prove he has three bananas when he has only two and who ends up with no bananas since the other two comics take the first and second ones.)

Although audiences came mainly for the girls—from the beginning they dressed more skimpily and behaved more lasciviously than in vaudeville or British burlesque—the comedy was often memorable, if determinedly blue. Over the years, routines were developed, shared, stolen, and repeated over and over again by burlesque and vaudeville comics around the country. (When done by vaudevillians, the material had to be cleaned up a bit.) Everything was performed straight out, the comics even occasionally going into the audience. (The girls would sometimes move out onto a runway to get closer to the audience—but never so close that they could be easily touched.) Eventually circuits, like vaudeville circuits but known as *wheels*, were set up around the country, and performers were booked by the season. The Minskys were burlesque's most famous producers.

Except for some very seedy leftovers, burlesque was dead by the 1940s—it was banned in New York in the 1930s—and buried in the 1950s by Milton Berle's live, hour-long TV show, a weekly mix of vaudeville acts, cleaned-up burlesque sketches, and Berle as top banana intruding on everything, but with no strippers. In 1979, Mickey Rooney and Ann Miller starred in the revue

Sugar Babies, which had a long run on Broadway followed by years of touring. It was a series of venerable burlesque routines, old songs—mostly by Jimmy McHugh and Dorothy Fields—and dances, with no strippers but with a fan dancer.

Many big stars got their start in burlesque, including Fanny Brice, Eddie Cantor, Red Skelton, Phil Silvers, Jackie Gleason, and Gypsy Rose Lee, whose rise from a kiddie vaudeville act to the most famous of all burlesque strippers is chronicled in the 1959 Jule Styne, Stephen Sondheim, and Arthur Laurents musical *Gypsy.*

During the late 1870s, the same years that saw the rise of Gilbert and Sullivan, a new American form, **farce-comedy,** was, like burlesque, attracting the less-sophisticated audiences. These shows, immediate forerunners of the musical comedy, were extensions of afterpieces but with semblances of an original plot instead of a parody. They were noisy and unstructured, the usually immigrant and minority humor was broad and physical, and the performers had no sense of a fourth wall between themselves and the audience. Farce-comedies were **star vehicles,** which means the talents and desires of the performers dictated shape and much of the content. Unlike operettas and extravaganzas, farce-comedies were set in contemporary, urban, lower-class, and lower-middle-class America, the home of their audiences, with no classical music, exotic locales, ballet dancers, or romance. As in vaudeville, the characters came complete with contemporary American dialects and slang, and the shows were meant as family entertainment. Comedy routines, pop songs, and specialty numbers rarely even pretended to grow out of the slight event that constituted the glue holding the piece together and that was constantly pushed aside or forgotten altogether. The form was patterned on the hugely successful 1823 British import *Tom and Jerry, or Life in London* (which spawned a number of what were called Tom and Jerry shows). In *Tom and Jerry,* a country cousin paid his city cousin a visit, and the two of them went to many places, met many people, and got into trouble wherever they went, but never so badly that the show couldn't stop regularly for songs, dances, specialty numbers, and comedy routines. The first American farce-comedy to make a hit was *The Brook: A Jolly Day at the Picnic,* presented in 1879 by Salsbury's Troubadours.

Edward (Ned) Harrigan (1844–1911, born in New York) and Anthony (Tony) Hart (1855–91, born in Worcester, Massachusetts) were the most popular figures in the development of the farce-comedy. They were Irish American minstrel and vaudeville headliners who'd teamed up in 1871, specializing in pop songs and dances, drag, and dialect comedy—especially Irish, blackface, and German. They were particularly popular with the many Irish Americans who'd moved to the United States because of the potato famine. Harrigan wrote most of the material for their shows, including the song lyrics, which were usually topical. The music, by David Braham (1838–1905, born in England), was invariably serviceable and rarely memorable. Harrigan and Braham (Harrigan's father-in-law) wrote over two hundred songs together. Much later, George M. Cohan, creator of what many consider to be the first successful American musicals, always acknowledged his debt to Harrigan, the creative force behind the team. In tribute, Cohan wrote the song "H-A-Double-R-I-G-A-N Spells Harrigan." (Harrigan was the father-in-law of Joshua Logan, an important director of Broadway and movie musicals during the golden age.)

Harrigan and Hart's first farce-comedy was developed from a vaudeville afterpiece. In 1875 the team had success with an extended Irish dialect afterpiece called *The Donovans*. It was about a search for a kidnapped child, which took the characters to many locations. Hart, who specialized in drag, played Mrs. Donovan. In 1876, having taken over managing the Theatre Comique in New York, they began developing their farce-comedies, building off what they had done in *The Donovans*.

In 1877—the year of the first Bell telephone and the first hand-cranked phonograph—Harrigan, Hart, and Braham created an extended sketch, *Old Lavender*, which was the first to use their Irish American characters, the Mulligan Guard, who reappeared in most of their shows from then on. *Old Lavender* was in one act, preceded by an act of vaudeville, as was *The Mulligan Guard's Picnic*, presented in 1878. Then, in 1879—the year *H.M.S. Pinafore* and *The Pirates of Penzance* arrived in New York—Harrigan and Hart produced the first of their two-act farce-comedies, *The Mulligan Guard's Ball*. During its four-month run, it was preceded by an act of vaudeville that changed every week. Their other 1879 shows were *The Mulligan Guard's Chowder* and *The Mulligan Guard's Christmas*. The bits and pieces that made up the bulk of these shows were strung onto an event such as a picnic, a dance, a boat trip, or a party. Harrigan always played an Irish character; Hart played several different ethnic characters in each show, many in drag or blackface. The songs were very contemporary and very American.

These shows weren't big on production values but focused rather on slapstick immigrant and minority humor, frequently centering on violent confrontations between Irish Americans and African Americans, with the Irish always coming out on top.

Harrigan broke up the act in 1885 because Hart's substance abuses had gotten the better of him. Harrigan and Braham continued doing some new shows but mostly revived old ones. Hart went into other people's shows but soon was in such bad shape he could no longer perform. By then farce-comedies were beginning to repeat themselves, and audiences were beginning to lose interest.

A major contributor to farce-comedy as it neared the end of its popularity was book and lyric writer Charles Hoyt. His biggest hit, *A Trip to Chinatown* (1890), with music by Percy Gaunt, is one of the last successes the form ever had. Two songs introduced in the show—"The Bowery" and "Reuben, Reuben (I've Been Thinking)"—were big hits that remained popular well into the twentieth century. As with many shows of the 1890s, *A Trip to Chinatown* played for a short time on Broadway, went on a national tour for a year, then reopened in New York in 1891 for a 657-performance run, Broadway's longest until *Irene* in 1919. It was revived on Broadway in 1894 and by Ziegfeld in 1908. A few other shows, such as *The Black Crook* and *Adonis*, returned even more frequently.

Backdrop: 1893–1900

National In 1893—the year of Chicago's Columbian Exposition—the U.S. stock market collapses and doesn't begin to recover until the Spanish-American War in 1898. Business and labor are increasingly at odds. Hundreds of workers go on strike in 1894 alone. The U.S. Supreme Court upholds racial segregation in 1896, the same year African American poet Paul Laurence Dunbar publishes *Lyrics of a Lowly Life*. As it becomes steadily more difficult for blacks to vote in Southern states, there are many race riots and lynchings. In 1900, Booker T. Washington publishes *Up from Slavery,* and Carry Moore Nation begins using a hatchet on saloons.

International America is establishing itself as a world power. In 1897, it annexes Hawaii. In 1898, the U.S. battleship *Maine* is blown up in Havana Harbor, escalating into the Spanish-American War, at the end of which Spain gives Cuba its independence and turns over Puerto Rico, Guam, and the Philippines to the United States. European empires are crumbling, Asian countries are getting stronger, and African countries are being exploited.

New Developments Science and industry make remarkable progress. The first open-heart surgery is performed, and Henry Ford road tests his first automobile. (By the end of the decade, U.S. auto production is up to 2,500 a year.) Marie and Pierre Curie isolate radium, the first radioactive element; Sigmund Freud publishes *The Interpretation of Dreams;* the mosquito carrying yellow fever is identified; and the compound for aspirin is perfected. The U.S. College Entrance Examination Board writes the first SATs. Products such as Tootsie Rolls, Cracker Jack, Jell-O, Michelob beer, and Pepsi-Cola are introduced in the United States, and the companies Dow Chemical and Goodyear are founded.

Tin Pan Alley

Joan Morris, in the insert to *After the Ball plus Highlights from Vaudeville*, writes:

> In 1892 Charles K. Harris wrote a ballad entitled "After the Ball," and its publication marked the beginning of popular music as big business in America. There had been hits before this—Stephen Foster's "Old Folks at Home" . . . had reached a sale of 130,000 copies. . . . "After the Ball" caused an earthquake by selling five million copies, and the music business in America would never again be the same. Suddenly it dawned on music-men that songs could

Pop Culture Popular songs include Maude Nugent's "Sweet Rosie O'Grady," the first song written by a woman to sell a million copies; Metz and Hayden's "There'll Be a Hot Time in the Old Town Tonight" and Black and Purvis's "When the Saints Go Marching In" (composers are always listed before lyricists). In 1896, Benjamin Robertson Harney introduces African American ragtime music to white America at Tony Pastor's in New York; its popularity is spread by other white vaudeville performers. The earliest published rag, "Mississippi Rag," in 1897, is by William H. Krell, also white. It's followed by Tom Turpin's "Harlem Rag," the first published rag by an African American. In 1899, the publication of "Original Rags" introduces the public to Scott Joplin, another African American, and the best and most famous of all ragtime composers; his "Maple Leaf Rag" soon follows.

Stage In 1894, stagehands form the first trade union in the entertainment industry, the show-business magazine *Billboard* begins publishing, and the first public striptease takes place in Paris. Russian playwright Anton Chekhov's *The Sea Gull* has its unsuccessful premiere, and French playwright Alfred Jarry's *Ubu Roi* has its scabrous and scandalous one. Konstantin Stanislavsky forms the Moscow Art Theater and directs a successful revival of *The Sea Gull;* he uses his methods for more realistic acting, establishing, among other things, the concept of the fourth wall between actors and audience. Puccini's *La Bohème* is produced. *The Grand Duke, or The Statutory Duel* is Gilbert and Sullivan's final collaboration, a flop. Sullivan dies in 1900. In that same year, Victor Herbert becomes conductor of the Pittsburgh Symphony Orchestra; *Florodora* opens in New York; and the United Booking Office, led by B. F. Keith, begins organizing vaudeville bookings around the country. (Eventually known as the Keith–Albee circuit, it's competitive with the Syndicate's circuit.)

Screen Motion pictures have their first public showing in America. A cathode ray tube invented in Germany begins the development of television.

be marketed . . . , and this realization led to the vast merchandising machinery of the 1890s sheet-music trade. . . . [A] song could be presented in many different contexts: as part of a minstrel show; played by the house orchestra in a restaurant, beer hall, resort, or dance hall; used in a vaudeville spot; or inserted in a current musical comedy.

Like many vaudeville and English music hall songs of the time, "After the Ball" tells its sad story of love betrayed in three long verses with a shorter chorus—a slow waltz in an ABA′C structure—repeated after each verse. (The verse of a song has no standard length. It serves a function similar to a recitative in opera and operetta; its lyrics set up what the song is about. Also, as in a recitative, the music of the verse sounds more conversational than the music of the chorus, helping the transition from spoken dialogue to song. The music of the verse isn't used in the chorus.) Soon after it was published, "After the Ball" was interpolated into *A Trip to Chinatown*. It was also used in Kern and Hammerstein's 1927 *Show Boat* as the song that makes its heroine a star.

Starting in the 1890s, the heart of the sheet-music business was located at Twenty-eighth Street between Broadway and Eighth Avenue in Manhattan, where most of the song publishers had their offices. In 1903—so one of the stories goes—the block got nicknamed Tin Pan Alley when songwriter/publisher Harry von Tilzer, having been asked by a reporter why his piano sounded so strange, explained that he had stuffed newspapers in it to muffle the sound from other tenants of the building, which made it sound a bit like a tin pan. On Tin Pan Alley, each publisher's office had small rooms where pianists (called **song pluggers**) could noisily peddle (plug) the company's wares to performers, producers, and anyone else who might be looking for new material. The customers would go from office to office until they found the song they wanted. When a star or a show picked up a song, that fact got featured on the cover of the sheet music to help promote it all over the country, especially for home use around the parlor piano. The Alley was a place where composers like Jerome Kern and George Gershwin got their starts as song pluggers, playing the publisher's new songs for potential customers and gradually adding their own early compositions to the mix. In the early twentieth century, the music of Broadway became vitally important to the Alley when pop hits were getting written for musicals and revues and not always directly for the publishers.

In 1894, George Edwardes's Gaiety Theatre Company came from London with its latest show, *A Gaiety Girl*, music by Sydney Jones, lyrics by Harry Greenbank, and libretto by Owen Hall. The company had first played New York successfully in 1888 and 1889 with British burlesques, which included the requisite large number of beautiful girls but which, though still parodies, differed from other burlesques in that the dialogue felt more contemporary; for one thing, it was in prose instead of rhyming couplets. However, *A Gaiety Girl* wasn't a British burlesque; it was billed as a musical comedy—a first. It resembled operetta in that, rather than being a parody, it told an original story—a slight one about a Gaiety chorus girl falsely accused of theft while a guest at a society party. One of the wealthy and handsome young men at the party falls in love with her at first sight, helps clear her name, and marries her. As in operettas, the musical numbers and comedy were fairly well connected to the story, though with room for some interpolated songs, comedy bits, and specialty numbers.

The resemblance to operetta was, however, less important to the show's success than were its differences. The tone was light and sophisticated, the characters young and attractive, the look and language contemporary (though British), and the songs and dances up-to-the-minute in style and sound. And there were the Gaiety Girls, perhaps the strongest reason for the show's success. They became the rage of New York, their behavior and clothing copied, their favors sought by young and old alike. (Men waiting at the stage door after the show were called stage-door Johnnies.) *A Gaiety Girl* was soon widely imitated; in particular, chorus girls more than ever became a large part of the mix that made up a musical evening. The earliest American musicals were mostly a combination of *A Gaiety Girl*'s contemporary story with the farce-comedy's more raucous, American style and sound.

Several more shows like *A Gaiety Girl* were imported during the rest of the 1890s. The most influential, brought over in 1900, was the musical comedy *Florodora*, with music by Leslie Stuart; lyrics by Stuart, Ernest Boyd-Jones, and Paul Rubens; and a book again by Owen Hall. It ran 505 performances before going on tour. Apparently the main reason for the show's success was the six Florodora Girls, along with a song sung by them and six gentlemen, beginning "Tell me, pretty maiden, are there any more at home like you?", which quickly became a hit song and a national catchphrase. The six perfectly matched women weighed 130 pounds each—slim for the time—and were all five feet four inches tall, long-waisted, and either brunettes or redheads. (There were crowds of stage-door Johnnies, and three of the women ended up marrying wealthy and influential men, hardly acceptable in high society till then.) Set mostly on Florodora, a mythical South Seas island where women wear grass skirts, the show started a fad for entertainments with similarly exotic locales and costumes.

The year 1894 saw two other important American musical theater firsts: the first operetta by Victor Herbert and the first revue. *Prince Ananias*

(55 performances), with lyrics and libretto by Francis Neilson, is an operetta with a long and clunky script set in sixteenth-century France. It was the Irish American composer Victor Herbert's first show. Already established as a classical music composer, he demanded and got an agreement with his producer that no changes could be made in the libretto or music without his consent—a contract condition for the rest of his career that effectively prevented interpolations by other composers and set a standard for Broadway composers that eventually became the rule. During the rest of the 1890s, Herbert wrote scores for seven more operettas and a farce-comedy. As we'll soon see, he eventually set a new standard for the American operetta with his 1910 *Naughty Marietta*.

The Passing Show (145 performances) had music by Ludwig Englander with sketches and lyrics by Sydney Rosenfeld, and was produced by George Lederer. It was the first American revue, patterned on an elaborate vaudeville form popular in Paris. (Spelled *review* at the time; the French spelling *revue* was soon preferred, since it was fancier.) Advertised as a "topical extravaganza" with a cast of one hundred, it was basically storyless, although it had a theme of satirizing events of the preceding year that tied the various elements together. The show had a respectable run, but the revue form didn't catch on till several years later, when Florenz Ziegfeld popularized both it and its French spelling. After Ziegfeld's success, the Shuberts, between 1912 and 1924, produced twelve editions of a revue they called *The Passing Show*, borrowing the title from the 1894 original.

In 1896, Florenz Ziegfeld produced his first Broadway show, a revival of Charles H. Hoyt's 1884 farce-comedy *A Parlor Match*. To star in it, he imported the celebrated French singer/dancer/comedienne Anna Held, whom he married, apparently never legally.

During the summer of 1896, a group of powerful New York producers, owners of vaudeville and legitimate theaters around the country, had a meeting.

The future members of the Theatrical Syndicate—Hayman and Frohman, Klaw and Erlanger, Nixon and Zimmerman—were quietly meeting to hammer out an official agreement. On August 1, they signed a secret agreement pooling their resources

Joseph Weber (1867–1942, born in New York) and **Lew Fields** (1867–1941, also born in New York), one of the most successful comic teams in vaudeville, created the burlesque-extravaganza. Weber was the tall, thin straight man, Fields the short, fat comic; both wore checked clothes, flat derbies, and whiskers on their chins. The team broke up in 1904; by then Weber had stopped talking to Fields. Fields became a successful Broadway star and producer of musical comedies. (His children, Herbert, Dorothy, and Joseph, also made significant contributions to the musical.) Weber continued producing and starring in burlesque-extravaganzas until 1907, when, like Fields, he began producing musical comedies, though less successfully than his former partner. The men revived their act in 1912 for 108 performances, then continued their separate ways.

and establishing an exclusive booking exchange for first-class theaters across the country. (Fields and Fields, 123)

The Orpheum circuit began operations the next year; it was the first of the competitive and very cutthroat vaudeville circuits to be set up. Performers were booked to tour the country by the season on one circuit and one circuit only. This soon also became true for touring legitimate and musical shows. It was the beginning of control of theaters across the country and of what was in them by what is known as **the Syndicate.** Within ten years, the control was nearly complete.

By the end of the century, public interest in both farce-comedy and operetta was basically dead in the United States. Farce-comedies were replaced in popularity in the mid-1890s by a new form that was appreciated by a wider audience, including, eventually, the carriage trade. The form was known as the **burlesque-extravaganza.**

Weber and Fields developed the burlesque-extravaganza on the road and brought it to New York in 1896, when they opened their Broadway Music Hall, which seated 665 people for a top ticket price of $2. The form was a family-friendly combination of farce-comedy, vaudeville, British burlesque, and extravaganza, most of the elements that soon recombined into early musicals and revues.

Weber and Fields had been performing lower-class immigrant humor in broad "Dutch" accents, touring the country with their own handpicked vaudeville company. Along with their jokes, they were known for violent physical comedy, like Laurel and Hardy, the Three Stooges, and Abbott and Costello after them. They were the first to throw a custard pie in someone's face for a laugh and the inventors of the gag "Who was that lady I saw you with last night?" (Response: "That was no lady. She was my wife.")

While Weber and Fields were developing the burlesque-extravaganza, the first half of the bill was straight vaudeville using the entire company, as had been the case with Harrigan and Hart's first farce-comedies. The other half was a parody of some popular new show, longer than an afterpiece, but shorter than full-length farce-comedies or British burlesques, with extravagant production values, other stars along with Weber and Fields, and, of course, girls. The first half soon became a parody as well,

Julian Mitchell (1854–1926, born in Long Branch, New Jersey) staged the original production of *A Trip to Chinatown* and later directed some of George M. Cohan's shows and some *Ziegfeld Follies.* He always made sure dances were well rehearsed—not always the case in those days—a practice he continued throughout his career, influencing other choreographers to do the same. Mitchell was deaf.

Lillian Russell (1861–1922, born Helen Louise Leonard in Clinton, Iowa) was a soprano introduced by Tony Pastor in 1880. Russell was soon too classy for vaudeville and left it to become a major Broadway star, beginning with Gilbert and Sullivan's *Patience*. She remained a star for over twenty years, as well known for her beauty, charm, and hourglass figure as for her singing voice and her serious approach to her work (though not, apparently, as much for her acting ability). The first American woman to become a superstar, she was the darling of the carriage trade, one of the reasons they began coming to Weber and Fields's burlesque-extravaganzas.

Harry B. Smith (1860–1936, born in Brooklyn) wrote all or part of 123 shows—operas, operettas, musicals, and revues—with many composers, including Jerome Kern and Irving Berlin. He was far more prolific than talented. Victor Herbert wrote thirteen shows with him, none of them likely to be revived.

discarding the opening act of vaudeville altogether, and the two halves were connected by a very loose parody plot. Julian Mitchell, who became the director/choreographer for Weber and Fields in 1897, even tried to integrate the dances.

Burlesque-extravaganzas could be considered the first American musical comedies, except that the scripts were parodies. Including both new shows and revivals, Weber and Fields usually opened three or four shows a year. *Whirl-i-gig* was the first full-length burlesque-extravaganza. Other titles included *Twirly Whirly* and *Fiddle-Dee-Dee*. Among Weber and Fields's costars in all three shows was Lillian Russell.

In 1898, theater tickets cost fifty cents to two dollars; vaudeville tickets cost twenty-five cents on average.

Clorindy, or The Origin of the Cakewalk, music by Will Marion Cook, book and lyrics by Paul Laurence Dunbar, and produced by Edward E. Rice, was an extended afterpiece and the first successful, African American musical theater work on Broadway. It ran on the roof garden of the Casino for most of the summer.

The Fortune Teller (40 performances), music by Victor Herbert, lyrics and libretto by Harry B. Smith, with Julian Mitchell as the director/choreographer, was the first Herbert operetta to put songs into what would become the standard American operetta repertory. Both numbers that endured, "Gypsy Love Song" and "Romany Life," are pseudo-Gypsy music, heavy with trilling sopranos. The leading woman played a fortune-teller and her look-alike. The show did its scheduled run on Broadway, then toured extensively. Herbert's music got generally good reviews, but Smith's book did not.

At the start of the twentieth century, scientific understanding of human history and the universe continued to develop and grow. As a result, traditional beliefs in all areas of human life were being questioned and doubted as never before. Music, theater, dance, painting, and the other fine arts were therefore also going through many changes, breaking old forms and rules to reflect these new ways of seeing the world. To people looking for what was new to go with the new century, more and more often vital young America seemed to be the answer. This vitality was evident in the world of musical entertainment, and Europe, in particular, was beginning to take notice. With the additions to the New York scene of Tin Pan Alley, the Gaiety musical comedies, and Weber and Fields's burlesque-extravaganzas, all the elements were in place that went into the simultaneous development of three musical theater forms: American versions of the musical comedy, the operetta, and the revue.

Suggested Watching and Listening

After the Ball plus Highlights from Vaudeville: Tin Pan Alley
The following is from Joan Morris and William Bolcom's Elektra/Nonesuch CD.
- "After the Ball" (vocals performed by Joan Morris with William Bolcom on the piano, and music and lyrics by Charles K. Harris)

The Great Ziegfeld
Robert Z. Leonard's 1936 movie, *The Great Ziegfeld* (available on Warner Brothers DVD), is a semifictional biography of the famed Broadway producer.
- "Florenz Ziegfeld Discovers Fanny Brice" (performed by William Powell, Virginia Bruce, and Fanny Brice): The sequence attempts to re-create the early twentieth-century burlesque show in which Jewish dialect comedienne Fanny Brice (cast as herself) was discovered by Ziegfeld. Her number, performed in the very broad style of burlesque, begins in front of the front drop (in 1). The curtain then opens to reveal another drop so that the introduction of the bored and overripe chorus girls is in 2. That drop opens to full stage for the end of the number.

Gypsy
This 1959 show is the story of Gypsy Rose Lee's career from vaudeville to burlesque, pushed along by Rose, the ultimate stage mother.
- Opening credits, backstage, "You Gotta Have a Gimmick" (performed by Christine Ebersole, Anna McNeely, and Linda Hart): In Emile Ardolino's 1993 TV version, with a re-creation of Jerome Robbins's original choreography (available on Artisan Home Entertainment DVD), the credit sequence includes a montage of real vaudeville and burlesque shows, with some shots of Gypsy Rose Lee herself. In act 2 of *Gypsy*, Rose's not-very-talented vaudeville act, fronted by her not-very-talented daughter Louise, accidentally gets booked into a flea-bitten burlesque house where Louise gets a new career as Gypsy Rose Lee. Three strippers tell her how to go about doing it with a gimmick.
- "Let Me Entertain You" (performed by Cynthia Gibb): Through a montage sequence, the show traces Gypsy's rise to fame from her first tentative appearance to her star appearances at Minsky's in New York. (She never took it all off, leaving on at least her pasties and G-string. What made her really different from other strippers was that she was elegant, smart, and funny.) By the time Gypsy uses "Let Me Entertain You" in this montage, we've heard it several times sung in a children's vaudeville act. Just as Louise is transformed into a star stripper, the song, without changing the notes or lyrics, is transformed into a stripper's number by changing the beat and the interpretation.

PART TWO

Early American Musical Comedies, Operettas, and Revues, 1901–1924

Overleaf: (*left*) *The Ziegfeld Follies* on Broadway; (*right*) Fanny Brice (1936)

George M. Cohan, Victor Herbert, and Florenz Ziegfeld Jr.

Give my regards to Broadway,
Remember me to Herald Square.
Tell all the gang on 42nd Street
That I will soon be there.
—"GIVE MY REGARDS TO BROADWAY,"
LITTLE JOHNNY JONES, LYRICS BY GEORGE M. COHAN

During the first two decades of the twentieth century, vaudeville was in its heyday, burlesque was continuing on its lewd and merry way, and Broadway was establishing itself as the hub of the American theater world. By the twenties, seeing a Broadway show in New York or on tour was one of the most popular things to do for an evening's entertainment no matter what your taste—unless you were poor or a member of a racial minority. (Until the twenties, African Americans were segregated to the balconies of "white" New York theaters.) Although extravaganzas still attracted anyone who could afford tickets, the English musical comedy, which had drawn both upper- and middle-class audiences, was losing steam, like the European operetta and the burlesque-extravaganza, and the minstrel show and farce-comedy were just about dead. There were, however, three new forms bringing customers back into Broadway theaters: American musical comedy, which appealed mostly to the burgeoning middle class; American operetta, which appealed mostly to the carriage trade; and revue, which appealed to both.

Early American Musical Comedies

Early American musical comedies got their light-headed tones from British musical comedies like *A Gaiety Girl* and from all the earlier American forms, such as minstrelsy, vaudeville, farce-comedies, burlesque-extravaganzas, and even American burlesque. Though meant mainly as middle-class entertainments, they had some appeal to upper- and lower-class audiences as well.

Not until Jerome Kern and Guy Bolton began writing their Princess musicals in 1915 did the musical comedy even start to have a real structure. Before that, dramatic coherence wasn't considered important; the shows were almost uniformly self-indulgent and shapeless. They were usually star vehicles to such an extent that, even after a show had opened, if a star found a new song in Tin Pan Alley, a new dance from vaudeville, a new routine, or a new joke, it could easily end up interpolated into the show that night, no matter how it got shoved in (a practice going back at least as far as Lillian Russell). As late as the 1920s, Al Jolson would often stop midway through the second act, tell the audience the rest of the plot, and then sing songs for an hour or so instead of finishing the show. He was adored by his audiences and hated by most of his colleagues. (In the 1996 revival of *Damn Yankees,* Jerry Lewis, who'd replaced Victor Garber as Mr. Applegate, the devil, stopped the show halfway through the second act to do an out-of-character, out-of-context, five-minute stand-up routine, which he continued doing during the entire post-Broadway tour. Some things in the history of the musical have never changed.)

The major exceptions to the semiformless early musicals were those by George M(ichael) Cohan (1878–1942), who was born on July 3 in Providence, Rhode Island, while his parents were on a vaudeville tour. He moved his birth date one day forward so he could be, as he put it in his song, "The Yankee Doodle Boy" from *Little Johnny Jones:*

> A Yankee Doodle do or die,
> A real live nephew of my Uncle Sam,
> Born on the Fourth of July.

Cohan joined his father, mother, and sister in their vaudeville act when he was three and soon became a star. By age fifteen, he was writing for the act. In 1901, he wrote the book, lyrics, and music for his first Broadway show, *The Governor's Son,* which he and his family starred in, followed by *Running for Office* in 1903. Expansions of the family's vaudeville sketches, both were flops, though successful on the road. In 1904, Cohan had his first hit, *Little Johnny Jones,* establishing him as a major force on Broadway; along with writing and starring in it with his family, he directed it. Eventually he also coproduced his and other people's shows. He composed most of his songs using the four chords he could play on the piano's black keys.

Little Johnny Jones (52 performances, followed by an extended tour) was billed as a musical play and, in publicity, a play with music. The show is a sentimental, melodramatic, star-powered story about a cocky, young, Irish American, working-class jockey who goes to England, where he's accused of throwing the English Derby. Once cleared of the charges at the end of act 2, he has to rescue his kidnapped fiancée in act 3. The plot is told in a lot of dialogue and, occasionally, in recitative. Most of the songs can be pulled out of context, although some of them help establish character and location. The show kept away from interpolated songs and extraneous comedy routines; laughs were incidental and came from character and situation—also true of the rest of Cohan's musicals. (The dances in his shows had little or no dramatic relevance.)

Cohan was in many ways the father of the American musical. In the years after *Little Johnny Jones,* he had many more successes—revues as well as musicals, once revues had become popular. His musicals had coherently structured scripts with contemporary American songs and dances, characters, sentiments, and language, including slang. By bringing his Irish American heritage and cocky, tough, down-to-earth vaudeville personality to Broadway, Cohan appealed to a broader audience than had been going to operettas and English musical comedies. His shows were, in fact, usually more popular on the road than on Broadway since critical standards were tougher in New York than in most other cities across the nation. (This was before Broadway was as much of a tourist draw as it later became.)

Cohan's most successful songs were usually either Irish or patriotic in flavor. As his career progressed, so did the intensity of his flag-waving, showing up at least as early as *Little Johnny Jones,* in which he first introduced himself as a "Yankee Doodle Dandy," and reaching a peak two years later in *George Washington, Jr.* with the song "You're a Grand Old Flag." Both songs are still favorites at patriotic events all over the country. (His zealous World War I march "Over There" was even recorded by opera star Enrico Caruso, singing in a nearly impenetrable Italian accent, and was popular again during World War II.) Oscar Hammerstein said:

Never was a plant more indigenous to a particular part of the earth than was George M. Cohan to the United States of his day. The whole nation was confident of its superiority, its moral virtue, its happy isolation from the intrigues of the "old country," from which many of our fathers and grandfathers had migrated.(Ken Bloom, *Broadway: An Encyclopedic Guide to the History, People, and Places of Times Square,* 70)

Unfortunately, Cohan didn't want to change with the times, wasn't interested in improvements being made in the form, and hated rag and jazz, so he began losing younger audiences after 1911, when rag started making inroads into young white America's listening and dancing preferences. He was also against the Actors' Equity union formed in 1913 and refused to join, making him the foe of many of his fellow theater people. (In all disputes he considered himself a producer and took management's side.) He was granted a waiver out of respect for his contributions to Broadway and was allowed to continue appearing in otherwise union shows.

From 1911 on, Cohan wrote and appeared in fewer musicals, concentrating more on producing and directing them and on writing and acting in straight plays and occasional revues. He also acted in shows by others, including creating the role of the father in Eugene O'Neill's only comedy, *Ah, Wilderness!* He came out of retirement in 1937 for his last successful stage appearance—Richard Rodgers, Lorenz Hart, George S. Kaufman, and Moss Hart's musical satire *I'd Rather Be Right,* in which he played President Franklin Roosevelt, whom Cohan, as a good Republican, hated.

Cohan is remembered chiefly because of the Hollywood biography. But because his shows are largely forgotten, he is never considered with the other giants of musical comedy. . . . Cohan's output is enormous and was very influential at the time. He wrote some of our most enduring standards and his melodies are as catchy and tuneful as any. (Ken Bloom, *American Song: The Complete Musical Theatre Companion* [1900–1984], 413)

James Cagney played Cohan in Curtiz's 1942 Hollywood biography *Yankee Doodle Dandy,* costarring Joan Leslie as his wife and Walter Huston as his father. In 1968, Joel Grey starred with Bernadette Peters in the Broadway musical biography *George M!* with book by the Pascals and Michael Stewart, directed and choreographed by Joe Layton. Cohan songs serve as the scores for both the movie and the stage show.

American Operettas

The enormously successful American premieres of *The Merry Widow* in 1907 and *The Chocolate Soldier* in 1909 revived the popularity of the operetta and led to the premiere of Victor Herbert and Rida Johnson Young's American operetta *Naughty Marietta* in 1910. After that, wealthier and better educated audiences began regularly attending expensively produced American operettas, often referred to as "light operas," which were more romantic and far less satiric than Gilbert and Sullivan's works and lighter musically than their Viennese counterparts. The plots tended to be stock tales of brave heroes and beautiful heroines encountering romance and adventure in exotic and/or historical settings. There was always a contrasting subplot, and plots were dealt with as economically as possible in dialogue and recitative, leaving plenty of room for expanded musical numbers.

The music sounded as if it could have been written in Europe; in fact, European expatriates trained as classical musicians were most often the composers. Although the music, the performers, and the occasional spectacle drew in audiences, it was the libretto that was written first for American operettas, as for their European counterparts. In the best of these works (many of them with books by Otto Harbach and/or Oscar Hammerstein II), story, music, comedy, spectacle, and even some of the occasional dances were integrated into a fairly coherent whole, once you accepted the often silly and melodramatic plots and the often corny comedy scenes.

Herbert's music had such diverse influences as Offenbach, Viennese operetta, Gilbert and Sullivan, and some of the pre-jazz, American-pop, song-and-dance forms of the time. Herbert often added songs to other composers' shows even though he didn't allow anyone else's into his. Although he composed shows in many styles, only his operettas are still occasionally revived. When they are, the plots seem preposterous, and the dialogue sounds extremely stilted and banal. The librettos of most operettas—and the books of most musicals, particularly before Rodgers and Hammerstein—were written by craftsmen with assorted levels of competence and little originality; their work was often no better than functional. Music was the most important element in all Herbert's shows; even when new, the shows clearly had better music than their scripts and lyrics deserved. (Some feel the same is true of Andrew Lloyd Webber's shows.) Many of Herbert's songs became non-jazz standards, still occasionally sung on recital programs.

Andrew Stone's 1939 Hollywood pseudo-biography *The Great Victor Herbert* features twenty-eight Herbert songs. The plot has to do with a totally fictional and mildly tempestuous romance between characters played by Allan Jones and Mary Martin; Walter

Victor Herbert (1859–1924, born in Dublin, Ireland) came to America in 1886 to play cello in the Metropolitan Opera Orchestra. He became a highly respected conductor and composer of classical music, including two operas. However, he's remembered best for songs from some of his forty-four shows and as the first important composer of American operettas. Starting with *Prince Ananias* in 1894, Herbert wrote operettas, extravaganzas, musical comedies, farce-comedies, vaudeville shows, and revues. Along with *Naughty Marietta*, among his most successful shows were *Babes in Toyland* (1903), *The Red Mill* (1906), and *Sweethearts* (1913). Herbert was active in the forming of ASCAP—the American Society of Composers and Publishers—and helped with the Supreme Court case that gave writers the right to royalties for performances of their songs.

Rida Johnson Young (1869–1926, born in Baltimore, Maryland), one of the first important women in American musical theater, sometimes wrote the books of her shows, sometimes the lyrics, sometimes both. She also wrote lyrics for several popular songs, including "Mother Machree," a ballad beloved by Irish tenors for decades. *Naughty Marietta* was her first big Broadway hit.

Connolly plays the rather avuncular Herbert, who solves their problems for them.

Naughty Marietta (136 performances)—music by Herbert, lyrics and libretto by Rida Johnson Young, produced by Oscar Hammerstein I—is the model for most of the successful American operettas that followed it. Its key features include a romantic plot, a comic subplot, adventure and heroism, faith in democracy, an exotic historical setting—French colonial Louisiana—and a runaway princess in disguise. Although written with opera singers in mind for the leads, the lyrics are more colloquially American, the rhythms jauntier than those in European scores of the same period. The hero and heroine are in an adversarial relationship from the beginning: she's an arrogant aristocrat, he a chauvinist democrat. Soon they realize they've been falling in love all along. Their relationship is like that of Laurey and Curly in *Oklahoma!* (The cliché is usually either love at first sight or antagonism at first sight that leads to love. Miranda and Ferdinand in Shakespeare's *The Tempest* and Beatrice and Benedick in *Much Ado About Nothing* are among the many prototypes of these two patterns.) As always in American operettas—and in Rodgers and Hammerstein's musical plays—a strong belief in democratic values is at the heart of the show.

W. S. Van Dyke II's 1935 MGM version of *Naughty Marietta* rewrote the story, making it even worse, as was usual when operettas were adapted to Hollywood. For one thing, in order to shorten the shows, the films usually dispensed with the comic subplot, leaving too little relief from the romantic and often melodramatic main plot. This obliged the writers to give the main plot more humor, and they ended up rewriting nearly everything, usually changing without improving, and leaving out big chunks of the score in the process, including most, if not all, of the ensemble and chorus numbers. *Naughty Marietta* was the first movie to costar Jeanette MacDonald and Nelson Eddy in what became a financially successful series of movie operettas during the rest of the decade. MacDonald, already a star, and Eddy, a newcomer, became almost as popular a box-office team as Ginger Rogers and Fred Astaire, appealing in part to the same audience in a time when pop culture was not so fractured.

Although younger people found the American operetta form attractive at first, many of them soon grew weary of its rather old-world music and unbelievable plots, which diminished the possibility of building new audiences once the older ones started dying out. Operetta's popularity began fading in the twenties as jazz took over Broadway and pop music; by the early thirties, the form was becoming a commercial risk. It eventually faded away into tacky road shows and is now seen only in occasional revivals by opera, light opera, and operetta companies. But the form didn't die. It's been revived in various guises, with more contemporary sounds, believable situations, and naturalistic characters. It's the form not only of Rodgers and Hammerstein's shows but also of Lerner and Loewe's, Lloyd Webber's, and Schönberg and Boublil's, to name a few of its later proponents. Most of their shows even take place in the past and/or in exotic locales, like Rodgers and Hammerstein's Bali Ha'i in *South Pacific* and nineteenth-century Siam in *The King and I,* Lerner and Loewe's *Camelot* and *Brigadoon,* and the nineteenth-century Paris of *The Phantom of the Opera* and *Les Misérables*. We no longer call them operettas, however, so the term itself has dropped out of fashion.

Revues

Revues were a series of production numbers, songs, specialty acts, and comedy sketches and routines, all driven by the producer on the strength of his stars, composers, designers, writers, and chorus girls (not necessarily in that order). Revues were far more sophisticated and expensively produced than vaudeville, and performers reappeared several times during the evening as in American burlesque, giving revues a stronger sense of structure than vaudeville had. The biggest difference between revues and the early musicals was that musicals occasionally, if somewhat unwillingly, stopped for the story. The earliest revues usually had, at most, a couple of characters who moved from place to place as in farce-comedies, very loosely tying the individual scenes and numbers together. The first of Ziegfeld's *Follies,* for example, had as its glue Pocahontas and Captain John Smith being introduced to present-day America. Soon, however, revues didn't even have continuing characters; once in a while a theme might tie the pieces together, but rarely even that.

Florenz Ziegfeld

Although the first American revue was *The Passing Show* in 1894, the form didn't really become commercially viable until Florenz Ziegfeld established his *Ziegfeld Follies* in 1907. Ziegfeld didn't actually add his name to the show's title until 1911 and even later added the motto "Glorifying the American

Girl" and a theme song, Irving Berlin's "A Pretty Girl Is Like a Melody," written for the *Ziegfeld Follies of 1919*. Its chorus is in an ABA' C form:

A: A pretty girl is like a melody
That haunts you night and day;

B: Just like the strain of a haunting refrain,
She'll start upon a marathon
And run around your brain.

A': You can't escape, she's in your memory
By morning, night, and noon;

C: She will leave you and then
Come back again:
A pretty girl is just like a pretty tune.

Always using the best talent available, Ziegfeld produced such musical comedies as Kern, Wodehouse, and Grey's 1920 *Sally*, and the Gershwins, Romberg, and Wodehouse's 1927 *Rosalie*, both starring Marilyn Miller; the Gershwins and Kahn's 1929 *Show Girl*, starring Ruby Keeler, Jimmy Durante, and Duke Ellington and his orchestra; Donaldson and Kahn's 1928 *Whoopee*, with Eddie Cantor and Ruth Etting; and Rodgers and Hart's 1926 *Betsy* and their 1930 *Simple Simon*, with Ed Wynn and Etting. Ziegfeld also produced such operettas as Friml, Wodehouse, and Grey's 1928 *The Three Musketeers* and Noël Coward's 1929 *Bitter Sweet*.

Ziegfeld was more a showman than an innovator. Even so, his dozens of productions, taken together, represent a microcosm of how the musical comedy, the operetta, and the revue began combining in ways that eventually led to the musical plays of Rodgers and Hammerstein. His shows even include Kern and Hammerstein's 1927 musical play *Show Boat*, the first real harbinger of the future development of the form. (The credit goes to Kern and Hammerstein, who stuck to their guns whenever Ziegfeld tried to make them change things to be more like other shows of the time.)

Mostly though, Ziegfeld is famous for the *Follies* and other similar revues. There were twenty-one editions of the *Follies* during his lifetime and two more after his death, produced by the Shuberts and supervised by Ziegfeld's widow, Billie Burke (best remembered as Glinda, the good witch, in the 1939 movie *The*

Florenz Ziegfeld Jr. (1867–1932, born in Chicago) was the son of the president of the Chicago Musical College (later incorporated into the music department of Roosevelt University). Ziegfeld's first success was his national and European presentation of strongman Sandow the Great, beginning at the 1893 World's Columbian Exposition in Chicago. He went on to produce over sixty Broadway shows, most of them big and lavish—terms with which his productions became identified—and many of them revues. He was the first, and possibly the only, Broadway producer whose name was as famous as the names of his stars.

Wizard of Oz), whom he married after Anna Held left him. Burke let the Shuberts have the title because she needed the money to help pay off Ziegfeld's debts. Despite being one of the most successful producers in the history of Broadway—expert at spotting trends, talent, and beautiful women—Ziegfeld was often broke, since his extravagance as a producer often exceeded the box-office take. His gambling habits, the 1929 stock market crash, and gifts to women who were not his wife didn't help, the latter being why Held left him.

The idea for the *Follies*, initiated by Held (whom Ziegfeld made famous by, among other things, having her photographed taking milk baths), was to imitate the French form of vaudeville as seen at the Folies Bergère, with its elaborate decor, sophisticated attitude, contemporary subject matter, topflight performers, and beautiful **showgirls** (the tall ones, often seminude in Paris, who just stood or walked and didn't sing or dance). Broadway choruses also had shorter singing girls (**mediums**) and even shorter dancing girls (**ponies**). Male dancers were called **hoofers,** although the term sometimes refers to musical-theater dancers in general. Choreographer Julian Mitchell did most of his major work for Ziegfeld's shows.

The first *Follies* opened on the roof of the New York Theatre on July 9, 1907. It was a hit and soon moved to street level and then out on tour. Although it was less risqué than the Folies Bergère, the fifty chorus girls did show their bloomers. A new edition immediately became an annual event until 1925, with several more through the rest of the decade and into the thirties. The shows got more elaborate as they got more successful. They also had several headliners instead of vaudeville's usual one or two, with the stars working together as well as separately, making the shows that much more attractive at the box office. The form really was a cleaned-up, glamorized variation on American burlesque—without strippers—as much as it was glorified vaudeville.

Among the stars in various editions of the *Follies* were Anna Held, Nora Bayes, Fanny Brice, Sophie Tucker, Bert Williams, the Dolly Sisters, Helen Morgan, Ed Wynn, Eddie Cantor, Marilyn Miller, Olsen and Johnson, Gallagher and Shean, Ruth Etting, Will Rogers, Buck and Bubbles, Paul Whiteman and his orchestra, and W. C. Fields. The *Follies* also employed such innovative designers as Joseph Urban and Erté, and such important choreographers as Michel Fokine and Albertina Rasch.

[In] devising a unique and extremely popular revue format, Ziegfeld gave
vaudeville a venue of esteem next to rather than within the musical. While Victor Herbert was purging the musical of vaudeville numbers, while George M.
Cohan was purging it of storyless comics, . . . Ziegfeld gave their victims a
place to land. . . . All revues before Ziegfeld were little better than vaudeville

with a title. The *Follies* gave revues dignity and latitude. (Ethan Mordden, *Broadway Babies: The People Who Made the American Musical*, 35)

Because of the *Follies*, large-scale revues quickly became the most popular kind of musical evening on Broadway and stayed so well into the twenties. The *Follies* had many imitators, none as lavish or with quite as many big stars per show. The two most successful series after Ziegfeld's were the Shuberts' *The Passing Show*, beginning in 1912 (twelve editions, plus two that closed out of town), and *George White's Scandals*, beginning in 1919 (thirteen editions).

Broadway revues—at least the best of them—were more elegant, elaborate, and literate than early musicals, which satisfied the upper class and older audiences, and more contemporary American in sound, setting, and comedy than operettas, which satisfied the middle class and younger audiences. In fact, a key reason for the popularity of the revue was its use of the changing sounds of pop music. When syncopated ragtime (and then jazz) came into fashion, they were first heard on Broadway in revues. Many of the successful songwriters of the golden age of the Broadway song (1925–39) got their start in revues; since these shows usually had songs by several composers and lyricists anyway, producers were willing to throw in one or two by novices, giving them invaluable experience in the writing of show songs. And because the form paid special attention to songs that suited current tastes, Tin Pan Alley soon paid special attention to revues, strengthening the bond between Broadway and the Alley. The form began losing its appeal during the late twenties, and its cost-effectiveness during the Depression.

Meanwhile, in the twenties, **intimate revues** (smaller, less expensive, more satiric than the Broadway revue form) began appearing regularly off-Broadway, in cabarets and nightclubs, and eventually on Broadway as well. During the thirties, this version of the form was more popular than the big shows. (By then, musical comedies had supplanted either revue form in popularity.) Some of the most successful of Broadway's intimate revues were Arthur Schwartz and Howard Dietz's *The Little Show* and *The Band Wagon* and Irving Berlin's *As Thousands Cheer*. The form is still produced fairly regularly off-Broadway, in theaters and cabarets,

Lee (1876–1905), **Sam S.** (1873–1953), and **J. J. Shubert** (1878–1963, all born in Lithuania with the last name Szemanski) leased a New York theater, the Herald Square, in 1900. It was the first of a chain that grew to almost one hundred nationwide. They produced their first show in 1901 and quickly became known as ruthless tyrants who cared little about art and culture, preferring instead to appeal to the lowest common denominator in Broadway audiences. They eventually produced over five hundred shows. To their credit, the Shuberts took on the Syndicate and Keith-Albee chains and, by the twenties, had destroyed those groups' cross-country theater monopolies. They created their own instead, which survived until the fifties.

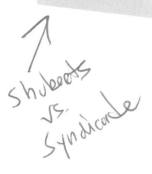

and by improvisational groups all over the country; *Saturday Night Live,* among other shows, does a weekly TV version of it.

The big Broadway revue—stars, large casts, big production values, up-to-the-minute comedy, songs, and dances—disappeared soon after the arrival of national television in the late forties. Sid Caesar's *Your Show of Shows,* for example, was an hour-and-a-half revue that came into homes free on Saturday nights, live and in prime time. Although Las Vegas still does versions of the big revues, the only revues that now get produced on Broadway are closer in size and production values to the intimate ones. They're actually different from both kinds of revues, since they're usually retrospectives of a single composer, lyricist, or songwriting team, with no sketches and often no dialogue, also true of many off-Broadway revues.

Unlike operettas, early musicals and revues felt contemporary and American. The two forms even shared stars, writers, composers, directors, choreographers, designers, and producers. They also shared a sense of wildness and unpredictability that was part of why audiences loved them: they had a feeling of spontaneity that gave each audience the idea that this wasn't exactly the same way it had been done the night before. And they had performers whose personalities and styles played all the way to the back row of the balcony in those days before amplification.

Vaudeville performers moved into revues and musicals when they could; the pay was better, and the shows stayed longer in one place. Although raucous, bawdy burlesque was still intended largely for lower-class, non-Broadway, male audiences and for horny teenagers of any economic class, its best comics were also soon moving up to revues and musicals. They cleaned up their humor enough to get by and, in the process, broadened the appeal of revues and musical comedies even more.

The old-style revue is dead, and its freewheeling spirit has nearly disappeared as the musical comedy has evolved into integrated and far more artful current forms (examples of which are called musical plays, musical dramas, concept musicals, pop operas, rock operas, or simply musicals, but rarely musical comedies).

> [Stephen] Sondheim . . . has a wistful fondness for the early decades of the musical, before Rodgers and Hammerstein's innovations made it requisite that a show have a strong narrative book from which all the songs convincingly emerge. "In the time of the Gershwins, the vitality was fabulous," Mr. Sondheim said. "Everything didn't depend on money. No art forms today have that kind of vitality, where people are having fun just trying things." (Anthony Tommasini, "A Crowd of Old Musicals Squeezes the New," *New York Times,* 1)

Perhaps it's time to start the cycle all over again with some big, old-style, Broadway revues.

Suggested Watching and Listening

Funny Girl
This is William Wyler's 1968 movie version of Jule Styne, Bob Merrill, and Isobel Lennart's Broadway 1964 musical biography (available on Columbia Pictures DVD).
- "His Love Makes Me Beautiful" (performed by Barbra Streisand as Fanny Brice and Walter Pidgeon as Florenz Ziegfeld): Fanny Brice is new to the *Follies*. In this sequence, Ziegfeld has cast her as the beautiful bride in a production number. When she protests that she's a funny girl, he orders her to do it or get fired. She does it but turns it into a comic triumph. (The incident didn't really happen.) Although the number was written for the musical, it's a fairly accurate re-creation of how a Ziegfeld finale might have been staged. (The hair and makeup are very 1960s, though, rather than early 1900s.)

Naughty Marietta
This version is from a 1955 live, black-and-white TV broadcast, available on Video Artists International DVD.
- "Tramp! Tramp! Tramp! (The Boys Are Marching)" (performed by Alfred Drake and the boys): There's a song like this for the hero and the male chorus in almost every successful American operetta; the macho male chorus was very important to the form. Alfred Drake was Curly in the original production of *Oklahoma!*
- "Italian Street Song" (performed by Patrice Munsel): Patrice Munsel, who plays Marietta, was a Metropolitan Opera star. For years, this song was a staple of every would-be lyric soprano in the world. Its lyrics include "Zing zing zizzy zizzy zing zing zing boom-ay," often performed while the singer beat mercilessly on a tambourine.
- "Ah! Sweet Mystery of Life" (performed by Patrice Munsel and Alfred Drake): Marietta has told the hero that she has been searching for the right lyrics to a song that has been haunting her—a song about the mystery of life—and she's sworn that she will only love the man who can finish it, which of course he does. At the end, love triumphs over avarice, democracy over aristocracy. (Jeanette MacDonald's husband, the actor Gene Raymond, played her recording of this song at her funeral.)

The Jeanette MacDonald and Nelson Eddy movie version is also available on video.

Yankee Doodle Dandy: George M. Cohan
This is the 1942 movie biography of George M. Cohan, who was still alive when it was made (available on Warner Brothers DVD).
- "The Yankee Doodle Boy" (performed by James Cagney and the Company)
- "Give My Regards to Broadway" (performed by James Cagney, Joan Leslie, and the company): There's a sequence purporting to be part of the first performance of *Little Johnny Jones* in 1904. The movie re-creation includes what was at the time a very famous stage effect at the end of the second of the show's three acts: Johnny, played by Cohan, is waiting at the dock for a signal that proof has been found showing he didn't throw the Derby. The signal is sent by a rocket shot from a miniature boat floating across the

back of the stage. At the time, the effect was quite an elaborate one for a musical not purporting to be an extravaganza; it caused a sensation and helped sell tickets. Cagney, who began as a Broadway hoofer, became famous in movies playing gangsters and tough guys and made very few movie musicals; he won an Academy Award for this one. His dancing style in the movie is apparently closer to his own than to Cohan's.

Ziegfeld Follies of 1919

For this show, Florenz Ziegfeld asked Irving Berlin to write a song to go with a number of expensive costumes he'd ordered, and Berlin's "A Pretty Girl Is Like a Melody" soon became Ziegfeld's theme song.

- "A Pretty Girl Is Like a Melody" (performed by Dennis Morgan dubbed by Tony Martin, with music and lyrics by Irving Berlin): It's used in a spectacular sequence from Robert Z. Leonard's 1936 *The Great Ziegfeld* (available on Warner Home Video DVD), a Hollywood magnification of a typical Ziegfeld production number. As in the original stage version, more and more and then more pretty girls appear, with no rhyme or reason to what country or historical period the next set of costumes represents or for what comes next musically—from Berlin to Mozart, Puccini, Gershwin and back to Berlin, with other stops along the way. The singer in the film, Stanley Morner, later became a star as Dennis Morgan. He could sing quite well, but was inexplicably dubbed in the movie by Tony Martin.

From *Babes* in *Joyland* to "*Alexander's Ragtime Band*"

The real American folk song is a rag—
A mental jag—
A rhythmic tonic for the chronic blues.
The critics called it a joke song, but now
They've changed their tune
And they like it somehow.
For it's inoculated
With a syncopated
Sort of meter,
Sweeter
Than a classic strain
—"THE REAL AMERICAN FOLK SONG (IS A RAG),"
LADIES FIRST, LYRICS BY IRA GERSHWIN

In 1901, about twenty-five musical shows of one form or another opened in New York, including Ziegfeld's *The Little Duchess,* with chorus girls taking off their stockings on stage. By 1911, the number of shows had doubled, peaking in 1907 with close to seventy musical evenings. The United States then entered a brief economic depression, meaning that fewer risks were taken as audience numbers dwindled slightly.

In 1902, *New York Times* publisher Adolph S. Ochs bought the small triangle of land connecting Broadway, Seventh Avenue, and Forty-second Street and built the Times Tower. The area, known as Longacre Square, was renamed Times Square in 1904. With the success of Weber and Fields's Broadway Music Hall and other theaters and restaurants in the area, Times Square quickly became the center of the theater district.

Ned Wayburn (1874–1942, born in Pittsburgh, Pennsylvania) was one of the first Broadway director/choreographers. He was responsible for many early shows, particularly revues, including several *Ziegfeld Follies*. Wayburn, like Julian Mitchell, insisted that the choruses rehearse far more rigorously than was the norm at the time. In 1905 he founded the Studio of Stage Dancing.

The Wizard of Oz

MUSIC: A. Baldwin Sloane and Paul Tietjens

LYRICS/BOOK: L. Frank Baum, adapted from his 1900 children's book

DIRECTOR: Julian Mitchell

CHOREOGRAPHER: Julian Mitchell

PRODUCER: Fred R. Hamlin

CAST INCLUDES: the vaudeville team of David Montgomery as the Tin Woodman and Fred Stone as Scarecrow

PERFORMANCES: 293

Babes in Toyland

MUSIC: Victor Herbert

LYRICS/LIBRETTO: Glen MacDonough

DIRECTOR: Julian Mitchell

CHOREOGRAPHER: Julian Mitchell

PRODUCERS: Fred R. Hamlin and Julian Mitchell

PERFORMANCES: 192 after a successful Chicago run

In 1903, on Broadway, choreographer Ned Wayburn replaced wooden clogs by putting metal taps on lighter-weight dancing shoes (sometimes said to have happened in 1902).

Weber, Fields, and Lillian Russell opened at the Music Hall in the musical extravaganza *Whoop-Dee-Doo* (151 performances). Weber and Fields had come to depend less on immigrant humor, but they kept their knockabout style. Fields was tiring of it.

Running for Office, George M. Cohan's second musical, closed after forty-eight performances. It then went on a very successful road tour. It costarred Cohan, his father, Jerry, his mother, Helen, his sister, Josie, and his wife, Ethel Levey.

The Wizard of Oz was billed as a musical extravaganza for the whole family and had many spectacular stage effects. There was no Cowardly Lion as a major character in this version, as there is in the 1939 movie musical, which has a very different script and score. In the 1903 musical, for instance, Dorothy landed in Oz with her pet cow Imogene rather than with her pet dog Toto. Even though the songs weren't very good, the show was a huge hit. Within months, there were several attempts to cash in on its success. The most successful, with the same producer and director/choreographer and opening at the same theater, was *Babes in Toyland.*

Herbert's first show since becoming the conductor of the Pittsburgh Symphony, *Babes in Toyland* was a combination of extravaganza—with many elaborate scenic effects—and operetta, although the charming score is simpler and closer to contemporary pop than usual for operetta. In the plot, involving many nursery rhyme characters, Little Bo Peep loses her sheep as part of the villain Barnaby's plot to abduct and marry her. Little Boy Blue, who loves her and whom she loves in return, foils Barnaby at the end, with the help of the Toy Maker and his troop of toy soldiers. *Babes in Toyland* was Herbert's eleventh show, and the first to endure; for years, almost everyone knew its sweet, slow waltz "Toyland" and its "March of the Toys." After its first Broadway run, the show embarked on an extensive series of tours and revivals and is still revived occasionally at Christmastime.

Laurel and Hardy and Walt Disney made movie versions of *Babes in Toyland* in 1934 and 1961, respectively. Disney's starred Tommy Sands and Annette Funicello; Barnaby was played by Ray Bolger, the then-aging **eccentric dancer** (a dancer who uses extreme leg and body flexibility in comic dances). Bolger was a star of revues, musicals, and movies, and he is best known for playing Scarecrow in the 1939 movie of *The Wizard of Oz*. The Toy Maker in Disney's version of *Babes in Toyland* was played by the even older Ed Wynn, a tremendously popular star of vaudeville, revue, musical comedy, radio, and early TV, billed as the Perfect Fool. He was also the laughing-gas man in Disney's 1964 *Mary Poppins*. (Wynn's 1930s radio show was the first to use a live audience; a large part of his humor was visual, and he wanted to be sure the audience at home knew that what he was doing was funny.) There was a terrible 1986 TV movie of *Babes in Toyland*, directed by Clive Donner, with Drew Barrymore, Keanu Reeves, and Pat Morita in the cast. It used only two of Herbert's songs, the rest having been supplied—inadequately—by Leslie Bricusse.

In Dahomey was the first musical comedy both written and performed by African Americans to play Broadway. After its Broad-

In Dahomey

MUSIC: Will Marion Cook and James Vaughn

LYRICS: Paul Laurence Dunbar and Alex Rogers

LIBRETTO: J. A. Shipp

DIRECTOR: J. A. Shipp

CAST INCLUDES: Bert Williams and George Walker

PERFORMANCES: 53

Backdrop: 1901–1911

National President McKinley is assassinated, and Theodore Roosevelt becomes president. The United States helps negotiate a peace treaty between Japan and Russia and starts work on the Panama Canal. The FBI is established. The San Francisco earthquake and fire destroy two-thirds of the city. The NAACP is founded. The 1907 Wall Street panic is the third in fourteen years; America enters a depression. More than 9 million foreign immigrants enter the United States during this decade, 1.29 million in 1907 alone. A new migration of Southern African Americans begins, bringing more than two million north by 1917. Oklahoma becomes the forty-sixth state.

International Belief in Communism is growing in Russia, especially after the 1905 uprising, and in China, after Sun Yat-sen overthrows the Qing dynasty in 1911. Mohandas Gandhi launches his campaign of passive resistance against the British regime in India.

way run, *In Dahomey* toured London and was revived on Broadway in 1904 and off-Broadway in 1999.

In 1904, Weber and Fields broke up their comedy act and ended production of their burlesque-extravaganzas. *Lady Teazle,* the first major production of the Shubert brothers, was a musical adaptation of Sheridan's 1777 British comedy *The School for Scandal.* Along with Lillian Russell, it had eighty-six chorus girls, none of whom appeared in the cast list of the original play. Also that year, nineteen-year-old Jerome Kern's first Broadway songs were interpolated into *Mr. Wix of Wickham,* an imported British musical. His first hit song, "How'd You Like to Spoon with Me?" was interpolated into *The Earl and the Girl* in 1905.

With *Little Johnny Jones,* George M. Cohan began his long-standing partnership with Sam H. Harris (1872–1941, born in New York), who produced it. Cohan's costars were his father, mother, and wife; his sister and her husband had gone into another show. After its successful road tour during which Cohan revised and improved it, *Little Johnny Jones* had a four-month Broadway revival and still another revival in 1907. There was a flop Broadway revisal in 1982, with Donny Osmond as Johnny. (David Cassidy played the role for a while during the show's long tryout tour.) Cohan and Harris eventually coproduced all of Cohan's shows and others' shows as well. The partnership ended when Cohan refused to join Actors' Equity. Harris continued

New Developments Einstein publishes his first paper on the theory of relativity. Psychiatry has its first international convention; Carl Jung publishes *Psychology of Dementia Praecox.* The first airplanes fly. The SS *Lusitania,* the world's largest ocean liner, and the SS *Mauritania* are launched; in 1910, the *Mauritania* sets a new transatlantic speed record. Explorers reach the North and South poles and the Incan city of Macchu Picchu. The electrocardiograph, the Wassermann test for syphilis, neon signs, and the Geiger counter are developed. Maytag washers, Hoover vacuum cleaners, Rolls-Royces, Mack trucks, and the Model T Ford are introduced. The Gulf Oil Company and Planters Nut and Chocolate Company are founded. The Neiman-Marcus department store opens in Dallas.

Sports In 1908, Jack Johnson is the first African American to win the world heavyweight boxing championship. In 1910, he retains his title against James J. Jeffries, widely known as the Great White Hope, and race riots ensue in several parts of the country. (Johnson's story is the subject of Howard Sackler's 1968 play *The Great White Hope* and its 1970 movie version, both with James Earl Jones and Jane Alexander.) Baseball's first World Series is held, as are the first Grand Prix and Indianapolis 500 auto races. Auction bridge is invented.

producing both by himself and with others, including shows by Irving Berlin, the Gershwins, Cole Porter, Rodgers and Hart, and Kurt Weill.

In 1906, Harry K. Thaw, husband of chorus girl Evelyn Nesbitt, shot her lover, architect Stanford White. It was dubbed the "crime of the century," and Nesbitt cashed in on it to become a vaudeville star. (It is one of the story strands of the 1998 musical *Ragtime*.) Ziegfeld starred Anna Held in *A Parisian Model*. The two remaining Shubert brothers—Sam, the most creative, was killed in a train wreck in 1905—took over New York's gigantic Hippodrome theater, built in 1905 for staging spectacles. The Hippodrome seated 5,200 people; it had a permanent ballet company of 200, 400 chorus women, and 100 chorus men. The stage, 110 feet deep and 200 feet wide, was divided into twelve sections, each of which could be raised and lowered by hydraulics. Its water tank could float boats or catch a waterfall. There was a menagerie under the stage where the elephants and other animals were kept. The success of the Hippodrome led to the production of many extravagant spectacles on Broadway all the way into the twenties. Located on Sixth Avenue (Avenue of the Americas) between

Bert Williams (1874–1922, born Egbert Williams in Antigua, British West Indies) and his partner, George Walker, were a legendary minstrel and vaudeville, comedy and dance act who performed in blackface. They were the first African Americans to make recordings. After Walker retired in 1909 due to ill health, Williams, who had been the straight man in the act, became the first black star of the *Follies*, and, thus, the first black to appear in an otherwise white Broadway show. Light-skinned, he continued wearing blackface, which he considered essential to his comic character, a gloomy and slow-moving innocent trying to make it in the big city and usually getting the worst of it. (What seemed funny then has a far different resonance now.)

Art Among painters trying new techniques, including abstractionism and surrealism, or expanding old ones are such diverse talents as Monet, Renoir, Picasso, Chagall, Munch, Braque, Dufy, Utrillo, Matisse, Kandinsky, Modigliani, Rouault, Rivera, Rousseau, Klimt, and Remington. The Ashcan School of Art is founded in Philadelphia. Architect Frank Lloyd Wright designs the Ward Willitts House, the Robie House, the Larkin Building, and the Unity Temple.

Music/Dance Classical composers expanding, breaking, or following traditional forms and tonalities include Ravel, Elgar, Sibelius, Rachmaninoff, Stravinsky (whose ballets *The Firebird* and *Petrouchka* cause major sensations at their premieres in Paris), Mahler, and Richard Strauss. Anna Pavlova, the most famous ballerina of the day, introduces "The Dying Swan" in St. Petersburg. Ruth St. Denis introduces modern dance, and Isadora Duncan begins performing her interpretive dances inspired by Greek art.

Publications The first major black newspaper, the *Chicago Defender*, begins publication in 1905, as do the weekly show business bible *Variety*, the *Christian Science Monitor*, *Women's Wear Daily*, and Bud Fisher's *Mutt and Jeff*, the first daily comic strip with continuing characters. Emma Goldman

Forty-third and Forty-fourth streets, the Hippodrome was torn down in 1939 and is now a parking lot.

George M. Cohan wrote and directed two musicals in 1906. *George Washington, Jr.* (81 performances) starred Cohan, his father, his mother, and his wife, and included "You're a Grand Old Flag," the first song written for a show to sell over a million copies of sheet music. (The title was originally the more slangy "You're a Grand Old Rag," but when people said "rag" was disrespectful, Cohan changed it.) *Forty-five Minutes from Broadway* (90 performances)—the first time Cohan didn't write a part for himself—starred Fay Templeton, made a star of Victor Moore, and included Cohan's famous Irish ballad "Mary's a Grand Old Name." Both shows toured extensively.

The producer Charles Dillingham was Ziegfeld's closest competitor for lavish productions. *The Red Mill* was the first Broadway show to advertise with a moving electric sign. An operetta combined with musical comedy elements about two clownish Americans traveling through Europe, its stars were the comics instead of the traditional romantic leads of other operettas—a step toward the American musical comedy. (The show is occasionally classified as a musical comedy.) It was one of Herbert's biggest

Victor Moore (1876–1962, born in Hammonton, New Jersey) was usually cast as an easily confused little man caught up in some kind of intrigue. After *Forty-five Minutes from Broadway* and its sequel in 1907, he toured with his wife in vaudeville. In 1926, he reestablished himself on Broadway in the Gershwins' *Oh, Kay!* By the forties, his work was mostly in movies and then on TV.

(a character in the 1998 musical *Ragtime*) and Alexander Berkman found *Mother Earth,* an anarchist journal. The first Pulitzer Prizes are awarded. There are novels and stories by Mann, Hesse, James, Conrad, Forster, Wharton, London, Sinclair, Dreiser, O. Henry, Stein, and Colette. W. E. B. DuBois publishes *The Souls of Black Folks.*

Radio   Guglielmo Marconi sends a wireless message across the Atlantic, the beginning of what will become radio. Lee De Forest develops a tube permitting its final development. The first broadcast, transmitted from Brant Rock, Massachusetts, is picked up by all the ships within hundreds of miles.

Pop Culture   The tango, a South American dance, becomes popular in the United States and Europe. Ragtime and jazz are moving north. The Victor Talking Machine Company begins massproducing Victrola record players, and records begin to help sell new songs. Popular songs include Cowan's "Waltzing Matilda," Cannon's "Frankie and Johnny," Burnett and Norton's "My Melancholy Baby," Conn and Edwards's "School Days," Ayer and Brown's "Oh, You Beautiful Doll," Zimmerman and Miles's "Anchors Aweigh" (adopted by the U.S. Navy), Gruber's "The Caissons Go Rolling Along" hits. (In 1905, his *Mlle. Modiste,* with its famous waltz "Kiss Me Again," had run 262 performances.) In *The Red Mill,* Herbert proved he was able to compose successful vaudeville-style songs, particularly with his soft-shoe number "The Streets of New York" ("In Old New York"). Although the comic songs in almost any operetta date the fastest, the baritone number "Every Day Is Ladies' Day with Me" is an exception, if you can get past the extreme sexism traditional for that time.

In 1907, the members of the Syndicate were indicted for violating antitrust laws, but the case was thrown out of court. Jerome Kern was regularly adding songs to European imports, something producers insisted on doing in order to make imports feel more American. Weber and Fields opened in separate shows; Fields's was a hit, Weber's a flop.

The Merry Widow (416 performances) opened that year in New York and rejuvenated the popularity of romantic Viennese operetta, with productions touring the country and the rest of the Western world. When *The Merry Widow* premiered in the United States, it also inspired a long-lasting national fad for **ballroom dancing,** a major feature of its staging, which requires couples to dance close in each other's arms.

The Red Mill

MUSIC: Victor Herbert

LYRICS/LIBRETTO: Henry Blossom

PRODUCER: Charles Dillingham

CAST INCLUDES: David Montgomery and Fred Stone (stars of the 1903 *The Wizard of Oz*)

PERFORMANCES: 274

(adopted by the U.S. Army), Armstrong and Gerard's "Sweet Adeline," Taylor's "Down by the Old Mill Stream," Friedman and Whitson's "Let Me Call You Sweetheart," von Tilzer and Dillon's "I Want a Girl Just Like the Girl That Married Dear Old Dad" (all four barbershop quartet favorites), von Tilzer and Norworth's "Take Me Out to the Ball Game," and Irving Berlin's "Marie of Sunny Italy," the first time he uses the name Irving Berlin.

Stage   There are plays by Chekhov (who dies in 1903), Strindberg, Feydeau, Barrie, Synge, and Shaw. Chicago's Iroquois Theatre burns in 1903, killing over six hundred people; new theater fire code rules and regulations sweep the country. Dublin's Abbey Theatre opens and London's Royal Academy of Dramatic Art is founded.

Screen   The movie industry is gearing up. *The Great Train Robbery* is the first movie to tell a story. Bell and Howell Company develops a process for mass-printing copies of movies. Mack Sennett opens the Keystone Company and begins making knockabout comedies; many acrobatic vaudeville comedians soon find a new and more lucrative arena for their talents.

In *The Merry Widow* the ballroom dance was glorified as a symbol of romantic love and placed in the focus of attention. . . . It dealt a death blow to the marches, drills, and empty convolutions that had punctuated musical-comedy performances until then. It opened the way for Vernon and Irene Castle, the tango, the turkey trot, and the fox-trot. It humanized dancing, and made it warm, immediate, and personal. (Smith and Litton, 88–89)

Cohan's *The Honeymooners* (167 performances), a rewrite of his 1903 flop *Running for Office*, starred Cohan, his father, and his mother. His *The Talk of New York* (157 performances) starred Victor Moore as the same character he had played in Cohan's *Forty-five Minutes from Broadway*. Both shows toured successfully.

Ziegfeld's *Follies of 1907* (70 performances), subtitled *Another One of Those Things, in 13 Acts*, was the revue's first edition, had a minimal plot by Harry B. Smith to tie together the various acts, was choreographed by Julian Mitchell, and starred Nora Bayes, Anna Held, and fifty "Anna Held Girls." The New York Theatre's roof, where it played before going off on a successful tour, was rechristened the Jardin de Paris. There were weekly changes in the program.

Because of the depression that started in 1908, poorer people in particular deserted the theater for much cheaper silent movies. That year, Lew Fields had a hit burlesque of *The Merry Widow*. Al Jolson joined Lew Dockstader's Minstrels. Variety entrepreneur Tony Pastor died.

Cohan's *Fifty Miles from Boston* (32 performances) was the first of his three shows for the year. He wrote, directed, and coproduced it, but he didn't appear in it. The score included the song "H-A-Double-R-I-G-A-N Spells Harrigan" in tribute to Ned Harrigan of Harrigan and Hart, who was in the audience with Cohan on opening night. It was basically a play with music; all the songs were in the third act.

In Ziegfeld's *Follies of 1908* (120 performances), vaudeville star Nora Bayes and her then husband Jack Norworth introduced their classic "Shine On, Harvest Moon." (Bayes sang it in every show she was in from then on, whether it fit in or not. By the next year, when she sang it in the new edition of the *Follies*, it was credited entirely to her.) Like "After the Ball" and many other vaudeville and early revue songs, it tells a story in the verses, with each verse followed by a repeated chorus commenting on the story. The sixteen-bar chorus of "Shine On, Harvest Moon" is in an ABAC structure. (By then, some songs were being written with a thirty-two-bar chorus. As choruses got longer, verses got shorter.) Even though its lyrics were clearly intended to be sung by a man ("Shine on . . . for me and my gal"), if a singer liked the song, that often didn't matter. Besides, the verse usually made the sex of the character singing the song clear, regardless of the sex of the singer. Even more frequently, the chorus was written without any reference to gender or could be sung by either sex with a few simple changes of nouns or pronouns. (If a song written for a musical was considered a potential hit, any story elements and gendered words would most likely be in the verse, which could be dropped if the song was sung out of the context of the show.)

In 1910, the Palladium, London's leading vaudeville and revue house, opened. Playing there was the equivalent of playing the Palace, which opened in New York three years later. A U.S. copyright law that included protection for composers and music publishers went into effect. African American composer-lyricist Shelton Brooks published his bluesy, occasionally syncopated "Some of These Days," an enormous leap in style, tone, and content from "Shine On, Harvest Moon" only two years earlier.

["Some of These Days" is] truly a landmark in popular music, perhaps *the* landmark of the transition era. It was completely unlike most songs of its time. . . . It is a straightforward, well-written rhythm ballad, melodically and harmonically . . . [and] has the unusual form of *ABCD*. (Alec Wilder, *American Popular Song: The Great Innovators, 1900–1950*, 14)

Also that year, Herbert and Johnson's *Naughty Marietta* premiered, and Cohan's first nonmusical play, *Get-Rich-Quick Wallingford*, was a hit and ran 424 performances.

The *Follies of 1910* (88 performances) had music mostly by Gus Edwards and lyrics and book mostly by Harry B. Smith. The production values were getting noticeably more lavish. Two frequent *Follies* performers were introduced: Fanny Brice (1891–1951, born Fanny Borach in New York), the Yiddish-dialect, burlesque comedienne, who sang Irving Berlin's "Good-bye, Becky Cohen"; and Bert Williams, who sang his signature song "Nobody," written in 1905 for Walker and his vaudeville act. As mentioned before, it was in the *Follies of 1910* that Williams became the first black in a white show on Broadway. At first the other stars refused to appear onstage with him, but once they saw him perform, they rapidly changed their minds. Williams was an almost yearly *Follies* star until 1919. However, it was in his contract that he wouldn't appear onstage with a woman lest there be any kind of uproar and that the show wouldn't tour the South.

In 1911, Gilbert of Gilbert and Sullivan, Harrigan of Harrigan and

Hart, and Walker of Williams and Walker died. Cecil Smith and Glenn Litton describe the situation of musical theater at this time:

> At the beginning of the second decade of this century, the musical stage had again encountered the doldrums. New hits seemed like repetitions of old ones. . . . A gap had opened between the carriage trade and the mass audience, which adored its whirly-girly shows and wanted no traffic with art. During the next few years Broadway kept only an attenuated hold upon its audience of cultivated patrons. (Smith and Litton, 93)

George White (1890–1968, born George Weitz in New York) began to produce his *Scandals,* one of the most popular series of revues in imitation of Ziegfeld's, in 1919. With a better ear for new pop music than Ziegfeld had, he hired, among many others, George Gershwin and the songwriting team of Henderson, DeSylva, and Brown.

The Shuberts opened their Winter Garden Theatre with *La Belle Paree* (104 performances), a revue with music by Jerome Kern and others, lyrics by Edward Madden and others, and sketches by Edgar Smith. It was Al Jolson's Broadway debut. The Shuberts and Jolson did ten more shows together between 1911 and 1927, when Jolson's movie *The Jazz Singer* was released and he switched to Hollywood.

Ziegfeld Follies of 1911, the last to open on the roof of the New York Theatre, was the first to bear Ziegfeld's name in the title. It had songs by Jerome Kern and Irving Berlin, among others, and ran 80 performances before touring. Its stars included Fanny Brice, Bert Williams, the dancing twin Dolly Sisters, comic Leon Errol, and vaudeville dancer George White.

"Alexander's Ragtime Band"

Just as "After the Ball" revolutionized the pop-music publishing business, Irving Berlin's 1911 song "Alexander's Ragtime Band" revolutionized pop music itself by introducing ragtime to white America in sheet music and on records. (Brooks's 1910 "Some of These Days" had been a step along the way, though it never achieved anything like the popularity or influence of Berlin's song.) The new sound soon became what most young people wanted to hear for dancing and romancing.

A huge Tin Pan Alley hit—it took Berlin eighteen minutes to write it—the song isn't a rag; it's a syncopated march about rag. It was the **syncopation** (a shift in accent onto a beat that isn't normally accented, usually in a succession of eighth note, quarter note, eighth note) and the **pickup notes** (which start a musical phrase before instead of on the beat) that were new and exciting and presented interesting ideas for dancing. The verse is short, setting up what the song is about. The chorus, in thirty-two bars, has an ABAC structure. (The lyrics are in a "Negro" dialect. At the time the name Alexander, like Rastus, Rufus, and Jemima, clearly referred to an African American. That connotation for the name soon disappeared.)

Oh, ma honey, oh, ma honey,
Better hurry and let's meander,
Ain't you goin', ain't you goin',
To the leader man, ragged meter man?
Oh, ma honey, oh, ma honey,
Let me take you to Alexander's
Grand stand, brass band,
Ain't you comin' along?

CHORUS:

A: Come on and hear, come on and hear
   Alexander's Ragtime Band.
   Come on and hear, come on and hear,
   It's the best band in the land.
B: They can play a bugle call like you never heard
      before,
   So natural that you want to go to war,
   That's just the bestest band what am,
   Honey lamb.
A: Come on along, come on along,
   Let me take you by the hand,
   Up to the man, up to the man
   Who's the leader of the band,
C: And if you care to hear the "Swanee River" played
      in ragtime,
   Come on and hear, come on and hear
   Alexander's Ragtime Band.

In the first and third lines of the first A, "come on" and "and" are on syncopated pickup notes twice. Then, in the B section, the melody of the first three lines imitates a bugle call. It's also become fairly common to change "want to go to war" to "want to hear some more." Toward the end, in the C section, the music "quotes" Stephen Foster's "Swanee River"; familiarity with the original was assumed. In the 1938 movie *Alexander's Ragtime Band,* there is a very fictional account of how "Alexander's Ragtime Band" first started becoming a national craze.

Since musical comedies and revues tried to keep up with new fads in song and dance styles, and, since suddenly the sounds and syncopations of ragtime were what people wanted in their pop music, the Broadway sound had to adjust. Victor Herbert's music soon seemed old-fashioned; as with Cohan, much of his later output was unsuccessful. Meanwhile, Berlin was writing syncopation into his Broadway revues as well as into his Tin Pan Alley songs, and Jerome Kern was experimenting with a new form for the musical comedy. An era of significant growth was beginning to take shape in American musical theater, as in American society itself.

Suggested Watching and Listening

After the Ball plus Highlights from Vaudeville
This is Joan Morris and William Bolcom's Elektra/Nonesuch CD, which includes the following song, originally from the show *Ziegfeld Follies of 1908.*
- "Shine On, Harvest Moon" (performed by Joan Morris and William Bolcom, with music by Nora Bayes and Jack Norworth and lyrics by Jack Norworth)

"Alexander's Ragtime Band"
The music and lyrics for the 1911 song were written by Irving Berlin. The following version is Bessie Smith's 1927 recording of the song, available on Four Star CD.
- "Alexander's Ragtime Band" (performed by Bessie Smith with Joe Smith on the cornet, Jimmy Harrison on the trombone, Coleman Hawkins on the clarinet, Fletcher Henderson on the piano, and Charlie Dixon on the banjo): In this version, Smith sings "go down there" for "meander" in the verse, losing a rhyme with "Alexander." In the B of the chorus, she sings "best band in the land" for "bestest band what am," softening the "Negro" dialect. That change has since become traditional.

Sophie Tucker: Jazz Age Hot Mama
This is a Take Two CD recording featuring the following song.
- "Some of These Days" (performed by Sophie Tucker and Ted Lewis and his band, with music and lyrics by Shelton Brooks): This is a 1926 recording of the 1910 song. Tucker, more often seen in vaudeville and nightclubs than on Broadway, used Brooks's "Some of These Days" as her signature song. She was also known for including off-color songs in her act. During her long career, she was billed as "the last of the red-hot mamas";

her singing style resembled that of the great blues singer Bessie Smith. There was some of Jolson's style in it too but with a sense of humor and without blackface—although she did wear it briefly at the start of her vaudeville career. Tucker was featured in the *Follies of 1909* until Nora Bayes had her fired for being too good.

From The Firefly to Yip-Yip-Yaphank

Bit by bit, putting it together . . .
Piece by piece, only way to make a work of art.
Every moment makes a contribution,
Every little detail plays a part.
Having just the vision's no solution,
Everything depends on execution,
Putting it together, that's what counts.

—"PUTTING IT TOGETHER,"

SUNDAY IN THE PARK WITH GEORGE, LYRICS BY STEPHEN SONDHEIM

Between 1912 and 1918, musical entertainments changed almost as rapidly as the times themselves. With the start of World War I, producers stopped importing shows from Europe. American operetta and revue reached full flower. Theatrical design elements were coordinated. Unions for the protection of actors, composers, authors, and publishers were formed. And, most important to the development of the musical during this time, Irving Berlin brought ragtime to Broadway, and Jerome Kern, Guy Bolton, and P. G. Wodehouse reconceived the European operetta as an intimate, lighthearted, and structured American musical comedy.

One great figure to emerge during the early 1900s was Irving Berlin.

He began his Broadway career interpolating songs into other people's shows. He also got songs into vaudeville acts and anywhere else he could. The 1911 song "Alexander's Ragtime Band" was Berlin's first big pop hit. His chance to write songs for a whole Broadway score then came in 1914 with *Watch Your Step: The First All-Syncopated Musical,* with the script by Harry B.

Irving Berlin (1888–1989, born Israel Baline in Russia), the youngest of eight children, immigrated with his family in 1893 to the tenements of New York's Lower East Side. When he was thirteen, his father died, and Berlin started earning his own way. While working as a singing waiter in 1907, he wrote the lyrics for his first published song, "Marie from Sunny Italy," with music by M. Nicholson. Soon Berlin, like Cohan, was writing both music and lyrics. Also, like Cohan, Berlin couldn't read music; he taught himself to compose by picking out tunes on a piano's black keys. He eventually had a piano built with a lever that could move the keyboard to different hammers, allowing him to change key signatures while still only playing in the key of F#. That piano's now in the Smithsonian.

Vernon Castle (1887–1918, born Vernon Blyth in Norwich, England) and **Irene Castle** (1893–1969, born Irene Foote in New Rochelle, New York) were the most influential ballroom dancers of the time. They had their first success in Paris; then they conquered the United States. They introduced and/or popularized many dances; were refined, sophisticated, and graceful; and made ballroom dancing respectable and popular, especially among the upper classes.

Smith. Featuring ballroom dancers Vernon and Irene Castle, it began a ragtime craze on Broadway. Berlin was an excellent businessman and soon had his own publishing house in Tin Pan Alley.

From then on, Berlin wrote regularly for Broadway and Tin Pan Alley, and for movies as well once sound came in. He wrote twenty-one scores for Broadway, fourteen of them revues. His best and most successful musical was the 1946 *Annie Get Your Gun*. Songs from Berlin's musicals were usually easy to remove from their original contexts if they became pop hits or got recycled into movies. He wrote in an amazing number of styles and had more hits than any other composer in the world. His catalogue includes such traditional songs as "White Christmas," "Easter Parade," and "God Bless America."

> During the six decades of his career, he was the composer most able to chart America's taste in popular song and he influenced scores of others in his field. . . . His more than 800 songs captured the spirit of the nation unlike those of any other songwriter. . . . Berlin remains America's most popular composer. . . . His contributions to Broadway were often entertaining and usually profitable—not a bad combination. But Berlin rarely attempted well-rounded musical theatre scores; he always seemed more interested in parades of song hits, which kept his publisher (i.e., himself) happy. . . . In 1914 Kern and Berlin . . . led Broadway into a new era. While Kern made musico-dramatic innovation his lifelong quest, Berlin seemed content just writing song hit after song hit. (Bloom, 42–44)

Another musical figure to start his career during this time was Jerome Kern.

Kern made his first big hit and first lasting contribution to the pop song repertory with "They Didn't Believe Me," interpolated into the British import *The Girl from Utah* in 1914, the same year that Berlin wrote his first full Broadway score. As lyrical musically as operetta but simpler melodically and with more conversational lyrics, "They Didn't Believe Me," a thirty-two-bar ABA'C song, doesn't require an operatic voice or range. (A man could perform it by changing a few words: "handsomest boy" to "loveliest girl" and "You're the man whose wife some day I'll be" to "I'm the man whose wife some day you'll be.")

Written in 4/4 time, it signaled the beginning of the end of the reign of the waltz.

Kern almost always wrote his music first and refused to change a note to accommodate his lyricists. This sometimes led to rather awkward language and phrasing in his songs. (He was in general known to be very difficult.) During his career he contributed songs to over 130 shows of many kinds, including revues and such gigantic Ziegfeld creations as *Sally* (1920) and *Sunny* (1925), both shaped to the talents of Broadway dancing superstar Marilyn Miller.

And there was *Show Boat* with Hammerstein in 1927. Hammerstein was looking for the same kinds of integrated shows that Kern was. They were the ideal collaborators for this major development, the first real forging of the musical comedy and the operetta into the musical play. After 1927, most of Kern's work was done in Hollywood. He made only occasional returns to Broadway, always with more traditional fare than *Show Boat*, although he continued experimenting with combinations of the musical comedy and the operetta. He was in New York in 1945 to write the music for *Annie Get Your Gun*, but died before work could begin. To replace him, producers Rodgers and Hammerstein hired Irving Berlin, a fitting choice. It was Kern who, when asked to assess Berlin's place in American music, said, "Irving Berlin has no place in American music. He *is* American music."

In 1915, partly as a matter of economics, musicals began to develop a more structured script when Kern and Guy Bolton were hired to write the first of the small-scale, intimate musical comedies that came to be known as the **Princess musicals**. Those who discount the contributions of Cohan call Kern the father of the American musical, largely because of these shows (and, of course, *Show Boat*). With them, Kern got his first chance to bring what he'd learned from European operettas into the American musical comedy. He wanted the musical to be coherent, he wanted the musical numbers to help carry on the action of the play and be true to the characters who sing them, and he wanted the characters and situations to be realistic, American, and contemporary.

The Princess musicals, produced by F. Ray Comstock and Elizabeth Marbury, were written for the 299-seat, cost-conscious Princess Theatre, located at Thirty-ninth Street and Sixth Avenue.

Jerome David Kern (1885–1945) was born into a middle-class Jewish family in New York. Although his father wanted him to go into business, he was constitutionally incapable of doing so. He began as a song plugger in Tin Pan Alley, playing his own music whenever possible. A Weber and Fields show first used one of Kern's songs, and his songs were soon being interpolated into imported shows. After spending time in Europe, where he placed songs into London shows, Kern returned home, played rehearsal piano for some shows, and again was able to have his songs interpolated into European imports. From working on these shows, he learned to combine Europeanisms and Americanisms into a romantic sound uniquely his own. Known as the Great Melodist, he wrote scores for over thirty musicals, including *Show Boat*.

Guy Bolton (1884–1979, born of American parents in Broxbourne, England) moved with his family to the United States when he was a child. Bolton wrote the books for fifty-seven musicals with such songwriters as the Gershwins, Cole Porter, and Rodgers and Hart.

There were seven Princess musicals altogether over a four-year period, though only four actually played the Princess. They were
trivial, lightweight farces, funnier and more sophisticated than
Cohan's sentimental, melodramatic star vehicles, but, like Cohan's shows, they had no interpolations, musical or comic. Budget and space demands required the shows to have small choruses
(only twelve girls), one set per act, and no expensive stars. Kern
and Bolton, eventually joined by P. G. Wodehouse, used these limitations to integrate the scores and scripts into reasonably coherent, two-act stories written for an ensemble rather than for stars
and supporting players. This was accomplished in several ways: a
romantic main plot and a comic subplot; songs and comedy
scenes keyed to character and situation; musical numbers carefully organized for variety and to make certain that each performer got a chance in the spotlight; many reprises of songs to
help structure the shows; and dialogue that flowed fairly effort-
lessly into music and back again. All this was accomplished without the stretching, pulling, and ignoring of the script necessary to
satisfy the whims of stars.

Since the Princess was small, performers were directed to
keep everything intimate, making their performances seem
more natural than usual. This included the singing: since the orchestra was also small—the pit held a maximum of eleven
players—softer-than-usual singing could be easily heard. Another innovation was that the members of the chorus had individual personalities and costumes, and they all had to both sing
and dance. (In musicals of the time, there was usually a large
singing chorus and a separate, smaller dancing one, a practice
which still often holds true. Nowadays, however, with fewer chorus members in the budget, the dancers are expected to be able
to sing at least adequately, and the singers usually have to do
some dancing.) Richard Rodgers said the Princess shows gave
"to a small audience the feeling that the whole composition of
the evening had been created for the two ears of the single lis-
tener. The effect was one of intimacy and warmth and something quite rare and memorable." (Goodfriend, 16)

The first Princess musical, *Nobody Home*, was imported from
London, where it had been called *Mr. Popple of Ippleton* (two
acts, one set each). Kern and Schuyler Greene, the original
British writer, were hired to adapt the show for American audiences. After a disastrous preview, *Nobody Home* closed down for

**P. G. (Pelham Grenville)
Wodehouse** (1881–1975,
born in Guildford, England) wrote
witty, slangy, intelligent lyrics,
a big step in making songs
more characterful and more
contemporary, moving them
away from *moon-June-spoon-
tune* rhymes and the *thou, alas*
stilted language typical of late
nineteenth- and early twentieth-
century lyrics. Today, Wodehouse
is largely remembered as the
author of many lightweight,
comic novels and stories about
silly upper-class Englishmen and
their servants, including several
about the gentleman's
gentleman Jeeves and his dim-
witted master Bertie Wooster
(one of which was adapted into
By Jeeves, a musical by Andrew
Lloyd Webber and Alan
Ayckbourn that ran only 73
performances in 2001).
Wodehouse's first Broadway
lyrics were for *Miss
Springtime* in 1916.

two weeks, and Bolton was hired to rewrite the book while Kern wrote an entirely new score. His new music was close to operetta, but with a ragtime wash. This time the show was a success, soon followed by *Very Good Eddie,* the first original Princess show, which had seven lyricists and a book adapted by Philip Bartholomae and Bolton from a farce by Bartholomae. The music was even further away from operetta than that in *Nobody Home.* The lightweight story centers around mistaken relationships, a standard plot device in these musicals.

Kern and Bolton felt that having only one lyricist would lead to even greater coherence between script and songs, so they chose Wodehouse for their next show. He also cowrote the books for the shows with Bolton from then on. *Oh, Boy!* (1917), the most successful of them, ran 463 performances before going on a lucrative road tour. It's a light farce about innocent but suspicious-looking behavior among engaged and married couples.

Leave It to Jane (also 1917, based on George Ade's 1904 play *The College Widow*) is a Princess musical that didn't open at the Princess since *Oh, Boy!* was still running there. *Leave It to Jane* ran 167 performances to sold-out houses before touring. This slightly-larger-than-Princess-style musical comedy was the first college football musical and the prototype for many more, including *Good News!* (1927) and *Too Many Girls* (1939). The main story of these shows usually focused on whether or not the smartest girl in school could help the big football star pass an exam so he could win the big game for the home team and whether or not the two fall in love. The answers were obvious. There was a 1959 off-Broadway revival of *Leave it to Jane* that ran two years.

Kern, Bolton, and Wodehouse amicably broke up their partnership after *Oh, Lady! Lady!* in 1918; they were all doing other projects in addition to working together and felt they had done enough Princess shows. All these shows' innovations were seen as revolutionary by the people who made musicals, especially since the shows remained very successful even when done in bigger houses than the Princess or on tour. Since these shows were light-headed, boy-meets-girl musical comedies, they didn't influence new shows to become more meaningful. Well into the thirties, show after show was still full of silliness and good-natured fun. And even though many of them were at least somewhat subject to the talents and whims of stars, most shows had more structure and story than before—if only by a little—thanks to the Princess musicals.

Even with all the new developments in the musical, thanks to *The Merry Widow* and *Naughty Marietta,* romantic operettas set in far-off lands and times were also in vogue; between 1911 and 1917, Victor Herbert alone

Rudolf Friml (1879–1972, born in Prague) first came to America in 1901 as the piano accompanist for violinist Jan Kubelik and returned permanently in 1906. He wrote music for over twenty shows, more successfully for operettas than for musical comedies and revues, although he contributed songs to many of the latter, including those of Ziegfeld. When jazz completely overtook Broadway's music, Friml fled to Hollywood, where he could ignore it, and died there. Some of the songs from his operettas were among the most popular hits of the day. His first hit was *The Firefly*, written with Otto Harbach in 1912, and his most enduring is the 1924 operetta *Rose-Marie*, with lyrics and libretto by Harbach and Hammerstein.

wrote thirteen of these types of shows, five of them hits. His most important successors, Rudolf Friml and Sigmund Romberg, were also European born and trained and were most comfortable with European musical structures, rhythms, and harmonies. They both were more romantically inclined than Herbert.

> Among Herbert, Friml, and Romberg an epoch on the Broadway stage came and passed. Their music was popular in restaurants, cafes, and concerts. Their European-influenced music, written for the finest voices on the lyric theatre stage of the time, brought lush orchestrations, Viennese waltzes, and sophisticated harmonics to Broadway. (Denny Martin Flinn, *Musical! A Grand Tour*, 92)

In 1912, German director/designer Max Reinhardt (1873–1943) brought his concept of unifying all the visual elements of a production to the United States. For him, the sets, lights, and costumes had to work together to focus the audience's attention on the central action. The scenery should be designed to be enhanced by the lighting and the costumes designed and colored to be in sync with the sets and lights. (Most Broadway designers of the time went their separate ways, and the results often clashed with each other and sometimes even with the show they were working on.) Reinhardt also built an apron in front of the

Backdrop: 1912–1918

National U.S. suffragettes march on Washington, D.C., in 1913; men along the route incite a riot. Union leader Joe Hill is tried for murder, executed, and becomes a legendary hero in the growing discord between labor and management. The Sixteenth Amendment, providing a graduated income tax, is instituted. By 1917, the United States has over forty thousand millionaires. Race riots in East St. Louis, Illinois, in 1917, leave thirty-nine dead and hundreds injured; this leads to a silent walk down Fifth proscenium and a runway over the orchestra in order to bring the actors out into the auditorium. His concepts changed the very nature of theatrical design.

The Red Petticoat (61 performances) was Kern's first full Broadway score. *Roly Poly,* Weber and Fields's reunion and their last burlesque-extravaganza, costarred Nora Bayes, still singing "Shine On, Harvest Moon." *Ziegfeld Follies of 1912* starred Bert Williams and Leon Errol, had bare-legged chorus girls, was the first to open on the ground floor rather than the roof, and ran 88 performances before touring. It was rivaled by the first of the annual Shubert revues, called *The Passing Show* after that original Broadway revue in 1894. It had an eighty-girl chorus and ran 136 performances. The first act was a ballet, the second a Weber Fields–style burlesque-extravaganza staged and choreographed by Ned Wayburn.

The Firefly (120 performances), with music by Friml and libretto by Otto Harbach (Hauerback), was produced by Arthur Hammerstein (Oscar II's uncle) and directed by Fred G. Latham. It was Friml's first show, an operetta about an Italian street singer who, after many adventures and disguises, ends up a famous opera singer. It was a huge success. Friml got the job when Victor Herbert walked out because of major disagreements with Emma Trentini, the star soprano, who also starred in Herbert's *Naughty Marietta.* Revived fairly frequently for many years, *The Firefly* seems to have disappeared altogether now. Robert Z.

Sigmund Romberg (1887–1951, born in Hungary) moved to America in 1909. He wrote music for nearly sixty shows, much of it churned out for the Shuberts. Romberg and Rida Johnson Young had contracts with the Shuberts that allowed the Shuberts to keep all the rights and royalties to their work. Romberg eventually became successful enough to break free from the Shuberts. He wrote revues and musicals, including some for Ziegfeld, but, like Friml, he was most comfortable and successful with operettas. Also like Friml, he hated jazz and other contemporary sounds. He too went to Hollywood in the thirties, where he did quite well, but unlike Friml, he occasionally returned to Broadway. Among the Romberg operettas still produced are *The Student Prince* (1924), *The Desert Song* (1926), and *The New Moon* (1928).

Avenue in New York by W. E. B. DuBois, James Weldon Johnson, and fifteen thousand others. The Universal Negro Improvement Association and the Anti-Defamation League are formed. The Lincoln Memorial in Washington, D.C., is completed. In 1918, for the third time, the U.S. Senate rejects an amendment granting women the vote.

International The luxury liner SS *Titanic* hits an iceberg in the North Atlantic and sinks on its first trip in 1912; 1,513 die (source and title in 1997 of both the movie and the musical). In 1914, Archduke Franz Ferdinand, heir to the Austrian throne, and his wife are assassinated in Sarajevo; World War I begins in Europe. A German submarine sinks the U.S. passenger ship SS *Lusitania* in 1915, killing

Leonard's 1937 movie version, starring Jeanette MacDonald, has Allan Jones singing "The Donkey Serenade," which became very famous but wasn't in the original operetta.

By 1913, the Times Square area was firmly established as the center of the theater district. Almost every successful show went on tour. The Shubert Theatre opened, and with it Shubert Alley, which created a walking path between Forty-fourth and Forty-fifth streets, halfway between Broadway and Eighth Avenue. The United Booking Office—the powerful vaudeville chain of B. F. Keith and Edward F. Albee (the playwright's adoptive grandfather)—opened the 1,736-seat Palace Theatre in Times Square; tickets were two dollars. Almost immediately, the Palace assumed its position as the most important vaudeville house in North America. Actors' Equity Association, the theater actors' union, was formally activated, and chorus girls also formed a union.

Vernon and Irene Castle were featured in the Broadway musical comedy *The Sunshine Girl* (160 performances), in which they did the turkey trot and the tango. Afterwards, waltzes and other European dances were replaced onstage by ballroom dances from the Americas.

Ziegfeld Follies of 1913 (96 performances), starring Leon Errol, was presented at the New Amsterdam Theatre, where most of the remaining editions were also produced. The Shuberts' *The*

Otto Harbach (1873–1963, born Otto Abels Hauerback in Salt Lake City, Utah) changed his name when the United States entered World War I with Germany. He was a major force in the development of integrated lyrics and librettos for operettas and musicals. His first Broadway success as a lyricist came in 1908 with the musical comedy *Three Twins*, written with composer Karl Hoschna, which included the hit song "Cuddle Up a Little Closer, Lovey Mine." Harbach collaborated on ten shows with Friml and wrote with such other composers as Romberg, Kern, Vincent Youmans, and George Gershwin. Among his most successful shows were *No, No, Nanette, Rose-Marie, The Desert Song,* and *Roberta.* He became Oscar Hammerstein II's teacher and mentor.

1,198 people. In 1917, Germany begins unrestricted submarine warfare, and the United States enters World War I. The United States moves troops and businesses into Central and South America. Puerto Rico and the Virgin Islands become U.S. territories. The Panama Canal opens. The 1917 Russian revolution ends the three-hundred-year Romanov dynasty; in 1918, the entire Romanov family is executed by the Bolsheviks, although some claim Anastasia, the youngest daughter, survived. (In 1954, Bolton and Maurette wrote the play *Anastasia,* about a woman who may be the surviving princess; it was adapted into the flop 1965 musical *Anya*).

New Developments Margaret Sanger introduces the term *birth control.* The passenger pigeon becomes extinct. Parcel post and regular airmail service begin. Ford cuts the assembly time of autos to under two hours, making them affordable to many more people. Long-distance phone links between New York and San Francisco are opened, and the Teletype machine further expands communication capabilities. The Merrill Lynch brokerage firm and the Greyhound Bus Company begin operations. The pop-up toaster,

Passing Show of 1913 (116 performances) had a runway and was staged by Ned Wayburn. It included parodies of current Broadway shows, Monaco and McCarthy's hit song "You Made Me Love You (I Didn't Want to Do It)," and such dances as the tango, the turkey trot, and the cakewalk.

Sweethearts (136 performances), with music by Victor Herbert, lyrics by Robert B. Smith, and libretto by Harry B. Smith and Fred De Gresac, was the most successful show Herbert wrote with Smith. The title song, a waltz, became a pop hit. In 1938, the operetta was turned into a Jeanette MacDonald and Nelson Eddy movie, even less faithful to the original than usual for Hollywood.

In 1914, the American Society of Composers, Authors, and Publishers (ASCAP) was founded, largely at the instigation of Victor Herbert. It defended its members against illegal performances and other copyright violations, and it collected royalties. Grossinger's Resort opened in the Catskill Mountains as a summer vacation retreat for New York laborers. Over the years, it and other resorts that opened in the area served as starting places for many performers who soon became famous. (The area became known as the "borscht belt" since most of the audiences and performers were Jewish.) The Shuberts gave up producing at the Hippodrome, which Charles Dillingham then took over. Kern's songs were interpolated into the British musical *The Girl from Utah* (120 performances). They made the show a hit, and "They Didn't Believe Me" established Kern's reputation.

The revue form continued to grow in popularity, giving employment to many vaudeville performers. Cohan's revue *Hello, Broadway!* (123 perfor-

the Raggedy Ann doll, Quaker's Puffed Wheat and Puffed Rice breakfast cereals, Camel and Chesterfield cigarettes, and Life Savers (peppermint) go on the market. Clarence Birdseye begins freezing fish, Helena Rubinstein starts her cosmetics firm, and Coco Chanel designs and sells sportswear for women.

Sports The National Hockey League is organized. Notre Dame University student Knute Rockne, with his use of the forward pass, changes how football is played. The new Great White Hope, Jess Willard, defeats heavyweight champ Jack Johnson. Native American athlete and football player Jim Thorpe wins the pentathlon and the decathlon at the Fifth Olympiad; he's stripped of his medals when he admits to having played semiprofessional football for a summer.

Art The Dadaist movement, dedicated to the pursuit of anti-art and illogic, is founded in Switzerland and New York. Painters Edgar Degas and Gustav Klimt and sculptor Auguste Rodin die. Painters Gris, Kokoschka, Klee, O'Keeffe, Sargent, and Miró come into prominence. Georges Braque invents collage.

Marilyn Miller (1898–1936, born Mary Ellen Reynolds in Evansville, Indiana) switched to the *Follies* in 1918 and soon became one of Ziegfeld's biggest stars and one of the highest paid Broadway stars of the time. She was an excellent dancer with a charming personality and an almost adequate singing voice. Until Ziegfeld got her to change it, she spelled her first name *Marilynn*.

mances) lacked even a thread of a plot or continuing characters to tie the sketches and musical numbers together. *Ziegfeld Follies of 1914* (112 performances) starred Ed Wynn in his first nonvaudeville appearance, Leon Errol, and Bert Williams. Romberg's first show, the Shuberts' *The Whirl of the World* (161 performances), was a revue with lyrics and script by Harold Atteridge. *The Passing Show of 1914* (133 performances), music mostly by Romberg and lyrics mostly by Atteridge, had chorus girls with bare legs and arms and the first bare midriffs on Broadway; the show also introduced Marilyn Miller.

Watch Your Step: The First All-Syncopated Musical (175 performances), with a score by Irving Berlin and a book by Harry B. Smith, was produced by Charles Dillingham and starred Fanny Brice and the Castles. It was Berlin's first full Broadway score. Although billed as a syncopated musical, it had a plot that was so

The Armory Show introduces cubist and postimpressionist paintings to New York. Architect Walter Gropius opens his influential Bauhaus School in Weimar. Wright designs the Imperial Hotel in Tokyo; Gilbert designs the Woolworth Building in New York.

Music/Dance   Composer Claude Debussy dies. Composers De Falla, Bartók, and Prokofiev come into prominence. Vaslav Nijinsky—the most famous male ballet dancer of the day—dances Debussy's erotic *The Afternoon of a Faun* and choreographs Stravinsky's modernist ballet *Le Sacre du Printemps* (*The Rite of Spring*), which causes a riot at its Paris debut.

Publications   The *New Republic* and *Poetry* magazines begin publication. Novelists Henry James and Jack London die. Novelists Joyce, Lawrence, Woolf, Maugham, Cather, and Proust, and poets Eliot, Lindsay, Millay, Frost, and Sandburg become prominent. Italian educator Maria Montessori's *The Montessori Method* and James Weldon Johnson's *The Autobiography of an Ex-Colored Man* are published.

Radio   AM radio is pioneered. Phonograph records begin selling in the millions.

Pop Culture   Scott Joplin dies, marking the end of pure ragtime, which has already peaked in popularity and is soon replaced by jazz. Jazz cornetist King Oliver moves to Chicago from New Orleans; his student Louis Armstrong joins him in 1922. Columbia Records releases the first jazz recording, Shelton Brooks's "The Darktown Strutters' Ball" ("I'll be down to get you in a taxi, honey"). Jolson begins his recording career. Berlin forms his own music publishing business; among his new songs are "When That Midnight Choo Choo Leaves for Alabam'" and "That International Rag." Other pop songs include Yale sophomore Cole Porter's "Bulldog" and "Bingo Eli Yale" for the football team, Wenrich and Madden's "(On) Moonlight Bay" (another barbershop quartet favorite), Fisher and thin, it was almost a revue; the program read "Book (if any) by Harry B. Smith." The show's biggest hit song, "Play a Simple Melody," is the first of several two-part songs Berlin wrote with a ballad-like melody and a contrasting, fast, syncopated one. Each melody was sung separately, then together. The Castles danced the tango, the fox-trot (which replaced the turkey trot), the one-step, and the Castle Walk. The dance craze was starting to lose business for Broadway; people went out dancing instead of going to shows.

In 1915, going to the theater began to appeal to younger audiences again. In that year, Broadway entered an era of great prosperity that continued and grew until the 1929 stock market crash. Because of the war in Europe, Viennese operettas soon disappeared from U.S. stages. American operettas continued to find favor, however, and musical comedies were becoming almost as popular as revues.

Also during the year, an antitrust suit against the United Booking Office

Bryan's "Peg o' My Heart," Smith and Burris's "Ballin' the Jack," Handy's "St. Louis Blues" (the definitive blues song of the period), Bowman's "12th Street Rag," Carroll and Atteridge's "By the Beautiful Sea," Black's "Paper Doll," Morse and Johnson's "M-O-T-H-E-R (M is for the million things she gave me)," LaRocca's "Tiger Rag," Meyer, Leslie, and Goetz's "For Me and My Gal," Cohan's "Over There" (introduced by Nora Bayes), Alford's "Colonel Bogey March," Jones, Powell, and Asaf's "Pack Up Your Troubles in Your Old Kit Bag," Taylor and Olsen's "You're in the Army Now," and many other war-related songs.

Stage London's Old Vic Shakespeare Company opens, as does Shaw's *Pygmalion* (adapted in 1956 into the musical *My Fair Lady*). The Yiddish Art Theatre and the Provincetown Playhouse (the first New York producers of Eugene O'Neill's plays) open off-Broadway.

Screen Universal Pictures Corporation is formed and is the first studio to promote its stars as much as its movies. About five million Americans go to the movies every day. DeMille's *The Squaw Man* is the first full-length film made in Hollywood. Innovative director D. W. Griffith relocates his movie company there. Lasky, Goldwyn, and DeMille found the Jesse L. Lasky Feature Play Company, which becomes Paramount Pictures in 1932, and the Warner brothers and Louis B. Mayer open their studios. Movie theaters open in the Times Square area. Mack Sennett produces Charlie Chaplin's first movies; within a short time, Chaplin's salary reaches a million dollars. Movies include Sennett's *Tillie's Punctured Romance,* with Chaplin, Marie Dressler, and Mabel Normand. (Sennett and Normand's unhappy love story is the subject of the 1974 musical *Mack and Mabel*). D. W. Griffith's *The Birth of a Nation* premieres; it includes close-ups, panning shots, flashbacks, and a moving camera. It creates a sensation, revolutionizes filmmaking, and causes race riots with its glorification of the Ku Klux Klan, the "nation" born after the Civil War. (The Klan itself is reborn in Georgia during the year.)

Joseph Urban (1872–1933, born in Vienna) arrived in America already a well-known architectural designer. He was a follower of the unified methods of European director/designer Max Reinhardt and known for his bold color schemes, pointillistic approach to lighting and set painting, color-coordinated sets, and an architectural—as opposed to painted—approach to perspective. Along with Reinhardt and Diaghilev's Ballets Russes, Urban helped bring the art nouveau and art deco movements to Broadway. One of the most influential and sought-after designers of his generation, he did over sixty Ziegfeld productions alone. He was also an architect and interior designer (of the elaborate Ziegfeld Theatre and others) and even worked on several movies.

(Keith-Albee) was dismissed. The Marx Brothers (central characters in the 1970 musical *Minnie's Boys*), Fanny Brice, escape artist Harry Houdini (a character in the 1998 musical *Ragtime*), and a reunited Weber and Fields were among the headliners who played the Palace. Cole Porter's first Broadway song, "Esmeralda," was interpolated into the musical *Hands Up*.

It was an important year for the musical, with the premieres of the first two Princess musicals, *Nobody Home* (135 performances) and *Very Good Eddie* (341 performances), and the addition of Joseph Urban's designs to the *Follies*.

Ziegfeld Follies of 1915 (104 performances) was director/choreographer Julian Mitchell's last *Follies* for a while and starred W. C. Fields in his *Follies* debut, Ed Wynn, Bert Williams, Leon Errol, and George White. The 1916 edition, also designed by Urban, was the first to be staged by Ned Wayburn and starred Will Rogers (the central character in the 1991 concept musical *The Will Rogers Follies*) in his first *Follies*, W. C. Fields, Bert Williams, and Fanny Brice.

Berlin and Harry B. Smith's revue *Stop! Look! Listen!* (105 performances) had among its songs the romantic "The Girl on the Magazine Cover" and the syncopated "I Love a Piano." *The Passing Show of 1915* (145 performances) again featured Marilyn Miller. The 1916 edition starred Ed Wynn and included Van Alstyne and Kahn's "Pretty Baby" and George Gershwin's first Broadway songs.

In 1917, the top Broadway ticket price averaged $3, and a musical averaged $25,000 to produce. The Shuberts owned theaters in almost every major American city. Jolson was the highest paid performer on the musical stage.

Ziegfeld Follies of 1917 (111 performances) was directed and choreographed by Ned Wayburn and starred Fanny Brice, W. C. Fields, Will Rogers, Bert Williams, and comic Eddie Cantor (1892–1964, born Edward Israel Iskowitz in New York) in his *Follies* debut. Cantor began in vaudeville doing blackface and later was a star of musicals, movies, radio, and early TV. (He also founded the March of Dimes, among his many charitable works.) The 1917 *Follies* had a patriotic Victor Herbert finale, cost $90,000 to produce, and was—like many of the subsequent editions of the revue—designed by Urban. *The Passing Show of 1917* (196 performances) had music mostly by Romberg and lyrics mostly by Harold Atteridge. *Over the Top* was a revue with music also mostly by Romberg.

Have a Heart (76 performances) was the first show Kern, Bolton, and Wodehouse worked on together, a sort of tryout before their first Princess musical. During the year, they also wrote the Princess musicals *Oh, Boy!* and *Leave It to Jane*. Ticket prices at the Princess rose from $1.50 to $3.50, a new high. Kern also did *Love o' Mike* (192 performances), with lyrics by Harold B. Smith and book by Thomas Sydney. He and Victor Herbert both wrote songs for *Miss 1917*, with lyrics by Wodehouse, book by Bolton and Wodehouse, and with George Gershwin as the show's rehearsal pianist. Kern, a busy man in 1917, also interpolated songs into the Viennese operetta *The Riviera Girl*.

Eileen (64 performances), with music by Victor Herbert and lyrics and libretto by Henry Blossom, was Herbert's personal favorite operetta, set in his native Ireland. The show's "Thine Alone" became a song sung at countless American weddings.

Maytime (492 performances) had music by Sigmund Romberg, libretto by Rida Johnson Young and Cyrus Wood, and was produced by the Shuberts. It was Romberg's first true operetta—although billed as a musical play so it wouldn't be thought of as German—and it was one of Johnson's and his biggest hits under their Shubert contracts. For a while, the Shuberts, never at a loss for how to make more money quickly, had two Broadway productions of it running across the street from each other. (The Shuberts eventually became infamous for sending out multiple tacky-looking productions of hit operettas on endless tours.) *Maytime*, a sentimental tale of true love forced apart by the rules of society, was the basis of a 1937 movie with Jeanette MacDonald, Nelson Eddy, John Barrymore, and with an entirely different story.

In 1918, dancer Vernon Castle enlisted and was killed shortly before the end of World War I. The Original Dixieland Jazz Band toured Europe, increasing foreign interest in jazz. A standard Actors' Equity contract was established, and vaudeville managers stopped booking performers born in Germany. Paul Keith died, leaving the Keith-Albee circuit fully in E. F. Albee's control. At that time, "25,000 performers [were] now touring in 4,000 vaudeville theatres in the United States. They are booked on the Keith (eastern) or Orpheum (western) 'circuit,' with a

Fred (1899–1987) and **Adele** (1897–1981) **Astaire**, brother and sister dancing partners, were introduced to Broadway in *Over the Top*. Born in Omaha, Nebraska, they started in vaudeville at the ages of five and seven, where they became major stars before moving on to Broadway revues and musicals. After Adele retired in 1932 to get married, Fred went on to a brief solo career, followed by fame and fortune in Hollywood.

gig at the Palace Theatre in New York City as the ultimate and most desirable goal" (Lax and Smith, 41).

George and Ira Gershwin (with Ira writing as Arthur Francis) had their first song as a team sung on Broadway, "The Real American Folk Song Is a Rag," in *Ladies First,* starring Nora Bayes. *Ziegfeld Follies of 1918* (151 performances) starred Will Rogers, Marilyn Miller (her first for Ziegfeld), Eddie Cantor, W. C. Fields, and seventy-four chorus girls, had songs by Berlin and B. G. DeSylva (among others), and cost $100,000 to produce. *The Passing Show of 1918* (124 performances) starred the Astaires and had music mostly by Romberg and Jean Schwartz and lyrics mostly by Harold Atteridge. The last of Kern's Princess musicals with Wodehouse and Bolton was *Oh, Lady! Lady!* (219 performances). The song "Bill" was dropped before opening, from *Zip Goes a Million* in 1919, and from *Sally,* but was used in *Show Boat* in 1927 with the lyrics revised by Hammerstein.

Sinbad (164 performances), with music by Romberg and others and produced at the Shuberts' Winter Garden Theatre, starred Jolson as Gus, his usual blackface character. He interpolated Donaldson, Young, and Lewis's "My Mammy" and Schwartz, Young, and Lewis's "Rock-a-Bye Your Baby with a Dixie Melody," and had a runway built to get closer to his audience. During the following tour, he interpolated George Gershwin and Irving Caesar's "Swanee," which skyrocketed their careers.

Yip-Yip-Yaphank had songs by Berlin, who was in the cast along with 350 other members of the U.S. Armed Forces. The revue, about life in the army and staged like a giant minstrel show, was produced by the United States and ran thirty-two performances on Broadway before touring to raise money for the war effort. As in minstrel shows, men in drag played all the women's roles. Berlin created the show while stationed at Camp Upton, in the town of Yaphank on Long Island. At the end of the last Broadway performance, the entire cast marched off through the audience, out of the theater, and down to the boat that took them overseas. The event was re-created in the 1943 movie *This Is the Army.* Stephen Suskin, in *Berlin, Rodgers, Hart, and Hammerstein: A Complete Song Catalogue,* notes:

> For the first time Berlin was writing about a specific subject, rather than just trying to come up with songs that would sell. This made a difference, one that would remain in evidence through the rest of his career. . . . *Yaphank* featured . . . Berlin himself, singing "Oh, How I Hate to Get Up in the Morning." . . . This was not a typical Tin Pan Alley tune, but real, universal, and funny. And a big hit. . . . Then there was "God Bless America," which was withdrawn and remained unheard for twenty years. (Suskin, 3)

❖

The score also includes the hit song "Mandy."

On November 11, the armistice was signed. Over nine million people died in World War I, and about twenty million were wounded. Europe could never return to its old ways. Monarchy had become essentially meaningless; democracy, socialism, and communism were now the ways of the Western world. The United States had become a major international power and set about celebrating that in every way possible.

Suggested Watching and Listening

Easter Parade: Early Berlin Hit Songs
In director Charles Walters's 1948 *Easter Parade* (available on Warner Home Video DVD), with a score of old and new Berlin songs, Judy Garland and Fred Astaire play a vaudeville team. (*Holiday Inn* in 1942 and *Blue Skies* in 1946 also have scores of old and new Berlin songs, and they costar Astaire and Bing Crosby playing vaudeville teams.)
- "I Love a Piano" (from *Stop! Look! Listen!,* 1915)
- "Snookey Ookums" (1913)
- "The Ragtime Violin" (1911)
- "When That Midnight Choo Choo Leaves for Alabam'" (1912)

In this sequence, Astaire and Garland do four early Berlin hits (three of them written directly for Tin Pan Alley).

Irving Berlin's America
This PBS "Think Tank" show, narrated by Sandy Duncan and made shortly before Berlin's death, contains a great deal of biographical information and excerpts from many of Berlin's songs done by their originators and other top stars. A&E's *Biography* also has a documentary on Berlin called *Irving Berlin: An American Song* (available on A&E DVD).

The Jolson Story
This is a 1946 biography of Al Jolson, available on Columbia Pictures DVD.
- "Swanee" (performed by Al Jolson): It's from the show *Sinbad*. Filmed at a distance, Jolson himself performs the Gershwin song in blackface.

The Story of Vernon and Irene Castle
Director H. C. Potter's 1939 pseudo-biography (available on Turner Home Entertainment DVD) stars Fred Astaire and Ginger Rogers in the last of their RKO musicals together. It has an accurate re-creation of some of the Castles' dances, personally supervised by Irene Castle, who made sure they got it exactly right (although she was apparently mostly concerned with what clothes Rogers wore).
- "The Castle Walk," "The Tango," "The Fox-Trot," "The Polka," and "The Maxixe" (all performed in this montage sequence by Ginger Rogers and Fred Astaire): The sequence also includes a montage showing how incredibly famous and influential the Castles became.

Till the Clouds Roll By

This film (available on Warner Home Video DVD) is director Richard Whorf's 1946 all-star pseudo-biography of Jerome Kern.

- "How'd You Like to Spoon with Me?" (performed by Angela Lansbury and the chorus with lyrics by Edward Laska): This typical English music hall song is performed in the film while Kern is still living in London. It was actually sung in *The Earl and the Girl,* written in 1905 after he'd already returned to the United States. "Spoon" was slang for kissing and hugging. (Angela Lansbury's years in Hollywood were very different from her years on Broadway or as Jessica Fletcher on her TV show *Murder, She Wrote.*)
- "They Didn't Believe Me" (performed by Dinah Shore with lyrics by Herbert Reynolds): This performance, from the show *The Girl from Utah,* is also in *Till the Clouds Roll By,* as is the following number.
- "Till the Clouds Roll By" (performed by June Allyson, Ray McDonald, and the chorus): This song is from the show *Oh Boy!* It's known as a charm song (a term coined by Alec Wilder) with one of Kern's many lilting melodies.

From The Scandals of 1919 to the Cotton Club

Though you're only seventeen
Far too much of life you've seen,
Syncopated child.
Maybe if you only knew
Where your path was leading to
You'd become less wild.
But I know it's vain
Trying to explain
While there's this insane
Music in your brain.
— "DANCE LITTLE LADY,"
THIS YEAR OF GRACE, LYRICS BY NOËL COWARD

In 1919, the United States was moving into the Jazz Age. American operettas were losing audiences, especially younger ones (as were shows like Cohan's) because they ignored the contemporary American rhythms set by Berlin, Kern, and Tin Pan Alley. However, musical comedies and, especially, revues thrived and grew stronger in the flapper-and-bootleg-gin era. They were urban, urbane, and about looking for fun and love in some form or other. They were youthful, unruly, anarchic, sexy, and crazy. They had stars, hit songs, good dances, expert comedians, good-humored satire, designs that set art and fashion trends, lots of girls, mostly cardboard characters, and a wide-ranging audience appeal.

The pleasure-seeking, Prohibition-despising, boom-rich American public enabled the musical theatre to revel in a decade of luxury and wastefulness and irresponsibility such as it had never known before, and will probably never know again in our time. Money was available to produce anything with the slightest prospect of success, and audiences were lenient, easily amused, and generous with their patronage. (Smith and Litton, 125)

The musicals didn't have much in the way of books, but that had no effect on whether a show was a hit. Star vehicles, in slightly more sophisticated and structured guises, continued as the form of choice for most musicals and were therefore tailored to specific and frequently unique talents. As late as 1924, in *Lady, Be Good!* the Gershwins, Bolton, and Thompson had to accommodate the clause written into all Cliff "Ukulele Ike" Edwards's contracts that said he'd do his ukulele specialty sometime between 10:00 and 10:15 P.M.—regardless. The same accommodation had to be made in Kern, Harbach, and Hammerstein's 1925 *Sunny,* and Edwards wasn't even the biggest star of either show. (Edwards is best remembered as the voice of Jiminy Cricket in Disney's 1940 *Pinocchio.*)

None of that lack of structure or even coherence mattered to audiences at the time, partly because of the stars, laughs, and spectacle and partly because both musicals and revues regularly produced the kinds of songs people wanted to hear. Broadway composers—Berlin and Kern in particular—were becoming as big stars as the performers of their songs.

In this atmosphere, new talent was nurtured and allowed to learn while doing. In the first five years after the war, such important contributors to the American musical as Hammerstein, Vincent Youmans, the Gershwins, and Rodgers and Hart began their Broadway careers, and Cole Porter had his first success. (His first show, *See America First,* written with T. Lawrason Riggs, was a 15-performance flop in 1916, after which the wealthy Porter retreated to Europe for several years to lick his wounds.)

Through the first half of the twenties, revue was the most popular and jazziest form of entertainment on Broadway. Both Ziegfeld and the Shuberts produced revues in addition to the *Follies* and *The Passing Show* each year, and other producers tried their luck as well. Among the most successful of the new annual shows were Berlin's four *Music Box Revues, George White's Scandals,* and *Earl Carroll's Vanities.* None of them, including the Shubert revues, achieved the same degree of fame and splendor as

Vincent Youmans (1898–1946, born in New York) began as a Tin Pan Alley song plugger and rehearsal pianist. His first Broadway show was *Two Little Girls in Blue* (1921). Youmans's two biggest hits were *No, No, Nanette* (1925) and *Hit the Deck* (1927). He became a producer as well. Unfortunately, he also became a difficult alcoholic. His shows followed the jazzy musical comedy formulas of the day. After the 1929 stock market crash, Youmans changed to a more romantic, less jazz-based sound more suitable to the new times. Nonetheless, his last Broadway shows were flops, and soon no one wanted to hire him. He moved to Hollywood, where his last score was for the 1933 movie *Flying Down to Rio,* the first pairing of Fred Astaire and Ginger Rogers. Youmans contracted tuberculosis and died in 1946. He wrote fewer than a hundred songs.

the *Follies*. In fact, the Shubert and Earl Carroll shows were decidedly cheaper, both in money spent and in taste exhibited; by 1922, they had added partial female nudity.

Several smaller, more intimate revues were also successful, including *The Greenwich Village Follies* and *The Grand Street Follies*. Simply produced, witty, frequently satirical, and ensemble-oriented, they didn't depend on showgirls, stars, and spectacle to bring in business but rather on the talents of their young writers and performers. Some were produced on Broadway, some in smaller, nonunion theaters scattered around town and later known as "off-Broadway." These shows were prototypes of the revues more popular in the thirties, when the big revues lost steam and got more expensive.

In 1919, Actors' Equity won its first strike; many shows closed during the strike and weren't able to reopen after it was settled. Most producers—including Cohan's partner, Sam H. Harris, who headed the new Producing Managers Association—accepted the union. Cohan didn't; his partnership with Harris ended in 1920. The settlement raised production costs; top ticket prices were $3.50.

Backdrop: 1919–1923

National By 1919, more people are living in cities than in rural areas. Warren G. Harding is elected president in 1920; he dies in 1923—some say conveniently—just as his administration's Teapot Dome scandal is erupting. Calvin Coolidge becomes president. The Eighteenth Amendment prohibiting the sale of alcoholic beverages goes into effect; Prohibition begins in 1920. Congress adopts the Nineteenth Amendment, giving women the vote. The Supreme Court rules that a minimum wage law for women is unconstitutional. The League of Women Voters and the American Civil Liberties Union are formed. Nearly a million immigrants enter the country during 1921. United States Steel reduces its working day to eight hours. In 1922, business improves, led by the auto industry, and prosperity begins building throughout the country. There are race riots in twenty-six cities, and four million U.S. laborers strike or are locked out. There's Klan-created violence in the South; in 1923, in Indiana, two hundred thousand attend a tristate Klan meeting.

International The Treaty of Versailles makes Germany solely responsible for starting World War I, placing the defeated country in enormous debt. A resolution is adopted by the Versailles Peace Conference to form the League of Nations. The U.S. Senate rejects the Treaty of Versailles and the League of Nations. The Sinn Féin Party organizes the Irish Republican Army (IRA) and begins a war with the British regular

Broadway revues of this year included *The Scandals of 1919* (128 performances), the first of the annual George White revues which copied Ziegfeld's formula but were heavier on contemporary dance styles. It had music by Richard Whiting and Herbert Spencer and book and lyrics by White and Arthur Jackson. White was also one of the stars, the producer, and choreographer. He added his name to the title of the show in 1922.

The Greenwich Village Follies (232 performances), the first in a series of more intimate, sophisticated revues created by John Murray Anderson, had satiric sketches and avant-garde dancers and designers as its main selling points. The first two editions were produced in Greenwich Village, then moved to Broadway. Beginning in 1921 they opened directly on Broadway, where increasingly less sophisticated editions appeared until 1928. The first edition was able to continue running during the Equity strike because it was a non-Equity show.

Ziegfeld Follies of 1919 (171 performances) starred Bert Williams and Marilyn Miller in their last *Follies,* and Eddie Cantor. For the first time, Ziegfeld hired one person, Irving Berlin, to write the bulk of the songs. There were

army. Benito Mussolini forms a fascist party in Italy. Lenin initiates the first Russian, forced-labor camp. Germany's stock market collapses. In 1923, in Munich, Adolf Hitler stages his Beer Hall Putsch, which fails.

New Developments   Joan of Arc is canonized. Evangelist Aimee Semple McPherson, founder of the International Church of the Four-Square Gospel, opens the five-thousand-seat Angelus Temple in Los Angeles, which features a rotating, illuminated cross visible for fifty miles. Studies of eclipses of the sun confirm Einstein's theory of relativity. Margaret Sanger founds the American Birth Control League. Insulin and tetanus shots are developed. King Tutankhamen's tomb is discovered in Egypt. Pan American World Airways, RCA, and Zenith Radio begin operations. Dial telephones, Drano, Johnson and Johnson Band-Aids, Arrow shirts, Wise potato chips, and Mounds and Baby Ruth (named for former president Cleveland's daughter) candy bars are introduced. The first Miss America is crowned in Atlantic City.

Sports   Baseball's Babe Ruth is sold by the Boston Red Sox to the New York Yankees. The Cincinnati Reds defeat the Chicago White Sox in the World Series, creating strong suspicion that the Sox were paid to throw the series; eight "Black" Sox are found guilty. The National Football League is organized.

Art   Impressionist Pierre Renoir dies. Naum Gabo begins experiments in kinetic art.

Music/Dance   Opera tenor Enrico Caruso dies. The Hollywood Bowl opens. Milhaud, in his score for the ballet *La Création du Monde* (*The Creation of the World*), is the first to incorporate jazz into classical music. Arnold Schoenberg writes his first twelve-tone music. Isadora Duncan opens a dance school in Moscow.

EARLY AMERICAN MUSICAL COMEDIES, OPERETTAS, AND REVUES, 1901–1924 interpolations, however, including Donaldson, Lewis, and Young's song "How Ya Gonna Keep 'Em Down on the Farm (After They've Seen Paree)?" about soldiers returning from Europe after the armistice, as well as a Victor Herbert circus ballet. Berlin's songs included "Oh, How I Hate to Get Up in the Morning" and "Mandy," both from *Yip-Yip-Yaphank;* "I've Got My Captain Working for Me Now," another song appropriate to the year after the end of the war; "You'd Be Surprised," sung by Cantor ("He's not so good in a crowd, but when you get him alone, you'd be surprised"); and "A Pretty Girl Is Like a Melody," Ziegfeld's eventual theme song.

The Passing Show of 1919 (280 performances) had music mostly by Romberg and lyrics mostly by Harold Atteridge, with Kenbrovin and Kellette's "I'm Forever Blowing Bubbles" among the interpolations. It was with this show that Romberg ended his contract with the Shuberts and became an independent agent, but with frequent returns to the fold.

Cole Porter's "Old-Fashioned Garden," a sentimental ballad, was his first hit song; it was in his score for *Hitchy-Koo of 1919*, a Broadway revue produced by Raymond Hitchcock, with annual editions from 1917 to 1920.

Publications Walter Winchell begins his eventually powerful career as a gossip columnist with a column for the *Vaudeville News. Reader's Digest, Better Homes and Gardens,* and *Time* magazines begin publication. Novelist Marcel Proust dies. Inspirational books such as Buber's *I and Thou* and Gibran's *The Prophet* are published. Other new books and poetry examining the way things are in the postwar world include Mencken's *The American Language,* Spengler's *The Decline of the West,* Yeats's *The Wild Swans at Coole* and Eliot's "The Waste Land," Lewis's *Main Street* and *Babbitt,* Wharton's *The Age of Innocence,* Lawrence's *Women in Love,* Joyce's *Ulysses* (banned in the United States until 1934), Hesse's *Siddhartha,* and Fitzgerald's *This Side of Paradise* (called the defining novel of the Jazz Age), *The Beautiful and Damned,* and *Tales of the Jazz Age.*

Radio Acoustical recording onto wax replaces the electric recording horn. The first paid radio commercials are aired. The A. C. Nielsen Company begins doing market research; its ratings system becomes a widely accepted measure for determining the popularity of radio programs and, eventually, TV shows, greatly influencing which get renewed and which get canceled. The British Broadcasting Company (BBC) begins operations. Americans now own eight hundred thousand radios.

Pop Culture Jazz musicians such as Jelly Roll Morton (subject of the 1992 musical *Jelly's Last Jam*) and Paul Whiteman tour Europe. African American composer/arranger Fletcher Henderson, later an important part of Benny Goodman's orchestra, opens at the Club Alabama in Manhattan. Louis Armstrong arrives in Chicago to join King Oliver's band. Bix Beiderbecke organizes his jazz band there. Blues singers Bessie Smith and "Ma" Rainey make their first recordings. Mary Louise "Texas" Guinan opens her famous Prohibition-era New York nightclub, welcoming customers with the phrase "Hello, suckers!"

Porter also wrote the music and lyrics for a 1922 edition, which closed out of town; it was the only one of the series produced by the Shuberts.

The most successful show of the year was the new musical *Irene* (675 performances), with music by Harry Tierney, lyrics by Joseph McCarthy, and book by James Montgomery. It was a sentimental, feel-good Cinderella story about a poor Irish American heroine who ends up marrying a millionaire. Its score included the top hit song of the year, the tender waltz "(In My Sweet Little) Alice Blue Gown." (The shade of blue in the title refers to a color named in tribute to Theodore Roosevelt's daughter Alice.) The record-breaking run—it beat the 1874 *Evangeline*—was partly based on the success of that one song. A 1973 revisal (605 performances) starring Debbie Reynolds was directed by Gower Champion and choreographed by Peter Gennaro. There were also 1926 (silent) and 1940 film versions.

A Lonely Romeo (87 performances), with music by Malvin F. Franklin, lyrics by Robert B. Smith, and a book by Harry B. Smith and Lew Fields (who also starred), was produced by the Shuberts. Richard Rodgers and Lorenz Hart's first Broadway song, "Any Old Place with You," was interpolated. Lew Fields found it through his son Herbert, who was doing college shows with Rodgers and Hart. The song is about places to go on a honeymoon and gives a taste of Hart's style and wit in embryo form. The first chorus goes:

New York's Roseland Ballroom opens. The city's musicians form a union. Pop songs include Piron's "I Wish I Could Shimmy Like My Sister Kate," von Tilzer and Fleeson's "I'll Be with You in Apple Blossom Time" (popular again during World War II, when many men and women were overseas), Handy's "Careless Love," Silver and Cohn's "Yes, We Have No Bananas," Creamer and Layton's "Way Down Yonder in New Orleans," Fisher's "Chicago (That Toddlin' Town)," George Gershwin and DeSylva's "(Please) Do It Again!" Whiting, Kahn, and Egan's "Ain't We Got Fun?" Donaldson and Kahn's "My Buddy," and Jones and Kahn's "I'll See You in My Dreams." (Gus Kahn wrote the lyrics for many Tin Pan Alley standards, but had little to do with Broadway.)

Stage Stanislavsky's Moscow Art Theatre begins a European tour to introduce his new acting techniques internationally; they play New York in 1923. Emmett Kelly joins Ringling Brothers, Barnum, and Bailey and starts his fifty-year career as a circus clown. Lindy's restaurant opens in New York and becomes a favorite Broadway hangout; Lindy's (called Mindy's) cheesecake is the subject of the bet that ties together the two plots of the 1950 musical *Guys and Dolls*. The Theatre Guild produces Molnár's *Liliom* (adapted in 1945 into *Carousel*). Among the new plays dealing with the same subject matter as the new books are O'Neill's *The Emperor Jones, The Hairy Ape, Beyond the Horizon* (his Pulitzer Prize–winning, first full-length drama and his first on Broadway), and his Pulitzer Prize–winning *Anna*

We'll melt in Syria,
Freeze in Siberia,
Negligee in Timbuktu.
In dreamy Portugal
I'm goin' to court you, gal.
Ancient Rome we'll paint anew.
Life would be cheerier,
On Lake Superior.
How would Pekin do?
I'm goin' to corner ya
In California.
Any old place with you.

The second chorus ends:

I'll go to hell for ya,
Or Philadelphia,
Any old place with you.

There was a third chorus as well. It's a **list song** (also known as a **catalog song**), which means it makes its point with a series of examples—a list.

Christie (source of the 1957 musical *New Girl in Town*). Also produced are Rice's *The Adding Machine;* Pirandello's *Six Characters in Search of an Author* and *Henry IV;* Shaw's *Heartbreak House* and *Saint Joan;* O'Casey's first play, *The Shadow of a Gunman;* and Brecht's first plays, *Baal, Drums in the Night,* and *In the Jungle of Cities.* Anne Nichols's silly romantic comedy about a Jewish-Catholic marriage, *Abie's Irish Rose,* opens and, though trashed by most critics, runs eight years and sets a Broadway record of 2,532 performances.

Screen Lee De Forest demonstrates a process for movies with sound. Eastman Kodak puts the first 16 mm camera on the market. Chaplin, Griffith, Mary Pickford, and Douglas Fairbanks form the United Artists picture company. A scandal involving silent movie comedian Fatty Arbuckle destroys his career and reveals for the first time to an outraged U.S. public that there's drug and alcohol abuse in Hollywood. New movies include the expressionist nightmare *The Cabinet of Dr. Caligari; The Sheik, The Four Horsemen of the Apocalypse,* and *Blood and Sand,* all with Rudolph Valentino (whose popularity inspires Snyder, Harry B. Smith, and Wheeler's pop song "(I'm) The Sheik of Araby"); Max Schreck as a vampire in Murnau's *Nosferatu;* Dorothy and Lillian Gish as sisters (one of them blind) caught up in the French Revolution in Griffith's *Orphans of the Storm;* Harold Lloyd hanging off a clock in *Safety Last;* Lon Chaney as *The Hunchback of Notre Dame;* and DeMille's silent version of *The Ten Commandments.*

La! La! Lucille (104 performances) featured music by George Gershwin, lyrics by Arthur J. Jackson and B. G. DeSylva, and a book by Fred Jackson; it was produced by Alex A. Aarons and George B. Seitz. Gershwin's first Broadway musical, it gave little hint of the groundbreaking scores to come. Also Aarons's first show, it was a door-slamming bedroom farce about a will that requires a man to divorce his wife before he can claim his large inheritance. He divorces her, gets the inheritance, then remarries her. The show was billed as "The New Up-to-the-Minute Musical Comedy of Class and Distinction." The score's most successful song was "There's More to the Kiss than the *X X X*," with lyrics by Irving Caesar.

Ziegfeld Follies of 1920 (123 performances)—with songs by Berlin and Herbert, among others, and starring Fanny Brice, W. C. Fields, and Van and Schenck—was one of four revues of 1920 with Ziegfeld's name in the title. The Shuberts produced nineteen shows during the 1920–21 season. George White's *Scandals* (1920, 120 performances) had music by George Gershwin and lyrics by Arthur Jackson. Gershwin wrote for the *Scandals* until 1924; very few of the songs he wrote during those years entered the standard repertory.

Always *You* (66 performances), with music by Herbert Stothart, had Oscar Hammerstein II's first libretto and lyrics for an operetta. It was produced by his uncle Arthur. Stothart and Hammerstein also wrote *Tickle Me* and *Jimmie,* both with Otto Harbach and Frank Mandel as coauthors.

Another show of 1920, *Poor Little Ritz Girl* (93 performances), had music by Richard Rodgers and Sigmund Romberg, lyrics by Lorenz Hart and Alex Gerber, and book by Lew Fields (also the producer) and George Campbell. Fields hired Rodgers and Hart to write their first full Broadway score after having used "Any Old Place with You" in *A Lonely Romeo*. During out-of-town tryouts, however, he cut eight of their songs and had Romberg and Gerber write new ones. Many critics noticed the difference between Romberg's European romantic style and Rodgers's harder, brighter American sound and seemed fairly split about how they felt about it. After this show, Rodgers and Hart had a hard time selling any songs until 1925.

Like *Irene, Sally* was a Cinderella story, this one about a dishwasher who ends up a *Follies* star. Kern was moving back and

Sally

MUSIC: Jerome Kern, with the ballet finale by Victor Herbert

LYRICS: Clifford Grey and P. G. Wodehouse

BOOK: Guy Bolton

DESIGNERS: Joseph Urban (sets) and Alice O'Neil (costumes)

PRODUCER: Florenz Ziegfeld

CAST INCLUDES: Marilyn Miller and the comic actors Leon Errol and Walter Catlett, with Helen Morgan in the chorus

PERFORMANCES: 570

forth between the older, sentimental musicals and more up-to-date ones; *Sally* was some of each. The score included the enormous hit "Look for the Silver Lining," with lyrics by B. G. DeSylva. This was the show that made Miller one of the biggest and highest paid stars of the twenties. She re-created her role in a 1929 film version. There was an unsuccessful 1948 revival.

In 1921, as a sign of the times, Chicago's State-Lake vaudeville house began running a feature film along with its vaudeville acts, and the Hippodrome had movies instead of a show during the summer months. The top Broadway ticket price was $5.50 for Berlin's *Music Box Revue*. Women began smoking in theater lobbies, though never outside.

Ziegfeld Follies of 1921 (123 performances) had songs by B. G. DeSylva, Rudolf Friml, and Victor Herbert, among others; was designed by Joseph Urban; and starred Fanny Brice, W. C. Fields, and Van and Schenck. It was the first *Follies* to cost over $125,000 to produce, more than twice as much as the average cost for a musical. Brice's songs included "Second-Hand Rose," by Hanley and Clarke, and "My Man," by Yvain and Jacques-Charles, with English lyrics by Pollock. Although Brice was mainly a Jewish-dialect comedienne, she also sang an occasional ballad or **torch song,** such as "My Man." (In the slang of the day, a person who loved someone without reciprocation *carried a torch,* so a torch song is a sentimental song of unrequited love.) Brice was one of the first who truly acted these songs line by line as if they were monologues in a play.

The Passing Show of 1921 (191 performances) included a song entitled "Beautiful Girls Are Like Opium."

> In putting the *Follies* together . . . Ziegfeld spared no expense. In putting on the *Passing Shows* the Shuberts spared all expense. . . . The sets were mainly culled from previous Shubert shows and the costumes too had previous incarnations in countless Shubert productions. Where Ziegfeld would have songs written to fit sets yet to be built, the Shuberts would assign Harold Atteridge the task of writing sketches for the same sets over and over in a variety of shows. Composers would be sent down to the Shubert warehouse for inspiration. (Bloom, *American Song,* 565)

George White's *Scandals* (1921, 97 performances) had music by George Gershwin and lyrics by Arthur Jackson. *The Perfect Fool* (275 performances), a revue written by and starring Ed Wynn with interpolations by Gershwin and Irving Caesar, had a title that gave Wynn the catchphrase he was known by for the rest of his career.

Music Box Revue (440 performances), which cost well over $180,000 to produce, was the first of four annual revues coproduced by Berlin and Sam H. Harris. It was the opening attraction of their new Broadway theater, the Music Box (still a flourishing Broadway house). Because the theater was smaller than most Broadway houses, the *Music Box Revues,* though lavishly produced, became a middle ground between the big Ziegfeld-type shows and the more intimate revues of the thirties. Berlin wrote the scores for all four editions and appeared in this one. Among the songs were the syncopated "Everybody Step" and the romantic "Say It with Music," the theme song for all four revues.

Bombo (218 performances before going out on a long tour) had music by Sigmund Romberg and book and lyrics by Harold Atteridge. A revue with a tiny plot, it was produced by the Shuberts and starred Al Jolson in blackface. During the run, he interpolated such songs as Rose, Jolson, and DeSylva's "Avalon"; Meyer, Jolson, and DeSylva's "California, Here I Come" (added on the road); Russo, Kahn, and Erdman's "Toot, Toot, Tootsie (Goo' Bye)"; and Silvers and Yellen's "April Showers." All became pop hits.

Shuffle Along of 1921

MUSIC: Eubie Blake

LYRICS: Noble Sissle

BOOK: Flournoy Miller and Aubrey Lyles, based on their vaudeville sketch

DIRECTOR: Walter Brooks

PRODUCER: Nikko Producing Company

CAST (ALL AFRICAN AMERICAN) INCLUDES: the four creators and the teenage Josephine Baker

PERFORMANCES: 504 on Broadway, after first opening in Harlem

Shuffle Along of 1921, a revue tied together with a minimal plot about the candidates for mayor in the mythical town of Jimtown, was an early sign of the African American period of creativity—particularly literary—known as the Harlem Renaissance.

> Nearly all activity in black shows on Broadway [had come] to an end around 1909. . . . With the migration of Southern blacks . . . racial tension in New York had increased significantly. Bert Williams was the only black performer to find employment in mainstream theater (and as a result no longer appeared in black shows), and while many other black performers were working in Harlem and other cities around the country, on the whole white audiences still preferred to see blacks portrayed by whites. . . . *Shuffle Along* helped to change that, and was the first all-black show to play on Broadway in twelve years. (Gruber, *Original Cast! The Early Years,* 46)

For the first time, black audience members were allowed seating on part of the main floor. The show's biggest hit songs were the fox-trot number "I'm Just Wild About Harry" (taken up as a campaign song for Harry Truman in 1948), the ballad "Love Will Find a Way," and "Baltimore Buzz."

Two Little Girls in Blue (135 performances) had music by Vincent Youmans and Paul Lannin, lyrics mostly by Arthur Francis (Ira Gershwin), and book by Fred Jackson. Ned Wayburn was the director/choreographer. It was Youmans's and Gershwin's first musical comedy. Its hit song, "Oh Me! Oh My!" showed Gershwin's wit and style very much in embryo form:

> Oh me! Oh my! Oh you!
> No other girl will do.
> Cares would be forever ended,
> And this world would be so splendid,
> If you cared enough, dear,
> To be true.
> Oh me! Oh my! Oh you!
> Those lips! Those eyes of blue!
> You're so lovely; you're so sweet;
> You simply lift me off my feet.
> Oh me! Oh my! Oh you-oo.

Blossom Time (592 performances) had music by Sigmund Romberg, lyrics and libretto by Dorothy Donnelly, and was produced by the Shuberts. A hugely popular operetta, it was a fictional episode in the life of early nineteenth-century classical composer Franz Schubert, adapted from a German operetta and known in London as *Lilac Time*, with much of the music based on Schubert melodies. Romberg and Donnelly did a major rewrite of the original. Among *Blossom Time*'s most familiar numbers were "Serenade," with music from one of Schubert's most familiar songs, and "Song of Love," adapted from the second theme of the first movement of his "Unfinished Symphony." The second-longest-running musical evening of the decade, the show became a Shubert staple on the road for many years in notoriously flimsier and undercast productions. Dorothy Donnelly (1880–1928) was an actress before turning to writing books and lyrics as well as straight plays. She created the title role in the American premiere of Shaw's *Candida* and wrote the W. C. Fields comedy *Poppy*.

Eubie (James Hubert) Blake (1883–1983, born in Baltimore, Maryland) and **Noble Sissle** (1889–1975, born in Indianapolis, Indiana) composer and lyricist, respectively, teamed up after the war and became a popular vaudeville act known as the Dixie Duo, singing and playing their own songs. They dressed in tuxedos and were the first African American vaudevillians not to wear blackface.

In 1922, megastar Lillian Russell and vaudeville and *Follies* star Bert Williams died. Also, both theaters and vaudeville houses began suffering as radio kept more people home. *Better Times* was the eighteenth of the annual gigantic Hippodrome shows, and the last; no one would take over when producer Dillingham decided he'd done it for long enough.

Ziegfeld Follies of 1922 (426 performances) had cowboy humorist Will Rogers and the comedy team of Ole Olsen and Chic Johnson (lots of physical comedy, dumb jokes, and silly running gags) among its stars. It was the first edition of the revue to use the slogan "Glorifying the American Girl." Ballet's Michel Fokine was one of the choreographers, Urban designed the sets, and Gallagher and Shean sang their vaudeville patter song "Mr. Gallagher and Mr. Shean." Among many other songs was Herbert and DeSylva's waltz "A Kiss in the Dark." It had already been used earlier in the year in the operetta *Orange Blossoms*—the last of Herbert's shows produced during his lifetime—and it is still sung occasionally on recital programs.

The Passing Show of 1922 (95 performances) starred vaudevillian Fred Allen (later a popular radio comedian) and included Donaldson and Kahn's "(Nothing Could Be Finer Than to Be in) Carolina in the Morning." It was by this point that the Shuberts had partial female nudity in their revues.

Also this year, Berlin and Harris's second *Music Box Revue* (330 performances) introduced the dancer Ruth Page and the vaudeville comedy team of Bobby Clark and Paul McCullough to Broadway. (Clark went on to become a major Broadway star on his own after McCullough's death.) The score included Berlin's "Pack Up Your Sins (and Go to the Devil)."

George White's Scandals (1922, 168 performances) was the first to have White's name in the title. He also starred in it with W. C. Fields and Paul Whiteman and his orchestra. George Gershwin's score included "(I'll Build a) Stairway to Paradise," one of the earliest of his songs still sung occasionally; it has lyrics by B. G. DeSylva and Ira Gershwin, using his pseudonym, Arthur Francis. French artist Erté's costumes brought art deco styles to the show.

George M. Cohan's sentimental musical *Little Nellie Kelly*, his longest-running show (276 performances), seemed old-fashioned even at the time; the average age of his audience was rising rapidly.

In 1923, the African American musical comedy *Runnin' Wild* (167 performances), produced by George White, had music by James P. Johnson and lyrics by Cecil Mack. The book was by Flournoy Miller and Aubrey Lyles, who'd both written the book for and costarred in *Shuffle Along of 1921* and who starred in this show as well. The plot, just as with *Shuffle Along*, was a particularly thin excuse for comedy routines and musical numbers. The show introduced the Charleston, which started a national dance craze.

Kid Boots (479 performances) had music by Harry Tierney, lyrics by Joseph McCarthy, and book by Otto Harbach and William Anthony McGuire. Produced by Ziegfeld that year, it starred Eddie Cantor. A big hit, the plot had something to do with bootleggers and something to do with golf. Most of the songs were by the men who wrote *Irene,* but Cantor interpolated DeSylva and Meyer's "If You Knew Susie," which was passed on to Cantor by Jolson, and Henderson, DeSylva, and Green's "(I'm) Alabamy Bound." Both songs became pop hits. (Note the increasing frequency of DeSylva's name.) Cantor made a silent film version of the show in 1926.

Wildflower (477 performances)—produced by Arthur Hammerstein, with music by Vincent Youmans and Herbert Stothart and book and lyrics by Otto Harbach and Oscar Hammerstein—was the real beginning of Harbach's tutelage of Hammerstein. The show, about a young maid with a bad temper who must control it for six months to inherit a lot of money, was the first hit for both Youmans and Hammerstein.

By 1923 there was nearly a glut of revues on Broadway. There was a *Follies* with some of the music by Friml, starring Fanny Brice and the Paul Whiteman Orchestra; a *Scandals,* which was beginning to fade in popularity, with songs by Gershwin, DeSylva, Goetz, and Ballard MacDonald; and a *Passing Show* with some of the music by Romberg. *Artists and Models of 1923,* the first in a series of sleazy Shubert revues running intermittently until 1930, had female nudes who moved; until this show, nudes on stage didn't. *Vanities of 1923,* the first of nine produced by Earl Carroll until 1932, was less classy than the *Scandals,* a bit classier than the Shubert revues; the first edition had nudity (added after *Artists and Models* opened) and 108 girls on a revolving staircase. In 1924, Carroll added his name to the title.

Music Box Revue (third edition) ran 277 performances, had songs by Berlin, was directed by Hassard Short, and was produced by Sam H. Harris. It starred opera singer Grace Moore and critic and humorist Robert Benchley, who—along with George S. Kaufman—wrote some of the sketches, including Benchley's "Treasurer's Report" and Kaufman's "If Men Played Cards as Women Do."

The score of the third *Music Box Revue* included "What'll I Do?" which was not originally written for the show. For many people, the song has come to represent the underlying sadness of the Roaring Twenties. (It was used prominently in the score for the 1974 film version of Fitzgerald's tragic Jazz-Age novel *The Great Gatsby.*) It has a verse and a thirty-two-bar AABA chorus.

> Gone is the romance that was so divine;
> 'Tis broken and cannot be mended.

You must go your way and I must go mine,
But now that our love dreams have ended,

CHORUS:

A: What'll I do
When you are far away
And I am blue,
What'll I do?
A: What'll I do
When I am wond'ring who
Is kissing you,
What'll I do?
B: What'll I do
With just a photograph
To tell my troubles to,
A: When I'm alone
With only dreams of you
That won't come true,
What'll I do?

The complexity of the rhyming words and sounds is concealed by the ordinariness of the language Berlin used, one of his greatest skills. His lyrics are often accused of being simplistic because he used simple, everyday vocabulary to express his very human, and often sophisticated, thoughts and feelings. (The same is true for Hammerstein when he wrote with Rodgers.) Albert Williams observes:

> Note the unusually long phrasing of both the melody and the lyrics. The long phrases are written with no interior punctuation—commas, etc.—as a guide to phrasing and interpretation, and are followed in each of the A's by an abrupt, short second line. (Singers should always take note of punctuation in a lyric.) Though of course these phrases can be, and often are, sung with interior pauses for breath, the song is best conveyed without these pauses. (Williams, personal communication)

The *Grand Street Follies*, produced at the Neighborhood Playhouse, was the first of an annual series of intimate, intelligent, off-Broadway revues that continued until 1929.

Hassard (Hubert) Short (1877–1956, born in England) was a director and a designer. Along with three of the *Music Box Revues* and other Berlin shows, he worked on several innovative revues of the thirties as well as shows by Kern, Hammerstein, Porter, and many others.

Jimmy McHugh (1894–1969, born in Boston) wrote music and, for a while, worked with lyricist Dorothy Fields. Their career together took off while they were writing songs for the Cotton Club. They quickly moved to Broadway, where their first score was for *Blackbirds of 1928*, an African American revue. Soon after that they went to Hollywood, where they wrote several successful songs, including the lyrics for the new songs Jerome Kern added to the 1935 film version of Harbach's and his 1933 musical *Roberta*. (Fields did the lyrics alone, but McHugh's contract got him co-lyricist credit.) Shortly thereafter, McHugh and Fields split up and teamed with others. McHugh stayed mostly in Hollywood, and his career went rather downhill after the breakup.

The Cotton Club in Harlem had a frequently changing, all-black revue. Owned by white gangsters, it catered to a whites-only audience, preferred light-skinned African Americans as its entertainers, and was a favorite late-night spot for many years, featuring such great talent as Duke Ellington, Cab Calloway, Ethel Waters, Lena Horne, and the Nicholas Brothers. Along with Ellington and Calloway, songs were written by, among others, the white teams of Jimmy McHugh and Dorothy Fields, and Harold Arlen and Ted Koehler.

Duke Ellington and Harold Arlen were jazz-based composers of many memorable songs. Other than the Cotton Club revues, Ellington almost never composed for the stage, and many of Arlen's biggest hit songs came from Hollywood movies and unsuccessful musicals. Even so, both so enriched the repertory that it's important to know their work. Both men worked with several different lyricists.

Edward Kennedy "Duke" Ellington (1899–1974, born in Washington, D.C.) was one of the most innovative of all jazz musicians. He moved to New York in his twenties, where he and his orchestra were booked almost immediately into the Cotton Club. From 1926 to 1974, the band played there or in bookings around the country. Ellington's songs usually started as instrumentals written for the band, with additions to the tunes and arrangements often made by others. Lyrics were added later, sometimes much later. During his career, Ellington was continuously pushing the boundaries of jazz. His forty-seven-minute orchestral suite "Black, Brown, and Beige" premiered at Carnegie Hall in 1943. Just like George Gershwin and Leonard Bernstein, he was too pop for the classical critics and too classical for the pop critics. In the late forties, the bebop sounds of musicians like Dizzy Gillespie and Charlie "Bird" Parker replaced big-band jazz in popularity. Ellington didn't like the cooler, less danceable style and wasn't interested in "moving" with the times. He lost much of his audience, but his career was rejuvenated in 1956 at the Newport Jazz Festival. The 1981 Broadway revue *Sophisticated Ladies* was an all-dancing, all-singing collection of Ellington songs.

Harold Arlen (1905–86, born Hyman Arluck in Buffalo, New York) was known as a "songwriters' songwriter." He had as many hit songs as Gershwin, Porter, or Rodgers, but his name never became as familiar to the general audience. He did, however, have an enormous influence on his fellow artists. He

Dorothy Fields (1904–74, born in Allenhurst, New Jersey), the daughter of Lew Fields, wrote lyrics and, eventually, books. After the breakup with Jimmy McHugh, she wrote lyrics and/or books for Kern, Porter, Romberg, Arthur Schwartz, and Cy Coleman, among others. Together, Fields and her brother Herbert wrote the books for eight shows, including Berlin's 1946 *Annie Get Your Gun*. She was one of the most successful writers in the history of Broadway because she had the ability to adapt to the changing times throughout her career, which continued up to such shows as *Sweet Charity* in 1966 and *Seesaw* in 1973. Her working career lasted over forty-five years.

formed his own jazz trio—"The Snappy Trio"—when still a teenager, for which he played piano, sang, and wrote the arrangements. He moved to New York in 1925 to begin a singing career in vaudeville. Because of their first hit, "Get Happy" in the 1930 *Nine-Fifteen Revue,* Arlen and lyricist Ted Koehler followed McHugh and Fields as writers-in-residence at the Cotton Club, for which they wrote songs until 1934. By then, Arlen had moved on to Broadway. He wrote revues, musicals, pop songs, and movie musicals. His musicals were rarely successful, although they included some great songs. (Pay particular attention to the bridges of his songs; they're often quite amazing.) Both he and E. Y. Harburg won an Academy Award in 1939 for "Over the Rainbow." Along with the score for the movie of *The Wizard of Oz,* among his many hit songs are "Stormy Weather," "One for My Baby (And One More for the Road)," "Blues in the Night," "I've Got the World on a String," "Any Place I Hang My Hat Is Home," "Come Rain or Come Shine," and "It's Only a Paper Moon."

Suggested Watching and Listening

An American in Paris
Director Vincente Minnelli's 1951 movie *An American in Paris* (available on Warner Home Video DVD) has a score of old Gershwin songs.

- "(I'll Build a) Stairway to Paradise" (performed by Georges Guetary): This number, from *George White's Scandals* (1922), takes place in MGM's overproduced idea of the Folies Bergère, with French cabaret performer Georges Guetary singing the song. In the movie sequence, the nonmoving showgirls on the light fixtures would have been even more scantily dressed, especially at the Folies Bergère or a Shubert show.

Broadway: The American Musical
In this PBS series (available in a wide-screen box set on PBS Paramount DVD), the second episode, "Episode 2: Syncopated City (1919–1933)," is important to watch.

Funny Girl
The 1968 movie version of the musical *Funny Girl*—about Fanny Brice—is available on Columbia Pictures DVD.

- "My Man" (performed by Barbra Streisand): Hardly politically correct, the lyrics of this 1920 French cabaret song were not so much translated as rewritten by Pollock for Fanny Brice to sing in *Ziegfeld Follies of 1921.* (The song became identified with her well-publicized problems with her first husband, gambler Nicky Arnstein.) It's about a woman who loves her man despite the fact that he abuses her, is unfaithful, and apparently sends her out on the street to earn money for him. Although "My Man" isn't used in the stage version of *Funny Girl* (which has an entirely original score), Streisand does sing much of it at the end of the movie, leaving out the verse, which sets up the abusive part of the relationship.

Music Box Revue (Third Edition)

The following song from the 1923 *Music Box Revue* is available on Linda Ronstadt's CD *'Round Midnight,* available on Elektra/Asylum CD.

- "What'll I Do?" (performed by Linda Ronstadt with Nelson Riddle and his orchestra)

On the Road with Duke Ellington

This is an excellent biography of Duke Ellington, directed by filmmaker Robert Drew (available on A&E/Docurama DVD).

Somewhere over the Rainbow: Harold Arlen

This is an excellent biographical documentary from 1999, with appearances by Arlen, Tony Bennett, Judy Garland, Bing Crosby, and others. It's available on Winstar Home Entertainment DVD.

Sophisticated Ladies

Sophisticated Ladies is the 1981 original-cast, Broadway revue of Duke Ellington's songs, which was taped live in 1982 and is available on Kultur DVD. It includes the following combination of two of his songs.

- "I've Got It Bad and That Ain't Good" (performed by Phyllis Hyman, and written by Ellington and Paul Francis Webster in 1941), coupled with "Mood Indigo" (performed by Terri Klausner, and written by Duke Ellington, Albany Bigard, and Irving Mills in 1931)

Summer Stock

This 1950 movie (available on Warner Home Video DVD) contains the following Harold Arlen song from the show *Nine-Fifteen Revue.*

- "Get Happy" (performed by Judy Garland): Arlen converted the song from a piano vamp he'd written while working as a rehearsal pianist. This version became identified with Garland, as did the costume she wore. She'd already been fired; this was the last thing she filmed under her MGM contract, many pounds lighter than in the rest of the movie.

Till the Clouds Roll By

This 1946 pseudo-biography of Jerome Kern (available on Warner Home Video DVD) contains the following song from the 1920 show *Sally.*

- "Look for the Silver Lining" (performed by Judy Garland): The big hit of the show, Kern and DeSylva's sentimental ABA'C ballad was used earlier in *Zip Goes a Million,* which closed out of town. Garland sings a very slow version of the song in this "biography," in which she plays Marilyn Miller without looking or sounding the least bit like her.

From *Lady, Be Good!* to *Rose-Marie*

I'm a little jazz bird,
And I'm telling you to be one, too.
For a little jazz bird
Is in Heaven when he's singing "blue."

—"LITTLE JAZZ BIRD,"

LADY, BE GOOD! LYRICS BY IRA GERSHWIN

During the twenties, the most famous brothers in the history of the American musical started their careers: George and Ira Gershwin.

George Gershwin published his first song, "When You Want 'Em, You Can't Get 'Em (When You Got 'Em, You Don't Want 'Em)," with lyrics by Murray Roth, when he was eighteen. That same year he placed the song "The Making of a Girl," cowritten with Romberg and Harold Atteridge, in *The Passing Show of 1916*. After his first hit song (thanks to Jolson), "Swanee," two years later, and his first full Broadway score, *La! La! Lucille!* in 1919, he wrote songs and scores for both revues and musicals—often with B. G. DeSylva— and began to incorporate jazz into his music.

There were some minor hits, but two works in 1924 assured George and Ira's success: *Rhapsody in Blue* and *Lady, Be Good!* George was equally passionate about writing jazz and classical music and wanted to be recognized for both. In 1924, his jazz concerto *Rhapsody in Blue* premiered at New York's Aeolian Hall, performed by Paul Whiteman and his orchestra with Gershwin himself as soloist. A classical piece using jazz rhythms and harmonies, it caused a sensation, as did George's skill at the keyboard.

Later in 1924, the musical comedy *Lady, Be Good!* was the first complete Broadway score with music and lyrics by George and Ira writing together, and

George Gershwin (1898–1937, born Jacob Gershovitz in New York) was the son of immigrant parents. His father bought a piano for his brother Ira to take lessons, but young George, unbeknownst to his family, had already taught himself how to play, so he started the lessons instead. In 1912, he began studying with Charles Hambitzer, who was very important to his understanding of music and theory and to his extraordinary technique as a pianist. George soon fell in love with jazz and the music of Kern and Berlin. He quit school at fifteen to become a song plugger. He was also pianist for Nora Bayes (still singing "Shine On, Harvest Moon") and rehearsal pianist for Kern and Herbert's *Miss 1917.* By then he was selling his own songs.

Ira Gershwin (1896–1983, born Israel Gershovitz in New York) was George's protective older brother. While George concentrated on composing, Ira was establishing a career as a lyricist, using the name Arthur Francis (the names of his sister and his other brother). His first song with George was "The Real American Folk Song (Is a Rag)," which was used in Nora Bayes's 1918 musical *Ladies First.* George and Ira continued writing together occasionally, and then regularly starting in 1924.

with Ira using his real name. (From then on, George always wrote with Ira.) The show is credited with cementing jazz as the new music of Broadway. Jazz had already made inroads into the revue form by then, particularly through some of Berlin's songs and several of the songs in *Shuffle Along of 1921.* But George's harmonic and rhythmic inventiveness and use of **blue notes** (flatted notes, most often the third or seventh notes of a chord that are normally not flatted in the key signature), coupled with Ira's witty and slangy lyrics, set a new style for the musical comedy as immediate to twenties audiences as the Princess shows had been to those of the previous decade. The songs were the kind young people were already dancing and romancing to, only better and with better lyrics.

During the remainder of the twenties, the Gershwins wrote several hit musical comedies, all lightweight, loosely structured, and conventional, but with many memorable songs. George continued writing classical music as well, including *Concerto in F* and the orchestral tone poem *An American in Paris.* Like Ellington, he was always frustrated by the snobbish attitude most of the important classical music critics displayed toward his serious music at the time.

By the thirties, George and Ira Gershwin's shows were getting more satiric and more experimental, including the Pulitzer Prize–winning *Of Thee I Sing* in 1931, which demonstrated George's move toward a true blending of his popular and classical styles. During this decade, the brothers spent most of their time in Hollywood; George only wrote three more shows for Broadway after *Of Thee I Sing:* two flop musicals and the folk opera *Porgy and Bess,* also a flop in its original production. Ira wrote lyrics for all three (collaborating with DuBose Heyward on *Porgy and Bess*) and for the revues *Life Begins at 8:40,* written with Harold Arlen and E. Y. Harburg, and *Ziegfeld Follies of 1936,* with music by Vernon Duke.

Then, in Hollywood in 1937, George died of a brain tumor at the age of thirty-eight. Ira continued writing lyrics both for Broadway (including *Lady in the Dark,* with Kurt Weill, in 1940) and for Hollywood (including, with Harold Arlen, Judy Garland's 1954 remake of *A Star Is Born*). He too died in Hollywood.

In 1924, Victor Herbert and Giacomo Puccini died. Also during the year, *Lady, Be Good!* premiered.

The show is about a brother and sister who get evicted unfairly and set up their apartment outside the building. There are strange legal maneuvers, millionaires mistaken for hobos, and true love at the end. Along with being the Gershwins' first hit musical together, it was the first teaming of Aarons and Freedley, who went on to produce many Broadway shows, including most of the Gershwins'. Not only did *Lady, Be Good!* make jazz the king of the Broadway musical, but, with its debut ten months after the sensation created by *Rhapsody in Blue,* it also made the Gershwins wealthy and a household name. The score is filled with complex rhythms incorporated into what became Broadway's version of the blues, which is tinged with Jewish inflections. Among the show's hit songs, as successful for Ira's colloquial and clever lyrics as for George's music, are the title song, "The Half of It, Dearie, Blues," and "Fascinating Rhythm." ("The Man I Love," written for the show, was dropped before opening; dropped from *Rosalie* in 1928; put into the 1927 version of *Strike Up the Band,* which closed out of town; and dropped when that show was rewritten in 1930. The song became a stand-alone pop hit without ever making it to Broadway.) MGM's 1941 movie *Lady, Be Good!* bears no relation to the script of the original show and keeps only a couple of its songs.

Sitting Pretty (95 performances) was a reteaming of Kern, Wodehouse, and Bolton. The show had its charms, and Kern's score was lovely, but he was ready for something more innovative than another lightweight, musical-comedy farce.

In 1924, there were also many revues, including *Ziegfeld Follies of 1924* (401 performances, the longest run of any of the *Follies*), which starred W. C. Fields, Will Rogers, and Vivienne Segal. Most of its songs were by Tierney and McCarthy, the six set designers included Urban, the four costume designers included Erté, and the show continued as *Ziegfeld Follies of 1925.*

The Passing Show of 1924 (106 performances) was the last of its series. Romberg wrote some of the music. Two more attempts by the Shuberts to revive the series, one in 1932 and one in 1945, closed out of town. *Music Box Revue* (4th edition, 184 performances) was the last of Berlin and Harris's revues at their Music Box Theatre. Directed by John Murray Anderson and Harris, it starred Fanny Brice, Grace Moore, and the comedy team of Bobby Clark and Paul McCullough. Included in its score was Berlin's hit waltz-ballad "All Alone." *George White's*

Lady, Be Good!

MUSIC: George Gershwin

LYRICS: Ira Gershwin

BOOK: Guy Bolton and Fred Thompson

PRODUCERS: Alex A. Aarons and Vinton Freedley

CAST INCLUDES: the Astaires, comic actor Walter Catlett, and Cliff "Ukulele Ike" Edwards (with his 10:00–10:15 PM ukulele number— "Little Jazz Bird")

PERFORMANCES: 330

Scandals (1924, 198 performances) had music by Gershwin, lyrics by DeSylva, and costumes by Erté. It was George Gershwin's last *Scandals;* White wouldn't give him a raise. The show had one of the few Gershwin songs from these revues to enter the permanent repertory: "Somebody Loves Me."

The Greenwich Village Follies (1924) was an intimate revue with music and lyrics by Cole Porter (including "I'm in Love Again") and sketches by Lew Fields and Irving Caesar, among others. It was directed by Fields and John Murray Anderson and ran 131 performances. *Charlot's Revue* (298 performances), imported from London, introduced Beatrice Lillie, Jack Buchanan, and Gertrude Lawrence to America. Small, smart, and sophisticated, it's often called the first intimate revue on Broadway, smaller in cast and production values than even the Berlin-Harris *Music Box Revues.* The score included three songs by Noël Coward and one by Eubie Blake and Noble Sissle. *I'll Say She Is* (131 performances) was the "musical comedy revue" that brought the four Marx Brothers from vaudeville to Broadway. Its music was by Tom Johnstone and its script—what the Marx Brothers used of it— and lyrics by Will B. Johnstone. It made the brothers the toast of the town.

Backdrop: 1924

National   Calvin Coolidge is reelected president. A bill is passed limiting immigration and excluding all Japanese. J. Edgar Hoover is appointed head of the FBI. Chicago teenagers Nathan Leopold and Richard Loeb confess to the thrill killing of fourteen-year-old Bobby Franks, soon called the Crime of the Century. In a sensational trial, both men are saved from hanging by defense attorney Clarence Darrow. Hymie Weiss takes over Chicago's O'Banion mob. A battle for control of bootleg liquor begins between Johnny Torrio and Al Capone, who wins.

International   Lenin dies. A power struggle for control of the Soviet Union begins between Leon Trotsky and Joseph Stalin, who wins.

New Developments   Two planes fly around the world, the first U.S. diesel locomotive begins its run, and Chrysler manufactures its first automobile. Saks Fifth Avenue opens, Kleenex and Wheaties are introduced, IBM is organized, and the first Winter Olympics are held.

Publications   Walter Winchell begins his daily newspaper column. The comic strip *Little Orphan Annie* (source of the 1977 musical *Annie*) begins publication. Novelists Joseph Conrad and Franz Kafka

Although the majority of the musical evenings opening during this year were revues, the biggest hits (along with the *Follies*) were *Lady, Be Good!* and a couple of operettas. Despite the great popularity of revues and musical comedies throughout the twenties (when most shows could pay off their entire investment in less than three months), there was still an audience for American operettas, and many new ones were produced along with the occasional revivals. Even with a noticeable drop-off in new operettas after 1929, when the majority of the form's older audiences lost their money in the stock market crash, the hits from the first three decades of the century continued to tour for years, and many of them were made into movies during the thirties.

Perhaps the most romantic of all American operettas, *The Student Prince*, in its original Broadway production, was the longest-running musical evening of the twenties and the biggest hit of Romberg's career. The story is about the love affair between a

The Student Prince

MUSIC: Sigmund Romberg

LYRICS/LIBRETTO: Dorothy Donnelly, adapted from the play *Old Heidelberg* by Rudolf Bleichman

PRODUCERS: the Shuberts

CAST INCLUDES: Howard Marsh and Ilse Marvenga

PERFORMANCES: 608

die. Among the new books are Stanislavsky's *My Life in Art*, Breton's *Manifesto of Surrealism*, Mann's *The Magic Mountain*, Forster's *A Passage to India*, and Hemingway's first book of stories, *In Our Time*.

Radio   There are 2.5 million radios in America.

Pop Culture   Jazz cornetist Bix Beiderbecke makes his first recording. The Music Corporation of America (MCA) is established and begins its rise to show-business power by booking bands for one-night stands; eventually MCA signs up leading swing bands, vaudeville acts, movie stars, and many other big names. Pop songs of the year include Berlin's "Lazy," and Jones and Kahn's "It Had to Be You" and "The One I Love Belongs to Somebody Else."

Stage   O'Casey's *Juno and the Paycock* (source of the flop 1959 musical *Juno*), O'Neill's *Desire under the Elms*, and Howard's Pulitzer Prize–winning *They Knew What They Wanted* (source of the hit 1956 musical *The Most Happy Fella*) have their premieres.

Screen   Metro-Goldwyn-Mayer and Columbia Pictures are founded. New movies include Murnau's *The Last Laugh*, von Stroheim's *Greed*, Keaton's *Sherlock, Jr.* and *The Navigator*, and the first *Our Gang* short.

prince and an innkeeper's daughter while he is studying at Heidelberg University in 1860. At the end, he has to leave her to return home to his responsibilities and a politically motivated marriage to a woman also in love with someone else, but he has felt true love and has even learned about the needs of the "little" people.

The show has waltzes, drinking songs, operatic ensembles— you'd hardly know it wasn't turn-of-the-century Viennese. (It opened the night after the jazz-age *Lady, Be Good!*) *The Student Prince* toured for years and was made into movies in 1927 (silent) and 1954 (with Mario Lanza on the sound track but not on screen). It's still done by light opera companies everywhere. The score includes "Drinking Song" (the "Tramp! Tramp! Tramp!" of the show), sung by the men of the chorus, who are not brave heroes this time, just manly students out to have a good time. Also in the score are the waltz "Deep in My Heart, Dear" and the romantic "Serenade."

Rose-Marie

MUSIC: Rudolf Friml (with additional music by Herbert Stothart)

LYRICS/LIBRETTO: Otto Harbach and Oscar Hammerstein

PRODUCER: Arthur Hammerstein

CAST INCLUDES: Dennis King and Mary Ellis

PERFORMANCES: 557 on Broadway, 851 in London, and 1,250 in Paris

Rose-Marie is another operetta that became a permanent part of the repertory. It was the biggest financial success in Broadway history until *Oklahoma!* in 1943. *Rose-Marie* is about a part-Indian woman, a singer in a small hotel in the Canadian Rockies, who falls in love with a man accused of murder. He's eventually cleared of all suspicions of guilt by the Mounties, just in time for a happy ending. It's been filmed three times: 1928 (silent), with Joan Crawford; 1936, starring Jeanette MacDonald, Nelson Eddy, and James Stewart in a story with major changes, including making the outlaw Rose-Marie's brother rather than her lover so she could end up with Eddy, who plays the manly Mountie; and 1954, a slightly more faithful though rather dull version, starring Ann Blyth, Howard Keel, Fernando Lamas, and Bert Lahr (star of burlesque, revue, and musical comedy, fondly remembered as the Cowardly Lion in *The Wizard of Oz*) as the comic lead. One of Friml's best scores, it includes the cheerfully romantic title song, "Song of the Mounties" (the "Tramp! Tramp! Tramp!" of the show), and "Indian Love Call," probably the most frequently parodied piece of music in all American operetta. ("When I'm calling you-ou-ou-ou-ou-ou-ou" is the first line of the chorus.)

It was in operetta that Oscar Hammerstein first made his mark. He credited Otto Harbach with being his mentor, the person who taught him that the script must come first. By the time he wrote *Rose-Marie* with Friml and Harbach, Hammerstein was already publicly announcing his search for better ways to integrate music and dance into the stories of his shows. He wrote in the program note for *Rose-Marie*, "The musical numbers of this play are such an integral part of the action that we do not think we should list them as separate episodes." Not really true, but Hammerstein was closer than most and well on his way to *Show Boat* and *Oklahoma!* Until he began his collaboration with Rodgers, he wrote his lyrics to already existing music, which made the task of adjusting the lyrics to the needs of the book and the characters that much more difficult. (Rodgers, until his collaboration with Hammerstein, always wrote the music first.)

> Hammerstein was involved with most of the trendsetting or record-breaking musicals until the 1950s. While his individual contributions may not have been the primary reasons for a show's success, his influence extended far beyond his own credited contributions. One problem people have in assessing Hammerstein's importance is their lack of historical perspective. Hammerstein's career was so long and covered so many styles of writing, it's inevitable that some of his contributions are dated. . . . This doesn't excuse his occasional lapses of quality but considering the quantity of his career his record is amazing. (Bloom, *American Song*, 129)

With *Lady, Be Good!* jazz permanently replaced ragtime as the music of choice in musicals and revues, both on Broadway and on tour. After this show, the musical comedy also began its ascendancy over the revue in popularity. Throughout the rest of the twenties and well into the thirties, Broadway shows were responsible for many of the pop hits of the year. Of course, with the arrival of sound to movies in 1927, Hollywood began to produce hit songs too, many of them by Broadway songwriters who'd gone out West for the money and the sun. Nevertheless, the period from the mid-twenties to the end of the thirties can easily be thought of as the golden age of the Broadway song.

Suggested Watching and Listening

George Gershwin Remembered
This 1987 American Masters Program biography is written and produced by Peter Adam and available on A&E Home Video VHS. It's a clear and thorough examination of George Gershwin's life and career, with much on his brother Ira as well. It has interesting film clips, photos, and interviews with people who knew and worked with them. It also contains several clips from the 1945 movie *Rhapsody in Blue,* a highly fictionalized re-creation of George's life. Robert Alda (Alan's father and the original Sky Masterson in *Guys and Dolls*) played Gershwin; Al Jolson and Paul Whiteman, among others, played themselves.

Virgil Thomson, interviewed in the documentary, was a noted composer, musicologist, and critic. His snobbishness (as well as his jealousy and, possibly, anti-Semitism) never allowed him to accept Gershwin's classical music as anything but the dabblings of a pop composer, as he makes clear in the documentary. Also interviewed is Leonard Bernstein, another composer of both classical music and Broadway shows, who received the same kind of reaction to his serious music from classical music critics and musicologists (as did Duke Ellington). These days, the music of all three is performed and recorded far more regularly than is, for example, Thomson's.

Lady, Be Good!

The 1992 Elektra/Nonesuch CD recording of this 1924 show is a reconstruction of the complete score, using the original orchestrations by Stephen Jones as overseen by Gershwin. All the following suggestions are from that recording.

- "Fascinating Rhythm" (performed by John Pizzarelli, Lara Teeter, Ann Morrison, and the ensemble): "Fascinating Rhythm," more than any other song in the show, proclaimed the new Broadway sound and became a huge hit. The number, which runs seven and a half minutes, begins as a first-act solo for Ukulele Ike's character, then becomes a dance and duet for Fred and Adele Astaire's characters, and ends with the whole ensemble participating.
- "The Half of It, Dearie, Blues" (performed by Lara Teeter, Michelle Nicastro, and the ensemble): It starts as a duet; the Astaire character sings a verse and chorus, and the woman he's in love with sings a verse and chorus; then the ensemble appears and sings a chorus, Astaire's character has a tap solo, and everybody does a final chorus. (As with "Fascinating Rhythm," the tune is repeated so many times during the number, it would have been nearly impossible not to be able to hum it while leaving the theater.) The orchestration includes a muted jazz trumpet and blue notes, another prime example of the new Broadway sound. Here are Ira Gershwin's slangy and clever lyrics for the Astaire character's verse and chorus:

Each time you trill a song with Bill
Or look at Will, I get a chill—
I'm gloomy.
I won't recall the names of all
The men who fall—It's all appall-
Ing to me.
Of course, I really cannot blame them a bit,
For you're a hit wherever you flit.
I know it's so, but, dearie, oh!
You'll never know the blues that go
Right through me.

Chorus: I've got the You-Don't-Know-the-Half-of-It-Dearie Blues.
      The trouble is you have so many from whom to choose.
      If you should marry
      Tom, Dick, or Harry,
      Life would be the bunk—
      I'd become a monk.
      I've got the You-Don't-Know-the-Half-of-It-Dearie Blues!

In the fourth and fifth lines of the verse, the rhymes *all* and *appall*-ing—typical of Ira's easy wit—are called **cross-line rhymes.**

- "Oh, Lady Be Good!" (performed by Jason Alexander, Ann Morrison, and the girls): The title song has a verse and an AABA chorus. In it, the comic lead switches what he wants: in the first verse and chorus he wants a favor from his friend Susie, Adele Astaire's character; in the second verse and chorus he wants a date with any or all of the girls who have suddenly appeared.

The Student Prince

The show is available as a 1954 movie on MGM/Warner DVD.

- "Serenade" (performed by Mario Lanza): Mario Lanza started out as a truck driver, trained briefly for opera, was cast as a truck driver with an operatic voice in MGM's 1949 *That Midnight Kiss,* and became a movie star. He remained one until he got too fat and too frequently drunk, which is why only his singing voice was used in the 1954 movie. He died of a heart attack when he was thirty-eight years old.

PART THREE

Overleaf: (*left*) *Show Boat* (1927); (*right*) *Of Thee I Sing* (1931)

From The Garrick Gaieties to Strike Up the Band

We're gonna go down where
Ladies' backs are bare
And the farm girls all go astray;
Our old clothes are dowdy,
We want to be rowdy,
And so we'll say Howdy to Broadway.
—"HOWDY TO BROADWAY,"
PEGGY-ANN, LYRICS BY LORENZ HART

Musical comedies continued to gain in popularity on Broadway and on the road during the late twenties and into the thirties, as did intimate revues, which were gradually replacing the big ones. With few exceptions, musical comedies of the late twenties were written to formula: high-energy opening choruses featuring the girls, opening scenes that told the audience everything they needed to know to get the minimal stories rolling, predictable plots that could stop at any time for only slightly integrated songs and comedy sequences, dances that had no bearing on character or plot, and whole shows tailored to the talents of the stars. By the end of the twenties, a hit pop song was as likely to come from a show as from Tin Pan Alley directly. Berlin, Kern, Youmans, the Gershwins, Rodgers and Hart, Cole Porter, and the team of Henderson, DeSylva, and Brown (among others) had hit shows and songs during the last five years of the decade that put their names up in lights alongside those of the star performers and producers. Their music was jazz-based and their lyrics less mundane, more colloquial, often more witty (or at least smart-alecky), and, on occasion, even more specific to the situation and the psychology of the character singing the song than had been the norm. Because of the growing power of ASCAP, there were also fewer interpolations, so shows tended to sound more integrated. Even the revues, taking the lead from George White, were now mostly one-composer shows.

Vaudeville was in trouble; most vaudeville houses were now showing movies as well—some of them exclusively—particularly after sound took over in Hollywood starting in late 1927. Even though the popularity of operettas was diminishing rapidly, and the form had pretty much lost the possibility of building new younger audiences, Romberg had two of his biggest hits during the late twenties, both written with Hammerstein, and Friml had one. Then, after Hollywood's love affair with the form began in the thirties, allowing audiences to see what they didn't know were highly bastardized versions of operettas at a neighborhood movie theater for twenty-five cents or less, almost no new ones were produced. However, older operettas (mainly Shubert shows) and vaudeville units continued touring through the thirties and into the forties, playing big cities and small towns alike and getting tackier all the time. Operetta under that name was dead by the late forties, by which time it had been reconstructed into the musical play—around the same time that vaudeville began to disappear entirely into television.

By the mid-twenties, almost all pop songs, whether written for shows or for Tin Pan Alley, had a thirty-two-bar chorus divided into four eight-bar sections. (The term **refrain** is sometimes used to mean the chorus of a pop song, but some musicians and musicologists use it to mean just the A of the chorus. To prevent confusion, we'll avoid either use of the term except in quoted material. The B, or bridge, of a song is sometimes called the **release,** because it's a release from the main melody. We'll continue calling it the bridge; it "bridges" two A's.) The most frequently used thirty-two-bar form was the AABA structure. The other most frequently used structure—ABAC—was more often an **ABAC/A,** just to complicate things a little further. The last part of the C often returned to the beginning of the music or lyrics (or both) of the A's, making the C into a C/A and thus giving the song a sense of completion, of coming back full circle. For instance, the C in "Alexander's Ragtime Band" begins with:

> And if you want to hear that "Swanee River"
> Played in ragtime

and then returns to the words and music of the top of the A:

Lorenz Hart (1895–1943, born in New York) claimed Gilbert and Wodehouse as early influences on his work. He began his career by translating German operettas for the Shuberts. Extremely troubled and undisciplined, he was four foot ten (not counting his elevator shoes), had a head too big for his body, had severe substance-abuse problems, and was a homosexual in a time when it was necessary to remain closeted. All of this contributed to his early death and also to the psychological depth and complexity of his sophisticated lyrics. Rodgers often had to lock him up like a prisoner to get any work out of him and always had to write the music first. (Once when Hart was hospitalized, Rodgers had a piano installed in the next room in order to meet a deadline.)

Come on and hear, come on and hear,
Alexander's Ragtime Band.

Gershwin's "Fascinating Rhythm" is another example.

The dramatic or emotional climax of an AABA song usually comes at the end of the bridge as the song returns to the third A; the climax of an ABAC song typically comes at the end of the second A leading into the C. In both cases that means the climax generally occurs as the song goes into its last eight bars. (A good example: the B in Cole Porter's "I Get a Kick Out of You" ends with the singer admitting that "you obviously don't adore me," an emotional climax, which the performer can move away from in the final A by "flying too high with some guy in the sky" as the vocal line literally takes the singer up higher in the final A.) No matter what might be usual, however, and no matter what the form, in a well-written song the combination of music and lyrics will tell the performer where the climax comes. If it doesn't, the singer must invent one in order to give the song dramatic shape.

There are, of course, quite a few great songs that are exceptions to the thirty-two-bar forms, including Cole Porter's 108-bar "Begin the Beguine." (Berlin, always interested in business, often asked Porter how "that long song" of his was doing, wondering whether it was still bringing in money on royalties. It was. Berlin himself wrote the seventy-two-bar "Cheek to Cheek," which also did well for years.) However, most of the hit songs of the golden age of the Broadway song kept to thirty-two bars and were usually either AABA, ABAC, or ABAC/A.

Richard Rodgers, Lorenz Hart, and Herbert Fields

Rodgers and Hart met and began writing together in 1919, the year Lew Fields put their "Any Old Place with You" into *A Lonely Romeo*. Until *Oklahoma!* in 1943, neither wrote songs with anyone else; Hart never did, except when translating operetta lyrics.

Hart [advanced] the art of lyric writing by leaps and bounds through intricate wordplay, wit, lithe rhymes, insight, intimacy, and, to be sure, his romantic honesty. . . . [He brought] show-tune lyrics out of their dittyfied, doggerel past and [gave] them a new adult respectability, writing about a real emotional world. . . . [Rodgers's] irresistibly fetching melodies and soaring ballads often contradict and point up Hart's acerbic lyrics and make their songs . . . accessible, instantly lovable and immortal. (Gerald Nachman, "Lorenz Hart: Little Boy Blue," *Theatre Week*, 35–36)

Herbert Fields (1897–1958, born in New York), during his very successful career as a book writer for musicals, wrote seven shows with Rodgers and Hart and seven with Cole Porter, as well as shows with Romberg, Berlin, and the Gershwins, among others. His stories and dialogue were known for being somewhat racier than the norm for the time. In the last part of his career, he wrote eight shows with his sister Dorothy, including the book of Berlin's *Annie Get Your Gun*. Their brother Joseph (1895–1966) cowrote the books for *Wonderful Town* and *Gentlemen Prefer Blondes* as well as several plays. Broadway owes a lot to Lew Fields and his children.

In 1920, Rodgers and Hart wrote songs for the Columbia University Players' Varsity Show *Fly with Me,* as did Oscar Hammerstein II; Lew Fields's son Herbert choreographed it. After half of Rodgers and Hart's songs were cut from *Poor Little Ritz Girl* in 1920, they went back to writing university and amateur shows and were almost ready to give up. Then, in 1925, their big break came with the intimate revue *The Garrick Gaieties,* which led directly to the production of their first complete score for a musical, *Dearest Enemy.* Lew Fields produced their next two shows; his son Herbert wrote the books for all three.

Rodgers and Hart wrote music and lyrics for well over thirty musicals and revues and for several movies. Hart was the first American lyricist to get equal billing with the composer. Unlike most of their predecessors and contemporaries, Rodgers and Hart didn't write for Tin Pan Alley; their songs were originally written for shows or movies, whether they ended up being used or not. ("Blue Moon," for example, was written for a movie, cut from it, went through several lyrics changes, was finally published as a separate song, and became a stand-alone pop hit.)

Most of their shows had formula books with good tunes, clever lyrics, and even moments of true emotion. They also sometimes looked for more innovative ways to approach the form. *Peggy-Ann* (1926) was partly expressionistic and dealt with Freudian theories before they'd become fashionable. It also had no opening chorus and no singing at all for the first twenty minutes—also true of their satiric, semi-musical, semi-concept show *I'd Rather Be Right* (1937). In Hollywood from 1931 to 1935, they wrote rhythmic, rhymed dialogue as lead-ins to some of their songs, never tried before in a movie (and rarely since).

They also experimented with the use of dance in some of their later musicals. George Balanchine did some storytelling with his choreography for three of their shows: *On Your Toes* (1936), *Babes in Arms* (1937), and *I Married an Angel* (1938). With writer/director George Abbott, they even adapted Shakespeare into a musical comedy, turning *The Comedy of Errors* into the 1938 hit *The Boys from Syracuse,* leaving in only one line of the original play. And in 1940, their controversial adaptation—with Abbott and John O'Hara of O'Hara's hard-boiled *New Yorker* stories about *Pal Joey*—was the most frank, adult, and realistic treatment of sex and sleaze yet seen in a Broadway musical. Set among the low-life denizens of a seedy Chicago nightclub, it also had unpleasant central characters and a rather down ending, basically unheard of in the musical until then. Furthermore, many of the show's songs reveal character and help carry the story forward; even the nightclub numbers help define character and atmosphere in much the same way they do in the 1966 musical drama and semiconcept show *Cabaret.* By the forties, Hart was getting difficult to find, let alone work with. The team's last new show together was *By Jupiter* in 1942. Then Hart turned down *Oklahoma!* and the rest is a new chapter in Broadway history.

Ray Henderson, B. G. DeSylva, and Lew Brown

Working within the song and show formulas of the day, the team—who were brought together by George White—had six hit shows in a row, most famously *Good News!* in 1927. Their partnership ended when their songs no longer suited the mood of the times. We've already encountered some of DeSylva's work with Gershwin, Kern, and Herbert. He also wrote lyrics for such hits popularized by Al Jolson or Eddie Cantor as "April Showers," "California, Here I Come," and "If You Knew Susie" (for which he also wrote the music). After dropping out of the team in 1931, he worked in Hollywood, even producing some of little Shirley Temple's movies. He then returned to New York, where he co-wrote the book and produced Cole Porter's 1939 *DuBarry Was a Lady* and 1940 *Panama Hattie,* and produced Irving Berlin's 1940 *Louisiana Purchase.* He then quit Broadway and writing altogether and became an executive producer at Paramount Pictures. Brown and Henderson wrote the songs for *George White's Scandals* (1931), including the big hit tune "Life Is Just a Bowl of Cherries." They both continued their musical careers sporadically through the thirties and into the forties, sometimes working together, sometimes working with others. But they never again achieved the kind of success they'd enjoyed when part of the trio.

In 1925, New York police raided Minsky's burlesque house. The intimate *Charlot's Revue of 1926* (138 performances) opened in late 1925, again starring Beatrice Lillie, Gertrude Lawrence, and Jack Buchanan.

The Garrick Gaieties, originally done in 1925 by the junior members of the Theatre Guild as a Sunday-night fund-raiser for some

Ray Henderson (1896–1970, born G. Raymond Brost in Buffalo, New York), **George Gard (B. G. "Buddy") DeSylva** (1895–1950, born in New York) and **Lew Brown** (1893–1958, born Lewis Brownstein in Russia) wrote some of the most successful shows and songs of the twenties. Their first song together was "It All Depends on You" for the 1925 musical *Big Boy,* and their first score together was *George White's Scandals* (1925). Although Henderson, a former song plugger, was officially the composer, the other two often worked on the music and Henderson on the lyrics. Henderson usually composed short, repetitive phrases that could wear thin rapidly. An example is the 1925 flapper song "Five Foot Two, Eyes of Blue (Has Anybody Seen My Gal?)," written with Lewis and Young.

The Garrick Gaieties

MUSIC: Richard Rodgers

LYRICS: Lorenz Hart

SKETCHES: Morrie Ryskind and several others

DIRECTOR: Philip Loeb

STAGE MANAGER: Harold Clurman

CHOREOGRAPHER: Herbert Fields

PRODUCER: the Theatre Guild

CAST INCLUDES: Philip Loeb, Lee Strasberg, and Sanford Meisner

PERFORMANCES: 211

new curtains, was so successful that it was booked for a regular run. The show was an intimate revue with sketches and songs satirizing the guild and its productions as well as current events, including the Scopes "Monkey Trial." Rather than depending on spectacle and girls for success, the show depended on its talent. (Clurman, Strasberg, and Meisner were later instrumental in founding the Group Theatre and in bringing Stanislavsky's acting techniques to America.) The *Gaieties* was, with *Charlot's Revue*, the beginning of the ascendancy of the intimate revue; within the next few years, the extravagant revues were clearly on the way out. The show was also Rodgers and Hart's big break and included their first hit, the charm song "Manhattan." It was written in 1922 for an unproduced show called *Winkle Town*, with songs

Backdrop: 1925–1927

National   President Calvin Coolidge says "The business of America is business." Forty thousand Ku Klux Klan members parade in Washington, D.C. Detroit's Father Charles Edward Coughlin starts radio broadcasts preaching extreme conservatism and racial bigotry. Italian immigrant anarchists Nicola Sacco and Bartolomeo Vanzetti are executed in Massachusetts despite worldwide protests of their innocence; they're granted posthumous pardons in 1977. In the Dayton, Tennessee, "Monkey Trial," John Scopes is found guilty for teaching Darwinian evolution to his students; he is defended by Clarence Darrow and prosecuted by William Jennings Bryan. Ford Motor Company starts a five-day work week. Al Capone, now boss of Chicago's bootleggers, has a personal income of $105 million; the Supreme Court rules that illegal income can be taxed. The Florida land boom falls apart when it's revealed that many of the purchased properties are on swampland. (The land boom is the subject of the musicals *Tip-Toes* and *The Cocoanuts*.) Reporters and tourists from all over the country descend on a cave in Kentucky where Floyd Collins is trapped for eighteen days; rescuers are too late to save him. (The 1996 off-Broadway musical *Floyd Collins* is based on the event.)

International   Stalin takes over as head of the Soviet Union and expels Trotsky from the Communist Party. Benito Mussolini and his Fascist Party take power in Italy. Hirohito becomes emperor of Japan. The first part of Adolf Hitler's *Mein Kampf* (*My Struggle*) is published.

New Developments   The first liquid-fuel rocket is launched. Phone service between London and New York begins. Charles Lindbergh makes the first nonstop, solo, transatlantic flight, going from Long by Rodgers and Hart and book by Hammerstein and Herbert Fields. A love song that never mentions love, "Manhattan" is a list song with a verse and four choruses. Each chorus has a new set of lyrics about what's wonderful in New York for a young couple too poor to leave town in the summer. For example:

> We'll have Manhattan,
> The Bronx and Staten
> Island too.
> It's lovely going through
> The zoo.

Dearest Enemy (286 performances) was the first musical comedy with a score entirely by Rodgers and Hart. The book was by Herbert Fields, and

Island, New York, to Paris. Gertrude Ederle is the first woman to swim the English Channel. Gene Tunney beats Jack Dempsey and becomes world heavyweight boxing champ. Babe Ruth hits his sixtieth home run of the season in 1927, a record not beaten until 1961.

Art   Artists Mary Cassatt and Claude Monet die. Monet's water lily paintings are exhibited. There are new paintings by O'Keeffe, Mondrian, Chagall, Miró, Kandinsky, Munch, Kokoschka, and Magritte, among others. Sculptor Henry Moore completes his *Draped Reclining Figure.* The first art deco exhibit is held in Paris.

Music/Dance   Weill and Brecht's singspiel *Mahagonny* premieres in Germany; in 1930, they turn it into the pop opera *The Rise and Fall of the City of Mahagonny.* Berg's opera *Wozzeck,* Shostakovich's Symphony no. 1, Vaughan Williams's Concerto for Violin and Orchestra, Ravel's *Bolero,* and Gershwin's Concerto in F premiere. Modern dance exponent Martha Graham gives her first major concert. Dancer Isadora Duncan is strangled when her long scarf gets caught in an auto wheel.

Publications   The *New Yorker* and *Cosmopolitan* magazines begin publication. Also published are Fowler's *Dictionary of Modern English,* Lawrence (of Arabia)'s *Seven Pillars of Wisdom,* and poets Hughes's *The Weary Blues* and Parker's *Enough Rope.* Many new novels question the nature of our existence and our beliefs, including Kafka's posthumous *The Trial* and *Amerika,* Woolf's *Mrs. Dalloway* and *To the Lighthouse,* Dreiser's *An American Tragedy,* Fitzgerald's *The Great Gatsby,* Hemingway's first novel, *The Sun Also Rises,* and Cather's *Death Comes for the Archbishop.* Also new are Milne's *Winnie-the-Pooh,* Piper's *The Little Engine That Could,* Loos's *Gentlemen Prefer Blondes* (adapted into a musical in 1949), and Ferber's *Show Boat* (adapted into the musical play in 1927).

John Murray Anderson was one of the three directors. It was written before *The Garrick Gaieties* but didn't get produced until after the *Gaieties* was a hit. *Dearest Enemy* was a three-act, three-set sex farce based on a real event that took place during the Revolutionary War, when a group of women delayed the British troops overnight while the American troops managed an escape. Its biggest hit tune was "Here in My Arms."

> With his lyrics for this show Hart made public once and for all his unique, bittersweet cynicism. It was a view of the world he retained, only slightly altered, to the end of his career, and it gave his body of rhymes a philosophic backbone not found in any other major lyricists. (Bordman, 404)

Another big hit during this year was *No, No, Nanette!* (321 performances), featuring music by Youmans, lyrics mostly by Irving Caesar, and a book by Harbach and Frank Mandel. The show is a three-act, three-set, lighthearted, totally conventional, girl-meets-loses-gets-boy comedy, but with a jazzy, quintessentially twenties score and a jazz-baby title character. (**Jazz-babies** was a term for young women of the Roaring Twenties.) The show was so successful on the road before coming to New York—including a year in Chicago—that it opened on Broadway with two touring companies and a London production

Radio/TV   The National Broadcasting Company (NBC) is founded and soon splits into two networks, Blue and Red. The Columbia Broadcasting System (CBS) radio network goes on the air. Television is demonstrated for the first time.

Pop Culture   Recordings by Jelly Roll Morton help popularize jazz. Louis Armstrong begins his recording career. Duke Ellington and his band begin a five-year booking at the Cotton Club, recommended by composer Jimmy McHugh. Gospel singer Mahalia Jackson moves to Chicago. The first electric jukeboxes (also called nickelodeons because it costs a nickel to play a three-minute record) are installed. The spiritual "He's Got the Whole World in His Hands" is published. The radio program *WSM Barn Dance* begins broadcasts from Nashville; in 1927, it becomes the *Grand Ole Opry*. The fox-trot becomes a popular ballroom dance. Pop songs include Bernie, Pinkard, and Casey's "Sweet Georgia Brown"; Henderson, DeSylva, and Green's "Alabamy Bound"; Hanley and DeSylva's "(You Must Have Been a) Beautiful Baby"; Henderson and Dixon's "Bye Bye Blackbird"; Robinson and Hayes's union song "I Dreamed I Saw Joe Hill Last Night"; Berlin's "Remember" and "Always"(two of his most enduring ballads); Ager and Yellen's "Ain't She Sweet"; Donaldson and Kahn's "Yes, Sir, That's My Baby!" and Donaldson and Whiting's "My Blue Heaven" (which sells a million records in Gene Austin's recording).

already in operation. Along with such songs as "Too Many Rings around Rosie" and "You Can Dance with Any Girl at All," the score included two numbers that became standards: "I Want to Be Happy" and "Tea for Two," both written while the show was in trouble out of town. Irving Caesar wrote a set of **dummy lyrics** (easy rhymes to indicate rhythm and structure, and meant to be rewritten later) for "Tea for Two" so that Youmans could work out the tune. They kept the dummy lyrics:

> Picture you upon my knee,
> Just tea for two, and two for tea,
> Just me for you
> And you for me alone.

The song has a verse and an ABA'C/A chorus. It starts as a duet for the **juvenile** and the **ingenue** (the standard character descriptions for the young romantic leads) and then turns into a production number for the entire ensemble. By the time it's over, the song has been heard enough times to be firmly implanted in the audience's memory. The couple singing "I Want to Be Happy" is a millionaire who's the center of the comic subplot and his ward, Nanette. (It can be taken as a love song out of context.) In the show, he sings a verse,

Stage The Dramatists Guild establishes minimums, control of rights, and rules for creative control. Sardi's, the legendary Broadway restaurant, opens on Forty-fourth Street. Noël Coward debuts on Broadway in his play *The Vortex*. Other new plays include O'Casey's *The Plough and the Stars*, Brecht's *A Man's a Man*, Watkins's *Chicago* (basis of the 1975 musical and the 2002 movie musical), and the Heywards' *Porgy* (adapted in 1935 into *Porgy and Bess*).

Screen Grauman's Chinese Theatre opens in Hollywood; movie stars put their footprints in cement outside. There are more than 750 films produced in 1926 alone; *Don Juan* is the first to have a synchronized music and sound-effects track. Musical shorts with sound are released. New silent films include *The Big Parade; Ben Hur;* Chaplin's *The Gold Rush;* Eisenstein's *Ten Days That Shook the World* and *The Battleship Potemkin*, with its influential use of montage as an editing technique; Lang's *Metropolis;* Gance's *Napoleon;* Keaton's *The General;* Emil Jannings in *The Way of All Flesh;* Janet Gaynor in *Sunrise* and *Seventh Heaven;* and *Wings*, which wins the first Academy Award for best picture. Gaynor and Jannings win the first awards for best actress and actor. Thirty-one-year-old Rudolph Valentino finishes *The Son of the Sheik* just before his death from peritonitis; over one hundred thousand mourners are at his funeral. The first feature-length film with talking and singing, *The Jazz Singer*, starring Al Jolson, opens on October 6, 1927, and, although it has only a few dialogue and music sequences, it creates such a sensation that within two years the silent movie is history.

followed by an AABA chorus; then she sings the verse with different lyrics, followed by the same chorus. Burt Shevelove's 1971 revisal of the show (861 performances) began a wave of nostalgic revivals starring old movie actors (Ruby Keeler in this one, still watching her feet while tapping).

The first time Kern and Hammerstein worked together, they had to tailor the show to the talents of their stars. *Sunny* is about a circus performer who stows away on a boat to be near the man she loves. With its circus acts and lavish production values, it cost $500,000 to produce, sending the standard $4 top ticket price up to $5. As with the 1920 *Sally*, its long run was largely attributable to the popularity of Marilyn Miller and of Kern's score, which includes the up-tempo title song and the two-step "Who?" Miller starred in a 1930 movie version.

Tip-Toes (194 performances) has songs by the Gershwins and book by Guy Bolton and Fred Thompson, was produced by Aarons and Freedley, and starred Jeanette MacDonald. The musical tells a lightweight story about looking for love and wealth in Florida during the land boom. Among its now-standard pop songs are "Sweet and Low-Down," "Looking for a Boy," and "That Certain Feeling."

The Cocoanuts (375 performances), produced by Sam H. Harris, was the second of the Marx Brothers' three Broadway shows, with straight woman Margaret Dumont also in the cast. It's about hotels and swampland in Florida, and includes Groucho and Chico's famous "Why a duck?" routine. Irving Berlin's score is generally undistinguished. He wrote the song "Always" for this show, but cynical director/book writer George S. Kaufman (assisted on the book by Morrie Ryskind) couldn't accept the concept of "I'll be loving you always." He suggested changing the lyric to "I'll be loving you Thursday." Berlin dropped the song from the show and published it separately. It quickly became a standard.

A shortened version of the original production of *The Cocoanuts* was filmed at New York's Long Island Studios in 1929. (It is available on Image Entertainment DVD.) Berlin contributed three new songs for it by long-distance phone. The show was revived off-Broadway in 1996. (The problem with reviving the Marx Brothers' shows is that the actors have to play the Marx Brothers in order for the material to work.)

Sunny

MUSIC: Jerome Kern
LYRICS/BOOK: Otto Harbach and Oscar Hammerstein II
DIRECTOR: Hassard Short
CHOREOGRAPHERS: several, including Fred Astaire
PRODUCER: Charles Dillingham
CAST INCLUDES: Marilyn Miller, Clifton Webb, and Cliff "Ukulele Ike" Edwards
PERFORMANCES: 517

George S. Kaufman

(1889–1961, born in Pittsburgh, Pennsylvania) was one of the most successful and influential writers and directors of theater, particularly in the twenties and thirties. He continued his career well into the fifties, when he directed the original production of *Guys and Dolls* and cowrote the book for Cole Porter's *Silk Stockings*. He usually wrote with collaborators, including Moss Hart (no relation to Lorenz), Edna Ferber, and Morrie Ryskind. He was also one of the wittiest members of the famed Algonquin Round Table and, besides Harpo Marx, one of the only ones not to destroy himself with drink.

The Vagabond King (511 performances) was Friml's next show after *Rose-Marie*, this time with lyrics by Brian Hooker. The show used to be revived frequently. Adapted by Hooker, Russell Janney, and William H. Post from Justin Huntley McCarthy's *If I Were King*, it's a romantic adventure about fifteenth-century French poet and thief François Villon (played by Dennis King), who's made king for a day. The show is formula-ridden, but the music is pretty. The score includes "Only a Rose" (which Groucho liked to parody) and "Song of the Vagabonds," one of the most famous of all the "Tramp! Tramp! Tramp!" songs. The 1930 film version starred Jeanette MacDonald, with Dennis King recreating his original role; the unsuccessful 1956 remake starred Kathryn Grayson and Oreste.

In 1926, lyricist/book-writer Rida Johnson Young passed away as did escape artist and vaudeville performer Harry Houdini (a character in the musical *Ragtime*), who died of peritonitis. Over the next few years, there were successful revivals of several Gilbert and Sullivan operettas. Black entertainer Josephine Baker, unable to find suitable work in the United States, moved to Paris, opened her own jazz club at the age of twenty, and became famous, partly for her nude dances.

There were three Rodgers and Hart shows on Broadway during that year. *The Girl Friend* (301 performances) was about a farm boy being trained by his girlfriend for a bicycle race. The score included the hit song "The Blue Room," an AA′BA′ song, described by Alec Wilder in *American Popular Song* as "the first instance of a Rodgers stylistic device which he continued to use throughout his career, that of returning to a series of notes, usually two, while building a design with other notes" (p. 169).

Peggy-Ann (354 performances) contained several nightmarish, Freudian dream sequences. Included in the score was the up-tempo "Where's That Rainbow?" Both *The Girl Friend* and *Peggy-Ann* had books by Herbert Fields and were produced by his father, Lew. *Betsy* (39 performances, a flop) had a book by Irving Caesar, David Freedman, and William Anthony McGuire; was produced by Ziegfeld, with designs by Urban, among others; and starred Al Shean without Gallagher. (Shean was the Marx Brothers' uncle, who helped them at the start of their vaudeville career.) Ziegfeld added Berlin's "Blue Skies" on opening night without warning Rodgers and Hart in advance; they didn't appreciate it, especially since it got the biggest applause of the evening and several encores, despite the fact that Belle Baker forgot the lyrics. (Berlin stood up in the audience and sang them for her.) It's an AABA song, also sung by Jolson in the first talking picture, the 1927 *The Jazz Singer*. The score of *Betsy* included "This Funny World," perhaps Hart's truest expression of how he felt about life; he wasn't a happy man.

A: This funny world
Makes fun of the things that you strive for.
This funny world
Can laugh at the dreams you're alive for.

B: If you're beaten, conceal it!
There's no pity for you.
For the world cannot feel it.
Just keep to yourself.
Weep to yourself.

A': This funny world
Can turn right around and forget you.
It's always sure
To roll right along when you're through.

C/A: If you are broke you shouldn't mind.
It's all a joke, for you will find
This funny world is making fun of you.

Gertrude Lawrence
(1898–1952, born Gertrude Klasen in London) was a prominent star on both sides of the Atlantic. Charismatic and an excellent comic actor, her talents didn't include a very large or impressive singing voice; that too was part of her charm. Kurt Weill, Ira Gershwin, and Moss Hart's *Lady in the Dark* was written for her, as was the role of Anna in Rodgers and Hammerstein's *The King and I.*

Peggy-Ann and *Betsy* opened on consecutive nights. In 1926, Rodgers and Hart also wrote the songs for *Lido Lady,* produced in London, and for three revues, including the 1926 *Garrick Gaieties,* which had the hit song "Mountain Greenery."

Oh, Kay!
MUSIC/LYRICS: the Gershwins
BOOK: Guy Bolton and P. G. Wodehouse
PRODUCERS: Alex A. Aarons and Vinton Freedley
CAST INCLUDES: Gertrude Lawrence and Victor Moore
PERFORMANCES: 256

Written for British star Gertrude Lawrence and comic actor Victor Moore, *Oh, Kay!* is about bootleggers on Long Island. It's still occasionally revived, though usually with major rewrites and added Gershwin songs. Along with such standards as "Maybe," "Clap Yo' Hands," "Fidgety Feet," and "Do, Do, Do," the score includes "Someone to Watch Over Me," one of the most frequently performed songs in the entire pop repertory; it has a verse and an AABA chorus. (Lawrence sang it on stage while holding a doll given to her by George Gershwin.)

George White's Scandals (1926) was Henderson, DeSylva, and Brown's second show as a team and their second *Scandals;* it was the most successful of the series (432 performances). Among the songs were "The Birth of the Blues" and "The Black Bottom," which became a national dance craze as popular as the Charleston. The score also included Gershwin's *Rhapsody in Blue* and other interpolations. At that point, the top ticket price was up to $5.50.

The Desert Song was Romberg's next hit after The Student Prince and gave Hammerstein and Harbach another huge hit two years after Rose-Marie. The formula libretto is about a masked outlaw named the Red Shadow, who, when out of disguise, pretends to be rather empty-headed. The Desert Song is probably Romberg's lushest and most beautiful score, the first of two very successful collaborations with Hammerstein. There have been three movie versions (1929, 1944, and 1953) and countless touring productions; it's still performed by opera and light opera companies. Included in the score are the title song, "One Alone," "Romance," and "Ho! (The Riff Song)"—the show's "Tramp! Tramp! Tramp!"

In 1927, many of the most popular songs of the year came from Broadway. The Orpheum and Keith-Albee vaudeville circuits merged. New York had twenty-four daily newspapers; they all covered the 268 Broadway shows that opened during the year, twenty during the week of Christmas alone. Among the more than fifty musicals and revues opening in New York in 1927 was The Merry Monahans, which was George M. Cohan's last appearance in one of his own musicals.

Ziegfeld Follies of 1927 (167 performances) was the first new Follies in two years and the last for four; most of Ziegfeld's imitators had already folded. Designed by Urban, it starred Eddie Cantor and Ruth Etting. Cantor and Harold Atteridge wrote the sketches and Berlin wrote most of the songs, including "Ooh, Maybe It's You" and "Shaking the Blues Away."

Africana (77 performances) was an African American revue in which Ethel Waters made her Broadway debut; she interpolated Akst, Lewis, and Young's "Dinah," which she'd recorded in 1925.

A musical comedy about sailors and their girlfriends, Hit the Deck! (352 performances) was Youmans's last Broadway success; by then, he'd become very difficult to work with. The hit tunes included "Sometimes I'm Happy" and "Hallelujah!" The 1955 movie—starring Jane Powell, Tony Martin, Debbie Reynolds, Ann Miller, Vic Damone, and Russ Tamblyn—changed the story and used Youmans songs from various sources.

Rio Rita was the first show to play at the spectacular, new, Urban-designed Ziegfeld Theatre (the second was Show Boat, which was supposed to be first but wasn't ready in time) with the highest

The Desert Song
MUSIC: Sigmund Romberg
LYRICS: Oscar Hammerstein II and Otto Harbach
LIBRETTO: Hammerstein, Harbach, and Frank Mandel
PRODUCERS: Mandel and Laurence Schwab
CAST INCLUDES: Robert Halliday and Vivienne Segal
PERFORMANCES: 465

Hit the Deck!
MUSIC: Vincent Youmans
LYRICS: Leo Robin and Clifford Grey
BOOK: Herbert Fields
DIRECTORS: Lew Fields and Alexander Leftwich
PRODUCERS: Vincent Youmans and Lew Fields
CAST INCLUDES: Charles King
PERFORMANCES: 352

Rio Rita
MUSIC: Harry Tierney
LYRICS: Joseph McCarthy
BOOK: Guy Bolton and Fred Thompson
CHOREOGRAPHERS: Sammy Lee and Albertina Rasch
DESIGNER: Joseph Urban (sets)
PRODUCER: Florenz Ziegfeld
CAST INCLUDES: the comedy team of Bert Wheeler and Robert Woolsey
PERFORMANCES: 494

Ethel Waters (1900–77, born in Chester, Pennsylvania), starting in 1917, was a star on the African American vaudeville circuit called the Theater Owners Booking Association (T.O.B.A., which the performers often said stood for "Tough on Black Asses"). During the early part of her career she was known as "Sweet Mama Stringbean" and usually sang and recorded the blues. Waters became a Broadway star with *Africana*, appearing for many years in both all-black and integrated shows (mostly revues) and headlining at the Cotton Club. She made several movies and, in the later part of her career, acted in dramatic roles on Broadway and in Hollywood.

A Connecticut Yankee

MUSIC/LYRICS: Richard Rodgers and Lorenz Hart

BOOK: Herbert Fields, based on Mark Twain's *A Connecticut Yankee in King Arthur's Court*

DIRECTOR: Alexander Leftwich

CHOREOGRAPHER: Busby Berkeley

PRODUCERS: Lew Fields and Lyle D. Andrews

CAST INCLUDES: William Gaxton

PERFORMANCES: 418

ticket price of the day: $5.50. It was a mixture of a musical comedy, an operetta, and an extravaganza, and it was Tierney and McCarthy's biggest hit since *Irene* in 1919. Wheeler and Woolsey were in the 1929 movie version; Abbott and Costello were in the 1942 remake.

In 1927, *Good News* (557 performances) was Henderson, De-Sylva, and Brown's first musical comedy, with book by Laurence Schwab and DeSylva. Like the Princess musical *Leave It to Jane*, it's a college football story. The score includes the title song, the charm song "The Best Things in Life Are Free," and "The Varsity Drag," which created another huge dance craze; all three became enormous pop hits. Because of the show's success at capturing the mood and music of the flapper generation, Henderson, DeSylva, and Brown were the first Broadway team brought to Hollywood. A 1930 film of the show used many from the original Broadway cast. There was a 1947 remake (available on Warner Home Video DVD), considerably rewritten by Betty Comden and Adolph Green, starring June Allyson and Peter Lawford. A 1974 Broadway revisal, trying to cash in on the nostalgia craze set off by the 1971 revisal of *No, No, Nanette*, closed in two weeks.

A Connecticut Yankee was Rodgers and Hart's eighth hit in three years (and the biggest for Rodgers, Hart, and Fields together) and their last Broadway success until 1936. (They revised and revived it in 1943, for which Hart wrote his last lyrics.) It's about a contemporary man who's knocked over the head with a champagne bottle and dreams that he's back in Camelot. Among the hit songs were "Thou Swell" and "My Heart Stood Still," which Rodgers and Hart wrote for a 1927 London revue called *One Damn Thing After Another*, then added it to *A Connecticut Yankee*.

Funny Face (250 performances), with a score by the Gershwins and book by Fred Thompson and Paul Gerard Smith, was produced by Aarons and Freedley and starred the Astaires and Victor Moore. Written to the talents of the stars, it has a nonsensical story about attempts to steal some jewels belonging to the heroine. The Gershwins wrote several hit songs for the show, including the title song, "He Loves and She Loves," "My One and Only," "'S Wonderful," "The Babbitt and the Bromide," and "How Long Has This Been Going On?" (dropped before opening, then used a month later in the otherwise undistinguished

Rosalie, produced by Ziegfeld for Marilyn Miller). *Funny Face* was completely rewritten in 1983 into the successful and equally nonsensical musical *My One and Only,* with considerable changes to the script and the addition of Gershwin songs from other sources. The 1957 movie *Funny Face* (available on Paramount VHS) was directed by Stanley Donen and stars Fred Astaire and Audrey Hepburn (who started as a dancer). It has a completely different story and some songs not by the Gershwins. Hepburn sings "How Long Has This Been Going On?" in the film.

Strike Up the Band, despite a score by the Gershwins and a book by George S. Kaufman, closed out of town. An antiwar satire (Kaufman once defined satire as what closes on Saturday night), the show was about big business maneuverings that force America into war with Switzerland over tariffs on cheese. Halfway between a musical comedy and an American Gilbert and Sullivan operetta and with some revue elements thrown in, it was basically the only twenties musical besides *Show Boat* with something to say. The score includes the title song and the great ballad "The Man I Love." It was revised and got to Broadway in 1930 with the war over chocolate instead of cheese.

1927 was a great year for the frivolous musical comedy, although the big Broadway revue and the operetta were nearing their ends. Since *Strike Up the Band* closed out of town, Kern and Hammerstein's *Show Boat* was, however, the only truly innovative show of the year—and of the decade—to play New York. Thus, it gets its own chapter.

> **William Gaxton** (1893–1963, born Arturo Gaxiola in San Francisco) was a strong Broadway presence throughout the thirties; he starred with Victor Moore in the Gershwins' *Of Thee I Sing* and with Ethel Merman and Moore in Porter's *Anything Goes,* among many other shows. (Altogether, he and Moore costarred in seven shows.) An unlikely type for a hero, he seemed more like a con man.

Suggested Watching And Listening

Ella Fitzgerald Sings The Irving Berlin Songbook
The following song is from Fitzgerald's recording of *The Irving Berlin Songbook,* vol. 2, available on Verve Records CD.
- "Blue Skies" (performed by Ella Fitzgerald): It was added to Rodgers and Hart's show *Betsy* on opening night. Fitzgerald does a long scat on the recording.

The Glory of Gershwin
This 1994 CD *The Glory of Gershwin* is available from Mercury Records. It includes the following song from the show *Oh, Kay!*
- "Someone to Watch Over Me" (performed by Elton John)

No, No, Nanette!

The recording is from the original-cast CD of the 1971 Broadway revisal, available on Columbia (USA) CD.

- "Tea for Two" (performed by Roger Rathburn and Susan Watson).

Richard Rodgers: The Sweetest Sounds

This is part of the *American Masters: Legends of Broadway* PBS biography series (available in a box set on Winstar DVD) and was directed by Roger M. Sherman. The first half covers Rodgers's career with Lorenz Hart.

The Rodgers and Hart Songbook

This is Ella Fitzgerald's 1956 version of the *Rodgers and Hart Songbook,* vol. 2, available on Verve Records CD.

- "Manhattan" (performed by Ella Fitzgerald): In this song from the show *The Garrick Gaieties,* Fitzgerald sings the verse and two choruses; unlike many others, Fitzgerald almost always sang the verses of songs. (If you're a singer, don't take a breath in the middle of a word the way she does. She's Ella Fitzgerald; you're not.)

Strike Up the Band

This Elektra/Nonesuch CD is a 1991 reconstruction of the original 1927 score and orchestrations. The show includes the following songs.

- "The Man I Love" (performed by Rebecca Luker and Brent Barrett): It's an AABA song that Luker and Barrett perform exactly as written for the show, paying special attention to the dotted rhythms. (Many phrases in the song start with a very short note—a sixteenth note—followed by a long note—a dotted eighth note. These rhythms are smoothed out by most pop singers to be closer to two eighth notes.) The number is over six minutes long, including dialogue, her verse and chorus, and his chorus ("The Girl I Love"), which ends with both singing together. (The song is rarely sung by men out of context.) Rebecca Luker played Magnolia in the 1995 Broadway revisal of *Show Boat* and Maria in the 1998 revival of *The Sound of Music.*
- "Strike Up the Band" (performed by Jason Graae and the chorus and danced by Randy Skinner): The song makes fun of patriotism forty years before it became fashionable to do so. Without the verse, you'd never know it was satiric. It's often used out of context—and without the verse—as a truly patriotic number. Here's the verse:

We fought in 1917,
Rum ta ta tum, tum, tum!
And drove the tyrant from the scene—
Rum ta ta tum, tum, tum!
We're in a bigger, better war
For your patriotic pastime.
We don't know what we're fighting for—
But we didn't know the last time!
So load the cannon! Draw the blade!
Rum ta ta tum, tum, tum!
Come on and join the Big Parade!

Rum ta ta tum, tum,
Rum ta ta tum, tum,
Rum ta ta tum, tum, tum!

This Funny World: Songs by Lorenz Hart

This is Mary Cleere Haran's Varese Sarabande CD, which is a collection of songs by Rodgers and Hart.

- "This Funny World" (performed by Mary Cleere Haran): It's from the show *Betsy*.

Till the Clouds Roll By

The versions of the following songs are from the movie *Till the Clouds Roll By,* which features Judy Garland as Marilyn Miller and is available on Warner Home Video DVD.

- "Sunny" (performed by Judy Garland and the chorus)
- "Who?" (performed by Judy Garland and the chorus): The two-step "Who?" was one of Kern's biggest hits.

Ziegfeld Follies

The following song from the show *Funny Face* is included in the 1946 movie revue *Ziegfeld Follies,* directed by Lemuel Ayers and available on Warner Home Video DVD.

- "The Babbitt and the Bromide" (performed by Fred Astaire and Gene Kelly): "Babbitt" (the title character of Sinclair Lewis's 1922 novel) and "bromide" (an overused saying or expression) were slang terms for rigidly conventional, middle-class businessmen. (Hollywood always prerecorded songs for movies; the singers mouthed them on camera rather than singing them over and over again for every "take" of every camera angle. Since there were, therefore, no microphones used during the shooting, taps were post-recorded.)

Ziegfeld Follies of 1927

This show included the following song.

- "Shaking the Blues Away" (performed by Doris Day): This version is from director Charles Vidor's 1955 *Love Me or Leave Me* (available on MGM/Warner Home Video DVD), a fairly accurate biographical film starring Doris Day as Ruth Etting and James Cagney in a nonsinging, nondancing role as the gangster who loved her. Ann Miller does a sizzling tap to the song in the 1948 movie *Easter Parade*. (She was known as the fastest tapper in the world.)

Show Boat

Life upon the wicked stage
Ain't ever what a girl supposes;
Stage door Johnnies aren't rag-
Ing over you with gems and roses.
—"LIFE UPON THE WICKED STAGE,"
SHOW BOAT, LYRICS BY OSCAR HAMMERSTEIN II

Show Boat was enormous, with a chorus of nearly a hundred people, many lavish scenes, and a magnificent Urban design. (A 1932 revival was Ziegfeld's last production.) It was also long—over three hours uncut—and complex. Structurally an operetta, with songs that make it feel like a musical, albeit a serious one, it has three-dimensional characters and even includes long dramatic scenes without any music at all, except for underscoring. Musical theater historian Miles Kreuger describes it as:

> The first musical in which a leading character grew and matured as she faced the adversities of life; the first musical to present a panoramic history of America from the Mississippi levees of the 1880s to the Broadway of the 1920s; the first to depict alcoholism in a poignant, rather than a farcical, manner; the first to deal with wife desertion, miscegenation, and the contrasting dreams and life styles of black and white people living side-by-side along the river.

It was also the first musical to have black and white principals and choruses singing together onstage. Albert Williams notes:

> This was a vital aspect of the show, which examined the parallel and sometimes intersecting lives of white and black Americans and the way American culture has been shaped by the interaction of the two. In a truly epic way, *Show*

Boat uses the emotional and social conditions of its characters, black and white, to reflect on American history on a grand scale during a specific, crucial era of transition—from the Gilded Age to the Jazz Age. (Williams, personal communication)

Show Boat—An American Musical Play

MUSIC: Jerome Kern

LYRICS/BOOK: Oscar Hammerstein, adapted from Edna Ferber's 1926 novel

DIRECTORS: Oscar Hammerstein, Jerome Kern, and Zeke Colvan (stage manager)

ORCHESTRATOR: Robert Russell Bennett

CHOREOGRAPHER: Sammy Lee

DESIGNERS: Joseph Urban (sets) and John Harkrider (costumes)

PRODUCER: Florenz Ziegfeld

CAST INCLUDES: Charles Winninger, Helen Morgan, Norma Terris, Edna May Oliver, Sammy White, and Jules Bledsoe

PERFORMANCES: 575 on Broadway, 350 in London, and 910 in a 1971 London revival

Show Boat is a backstage family chronicle that traces five couples over a forty-year period, moving from Natchez, Mississippi, to Chicago and back. Along the way, it also follows the development of American theater from showboats to vaudeville to Broadway, as reflected in the lives of three generations of women, which center on Magnolia Hawks in the middle generation. It is, for the times, a seamless collaboration between Kern and Hammerstein, who, for the first time, wrote both book and lyrics without other collaborators. (As often retold, the hostess at a party introduced Mrs. Kern as the wife of the man who wrote "Ol' Man River." Mrs. Hammerstein said, "No, he didn't. Her husband wrote 'Dum dum dee dum, da dum dum dee dum.' My husband wrote 'Ol' man river, dat ol' man river.' ") The humor in the show comes out of character and situation, as do the lyrics, making audiences keep the plot in mind while enjoying the musical numbers. The music and dances—including interpolations of real period songs and dances—change styles to reflect the trends of the passing years. (During the period from 1925 to 1927, Sammy Lee also did the dances for *Betsy, Tip-Toes, No, No, Nanette!, The Cocoanuts, Oh, Kay!, Rio Rita, Ziegfeld Follies of 1927,* and five other shows.) The music in *Show Boat*—and there's a lot of it—is therefore part operetta, part vaudeville and show tunes, part distillations of Negro spirituals and work songs, and part rag and jazz. There's also a great deal of underscoring using themes from the musical numbers, further helping to unify the show.

Although the black characters in *Show Boat* were the first to be treated seriously on white Broadway, some of the language and attitudes are today seen as unintentionally racist. Also, some characters are now considered stereotypes, there are some awkward transitions and creaky plot devices—it often depends on characters showing up by coincidence just when they're needed to move the plot along—and the show is too long, particularly in the second act. With five stories to tell, *Show Boat*'s first tryout in Washington, D.C., ran almost four and a half hours. There was a lot of cutting and fixing on the road before it opened on Broadway six weeks later. The three movie versions (1929, 1936, and 1951) and most revivals have continued to tinker with the show, restoring or cutting scenes and numbers and trying to rid the book of its creaky and unintentionally racist elements. Kern and Hammerstein themselves made changes for the 1936 film and for a 1946 Broadway revival. Kern wrote new songs for both. Technology had advanced far enough by 1946 that Hammerstein could cut several short scenes he'd written to be played in 1 while the sets were being changed. Harold Prince's hit 1994 revival drew on the novel as well as on Hammerstein's script, with cuts and changes to make the show acceptable to the more politically and psychologically aware audiences of the nineties.

The Magnolia Hawks and Gaylord Ravenal main plot is a love story; they meet and fall in love in the first scene, soon become the leads in the show on the showboat (the *Cotton Blossom*), and marry at the end of the first act (which is when most musicals would have ended). Things turn very unhappy for them through most of the second act after they leave the *Cotton Blossom* for Chicago. A gambler, Ravenal eventually goes broke and, unable to face his responsibilities, he deserts Magnolia, leaving her to support herself and their child, Kim.

The Julie LaVerne and Steve Baker tragic subplot (they are the original leads in the *Cotton Blossom*'s show) is about an interracial marriage. (Miscegenation was illegal in the 1880s and for quite a while after in the South, where it was also illegal for blacks to perform onstage with whites.) Once it's revealed that Julie is half black but passing as white, she and Steve have to leave the boat; they too end up in Chicago, where he deserts her. Julie becomes an alcoholic and—in the novel—a prostitute. Although both have been deserted, Magnolia and Julie love their men no matter what. (Both sing "Can't Help Lovin' Dat Man.") Julie's life is destroyed; Magnolia endures and becomes a vaudeville star. Steve never returns; neither does Ravenal in the novel, although he does, after an absence of over twenty years, in the musical. His return feels tacked on to make a happy ending.

In the comic subplot, Ellie May Shipley hesitates about marrying Frank Schultz. (Both are actors and dancers in the boat's show.) When she finally gives in, they leave the *Cotton Blossom* to pursue a career as a dance team. The only couple who leave the boat and succeed in staying together and maintaining a career, they're living in Hollywood at the end of the show, managing their son's career as a child silent-movie star. Two older couples,

Robert Russell Bennett (1894–1981, born in Kansas City, Missouri), at least partly responsible for over three hundred shows, was Broadway's most important orchestrator; during the twenties alone, he worked on up to twenty-two shows a season. He did shows for Kern, Berlin, Porter, Gershwin, Rodgers (including seven of the shows he wrote with Hammerstein), Burton Lane, Frederick Loewe, and Arthur Schwartz, among many others. He was a huge influence on what we think of today as the Broadway sound. Other significant orchestrators over the years include Hans Spialek, Hershy Kay, and Jonathan Tunick.

both also comic, stay together and on the boat: Parthy and Andy Hawks, who are white and who own the boat, and Queenie and Joe, who are black and who work on it. Both women love their men but browbeat them mercilessly—which has little or no effect on them. (Andy is the comic lead, often played by the biggest star in the cast.)

The five stories parallel and tie into each other at various points in the action, and all get a lot of stage time. Eventually, so does Kim, who is seen first as a child in the second act when Ravenal bids her a very sentimental farewell before disappearing. We meet Kim as an adult in the last scene when she has become a Broadway star (of musicals in the show, but of dramas in the novel, which was patterned after the famed actress Katherine Cornell, whose nickname was Kit). Kim gets the **eleven o'clock number.** (This is the last big number in most Broadway musicals, which rouses the audience to a peak of pleasure and applause before the story is resolved—usually in dialogue scenes. Then, after the singing of a short reprise of one or two tunes from earlier in the show, everyone goes home happy. Since curtain time was 8:40 P.M., eleven o'clock was usually about ten minutes before the end of the show. "Oklahoma!" was the eleven o'clock number Mamoulian was missing until it was added out of town.) *Show Boat* also has many small roles as well as both white and black singing and dancing choruses. Along with being huge and expensive, the show is difficult to cast. Magnolia (soprano), Ravenal (high baritone), and Joe (bass) need light operetta voices and the ability to act believably in both song and dialogue while aging forty years. (The role of Joe was written for famed bass Paul Robeson, but he wasn't available for the original production. He did, however, play it in the original London production and in the 1936 movie.) Magnolia is a particularly difficult role: she matures noticeably while going through a wide range of emotions. (Naturalistic acting and operetta-trained voices don't always go together in one person.) Queenie has to be funny and able to **belt** (sing high and loud in chest voice, like Ethel Merman, who's probably the most famous of all Broadway belters).

The tragic Julie was written for Helen Morgan's pop soprano voice and natural acting instincts. (The original keys of her numbers are often lowered for other women doing the role.) Steve doesn't sing but has to participate in a convincing fistfight as well as be at the center of the most dramatic scene in the show, the so-called Miscegenation Scene, when it's revealed that Julie is half black. Ellie and Frank need to sing well for dancers (Ellie more so than Frank), and they have to do both comic and serious acting.

Captain Andy can **talk-sing** his music but must be an expert comic actor. In talk-singing, the performer sings some of the lyrics—those within his or her vocal range—and speaks the rest semi-rhythmically. The orchestration usually includes the melody, particularly of those sections the performer speaks. It's the style used by Rex Harrison as Professor Higgins in *My Fair Lady* and by Richard Burton as King Arthur in *Camelot*.

The original Parthy, who must try to make a rather unlikable character more likable, didn't sing. In revivals the character usually does a chorus of "Why Do I Love You?" with Andy, as she does in the 1936 film; it's not difficult, has a fairly limited vocal range, and gives them a gentle moment together. In Prince's revival, she sang it to the newly born Kim in a scene that isn't in the original show but is in the 1936 movie without the song. The lyrics make no sense sung to a one-hour-old child:

> Why do I love you?
> Why do you love me?
> Why should there be two
> Happy as we?

It does give a badly needed moment of warmth to Parthy, but at a peculiar cost.

The adult Kim, beginning with the first production, is traditionally played by the same actress who plays Magnolia, although not in Prince's production. Mother and daughter are onstage at the same time for only a brief moment at the very end of the show. At that point, Kim has no lines and is therefore usually played by someone in matching wig and costume staged in shadows. Although Kim isn't a large role, she must carry the eleven o'clock number, which has varied from production to production. The original Magnolia/Kim, Norma Terris, did a jazzed-up reprise of "Why Do I Love You?" interspersed with her specialty: imitations of famous Broadway stars. Kern wrote "Nobody Else but Me" for the spot in the 1946 revival; it's the last song he wrote. In most later revivals, Kim does a Charleston version of "Why Do I Love You?" with Parthy, Queenie, and the choruses joining in, making it a high-energy dance number. Notable songs from the show also include Ellie and the chorus of white women's "Life upon the Wicked Stage" and Ellie and Frank's "I Might Fall Back on You," both comedy numbers; Julie's torch song "Bill"; and Magnolia and Ravenal's first-act duet "Make Believe." In his *New York Times* article "A Proud Flagship Keeps On Rollin' in Deeper Currents," Ethan Mordden writes:

> When it was new, the work marked the resolution of two conflicts that had vexed American culture for some 50 years. . . . One was the battle between vaudeville fun and cogent storytelling for prominence as the nation's dominant form in musical theater; the other was the theater world's use of the stage as a socially liberalizing force despite resistance by reactionaries. The twenties saw a last stand between censors and innovators—not only Shaw, Ibsen and O'Neill but Mae West, who spent 10 days in jail as the author of [her play] *Sex* the year *Show Boat*

opened. . . . Today, of course, the American musical has tamed its vaudeville spirit, and the theater . . . deals freely with social issues. (Mordden, 22)

Show Boat is about many things, but one theme ties everything together: people's need for a sense of community and continuity in their lives, and in the world, to help them face the difficulties that life always brings. Captain Andy, for example, frequently says that everyone on the boat should be "one big happy family"—a recurring theme in Hammerstein's work. Show business, a common metaphor in musicals (as in such later shows as *Gypsy, Cabaret,* and *A Chorus Line,* although for very different purposes) is used in *Show Boat* as a metaphor not only for an extended family but also for America as a whole, including the plight of African Americans during the forty years the show covers. *Show Boat* places a great deal of emphasis on the too-slowly-changing life of blacks in the post–Civil War South at the same time that their music was rapidly being adapted by white musicians. And there's Joe's song "Ol' Man River," reprised several times during the show; in the song, the river represents the relentless, unchanging, and uncaring passage of time ("He jes' keeps rollin' along"), and at the same time, it is saying that the injustices of mankind didn't change much either from the 1880s to the 1920s. (The song also helps tie together the rather episodic structure of the second act. The first act, in eight scenes, takes place over a three-week period in the late 1880s. The second act, in nine scenes, begins in 1893 and covers thirty-four years.)

> Notice too the running theme of illusion/reality—the idea that life itself is a "wicked stage" on which people play roles in an often futile attempt to control their conditions and destinies. Take Ravenal and Magnolia's courtship—the "Make Believe" duet and their first embrace during a rehearsal: all role-playing, as is Ravenal's pretense to being a Southern aristocrat. The theme takes on special resonance when combined with the show's racial concerns. Julie is a mulatto "passing" for white; Magnolia gets her job at the Trocadero by singing "black" (the way she learned from Julie). Magnolia succeeds by adapting black culture, while Julie is destroyed for adopting a white persona. (Williams, personal communication)

Depression-era audiences didn't want to take their musical entertainments that seriously. So *Show Boat* had no immediate imitators, though it was the prototype for Rodgers and Hammerstein's trendsetting shows, beginning with *Oklahoma!* in 1943. The show did, however, prove that the musical could tell a serious, complex, coherent, adult dramatic story without sounding like an opera, the first true blending of the musical comedy and the operetta. It deserves its U.S. postage stamp.

Suggested Watching and Listening

Show Boat

If you can find it, the Paper Mill Playhouse 1989 production of *Show Boat,* taped live before an audience and broadcast on PBS's "Great Performances," is a smallish but virtually complete revival.

In act 1, scene 1, we're on the levee at Natchez, Mississippi, in the late 1880s. The show opens with the black chorus singing about their hard life working on the Mississippi. (The number, based on African American rhythms, is slowed down much later in the scene to become the verse of "Ol' Man River.")

- *"Cotton Blossom"* (performed by the choruses): The white chorus enters and their music moves from operetta to minstrel-show style on *"Cotton Blossom"* (later inverted to become the first A of "Ol' Man River"), as both choruses sing together while waiting for Captain Andy, whose boat, the *Cotton Blossom,* is just tying up on the levee. Pete, the engineer, notices that Queenie, the black cook (Ellia English), is wearing a brooch he gave Julie, the boat's star; he's furious.

- "Captain Andy's Entrance" and "Ballyhoo" (performed by Eddie Bracken and the company): Captain Andy is given a syncopated star entrance. (A ballyhoo is a pitchman's routine.) Here, Andy introduces us to the principal players in his show, a three-act melodrama and an olio. We meet Ellie and Frank (Lenora Nemetz and Lee Roy Reams), who act in the melodrama and dance in the olio, and Julie and Steve (Shelly Burch and Robert Jensen), the heroine and hero of the melodrama. We also meet Andy's mean-tempered wife Parthy (Marsha Bagwell), who runs the business and orders everyone around, especially Andy. When Pete confronts Julie about the brooch, Steve starts a fistfight with him. (Most of the dialogue and action in the scene is underscored, helping sustain or change the mood.) Andy fires Pete, who swears revenge.

Gaylord Ravenal, a riverboat gambler who pretends to come from a well-placed Southern family, enters. Sheriff Vallon warns him that he can only stay for twenty-four hours or he'll get thrown in jail. (We learn later that he once shot a man in self-defense and isn't allowed in town.)

- "Where's the Mate for Me?" (performed by Richard White): Ravenal's opening song makes clear that he's an aimless drifter. He never even finishes it, interrupted by some bad offstage piano playing by Magnolia, the Hawks' young daughter, who's practicing between lessons with Julie. Magnolia then enters on the deck above him. Magnolia and Gaylord are immediately attracted to each other. She's not supposed to talk to strangers, but he convinces her to pretend they know each other.

- "Make Believe" (performed by Richard White and Rebecca Baxter): It's pop-styled, romantic operetta music, suitable to the period in which the scene takes place. The couple are like an American Romeo and Juliet at their first meeting, and the staging of her up on deck and him down on the levee mirrors Shakespeare's balcony scene. Sheriff Vallon interrupts and takes Ravenal off because the judge wants to talk to him.

Suggestions for the rest of the scene (or for the beginning as well if you can't find the Paper Mill Playhouse version) and for the others below are from the 1936 movie directed by James Whale, available on MGM VHS.

Queenie's husband, Joe, who also works on the boat, has overheard Magnolia and Ravenal's flirtation. Magnolia asks him what he thinks of Ravenal. He tells her she might as well ask the river what he thinks because "he knows all about everything," setting up his famous solo.

- "Ol' Man River" (performed by Paul Robeson from the original London company and the black men's chorus): The song and its regular reappearance throughout the rest of the show were Hammerstein's idea; he needed something "in 1" while the set was being changed. By the end of the first scene we've met all five central couples and gotten their stories going. We've also heard two songs that became pop standards: "Make Believe" and "Ol' Man River."

In act 1, scene 2, we're in the kitchen pantry of the *Cotton Blossom* a half hour later. Magnolia tells Julie about Ravenal; Julie recognizes that Magnolia (Irene Dunne from the original touring company) already feels toward him the way she herself feels toward Steve. At Magnolia's urging, she sings the following song.

- "Can't Help Lovin' Dat Man" (performed by Helen Morgan from the original cast): The song, another standard, furthers the plot considerably. In it, Julie shows how she feels about Steve but also accidentally reveals to Queenie (Hattie McDaniel from the original West Coast company) that she knows a song supposedly only known by blacks. The solo becomes a duet for Queenie and Joe (about how lazy Joe is, replaced in Prince's revival by a repeat of Julie's lyrics) and finally a huge number for Julie, Magnolia, Queenie, Joe, and the singing and dancing black choruses, all singing and doing the shuffle. (Although it looks rather ludicrous now, in 1927 it was quite daring to have a white woman doing the shuffle.) The 1936 movie has the complete scene.

In act 1, scene 4 (the Miscegenation Scene), it's later that day in the *Cotton Blossom* auditorium (we can see the stage and part of the audience section). Andy is holding a rehearsal of the melodrama "The Parson's Bride" with Parthy (Helen Westley) keeping an eagle eye on him.

At the first preview, the scene opened with "Mis'ry's Comin' Round," a six-minute number for Queenie, Joe, Julie, and the black chorus while getting things ready for the evening's show. In it they sing "spiritual style" of their fear that tragedy is pursuing them. The number unfortunately had to be cut for length, but it's a powerful statement for the times about the African American condition. Prince reinstated it.

Ellie (Queenie Smith) interrupts the rehearsal to tell Steve (Donald Cook) that Pete has told the sheriff there's a case of miscegenation on the boat. Steve cuts Julie's finger and sucks a few drops of her blood. When the sheriff arrives to arrest the couple, Steve says he has Negro blood in him, so the marriage is legal. (Even one drop made him black in Natchez.) The sheriff doesn't arrest them but tells them they can't continue performing with whites. Julie and Steve leave the boat. Captain Andy, over Parthy's loud protests, has Magnolia take over Julie's roles. Gaylord Ravenal (Allan Jones) shows up looking for passage out of town just as Andy is trying to figure out who'll replace Steve—one of the many coincidences in the plot. As Joe sings a reprise of "Ol' Man River," Andy hires Ravenal and begins rehearsing a scene between him and Magnolia that ends in a kiss much too realistic for Parthy.

This scene is like nothing before it in the history of the musical—a nearly fifteen-minute sequence alternating between heavy drama and comedy and with no music except underscoring (unless the production uses "Mis'ry's Comin' Round," making it a twenty-minute scene). It's also unusual that, after being so prominent for the first half of the first act, Julie isn't seen again until the middle of the second act, and Steve never reappears at all. The 1936 movie has the scene nearly word for word as in the original. The underscoring is partly "Mis'ry's Comin' Round."

Act 2, scene 4 is set at the Trocadero nightclub in Chicago on December 30, 1904. After a short rehearsal number for the white female dance chorus, accompanied by John Philip Sousa's "The Washington Post March" played on an onstage piano, Julie, the star of the show, rehearses her new song. (It's the first time we've seen her since she and Steve left the showboat.) Steve has disappeared, and Julie has become an alcoholic who's known to go on week-long benders.

- ■ "Bill" (performed by Helen Morgan): It's Julie's torch song, suitable to the period in which the scene is set. It's showing us that she still feels the same way about Steve: she can't help loving him. ("Bill" was originally written by Kern and Wodehouse for the 1918 *Oh Lady! Lady!* but dropped before opening. For *Show Boat,* Hammerstein did a large rewrite on the lyrics but insisted that Wodehouse get sole program credit.) Helen Morgan sings it in the 1936 movie nine years after she became a star singing it on Broadway.

After "Bill," Julie exits to get another drink. Frank (Sammy White from the original cast), who coincidentally has been booked into the club with Ellie, brings in Magnolia, whom he ran into through another coincidence and who needs a job after being deserted by Ravenal.

- ■ "Can't Help Lovin' Dat Man" (performed by Irene Dunne): Magnolia auditions with a reprise of the song. Julie sees her and hides, embarrassed, before Magnolia can see her. Realizing Magnolia needs a job, Julie walks out. (This is her last scene; in Prince's revisal, we later see in a crossover that she's become a street person.) Magnolia, never learning of Julie's sacrifice, gets the now-vacant singer's job after singing "Can't Help Lovin' Dat Man" again, this time in a rag version, while Frank improvises a dance to it.

In act 2, scene 6, it's New Year's Eve. (As with the *Cotton Blossom* auditorium in act 1, we can see both the stage and the audience.) The first act of the Trocadero's show is a Parisian "Apache Dance" performed by a sister act to Offenbach's "Valse des Rayons." (All the music in the scene is interpolated; it was Kern's idea to use music that could have been used in 1904.) The next act is Frank and Ellie singing Joseph E. Howard's 1904 song "Good-bye, My Lady Love" and doing a cakewalk. Captain Andy enters—another coincidence. He's come on a visit with Parthy, knowing nothing about what's happened to Magnolia. Having given up trying to find her, he's left Parthy at their hotel and enters the Trocadero with some women he's picked up as drinking companions. (It's Andy's comic drunk scene. He also has a big comic scene in the first act where he has to play all the roles in the showboat's melodrama.) Magnolia is introduced; the audience, angry that it's not Julie, heckles her and, frightened, she can barely sing her song: Charles K. Harris's best-selling 1892 ballad "After the Ball." Andy quiets the audience; Magnolia sings out and becomes an instant success. In this scene, along with the father-daughter reunion, we see the beginning of Magnolia's rise to stardom. The scene is relatively complete in the 1936 movie.

The show then jumps to 1925. By yet another coincidence, Andy runs into Ravenal and invites him to the boat, where Ellie and Frank are coincidentally visiting, and where Ravenal is reunited with Magnolia right after their daughter, Kim, leads the eleven o'clock number.

From The New Moon to The Little Show

Birds do it, bees do it,

Even educated fleas do it,

Let's do it, let's fall in love.

In Spain, the best upper sets do it,

Lithuanians and Letts do it,

Let's do it, let's fall in love.

The Dutch in old Amsterdam do it,

Not to mention the Finns,

Folks in Siam do it,

Think of Siamese twins.

—"LET'S DO IT (LET'S FALL IN LOVE)," *PARIS*, LYRICS BY COLE PORTER

Like Irving Berlin, Cole Porter wrote both words and music, including the football and varsity show songs he wrote while at Yale. He placed songs in London shows starting in 1918 and in American shows a year later. His first hit song was the sentimental "Old Fashioned Garden" in the 1919 revue *Hitchy-Koo*. His first pop standard, "Let's Do It (Let's Fall in Love)," in the 1928 musical *Paris*, was the first hit song to proclaim openly that sex was fun. (Calling it "falling in love" didn't fool anyone and wasn't meant to.) Porter, already a favorite member of the social upper crust of New York and Europe, soon became a celebrity as well. From then into the fifties, he wrote the scores for over two dozen musicals and movies, including *Gay Divorce, Anything Goes,* and *DuBarry Was a Lady.*

Of all the composers and lyricists on Broadway, Cole Porter was the most urbane and sophisticated and at times the silliest. . . . His wealth and social con-

Cole Porter (1891–1964), unlike most Broadway songwriters of the time, came from a very wealthy family, wasn't Jewish, and was born in Peru, Indiana. Although he began writing songs at age ten, Porter went to Yale to become a lawyer. His first song in a Broadway show, "Esmeralda," was interpolated into the 1915 musical *Hands Up*. His first full Broadway score, *See America First*, a "patriotic-comic opera" written with a Yale schoolmate, closed after fifteen performances. Porter, discouraged, toured the world for three years, finally settling in Paris. In 1919, he married Linda Lee Thomas, a socialite even richer than he. Theirs was a close relationship, but neither wanted a sexual one. With their combined fortunes, the Porters lived elegantly on both continents.

tacts made him the spokesperson and satirist of the upper classes. . . . He also spoke to the average person, as witnessed by the hundreds of popular songs to his credit. . . . His melodies were uniquely his own and not based on clichéd musical forms currently in vogue. His lyrics, too, showed added layers of emotion. (Bloom, *Broadway: An Encyclopedic Guide*, 286)

In 1937, Porter's horse reared and fell on him, crushing both his legs. He was in pain for the rest of his life, enduring almost forty operations and eventually having to be carried from room to room. He continued writing hit shows and songs, but they became increasingly paler reflections of his earlier work. By 1946, it looked as if his career was finished. Then in 1948, he had his biggest hit and his most original show, *Kiss Me, Kate*, followed by such other successes as *Can-Can* and *Silk Stockings*.

Porter's shows were in no way innovative; they followed the trends of the times. The books of his shows before *Oklahoma!* were standard, musical-comedy star vehicles, written for performers like Ethel Merman, Bert Lahr, Jimmy Durante, Bob Hope, William Gaxton, Victor Moore, and Sophie Tucker. His later shows, though still musical comedies, were better integrated and characterized because they took their example from the new standards set by Rodgers and Hammerstein. However, throughout his career, Porter wrote songs in ways that frequently broke the traditional forms and structures. His music was complex and sophisticated, often using Latin rhythms and long **chromatic lines.** (When music moves chromatically, it progresses up or down the scale by half steps, which frequently gives it a sensual feeling.) His lyrics were among the best ever written for Broadway, often attaining an emotional depth and a skill at wit and imagery far beyond those of any of his contemporaries.

I find Rodgers warmer, Arlen more hip, Gershwin more direct, Berlin more practical. But no one can deny that Porter added a certain theatrical elegance, as well as interest and sophistication, wit, and musical complexity to the popular song form. And for this we are deeply indebted. (Wilder, 252)

In 1928, Rudy Vallee opened at New York's Heigh-Ho Club with his band, introducing a new style of pop singing: **crooning.** Rather than projecting his voice out into the house, he amplified it by singing through a megaphone, thereby keeping the sound more intimate. He soon began radio broadcasts from the club, starting them with "Heigh ho, everybody."

> With the advent of electrical recording, the use of microphones, and a [radio]
> in every home, the scene was set for a smoother, more elegant style of singing—
> informed by jazz, though not exactly jazz singing. It was the age of crooning,
> and it lasted from the emergence of the first great exponent of the art—Bing
> Crosby . . . until rock and roll changed the course of popular music once again.
> Crosby originally worked as a band singer for the Paul Whiteman Orchestra . . .
> but it was the influence of Louis Armstrong that helped create his style, incorporating Armstrong's manner of swinging and scatting certain phrases into what
> was essentially a confidential, intimate style of singing. . . . Crosby and his contemporaries . . . caressed words, made lyrics meaningful, used turns of phrase to
> suggest something eloquent beyond the words of the song sheet. Alongside
> their rise to eminence, popular songwriting itself found a new sophistication.
> (Richard Crook, "Crooners and Torchsingers," *Gramophone*, 102)

Backdrop: 1928–1929

National   Herbert Hoover is elected president. Huey Long becomes governor of Louisiana. Signs of drought begin to appear in the Southwest and upper Great Plains. In the 1929 St. Valentine's Day Massacre, Al Capone's men machine-gun down seven members of Bugs Moran's gang in a Chicago garage at 2122 North Clark Street.

International   Trotsky is expelled from the USSR and Stalin's first five-year plan begins. Chiang Kai-shek is elected president of China. Hitler moves Himmler up in the hierarchy of the Nazi Party. The "Kingdom of Serbs, Croats, and Slovenes" changes its name to Yugoslavia. The Lateran Treaty establishes the independence of Vatican City.

New Developments   Penicillin's antibacterial properties are discovered. Vitamin C is isolated. Blue Cross health insurance is organized. Magnetic tape is invented. German movie producer Louis Blattner designs the first tape recorder. After setting sixty-seven world records and winning three gold medals, U.S. Olympic swimmer Johnny Weissmuller retires to Hollywood and stars in nineteen Tarzan movies.

Art   New York's Museum of Modern Art opens. There are new paintings by, among others, Dalí, Hopper, Picasso, Klee, Rivera, and Wood. Construction begins on the Empire State Building, completed in 1931.

Bing Crosby had his first hit record, Barris and Clifford's "I Surrender Dear," in 1928. The Mills Brothers also made their first recording that same year.

Also during 1928, performer/songwriter Nora Bayes and playwright/lyricist Dorothy Donnelly died. Kurt Weill and Bertolt Brecht's *Die Dreigroschenoper* (*The Threepenny Opera*) premiered in Berlin starring Weill's wife, Lotte Lenya; it flopped in New York. Then, in 1954, it had an extremely successful and influential off-Broadway production in an English version by Marc Blitzstein and again starring Lenya.

The New Moon

MUSIC: Sigmund Romberg

LYRICS: Oscar Hammerstein

LIBRETTO/DIRECTORS: Frank Mandel, Oscar Hammerstein, and Laurence Schwab

PRODUCERS: Frank Mandel and Laurence Schwab

CAST INCLUDES: Robert Halliday and Evelyn Herbert

PERFORMANCES: 519

When *The New Moon*—which closed down for eight months after its out-of-town tryout in Philadelphia—finally opened, it was an enormous hit and is still revived occasionally. The music is well-written, traditional American operetta fare, very romantic and often quite beautiful. The libretto fits everything together quite sensibly and smoothly for the times, and the show has an isolationist view of democracy very much in keeping with the mood

Music/Dance Modern dancer/choreographer Martha Graham forms her dance troupe. Gershwin's tone poem for orchestra *An American in Paris* premieres at Carnegie Hall; the score includes the use of real French taxicab horns. (Most Broadway composers have always left the orchestrations of their scores to others; Gershwin orchestrated *An American in Paris* himself and soon began doing some orchestrating for his musicals as well.) Minnelli's 1951 movie *An American in Paris,* with Gene Kelly and Leslie Caron, ends with a ballet choreographed to the score and designed as a series of French impressionist paintings.

Publications *Business Week* begins publication. Anthropologist Margaret Mead's *Coming of Age in Samoa* and the twelve-volume *Oxford English Dictionary* are published, as are poets Benét's *John Brown's Body,* Yeats's *The Tower,* and Pound's *Canto II.* New novels, some more concerned with the world, some with the individual, include Lawrence's last novel, *Lady Chatterley's Lover* (banned in the United States until 1959), Waugh's *Decline and Fall,* Woolf's *Orlando,* the seventh and final volume of Proust's *Remembrance of Things Past,* Remarque's *All Quiet on the Western Front,* Wolfe's *Look Homeward, Angel,* Faulkner's *As I Lay Dying* and *The Sound and the Fury,* Hemingway's *A Farewell to Arms,* and Hesse's *Steppenwolf.*

Radio/TV General Electric begins occasional television broadcasts. Radio show *Amos 'n' Andy* debuts on Chicago's WMAQ. A situation comedy with white actors playing stereotypical black characters straight out of minstrel shows and vaudeville, it becomes so popular that, in the 1930s, neighborhood movie theaters throughout the country interrupt films to play it in order to keep people from staying home to listen. *Amos 'n' Andy* moved to TV in 1949 with the characters intact, though played by black actors. Protests from the NAACP and other organizations eventually got it off the air.

of its audience. *The New Moon* is set mostly in New Orleans in 1792 and deals with people fleeing the results of the French Revolution. They want to start their own new world (a democracy, of course) on an island far away. The show has a romantic main-plot triangle and a comic subplot quadrangle, and there's a second hero involved in a melodramatic adventure story tying the whole thing together. Various people are in disguise at various times for various reasons. Among the most famous numbers are "One Kiss"; "Wanting You"; "Softly, as in a Morning Sunrise"; "Lover, Come Back to Me," which became a pop standard often performed in jazz arrangements; and "Stout-Hearted Men," the "Tramp! Tramp! Tramp!" of the show and operetta's idea of the American male ideal summed up in one song. (Barbra Streisand made a recording of it. When a woman sings, "Give me some men who are stout-hearted men who will fight for the right they adore," the lyrics take on a whole new meaning.) After *The New Moon*, Romberg and Hammerstein continued to collaborate occasionally, but their later shows didn't achieve the great or lasting success of this show or of *The Desert Song*. There's a 1940 Jeanette MacDonald and Nelson Eddy film version of *The New Moon*, unfaithful as ever to the original.

Pop Culture   Lawrence Welk and his band start playing "champagne music" and continue doing so for fifty years. Guy Lombardo's Royal Canadians dance band opens in New York with "the sweetest music this side of heaven." *Billboard* publishes its first chart of the week's most popular songs. Pop songs include Ahlert and Turk's "I'll Get By" and "Mean to Me," Van Boskerck's "Semper Paratus (Coast Guard March)," Williams's "Basin St. Blues," Primrose's "St. James Infirmary," Carmichael and Parish's great standard "Star Dust" (the most frequently recorded pop song), and Waller and Razaf's "Honeysuckle Rose."

Stage   Harold Clurman begins organizing what will become the Group Theatre. New York sees its first production of Chekhov's *Uncle Vanya*. Among the new plays are Hecht and MacArthur's *The Front Page*, Barry's *Holiday*, Treadwell's expressionist *Machinal*, Rice's *Street Scene* (adapted into the 1947 pop opera), and O'Neill's third Pulitzer Prize–winning play, the five-hour, nine-act *Strange Interlude* (with a dinner break), which has characters speaking their inner thoughts while the other characters freeze, and which gets parodied by Groucho Marx in the musical *Animal Crackers*.

Screen   George Eastman shows the first color movies. After two silent animated Mickey Mouse cartoons, Disney introduces Mickey's voice (done by Disney himself) in *Steamboat Willie*, the first cartoon with a sound track. New silent feature films include Dryer's *The Passion of Joan of Arc*, Pabst's *Pandora's Box*, Buñuel and Dalí's surrealist *Un Chien Andalou*, and Keaton's *Steamboat Bill, Jr.*

The Three Musketeers

MUSIC: Rudolf Friml

LYRICS: P. G. Wodehouse and Clifford Grey

LIBRETTO/DIRECTOR: William Anthony McGuire, adapted from the first half of the novel by Alexandre Dumas

CHOREOGRAPHERS: Richard Boleslavsky and Albertina Rasch

DESIGNERS: Joseph Urban (sets) and John W. Harkrider (costumes)

PRODUCER: Florenz Ziegfeld

CAST INCLUDES: Dennis King and Vivienne Segal

PERFORMANCES: 319

The operetta *The Three Musketeers*, extravagantly produced by Ziegfeld, was a success but depended on more of the same operetta formulas. Friml's next two shows flopped; he moved to Hollywood in 1934 and wrote little in the last thirty-eight years of his life.

In 1928, Cohan's *Billie* (112 performances) had his last Broadway score. Rodgers and Hart had three shows that year. *Present Arms* (155 performances), about marines and their girls, was choreographed by Busby Berkeley (who was also in it). The book was written by Herbert Fields, and the show was produced by Lew Fields. A movie version called *Leathernecking* was released in 1930. The show's most famous song is "You Took Advantage of Me." *She's My Baby* (a 71-performance flop) has a book by Guy Bolton, Bert Kalmar, and Harry Ruby, and was produced by Charles Dillingham. The show starred Beatrice Lillie, Clifton Webb, and Irene Dunne. It's about a man trying to borrow money from his uncle by pretending he's married to his maid. Lew Fields also produced Rodgers, Hart, and Herbert Fields's *Chee-Chee* (a 31-performance flop), set in China, about the son of the Grand Eunuch trying to avoid castration, a new subject for the musical both then and now. It was the last show Lew Fields did with Rodgers and Hart. Herbert did one more in 1931.

Paris (195 performances), score by Cole Porter and book by Martin Brown, was billed as a "musicomedy." Porter's score is one of his jazziest. He replaced the song "Let's Misbehave" before opening with "Let's Do It (Let's Fall in Love)"; it's a list song with a verse and five choruses of AA'BA. (Porter wrote many witty and frequently suggestive, or downright dirty, list songs.)

Nearly sixty movie musicals and revues are made during the two years, most of them in 1929. Among them is Jolson in *The Singing Fool*, with a score by Henderson, DeSylva, and Brown featuring "Sonny Boy" and "I'm Sittin' on Top of the World," and *The Awakening*, with Berlin's "Marie" in its score. Berlin's first full movie score is for *Puttin' On the Ritz*, starring Harry Richman; the title song is one of Berlin's biggest hits. Among other musicals are Helen Morgan in Mamoulian's *Applause;* an adaptation of *The Desert Song*, the first "all-talking and singing operetta" (the film has been lost); *The Gold Diggers of Broadway*, which introduces Burke and Dubin's "Tip Toe Through the Tulips"; *Hallelujah*, with an African American cast; Jeanette MacDonald and Maurice Chevalier in *The Love Parade; Sunny Side*

Whoopee is about a hypochondriac taking a rest cure out West who accidentally gets involved in the difficulties the characters in the romantic subplot are having getting married. It was tailored to the talents of noisy and highly energetic singer/comedian Eddie Cantor, who even got to do a blackface number in the second act when an explosion blackened his face. Ruth Etting's role in the show was extraneous to both the comic plot and the romantic subplot; she was there to sing a couple of songs, usually in 1 while the set was being changed. Composer Walter Donaldson wrote mainly for Tin Pan Alley; this show was one of only two he wrote for Broadway and was his only success. He wrote the music for such pop hits as "Yes, Sir, That's My Baby," "Carolina in the Morning," and "My Blue Heaven." The score for Whoopee includes "Makin' Whoopee," "My Baby Just Cares for Me," and "Love Me or Leave Me," a torch song for Etting still sung frequently and the title of her 1955 movie biography starring Doris Day.

Ziegfeld closed Whoopee early; after the 1929 stock market crash, he needed the money from a Hollywood deal. The 1930 movie version, in early Technicolor and with most of the Broadway cast, was coproduced by Ziegfeld and choreographed by Busby Berkeley. It cut out Etting's role but otherwise remained often painfully faithful to the Broadway production. Berkeley's dances (his first for film) partly reflected his Broadway style and partly foreshadowed the style of camera choreography he soon developed in such films as 42nd Street and the Gold Diggers series. He didn't return to Broadway until the 1971 revisal of No, No, Nanette! By then, he was too old to do much but pose for photographs.

Animal Crackers was the Marx Brothers' last show before moving to Hollywood permanently. The plot, to dignify it slightly by

Whoopee

MUSIC: Walter Donaldson
LYRICS: Gus Kahn
BOOK: William Anthony McGuire, adapted from Owen Davis's 1923 play The Nervous Wreck
DIRECTOR: Seymour Feliz and William Anthony McGuire
PRODUCER: Florenz Ziegfeld
DESIGNERS: Joseph Urban (sets) and John Harkrider (costumes)
CAST INCLUDES: Eddie Cantor and Ruth Etting
PERFORMANCES: 407

Animal Crackers

MUSIC/LYRICS: Bert Kalmar and Harry Ruby
BOOK: George S. Kaufman and Morrie Ryskind
PRODUCER: Sam H. Harris
CAST INCLUDES: the Marx Brothers and Margaret Dumont
PERFORMANCES: 213

Up, with a Henderson, DeSylva, and Brown score that includes "(Keep Your) Sunny Side Up"; and On with the Show, in which Ethel Waters sings Akst and Clarke's "Am I Blue?" The Broadway Melody ("100% All Talking + All Singing + All Dancing!") wins the Academy Award for best movie of 1929—hard to believe if you view it now. (In the score are Brown and Freed's "You Were Meant for Me" and "The Wedding of the Painted Doll," both used in the 1952 Singin' in the Rain, which has a score of their old songs; they mostly wrote for the movies. Freed later produced many of MGM's most famous musicals of the 1940s and 1950s.)

calling it that, is constantly interrupted for irrelevant comedy scenes as well as for songs and dances. The score includes "Hooray for Captain Spaulding," which became Groucho's theme music on his radio and TV shows *You Bet Your Life.* As with *The Cocoanuts, Animal Crackers* was filmed on a sound stage on Long Island and shot, with cuts, almost exactly as performed on stage. (There was rarely a fourth wall between the comics and the audience in early musical comedies. Groucho often played to the camera at those moments when, on stage, he would have played out to the audience, as in the sequence in *Animal Crackers* parodying one of O'Neill's "strange interludes.")

Rosalie

MUSIC: George Gershwin and Sigmund Romberg

LYRICS: P. G. Wodehouse and Ira Gershwin

BOOK: Guy Bolton and William Anthony McGuire

DIRECTOR: William Anthony McGuire

DESIGNER: Joseph Urban (sets)

PRODUCER: Florenz Ziegfeld

CAST INCLUDES: Marilyn Miller and Frank Morgan (the Wizard of Oz in the 1939 movie)

PERFORMANCES: 327

Another vehicle for Marilyn Miller, *Rosalie* ran on the strength of her star appeal. The Gershwins' "How Long Has This Been Going On?" dropped from *Funny Face,* is in the score. Van Dyke II's 1937 movie with the same title, starring Eleanor Powell, Nelson Eddy, and Morgan, has songs by Cole Porter.

In *Hold Everything!* Bert Lahr played a punch-drunk, inept fighter, and it made him a Broadway star. The show includes the hit tune "You're the Cream in My Coffee." There was a 1930 movie version with a different cast, script, and score.

Henderson, DeSylva, and Brown also wrote the score for *George White's Scandals* (1928, 240 performances), starring W. C. Fields and Harry Richman; it was their last score for the series and produced no hit songs. There was no *Follies* during the year. *This Year of Grace,* by Noël Coward (1899–1973, born in Teddington, England), ran 316 performances in London, 158 on Broadway. It was the revue in which the very sophisticated and talented British playwright, songwriter, and actor made his American musical theater debut, costarring with Beatrice Lillie. Among the songs are "Dance Little Lady" and "A Room with a View." Coward wrote book, music, and lyrics for all his plays, musicals, and operettas.

Hold Everything!

MUSIC/LYRICS: Ray Henderson, B. G. DeSylva, and Lew Brown

BOOK: John McGowan and B. G. DeSylva

DIRECTORS: Jack Haskell and Sam Rose

DESIGNERS: Henry Dreyfuss (sets) and Kiviette (costumes)

PRODUCERS: Alex A. Aarons and Vinton Freedley, branching out from the Gershwins

CAST INCLUDES: Bert Lahr and Victor Moore

PERFORMANCES: 413

McHugh and Fields's first score for Broadway, and one of the biggest hits of all the African American Broadway revues, *Blackbirds of 1928* was created entirely by whites. The production values were minimal, so success depended on the performers and writers. The show was fifty-year-old Bill "Bojangles" Robinson's

Broadway debut. The score included "I Can't Give You Anything but Love, Baby," "Diga Diga Do," and "Doin' the New Low Down," Robinson's solo. It included his signature tap dance up and down a staircase, a routine that he later taught Shirley Temple and that they performed in some of their movies together. A few less-successful sequels to *Blackbirds of 1928* featured stars such as Ethel Waters and Lena Horne.

By 1929, there were only about three hundred vaudeville houses left in America, down from about fifteen hundred in 1925. Ziegfeld, Jolson, and Cantor were among those ruined by the stock market crash. Johann Strauss's *Die Fledermaus,* retitled *A Wonderful Night* (125 performances), finally became a success in America. Weill and Brecht's *Happy End* premiered in Berlin; the score included "Surabaya Johnny," "The Bilbao Song," and "The Sailor's Tango."

Noël Coward's operetta *Bitter Sweet* opened that year in London (697 performances) before being produced on Broadway by Ziegfeld (157 performances). The songs "I'll See You Again," "Zigeuner," "I'll Follow My Secret Heart," and "If Love Were All" are part of the enduring Coward repertory. It was filmed in 1933 and, with Jeanette McDonald and Nelson Eddy, in 1940 (which made Coward weep, he thought it was so terrible).

Like many other well-received shows of 1929, *Show Girl* had to close because of the stock market crash. Like *Sally,* it's about a young woman's rise to stardom in a Ziegfeld show. It includes a ballet to "An American in Paris" as well as the song "Liza," which Jolson sang from the audience on opening night because he thought his young wife, Ruby Keeler, was so nervous she wouldn't be able to sing out. Keeler has been quoted as saying that she wasn't nervous at all. Jolson liked to be noticed, even at his wife's opening night.

That year, *Follow Thru* (403 performances) was the next Henderson, DeSylva, and Brown hit. Having already done college football and boxing, this time the team took on golf, centering on women golfers at a country club. The hit tune was "Button Up Your Overcoat." The book was by Laurence Schwab and DeSylva, and the show starred Jack Haley and Eleanor Powell. (Jack Haley was the Tin Man in the 1939 *The Wizard of Oz*. All

Blackbirds of 1928

MUSIC/LYRICS: Jimmy McHugh and Dorothy Fields
DIRECTOR/PRODUCER: Lew Leslie
CAST INCLUDES: Bill "Bojangles" Robinson, Mantan Moreland, and Adelaide Hall
PERFORMANCES: 518

Show Girl

MUSIC: mostly George Gershwin
LYRICS: mostly Ira Gershwin and Gus Kahn
BOOK: William Anthony McGuire
DIRECTOR: William Anthony McGuire
CHOREOGRAPHERS: Bobby Connolly and Albertina Rasch
DESIGNERS: Joseph Urban (sets) and John Harkrider (costumes)
PRODUCER: Florenz Ziegfeld
CAST INCLUDES: Ruby Keeler, Eddie Foy Jr., and the team of Clayton, Jackson, and (Jimmy) Durante, with Duke Ellington and his orchestra in the pit
PERFORMANCES: 111

Bert Lahr (1895–1967, born Irving Lahrheim in New York) came from vaudeville and burlesque. Most of his characters were aggressively inept. Much of his career was spent on the stage, mostly in musicals and revues, but he also played Estragon in Samuel Beckett's *Waiting for Godot*. He made a few movies but never quite learned how to scale down his outsized stage performances, and he is best remembered as the Cowardly Lion in *The Wizard of Oz*, where he didn't have to do that.

the principal players in the movie except Judy Garland had been Broadway stars.)

Sweet Adeline (233 performances), produced by Arthur Hammerstein, was the first collaboration of Jerome Kern and Oscar Hammerstein after *Show Boat* and was written for Helen Morgan after her success in that show. It's the story of a young woman's rise to fame from the Bowery to Broadway in the 1890s. The score contains an excellent ballad, "Don't Ever Leave Me," and the torch song "Why Was I Born?" The show could have run longer were it not for the stock market crash.

Rodgers and Hart had two shows, both financial flops: *Spring Is Here* (104 performances), its biggest hit song being "With a Song in My Heart," and *Heads Up!* (144 performances), with its most famous song being "A Ship Without a Sail."

A deeply flawed book and the stock market crash during this time were most responsible for the thirty-six-performance Vincent Youmans flop *Great Day!* By then, Youmans had changed to a much more romantic style, suitable for crooning. Along with the high-energy title number, the show boasted the hit ballads "More Than You Know" and "Without a Song."

Fifty Million Frenchmen (254 performances) was the first of seven consecutive hits Cole Porter wrote with Herbert Fields. (Maybe Rodgers and Hart should have continued with him.) It starred William Gaxton and Helen Broderick. The score includes "You've Got That Thing," "Find Me a Primitive Man," and "You Do Something to Me," another of Porter's chromatic, suggestive songs. Director Monty Woolley, a Yale classmate of Porter's, eventually became an actor on Broadway and in Hollywood. He created the title role in Kaufman and Moss Hart's *The Man Who Came to Dinner* and played it in the movie as well. The 1931 movie of *Fifty Million Frenchmen* dropped the score.

Wake Up and Dream (136 performances) had another Porter score and a book by John Hastings Turner. The show first played 263 performances in London, with choreography by George Balanchine. British star Jessie Matthews starred both in London and in New York; her costar Jack Buchanan co-choreographed the American version with Tilly Losch. The show closed early, partly because of the stock market crash, partly because Matthews didn't catch on with American audiences. Among the songs were "I'm a Gigolo" and "What Is This Thing Called

Love?", which, like many of Porter's best love songs, displays his talent for sensuous melodies and rhythms.

George White's Scandals (1929, 161 performances) had songs by Irving Caesar, Cliff Friend, and White, and it repeated "The Black Bottom" and other Henderson, DeSylva, and Brown songs. White produced only three more *Scandals,* two in the thirties and one in the early forties.

Hot Chocolates (228 performances) had music mostly by Thomas "Fats" Waller and Harry Brooks, lyrics by Andy Razaf, sketches by Eddie Green, and it starred Cab Calloway. The African American revue had Louis Armstrong in the band and onstage for a solo in one of Waller's biggest hits, "Ain't Misbe-havin'." The score also included "Black and Blue."

Like the *Garrick Gaieties,* the revue *The Little Show* began as a se-ries of Sunday-night concerts but was so successful it moved to a regular Broadway run at the end of the twenties. Unlike the *Gai-eties, The Little Show* had a fairly lavish and beautifully designed production and three stars. Among the songs were "Can't We Be Friends?" by Kay Swift and Paul James, "Moanin' Low" by Ralph Rainger and Dietz, and Schwartz and Dietz's "I Guess I'll Have to Change My Plans." *The Little Show* is generally thought of as another strong reason for the rise in popularity of the intimate Broadway revue.

Composer Arthur Schwartz (1900–84, born in Brooklyn) and lyricist Howard Dietz (1896–1983, born in New York) wrote twelve shows together. Their on-again, off-again collaboration began with *The Little Show* and continued into the sixties. Their very successful and influential 1931 revue *The Band Wagon* brought the form to Broadway in a new way: Dietz described it as "combining the sophistication and intelligence of the intimate revue with the opulence of a Ziegfeld extravaganza." Among other Schwartz and Dietz thirties revues were: *Flying Colors* (1932); *At Home Abroad* (1935), starring Beatrice Lillie and Ethel Waters and designed by Vincente Minnelli; and *The Show Is On* (1936), starring Lillie and directed and designed by Minnelli. Schwartz, who was a lawyer before his songwriting career took off, also worked on revues and book musicals with such lyricists as Dorothy Fields and Ira Gershwin; his musicals were never as successful as his revues. Dietz wrote lyrics for Kern, McHugh,

Thomas Wright "Fats" Waller (1904–43, born in New York) was famous for his jazz-stride piano style. He was also a singer and a composer, and he was funny. Among his most frequent collaborators was **Andy Razaf** (1895–1973), one of the few black lyricists of the first half of the century whose work has endured. They wrote little for the stage; most of their songs, such as "Honey-suckle Rose," were for the pop market. The extremely success-ful 1978 five-person revue *Ain't Misbehavin'* was a collection of songs either written by or associ-ated with Waller.

The Little Show

MUSIC: Arthur Schwartz

LYRICS: Howard Dietz

SKETCHES: Howard Dietz, George S. Kaufman, and others

DIRECTORS: Alexander Leftwich and Dwight Deere Wiman

CHOREOGRAPHER: Danny Dare

DESIGNERS: Jo Mielziner (sets) and Ruth Brenner (costumes)

PRODUCERS: William A. Brady, Tom Weatherly, and Dwight Deere Wiman

CAST INCLUDES: Clifton Webb, Libby Holman, and Fred Allen

PERFORMANCES: 321

Jo Mielziner (1900–76, born in France), one of the most important Broadway designers after Urban, worked on such plays as *The Glass Menagerie*, *A Streetcar Named Desire*, and *Death of a Salesman*. He was also the designer of the first productions of *Of Thee I Sing*, *Pal Joey*, *Annie Get Your Gun*, *Carousel*, *South Pacific*, *The King and I*, *Guys and Dolls*, and *Gypsy*, among many other musicals.

and Vernon Duke, among others. He was the head of publicity at MGM—he'd created the MGM lion while still an advertising executive—and considered songwriting his sideline until he retired and realized how much he was collecting on royalties.

The Wall Street stock market crashed on Tuesday, October 29, 1929—the show-business weekly *Variety*'s famous headline was "Wall St. Lays an Egg"—and the United States moved into the Great Depression. The crash led to tighter budgeting of shows and made it difficult to find financing for new ideas—in fact, for anything that didn't seem like a sure thing. And Hollywood was beckoning the best of Broadway's talent to come to California, where there was sun, fun, and lots of money. By the end of 1929, one out of five Broadway theaters was empty.

Suggested Watching and Listening

Ain't Misbehavin'
This is a 1978 original Broadway cast recording, available in a two-disc CD set from RCA Victor Broadway. It was a five-person revue, which was later videotaped in a Las Vegas nightclub. The following songs are from the show *Hot Chocolates*.
- "Black and Blue" (performed by Nell Carter, André DeShields, Armelia McQueen, Ken Page, and Charlaine Woodard)
- "Ain't Misbehavin'" (performed by Fats Waller): Waller actually sings this version of the title song in the 1943 movie *Stormy Weather* (available on 20th Century Fox DVD).

Animal Crackers
This Marx Brothers farce was made into a 1930 movie directed by Victor Heerman. It's available on Universal Studios DVD.

The Band Wagon
This 1953 Vincente Minnelli film, available on MGM/Warner Home Video DVD, has a score of old and new Schwartz and Dietz songs, including "I Guess I'll Have to Change My Plans" (performed by Fred Astaire and Jack Buchanan) from *The Little Show*.

The Cole Porter Songbook: Night and Day
This is available on Verve Records CD. The following song is from the 1928 show *Paris*.
- "Let's Do It (Let's Fall in Love)" (vocals performed by Louis Armstrong with Oscar Peterson on piano, Herb Ellis on guitar, Ray Brown on bass, and Louis Bellson on drums): Armstrong's version has the verse and four choruses at a slower tempo than usual, relishing the lyrics in his usual way.

Puttin' on the Ritz
Fred Astaire sings a version of the title song of this 1929 show in the 1946 movie *Blue Skies*,

available on Universal DVD. The background dancers are also Astaire, done with trick photography long before digital techniques were invented.

Red, Hot+ Blue

These are videos of Cole Porter songs made in 1990 by pop singers as a fundraising effort to help fight AIDS. Released collectively as a two-disc DVD/CD set from Shout! Factory, they include the following song from the show *Fifty Million Frenchmen*.

- "You Do Something to Me" (performed by Sinead O'Connor)

Stormy Weather: The Cotton Club

In the 1943 movie *Stormy Weather,* available on 20th Century Fox Classics Collection DVD, both of the following numbers from the show *Blackbirds of 1928* are performed in Cotton Club–like settings.

- "Diga Diga Do" (performed by Lena Horne and the chorus)
- "I Can't Give You Anything but Love, Baby" (performed by Lena Horne, Bill "Bojangles" Robinson, and the chorus)

Till the Clouds Roll By

In this 1946 MGM movie (available on MGM/Warner Home Video DVD), the following song is from the show *Sweet Adeline*.

- "Why Was I Born?" (performed by Lena Horne)

Whoopee

The movie version of this show, directed by Thornton Freeland, is available on VHS from HBO Home Video.

You're the Top—The Cole Porter Story

It's a 1990 documentary produced by Alan Albert, available on Winstar Home Entertainment DVD.

The Gershwins and Irving Berlin in the 1930s

Let a smile be your umbrella,

For it's just an April show'r,

Even John D. Rockefeller

Is looking for the silver lining.

Mister Herbert Hoover

Says that now's the time to buy,

So let's have another cup of coffee

And let's have another piece o' pie.

—"LET'S HAVE ANOTHER CUP OF COFFEE,"

FACE THE MUSIC, LYRICS BY IRVING BERLIN

In the thirties, rather than buying theater tickets, a large and growing number of people were more likely to spend their diminished funds at double-feature movie theaters and on sheet music and 78 rpm records with a song on each side. People of all ages and backgrounds listened and danced to the hit tunes played on the radio, on records, on home pianos, in dance halls, and on jukeboxes across the country. In any given week, as many as half the top-ten songs on *Your Hit Parade* were from film and stage musicals. However, the songs of Hollywood were overtaking those of Broadway as the most popular music in the nation, and many Broadway composers were soon spending much of their time on the West Coast. Tin Pan Alley itself was beginning to look west.

In Hollywood, songwriters wrote songs—period—and earned great money doing it. They rarely had anything to do with how the songs were filmed or even how they were performed. Since few movies had more than five or six songs, songwriters often found themselves inactive and bored much of the time, even with good weather, comfortable surroundings, playing tennis on their own courts, and swimming in their own pools to while away the hours. Many of them returned to the theater at least occasionally. (By the forties, some Hollywood songwriters who'd never even written for the stage, such as Frank Loesser and Jule Styne, traveled east to take part in what would become Broadway's golden age.)

As Broadway ticket prices got more difficult to afford and production money got more difficult to find, fewer shows were produced and more of them lost money. Sophisticated silliness remained the musical entertainment of choice; a reflection of the times in the twenties, it then became escapist entertainment during the Depression. But even the silliness was tempered with a new kind of awareness of what the real world was like. Although usually still boy-meets-girl, more shows were about getting enough money to rise above that real world so boy could get girl and good could triumph over evil.

The star vehicle continued to reign supreme. Of course, with such composers and lyricists as Berlin, Kern, Hammerstein, Harbach, the Gershwins, Rodgers and Hart, and Porter, and with such performers as Fred Astaire, Ethel Waters, Ed Wynn, Eddie Cantor, Bob Hope, Bert Lahr, Ray Bolger, Ethel Merman, and Jimmy Durante—to name only a few—it was hard to go wrong. Even so, almost every famous name had flops as well as hits during the thirties; audiences were getting more discriminating about where they spent their money, and who the stars were didn't necessarily matter as much.

Star vehicles have never disappeared; they've been shaped for such performers as Mary Martin (*South Pacific* and *The Sound of Music*), Rosalind Russell (*Wonderful Town*), Phil Silvers (*Top Banana*), Sid Caesar (*Little Me*), Gwen Verdon (*Sweet Charity* and *Chicago*), Chita Rivera (*Kiss of the Spider Woman* and *The Rink*), Liza Minnelli (*The Rink* and *The Act*), Lauren Bacall (*Applause* and *Woman of the Year*), Katharine Hepburn (*Coco*), Julie Andrews (*Victor/Victoria*), and Nathan Lane (*The Producers*). They weren't all hits, but the stars' names did at least help advance sales on their shows, as did the names of such star songwriters as Rodgers and Hammerstein, and Lerner and Loewe.

The Gershwins in the Thirties

While the Depression steered audiences toward the much less high-priced movies, it also prompted the creators of stage musicals to imbue their work with greater artistry as well as heightened social and political awareness, often conveyed with satirical wit in musical comedies and intimate revues. (Albert Williams, personal communication)

Most people writing for the musical theater tried at least one or two satirical shows. (Kern, a notable exception, didn't seem interested in politics or satire.) Opening the way for the satirical musicals of the thirties were three shows by the Gershwins, Kaufman, and Ryskind: the new version of *Strike Up the Band*, the Pulitzer Prize–winning *Of Thee I Sing*, and its sequel, *Let 'Em Eat Cake*. All had strong points of view about democracy, government, big business, and the American way of life. To go along with the content, the shows' creators experimented with form: while still telling a thin story, they included revue-like sequences that illustrated the satiric ideas without furthering the plot. In fact the three shows were, in part, an early form of the concept musical, parodying various aspects of politics. They also differed from the usual musicals of the day: although they're certainly musical comedies, they have very demanding scores that are partly composed like comic operettas, with long through-composed sequences and complex harmonies. Huge portions of plot and character development are sung.

Strike Up the Band (191 performances) made it to Broadway in 1930 in a revised version of the 1927 show. This time it was about the United States at war with Switzerland over chocolate instead of cheese tariffs, apparently based on the assumption that chocolate is funnier. It was a far more topical subject in 1930 since the United States was raising its tariffs, other nations were raising theirs in reaction, and a world economic depression was setting in. Kaufman refused to work on the rewrite, which was done by Morrie Ryskind instead and which dropped "The Man I Love." The book was tailored to the silly sexual leerings of Broadway comic Bobby Clark, which made it more palatable to Broadway audiences than the original. Even though it was less complex than the first version and the action was changed to take place in a dream, the show was still too bitter to become a major hit. The pit band was led by Red Nichols and included soon-to-be big-band leaders Glenn Miller, Jimmy Dorsey, and Jack Teagarden.

Although *Strike Up the Band* is important historically, *Of Thee I Sing*—part musical comedy, part revue, part Gilbert and Sullivan-ish operetta—was far more popular and influential (and better). It was the first book and lyrics of a musical to be published as a hardcover book as well. It was also the first musical to

Of Thee I Sing

MUSIC/LYRICS: the Gershwins

BOOK: George S. Kaufman and Morrie Ryskind

DIRECTOR: George S. Kaufman

CHOREOGRAPHER: George Hale

ORCHESTRATORS: Robert Russell Bennett and William Daly

DESIGNERS: Jo Mielziner (sets) and Charles LeMaire (costumes)

PRODUCER: Sam H. Harris

CAST INCLUDES: William Gaxton and Victor Moore

PERFORMANCES: 441

win a Pulitzer Prize, which created a controversy since its composer wasn't included in the award; the Pulitzer rules were later changed.

> To a degree hitherto unknown in the musical-comedy theatre, the mood, pace, and placing of the musical numbers was an integral part of the construction of the play as a whole. If the music were removed, the structure would collapse. In its loud and raw way, *Of Thee I Sing* was a genuine music drama. (Smith and Litton, 162)

The show—which opened in 1931—is about fast-talking John P. Wintergreen, elected president of the United States on a campaign of "Love," and of the two women engaged to him; one is the woman he loves, the other the winner of a beauty contest whose prize is supposed to be marriage to him. The show's satiric content is as relevant today as it was seventy years ago. It centers around the shallowness and frequent meaninglessness of political campaigns and their slogans, and on the deviousness of some politicians and the stupidity of others. One of the political campaign numbers (which becomes a big tap dance) is the hit song "Love Is Sweeping the Country." The title song, a quote from "My Country, 'Tis of Thee," has a chorus that begins with the line "Of thee I sing, baby," making hash of the patriotism of the quote.

The subplot involves Vice President Alexander Throttlebottom—Victor Moore's standard character, a bewildered, naive person caught up in other people's intrigues; everyone has trouble recognizing him or remembering his name. He spends most of the show trying to find out what his job's responsibilities might be and solves the main plot problem by marrying the beauty-contest winner—his duty, according to the Constitution, when the president cannot.

> As *Show Boat* in the previous decade had brought a new maturity to the American operetta . . . *Of Thee I Sing* ushered in a refreshingly adult, if offbeat, approach to the native musical comedy. . . . The Gershwins' score was a real departure from their series of syncopated ditties for twenties musicals. In their interwoven succession of individual songs, recitatives, and complex extended musical scenes, they explored a new style of composition for the American musical theater that earned them the sobriquet "a jazz Gilbert and Sullivan." (Bowers, 26)

With this show George Gershwin moved closer to a true blending of his popular and classical styles. Working on it helped lead him away from the musical comedy altogether and toward *Porgy and Bess*, the first Broadway opera.

Let 'Em Eat Cake (90 performances) was an unsuccessful 1933 sequel to *Of Thee I Sing,* with another book by Kaufman and Ryskind and with Gaxton and Moore again playing Wintergreen and Throttlebottom. In the show, Wintergreen isn't re-elected and takes over the country as a Mussolini-like dictator. It was too mean-spirited for Broadway audiences of the time. It might be worth investigating for revival, although a couple of attempts in the eighties seemed to prove otherwise.

Besides the three political satires, the Gershwins wrote three other Broadway shows together during the thirties.

Girl Crazy opened in 1930, the same year as both the revised *Strike Up the Band* and the Gershwins' first movie score, *Delicious.* It's about a New York playboy sent by his father to Custerville, Arizona, to straighten up and sober up; instead he starts a night-club and gambling casino. Nineteen-year-old Ginger Rogers, in her second and last Broadway musical before going to Hollywood, played the ingenue he falls in love with. Kate Fothergill, the brassy, down-to-earth wife of the casino's manager, was the first musical role for Ethel Merman (1909–84, born Ethel Zimmerman in New York—her birth year has also been given as 1908 and 1912). It made her a star. Red Nichols's pit band again included Glen Miller, Jimmy Dorsey, and Jack Teagarden, as well as soon-to-be big-band leader Benny Goodman and drummer Gene Krupa.

Girl Crazy was adapted by Ken Ludwig in 1992 into the long-running musical *Crazy for You;* he rewrote the book considerably and added Gershwin songs from other sources. It's not much of a story either way, but it's a great score. The original included the ballad "But Not For Me," "(I'm) Bidin' My Time ('Cause That's the Kind of Guy I'm)," "Sam and Delilah" (Merman's first number), "Embraceable You," and "I Got Rhythm," the first-act finale, which made Merman a star—she held the high note for sixteen measures. (Cole Porter called her the Golden Foghorn; actually, her voice was more like a trumpet.) There were movie adaptations in 1933 and 1943. The 1943 version costarred Mickey Rooney and Judy Garland; its script was considerably changed.

Pardon My English, score by the Gershwins and book by Herbert Fields, produced by Aarons and Freedley in 1933 (the same year

Girl Crazy

MUSIC/LYRICS: the Gershwins

BOOK: Guy Bolton and John McGowan

DIRECTOR: Alexander Leftwich

CHOREOGRAPHER: George Hale

ORCHESTRATOR: Robert Russell Bennett

DESIGNERS: Donald Oenslager (sets) and Kiviette (costumes)

PRODUCERS: Alex A. Aarons and Vinton Freedley

CAST INCLUDES: Ginger Rogers and Ethel Merman

PERFORMANCES: 272

as *Let 'Em Eat Cake*) ran only 43 performances—making two Gershwin flops in one year. Aarons and Freedley broke up their producing partnership after the show closed.

Porgy and Bess

MUSIC: George Gershwin

LYRICS: Ira Gershwin and DuBose Heyward

LIBRETTO: DuBose Heyward, based on his novel *Porgy* and on the play he and Dorothy Heyward adapted from it

DIRECTOR: Rouben Mamoulian, who also directed the play

ORCHESTRATOR: George Gershwin

PRODUCER: the Theatre Guild

CAST INCLUDES: Todd Duncan, Anne Brown, Ford Buck, and John Bubbles (Buck and Bubbles were a well-known vaudeville act)

PERFORMANCES: 124

Porgy and Bess is a through-composed, American folk opera about life in Catfish Row, a very poor African American section of Charleston, South Carolina. Folk, ethnic, classical music, spirituals, recitative, jazz, and pop are combined and synthesized into the fabric of the score. (There's very little dancing.) George Gershwin, who spent many months before the 1935 premiere researching, composing, and orchestrating the score himself (with help from Robert Russell Bennett), finally succeeded in his dream of combining all the kinds of music he loved into a coherent whole, a true American folk opera. In general, Heyward wrote the lyrics for the first act, Ira Gershwin for the rest.

Almost an hour was cut from the original three and a half hours while the show was out of town—too much, by all accounts. Although it lost money in its original production, a 1942 revival, which changed the recitative to spoken dialogue and cut about thirty-five more minutes of the score, was a hit. It was filmed in 1959 by Otto Preminger, with a cast including Sidney Poitier and Dorothy Dandridge (who didn't do their own singing), Pearl Bailey, and Sammy Davis Jr. A 1953 revival starring opera singer Leontyne Price, William Warfield, and Cab Calloway restored the show to its original form, even including material cut from the original production, and went on a four-year world tour sponsored by the U.S. State Department. The Houston Grand Opera revival played Broadway in 1976 (122 performances) and recorded it; it was the first complete recording of the score. *Porgy and Bess* is now performed regularly in opera houses all over the world; it was added to the repertory of the Metropolitan Opera Company in 1985. (Gershwin had wanted the Met to produce it originally, but only if the entire cast was black, which the Met couldn't do; there were no blacks in the company.)

Included in the long, magnificent score are many songs that have become standards for jazz and pop artists including Billie Holiday, Sarah Vaughan, Ella Fitzgerald, Miles Davis, Nina Simone, Cleo Laine, and Ray Charles. Among them are "Summertime," "My Man's Gone Now," "I Got Plenty o' Nuttin'," "Bess,

E. Y. (Edgar) "Yip" Harburg (1898–1981, born Isidore Hochberg in New York) was a lyricist who wrote with Harold Arlen, Vernon Duke, Burton Lane, and others. He also occasionally cowrote the books for his shows. Among his most familiar lyrics are those for the 1939 movie *The Wizard of Oz* and the 1947 musical satire *Finian's Rainbow.*

You Is My Woman Now," "It Ain't Necessarily So," "I Loves You, Porgy," and "There's a Boat That's Leavin' Soon for New York." As was the case with most of Gershwin's serious work, the classical critics looked down on *Porgy and Bess* for being too popular, and the pop critics looked down on it for being too highbrow. Time has vindicated the work. After *Porgy and Bess*, Gershwin left for Hollywood, never to return.

Along with working on all of George's shows, Ira also wrote lyrics for two Broadway revues during the thirties.

Life Begins at 8:40 was a satirical revue—8:40 P.M. was curtain time on Broadway. The score includes "Let's Take a Walk Around the Block" and "Fun to Be Fooled."

The second *Follies* produced after Ziegfeld's death, *Ziegfeld Follies of 1936* was George Balanchine's first Broadway show. Among the songs were Sammy Fain and Jack Yellen's "Are You Havin' Any Fun?" and Duke and Gershwin's "I Can't Get Started," sung by Bob Hope. (During the run of the show, lewd comic Bobby Clark replaced Hope, who went into Kern's *Roberta*, then to Hollywood, never to return.) Josephine Baker returned from Paris to do the show, and burlesque queen Gypsy Rose Lee made her Broadway debut in it, as a late addition to the cast.

The Gershwins also wrote songs for several movies during the thirties. Their first was the 1931 *Delicious*, including the title song and "Blah, Blah, Blah." In 1937—the year of George's death—they wrote the score for Rogers and Astaire's *Shall We Dance*, including such standards as "They Can't Take That Away from Me," "(I've Got) Beginner's Luck," "They All Laughed," and "Let's Call the Whole Thing Off (You Say Eether and I Say Eyether)," for which the dance was performed on roller skates. Also in 1937, Astaire, George Burns, and Gracie Allen starred in *A Damsel in Distress*, with a score that includes two Gershwin standards: "A Foggy Day (in London Town)" and "Nice Work If You Can Get It." Released in 1938, *The Goldwyn Follies* had Gershwin songs, ballet sequences composed by Vernon Duke, and choreography by Balanchine. The score included "Love Walked In" and "Our Love Is Here to Stay," George Gershwin's last song.

Life Begins at 8:40

MUSIC: Harold Arlen

LYRICS: Ira Gershwin and E. Y. Harburg

SKETCHES: mostly David Freedman and E. Y. Harburg

DIRECTORS: John Murray Anderson and Philip Loeb

CHOREOGRAPHERS: Robert Alton and Charles Weidman

ORCHESTRATORS: Robert Russell Bennett, Hans Spialek, and Don Walker

DESIGNERS: Albert R. Johnson (sets), Kiviette and others (costumes)

PRODUCERS: the Shuberts

CAST INCLUDES: Bert Lahr and Ray Bolger

PERFORMANCES: 238

Ziegfeld Follies of 1936

MUSIC: mostly Vernon Duke

LYRICS: mostly Ira Gershwin

SKETCHES: David Freedman

DIRECTORS: John Murray Anderson and Edward Clarke Lilley

CHOREOGRAPHERS: George Balanchine and Robert Alton

ORCHESTRATORS: Robert Russell Bennett, Hans Spialek, Don Walker, and Conrad Salinger

DESIGNER: Vincente Minnelli (sets and costumes)

PRODUCERS: Billie Burke Ziegfeld and the Shuberts

CAST INCLUDES: Fanny Brice, Bob Hope, Eve Arden, Judy Canova, Gypsy Rose Lee, the Nicholas Brothers, and Josephine Baker

PERFORMANCES: 115

Berlin in the Thirties

Irving Berlin wrote two Broadway shows during the early thirties, a political satire and a topical revue. The rest of his time was spent in Hollywood.

Face the Music

MUSIC/LYRICS: Irving Berlin
BOOK: Moss Hart and Irving Berlin
DIRECTORS: George S. Kaufman and Hassard Short
CHOREOGRAPHER: Albertina Rasch
ORCHESTRATORS: three, including Robert Russell Bennett
DESIGNERS: Albert R. Johnson (sets) and Kiviette (costumes)
PRODUCER: Sam H. Harris
CAST INCLUDES: Mary Boland
PERFORMANCES: 166

Face the Music was one of the political satires opening soon after *Of Thee I Sing.* (Notice how often Kaufman was writer, director, or both for shows with satiric content.) *Face the Music* deals with rich people, political graft, police corruption, and producing a Broadway show. Berlin's score includes "Let's Have Another Cup of Coffee" and "Soft Lights and Sweet Music."

> His songs for the show are as unlike his 1920 music as his 1920 work was from his 1910 style. More than any other major American composer, Berlin's music mirrored the age in which it was written. . . . The longer lines and subtle, plaintive chordings and more subdued gaiety of the thirties are all evident in his *Face the Music* score. (Bordman, 475)

As Thousands Cheer, Berlin's most successful revue, was largely satiric with a concept that held everything together: each song and scene was introduced by projections of sections of the newspaper—the front page, the gossip column, the comics, the rotogravure, and so forth. (The rotogravure was the Sunday magazine section printed in a process known as rotogravure, done by etching on a copper cylinder so that it printed in copper color and white.) The show also included impersonations of people in the news.

As Thousands Cheer

MUSIC/LYRICS: Irving Berlin
SKETCHES: Irving Berlin and Moss Hart
DIRECTOR: Hassard Short
CHOREOGRAPHER: Albertina Rasch
ORCHESTRATORS: five listed, including Adolph Deutsch
DESIGNERS: Albert R. Johnson (sets), Irene Sharaff (costumes), and Hassard Short (lights)
PRODUCER: Sam H. Harris
CAST INCLUDES: Marilyn Miller (her last show), Clifton Webb, and Ethel Waters
PERFORMANCES: 390

As Thousands Cheer was Ethel Waters's first integrated show. During the twenties and thirties, African American performers on Broadway were more likely to be seen in revues than in musicals. In musicals, their roles were usually limited to stereotypes of "darkies"; except for *Show Boat* and *Porgy and Bess,* it was rare for book shows to give them the opportunity to sing even as unstereotyped a song as "Ol' Man River." For revues they could be something closer to themselves. In *As Thousands Cheer,* for instance, Waters sang the sexy "Heat Wave"—the weather report in the newspaper concept—and the bluesy "Supper Time," for which the headline projection was "Unknown Negro Lynched by Frenzied Mob," although the lyrics never say so directly.

A: Supper time—
    I should set the table,
    'Cause it's supper time;
    Somehow I'm not able,
    'Cause that man o' mine
    Ain't comin' home no more.

A': Supper time—
    Kids will soon be yellin'
    For their supper time;
    How'll I keep from tellin' that
    That man o' mine
    Ain't comin' home no more?

B: How'll I keep explainin'
    When they ask me where he's gone?
    How'll I keep from cryin'
    When I bring their supper on?
    How can I remind them
    To pray at their humble board?
    How can I be thankful
    When they start to thank the Lord?
    Lord!

A: Supper time,
    I should set the table
    'Cause it's supper time;
    Somehow I'm not able,
    'Cause that man of mine . . .
    Ain't comin' home no more.

Moss Hart (1904–61, born in New York) had one of the most successful careers in Broadway history, beginning with his first comedy, *Once in a Lifetime*, a satire on the coming of sound to Hollywood, written with George S. Kaufman in 1930. Besides his comedies with Kaufman (such as *You Can't Take It with You* and *The Man Who Came to Dinner*) he wrote several other plays and musicals, including *Lady in the Dark*, with Kurt Weill and Ira Gershwin, and directed Lerner and Loewe's *My Fair Lady* and *Camelot*. (He often had an unbilled hand in writing shows while they were in rehearsals and previews.) He was married to musical-comedy actress Kitty Carlisle, who played the female lead in the Marx Brothers' movie *A Night at the Opera*.

Also from *As Thousands Cheer* is "Easter Parade" ("And we'll find that we're in the rotogravure").

In 1933 Berlin went to Hollywood and didn't return to Broadway until 1940. As with the Gershwins (and Kern), many of the songs he wrote for films were hits. He wrote songs for nine movies during the thirties, three of them starring Astaire and Rogers. The 1935 *Top Hat* includes "No Strings," "Isn't This a Lovely Day (To Be Caught in the Rain)?" and "Top Hat, White Tie, and Tails," which became almost a signature tune for Astaire. It has a verse in very jagged syncopation and an AABA chorus in which the B section has a similarly jagged feel while the A is much smoother. This provided Astaire with more rhythmic variety; Berlin knew how to write dance numbers. (Composers loved to write for Astaire. Although he didn't have a great voice, his rhythm and intonation were impeccable, as was his diction. The lyrics were a more important part of his performance style than they were for many of his contemporaries; he made the words determine how he sang the notes rather than the other way round, which was more usual. It was therefore said that he "sang off the words.")

Also in the score of *Top Hat* is "Cheek to Cheek," a seventy-two-bar AABBCA song, with the A's having sixteen bars each instead of the usual eight. A change in rhythm similar to that in "Top Hat, White Tie, and Tails" appears in the B of "Cheek to Cheek," its syncopation contrasted with the romantic flow of both the A and the C. Furthermore, the C is even smoother and more flowingly romantic than the A, providing more variety as well as an emotional peak to the song.

Berlin's 1936 score for the Astaire-Rogers movie *Follow the Fleet* (also the year of their *Swing Time,* with songs by Kern and Dorothy Fields) contains "We Saw the Sea," "Let Yourself Go," "I'd Rather Lead a Band," "I'm Putting All My Eggs in One Basket," and "Let's Face the Music and Dance," which suggests, very romantically, in a show within the movie, how to deal with the unpleasant facts of the stock market crash and the Depression.

> There may be trouble ahead,
> But while there's moonlight and music
> And love and romance,
> Let's face the music and dance.
> Before the fiddlers have fled,
> Before they ask us to pay the bill,
> And while we still have the chance,
> Let's face the music and dance.

The staging of the song makes it specific, with both Astaire and Rogers broke and contemplating suicide. (There were twenty-one thousand suicides in America in 1932 alone.) The story of *Follow the Fleet,* like most of the other Astaire-Rogers movies, is in the standard format of the stage musicals of the twenties and thirties: stars plus comedians plus a romantic farce plot built on a series of coincidences and misunderstandings, frequently with characters involved in show business. (These movies rarely had choruses, and when they did, they were almost always in the context of a show being performed within the movie.) The scripts, though largely a series of excuses for songs, dances, and comedy sequences, were always built on a solidly constructed albeit lightweight and farcical plot. *Follow the Fleet* even includes a subplot for Randolph Scott and Harriet Hilliard—later Harriet Nelson, wife of Ozzie and mother of David and Ricky in life and on their TV sitcom.

As with stage musicals, the stars of thirties movie musicals were usually chosen before anything was written for them, and the big songs could be pulled out of context and turned into pop hits since the lyrics were rarely show-specific. What was unusual, however, in the Astaire-Rogers movies was that the plot was usually furthered by their dances together; dancing together was how they fell in love and how they courted. To the majority of Americans, this was real musical comedy—better than most of the talent you could see on stage and for much cheaper tickets.

In 1937, Berlin's score for *On the Avenue,* a Dick Powell and Alice Faye movie, had "I've Got My Love to Keep Me Warm" and "This Year's Kisses." In 1938, Astaire and Rogers starred in *Carefree,* which featured "I Used to Be Color Blind" and "Change Partners" in its Berlin score. The same year, Alice Faye, Tyrone Power, Don Ameche, and Ethel Merman starred in *Alexander's Ragtime Band,* which had twenty-three Berlin songs old and new, including the title song, "Blue Skies," "A Pretty Girl Is like a Melody," "Say It with Music," "Oh, How I Hate to Get Up in the Morning," "Remember," and "All Alone."

The Band Wagon

MUSIC: Arthur Schwartz

LYRICS: Howard Dietz

SKETCHES: George S. Kaufman and Howard Dietz

DIRECTOR: Hassard Short

ORCHESTRATOR: Robert Russell Bennett

CHOREOGRAPHER: Albertina Rasch

DESIGNER: Albert Johnson (sets), Kiviette (costumes), and Hassard Short (lights)

PRODUCER: Max Gordon

CAST INCLUDES: the Astaires, Helen Broderick, and Frank Morgan

PERFORMANCES: 260

The Intimate Revue

There were satirical musicals throughout the decade besides those by the Gershwins and Berlin, but—as was the case with *Life Begins at 8:40* and *As Thousands Cheer*—satire was prevalent in the intimate revues that came into prominence in the early thirties, many of them written by some of the best composers, lyricists, and sketch writers in the business.

Boris Aronson (1898–1980, born in Kiev) came to America in 1923 and began designing sets for Broadway with *Walk a Little Faster.* Along with many plays, he designed such musicals as *Cabin in the Sky, Fiddler on the Roof, Cabaret, Company, Follies,* and *A Little Night Music.*

> The wildly extroverted jazz and florid romance of the twenties gave way to both the subdued, introspective material and strident muckraking of the early thirties. The great [revues] were dead. . . . While operetta was so moribund as to be for all practical purposes dead, the more intimate, thoughtful revue was obviously here to stay for a while. (Bordman, 460)

The Band Wagon was the most famous and possibly the best of the thirties revues. Johnson's elaborate design was notable for its double revolving stage, an active part of many of the num-

Vernon Duke (1903–69, born Vladimir Dukelsky in Parfianovka, Russia) fled the 1917 revolution and arrived in the United States in 1929 after working on some British musicals. He used the name Vernon Duke for his popular songs, his real name for his classical music; he is much better known as Vernon Duke. He tended to write hit tunes rather than hit musicals and was more comfortable writing for revues. His most successful book musical was the 1940 *Cabin in the Sky.*

Walk a Little Faster

MUSIC: Vernon Duke
LYRICS: E. Y. Harburg
SKETCHES: S. J. Perelman and Robert McGunigle
DIRECTOR: Monty Woolley
CHOREOGRAPHER: Albertina Rasch
ORCHESTRATORS: Robert Russell Bennett and Conrad Salinger
DESIGNERS: Boris Aronson (sets) and Kiviette (costumes)
PRODUCER: Courtney Burr
CAST INCLUDES: Beatrice Lillie and Bobby Clark
PERFORMANCES: 121

bers and the first revolving stage in a Broadway musical evening. It was also the first Broadway show to hang stage lights from the balcony, replacing footlights. *The Band Wagon* was Adele Astaire's last show; she retired to get married, leaving her brother to go it alone. The score includes "I Love Louisa," "New Sun in the Sky," and the highly romantic "Dancing in the Dark." There was a 1953 MGM movie called *The Band Wagon* that used a Schwartz and Dietz score of old and new songs. (They wrote "That's Entertainment" for the film.) The movie is a funny and very fictional version of how a show called *The Band Wagon* gets written and produced. It starred Fred Astaire, Cyd Charisse, Nanette Fabray, Oscar Levant, and the British performer Jack Buchanan, who was in Schwartz and Dietz's 1937 musical comedy *Between the Devil.* The movie was written by Betty Comden and Adolph Green (who based the Fabray and Levant characters on themselves), directed by Vincente Minnelli, and choreographed by Michael Kidd. (The year before, Comden and Green had taken a bunch of old Brown and Freed songs and written the script of *Singin' in the Rain* around them.)

Walk a Little Faster, a revue and Duke's first whole Broadway show, introduced his first big hit, "April in Paris." Another of his enduring songs, for which he also wrote the lyrics, is "Autumn in New York" in the 1934 revue *Thumbs Up!*

Besides having many hit songs, these literate, intimate revues were among the most innovative of the period, developing a form that has lasted to the present in cabarets and small theaters everywhere, though rarely on Broadway anymore.

Suggested Watching and Listening

The Band Wagon
The 1953 movie *The Band Wagon* (available on MGM DVD) includes the song "New Sun in the Sky," performed by Cyd Charisse dubbed by India Adams. (Charisse never did her own singing.)

Berlin in the Thirties
The following suggestions are songs by Irving Berlin from various shows during this decade.
- "Supper Time" (performed by Eileen Farrell): This version of the song (originally from the show *As Thousands Cheer*) is available on the Sony Masterworks CD *The Eileen Farrell Album.*

- "Heat Wave" (performed by Ethel Waters): It's structured with a verse and an AABA chorus. The chorus is followed by a short patter:

It's so hot,
The weatherman will
Tell you a record's been made.
It's so hot,
A coat of tan will
Cover your face in the shade.
It's so hot,
The coldest maiden
Feels just as warm as a bride.
It's so hot,
A chicken laid an
Egg on the street—and it fried.

That's followed by a repeat of the first and last A's. Waters's recording is available on Paul Gruber's *Original Cast! The Thirties*.

- "Let's Face the Music and Dance" (performed by Fred Astaire and Ginger Rogers): This version from the show *Follow the Fleet* is available on Warner Brothers DVD. As much as any of the Astaire-Rogers dances, this one epitomizes their mystique. Katharine Hepburn said he gave her class and she gave him sex appeal. (They were also skilled at comic numbers.) A blonde Lucille Ball is on Astaire's right at the gambling table at the top of the number.

Broadway: The American Musical

This is a PBS series directed by Michael Kantor and available in a wide-screen, box set from PBS Paramount DVD. This would be a good time to watch "Episode 3: I Got Plenty o' Nuttin' (1930–1942)."

The Gershwins in the Thirties

The following suggestions are songs from *Girl Crazy*.

- "Embraceable You" (performed by Judy Garland and the men's chorus): A charm song written in 1929 for the unproduced Ziegfeld musical *Ming Toy,* it has a verse and an ABAC/A chorus; the end of the C echoes the beginning of the A. In the Garland version from the 1943 MGM movie of *Girl Crazy* (available on MGM/Warner Home Video VHS), the chorus is sung a second time in a forties swing version, then repeated three more times, mostly as a dance break.
- "But Not for Me" (performed by Judy Garland): A great Gershwin ballad, it's sung by Garland in the 1943 movie.
- "I Got Rhythm" (performed by Ethel Merman and also by Judy Garland, Mickey Rooney, and Tommy Dorsey and his orchestra): Merman's recording is on *Original Cast! The Thirties* (MET CD). The Garland-Rooney-Dorsey swing version is from the 1943 movie adaptation; the sequence was directed by Busby Berkeley.

Porgy and Bess

The listed selections are from the 1989 Glyndebourne Festival Opera production, filmed for the BBC, conducted by Simon Rattle, and directed by Trevor Nunn. (The 1993 film adaptation is available on EMI DVD.)

- "Summertime" (performed by Paula Ingram and sung by Harolyn Blackwell): "Summertime," a folklike, sixteen-bar song with two choruses and a coda, is a lullaby sung by Clara, a character in one of several subplots. It's the first solo singing we hear in the show. Bess reprises it at the top of act 3, having taken over care of the baby after his parents' deaths in the storm that ends act 2.
- "My Man's Gone Now" (performed by Cynthia Clarey and the chorus): Sung by another supporting character, Serena, at the funeral of her murdered husband, it's a synthesis of opera and African American religious music.
- "Bess, You Is My Woman Now" (performed by Willard White and Cynthia Hayman): Bess was a cocaine-sniffing tramp until she took up with Porgy and changed her ways. Porgy, a cripple, wants her to go to the church picnic and have fun for both of them.
- "It Ain't Necessarily So" (performed by Damon Evans): Sportin' Life, who sings this, is one of the villains; he deals cocaine ("happy dust"). In this song, he's making fun of religion at the church picnic by exploding some biblical stories. The music combines jazz with mock African American chanting.

There's also a CD of excerpts from the 1953 revival of the show, which starred Leontyne Price and William Warfield. It's available as an RCA CD entitled *Porgy and Bess: Highlights*.

Ziegfeld Follies of 1936

The Nicholas Brothers never recorded songs from the *Follies*. The following number is from the 1943 movie *Stormy Weather* (available on 20th Century Fox DVD).

- "Jumpin' Jive" (written by Cab Calloway and Jack Palmer in 1939 and performed by the Nicholas Brothers, Cab Calloway and his band in the 1943 movie): This is one of the most impressive of the Nicholas Brothers' acrobatic tap dances.

Kern, Rodgers and Hart, and Cole Porter in the 1930s

They used to tell me I was building a dream
With peace and glory ahead.
Why should I be standing in line
Just waiting for bread?

Once I built a railroad
Made it run,
Made it race against time.
Once I built a railroad
Now it's done.
Brother, can you spare a dime?
—"BROTHER, CAN YOU SPARE A DIME?" *AMERICANA,*
LYRICS BY E. Y. HARBURG

Kern in the Thirties

Jerome Kern spent most of the thirties in Hollywood; he wrote only four musicals for Broadway, plus one for London and one that closed out of town. *The Cat and the Fiddle* (1931, 395 performances), with book and lyrics by Otto Harbach, was the last time Kern did any real experimenting with the form. It's about a female American pop composer in love and in conflict with a male Romanian opera composer, and the score, including "She Didn't Say Yes," "Poor Pierrot," and "The Night Was Made for Love," mixes the two musical styles.

[It had] no chorus-girl line, no synthetic comedy scenes, no set production numbers, no spectacle. The characters were believable human beings. The music progressed gracefully out of the context. (David Ewen, *New Complete Book of the American Musical Theater,* 64)

A movie version, starring Jeanette MacDonald, was made in 1934.

Music in the Air (1932, 342 performances), with book, lyrics, and direction by Oscar Hammerstein, is about a European composer trying to get a song published. It breaks no new ground but has a lovely Kern score, including "There's a Hill Beyond a Hill," "The Song Is You," and "I've Told Ev'ry Little Star," which Hammerstein sang to Kern as he was dying:

> I've told ev'ry little star
> Just how sweet I think you are—
> Why haven't I told you?

Like *The Cat and the Fiddle,* much of the show was told through music.

Roberta (1933, 295 performances), with book and lyrics by Otto Harbach, was adapted from Alice Duer Miller's novel *Gowns by Roberta;* was directed by Hassard Short; and had in its cast Lyda Roberti, Bob Hope, Sydney Greenstreet, George Murphy, and Fred MacMurray. A traditional musical set in Paris, it's about a dress designer, some former Russian royalty, and an American college football star who inherits the designer's shop. It was more romantic than comic and was almost a flop, but it eventually caught on because of the popularity of Kern's score and the draw of its fashions, which were changed with the seasons. In its score were "Smoke Gets in Your Eyes," "Yesterdays," and "The Touch of Your Hand." The songs "Lovely to Look At," "I'll Be Hard to Handle," and "I Won't Dance" were written by Kern and Dorothy Fields (and Jimmy McHugh) for the 1935 movie starring Irene Dunne, Astaire, and Rogers. There was also a 1952 remake, retitled *Lovely to Look At,* with Kathryn Grayson, Howard Keel, Red Skelton, Marge and Gower Champion, and Ann Miller.

After *Roberta,* Kern went to Hollywood; it was six years before his next Broadway show, also his last. *Very Warm for May* had book and lyrics by Hammerstein, who codirected it with Hassard Short and Vincente Minnelli. A flop closing after only fifty-nine performances, it's about a young woman whose former vaudevillian parents want her to go to college but who runs away to join a summer-stock theater. Apparently the show suffered a lot from changes demanded by producer Max Gordon while the show was in out-of-town tryouts. The score includes "All the Things You Are," which many, including Stephen Sondheim, consider one of the best theater songs ever written.

After *Very Warm for May,* Kern returned to Hollywood. He came back to New York for the 1946 revival of *Show Boat* (for which he wrote his last songs) and to write the score for *Annie Get Your Gun,* but he died before starting on it.

During the thirties, Kern wrote songs for eleven movies, both produced and unproduced. Kern, Harbach, and Hammerstein's 1925 *Sunny* was filmed in 1930; Harbach's and his *The Cat and the Fiddle* was filmed in 1934 and *Roberta* in 1935; and Hammerstein's and his *Music in the Air* was filmed in 1934, *Sweet Adeline* in 1935, and *Show Boat* in 1936. Also in 1936, Kern and Dorothy Fields wrote the score for the Astaire-Rogers *Swing Time*, featuring "Waltz in Swing Time," "Pick Yourself Up," "A Fine Romance (With No Kisses)," and "The Way You Look Tonight," which won an Oscar, making Fields the first woman to win for songwriting. Kern and Hammerstein wrote the score for the 1937 movie *High, Wide and Handsome*, directed by Rouben Mamoulian and starring Irene Dunne, and they won an Oscar for "The Last Time I Saw Paris," written for the 1941 movie *Lady, Be Good!*

Rodgers and Hart and George Abbott

Rodgers and Hart split their time between Hollywood and Broadway between 1930 and 1939, staying mostly in California until 1935, then returning to New York and Broadway for most of the rest of the thirties. They wrote nine Broadway musicals and many hit songs during the decade.

Simple Simon (135 performances)—with book by Ed Wynn and Guy Bolton, produced by Ziegfeld with sets by Urban, and starring Wynn and Ruth Etting—was a flop about a newspaper vendor who ignores all bad news stories and dreams himself into his favorite fairy tales. For the show, Rodgers and Hart wrote "Dancing on the Ceiling," cut before opening, then used the same year in their British musical *Ever Green*, a hit. Also in the score of *Simple Simon* is "Ten Cents a Dance," a character song sung by a dance-hall hostess looking for love. (The 1966 musical *Sweet Charity* centers around several dance-hall hostesses.) Dance halls charged ten cents a ticket for a dance with one of the hostesses, for whom prostitution was a major sideline career. Rodgers and Hart rarely wrote about this class of society; even their poor characters were usually of a higher social and economic class, and were likely to better themselves by the end of the show.

The team went to Hollywood after the flop of *Simple Simon;* their 1929 *Spring Is Here* was filmed that year. In 1931, they wrote *The Hot Heiress*, with screenplay by Herbert Fields, using underscored rhyming dialogue leading into such songs as "Nobody Loves a Riveter (But His Mother)." Having worked together again in Hollywood, Rodgers, Hart, and Fields decided to write another Broadway show, a satire on Hollywood: *America's Sweetheart* (135 performances at a loss), directed by Monty Woolley and starring Harriet Lake (later known as Ann Sothern). The score includes "I've Got Five Dollars," a cheerful duet for a young couple who intend to be happy regardless of monetary problems; it's more typical than "Ten Cents a Dance" of how Rodgers and Hart dealt with poor people.

Rodgers and Hart then returned to Hollywood and, in 1932, wrote the score for the George M. Cohan movie *The Phantom President* and for the Jeanette MacDonald and Maurice Chevalier movie *Love Me Tonight*, directed by Mamoulian, and including "Mimi," "Love Me Tonight," "Isn't It Romantic?" and "Lover." In 1933, they wrote the score for *Hallelujah, I'm a Bum*, starring Jolson, again with rhythmic, rhymed dialogue leading into songs.

The 1934 movie musical *Hollywood Party* (starring Jimmy Durante and Laurel and Hardy) had songs by Howard Dietz of Dietz and Schwartz, who also coproduced, and by Walter Donaldson, Gus Kahn, Arthur Freed, Nacio Herb Brown, and two by Rodgers and Hart. They wrote eleven others for the film as well, all of which were cut—including "Prayer," with a lyric about wishing to become a movie star, which Hart rewrote as "Manhattan Melodrama," then again as "Bad in Every Man," and then published it as "Blue Moon," with the familiar lyric. Also in 1934, Hart did English lyrics for *The Merry Widow*, a movie version of the Lehar operetta starring MacDonald and Chevalier. In 1935, *Mississippi*, starring Bing Crosby and W. C. Fields, had Rodgers and Hart songs, among which was "(It's) Easy to Remember (But So Hard to Forget)."

Jumbo

MUSIC/LYRICS: Richard Rodgers and Lorenz Hart

BOOK: Ben Hecht and Charles MacArthur

DIRECTORS: John Murray Anderson and George Abbott

ORCHESTRATORS: five, including Hans Spialek

PRODUCER: Billy Rose

CAST INCLUDES: Jimmy Durante, Paul Whiteman and his Orchestra, and a real elephant

PERFORMANCES: 233

Rodgers and Hart's return to Broadway in 1935 after four years in Hollywood was for the circus show *Jumbo*. It incorporated an entire circus and was the last show produced at the gigantic Hippodrome—an attempt to win back movie audiences with as much spectacle as possible. Hecht and MacArthur, best known as the authors of the hit play *The Front Page*, constructed a book about rival circus owners whose children fall in love. Although it had a long run, its preproduction and running costs were so high that *Jumbo* couldn't pay back its investment. Size was not the way to beat Hollywood; the investors lost $160,000. In the score are "The Most Beautiful Girl in the World," one of Rodgers's many lovely waltzes, "My Romance," and "Little Girl Blue." *Jumbo* was the first of several shows Rodgers and Hart did with George Abbott (billed as director and Anderson as stager, presumably because Anderson did both the choreography and the circus material). *Billy Rose's Jumbo* is a 1962 movie version of

Jumbo, directed by Charles Walter and starring Doris Day, Durante (in his original Broadway role), and Martha Raye.

George Abbott's signature on a show meant an insistence on structure and speed; the books of the shows he worked on were always tightly written and well constructed. He hated dance numbers because he felt they slowed down the pace and disturbed the onward thrust of the action; however, he was also instrumental in creating some of the earliest musicals in which dance told some of the story. Among his musicals were five by Rodgers and Hart; the first George Balanchine musical; the first two Bernstein, Comden, and Green shows; the first four Robbins musicals; both Adler and Ross shows; the first Fosse (as choreographer) and Prince (as producer) show; the first two Bock and Harnick collaborations; the first Styne, Loesser, Merrill, Mary Rodgers, and Sondheim shows; the first Kander and Ebb collaboration; and the last Berlin hit. All these artists and many more have acknowledged their debts to "Mr. Abbott," as he was always called.

With *On Your Toes,* produced in 1936, Balanchine first truly brought ballet to the musical stage—one in each act, as a matter of fact. He was also the first to be billed as choreographer rather than dance director. The show is about a struggling Russian ballet company and a young hoofer turned music professor who helps them become successful in America, despite problems with a hit man. The two ballets (each of which tells a story) are at least tangentially attached to the plot instead of being just dance numbers; they are the "Princess Zenobia Ballet" and "Slaughter on Tenth Avenue." Rodgers wrote new music for these ballets, rather than following the usual practice of having an arranger do the dance numbers out of tunes from the show. Also in the score of *On Your Toes* are the title song, "Too Good for the Average Man," "It's Got to Be Love (It Couldn't Be Tonsillitis)," "Glad to Be Unhappy," and the show's biggest hit, "There's a Small Hotel." The 1939 movie version used only a small part of Rodgers and Hart's excellent score. There was a successful Broadway revival in 1982, directed by Abbott when he was ninety-two years old; it used Spialek's original orchestrations.

Babes in Arms (1937) is the original "Hey, kids, we can do the show right here in the barn" musical, and it is still revived periodically

George Abbott (1887–1995, born in Forestville, New York) started as an actor but eventually established himself as a writer/director with the 1926 hit melodrama *Broadway*. He only occasionally returned to acting. Abbott had written and directed many Broadway hits before directing *Jumbo*, his first musical. By 1964, he had staged close to thirty musical comedies, almost all of them hits, and had influenced many of our best musical theater artists. He also wrote or cowrote the books for many of the musicals he directed. He worked on more than 120 shows during his lifetime and died at the age of 108, having remained active till the end.

On Your Toes

MUSIC/LYRICS: Richard Rodgers and Lorenz Hart

BOOK: Richard Rodgers, Lorenz Hart, and George Abbott

DIRECTORS: George Abbott and Worthington Miner

CHOREOGRAPHER: George Balanchine

ORCHESTRATOR: Hans Spialek

DESIGNERS: Jo Mielziner (sets) and Irene Sharaff (costumes)

PRODUCER: Dwight Deere Wiman

CAST INCLUDES: Ray Bolger

PERFORMANCES: 315

Babes in Arms

MUSIC/LYRICS: Richard Rodgers and Lorenz Hart

BOOK: Richard Rodgers and Lorenz Hart

DIRECTOR: Robert Sinclair

CHOREOGRAPHER: George Balanchine

ORCHESTRATOR: Hans Spialek

PRODUCER: Dwight Deere Wiman

CAST INCLUDES: Alfred Drake (Curly in *Oklahoma!* in 1943), Dan Dailey, and the Nicholas Brothers

PERFORMANCES: 289

George Balanchine (1904–83, born Georgi Balanchivadze in St. Petersburg, Russia), after rigorous training in ballet and music, was permitted to leave the Soviet Union in 1924 and, instead of returning home, joined the Ballets Russes in Paris. Balanchine arrived in New York in October 1933, and, sponsored by arts patron Lincoln Kirstein, he founded the School of American Ballet, which continues to thrive. He began choreographing for Broadway and brought ballet (including its use of mime) into the musical, using it to tell some of the story. Although he assembled several ballet companies, they eventually disbanded. In 1948, he found a permanent home when his troupe joined City Center as the New York City Ballet Company. Balanchine is now acclaimed as one of the foremost choreographers of all time.

around the country, though with extensive rewrites of the book. It's about a group of children whose parents, all vaudevillians, can't afford to take the kids with them on tour; the kids put on their own show to keep from being sent to a work farm. Their show flops, but the kids are saved from the farm with the help of a French pilot who makes a convenient emergency landing nearby. The cast was mostly made up of young unknowns. Along with having one of the first dream ballets, *Babes in Arms* had the most hit songs of any Rodgers and Hart score: "Where or When," "The Lady Is a Tramp," "I Wish I Were in Love Again," "Johnny One Note," and "My Funny Valentine," one of the most popular of the team's many romantic ballads. (There's a character named Valentine in the show.) The AA'BA″ song is an excellent example of how Rodgers's flowing romanticism supplies a subtext to Hart's wry lyrics:

Behold the way our fine-feathered friend
His virtue doth parade.
Thou knowest not, my dim-witted friend,
The picture thou hast made.
Thy vacant brow and thy tousled hair
Conceal thy good intent.
Thou noble, upright, truthful, sincere,
And slightly dopey gent—you're . . .

A: My funny Valentine,
     Sweet comic Valentine,
     You make me smile with my heart.

A′:   Your looks are laughable,
     Unphotographable,
     Yet you're my fav'rite work of art.

B: Is your figure less than Greek?
     Is your mouth a little weak?
     When you open it to speak
     Are you smart?

A″:   But don't change a hair for me,
     Not if you care for me,
     Stay, little Valentine, stay!
     Each day is Valentine's Day.

A 1939 movie of *Babes in Arms*, considerably rewritten, starred Mickey Rooney and Judy Garland, was directed by Busby Berkeley, and was the first in a popular series of Rooney-Garland-Berkeley, black-and-white movie musicals.

I'd Rather Be Right (also 1937, 289 performances) had a book by George S. Kaufman and Moss Hart and starred George M. Cohan. A political satire, it was Cohan's first appearance in a musical in ten years and his last Broadway success; he played President Franklin Delano Roosevelt. (Kaufman, who also directed, didn't like working with Rodgers and never did again. Nobody liked working with Cohan.) *I'd Rather Be Right* is the closest Rodgers and Hart came to writing an American Gilbert and Sullivan operetta and their only real political satire. It's a large-cast, semi-concept musical with a thin plot that barely holds together the revue-like sequences. Similar in structure to Kaufman and Ryskind's earlier musical satires written with the Gershwins, it has an even thinner plot.

Except for the opening ten minutes and the last two, the whole story takes place in a dream. A young man has been told by his boss that he won't get the raise he needs in order to get married until President Roosevelt balances the budget. While the young man and his girlfriend are listening to a concert in Central Park, he falls asleep and dreams that Roosevelt comes walking through the park, listens to his problem, and, during the rest of the show, tries several harebrained schemes to balance the budget, involving such groups as the cabinet, the Supreme Court, and all the women of America. (He suggests women give up cosmetics for a year, which brings them all on in a rage.) At the end, Roosevelt doesn't balance the budget, but the young couple decide to get married anyway.

Rodgers's sparkling score is part pop, part pseudo–Gilbert and Sullivan, and part parody (including a Bing Crosby–style crooner song sung by the secretary of the treasury over the radio, asking the public to buy government bonds). Aside from the charming "Have You Met Miss Jones?", very little of the score makes sense out of context. Huge as it is—and expensive as it would be to produce—the show is well worth considering for revival.

I Married an Angel (1938, 338 performances) has both score and book by Rodgers and Hart. The show, a fantasy—she really is an angel—was Joshua Logan's first assignment as a director of musicals. (He also helped with the script; Hart's drinking problems were getting worse.) Rhymed dialogue leads into several of the songs. The score includes the title song, the wistful romantic ballad "Spring Is Here," a "Honeymoon Ballet," and a ballet to "At the Roxy Music Hall," choreographed by Balanchine for his wife, Vera Zorina. There was a flop 1942 Jeanette MacDonald–Nelson Eddy movie, their last together.

The Boys from Syracuse

MUSIC/LYRICS: Richard Rodgers and Lorenz Hart

BOOK: George Abbott, adapted from Shakespeare's *The Comedy of Errors*

DIRECTOR/PRODUCER: George Abbott

CHOREOGRAPHER: George Balanchine

ORCHESTRATOR: Hans Spialek

DESIGNERS: Jo Mielziner (sets and lights) and Irene Sharaff (costumes)

CAST INCLUDES: Eddie Albert, Burl Ives, Teddy Hart (Lorenz's brother), and Jimmy Savio

PERFORMANCES: 235

Abbott was proud that he had kept only one Shakespeare line in the entire script of *The Boys from Syracuse*, (1938) a mistaken-identity farce involving two sets of identical twin brothers separated at birth, in which one set are the servants of the other. There was a 1940 movie version and a very successful 1963 off-Broadway revival. Rodgers and Hart's score includes "Falling in Love with Love," a lovely operetta-like ABAB′ waltz with very cynical lyrics and another excellent example of how the contrasts between the two men worked in favor of their collaboration. The very last line reveals the true emotional content of the song:

A: Falling in love with love
    Is falling for make-believe.
    Falling in love with love
    Is playing the fool.

B: Caring too much is such
    A juvenile fancy.
    Learning to trust is just
    For children in school.

A: I fell in love with love
    One night when the moon was full.
    I was unwise, with eyes
    Unable to see.

B': I fell in love with love,
    With love everlasting,
    But love fell out with me.

The lines "Falling in love with love / Is falling for make-believe" are a tongue-in-cheek reference to Kern and Hammerstein's *Show Boat* song "Make Believe." Also in the score are the big hit of the show, "This Can't Be Love (Because I Feel So Well)," and "Sing for Your Supper," an excellent double-entendre trio for the three leading women.

Too Many Girls (1939, 249 performances), book by George Marion Jr., was produced and directed by Abbott and choreographed by Robert Alton. Hart's drinking sprees and disappearances were increasing, and Rodgers had to write some of the lyrics. It's a college football musical and was made into a 1940 movie with Desi Arnaz and Eddie Bracken repeating their Broadway roles. (Lucille Ball, whose songs were dubbed, starred in the movie; that's when she met Arnaz.) The score includes "I Didn't Know What Time It Was."

Cole Porter in the Thirties

Cole Porter remained active on Broadway throughout the thirties; he also made occasional trips to Hollywood even after his riding accident. None of his thirties musicals were in any way innovative; however, like those of Rodgers and Hart, they did produce a great many hit songs.

The New Yorkers (1930, 168 performances), book by Herbert Fields, is a "sociological musical satire" dealing with Park Avenue society people and bootleggers who all end up in Miami. It's revue performer Jimmy Durante's first musical; he wrote his own songs for it. Among Porter's songs were "I Happen to Like New York" and "Love for Sale," sung by a prostitute. The song shocked and outraged as many as it pleased; it was banned from the radio for many years. (Like Rodgers and Hart, Porter rarely dealt with the poor.)

Gay Divorce, a two-act, two-set farce of mistaken identities (produced in 1932 when *gay* was still taken to mean "happy and high-spirited"), was Astaire's first show without his sister. He soon left for Hollywood, forcing the show to close early. In the score is "Night and Day," a famous example of Porter's Latin rhythms and chromatic intervals. It's a long song: verse, ABA'BCB'. (The end of the B echoes the beginning of the A.) The repetitions in the lyrics and notes of the verse set up the song's obsessive nature:

> Like the beat beat beat of the tom-tom
> When the jungle shadows fall,
> Like the tick tick tock of the stately clock
> As it stands against the wall.
> Like the drip drip drip of the raindrops
> When the sum'r show'r is through,
> So a voice within me keeps repeating
> You—You—You.

Gay Divorce

MUSIC/LYRICS: Cole Porter

BOOK: Kenneth Webb and Samuel Hoffenstein, adapted from a play by Dwight Taylor

DIRECTOR: Howard Lindsay

ORCHESTRATORS: Robert Russell Bennett and Hans Spialek

DESIGNERS: Jo Mielziner (sets) and Raymond Sovey (costumes)

PRODUCERS: Dwight Deere Wiman and Tom Weatherly

CAST INCLUDES: Fred Astaire

PERFORMANCES: 248

It's the only Porter song used in the 1934 Astaire-Rogers movie version. (Con Conrad and Herb Magidson's "The Continental," written for the movie, was the first song to win an Academy Award.) Hollywood changed the title from *Gay Divorce* to *The Gay Divorcee*, believing it's OK for a divorcée to be happy and high-spirited but not OK for the divorce itself to be referred to that way.

Anything Goes

MUSIC/LYRICS: Cole Porter
BOOK: Guy Bolton and P. G. Wodehouse, revised by Howard Lindsay and Russel Crouse
DIRECTOR: Howard Lindsay
CHOREOGRAPHER: Robert Alton
ORCHESTRATORS: Robert Russell Bennett and Hans Spialek
PRODUCER: Vinton Freedley
CAST INCLUDES: Ethel Merman, William Gaxton, and Victor Moore, with Vivian Vance
PERFORMANCES: 415

Robert Alton (1897–1957, born Robert Alton Hart in Bennington, Vermont) began as a hoofer. During his Broadway career, he did much to individualize dance routines by giving dancers solos and by breaking up the chorus line into smaller groups. He did dances for shows by Rodgers and Hart, Porter, and others, including *Anything Goes, Leave It to Me, Too Many Girls, DuBarry Was a Lady, Pal Joey, By Jupiter,* and *Me and Juliet.* He also directed dances for many MGM movie musicals, such as *The Harvey Girls, Till the Clouds Roll By, Good News, The Pirate, Easter Parade, Words and Music, Annie Get Your Gun,* and *White Christmas.*

Anything Goes (1934) was one of Porter's biggest hits and one of his best and most frequently revived shows (with a somewhat rewritten book). It's about love, gangsters, rich people, and showgirls on a boat to Europe. Bolton and Wodehouse's original book centered on a shipwreck, but the cruise boat *Morro Castle* caught fire in New Jersey two months before the show was to open, killing 125 people, and the book had to be redone without the wreck but with the requirement that it fit the already-written score. Bolton and Wodehouse weren't available, so Lindsay and Crouse took over the job. (It was their first collaboration. They went on to write, among many other successes, *Life with Father,* the longest-running play in Broadway history. They also wrote the book for Rodgers and Hammerstein's *The Sound of Music.* Actress Lindsay Crouse is Russel Crouse's daughter.)

Porter wrote half a dozen hits for the show: the title song, a list song with a verse and three choruses; "You're the Top," a list song with two verses, seven choruses, and an additional reprise chorus to end the first act; the sixty-four-bar, Latin-flavored "All Through the Night," another of Porter's songs that move in frequent chromatic lines; "Blow, Gabriel, Blow," a very rhythmic seventy-bar, pseudo-revival song; "I Get a Kick Out of You," Merman's opening number; and "Easy to Love," cut before opening but added to the score of the 1936 movie *Born to Dance,* where it's sung by James Stewart.

There was a 1936 movie version of *Anything Goes* retitled as *Tops Is the Limit,* with Bing Crosby and Merman. A 1956 movie called *Anything Goes* (with Crosby, Donald O'Connor, and Mitzi Gaynor) had no relation to the original story except that it was set on a boat and used some of the same songs. A successful Lincoln Center revival in 1987 had a new book (based on the original) by John Weidman and Russel Crouse's son, Timothy. It's this revised version that's most often produced now in regional and community theaters.

Jubilee (1935, 169 performances), with book by Moss Hart, starred Mary Boland, with fourteen-year-old Montgomery Clift in the cast. Porter and Hart wrote it while on a five-month cruise. About a royal family disguising themselves as commoners so they can live for a while like other people do, it closed early without paying back its investment because Boland left for Hollywood. The score contains a couple of Porter standards: "Begin the Beguine," probably the longest pop song ever—108 bars—and "Just One of Those Things," with a verse containing made-up quotes involving famous people, both real and fictional, and such great lyrics as in the chorus:

> It was just one of those nights,
> Just one of those fabulous flights,
> A trip to the moon on gossamer wings,
> Just one of those things.

Red, Hot and Blue! (1936, 183 performances) had a book by Lindsay and Crouse, and starred Ethel Merman, Jimmy Durante, and Bob Hope, with Vivian Vance. The title refers to a mark on the behind of a woman for whom the hero is searching; she got it by sitting on a waffle iron when she was a child. In the score were "Down in the Depths (On the Ninetieth Floor)," "Ridin' High," and "It's De-Lovely," another Porter list song.

Also in 1936, Porter's score for the Eleanor Powell, James Stewart, and Buddy Ebsen movie *Born to Dance* includes "I've Got You Under My Skin," a beguine with a fifty-six-bar chorus, and "Easy to Love." His 1937 film score for *Rosalie* (starring Eleanor Powell, Nelson Eddy, Ray Bolger, and Frank Morgan) includes the title song and "In the Still of the Night."

Leave It to Me! (1938, 291 performances) had a book by Bella and Sam Spewack (they later wrote the book for Porter's biggest hit, *Kiss Me, Kate*); it was adapted from their play *Clear All Wires*. The cast included William Gaxton, Victor Moore, Sophie Tucker, and Mary Martin, with Gene Kelly in the chorus. The show is about the mild-mannered American ambassador to Russia (Moore, of course), who wants to go home to the United States, and his pushy wife (Tucker in her only Broadway musical). Some of the songs became standards, the rest are second-rate. In the score are "Get Out of Town (Before It's Too Late, My Love)"; "Most Gentlemen Don't Like Love (They Just Like to Kick It Around)," a list song; and "My Heart Belongs to Daddy," also a list song. Mary Martin (1913–90, born in Weatherford, Texas), in her Broadway debut in a supporting role, did a refined strip while singing the song, and it made her a star. Among her later shows were *One Touch of Venus*, *South Pacific*, and *The Sound of Music*.

DuBarry Was a Lady (1939, 408 performances), book by Herbert Fields and B. G. DeSylva, was a hit starring Bert Lahr, Ethel Merman, and Betty Grable (her first Broadway lead). Most of the show is a dream: a washroom attendant (Lahr) accidentally downs a knockout drink and dreams he's Louis XV, the king of France at the time of Madame DuBarry. In the score is "But in the Morning, No," a double-entendre list song with a verse and ten choruses; only eight were performed, with the other two considered too vulgar even for Broadway at the time. Among the other songs were "Well, Did You Evah?" (a list song with four choruses, revised by Porter for the 1956 movie *High Society*) and "Friendship" (a list song with six choruses). When Merman left the show, she was replaced by Gypsy Rose Lee. The 1943 movie, with Red Skelton, Lucille Ball, and Gene Kelly, kept one of Porter's songs and had to clean the show up to such an extent that the original wasn't recognizable in what was left.

Suggested Watching and Listening

Cole Porter in the Thirties
The following suggestions are versions of Cole Porter songs from this decade.

- "Love for Sale" (performed by Ella Fitzgerald): Originally from the show *The New Yorkers,* Fitzgerald's version here includes the verse and is on her recording of *The Cole Porter Song Book* (disc 2, Verve Records CD). I'd recommend Billie Holiday's version as well, but she doesn't sing the verse.
- "Night and Day" (performed by Ginger Rogers and Fred Astaire): Astaire and Rogers immediately followed their featured appearance in the 1933 *Flying Down to Rio* with Mark Sandrich's movie *The Gay Divorcee* (Turner Home Entertainment DVD). It was the first time they got star billing, and "Night and Day" (from *The Gay Divorce*) was their first dance in the movie as well as the only Porter song in the movie.
- "Begin the Beguine" (performed by Fred Astaire and Eleanor Powell): The version of this song from the show *Jubilee* is on the Warner Brothers DVD *Broadway Melody of 1940.* It makes this long song considerably longer, given the number of times it's repeated. Astaire and Powell's final tap dance sequence on a shiny black floor is spectacular, one of the best ever filmed.
- "Just One of Those Things" (performed by Lena Horne): Horne's segment of *That's Entertainment III* (available on the 1994 Warner Brothers DVD) includes part of her performance of this song from the 1942 movie version of Cole Porter's *Panama Hattie.* Horne also talks about the difficulties of her career in Hollywood in the forties because she was African American. The segment includes part of Rodgers and Hart's "Where or When" from *Babes in Arms* (which she sang in *Words and Music*) and most of Arlen and Harburg's "Ain't It the Truth," written for the movie version of *Cabin in the Sky* but cut because the heads of MGM didn't want to show a black woman taking a bath on-screen. (It would have been just fine if she'd been white.) The song was used in Arlen and Harburg's 1957 musical *Jamaica,* starring Horne. The segment of *That's Entertainment III* ends with Annette Warren, Ava Gardner, and Horne all

singing parts of Kern and Hammerstein's "Can't Help Lovin' Dat Man," from *Show Boat.*

Jerome Kern in the Thirties
Roberta
The original 1935 movie version of *Roberta,* directed by William Seiter and starring Irene Dunne and Fred Astaire, is available on Warner Home Video DVD. The 1952 remake, *Lovely to Look At,* directed by Mervyn LeRoy and starring Kathryn Grayson and Red Skelton, is available on VHS and from MGM.

"Smoke Gets in Your Eyes" (performed by Marge and Gower Champion, and by Kathryn Grayson): The music was written for a tap dance in *Show Boat* but went unused. Kern then turned it into an AA'BA' ballad for *Roberta.* In the 1952 *Lovely to Look At,* the song is danced by the Champions several scenes before it's sung by Grayson. (Gower Champion later became an important Broadway director and choreographer. Among his many shows were *Hello, Dolly!* and *42nd Street.*)

Very Warm for May
"All the Things You Are" (performed by Tony Martin): An AA'BA" song, the A' is an extension of the A rather than a repeat or slight variation of it. Martin's version is in the movie *Till the Clouds Roll By* (available on MGM/Warner Home Video DVD).

Simple Simon
This show includes the song "Ten Cents a Dance." Doris Day sings a version of it in the 1955 Ruth Etting bio-pic *Love Me or Leave Me* (MGM DVD).

Words and Music: Richard Rodgers and Lorenz Hart
This highly fictionalized 1948 biography of Rodgers and Hart is available on MGM VHS. It stars Mickey Rooney as Hart, whose whole problem in the movie is that he's short. (He dies in the rain in front of a store window advertising elevator shoes.) The following three songs are from their show *Babes in Arms.*
- "The Lady Is a Tramp" (performed by Lena Horne): A list song with a verse and four AABA' choruses, "The Lady Is a Tramp" is about a woman considered a "tramp" (which can refer to a hobo who tramps around the country or a sexually promiscuous woman) because she doesn't live the way high society deems proper; clearly, she's the one who's right. Horne sings the verse and two choruses.
- "I Wish I Were in Love Again" (performed by Judy Garland and Mickey Rooney)
- "Johnny One Note" (performed by Judy Garland): Both of these numbers are also in *Words and Music;* Robert Alton directed the musical numbers. "Johnny One Note" is a great number for a belter. If you want to add it to your repertory, make sure Johnny's note is the strongest one at the top of your belt voice.

The Rodgers and Hart Songbook
This two-disc CD set (available from Verve Records) is sung by Ella Fitzgerald. Disc 2 contains the song "My Funny Valentine," also from *Babes in Arms.*

The Rise of Big Bands and Swing

Not so many summers ago
The Land of New Dealin' was feelin' so low
That even folks in darkest Washington
Knew something had to be done. . . .
Yet no one had a mumblin' word to say
'Cept Professor Cab Calloway.
But Cab, the Wise,
Rose and said to these guys,
"If you're fixin' to beat this ole thing,
As a Harlem resident,
Mister President,
I say, 'Give 'em Swing.' "
—"SWINGIN' THE JINX AWAY," *BORN TO DANCE,*
LYRICS BY COLE PORTER

Although there were a few important shows and some great songs during the thirties, it was a lean period in the development of the musical. Movies continued to attract many theater artists as well as audiences: over fifty movie musicals a year were released during the last half of the decade alone. The Depression continued to make it difficult for theater producers to find financing or take chances and for audiences to afford tickets. To make things even more difficult for Broadway business, younger audiences were beginning to prefer big-band swing over jazz.

Broadway never responded with the enthusiasm or imagination it had
brought to ragtime and jazz. . . . Swing was, to no small extent, unmelodic and

untheatrical. Its insistent, driving rhythms and strictly coordinated ensemble sounds were designed for what became known as "the big bands." . . . Even if swing had been more readily transferable, there is some cause to doubt its welcome would have been much heartier. Broadway was growing old. . . . The average age of Broadway's principal creators and stars was markedly higher than it had been twenty or forty years before. (Bordman, 493–94)

All of which sounds remarkably like what also started happening to Broadway in the sixties when rock and roll took over.

In 1930, fewer shows were being produced and even fewer of those were able to run long enough to pay back their investments. Producers were going broke (Lew Fields retired; Dillingham was bankrupt), critics were getting tougher, and audiences were getting choosier. Friml and Romberg had flop shows during the year, and there was a limited-run revival of *Babes in Toyland*.

Along with the Gershwins, Bolton, and McGowan's *Girl Crazy*, a big hit; the revised *Strike Up the Band*, a sort of hit; Rodgers and Hart, Wynn, and

Backdrop: 1930–1939

National By the end of 1930, unemployment reaches four and a half million in the United States. More than thirteen hundred banks close. By 1932, unemployment reaches nearly seventeen million, and there are thirty-four million Americans with no income at all. Nearly twenty thousand businesses go bankrupt. Breadlines form in many cities. Butter is twenty-eight cents a pound, eggs twenty-nine cents a dozen, and milk ten cents a quart; typical annual incomes are $3,382 for a physician; $1,227 for a public school teacher; and $216 for a hired farmhand. Democrat Franklin Delano Roosevelt, promising "a new deal for the American people," defeats President Hoover in the 1932 national elections. There's an unprecedented drought in the South and Midwest. For the first time, emigration from the United States exceeds immigration. Prohibition ends with the ratification of the Twenty-first Amendment. "The Star Spangled Banner" is designated the national anthem. Elijah Poole changes his name to Elijah Muhammad and establishes his first Black Muslim temple in Detroit. Al Capone, found guilty of tax evasion, is sent to jail for eleven years. Charles "Lucky" Luciano restructures the U.S. Mafia into a federation of "families." Charles A. Lindbergh's twenty-month-old son is kidnapped and later found dead; it's called the crime of the century, and Bruno Hauptmann is executed for it. Fiorello LaGuardia defeats New York's political machine and becomes mayor. (The early part of his career is detailed in the 1959 Pulitzer Prize–winning musical *Fiorello!*) U.S. Steel permits its workers to unionize. Henry Ford hires six hun-

Bolton's *Simple Simon,* a flop; and Porter and Field's *The New Yorkers,* an almost hit, 1930 was the year of such musicals as *Smiles,* with music by Youmans, lyrics by Harold Adamson and Mack Gordon, and book and direction by William Anthony McGuire. It was choreographed by Ned Wayburn, produced by Ziegfeld, and starred the Astaires, Marilyn Miller, Eddie Foy Jr., harmonica virtuoso Larry Adler, and Bob Hope. Even with that cast, it was a sixty-three-performance flop. The score included "Time on My Hands."

Flying High (355 performances) was Henderson, DeSylva, and Brown's last show together. Bert Lahr played a pilot who sets an all-time record for staying in the air because he can't figure out how to land the plane. Kate Smith played his girlfriend. It was filmed in 1931 with Lahr.

There were several new revues in 1930, including the new—and final—edition of *The Garrick Gaieties* (158 performances), produced by the Theatre Guild and with Sterling Holloway, Rosalind Russell, and Imogene Coca in the cast. It had Vernon Duke's first Broadway songs, including "I'm Only Human After All," with lyrics by E. Y. Harburg and Ira Gershwin. Also in the score was Johnny Mercer and Everett Miller's "Out of Breath (And Scared to Death)."

dred "goons" armed with guns and blackjacks to prevent the unionizing of his employees; Republic Steel and other industries do the same. Millionaires John D. Rockefeller and Andrew W. Mellon die. The Supreme Court upholds a minimum wage for women. The Daughters of the American Revolution won't let African American singer Marian Anderson give a concert in Washington's Constitution Hall; Eleanor Roosevelt arranges for her to sing at the Lincoln Memorial, where she draws an audience of seventy-five thousand. The New York World's Fair draws visitors from all over the world (but they don't go to the theater much).

International   Germany's National Socialist (Nazi) Party gains 207 seats in the Reichstag. Adolf Hitler becomes dictator of Germany. Germany evicts Jews from trade and industry, forces them to wear yellow stars, bars them from all public places, and opens the Buchenwald concentration camp. Japan and Germany withdraw from the League of Nations. Communist leader Stalin purges his political enemies; eight to ten million Soviet citizens will have died by the end of 1938. Japan invades China, killing hundreds of thousands of civilians. Italy withdraws from the League of Nations. The Spanish Civil War, led by General Francisco Franco, receives arms from Germany and Italy, while Russia supplies the Loyalists. There are many anti-Fascist American volunteers, known as the Lincoln Brigade, who fight for the Loyalists; by 1939, 3,100 Americans will have fought and half will have died. Most historians consider the Spanish Civil War a "tryout" for World War II. It ends with Franco's Fascists defeating the Loyalists. On September 1, 1939, Hitler invades Poland, marking the official start of World War II in Europe. The United States remains neutral.

Johnny Mercer (1909–76, born in Savannah, Georgia) sometimes wrote music, sometimes lyrics, sometimes both. He wrote lyrics for several hit songs with Harold Arlen in the forties, including "That Old Black Magic" and "One for My Baby (And One More for the Road)." He only occasionally wrote for Broadway.

Nine-Fifteen Revue (7 performances) had songs by Youmans, the Gershwins, Herbert, Friml, and Kay Swift, was choreographed by Busby Berkeley, and starred Ruth Etting. In its score was the first Broadway song by Arlen and Koehler, their first hit, "Get Happy." *The International Revue* (96 performances), score by Jimmy McHugh and Dorothy Fields, was also choreographed by Berkeley, starred Harry Richman and Gertrude Lawrence, and introduced such songs as "Exactly Like You" and the anti-Depression song "On the Sunny Side of the Street," which perfectly fit the mood of the times and was a big hit:

> Grab your coat and get your hat,
> Leave your worries on the doorstep.
> Just direct your feet
> To the sunny side of the street.

New Developments   Pluto is discovered and labeled a new planet. Inventor Thomas Alva Edison dies. Edwin Land invents Polaroid film. Nevada legalizes gambling and establishes a six-week residency for getting a divorce, greatly increasing tourism. Amelia Earhart is the first woman to make a solo flight across the Atlantic. Physicist Harold Urey pioneers the production of atomic energy by discovering heavy water. The atom is split, the neutron is discovered, and the first practical cyclotron is built. Amelia Earhart disappears on a Pacific flight from New Guinea and is never found. The first jet engine is built. General Motors introduces automatic transmission. Insulin is used successfully to treat diabetics. Xerography is pioneered.

Sports   Joe Louis knocks out James J. Braddock and wins the heavyweight championship. Louis is the first African American to hold the title since Jack Johnson lost it in 1915.

Art   Among new paintings are Wood's *American Gothic,* Hopper's *Early Sunday Morning,* Mondrian's *Composition in Red, Yellow, and Blue,* and Rivera's *Fall of Cuernavaca.* The Third Reich presents an exhibition of "degenerate art" in Munich that includes works by Van Gogh, Matisse, and Picasso. Picasso paints the mural *Guernica* in memory of the destruction of the Spanish town by bombs supplied by Germany. There are also new paintings by Klee, Miró, Braque, and Magritte. Walter Gropius brings his Bauhaus methods of architectural design to Harvard University. Alexander Calder creates stabiles and mobiles.

Music/Dance   In New York, Helmsley Winfield forms the New Negro Art Theatre Dance Group. Maurice Ravel dies. The NBC Symphony is formed for conductor Arturo Toscanini. Orff's *Carmina Burana* and Shostakovich's Symphony no. 5 premiere.

An intimate Broadway revue, *Three's a Crowd* was one of six shows to which Schwartz contributed songs in 1930. In its score were songs by Burton Lane and Vernon Duke (among others) as well as Johnny Green and Robert Sour's "Body and Soul" and Schwartz and Dietz's "Something to Remember You By."

At the beginning of 1931, half the Broadway theaters were empty. Bob Hope played the Palace for the first time; other headliners included Ed Wynn and Burns and Allen. There were brief revivals of such show as *The Student Prince, Blossom Time, The Mikado, HMS Pinafore,* and *The Pirates of Penzance.* Among the new musicals of 1931 were the Gershwins, Kaufman, and Ryskind's *Of Thee I Sing;* Kern and Harbach's "musical love story" *The Cat and the Fiddle;* and Rodgers, Hart, and Fields's flop *America's Sweetheart.* Shows by such artists as Romberg, Hammerstein, and Ryskind also flopped.

Along with Schwartz, Dietz, and Kaufman's hugely successful and elaborately intimate *The Band Wagon,* there were several

Three's a Crowd

MUSIC/LYRICS: Arthur Schwartz and Howard Dietz

SKETCHES: Howard Dietz, Groucho Marx, and others

DIRECTOR: Hassard Short

CHOREOGRAPHER: Albertina Rasch

DESIGNER: Kiviette (costumes)

PRODUCER: Max Gordon

CAST INCLUDES: Clifton Webb, Libby Holman, and Fred Allen, with Fred MacMurray

PERFORMANCES: 272

Publications   The Communist newspaper *The Daily Worker* begins publication in London. *Fortune, Newsweek, Esquire, Reader's Digest, Look,* and *Woman's Day* magazines and Chester Gould's comic strip *Dick Tracy* begin publication. Joyce's 1922 *Ulysses* is permitted publication in the United States. Among the new books are Freud's *Civilization and Its Discontents;* Stein's *The Autobiography of Alice B. Toklas;* Frost's *Collected Poems;* Porter's *Flowering Judas;* Hilton's *Lost Horizon;* West's *Miss Lonelyhearts;* Woolf's *The Waves;* Buck's *The Good Earth;* Faulkner's *Sanctuary* and *Light in August;* Miller's *The Tropic of Cancer* (banned in the United States until the 1960s); Huxley's cautionary novel *Brave New World;* Caldwell's *Tobacco Road;* Wilder's first Little House book, *Little House in the Big Woods;* De Brunhoff's *The Story of Babar;* Hammett's *The Maltese Falcon* and *The Thin Man* (the central characters but not the plot were used in the flop 1991 musical *Nick and Nora*); Steinbeck's *Of Mice and Men;* Hurston's *Their Eyes Were Watching God;* Eliot's *Collected Poems;* Tolkien's *The Hobbit;* and Dr. Seuss's *And to Think That I Saw It on Mulberry Street.*

Radio/TV   Electronic television and FM radio are developed. Vaudeville and revue comedians Jack Benny and Fred Allen begin their popular radio shows. The first transcontinental radio broadcast reports the arrival of the *Hindenburg,* a new German transatlantic zeppelin; it explodes on arrival at Lakehurst, New Jersey, killing thirty-six and ending transportation by hot-air balloon. Orson Welles causes a panic when he convinces thousands of people that Mars has invaded Earth with his Halloween radio broadcast of H. G. Welles's *The War of the Worlds.*

Pop Culture   Stereo recordings are patented. The popularity of the jukebox spreads through the country; favorite records can be played everywhere from fancy nightclubs to neighborhood soda shops.

new revues this year, including *Ziegfeld Follies of 1931* (165 performances), the last *Follies* produced by Ziegfeld and designed by Urban. It starred Ruth Etting, Harry Richman, Buck and Bubbles, and Helen Morgan.

George White's Scandals (1931, 204 performances), the last *Scandals* until 1936, had a score by Henderson and Brown (without DeSylva); sketches by White, Brown, Irving Caesar, and Harry Conn; and starred Ray Bolger, Ethel Merman, Rudy Vallee, and Eleanor Powell, with Alice Faye in the chorus. The score introduced the Depression-era hit "Life Is Just a Bowl of Cherries."

Rhythmania (music by Harold Arlen and lyrics by Ted Koehler) was a Cotton Club revue starring Aida Ward and Cab Calloway. Among its songs were "I Love a Parade" and "Between the Devil and the Deep Blue Sea." Arlen's first complete Broadway score, *You Said It* (192 performances), a college musical written with Jack Yellen and Sid Silvers, also premiered. None of its songs have endured.

Billy Rose's Crazy Quilt (67 performances), produced and directed by Rose and starring Fanny Brice (who also designed the costumes), had Warren, Rose, and Dixon's hit song "I Found a Million Dollar Baby (In a Five and Ten Cent Store)." Rose (1899–1966, born William Rosenberg) was Brice's second husband and a would-be Ziegfeld who often changed a word or two and claimed colyricist credit for songs in the shows he produced.

Record sales fall from 107 million in 1927 to 6 million. The South American rhumba, the samba, and the conga become popular on American dance floors. In 1938, Benny Goodman and his orchestra give the first swing concert at New York's Carnegie Hall; among the performers are Gene Krupa, Lionel Hampton, Harry James, Teddy Wilson, Count Basie, Bobby Hackett, Johnny Hodges, Lester Young, and Cootie Williams. Glenn Miller forms his swing band. Frank Sinatra becomes the singer for Harry James's band, leaving within a year to join Tommy Dorsey's band, and then, in 1942, starting on a solo career. Ella Fitzgerald begins her rise to stardom. Two new dances, the Big Apple and the Shag, are both ways of jitterbugging to swing bands. Pop songs include Carmichael and Washington's "The Nearness of You"; Carmichael and Gorrell's "Georgia on My Mind"; Carmichael and Mercer's "Lazy Bones"; Carmichael and Arodin's "(Up a) Lazy River"; McHugh and Fields's "Don't Blame Me"; Clare, Stept, and Palmer's "Please Don't Talk About Me When I'm Gone"; Turk, Ahlert, and Richman's "Walkin' My Baby Back Home"; Ellington, Mills, and Parish's "Sophisticated Lady" (Ellington said it took him thirty days to complete the tune); Ellington, Bigard, and Mills's "Mood Indigo" (Ellington said he wrote that tune in fifteen minutes); Ellington, Hoffman, and Mills's "It Don't Mean a Thing If It Ain't Got That Swing"; Calloway, Mills, and Gaskill's "Minnie the Moocher"; Fain and Brown's "That Old Feeling"; Sherman and Lewis's "(Potatoes Are Cheaper—Tomatoes Are Cheaper) Now's the Time to Fall in Love"; two Berlin ballads, "How Deep Is the Ocean" and "Say It Isn't So"; Waller and Razaf's "Keepin' Out of Mischief Now" and "The Joint Is Jumpin'"; Arlen, Harburg, and Rose's "It's Only a Paper Moon" (originally called "If You Believed in Me"); and Hupfeld's "As Time Goes By," interpolated into the 1931 musi-

In 1932, Florenz Ziegfeld died, a million dollars in debt.

> In his very last years sound movies came to offer more to please the eye than the richest Ziegfeld extravaganza could hope to match. They [also] forced a new microphoned style of singing and therefore of song that was essentially inimical to the stage. (Bordman, 477)

The death knell for vaudeville sounded when the Palace in New York added feature films to its bill; it soon closed down altogether and reopened in 1935 as a movie house. New York's Radio City Music Hall opened, with Ray Bolger heading the stage show; the biggest of all movie palaces, it seated sixty-two hundred people. Along with a major new motion picture, there was an elaborate stage show with precision dancers called the Rockettes.

Among the new musicals were Kern and Hammerstein's *Music in the Air,* Berlin and Moss Hart's *Face the Music,* and Porter, Webb, and Hoffenstein's *Gay Divorce.* Youmans's *Through the Years* closed after 20 performances; *Take a Chance* (243 performances), starring Ethel Merman and Jack Haley, also featured a few songs by Youmans, his last for Broadway. A hit revival of *Show Boat* (181 performances), with Paul Robeson as Joe, opened two months before Ziegfeld's death.

cal *Everybody's Welcome.* (It became a standard after Dooley Wilson, as Sam, sang and played it in the 1942 movie *Casablanca.*) Woody Guthrie, in sympathy with the labor movement, travels the country singing his songs, such as "This Land Is Your Land" and "So Long (It's Been Good to Know You)."

Stage The Group Theatre, formed by Harold Clurman, Cheryl Crawford, and Lee Strasberg, bases its work on the teachings of Stanislavsky; Kingsley's *Men in White* is its first hit. It also produces Odets's *Waiting for Lefty, Awake and Sing,* and *Golden Boy* (adapted in 1964 into a musical starring Sammy Davis Jr.). Humphrey Bogart plays Duke Mantee in Sherwood's *The Petrified Forest,* then goes to Hollywood to repeat the role in the movie version. Orson Welles directs his "voodoo" *Macbeth* with the Negro Theatre Unit of the Federal Theatre Project. Laurence Olivier joins London's Old Vic theater company. New plays include Pirandello's *Tonight We Improvise* and *As You Desire Me;* Lorca's *Blood Wedding;* Anouilh's *The Enchanted;* Kirkland's adaptation of Caldwell's *Tobacco Road* (3,182 performances); Connelly's *The Green Pastures;* Coward's *Private Lives* and *Design for Living;* Kaufman and Moss Hart's first collaboration, *Once in a Lifetime;* Ferber and Kaufman's *Dinner at Eight;* O'Neill's trilogy *Mourning Becomes Electra* and his *Ah, Wilderness* (adapted in 1959 into the musical *Take Me Along*); Drake's adaptation of Baum's *Grand Hotel* (adapted into a 1932 all-star movie and then, in 1989, into a musical); Hecht and MacArthur's *Twentieth Century,* directed by George Abbott (source of the 1978 musical *On the Twentieth Century*); and Riggs's *Green Grow the Lilacs* (source of *Oklahoma!*). Eugene O'Neill is the first dramatist and the second American to win the Nobel Prize. Dissatisfied with

Again, there were many revues in 1932, including Vernon Duke's first full Broadway score, *Walk a Little Faster*. *Flying Colors* (music by Schwartz; lyrics, sketches, and direction by Dietz; choreography by Albertina Rasch, who replaced Agnes de Mille; and produced by Max Gordon), starred Clifton Webb, Buddy Ebsen, Imogene Coca, Patsy Kelly, and harmonica virtuoso Larry Adler; it ran 188 performances after half-price tickets were offered. In the score were "A Shine on Your Shoes" and "Louisiana Hayride." *Cotton Club Parade: Twenty-first Edition* had music by Arlen; lyrics by Koehler, including "I've Got the World on a String"; and starred Aida Ward, the Nicholas Brothers, and Cab Calloway and his Orchestra. *Earl Carroll Vanities of 1932* (87 performances), designed by Vincente Minnelli and starring Milton Berle, introduced Arlen and Koehler's "I Gotta Right to Sing the Blues"; it was basically the last of the *Vanities* series.

In 1933, Joseph Urban died. The top Broadway ticket price was $4.40. The Ziegfeld Theatre became a movie house. Broadway business continued to plummet, and fewer revues were produced. Three notable ones were Berlin

the Pulitzers, the New York Drama Critics Circle is formed to give its own awards. The first award goes to Maxwell Anderson's *Winterset;* the Pulitzer goes to Robert E. Sherwood's *Idiot's Delight.* Other plays include Murray and Boretz's *Room Service,* Clare Booth's *The Women,* Kaufman and Moss Hart's *You Can't Take It with You* and *The Man Who Came to Dinner* (source of the flop 1967 musical *Sherry!*), Kaufman and Ferber's *Stage Door,* and Steinbeck's adaptation of his novel *Of Mice and Men,* directed by Kaufman. Also new are Lindsay and Crouse's *Life with Father* (3,224 performances, still the record for a straight play), Sherwood's *Abe Lincoln in Illinois,* Kingsley's *Dead End,* Saroyan's *The Time of Your Life,* Kober's *Having Wonderful Time* (source of the 1952 musical *Wish You Were Here,* with an onstage swimming pool), Hellman's *The Little Foxes* (source of Blitzstein's 1949 opera *Regina*), Barry's *The Philadelphia Story* (adapted in 1956 into the Cole Porter movie musical *High Society,* which was itself adapted into a flop Broadway musical in 1998), and Wilder's *Our Town* and *The Merchant of Yonkers* (which he rewrote in 1955 as *The Matchmaker,* source of the 1964 *Hello, Dolly!*).

Screen The first drive-in movie theater opens in Camden, New Jersey. Among the new movies are *Little Caesar* (which starts a craze for gangster films, such as *Public Enemy,* in which James Cagney pushes a grapefruit into Mae Clarke's face, and *Scarface,* in which Paul Muni plays a fictional version of Al Capone); *Dracula,* with Bela Lugosi, and *Frankenstein,* with Boris Karloff (which start a trend in monster movies); the first *Betty Boop* cartoon; an adaptation of Hecht and MacArthur's *The Front Page;* Chaplin's *City Lights,* with music and sound effects but no dialogue; *King Kong;* Greta Garbo in her first sound film, *Anna Christie,* adapted from the O'Neill play (adapted in 1957 into the musical *New Girl in Town*); Mamoulian's *Queen Christina,* with Garbo, and his *Dr. Jekyll and Mr. Hyde* (source of the 1997 musical *Jekyll and Hyde* since the original novel had no love interest); *The Private Life of Henry VIII,* which made and Hart's *As Thousands Cheer; Strike Me Pink* (105 performances), produced and with a score by Henderson and Brown and starring Jimmy Durante; and *Cotton Club Parade: Twenty-second Edition*, with songs by Arlen and Koehler and starring Ethel Waters and Ellington and his orchestra. The score included "Stormy Weather."

Among the musicals of 1933 were Kern and Harbach's *Roberta;* the Gershwins and Fields's flop *Pardon My English;* the Gershwins, Kaufman, and Ryskind's flop *Let 'Em Eat Cake;* and the American premiere of Kurt Weill and Bertolt Brecht's 1928 *The Threepenny Opera,* which had a twelve-performance run in an awkward translation. Also in 1933 Weill and Brecht fled Nazi Germany and George Balanchine settled in America.

In 1934, as part of President Roosevelt's New Deal, the federal government helped keep Broadway actors employed by putting up the money for free productions. Friml's last Broadway show, a flop, was produced. It was the year of Porter, Bolton, Wodehouse, Lindsay, and Crouse's *Anything Goes,* and of Arlen, Ira Gershwin, Harburg, and Freedman's revue *Life Begins at 8:40.* The Shuberts

a star of Charles Laughton; Laurel and Hardy in *Sons of the Desert;* and Mae West in *She Done Him Wrong* and *I'm No Angel.* (In 1934, in part because of West's movies, moral indignation at some movies' sexual content was running high in the United States. The Hays Office was created by the film industry to administer a production code in order to prevent threatened government censorship.) *Porky's Hare Hunt* introduces Bugs Bunny. Other new movies are *Grand Illusion, Lost Horizon* (adapted in 1973 into a flop movie musical with a second-rate Bacharach and David score), *Stage Door,* and *A Star Is Born* (adapted in 1954 into a Judy Garland movie musical with a score by Arlen and Gershwin, and in 1974 into a Barbra Streisand movie musical with a score by a lot of people, including Streisand herself). The year 1939 is one of the most successful and productive in Hollywood history. Among its many enduring movies are *Gone with the Wind, Mr. Smith Goes to Washington, Destry Rides Again, Stagecoach, Of Mice and Men, Dark Victory, Wuthering Heights,* and *You Can't Cheat an Honest Man.*

Nearly eighty movie musicals are released in 1930, including a reworking of the musical *Spring Is Here* and the first film versions of *The New Moon* and *The Vagabond King,* the first movie in two-color Technicolor. There are also film versions of the Marx Brothers in *Animal Crackers,* Marilyn Miller in *Sunny,* and Eddie Cantor in *Whoopee!* After the glut of movie musicals made in 1930, fewer than a dozen are made in 1931 and again in 1932; audiences got tired of the sameness. Among the new ones are Rodgers and Hart's first original movie score, *The Hot Heiress;* the Gershwins' first, *Delicious;* the Marx Brothers in *Monkey Business* (their first not adapted from one of their stage shows) and in *Horse Feathers;* and the first film version of *Girl Crazy.*

In 1933, movie musicals are popular again; there are over thirty released, as well as Disney's animated short *The Three Little Pigs,* from which the song "Who's Afraid of the Big Bad Wolf?" becomes an instant and Ziegfeld's widow, Billie Burke, produced *Ziegfeld Follies of 1934* (182 performances); it starred Fanny Brice. The first of the periodic series of revues called *New Faces* (148 performances) was produced by Leonard Sillman. There were seven altogether; this one introduced Henry Fonda, and later ones introduced Imogene Coca, Van Johnson, Eartha Kitt, Paul Lynde, Carol Lawrence, Robert Klein, and Madeline Kahn, among others.

There was a little development of the musical's form during the second half of the thirties, as in Rodgers and Hart's *On Your Toes,* which carried bits of the story into Balanchine's ballets. There was also some important experimenting with what kinds of shows could be musicalized: in 1935, the Gershwins and DuBose Heyward wrote *Porgy and Bess,* and in 1937, classically trained Marc Blitzstein (1905–64, born in Philadelphia, Pennsylvania) wrote *The Cradle Will Rock,* a deeply angry musical play with a complex, semiclassical score and a story that was a strong indictment of big business and the politics of poverty. According to Ken Bloom, "While other composers wanted us to forget the Depression with upbeat, optimistic tunes, Blitzstein frankly depicted the trouble America was in" (*American Song,* 142).

The Cradle Will Rock, a rather heavy-handed show, is a bitterly comic, politically and socially conscious, through-sung musical/operetta set in Steeltown, U.S.A. The city is run by the tycoon

The Cradle Will Rock

MUSIC/LYRICS/BOOK: Marc Blitzstein

DIRECTOR: Orson Welles

ORCHESTRATOR: Marc Blitzstein

PRODUCER: John Houseman and the Federal Theatre Project of the Works Progress Administration (the WPA)

CAST INCLUDES: Howard da Silva (Jud in *Oklahoma!* in 1943), Will Geer (the grandfather on the TV series *The Waltons*), Hiram Sherman, and Olive Stanton

PERFORMANCES: 184 eventually (after initially being shut down)

Depression-era hit. Three Warner Brothers hits, all choreographed by Busby Berkeley, are largely responsible for the boom in musicals and for helping deflate Broadway business; all three have spectacular, often dizzying production numbers. Among the Warren and Dubin songs in *42nd Street* are the title song, "Shuffle Off to Buffalo," and "You're Getting to Be a Habit with Me." Starring Warner Baxter, Dick Powell, and Ruby Keeler, it's the one with the famous line to the understudy (Keeler), who must take over on opening night, "You're going out a youngster, but you've got to come back a star." (The 1980 hit Broadway adaptation, which included other Warren and Dubin songs as well, was director/choreographer Gower Champion's last show.) The other two Busby Berkeley hits of the year are *Gold Diggers of 1933,* starring Powell and Joan Blondell, which features the Warren and Dubin songs "Pettin' in the Park" and "Shadow Waltz" and Ginger Rogers singing "We're in the Money" in pig Latin, and *Footlight Parade,* starring James Cagney, Blondell, Keeler, and Powell, which has songs by Fain and Kahal, including "By a Waterfall" and "Honeymoon Hotel." Among the other movie musicals of the year are the Marx Brothers in *Duck Soup* (Zeppo's last), Jolson in Rodgers and Hart's *Hallelujah,*

Mr. Mister, who's trying to keep out the unions by buying off newspapers, organized religions, educators, even gangsters. Because the show had leftist leanings, the WPA, under pressure from Congress, chickened out and locked the doors of the theater on opening day. (The arts have always been an easy target for politicians looking for notoriety.) The cast and a large part of the audience marched to an empty theater, where Blitzstein played the score on an onstage piano while the actors did their roles from the audience. Equity rules wouldn't allow them to perform on stage under the circumstances; some of the actors were afraid to participate even from their seats, so Blitzstein did their roles from the piano. (Tim Robbins's 1999 movie *Cradle Will Rock* is an attempt to re-create the event.) The show finally opened on Broadway in 1938, produced by Welles and John Houseman's Mercury Theatre. This time the actors did their roles from chairs onstage; it wasn't given a full production in New York until 1960. *The Cradle Will Rock* was the first show to get an original-cast recording, but on a small label with limited distribution.

There were two failed attempts at innovation during the late thirties by the expatriate Kurt Weill.

Weill constantly experimented with content, form, structure, and sound and eventually, in the late forties, moved into American opera. He worked hard to develop an American sound for his music that would "speak" to his adopted country.

Kurt Weill (1900–50) first established himself in his native Germany as a composer of classical music, then gained an international reputation as the creator (with Bertolt Brecht) of such satiric masterpieces as the political opera *The Rise and Fall of the City of Mahagonny*, *Happy End*, and *The Threepenny Opera*, which was written for musical theater performers, not opera singers. Weill was Jewish and had done his best-known work with Brecht, a Communist, so he sensibly fled the Nazis in 1933 (as did Brecht), and, after brief stops in Paris and London, arrived with his wife, Lotte Lenya, in New York, where he immediately began writing for Broadway.

I'm a Bum, and *Flying Down to Rio*, which has the last score by Youmans and lyrics by Eliscu and Kahn. It's the first teaming of Astaire and Rogers, dancing "The Carioca," which is their only number together. Among the nearly 150 new movie musicals released from 1935 through 1939 are Disney's first animated feature, *Snow White and the Seven Dwarfs*, with songs by Churchill and Morey, including "Some Day My Prince Will Come," "Heigh-Ho," and "Whistle While You Work"; *George White's 1935 Scandals*; adaptations of *Sweet Adeline*, *Roberta*, *Anything Goes*, *Show Boat*, *On Your Toes*, *The Firefly*, *The Great Waltz*, and *Babes in Arms* (the first of the Rooney-Garland-Berkeley series); *The Great Ziegfeld*, *The Great Victor Herbert*, and *Swanee River* (about Stephen Foster); six Shirley Temple movies, seven Astaire-Rogers musicals (with scores by Kern, Berlin, and the Gershwins, among others), five MacDonald-Eddy operettas, and three Marx Brothers comedies; Porter's score for *Rosalie*, Kern and Hammerstein's for *High, Wide and Handsome*, Berlin's for *On the Avenue* and *Alexander's Ragtime Band*, Rodgers and Hart's for *Mississippi*, the Gershwins' for *A Damsel in Distress*, and Arlen and Harburg's for *The Wizard of Oz*.

Joshua Logan (1908–88, born in Texarkana, Texas) directed plays, musicals, and movies, and occasionally wrote as well. He directed such shows as *Knickerbocker Holiday, This Is the Army, Annie Get Your Gun,* and *South Pacific* (which he also directed as a movie). Among the plays he directed were *Mister Roberts* (which he cowrote) and *Picnic* (which he also directed as a movie).

Therefore, the music he wrote in the United States differed from much of the music he'd written in Germany. Many fans of his German scores feel he sold out, but they don't understand that since he was searching for musical forms that allowed music and dialogue to flow naturally out of each other, he believed it was necessary to start with the popular music his audience danced to. (He once pointed out that classical composers like Bach, Beethoven, and Chopin made art out of the popular dance forms of the day.) Like Blitzstein, Weill did his own orchestrations and dance arrangements.

Weill's first two American musicals, *Johnny Johnson* and *Knickerbocker Holiday,* were flops, but he wasn't blamed; his talent was recognized by critics and theater professionals alike. The scores were considered too heavy for Broadway, but they were appropriate to their shows. Written by serious playwrights rather than by people experienced in the writing of musicals, the books and lyrics were preachy and heavy-handed, paralleling Weill's German shows too closely for American audiences.

Johnny Johnson (1936, 68 performances)—with book and lyrics by Paul Green, directed by Lee Strasberg, and produced by the Group Theatre—featured such members of the group ensemble as Lee J. Cobb, Robert Lewis, Luther Adler, and Elia Kazan. The show has an extremely angry, antiwar script, with a central character who is very Candide-like in his naivete. Although the show was a flop, Weill's talent was easy to see in the variety, scope, complexity, and inventiveness of the score, which carries much of the story and helps define character.

Knickerbocker Holiday (1938, 168 performances) had book and lyrics by Maxwell Anderson, was directed by Joshua Logan, produced by the Playwrights' Company, designed by Jo Mielziner, and starred Walter Huston. The book, by Pulitzer Prize–winning playwright Anderson, was only somewhat less heavy-handed than the book for *Johnny Johnson.* It's a satire on fascism set in seventeenth-century New Amsterdam when the Dutch ruled what would soon become New York. Though more successful than *Johnny Johnson,* and with a noticeably less operatic score—including Weill's first enduring American hit, "September Song"—the show was both a financial and a critical flop. Revivals have shown that it's the book that's at fault. Although Anderson was a successful playwright, he didn't understand how to write the book of a musical without weighing it down.

Weill understood the problem and switched to Ira Gershwin and Moss Hart as collaborators for his third show, *Lady in the Dark* (1941). In it, he further Americanized his sound and had his first Broadway hit.

In 1935, Will Rogers died in a plane crash, and Actors' Equity members won the right to rehearsal pay. Kurt Weill arrived in America. In the musical theater, it was the year of the Gershwins and Heyward's *Porgy and Bess;* Rodgers, Hart, Hecht, and MacArthur's *Jumbo;* and Porter and Moss Hart's *Jubilee.*

In 1936, lyricist/book-writer Harry B. Smith and Ziegfeld star Marilyn Miller died. *Variety* stopped publishing its separate section on vaudeville because there wasn't enough vaudeville left to warrant it. New musical evenings included Vernon Duke and Ira Gershwin's *Ziegfeld Follies of 1936;* Rodgers, Hart, Abbott, and Balanchine's *On Your Toes;* Porter, Lindsay, and Crouse's *Red, Hot and Blue!;* and Kurt Weill and Paul Green's *Johnny Johnson.*

In 1937, Cole Porter was crippled when his horse fell on him, and George Gershwin died. By that year, all the theaters on Forty-second Street had been converted to movie houses. The minimum pay for Broadway chorus members was $35 a week. Social and political thinking influenced several of the new Broadway musicals, including Blitzstein's *The Cradle Will Rock;* Rodgers, Hart, Kaufman, and Moss Hart's *I'd Rather Be Right;* and Rodgers and Hart's *Babes in Arms. Hooray for What?* (200 performances) had music by Arlen, lyrics by Harburg, book by Howard Lindsay (who also directed) and Russel Crouse, was produced by the Shuberts, had sets by Vincente Minnelli, and starred Ed Wynn, whose silliness took much of the sting out of a satire about the armaments race. In the score were "Moanin' in the Mornin' " and "Down with Love." Robert Alton replaced Agnes de Mille as choreographer. After the opening, Arlen returned to Hollywood until 1944.

> By the summer of 1937 the swing era was at its peak. The jazz era, which had reigned through the . . . twenties and, with a subdued, modified tone, continued through the early thirties, had drifted incontestably into history. . . . As an expression of popular musical speech, [swing] was more likely to be appropriated by and developed in Hollywood than on a stage catering to an increasingly older audience. (Bordman, 503)

There was also political and social content in several revues during this year, including *Pins and Needles* (1,108 performances), produced by Labor Stage Inc., with sketches by several people. The music and lyrics were by Harold Rome (1908–93, born in Hartford, Connecticut), whose later shows included *Call Me Mister, Wish You Were Here, Fanny, Destry Rides Again,* and *I Can*

Get It for You Wholesale. Pins and Needles was a funny, politically and socially conscious revue with a cast composed entirely of members of the singing, acting, and dancing classes of the International Ladies Garment Workers' Union (the ILGWU). Originally performed at the Labor Stage, the newly renamed Princess Theatre, the show was accompanied by two pianos. Among the songs were "Doing the Reactionary," "Sing Me a Song of Social Significance," and "Nobody Makes a Pass at Me," a comic song about a young woman who's done everything she can to seem more attractive to men by trying all the contemporary beauty products and self-help publications. The material was changed regularly to keep up with current events, and the show was subsequently presented as *Pins and Needles 1939* and *New Pins and Needles.*

Between the Devil (93 performances) had music by Schwartz, book and lyrics by Dietz, was directed by Hassard Short (among others), choreographed by Robert Alton, produced by the Shuberts, and starred Jack Buchanan. An unsuccessful musical comedy about a man who discovers after remarrying that his first wife isn't dead, the score includes "By Myself" and "Triplets," both included in the 1953 movie *The Bandwagon.*

Owing to charges of communism against the Federal Theatre Project, the House Un-American Activities Committee investigated it during the last years of the thirties. The project lost its funding in 1939. Most Broadway shows chose to ignore the outbreak of war in Europe by avoiding topicality altogether. The 1938–39 season was the first since 1902–3 to have fewer than a hundred shows of any kind on Broadway.

Other than Weill and Anderson's *Knickerbocker Holiday;* Porter's *You Never Know, Leave It to Me,* and *DuBarry Was a Lady;* and Rodgers and Hart's *I Married an Angel, The Boys from Syracuse,* and *Too Many Girls,* there were few new musical evenings during the last two years of the decade and even fewer that were successful. The biggest hit of 1938 was Ole Olsen and Chic Johnson's raucous and determinedly silly, slapstick revue *Hellzapoppin',* which ran 1,404 performances, a new record for a musical evening on Broadway, even though the music was unmemorable and definitely secondary to the wild goings-on. As Lehman Engle notes in *The American Musical Theater: A Consideration,* "*Hellzapoppin'* combined the least subtle elements of burlesque with the adolescent antics of a 1920s fraternity initiation." (p. 503) There was a 1941 movie version that captured some of the flavor of the show but was unfortunately often stifled by being tied to a dumb plot.

The D'Oyly Carte Company came over from London for a brief season of Gilbert and Sullivan operettas in 1939. Among the new shows of the year were *The Hot Mikado,* starring Bill Robinson, and *The Swing Mikado,* both adaptations of the Gilbert and Sullivan classic that featured black casts and contemporary arrangements of the score, and the last of *George White's Scandals* (120 performances), starring Ann Miller and the Three Stooges. *The Streets of Paris* (274 performances), one of the last revues produced by the Shuberts, had songs by Jimmy McHugh and Al Dubin, starred Bobby Clark, and had in its cast such future stars as Abbott and Costello, Gower Champion, and Carmen Miranda.

The musical, which looked and felt as if it were stagnating at the end of the thirties, was actually in a period of transition, trying to find some way of attracting new audiences. At the beginning of the forties, it was becoming clear that playing it safe as a way of doing business wasn't working. What to do instead wasn't clear yet, but it soon would be. In a very few years Broadway entered its golden age.

Suggested Watching and Listening

42nd Street
The complete movie version of *42nd Street* is available as part of the *Busby Berkeley Collection,* (available on Warner Brothers DVD), which includes the title song from this show.
- "42nd Street" (performed by Ruby Keeler and Dick Powell): This is the kind of elaborate production number Broadway could never duplicate, although it did occasionally try. The number is available on *The Busby Berkeley Disc.*

Knickerbocker Holiday
Although the show was a flop, it had one enduring hit.
- "September Song" (performed by Walter Huston): Huston's version is on *Original Cast! The Thirties* (MET CD). The song needs to be performed by an older person; it has alternate lyrics for a woman (recorded in the fifties by Weill's widow, Lotte Lenya).

Revue Songs
There were so many great songs written in the thirties that's it's difficult to make choices. Here are just a couple possibilities.
- "It Don't Mean a Thing If It Ain't Got That Swing" (performed by Phyllis Hyman, Gregg Burge, Hinton Battle, and the men): This 1932 number is in the 1981 Ellington revue *Sophisticated Ladies,* available on Kultur DVD.
- "Sophisticated Lady" (performed by Hinton Battle and Paula Kelly): This version is from the 1981 revue *Sophisticated Ladies.*

Stormy Weather
The following number comes from the twenty-second edition of *Cotton Club Parade.*
- "Stormy Weather" (performed by Lena Horne and Katherine Dunham and her company): In the 1943 movie *Stormy Weather,* Horne sings the verse after singing the chorus. Katherine Dunham was an important show choreographer in the thirties and forties, particularly because of her use of jazz ballet in her Broadway choreography.

PART FOUR

The Transitional Years, 1940–1945

Overleaf: (*left*) Van Johnson as a chorus boy and Joey (Gene Kelly) in *Pal Joey* (1940); (*right*) Julie Jordan (Jan Clayton) and Billy Bigelow (John Raitt) in *Carousel* (1945)

From *Pal Joey* to *Lady in the Dark*

Make City Hall a skating rink,

And push Wall Street in the drink,

But please, please,

I beg on my knees,

Don't monkey with old Broadway.

—"PLEASE DON'T MONKEY WITH BROADWAY,"

BROADWAY MELODY OF 1940, LYRICS BY COLE PORTER

Between 1940 and 1945, there weren't many new musicals of any real significance to the development of the form. In fact, there weren't many musicals at all during the war years, and most of them were mindless entertainments with the sole purpose of helping the public forget what was going on in the world. There were some landmarks along the way, though, leading to the golden age of the Broadway musical, including *Pal Joey, Lady in the Dark, One Touch of Venus,* and *On the Town,* as well as *Oklahoma!* and *Carousel.* In fact, some would say that the golden age had already begun.

There were also developments beginning to affect the sound of shows.

The orchestra had become louder—making use of heavier reeds (saxophones), more brass and percussion instruments, and virtuoso arrangements—and at the same time the solo singers became less vocal—first with respect to quality and then (as if to compensate for the deficiency) by the widespread adoption of new nonvocal singing styles. The vocal ensemble also began to diminish in size and vocal quality. The initial decreases in size were usually due to rising union minimums. . . . Beginning in 1939, to prevent a total blackout of the new "soft" vocal stage by the new "hard" orchestra, microphones were introduced, and in a short time no musical was done without them. . . . Six or seven microphones were spaced out evenly in the footlight troughs. Sometimes mikes were also hidden in scenery when singers had to perform at too great a distance from the forestage. For two decades this crude method of amplification sufficed. (Lehman Engle, *The American Musical Theater: A Consideration*, 70)

These days, of course, everyone wears body mikes or even visible head mikes.

Movie Musicals

A new standard for original movie musicals had been set with Disney's 1937 *Snow White and the Seven Dwarfs* and MGM's 1939 *The Wizard of Oz.* Though aimed at children, they were and still are enjoyed by adult audiences as well. They're tightly constructed, with songs and dances helping to define character and situation and with dialogue leading naturally into the musical numbers. Every song in *Snow White and the Seven Dwarfs* helps define character, situation, and mood; we learn as much about each individual dwarf, for instance, through their three songs (work, washing up, and entertaining them-

Backdrop: 1940–1941

National   Mount Rushmore National Monument is completed.

International   Hitler institutes "the final solution to the Jewish problem," and the Holocaust begins. Jewish settlers in Palestine use violence to fight for independence from Britain.

New Developments   The Ferrari and the Jeep are introduced. Penicillin and the first electron microscope are demonstrated. The Rh factor in blood is discovered. The first McDonald's hamburger stands open in California.

Art   Primitivist painter Grandma Moses has her first New York City show. New paintings include Hopper's *Nighthawks* and Pollock's *Bird*.

selves) as we do from their dialogue scenes, and Snow White's "I'm Wishing" and "Some Day My Prince Will Come" are the only way she allows herself to talk about what her life is like now.

Dorothy's only solo in *The Wizard of Oz* serves the same purpose. Louis B. Mayer, the head of MGM, wanted to cut "Over the Rainbow," thinking it slowed things down before Dorothy landed in Oz and the movie turned into full color. Fortunately, he was talked out of it, since the song tells us a lot about Dorothy and sets up her dream, which is the bulk of the movie; furthermore the music is used as underscoring throughout the film. And it's a great song.

Harburg wrote not only the lyrics for *The Wizard of Oz* but also the dialogue leading into the songs, making sure it all blended together seamlessly. The Munchkin sequence, for instance, is a connected series of songs, recitative, and rhymed and underscored dialogue, interrupted by the Wicked Witch of the West. Her exit leads naturally into "Follow the Yellow Brick Road" and "We're Off to See the Wizard." The film even has a subplot: how Scarecrow, Tin Man, and Lion get their brain, heart, and courage is a secondary story to how Dorothy gets back to Kansas. The two plots become one as the four join forces.

Music/Dance   George Balanchine and Lincoln Kirstin's American Ballet Theatre makes its New York debut.

Publications   F. Scott Fitzgerald dies. New books include McCullers's *The Heart Is a Lonely Hunter,* Hemingway's *For Whom the Bell Tolls,* Greene's *The Power and the Glory,* Wright's *Native Son,* and O'Hara's story collection *Pal Joey* (adapted into the musical the same year).

Radio/TV   There are radios in thirty million American homes. The Metropolitan Opera begins live weekly Saturday afternoon broadcasts sponsored by Texaco, whose backing continues through the 2002–3 season.

Pop Culture   The jitterbug, developed for the 4/4 syncopation of swing, is taking over dance floors. Pop hits include Raye, Prince, and Sheehy's boogie-woogie classic "Beat Me, Daddy, Eight to the Bar," Prince's "Boogie Woogie Bugle Boy" (popularized by the Andrews Sisters and, many years later, by Bette Midler singing all three parts of their arrangement), and three country and folk-flavored songs: Gene Autry's version of Leurs, Stock, and Rose's "Blueberry Hill," the Swanders' "Deep in the Heart of Texas," and Davis and Mitchell's "You Are My Sunshine." (Davis became governor of Louisiana in

Burton Lane (1912–97, born in New York) composed mostly for revues and movies until his first hit musical, *Finian's Rainbow,* in 1947. He then went back to Hollywood until 1965, when he and Alan Jay Lerner wrote *On a Clear Day You Can See Forever.* Among the many songs he wrote for Hollywood are "Everything I Have Is Yours" and "(I Like New York in June) How About You?" He and Lerner wrote the score for *Royal Wedding,* with Fred Astaire dancing on the walls and ceiling of his room.

Both *Snow White* and *The Wizard of Oz* (not forgetting the Astaire-Rogers movies) set a new standard for movie musicals. By the end of World War II the movie studios—MGM in particular—had begun turning out dozens of musicals a year; the best of them were well written and well structured, though usually lightweight romantic comedies or fantasies. In order to compete, Broadway had to dig deeper than whether girl is going to get boy or not, yet another impetus for the musical's entrance into its golden age.

In 1940, the top ticket price on Broadway was still $4.40. The Broadway Equity minimum rose to $50 a week. Katherine Dunham's dance company made its off-Broadway debut; having studied African and Caribbean movement and rituals, she brought aspects of them into her choreography. Among the new musical evenings were ice shows, water shows, cheaply produced revues and musical comedies, the last of the tawdry *Earl Carroll's Vanities,* a few better shows, and Jolson's return to Broadway in *Hold On to Your Hats* (158 performances), with a score by Burton Lane and E. Y. Harburg, book by Guy Bolton, among others, and Martha Raye as costar. The show closed early because Jolson didn't like New York's weather anymore and wanted to return to Los Angeles.

There was at least one important new show on Broadway in 1940: *Pal Joey.*

1942.) Berlin's "God Bless America" is fast becoming a second national anthem. Warren and Gordon's "Chattanooga Choo-Choo" sells over a million copies in Glenn Miller's recording, which gets the first gold record.

Stage The American Negro Theatre begins operations in Harlem. There are several new plays about the war in Europe, as well as Kaufman and Hart's *George Washington Slept Here,* Kesselring's *Arsenic and Old Lace,* Wright and Green's adaptation of Wright's *Native Son,* Brecht's *Mother Courage and Her Children,* Joseph Fields (Dorothy and Herbert's brother) and Chodorov's *My Sister Eileen* (which they adapted into the book of the 1953 musical *Wonderful Town*), and Coward's *Blithe Spirit* (adapted in 1964 into the musical *High Spirits*).

Screen *Citizen Kane* is released. There are over ninety new movie musicals, from low-budget second features to epics. Among them are Alice Faye in a very fictional biography of nineteenth-century star

By being more realistic and dramatic than earlier musical comedies, *Pal Joey* was a very important step in the development of the musical. Set mostly in a small-time Chicago nightclub, it explores the seamier side of show business. The show's antihero, Joey, is a two-bit hoofer and a heel. (The role made a star of Kelly and sent him directly to Hollywood.) Furthermore, Joey isn't changed or redeemed at the end nor is he any more self-aware—just defeated by even worse, more hard-boiled people than he is. He exits the show as sleazy and self-absorbed as ever.

The main plot is about a triangle, with Joey moving back and forth between Linda, the naive young chorus girl who loves him, and Vera, the wealthy and very hardened, older, married woman who keeps him. The story is coherently told, almost all the characters interact dramatically and have an effect on each other's lives, and the dialogue is sharp, concise, and characterful. Even the chorus girls are individualized. The show has a great deal of dancing. Most of the songs, including those in the nightclub show, help establish character and atmosphere.

The score includes "Joey Looks into the Future Ballet" (a dream ballet that closes the first act), "Zip" (which makes fun of Gypsy Rose Lee's intellectual pretensions and comes out of nowhere in the show; the idea for it may have been triggered by the presence of Lee's sister in the cast), "I Could Write a Book," an ABAC charm duet for Joey and Linda, "Den of Iniquity," a

Pal Joey

MUSIC/LYRICS: Richard Rodgers and Lorenz Hart

BOOK: John O'Hara, adapted from his thirteen *New Yorker* stories

DIRECTOR/PRODUCER: George Abbott

CHOREOGRAPHER: Robert Alton

ORCHESTRATOR: Hans Spialek

DESIGNER: Jo Mielziner (sets and lights)

CAST INCLUDES: Vivienne Segal, Gene Kelly, and June Havoc (Gypsy Rose Lee's sister, "Baby June"), with soon-to-be movie star Van Johnson and soon-to-be movie director Stanley Donen in the chorus

PERFORMANCES: 374

Lillian Russell; Faye and Betty Grable in *Tin Pan Alley,* set in the 1910s; Mickey Rooney (top box office star of 1939, 1940, and 1941) and Judy Garland in Berkeley's *Strike Up the Band* (which has no relation to the 1930 Gershwin satire except the title song without the verse); *Lady Be Good* (which has no relation to the 1924 Gershwin musical except the title and a couple of songs); *Ziegfeld Girl; Broadway Melody of 1940,* with a Porter score that includes "I Concentrate on You" and the Fred Astaire–Eleanor Powell version of "Begin the Beguine"; Astaire and Rita Hayworth in *You'll Never Get Rich,* with a Porter score; *They Met in Argentina,* with a less than memorable Rodgers and Hart score; *Sis Hopkins,* with a less than memorable Styne and Loesser score; and *Blues in the Night,* a musical drama with songs by Arlen and Mercer, two of which became standards, the title song and "This Time the Dream's on Me." The following Broadway musicals are made into movies: *Irene; The New Moon* and *Bitter Sweet,* starring MacDonald and Eddy; *Sunny; The Boys from Syracuse;* and *Too Many Girls,* one of the few times George Abbott directed a movie. The majority of the audiences who see these movies have never seen the originals; movies are almost all they know of any Broadway musicals.

sex duet for Joey and Vera, and "Bewitched," sung by Vera when she gets hooked on Joey. It's a list song with a verse, three AA'BA" choruses, and an encore half-chorus, with worldly, wise lyrics set to a romantic melody. The original lyrics were banned from the radio for many years. This is the second chorus:

Seen a lot—
I mean a lot—
But now I'm like sweet seventeen a lot—
Bewitched, bothered, and bewildered am I.
I'll sing to him,
Each spring to him,
And worship the trousers that cling to him—
Bewitched, bothered, and bewildered am I.
When he talks, he's seeking
Words to get off his chest.
Horizontally speaking,
He's at his very best.
Vexed again,
Perplexed again,
Thank God I can be oversexed again—
Bewitched, bothered, and bewildered am I.

There is also a reprise at the end of the show, when Vera is "bewitched, bothered, and bewildered no more."

Broadway audiences were not ready for *Pal Joey,* and it wasn't as big a success as it should have been. Its 1952 revival had greater success because in that post–World War II McCarthy era, cynicism was more acceptable to the American public. It was made into a movie in 1957 with Frank Sinatra, Rita Hayworth, and Kim Novak. The movie changed Joey from a not-overly-talented hoofer to a wonderful singer; gave "Zip" to a character who would never have sung it, let alone in public; cut much of the score and incorporated other Rodgers and Hart songs; and turned Joey into an honorable character at the end so he could walk off, literally, into the sunrise with Novak. In other words, the film was a greatly softened and deeply sentimentalized version of the show that served neither itself nor the original but had a lot of good Rodgers and Hart songs. Of course, this is hardly the only example of what Hollywood has done to Broadway musicals and, therefore, to most people's ideas of the shows.

Earlier in the year, Rodgers and Hart's *Higher and Higher* (108 performances), book by Gladys Hurlbut and Joshua Logan (who also directed it), opened. A traditional, featherweight musical comedy starring Jack Haley, it's about the servants of a bankrupt millionaire trying to save their jobs by getting one of them married to a wealthy man. The score includes the ballad "It Never Entered My Mind." The 1943 movie had a completely new score by Jimmy McHugh and Harold Adamson written for Sinatra.

Duke's only hit book show, *Cabin in the Sky* is a musical fantasy with an all-black cast. (Fantasy was soon to become as frequently recurring a musical genre as nostalgic Americana.) *Cabin in the Sky* is about a fight between God and the Devil for the soul of Little Joe Jackson, played by Wilson. The role of his loving wife—unfortunately named Petunia—who eventually saves him from the devil, was written for Waters. The score includes the title song, "Honey in the Honeycomb," and the hit "Taking a Chance on Love." In the 1943 film, directed by Vincente Minnelli (his first time as a movie director), Wilson was replaced by the more famous Eddie "Rochester" Anderson, and Dunham was replaced by Lena Horne. (Louis Armstrong and Duke Ellington were also in it.) Only three songs from the show were kept, and there were additional songs by Ellington and by Arlen and Harburg, including "Happiness Is (Just) a Thing Called Joe."

Berlin's first Broadway show since *As Thousands Cheer* in 1933, *Louisiana Purchase* is a political satire about a mild-mannered U.S. senator (Moore) sent to investigate corruption in Huey Long–like Louisiana politics. The plot centers on attempts by Gaxton's character, a lawyer, to fool or corrupt the senator. It was filmed in 1941 with the original stars, except for Gaxton, who was replaced by Bob Hope, already a big Hollywood star. The score, which includes some big-band swing, was recorded for the first time in 1998 from a concert staging, using the original orchestrations.

Panama Hattie is about a bar girl who won't marry the man she loves unless his young daughter accepts her.

> This is a typical Broadway show [of the time], where good performances, attractive production designs, a star or two, and a score with some good if unexceptional songs add up to a suc-

Cabin in the Sky

MUSIC: Vernon Duke
LYRICS: John Latouche
BOOK: Lynn Root
DIRECTORS: George Balanchine and Albert Lewis
CHOREOGRAPHERS: George Balanchine and Katherine Dunham
DESIGNER: Boris Aronson (sets and costumes)
PRODUCERS: Vinton Freedley and Albert Lewis
CAST INCLUDES: Ethel Waters, Dooley Wilson (Sam the piano player in *Casablanca*), Todd Duncan (the original Porgy in *Porgy and Bess*), and Katherine Dunham and her company in their Broadway debut
PERFORMANCES: 156

Louisiana Purchase

MUSIC/LYRICS: Irving Berlin
BOOK: Morrie Ryskind, from a story by B. G. DeSylva
DIRECTOR: Edgar MacGregor
CHOREOGRAPHERS: George Balanchine and Carl Randall
ORCHESTRATOR: Robert Russell Bennett
PRODUCER: B. G. DeSylva
CAST INCLUDES: William Gaxton, Victor Moore, Vera Zorina, and Irene Bordoni
PERFORMANCES: 444

Panama Hattie

MUSIC/LYRICS: Cole Porter

BOOK: Herbert Fields and
B. G. DeSylva

DIRECTOR: Edgar MacGregor

CHOREOGRAPHER: Robert Alton

ORCHESTRATORS: Robert Russell
Bennett, Hans Spialek, and Don
Walker

DESIGNER: Raoul Pène du Bois
(sets and lights)

PRODUCER: B. G. DeSylva

CAST INCLUDES: Ethel Merman,
with Arthur Treacher, Betty
Hutton, and June Allyson

PERFORMANCES: 501

cessful evening at the theatre. No fireworks here, but a wide range of competency and success can be classified as an entertaining evening. (Bloom, *American Song*, 556)

DeSylva went to Paramount Studios in Hollywood after this show. The 1942 movie, with Ann Sothern and Red Skelton, dropped most of the score and added Lena Horne singing "Just One of Those Things."

In 1941, Lew Fields—of Weber and Fields and father of Dorothy, Herbert, and Joseph—died, as did singer/actor Helen Morgan, and producer and former Cohan partner Sam H. Harris. The Yiddish Art Theatre closed after twenty-three years in operation. The Broadway chorus minimum went up to $40 a week.

During this year, a contract dispute between broadcasters and the American Society of Composers, Authors, and Publishers (ASCAP)—the organization founded to defend its members' performance rights and collect their royalties—caused a nine-month blackout of ASCAP-licensed songs on nearly seven hundred radio stations and led to the organizing of ASCAP's competitor Broadcast Music Inc. (BMI).

Along with the ice shows, there were tawdry girlie revues, a Romberg-Hammerstein flop, and other standard fare, including the return of Sophie Tucker, Eddie Cantor (who, like Jolson, left his show early because he missed the Los Angeles weather), Carmen Miranda, and Olsen and Johnson.

Jump for Joy, an all-black revue with music by Duke Ellington, was produced while Ellington and his orchestra were playing in Los Angeles. Although it was successful, the money couldn't be raised to move it to New York. The score included "Bli-Blip" (lyrics by Sid Kuller), "I've Got It Bad and That Ain't Good" and "Rocks in My Bed" (lyrics by Paul Francis Webster), "Just Squeeze Me" (lyrics by Lee Gaines and Ellington), and Ellington's theme song, "Take the 'A' Train" (music and lyrics by Billy Strayhorn, a lyricist and composer, who worked closely with Ellington for years).

Best Foot Forward

MUSIC/LYRICS: Hugh Martin and
Ralph Blane

BOOK: John Cecil Holm

DIRECTOR: George Abbott

CHOREOGRAPHER: Gene Kelly

ORCHESTRATORS: Hans Spialek and
Don Walker

DESIGNER: Jo Mielziner (sets and
lights)

PRODUCERS: George Abbott and
Richard Rodgers

CAST INCLUDES: Nancy Walker,
June Allyson, and Stanley
Donen

PERFORMANCES: 326

Best Foot Forward centers around a glamorous Hollywood star who shows up as the junior-prom date of a student at Winsocki High. It has some swing in its score and bears a strong resemblance in structure and pace to Rodgers and Hart's 1939 musical *Too Many Girls,* which had a fictional college named Pottawatomie and was also directed by Abbott. It was Martin and Blane's first and most successful Broadway score; they also wrote the score for the hit 1944 movie musical *Meet Me in St. Louis,* adapted into a stage musical in 1989. There was a 1943 movie of *Best Foot Forward* directed by Edward Buzzell, with a more or less new plot written for Lucille Ball, who played herself. Nancy Walker and June Allyson made their movie debuts in supporting roles. An off-Broadway revival in 1963 (224 performances) introduced Liza Minnelli to New York audiences.

Weill's first Broadway hit, *Lady in the Dark* was the first musical to deal with psychoanalysis as anything other than a joke; Hart's own successful analysis gave him the idea. He called it a musical play. It's still revived occasionally, even though its book is overlong, creaks slightly, and the solution to the heroine's problem is written from what is now a sexist point of view. The heroine, Liza Elliott, a powerful and unmarried fashion magazine executive, goes into analysis; she's having strange dreams that bother her so much that she can no longer make up her mind. "My Ship," a song from her childhood, haunts her throughout the show until she remembers it, thus resolving her psychological problems with her father. She is then free to give up "trying to be like a man" and turn the magazine over to Charley Johnson, with whom she's been fighting through the whole show. Of course she also realizes that he's the man she has loved all along, rather than the older, married father figure she's been sleeping with (Kendall Nesbitt), who now wants to divorce his wife and marry her, or the handsome movie star (Randy Curtis) she's attracted to. In 1941 terms, this means psychoanalysis has cured her (in about a week) and made her a whole woman, ready to take her rightful place in society as a glorified, wealthy housewife. (An easy rewrite makes her and Charley equals at the end.)

The show experimented mightily with the form and structure of the musical and was a key step in the musical being taken more seriously by critics and audiences alike. With the exception of "My Ship," completed only at the end of the show, the music is confined to three of Liza's dreams, told to her analyst. All three—a glamour dream, a wedding dream, and a circus dream—are extended musical sequences that turn at the end into nightmares. The rest of the evening is a long, straight play

Lady in the Dark

MUSIC: Kurt Weill
LYRICS: Ira Gershwin
BOOK: Moss Hart
DIRECTOR: Hassard Short
CHOREOGRAPHER: Albertina Rasch
ORCHESTRATOR: Kurt Weill
DESIGNERS: Harry Horner (sets), Hattie Carnegie and Irene Sharaff (costumes), and Hassard Short (lights)
PRODUCER: Sam H. Harris
CAST INCLUDES: Gertrude Lawrence, with Danny Kaye, Victor Mature, and Macdonald Carey
PERFORMANCES: 467

about Liza, her men, and her magazine; all the major characters in the play appear as characters in the dreams as well. The lavishly produced dream sequences—four revolving stages—are through-composed mini-musicals in different pop styles, with recitatives, choruses, underscored dialogue, songs, and dances. Along with "My Ship" (Liza's "Over the Rainbow" song), the score contains such numbers as "One Life to Live" (her declaration of how she intends to live), "Tschaikowsky" (Kaye's big number, in which he lists the names of fifty Russian composers—some made up—in an amazingly short period of time), and "The Saga of Jenny" (Liza's list song about the problems created by a woman who "would make up her mind"). Ginger Rogers starred in Leisen's 1944 movie, which leaves out almost the entire score. (Paramount paid nearly $300,000 for the rights.) There was a very successful 1998 revival in London, from which the complete score was recorded for the first time.

The show marked Gertrude Lawrence's heavily publicized return to Broadway after ten years at the highest salary ever paid a Broadway star at the time. Her salary plus her percentage of gross box office receipts came to $4,300 a week, and she demanded and got a three-week summer break. (She did only one more show after this, creating the role of Anna in *The King and I*). *Lady in the Dark* was Danny Kaye's first Broadway musical; he created a sensation in a flashy supporting role, playing a flamboyant gay.

Let's Face It

MUSIC/LYRICS: Cole Porter
BOOK: Dorothy and Herbert Fields, adapted from Russell Medcraft and Norma Mitchell's 1927 farce *Cradle Snatchers*
DIRECTOR: Edgar MacGregor
CHOREOGRAPHER: Charles Walters
ORCHESTRATORS: three, including Hans Spialek
DESIGNERS: Harry Horner (sets) and John Harkrider (costumes)
PRODUCER: Vinton Freedley
CAST INCLUDES: Danny Kaye, Eve Arden, Nanette Fabray, and Vivian Vance
PERFORMANCES: 547

Let's Face It was the first collaboration for siblings Herbert and Dorothy Fields (the beginning of a long-term partnership) and Danny Kaye's first starring role right out of *Lady in the Dark*. The show is about three married women who take revenge on their philandering husbands by seeking out three recent army inductees to be their lovers. Many plot complications ensue, including the three husbands' philandering with the girlfriends of the three inductees. The show was slightly timely, since the country was getting close to entering World War II and drafting men into the army. Among Porter's songs were two list songs for Kaye: "Farming," with a verse and five choruses, and "Let's Not Talk About Love," with two verses and three choruses, written to showcase Kaye's ability with tongue-twisting lyrics. This is part of the last chorus (the character has a Southern accent):

Let's write a tune that's playable, a ditty swing-and-swayable

Or say whatever's sayable, about the Tow'r of Ba-abel,

Let's cheer for the career of itty-bitty Betty Gra-able,

But let's not talk about love.

In case you play cards, I've got some right here,

So how about a game o' gin rummy, my dear?

Or if you feel warm and bathin' your whim,

Let's get in the all-together and enjoy a short swim,

No, honey, ah suspect you-all

Of bein' intellectual

And so, instead of gushin' on,

Let's have a big discussion on

Timidity, stupidity, solidity, frigidity,

Avidity, turbidity, Manhattan, and viscidity,

Fatality, morality, legality, finality,

Neutrality, reality, or Southern hospitality,

Pomposity, verbosity,

I'm losing my velocity,

But let's not talk about love.

It's a pseudo–W. S. Gilbert patter song, and the final list is meant to be done in one breath. Like many of Porter's lyrics (and Gilbert's) there are references to celebrities of the time. Kaye's wife, Sylvia Fine, also wrote songs for Kaye in the show, including "Melody in 4-F"; she wrote most of his material throughout his career. (Kaye also did "Melody in 4-F" in his first movie, *Up in Arms*). The 1943 Lanfield movie *Let's Face It,* starring Bob Hope, Betty Hutton, and Eve Arden, changed some of the plot and used only a couple of the show's songs.

On December 7, 1941, Japanese airplanes bombed Pearl Harbor, and the United States entered World War II, joining the Allies against the German-Japanese-Italian axis. Wartime jobs in factories, the military, and other related areas soon brought an end to the Depression, and there was a large-scale migration from rural to urban areas to get war work.

Suggested Watching and Listening

Cabin in the Sky
The 1943 movie of this show, directed by Vincente Minnelli, is available on Warner Brothers Home Video DVD.
- "Taking a Chance on Love" (performed by Ethel Waters, Eddie "Rochester" Anderson, and Archie Savage, with lyrics by Ted Fetter)

From This Moment On: The Songs of Cole Porter
This four-disc CD set is available on the Smithsonian Collection label. The following song is from the show *Let's Face It.*

- "Let's Not Talk About Love" (performed by Danny Kaye)

Lady in the Dark
This 1941 show includes the following number.

- "My Ship" (performed by Dawn Upshaw): This version is on Upshaw's Elektra/Nonesuch CD *I Wish It So.*

Pal Joey
The following songs are from the 1940 show.

- "I Could Write a Book" (performed by Peter Gallagher and Daisy Prince): It's on DRG Records CD, the original-cast recording of the 1995 City Center's Encores! series.
- "Bewitched, Bothered, and Bewildered" (performed by Vivienne Segal): It's on *Original Cast! The Forties: Part 1*, MET CD.

From *This Is the Army* to *Carousel*

This is the army, Mister Jones!—
No private rooms or telephones.
You had your breakfast in bed before,
But you won't have it there anymore.
This is the army, Mister Green!
We like the barracks nice and clean.
You had a housemaid to clean your floor,
But she won't help you out anymore.
—"THIS IS THE ARMY, MR. JONES," *THIS IS THE ARMY,*
LYRICS BY IRVING BERLIN

During the war years, Broadway business boomed, mostly with people—including military personnel—looking for mindless escapism, which is essentially what Broadway gave them. Four shows, however, were of major importance to the development of the form: *Oklahoma!* and *Carousel,* set in America's nostalgic past, which is reflected in their music; and *One Touch of Venus* and *On the Town,* set in up-to-the-minute New York City, which is reflected in their music. (Fantasy, the third most frequent setting, was usually combined with one of the two, as in both *Carousel* and *One Touch of Venus.*) Despite very different sounds and sensibilities, all four shows had well-constructed books with believable characters and situations, and in all four, dance played a vital role in telling story, shaping character, and establishing atmosphere.

In 1942, George M. Cohan and Joseph Weber of Weber and Fields died. Actors' Equity barred Communists and fascists from the union. Broadway's Stage Door Canteen, sponsored by the American Theatre Wing, opened. Both the Hollywood and the Stage Door canteens were open every night throughout the war. Military men and women on leave could get doughnuts and coffee served by volunteering stars, who not only provided entertainment but talked and danced with them as well. The Theatre Wing also sponsored *Lunchtime Follies,* a star-laden series of variety shows that entertained workers in plants like the Brooklyn shipyard during their lunch breaks.

Only about twenty musical evenings opened on Broadway that year. Among them were a 286-performance revival of *Porgy and Bess* (with the original leads), with some of the numbers cut and the recitative replaced with spoken dialogue; a 521-performance revival in English of Strauss's *Die Fledermaus* under the title *Rosalinda,* choreographed by Balanchine; and revivals of other operettas, including *The New Moon.* Vernon Duke, John Latouche, Joe E. Lewis, and Gower Champion were all involved in the musical *The Lady Comes Across.* Despite all that talent, the show turned out so badly it closed after only three performances.

This Is the Army, the first of a slew of shows inspired by the war effort, was Irving Berlin's World War II revue patterned after his 1918 *Yip-Yip-Yaphank.* Produced by the United States with some of its staging by Joshua Logan, it starred Berlin, with Burl Ives among an all-military cast of over 350. It ran 113 performances on Broadway before touring for the rest of the war. All proceeds from the show—estimated at about ten million—went to the Army

Backdrop: 1942–1945

National   By July 1, 1942, the United States is spending $150 million a day on the war effort. The government places 110,000 West Coast Japanese Americans in internment camps in remote areas, causing them to lose about $400 million in property. President Roosevelt is elected to an unprecedented fourth term. Italy surrenders unconditionally in 1943. On June 6, 1944—D-Day—Allied troops invade Normandy, and the war turns in favor of the Allies. Congressman J. William Fulbright drafts a resolution that begins the formation of the United Nations. The GI Bill of Rights, voted by Congress, will finance college educations and 4 percent home loans for millions of U.S. war veterans. There are race riots in Detroit and Harlem. President Roosevelt dies; Vice President Harry S. Truman becomes president. Mussolini is assassinated and Hitler commits suicide. World War II ends in Europe on May 8, 1945. The United States drops atomic bombs on Hiroshima and Nagasaki, and the war in the Pacific ends on August 14, 1945. About 55 million have died, most of them civilians; millions more are left maimed, displaced, and penniless.

Emergency Relief Fund. Among the songs were "I Left My Heart at the Stage Door Canteen," "This Is the Army, Mr. Jones," and Berlin singing "Oh, How I Hate to Get Up in the Morning," as he had in *Yip-Yip-Yaphank*. Curtiz's 1943 movie version added a story about the men in the show and starred Berlin, George Murphy, Kate Smith, and Ronald Reagan.

Star and Garter was a revue directed by Hassard Short, co-choreographed by Albertina Rasch, and produced by Michael Todd, with a score made up largely of previously performed songs by composers such as Berlin, Arlen, and Harold Rome. The show, which starred Gypsy Rose Lee and Bobby Clark, was semi-refined burlesque that appealed mostly to tired business-men and military men on leave; Todd called it a revue because burlesque had been outlawed in New York. It ran 605 performances at a top ticket price of $4.80.

By Jupiter, Rodgers and Hart's last new collaboration and longest-running show, was a farce set among the Amazons in mythological times, with Hippolyta, Hercules, and Theseus among its characters. The show closed earlier than it needed to so Bolger

By Jupiter

MUSIC/LYRICS/BOOK: Richard Rodgers and Lorenz Hart, adapted from Julian F. Thompson's 1932 play *The Warrior's Husband*

DIRECTOR: Joshua Logan

CHOREOGRAPHER: Robert Alton

DESIGNERS: Jo Mielziner (sets and lights) and Irene Sharaff (costumes)

PRODUCERS: Richard Rodgers and Dwight Deere Wiman

CAST INCLUDES: Ray Bolger

PERFORMANCES: 427

International The United States and Soviet Russia occupy Korea until a democracy can be estab-lished. The League of Arab States unites Egypt, Iraq, Jordan, Lebanon, Saudi Arabia, Syria, and Yemen.

New Developments The Pap test for cervical cancer is established. The first, general-purpose, digital computer is completed at Harvard University. Ballpoint pens are marketed. Grand Rapids, Michigan, is the first U.S. city to fluoridate its water. Penicillin and streptomycin are introduced com-mercially.

Art Among the new paintings are works by Braque and Bonnard. Abstract impressionism becomes the leading movement in painting into the 1960s; its painters, known as the New York School, include Pollock, Kline, de Kooning, and Rothko.

Music/Dance Twenty-five-year-old conductor Leonard Bernstein is a last-minute replacement for the ailing Bruno Walter on a Sunday broadcast concert of the New York Philharmonic and becomes an overnight celebrity; within a year he establishes himself as a symphonic and Broadway composer. In 1944, his *Jeremiah Symphony* and his ballet *Fancy Free*, choreographed and danced by Jerome Rob-bins, have their premieres. (*Fancy Free*, about three sailors on twenty-four-hour leave in New York, be-comes the inspiration for *On the Town* the same year.)

could go overseas to entertain the troops. The score included "Wait Till You See Her" (another lovely Rodgers waltz) and the duet "Ev'rything I've Got Belongs to You." The first chorus is sung by Hippolyta to Bolger as her husband; it's a good, comic, up-tempo number for a woman, which is hard to find.

> I have eyes for you to give you dirty looks.
> I have words that do not come from children's books.
> There's a trick with a knife I'm learning to do,
> And ev'rything I've got belongs to you.
> I've a powerful anesthesia in my fist,
> And the perfect wrist to give your neck a twist.
> There are hammerlock holds, I've mastered a few,
> And ev'rything I've got belongs to you.
> Share for share, share alike,
> You get struck each time I strike.
> You for me—me for me—
> I'll give you plenty of nothing.
> I'm not yours for better but for worse,
> And I've learned to give the well-known witches' curse.
> I've a terrible tongue, a temper for two,
> And ev'rything I've got belongs to you.

Publications   *Negro Digest* and *Ebony* magazine begin publication. New books during the war years, many of them philosophical in intent if not in form, include Camus' *The Myth of Sisyphus* and *The Stranger*, and Sartre's *Being and Nothingness;* Rand's *The Fountainhead;* Eliot's *Four Quartets;* Saint-Exupéry's *The Little Prince;* Wright's autobiography, *Black Boy;* Orwell's anticommunist allegory *Animal Farm;* Waugh's *Brideshead Revisited;* White's *Stuart Little;* and Welty's *The Robber Bridegroom* (adapted into a 1976 musical).

Radio/TV   NBC's Blue Network becomes the American Broadcasting Company (ABC). *Meet the Press* debuts on radio. By 1945, there are about five thousand TV sets in American homes.

Pop Culture   "The big bands begin to give way to the star solo vocalists. . . . 3,000 teenagers scream 'We want Frankie' [Sinatra] at New York's Paramount Theatre, with over 20,000 outside, spilling into Times Square. Within minutes the box office is destroyed, shop windows broken, and all pedestrian and vehicular traffic blocked. Inside the theatre girls swoon, scream and wave their undergarments, while outside 421 policemen try in vain to restore order." (Lax and Smith, 78)

Muddy Waters brings his blues sound from rural Mississippi to Chicago. Gospel singer Mahalia Jackson has her first hit record. Dizzy Gillespie breaks off on his own, and he and Charlie "Bird" Parker begin to

Most of the score was written while Hart was in the hospital, with Rodgers and a piano installed in the next room. *By Jupiter* had a successful off-Broadway revival in 1967, with additional material by Fred Ebb.

In 1943, Lorenz Hart, Fats Waller, and director/designer Max Reinhardt died. The Actors' Equity minimum went up to $57.50 on Broadway, and the top ticket price went up to $5.50. Another rather spare theatrical season saw revivals of such operettas as *The Student Prince, Blossom Time,* and *The Merry Widow,* and many flop revues and musical comedies, but there were several good new shows, including, of course, *Oklahoma!*

> Although it became obvious soon after *Oklahoma!* opened that a new era was under way, it took time for the show's effects to be manifest. Broadway could not react as quickly as it once did. Its great creative talents were getting old, many were elsewhere, and huge taxation on success militated against . . . writers creating two or three shows a year as they once had done. (Bordman, 537)

After a long dry spell, Hammerstein followed up *Oklahoma!* with another hit that year called *Carmen Jones* (502 performances), his resetting of Bizet's opera *Carmen* to the United States during World War II (for example, the cigarette factory became a parachute factory and the bullfighter became a

transform swing into bebop. Among the pop songs are Ellington and Russell's "Don't Get Around Much Anymore" and "Do Nothin' Till You Hear from Me," and Ellington, James, Hodges, and George's "I'm Beginning to See the Light"; Lilley and Loesser's "(I've Got Spurs That) Jingle Jangle Jingle"; Loesser's "Spring Will Be a Little Late This Year" and "Praise the Lord and Pass the Ammunition," one of many patriotic songs written throughout the war years by almost every pop composer; McHugh and Adamson's wartime anthem "Comin' In on a Wing and a Prayer"; Styne and Cahn's "I'll Walk Alone," "Saturday Night Is the Loneliest Night of the Week" (about waiting for the men to come back from overseas), "I've Heard That Song Before," and ("Kiss Me Once and Kiss Me Twice and Kiss Me Once Again,") "It's Been a Long, Long Time," a favorite of returning soldiers; and Drake, Hoffman, and Livingston's "Mairzy Doats."

Stage   New plays, many of them concerned with the human condition, include Sartre's *The Flies* and *No Exit;* Brecht's *The Good Person of Setzuan* and *Galileo;* Wilder's *The Skin of Our Teeth;* Lorca's posthumous *The House of Bernarda Alba;* Anouilh's *Antigone;* Giraudoux's *The Madwoman of Chaillot* (adapted in 1969 into the flop musical *Dear World*); Williams's first hit, *The Glass Menagerie;* and Van Druten's *I Remember Mama* (the source in 1979 of Rodgers's last musical).

Screen   Among the filmed adaptations of Broadway musicals are Abbott and Costello in a total redo of *Rio Rita;* a rewrite and modernization of *The Desert Song;* Bob Hope and Victor Moore in *Louisiana* prizefighter). Directed by Hassard Short and Charles Friedman, produced by Billy Rose and orchestrated by Robert Russell Bennett, it had an all-black cast. There was an original-cast recording, and it was filmed by Otto Preminger in 1954 with Dorothy Dandridge (dubbed by opera star Marilyn Horne), Harry Belafonte (dubbed by LeVern Hutcherson), Diahann Carroll (dubbed by Bernice Peterson), and Pearl Bailey.

One Touch of Venus is an intelligent, witty, and well-constructed fantasy. It's about a statue of Venus, the goddess of love, that comes to life when a young man puts his fiancée's engagement ring on its finger.

> [The show] told its tale with an unfailing sense of style and literate wit, never stopping to introduce extraneous bits of froth nor stopping to inject currently voguish elements of stripper burlesque. In keeping with the classic elegance of its heroine, its story was attractively simple. (Bordman, 538)

One Touch of Venus

MUSIC: Kurt Weill

LYRICS: Ogden Nash

BOOK: Ogden Nash and S. J. Perelman, adapted from F. Anstey's story "The Tinted Venus"

DIRECTOR: Elia Kazan

CHOREOGRAPHER: Agnes de Mille

ORCHESTRATOR: Kurt Weill

PRODUCERS: Cheryl Crawford and John Wildberg

CAST INCLUDES: Mary Martin and Kenny Baker

PERFORMANCES: 567

Purchase; Hope and Betty Hutton in *Let's Face It;* Ronald Reagan and George Murphy in a story-driven version of the revue *This Is the Army;* Mickey Rooney and Judy Garland in a reworking of *Girl Crazy;* Jeanette MacDonald and Nelson Eddy in their last movie together, *I Married an Angel,* a flop (movie operettas were out of fashion by now); Eddy in *Knickerbocker Holiday,* with only three songs left from the score; Ginger Rogers in *Lady in the Dark,* with almost none of the score left; Ann Sothern and Red Skelton in *Panama Hattie;* Gene Kelly, Lucille Ball, and Skelton in a reinvention of *DuBarry Was a Lady;* Ball in *Best Foot Forward; Higher and Higher* and *Something for the Boys,* both with entirely new scores by McHugh and Adamson; Minnelli's *Cabin in the Sky;* and *Earl Carroll's Vanities* and *George White's Scandals of 1945,* both B movies.

Movie musicals have become the most popular movie genre. Among the over 250 new ones are Cagney as Cohan in *Yankee Doodle Dandy;* Ann Sheridan as Nora Bayes in *Shine On, Harvest Moon,* a very fictionalized biography of the early *Ziegfeld Follies* star; Bing Crosby as Daniel Decatur Emmett in *Dixie,* a pseudo-biography of the nineteenth-century minstrel show producer; Robert Alda as George Gershwin in *Rhapsody in Blue;* Bill "Bojangles" Robinson, Lena Horne, and an all-star African American cast in *Stormy Weather;* Judy Garland and Gene Kelly (his first movie) in Berkeley's *For Me and My Gal,* about pre–World War I vaudeville; Bing Crosby and Fred Astaire as vaudeville performers in *Holiday Inn,* with a Berlin score of old and new songs, including "White Christmas," which wins the Academy Award for best song; Astaire and Rita Hayworth in *You Were Never Lovelier,* with a Kern and Mercer score featuring "I'm Old Fashioned" and "Dearly Beloved"; Hayworth and Kelly (dancing with his alter ego—his first innovative dance sequence for film, co-choreographed by Stanley Donen) in

Weill's second hit in a row, it was Mary Martin's first starring role on Broadway. (After being discovered in Porter's 1938 *Leave It to Me* singing "My Heart Belongs to Daddy," she went to Hollywood for a while but didn't like it much and returned to the stage. She had been in two shows that closed out of town and had turned down Laurey in *Oklahoma!* before taking on the role of Venus.)

Agnes de Mille's work on *Oklahoma!* got her hired for this show. It has two big ballets: "Forty Minutes to Lunch," which reveals much about the character of the newly revived Venus by showing her enjoying the world, the fashions, and the men of 1943 during lunch hour in midtown Manhattan; and "Venus in Ozone Heights," her dream of life in suburban Ozone Heights. (The dream ballet was becoming a tradition in musicals.) At the end of the number, Venus decides to return to being a statue rather than become a suburban housewife. Also in the score were the ballad "West Wind"; "The Trouble with Women," a comic barbershop number for four men who realize by the end that "the trouble with women is men"; "I'm a Stranger Here Myself," Venus's first number; and "That's Him," a charm song that Martin sang directly to the audience while sitting on a chair she'd pulled downstage. The hit tune of the show is "Speak Low," a fifty-six-bar AABA' song—the B is only eight bars—with a South American rhythm, an insinuating melody, and very wise lyrics:

Cover Girl, with songs by Kern and Ira Gershwin, including "Long Ago and Far Away"; Hayworth in *Tonight and Every Night,* with a score by Styne and Cahn; Styne and Cahn's score for *Anchors Aweigh,* with Kelly dancing with Jerry the animated mouse from the *Tom and Jerry* cartoons and Frank Sinatra as his fellow sailor crooning "I Fall in Love Too Easily"; Deanna Durbin in *Can't Help Singing,* with a score by Kern and Harburg; Dick Powell, Mary Martin, and Betty Hutton in *Happy Go Lucky,* with a score by McHugh and Loesser; Crosby and Hutton in *Here Come the Waves,* with an Arlen and Mercer score that introduces "Ac-cent-tchu-ate the Positive"; Hutton, Victor Moore, and every star on the Paramount lot in *Star Spangled Rhythm,* a movie about entertaining the troops, also scored by Arlen and Mercer, with the hit tunes "That Old Black Magic" and "Hit the Road to Dreamland"; Astaire as a pilot on leave in *The Sky's the Limit,* with an Arlen and Mercer score that has "My Shining Hour" and "One for My Baby"; Danny Kaye (his movie debut as a reluctant army draftee) and Dinah Shore in *Up in Arms,* with Kaye's songs by Fine and Liebman and Shore's by Arlen and Koehler; *Something to Shout About,* with "You'd Be So Nice to Come Home To" in its Porter score; and the patriotic Warner Brothers all-star *Thank Your Lucky Stars,* which has a score by Schwartz and Loesser and features Bette Davis singing "They're Either Too Young or Too Old," about the only men left at home during the war.

The most important movie musical of 1944 is Judy Garland in Vincente Minnelli's *Meet Me in St. Louis* (they later married), songs by Hugh Martin and Ralph Blane. It's the start of what came to be known as the MGM musical, many of them produced by lyricist Arthur Freed. While still writing songs for movies with Nacio Herb Brown, Freed worked on *The Wizard of Oz* as assistant producer. His first producing job was the Rooney-Garland-Berkeley *Babes in Arms.* His collaboration with Minnelli on *Meet Me in St. Louis*

A: Speak low when you speak, love,
   Our summer day
   Withers away
   Too soon, too soon.
   Speak low when you speak, love;
   Our moment is swift,
   Like ships adrift,
   We're swept apart too soon.

A: Speak low, darling, speak low,
   Love is a spark,
   Lost in the dark,
   Too soon, too soon.
   I feel, wherever I go,
   That tomorrow is near,
   Tomorrow is here
   And always too soon.

B: Time is so old, and love so brief,
   Love is pure gold, and time a thief.

A': We're late, darling, we're late,
   The curtain descends,
   Everything ends,
   Too soon, too soon.
   I wait, darling, I wait—
   Will you speak low to me,
   Speak love to me,
   And soon?

was a huge hit, leading MGM into its string of lavishly made musicals, many set in show business or in idealized mid-America, all of them vehicles for their stars. Like *Oklahoma!, Meet Me in St. Louis* deals with nostalgic Americana (St. Louis during the year of its 1903 World's Fair) and family values—favorite subjects of MGM studio head Louis B. Mayer. The original score includes two interpolated period songs (the title song and "Under the Bamboo Tree"), as well as "The Trolley Song," and "Have Yourself a Merry Little Christmas." Garland's first solo in the movie proved once and for all to movie audiences that she'd matured from longing for what's over the rainbow to longing for "The Boy Next Door." The show was adapted into a Broadway musical in 1989, with added songs by Martin and Blane from various sources. Walter Lang's *State Fair* (1945) has the only original Rodgers and Hammerstein

It's unfortunate that Ogden Nash (best known for his nonsense verse) didn't write more lyrics. There's a partial original-cast recording of *One Touch of Venus,* and it was filmed in 1948, leaving out most of Weill's score.

There was a revival of Rodgers, Hart, and Herbert Fields's 1927 *A Connecticut Yankee* (135 performances). Yet another fantasy, it had a few new songs, including "Can't You Do a Friend a Favor?" and "To Keep My Love Alive," Hart's last lyrics, a very funny list song with a verse, two choruses, and two encore choruses sung by the villainess, Morgan Le Fay, detailing her many marriages:

> I married many men,
> A ton of them,
> And yet I was untrue to none of them
> Because I bumped off ev'ry one of them
> To keep my love alive.

She then goes on to detail fifteen men, their bad habits, and how she killed each of them. Hart died five days after the opening.

Something for the Boys (422 performances) had a Cole Porter score (with no hits), a book by Dorothy and Herbert Fields (he also codirected with Hassard Short), was produced by Michael Todd, and starred Ethel Merman. To audiences during World War II, "for the boys" meant for men in military service. Merman played a girl living near an army base who can receive radio messages through the fillings in her teeth; she manages to save an airplane in danger of crashing.

Winged Victory (212 performances) was a semi-revue produced by the U.S. Army Air Forces with a score and orchestrations by David Rose, written and directed by Moss Hart, with a cast of 350 members of the Air Force, in-

film score. It stars Jeanne Crain, Dana Andrews, Dick Haymes, Vivian Blaine, and Charles Winninger (the original Captain Andy in *Show Boat*). From the novel by Phil Stong, it's about two love affairs (one ends happily, one bittersweetly), a pig contest, and a cooking contest set among farm folk attending the Iowa State Fair. Will Rogers starred in an earlier nonmusical movie version. The score includes "All I Owe Ioway," "It's a Grand Night for Singing," "That's for Me," and "It Might as Well Be Spring." (The last three became pop hits.) A 1962 remake starred Pat Boone, Bobby Darin, Ann-Margret, Tom Ewell, and Alice Faye attending the fair in Texas instead of Iowa. For the remake, Rodgers wrote lyrics as well as music for five new songs and, naturally, dropped "All I Owe Ioway." *State Fair* was made into a 1996 stage musical with the show back in Iowa.

Alan Jay Lerner (1918–86, born in New York) and **Frederick Loewe** (1904–88, born in Berlin) began their collaboration in 1942. Book writer/lyricist Lerner, born to wealthy parents and educated both in the United States and abroad, was just starting out in show business. Loewe, whose father created the role of the hero in *The Merry Widow*, arrived in this country at the age of twenty. Before composing, he was a busboy, a riding instructor, a boxer, a cowboy, and a beer-garden, shipboard, and rehearsal pianist. His first Broadway song was interpolated into a 1935 play, but he didn't achieve success until his teaming with Lerner, which produced such shows as *Brigadoon*, *My Fair Lady*, and *Camelot*.

On the Town

MUSIC: Leonard Bernstein

LYRICS/BOOK: Betty Comden and Adolph Green, from an idea by Jerome Robbins

DIRECTOR: George Abbott

CHOREOGRAPHER: Jerome Robbins

ORCHESTRATORS: Leonard Bernstein, Hershy Kay, Don Walker, Ted Royal, and Elliot Jacoby

DESIGNERS: Oliver Smith (sets), Alvin Colt (costumes), and Peggy Clark (lights)

PRODUCERS: Oliver Smith and Paul Feigay

CAST INCLUDES: Betty Comden, Adolph Green, and Nancy Walker

PERFORMANCES: 462

cluding Peter Lind Hayes, Karl Malden, Lee J. Cobb, Kevin McCarthy, Red Buttons, Ray Middleton, Barry Nelson, Edmond O'Brien, and George Reeves, all of whom had acting careers after the war, though only Middleton became a musical theater performer. The show follows three men through basic training and into combat. Like *This Is the Army*, it toured after its run on Broadway, raising money for the war effort. Cukor's 1944 movie version added more story.

The Shuberts' *Ziegfeld Follies of 1943* had music by Ray Henderson, Harold Rome, Vernon Duke, and others, and lyrics by Duke, Jack Yellen, Howard Dietz, and others. It had three directors, including John Murray Anderson; was choreographed by Robert Alton; starred Milton Berle; and ran 553 performances, the longest run of any *Follies*.

What's Up? (63 performances), Frederick Loewe and Alan Jay Lerner's first musical, was codirected and choreographed by Balanchine. About a sultan's plane crashing into an American girls' school and the amorous complications that ensue, it had a dream ballet and no particularly memorable songs. It was Balanchine's last try at directing.

By 1944, it cost a minimum of $100,000 to produce a musical on Broadway. Along with the mostly unsuccessful revivals of operettas, a few noteworthy new musicals were introduced.

On the Town was the first time working on Broadway for Bernstein, Robbins, Comden, and Green, an impressive group to make their debuts in one show. They all learned a lot from Abbott. Contemporary in place and time, *On the Town*, with a jazz- and swing-based score, was an expansion and reworking of the ballet *Fancy Free*, which Bernstein and Robbins had created earlier in the year. The show had a great deal of music, much of it danced, and was a major step on the way to Bernstein, Robbins, Sondheim, and Laurents's milestone 1957 dance-musical drama *West Side Story*.

Bernstein's use of dissonance and other techniques of contemporary music introduced a new sound to the musical. His many orchestral passages within songs and unconventional song structure perfectly complemented Comden and Green's vision of New York. (Bloom, *American Song*, 542)

On the Town tells the story of three sailors on a twenty-four-hour leave in New York during World War II and the three women they have romantic encounters with. Gabey, the central character, falls in love with the picture he sees on a subway train poster of the Miss Turnstiles of the month, Ivy Smith. He decides to find her from the poster's description of her work and interests. He and his friends Chip and Ozzie separate to widen the search. Chip meets taxi driver Brunhilde (Hildy) Esterhazy, who falls hard for him. Ozzie (played by Green) meets semi-nymphomaniac Claire de Loone (played by Comden) at the Museum of Natural History; they fall for each other despite Claire's being engaged. The two couples join the search for Ivy, who's found just in time, dancing at Coney Island. At dawn, the three couples bid each other farewell, the men return to their ship to go off to the war, and the next batch of sailors start their twenty-four-hour leave.

Although it wasn't the first show to use swing, *On the Town* showed clearly that the newest pop music could be translated into musical theater terms if the setting was sufficiently contemporary and "hep"—and if the show had a lot of dancing. The several ballets, such as "Times Square Dance," "Imaginary Coney Island Ballet," and "The Real Coney Island," helped create atmosphere, develop character, and tell story. Robbins's choreography—true of all his work—was based on the naturalistic movement proper to each character, time, and place. Among the show's songs are "New York, New York," "Come Up to My Place," "Lonely Town," "I Can Cook Too," "Lucky to Be Me," and "Some Other Time."

On the Town was filmed by MGM in 1949, using only part of Bernstein's score; new songs were written by Roger Edens with lyrics by Comden and Green. The movie starred Gene Kelly, Frank Sinatra, Ann Miller, Betty Garrett, Vera-Ellen, and Jules Munshin. There was an unsuccessful 1971 Broadway revival, and a 1997 revival that was semi-successful for a limited run in New York's Central Park but flopped quickly when it was brought to Broadway. Perhaps the show was too specific to its wartime setting to be an enduring classic, though the score still sounds quite wonderful.

Bloomer Girl, a musical about Civil War–period attitudes toward women's rights and toward blacks, had a strong, nostalgic book

Leonard Bernstein (1918–90, born in Lawrence, Massachusetts) returned to his career as a classical composer and conductor after *On the Town*, and made only a few (but important) subsequent forays into the musical to create scores for *Wonderful Town*, *West Side Story*, and *Candide*.

Jerome Robbins (1918–98, born Jerome Rabinowitz in New York) had been a dancer on Broadway and with the American Ballet Theatre before choreographing Bernstein's ballet *Fancy Free*. One of the twentieth century's most influential musical and ballet director/choreographers, he believed that dance is about relationships. Like de Mille and Balanchine before him, his Broadway choreography mixed ballet and popular dance styles. He choreographed fifteen Broadway musicals, and eventually directed them as well, including *High Button Shoes*, *Call Me Madam*, *The King and I*, *The Pajama Game*, *Peter Pan* (the first one he also directed), *West Side Story*, *Gypsy*, and *Fiddler on the Roof*, before returning almost exclusively to the world of the ballet. As a choreographer, he rarely seemed to repeat himself.

Betty Comden (1915–2006, born in Brooklyn) and **Adolph Green** (1915–2002, born in the Bronx) had been part of a nightclub act, the Revuers, which also included Judy Holliday. The team was still occasionally writing and performing into the twenty-first century. Among their works for the stage are *Wonderful Town, Bells Are Ringing, Hallelujah, Baby!, Applause, On the Twentieth Century,* and *The Will Rogers Follies.* Their screenplays include *Good News, Singin' in the Rain, The Band Wagon,* and *It's Always Fair Weather.* Most of their scripts are about big-city life and/or show business.

Bloomer Girl

MUSIC: Harold Arlen

LYRICS: E. Y. Harburg

BOOK: Fred Saidy and Sig Herzig, adapted from Dan James's play *Lilith*

DIRECTORS: E. Y. Harburg and William Schorr

CHOREOGRAPHER: Agnes de Mille

ORCHESTRATOR: Robert Russell Bennett

CAST INCLUDES: Celeste Holm, Dooley Wilson, and David Brooks

PERFORMANCES: 657

and a wonderful Arlen score. The central character, Evelina, is a Northern abolitionist who helps slaves escaping from the South. She's in love with a Southerner whom she eventually converts to her point of view about slavery. Evelina also supports both women's rights and her aunt Dolly Bloomer's campaign for women to replace hoopskirts with the more comfortable undergarment that came to be known as bloomers. The show might be worth considering for revival. As Ken Bloom has observed in *American Song, Bloomer Girl* is "certainly one of the most important yet strangely neglected shows in musical theatre history. Those who argue that musicals are nothing but fluff do not know *Bloomer Girl,* with its powerful statements about human rights presented in a most entertaining way" (Bloom, 75).

The score includes "Evelina," "Civil War Ballet" (a dramatic depiction of the women left at home while their men go off to war), "Right as the Rain," and "The Eagle and Me" (sung by a runaway slave). There's an original-cast recording.

Also during this year, *Mexican Hayride* (479 performances) debuted with a score by Cole Porter and a book by Dorothy and Herbert Fields (their third collaboration). It was directed by Hassard Short, produced by Michael Todd, orchestrated by Robert Russell Bennett, and starred Bobby Clark and June Havoc. Set in Mexico, the show is about an American bullfighter and her crooked cousin, who's hiding out from American justice. Like Porter's three previous shows, it was a hit, but also like those three, it seemed to hint that his riding accident had diminished his creative powers. Clark, the lascivious, knockabout comic, was popular enough for the show to run longer than it deserved, aided by Todd's production, which was suited for an old-fashioned extravaganza. *Mexican Hayride* was made into a 1948 Abbott and Costello movie without any of Porter's score, which included "I Love You," a beguine that became a pop hit.

Seven Lively Arts was a revue produced by Billy Rose (who took over and reopened the Urban-designed Ziegfeld Theatre for it). Despite a Cole Porter score, a ballet by Igor Stravinsky, great writers (Moss Hart, George S. Kaufman, and Ben Hecht, among others), a great cast (including Bert Lahr, Beatrice Lillie, ballet star Alicia Markova, Helen Gallagher, Dolores Gray, and Benny Goodman), Hassard Short among the directors, musical direction by Maurice Abravanel, choral direction by Robert

Shaw, and designs by Salvador Dalí, the show was a 183-performance flop, a sure sign of the fading of the Broadway revue form. In the score is the song "Ev'ry Time We Say Goodbye."

Tars and Spars was the Coast Guard's touring show. It had songs by Vernon Duke and Howard Dietz, was produced and directed by Max Liebman, was choreographed by Gower Champion and Ted Gary, and had Sid Caesar, Victor Mature, and Champion in the cast.

Song of Norway (860 performances) had music and lyrics by Robert Wright and George Forrest, based on the works of classical composer Edvard Grieg, with book by Milton Lazarus. A by-the-numbers throwback to European-style operettas of the twenties, it's a fictionalized biography about Norwegian composer Grieg, using operetta versions of his classical music—exactly what had been done to Franz Schubert in the 1921 *Blossom Time.* (Wright and Forrest spent much of their career adapting the music of classical composers into American operetta scores.) A new wave of operetta revivals, a lavish production, and wonderful George Balanchine choreography must have hit some responsive chord, since that's the only likely explanation for the success of *Song of Norway,* which was made into a really bad 1970 wide-screen movie.

In 1945, Jerome Kern died. The top ticket price went up to $6. Equity minimums rose to $60 a week for actors and $50 a week for chorus members. There were several operettas, old and new, including a revival of Victor Herbert's 1906 *The Red Mill* (531 performances). Although business was the best it had been since the twenties, besides *Carousel,* 1945 was a very lean year in the development of the musical.

Up in Central Park (504 performances) was Sigmund Romberg's first big hit since *The New Moon* in 1928, and his last successful show. Since it was a nostalgia piece set in nineteenth-century New York, his operetta-like romantic songs, the Currier and Ives ice-skating ballet, and the vaudeville-style comic numbers suited the period of the show. Dorothy Fields, who wrote the lyrics and cowrote the book with her brother Herbert, again displayed her ability to write differently for each show and each style. In the score is the hit ballad "Close as Pages in a Book." There was an original-cast recording and a 1948 Deanna Durbin movie.

The Firebrand of Florence (43 performances), music by Kurt Weill, lyrics by Ira Gershwin, book by Gershwin, Edwin Justus Mayer, and John Haggott from Mayer's 1924 play *The Firebrand,* starred Weill's wife, Lotte Lenya, and Earl Wrightson. A major flop set in Renaissance Italy, it centers around the exploits of real-life goldsmith, sculptor, and adventurer Benvenuto Cellini.

Composer Frederick Loewe and lyricist/book writer Alan Jay Lerner's *The Day Before Spring* (165 performances) was their second show together and their second flop. Going against the norm like its predecessor *What's Up?*, it's set in contemporary America, isn't a fantasy, and has a romantic rather than jazz or swing score. (Their next show, *Brigadoon* in 1947, a fantasy with a sweeping romantic score, was a hit.) *The Day Before Spring* is about people returning to their college campus for a tenth-year reunion, with predictable amorous results. Although the score has much to recommend it, the book is heavy-handed and periodically tedious. (Generally speaking, Lerner was a much more successful lyricist than book writer. His most successful book, *My Fair Lady,* is remarkably faithful to Shaw's play *Pygmalion,* from which it was adapted.)

Carousel

MUSIC: Richard Rodgers

LYRICS/BOOK: Oscar Hammerstein, based on the 1909 play *Liliom,* by Ferenc Molnár

DIRECTOR: Rouben Mamoulian

CHOREOGRAPHER: Agnes de Mille

ORCHESTRATOR: Don Walker

DESIGNERS: Jo Mielziner (sets and lights) and Miles White (costumes)

PRODUCER: The Theatre Guild

CAST INCLUDES: John Raitt and Jan Clayton

PERFORMANCES: 890

Carousel (Rodgers and Hammerstein's second hit in a row), like *Oklahoma!,* is a slice of Americana, this time set on the coast of Maine in the late nineteenth century. (*Liliom* is set in early twentieth-century Budapest.) Stephen Sondheim, explaining the importance of *Carousel* over *Oklahoma!* said that, while *Oklahoma!* is about whether Laurey will go to the box social with Curly or Jud, *Carousel* is about life and death.

> *Carousel* was the last hit musical to open during the war. From the discordant opening chords of its prologue to its moving (if sentimental) ending, Rodgers and Hammerstein managed to do the impossible—they followed an enormous hit show with one that was in many ways better than the first. And while the darkness of *Carousel* limited its run to a mere two years (and nearly another two on the road), to many—including the composer—it was their finest work. . . . Hammerstein could only write its libretto after he found a way to inject hope into the ending, but the play remains the story of two very sad people whose daughter inherits their problems. The bleakness of the show is what kept some critics (and audience members) from embracing it the way they did *Oklahoma!* It is also the factor that makes *Carousel* a far more original and important work. (Gruber, *Original Cast! The Forties: Part 1,* 83–84)

The show, a naturalistic romance, becomes a fantasy in the middle of the second act, which takes place in heaven. Billy Bigelow, the central male character, is a barker for a carnival carousel; he's also a vain blowhard, a drinker, a drifter, and a womanizer who occasionally hits his wife. When caught in a robbery attempt, he kills himself—a first in a musical—rather than face the loss of his freedom. He's sent back to earth for one day as a kind of ghost to help his troubled young daughter, who was born after he died. Despite his many character flaws, Billy is written so that his behavior is understandable and ultimately forgivable. Julie Jordan, the central female character, is strong, loving, and unintentionally, slightly masochistic.

> *Carousel's* story of ill-fated love is an interesting variation on *Show Boat* of a generation earlier. Billy Bigelow, like *Show Boat's* Gaylord Ravenal, is a fatally flawed weakling despite his romantic masculinity. Julie Jordan, like Magnolia, is an innocent youngster who falls in love in almost willful defiance of common sense. (After all, carousel barkers and riverboat gamblers are not exactly models of stability.) Both Julie and Magnolia are steadfast in their love, which is based in part on their protective feelings toward their vulnerable, troubled men. Written by a more mature Hammerstein for a more mature audience, *Carousel*—though still sentimentally optimistic—offers a more realistic depiction of such a relationship. *Show Boat* on stage even contrives a happy ending for Ravenal and Magnolia, but *Carousel* seems to admit that despite Billy and Julie's love, their relationship is untenable; only after Billy's death is a reconciliation possible, and then only on a spiritual plane. (Albert Williams, personal communication)

Instead of starting with the usual overture, the show opens with a ballet/mime set to "The Carousel Waltz." During this prologue, Billy Bigelow and Julie Jordan first meet and feel a mutual attraction, while the owner of the carousel and Billy's boss and mistress, Mrs. Mullin, watches jealously. The scene following the prologue is over half an hour long, constructed from dialogue, recitative, underscoring, and songs. It begins with a dialogue sequence during which Billy gets fired because of his attentions to Julie, and she agrees to meet him later. (It's love at first sight, though they don't know it yet.)

Carrie Pipperidge, Julie's best friend, sings "You're a Queer One, Julie Jordan," leading into her "When I Marry Mr. Snow," which sets up the comic secondary love story between Carrie and Mr. Snow, a straitlaced fisherman who smells of his calling. Billy returns. Carrie leaves for the mill where she and Julie work and live; if they don't return before curfew, they'll be fired. As Billy and Julie begin to talk, Julie's boss comes by and fires her for refusing to return to the mill in time. Then Billy and Julie begin the extended bench scene (they're sitting on one) during which they fall in love—a twelve-minute, through-composed sequence with underscored dialogue and recitative, a brief recall of "You're a Queer One, Julie Jordan" with different lyrics that lead into Julie's version of "If I Loved You," more underscored dialogue and recitative, Billy's version of "If I Loved You," a little more underscored dialogue, and a final kiss.

In the next scene, Julie and Billy are married. Billy remains a drifter, unemployed and unfaithful. The first act ends with the semi-operatic "Soliloquy," which has eight different melodies during its nearly eight-minute running time. Billy, having turned down an offer to join in on a robbery, learns that Julie is pregnant. During "Soliloquy" he dreams about the child, realizes he can't support it, and decides to participate in the robbery as a way of getting some money.

In act 2, Billy is caught during the robbery attempt, stabs himself, and dies in Julie's arms. To comfort her, Julie's cousin Nettie Fowler sings "You'll Never Walk Alone." (Hammerstein truly believed what the song says.) After fifteen years in purgatory, Billy is allowed one day on earth in order to achieve redemption. The problems of his and Julie's daughter, Louise, who has grown up poor and with the stigma of a father who was a thief and a suicide, are told through a second-act story ballet that Billy witnesses. Before the day is over, Billy is able to bring some peace to both Julie and Louise. Paul Gruber, in the *Original Cast!* series, commented:

> Though optimistic, its themes are complicated—the ability of humans to break the cycle of failure (and the cycle of abuse), and the harm that comes when people refuse to acknowledge their feelings for each other. To this, Agnes de Mille added another timely theme in her extraordinary dances. . . . De Mille's second-act ballet . . . tells us far more about Billy's daughter than Molnar did, making us care more about her at the end. (Gruber, *Original Cast! The Forties: Part 1*, 86)

Also in the score is "What's the Use of Wond'rin'," in which Julie says more or less the same thing that *Show Boat*'s Magnolia says in "Can't Help Lovin' Dat Man." There's an original-cast recording.

The 1956 movie version, directed by Henry King and choreographed by Rod Alexander, using de Mille's choreography for the second-act ballet, starred Gordon MacRae and Shirley Jones, who'd costarred in the movie version of *Oklahoma!* The movie considerably softens Billy's character.

London's National Theatre produced a revival in 1992 that played Broadway in 1994. Directed by noted stage and film director Nicholas Hytner and choreographed by ballet choreographer Kenneth MacMillan, it ran 337 performances before going on an extended tour. All the leads were young, sexually aware, and knew how to act; the cast was multiracial, the sets expressed more than they literally showed, and suddenly Rodgers and Hammerstein had been brought into the 1990s.

Just as *Oklahoma!* made Broadway's creators and critics sit up and take notice, *Carousel* proved once and for all that the form Rodgers and Hammerstein called the musical play—the form that made everything else dependent on the needs of the book—was the form that worked best. Not only that, but *Carousel* also showed that musicals didn't have to be comedies to succeed, an important thing to know given a noticeable change in the theater-going public. The scars of war were still fresh in the minds of returning veterans and their families, and the public's new awareness of such realities as the horror of the Holocaust, the possibility of atomic warfare, and the threat of communism led to an escalating sense of paranoia in the country. The world seemed to be a more serious and dangerous place than ever before, and the United States was directly in the middle of it all. It was *Carousel* that taught the creators of musicals that they needed to craft more dramatic situations and to dig more deeply into character in order to attract the more sober audiences of post–World War II America.

The golden age of the Broadway song had passed, but during the next twenty years there were many hit songs written for musicals and, more important, there were more durable and revivable shows produced than at any other time in the history of the form. The needs of the book and the integrity of the characters now regularly determined the placement and content of songs and comedy. Dance—largely because of Balanchine, de Mille, and Robbins—became an equal partner in the mix. The best shows, whether they traded in nostalgia or fantasy, or were absolutely up-to-the-minute, dealt with emotions as well as plot complications, and the characters had problems audiences could identify with. Some shows even had ideas and something genuine to say about the human condition. The golden age of the American musical had arrived.

Suggested Watching and Listening

Carousel
All the following recommendations for this 1945 show are from the 1956 movie, available in a two-disc set from 20th Century Fox DVD. The film version is directed by Henry King and stars Shirley Jones and Gordon MacRae.
- "Carousel Waltz," "Mister Snow," "If I Loved You (The Bench Scene)" (performed by Shirley Jones, Barbara Ruick, Audrey Christie, Gordon MacRae, John Dehner, and Richard Deacon): The "Carousel Waltz" sequence is considerably shortened and leaves out the choreography. There are also cuts in the scene that follows, including all of "You're a Queer One, Julie Jordan." The movie softens and sentimentalizes the entire show.
- "Soliloquy" (performed by Gordon MacRae)

- "You'll Never Walk Alone" (performed by Shirley Jones and Claramae Turner)
- "Louise's Ballet" (performed by Susan Luckey and Jacques D'Amboise): This is the only sequence in the film that uses de Mille's original choreography.

A Connecticut Yankee
Rodgers and Hart revived their 1927 musical *A Connecticut Yankee* in 1943.
- "To Keep My Love Alive" (performed by Vivienne Segal): Written for the revival, it's Hart's last lyrics. It's available on *Original Cast! The Forties: Part 1* (MET CD).

Musicals Great Musicals: The Arthur Freed Unit at MGM
It's a 1996 documentary directed by David Thompson and produced by PBS and the BBC that documents Arthur Freed's contributions to Hollywood musicals. It's available on Warner Brothers Home Video DVD as part of the two-disc edition of *Singin' in the Rain*.

One Touch of Venus
The following two songs are from Kurt Weill's show *One Touch of Venus*.
- "I'm a Stranger Here Myself" (performed by Ute Lemper): It's Venus's introductory song, very clearly setting up her amorous character and her confusion about contemporary men. It's available on the Decca CD *Ute Lemper Sings Kurt Weill*.
- "Speak Low" (performed by Lotte Lenya): Lenya's recording on the CBS Records Masterworks import CD *Lotte Lenya Sings Kurt Weill, Berlin, and American Theater Songs* was made in 1955, five years after Weill's death and after she'd starred in the successful off-Broadway revival of his show *The Threepenny Opera*. Her albums played a major part in establishing Weill's posthumous reputation in America.

On the Town
A 1993 concert version of the show with narration written and performed by Betty Comden and Adolph Green was videotaped in London and released as a laser disc by Deutsche Grammophon. The conductor and music director was Michael Tilson Thomas, accompanied by the London Voices and the London Symphony Orchestra. It was directed for the stage by Patricia Birch and for television by Christopher Swann.
- "I Feel Like I'm Not Out of Bed Yet" (performed by Samuel Ramey): The show opens with a reverse spin on *Oklahoma!*'s "Oh, What a Beautiful Mornin'," with a workman alone onstage in front of the Brooklyn Navy Yard complaining about having to be awake and on his way to work so early in the morning.
- "New York, New York" (performed by Thomas Hampson, Kurt Ollmann, and David Garrison): The three sailors, Gabey, Chip, and Ozzie, start their leave.
- "Come Up to My Place" (performed by Tyne Daly and Kurt Ollmann): Taxi driver Hildy and Chip meet.
- "Lonely Town" (performed by Thomas Hampson): Gabey, getting discouraged in his search for Miss Turnstiles, sings this ballad.
- "I Can Cook Too" (performed by Tyne Daly with additional lyrics by Bernstein): Hildy courts Chip with this swing tune.
- "Some Other Time" (performed by Tyne Daly, Kurt Ollmann, Frederica von Stade, and David Garrison): Chip and Hildy, Ozzie and Claire, the night coming to an end, start their good-byes with this beautiful quartet.

Red, Hot + Blue

These are videos of Porter songs (on Shout! Factory DVD) made in the 1990s as a fundraiser for AIDS. "Ev'ry Time We Say Goodbye," from the revue *Seven Lively Arts,* is a video of Annie Lennox that includes old home movies of Lennox and her brother, who died of AIDS.

- "Ev'ry Time We Say Goodbye" (performed by Annie Lennox): It's an ABA′B′ song, and the change from major to minor happens in the music at the same time that it happens in the lyrics.

PART FIVE

The Golden Age of the Broadway Musical, 1946–1964

Overleaf: (*top left*) The rumble in *West Side Story* (1957); (*bottom left*) Eliza Doolittle (Julie Andrews) and Henry Higgins (Rex Harrison) at the ball in *My Fair Lady* (1956); (*right*) The wedding dance from *Fiddler on the Roof* (1964)

From *Annie Get Your Gun* to *Brigadoon*

A change has come over us!
The whispered jokes,
The cracks that seemed funny
A few moments ago,
Aren't funny anymore.
This is no time for the humorous skeptic
Or the gloomy prophet.
This is a time for hope.
—"DEARLY BELOVED," *ALLEGRO*,
LYRICS BY OSCAR HAMMERSTEIN II

The last four years of the 1940s in the United States were both a time of recovery from the aftermath of World War II and the beginning of its involvement in the Cold War. The country's economy, sense of itself as a dominant world power, and paranoia were all growing.

By 1946, the overwhelming effect of Rodgers and Hammerstein's musical plays was apparent. Big revues, operettas, vaudeville, and burlesque were either dead or dying—although the operetta kept being erratically resuscitated—but the musical, after a rough patch in the thirties and early forties, was revitalized. Most of the important shows during the war years had been retreats from the present in one way or another. With the success of such innovative shows as *Oklahoma!*, *Carousel*, and *Bloomer Girl* (nostalgic Americana); *Lady in the Dark* and *One Touch of Venus* (dreams and fantasies set in the present); and *Pal Joey* and *On the Town* (contemporary urban America), in essence the Broadway musical had already entered its golden age, which is in part called that because so many of its shows have endured. During the last four years of the forties alone, seven shows opened that have more or less entered the permanent repertory: two fantasies—*Brigadoon* and *Finian's Rainbow; Kiss Me, Kate,* set in the present and in Elizabethan England; *Annie Get Your Gun,* set in nineteenth-century America; *Where's Charley?* set at the turn of the twentieth century; *Gentlemen Prefer Blondes,* set in the Roaring Twenties; and most successful of all—and the only one not a comedy—*South Pacific,* set on an exotic South Pacific island during World War II, with a romantic main plot and tragic subplot.

In 1946, Comedian W. C. Fields and composer Vincent Youmans died. *Oklahoma!* became the longest-running musical, beating *Hellzapoppin'.* About twenty-five musicals and revues opened, among which were a lavish 418-performance revival of *Show Boat* (for which Kern wrote his last song, a new one for Kim in the last scene) and a less successful revival of *The Desert Song.* There was also Raymond Scott, Bernard Hanighen, Will Irwin, and Sidney Howard's *Lute Song* (142 performances), directed by John Houseman, which introduced Yul Brynner to Broadway. The show starred Mary Martin, who later recommended Brynner to Rodgers and Hammerstein for the role of the King in *The King and I.*

Backdrop: 1946–1949

National Inflation begins and continues for decades. The minimum hourly wage rises from forty cents to seventy-five cents. Truman is reelected even though the polls (and the *Chicago Tribune*) proclaim Thomas E. Dewey the victor. Truman signs a bill ending racial segregation in the armed forces. The U.S. Defense Department is created, as is the Central Intelligence Agency (CIA). The Hollywood blacklist of about thee hundred alleged Communist sympathizers is compiled, and the Hollywood Ten are given short jail sentences. The Taft-Hartley Act is passed, restricting organized labor's power to strike. Returning veterans on the GI Bill of Rights begin the baby boom. Gangster Bugsy Siegel opens the Flamingo, the first big Las Vegas hotel.

International The United Nations General Assembly opens its first session in the new UN building in New York. The North Atlantic Treaty (NATO) is signed. Romania and Czechoslovakia become Communist states. The People's Republic of China is proclaimed, with Mao Zedong as chairman. The German Democratic Republic (East Germany) and Federal Republic of Germany (West Germany) are established. Paris recognizes Vietnam's independence. Siam is renamed Thailand. The Republic of Korea is proclaimed;

Kern was to write the score for *Annie Get Your Gun*, and Dorothy Fields was to write the lyrics as well as cowrite the book with her brother; the show was her idea. But Berlin, hired when Kern died, always wrote his own lyrics, so Fields agreed to stay on to cowrite only the book. Writing the score for a more integrated musical than anything he'd done before, Berlin crafted several songs that are truly character-specific. *Annie Get Your Gun* was Berlin's most successful and enduring show, with over half a dozen hit songs, including what has since become the entertainment world's unofficial anthem: "There's No Business Like Show Business." Dwight Blocker Bowers, in *American Musical Theater: Shows, Songs, and Stars*, comments:

> The 1940s were his most artistically expansive period, with works ranging from the patriotically oriented *Louisiana Purchase* (1940), *This Is the Army* (1942), and *Miss Liberty* (1949) to the brassy slice of Americana *Annie Get Your Gun* (1946). . . .
> Berlin's theatrical songs, like those he wrote for films, reflect

Annie Get Your Gun

MUSIC/LYRICS: Irving Berlin

BOOK: Herbert and Dorothy Fields

DIRECTOR: Joshua Logan

CHOREOGRAPHER: Helen Tamiris

ORCHESTRATORS: Robert Russell Bennett, Philip J. Lang, and Ted Royal

DESIGNERS: Jo Mielziner (sets and lights) and Lucinda Ballard (costumes)

PRODUCERS: Richard Rodgers and Oscar Hammerstein

CAST INCLUDES: Ethel Merman and Ray Middleton (Mary Martin and John Raitt starred in the national tour)

PERFORMANCES: 1,147 on Broadway

North Korea challenges the new regime, beginning what soon escalates into the Korean War. India and Burma gain independence from Great Britain. England recognizes Irish independence but keeps Northern Ireland within the United Kingdom. The State of Israel is proclaimed. Apartheid takes effect in South Africa. Newfoundland becomes the tenth Canadian province. Mahatma Gandhi is assassinated.

New Developments The Dead Sea Scrolls are discovered. A patent application is filed for a nuclear fusion (hydrogen) bomb. Penicillin is synthesized. Margaret Sanger founds the International Planned Parenthood Federation. Chicago's O'Hare Airport opens. Jets fly the Atlantic for the first time. The transistor is developed for Bell Laboratories. The first automobile air conditioner, Honda motorcycles, and radial tires are introduced, as are V-8 Juice, the Nikon and Polaroid Land cameras, commercial microwave ovens, Scrabble, Silly Putty, Tide detergent, Timex and Seiko watches, and Estée Lauder cosmetics. Baskin-Robbins begins selling ice cream in California, General Mills and Pillsbury begin marketing prepared cake mixes, and Sara Lee starts selling cheesecake. Paris couturier Louis Réard designs the two-piece bikini swimsuit, causing a sensation.

Sports Boxing great Joe Louis retires; Ezzard Charles beats Jersey Joe Walcott for the world heavyweight title. The Olympic Games are held for the first time since 1936. Bullfighter Manolete is killed in the ring. The Brooklyn Dodgers sign Jackie Robinson, the first black baseball player on a major league team.

both the eras in which they were written and a remarkable timelessness. (Bowers, 114)

Set in the mid-1880s, *Annie Get Your Gun* is a comedy based on the life of markswoman Phoebe "Annie Oakley" Moses of *Buffalo Bill's Wild West Show*, centering on her rocky love affair with competitive sharpshooter Frank Butler. Although written as a star vehicle for Merman, it's well structured in the Rodgers and Hammerstein tradition and has a nearly equal role for Butler. There's also a romantic subplot for the ingenue and juvenile, often cut from most revivals. (It was retained in the 1999 Broadway revival starring Bernadette Peters and Tom Wopat but was rewritten by Peter Stone to include some social commentary by making the juvenile a half-breed and the ingenue's sister a bigot—out of place in a show whose only purpose is to entertain.)

It isn't a perfect show in its original form. Its treatment of Native Americans is unconsciously racist (for example, in the song "I'm an Indian Too," which is correctly dropped from contemporary productions), some of the

Art   There are new paintings by, among others, Picasso, Matisse, Dubuffet, and Kokoschka. Jackson Pollock begins the school of action painting. Andrew Wyeth achieves fame with *Christina's World*. Robert Motherwell paints the first of his series Elegy to the Spanish Republic. Swiss sculptor Alberto Giacometti has a New York exhibition. American architect R. Buckminster Fuller designs Dymaxion House.

Music/Dance   The Communist Party rebukes Soviet composers Prokofiev, Shostakovich, and Khachaturian for their music, calling it "bourgeois decadence." New works include Richard Strauss's *Four Last Songs* and Barber's *Knoxville—Summer of 1915*. Balanchine choreographs Stravinsky's *Orpheus*, and de Mille choreographs Gould's Lizzie Borden ballet, *Fall River Legend*. Among the new operas are Britten's *Albert Herring* and Thomson and Stein's *The Mother of Us All*.

Publications   *U.S. News and World Report* and Walt Kelly's comic strip *Pogo* begin publication. Gertrude Stein dies. Newly published are Dr. Spock's *The Common Sense Book of Baby and Child Care*, *The Revised Standard Version of the New Testament*, Kinsey's *Sexual Behavior in the Human Male*, Shirley Jackson's "The Lottery," Mailer's *The Naked and the Dead*, Orwell's *1984*, de Beauvoir's *The Second Sex*, Camus' *The Plague*, Isherwood's *The Berlin Stories* (source of the 1966 musical *Cabaret*), Kazantzakis's *Zorba the Greek* (source of the 1968 musical *Zorba*), Paton's *Cry, the Beloved Country* (source of the 1949 musical *Lost in the Stars*), and Michener's *Tales of the South Pacific* (source of the 1949 musical *South Pacific*).

Radio/TV   Milton Berle's *Texaco Star Theater* premieres on network TV; it's so popular that many people buy TV sets to watch it. Ed Sullivan's TV variety show, originally called *The Toast of the Town*, humor seems cornier now, and the script creaks occasionally, especially in exposition and transition sections. Even so, the show is entertaining, has an excellent score, and is still revived frequently.

Along with "There's No Business Like Show Business," the score includes "Anything You Can Do (I Can Do Better)," the eleven o'clock number and a comic duet for Annie and Frank; "Doin' What Comes Natur'lly" and "You Cain't Get a Man with a Gun" (Annie's first two numbers, both comic and both character-specific); "The Girl That I Marry" (an intentionally sexist waltz sung by Frank, who soon falls in love with Annie, the exact opposite of the kind of fantasy woman he describes in the song); "My Defenses Are Down" (which Frank sings after he falls for her); "I Got the Sun in the Morning" and "I Got Lost in His Arms" (a pop hit, up-tempo song and an underrated ballad, both for Annie); and "They Say It's Wonderful" (a hit ballad and a duet for Annie and Frank). "An Old-Fashioned Wedding"—Berlin's last show song, a double duet with a romantic melody for Frank and a syncopated countermelody for Annie—was written for a 1966 revival, again starring Merman (old enough by then that the show was jokingly referred to as

makes its debut and continues broadcasting until 1971; the first show introduces Dean Martin and Jerry Lewis. *Hopalong Cassidy* is TV's first Western series, and *The Goldbergs* is the first situation comedy, moving over from radio, as does *Amos 'n' Andy*. The National Academy of Television Arts and Sciences announces the first Emmy Awards.

Pop Culture   With the advent of bebop in the late forties, jazz starts to be music to listen to rather than dance to, and audiences drop off. At the same time, singers are getting more popular than bands. Tillman's "Slippin' Around" is the first country-and-western song to reach the top ten. Other new pop songs are Stewart and King's "Tennessee Waltz," Ahbez's "Nature Boy," Strayhorn's "Lush Life," Louiguy and Piaf's "La Vie en Rose," Kosma, Prévert, and Mercer's "Autumn Leaves," Gross and Lawrence's "Tenderly," Livingston and Evans's "Mona Lisa," Loesser's "On a Slow Boat to China," Styne and Cahn's "Let It Snow, Let It Snow, Let It Snow," Tormé and Wells's "The Christmas Song" ("Chestnuts roasting on an open fire"), and Marks's "Rudolph, the Red-Nosed Reindeer."

Stage   Margo Jones's establishing of Theatre '47 in Dallas, Texas, and Nina Vance's of the Alley Theatre in Houston signal the beginning of the regional theater movement. Actors' Equity requires its officers to sign anti-Communist loyalty oaths. Equity and the League of New York Theatres threaten to boycott the National Theatre in Washington, D.C., if it doesn't end audience segregation; it converts to a movie house instead. The Actors' Studio is formed to teach acting through principles developed by Stanislavsky; Lee Strasberg takes over as artistic director. Among the new plays are O'Neill's *The Iceman Cometh*, Miller's *All My Sons* and *Death of a Salesman*, Williams's *A Streetcar Named Desire* and *Summer and Smoke*, Brecht's *The Caucasian Chalk Circle* and *Galileo*, and Genet's *The Maids*.

Granny Get Your Gun). There's an original-cast recording, one of the 1966 revival, and several more recent ones. George Sidney's movie, starring Betty Hutton and Howard Keel, was released in 1950. (Judy Garland was to have played Annie but was too ill to do it.)

Call Me Mister (734 performances), with music and lyrics by Harold Rome, was a very successful, post–World War II revue with a central theme of soldiers returning to civilian life. There's a partial original-cast recording, including "Goin' Home Train" and the big hit comic number "South America, Take It Away," which made Betty Garrett a star. Among the unknowns in the touring company were Bob Fosse, Carl Reiner, and Buddy Hackett.

St. Louis Woman was a flop with a weak book, a talented black cast, and a great Arlen score. Set in 1898 in the St. Louis African American community, the show centers around the free-and-easy Della and her love affair with Little Augie, a jockey trying to overcome a curse laid on him by Della's dying ex-boyfriend. It was Pearl Bailey's Broadway debut as the lead in the comic subplot. The score includes "Any Place I Hang My Hat Is Home," "I Had Myself a True Love," "Legalize My Name," and "Come Rain or Come Shine." There's an original-cast record-

St. Louis Woman

MUSIC: Harold Arlen

LYRICS: Johnny Mercer

BOOK: Countee Cullen and Arna Bontemps, from Bontemps's novel *God Sends Sunday*

DIRECTOR: Rouben Mamoulian

CHOREOGRAPHER: Charles Walters

DESIGNER: Lemuel Ayers (sets and costumes)

PRODUCER: Edward Gross

CAST INCLUDES: Juanita Hall, Pearl Bailey, and the Nicholas Brothers (Fayard and Harold)

PERFORMANCES: 113

Screen   Among the new movies are *It's a Wonderful Life, Miracle on 34th Street, The Big Sleep, Red River, The Treasure of the Sierra Madre, Adam's Rib, White Heat* ("Top of the world, Ma"), the ballet movie *The Red Shoes, The Third Man, Notorious,* Chaplin's *Monsieur Verdoux,* Olivier's *Hamlet,* Cocteau's *Beauty and the Beast,* and the beginning of Italian neorealism—de Sica's *Shoeshine* and *The Bicycle Thief* and Rossellini's *Open City.*

Most noteworthy of the approximately 150 new movie musicals produced during the four years are: *Centennial Summer,* Kern's last score, which includes "All Through the Day," with lyrics by Hammerstein; the all-star, pseudo-biography of Kern, *Till the Clouds Roll By;* the all-star, really pseudo-biography of Rodgers and Hart, *Words and Music;* Cary Grant in the almost entirely fictional Cole Porter biography *Night and Day; The Jolson Story* and *Jolson Sings Again;* June Haver in the pseudo-biography of Marilyn Miller *Look for the Silver Lining;* Minnelli's all-star revue *Ziegfeld Follies* and his *The Pirate,* with Judy Garland and Gene Kelly and songs by Porter, including "Be a Clown"; Bing

ing as well as a recording of the 1998 Encores! series concert starring Vanessa Williams.

There were flops by other celebrated songwriters as well. *Beggar's Holiday* (111 performances), with music by Duke Ellington and book and lyrics by John Latouche, was an unsuccessful attempt to update Gay's eighteenth-century, satiric ballad-opera *The Beggar's Opera* (also the source of *The Three-penny Opera*) by using an interracial cast. *Park Avenue*—music by Arthur Schwartz and lyrics by Ira Gershwin, with book by Nunnally Johnson and George S. Kaufman (who also directed)—was a 72-performance flop and Ira Gershwin's last Broadway show. *Around the World in Eighty Days*, adapted from the Jules Verne novel, had songs by Cole Porter and book and direction by Orson Welles, who also starred. A 75-performance flop—sometimes referred to as "Welles-apoppin' "—without a single Porter hit, it lost at least $400,000, a huge amount in 1946. Porter's career seemed to have taken a nosedive from which most experts felt he would never recover.

In 1947, songwriters Bert Kalmar and Walter Donaldson died. The first official off-Broadway theater, eventually named Circle in the Square, opened in Greenwich Village. The Tony Awards (named after Antoinette Perry, actor, director, and chair of the American Theatre Wing, who died in 1946) were established to honor the year's best on Broadway.

Although there were only about fifteen new musical evenings, including a double-bill of Gian-Carlo Menotti's operas *The Medium* and *The Telephone* (212

Crosby and Fred Astaire in *Blue Skies*, with twenty new and old songs by Berlin; Astaire and Garland in *Easter Parade*, choreographed by Alton, with seventeen old and new Berlin songs; the reunion after ten years of Rogers and Astaire in *The Barkleys of Broadway*, with a Comden and Green script; *The Shocking Miss Pilgrim*, with songs adapted by Kay Swift and Ira Gershwin from unpublished manuscripts by George Gershwin, with lyrics by Ira; Doris Day in *Romance on the High Seas*, choreographed by Berkeley, with a Styne and Cahn score that includes "It's Magic"; *Casbah*, with music by Arlen and lyrics by Robin; *The Perils of Pauline*, with a Loesser score that includes "I Wish I Didn't Love You So"; and *Neptune's Daughter*, with a Loesser score that has his Academy Award–winning "Baby, It's Cold Outside." Adaptations of musicals include: *Up in Central Park*; *One Touch of Venus*, leaving out most of the score; a remake of *Good News*, with new songs added by Edens, Blane, Martin, Comden, and Green (Comden and Green's first screenplay); and Gene Kelly and Frank Sinatra in *On the Town*, which uses very few of the original songs (and changes "New York, New York, a helluva town" to "New York, New York, a wonderful town") and adds new songs by Edens, Comden, and Green.

performances), 1947 was an important year with Lerner and Loewe's, Burton Lane's, and Jule Styne's first hits as well as what many consider Kurt Weill's best American score, for which he won a special Tony Award. There were also limited-run revivals of *Bloomer Girl* and *Up in Central Park,* as well as a revival of the 1913 operetta *Sweethearts.* The year ended with the arrival of the D'Oyly Carte Opera Company with an eighteen-week season of several Gilbert and Sullivan operettas in repertory.

Street Scene

MUSIC: Kurt Weill

LYRICS: Langston Hughes

BOOK: Elmer Rice, adapted from his 1929 play

DIRECTOR: Charles Friedman

CHOREOGRAPHER: Anna Sokolow

ORCHESTRATOR: Kurt Weill

DESIGNERS: Jo Mielziner (sets and lights) and Lucinda Ballard (costumes)

PRODUCERS: The Playwrights' Company and Dwight Deere Wiman

PERFORMANCES: 148

Street Scene deals with the poor residents of a tenement in New York, a sort of New York melting-pot variation of Catfish Row in *Porgy and Bess.* Faithful to Rice's original play, the main plots are about the Maurrant family—unfaithful wife and angry husband, daughter in love with the boy downstairs but with no money to get married. The husband shoots the wife and her lover; the daughter leaves to seek a better, if less moral, life. Many other residents of the building and the neighborhood also have their stories told. A nearly through-composed Broadway opera, it's now performed by opera companies around the world, even though much of the music sounds better sung by good musical-theater voices. (Some of the score is quite jazzy, and the very idiomatic language sounds strained when sung with operatic vocal production.) With *Street Scene,* Langston Hughes, a poet, tried song lyrics for the first time, and Elmer Rice, a dramatist, tried a musical theater book for the first time.

> Kurt Weill occupies the unique position as the composer who most successfully worked with the most unlikely of lyricists. Few lyricists are good poets and few poets understand the special skills lyric writing entails. But Weill worked with a host of poets and playwrights with little or no songwriting experience. What's even more remarkable is his high degree of success. (Bloom, *American Song,* 703)

Allegro

MUSIC: Richard Rodgers

LYRICS/BOOK: Oscar Hammerstein

DIRECTOR/CHOREOGRAPHER: Agnes de Mille

ORCHESTRATOR: Robert Russell Bennett

DESIGNERS: Jo Mielziner (sets and lights) and Lucinda Ballard (costumes)

PRODUCER: The Theatre Guild

CAST INCLUDES: John Battles and Lisa Kirk

PERFORMANCES: 315

Unfortunately the show was too serious and downbeat for 1947 audiences and was financially unsuccessful. There's a highlights recording with the original cast and two more-recent, complete recordings. The score includes "Ain't It Awful, the Heat?", "Ice Cream Sextet," "Wrapped in a Ribbon and Tied in a Bow," "Lonely House," "Wouldn't You Like to Be on Broadway?", "What

Good Would the Moon Be?" and "Moon-Faced, Starry-Eyed"—
and that's just a few of the numbers in the first act.

Allegro, the first Rodgers and Hammerstein show that wasn't
a big hit, was also their first not adapted from another source.
It's been called the first concept musical, although it has a more
linear story than most present-day concept musicals. (Stephen
Sondheim, a production assistant on the show, permanently established the concept musical as a viable form with George
Furth's and his 1970 *Company.* Like *Allegro,* his 1981 *Merrily
We Roll Along* deals with the loss of idealism.) *Allegro* tells a
parable-like tale about how an idealistic young man can become
corrupted by the attractions of money and society. The narrative
follows a small-town boy from birth through young manhood,
when he's an idealistic doctor, to almost middle age, when he's
become a corrupted, big-city society doctor. But it has a "there's
no place like home" happy ending. The chorus, which functions
as a sort of Greek chorus, both comments on the action and nar-
rates it, bridging the skips in chronology from birth in 1905 to
rebirth in the mid-1940s. The characters are intentionally drawn
more as prototypes than as the fully dimensioned human beings
in Rodgers and Hammerstein's earlier shows, which keeps the
audience from caring as much about what happens next. This
distancing—along with a certain amount of heavy-handedness
in the script and lyrics—works against the show's success despite
the variety, scope, and tunefulness of Rodgers's score, which is
divided among a lot of characters rather than Rodgers and
Hammerstein's usual practice of giving most of the songs to a
few principals. (De Mille was always more successful when she
just choreographed, which may be another reason for the
show's failure.) There's an abbreviated original-cast recording
that includes the title song, "A Fellow Needs a Girl," "So Far,"
and "The Gentleman Is a Dope." It would be well worth considering doing a revival—or a revisal—of the show.

Set in 1913 New Jersey during the era of silent movies and
the Model T, *High Button Shoes* is a nostalgic, lightweight
show about a con man (Phil Silvers) trying to bilk small-town
citizens. It's most famous for Robbins's Keystone Kops chase
ballet set on the boardwalk at Atlantic City. (He won a Tony for

Jule (Julius) Styne (1905–
94, born in London) came to
America when he was eight
years old. Before *High Button
Shoes,* he'd been a dance-band
pianist, arranger, and vocal
coach, and had become very
successful composing for
Hollywood and Tin Pan Alley.
Most of his pop hits—many for
Frank Sinatra—were written
with lyricist Sammy Cahn,
including "I've Heard That Song
Before," "Saturday Night (Is the
Loneliest Night of the Year)," and
the Oscar-winning "Three Coins in
the Fountain." Among Styne's
later musicals are *Gentlemen
Prefer Blondes, Bells Are
Ringing, Gypsy,* and *Funny Girl,*
all hits and all star vehicles with
a big, brassy, Broadway sound.

High Button Shoes

MUSIC: Jule Styne

LYRICS: Sammy Cahn

BOOK: Stephen Longstreet

DIRECTOR: George Abbott

CHOREOGRAPHER: Jerome Robbins

ORCHESTRATOR: Philip J. Lang

DESIGNERS: Oliver Smith (sets),
Miles White (costumes), and
Peggy Clark (lights)

PRODUCERS: Joseph Kipness and
Monte Proser

CAST INCLUDES: Phil Silvers, Nanette
Fabray, and Helen Gallagher

PERFORMANCES: 727

Finian's Rainbow

MUSIC: Burton Lane

LYRICS: E. Y. Harburg

BOOK: E. Y. Harburg and Fred Saidy

DIRECTOR: Bretaigne Windust

CHOREOGRAPHER: Michael Kidd (cowinner of the first Tony for choreography)

ORCHESTRATORS: Robert Russell Bennett and Don Walker

DESIGNERS: Jo Mielziner (sets and lights) and Eleanor Goldsmith (costumes)

PRODUCERS: William R. Katzell and Lee Sabinson

CAST INCLUDES: Ella Logan and David Wayne (winner of the first Tony for supporting actor in a musical)

PERFORMANCES: 725

Michael Kidd (1919–2007, born Milton Greenwald in New York), a dancer with American Ballet Theatre, got his first Broadway job with *Finian's Rainbow*. He went on to create the dances for such shows as *Guys and Dolls* (which he re-created for the movie) and *Can-Can* before also becoming a director for *Li'l Abner* and several other musicals—most of them less successful than the ones he'd only choreographed. His most memorable film dances were for *Seven Brides for Seven Brothers*. He, Gene Kelly, and Dan Dailey are the returning war veterans in the 1955 movie *It's Always Fair Weather*, with a script by Comden and Green.

it in 1948.) There's an original-cast recording of most of the pretty nostalgic score, including "Papa, Won't You Dance with Me?" (a polka) and "I Still Get Jealous" (a soft shoe). It's Jule Styne's second Broadway score—his first closed out of town.

Finian's Rainbow is a tuneful and witty satiric fantasy of the white South's attitude toward blacks and vice versa, rich people's attitude toward the poor and vice versa, and other subject matter new for the musical comedy. Although very liberal for its time, some of the satire feels a bit dated and unintentionally racist now. The show begins with Finian McLonergan and his daughter Sharon, having just left the fictional Glocca Morra, Ireland, arriving in the equally fictional Rainbow Valley, Missitucky, USA. Finian has stolen a leprechaun's pot of gold and plans to plant it at Fort Knox, where he thinks it will grow. Og, the leprechaun, has followed him. Sharon falls in love with union organizer Will Mahoney, and Og falls in love with both Sharon and Susan Mahoney, Will's mute sister, played by a dancer. During the show, the three wishes the pot can grant are used up, two by accidentally turning the bigoted white senator Billboard Rawkins into a black and eventually turning him white again. With the third wish, Og gives Susan the power of speech, even though using up the wishes makes him mortal. At the end, Sharon gets Will, Og gets Susan, and Finian leaves to go on looking for his rainbow and the pot of gold at its end.

Most agree that *Finian's Rainbow* is E. Y. Harburg's best work for Broadway. (The show flopped in London—too many American jokes and references.) In the score are the hit songs "How Are Things in Glocca Morra?", "Old Devil Moon," and "If This Isn't Love," as well as "Look to the Rainbow" and Og's "When I'm Not Near the Girl I Love (I Love the Girl I'm Near)," the eleven o'clock number. There's an original-cast recording as well as one of a 1960 revival. The show was filmed unsuccessfully by Francis Ford Coppola in 1968, starring sixty-nine-year-old Fred Astaire, Petula Clark, and Tommy Steele, and choreographed by Hermes Pan.

Brigadoon, Lerner and Loewe's third show together and their first hit, is a romantic fantasy set mostly in a small mythical Scottish town called Brigadoon. (Irish, Scottish, turn-of-the-century, fantastic, anything but contemporary America was the norm for hit musicals during this time, though not true for the few new revues.) The town rises out of the mists for one day every hundred years with the inhabitants only a day older each century. It thus escapes the unhappiness of the rest of the post–World War II world. The spell will be broken if any inhabitant leaves town. The show begins with two American war vets, Tommy Albright and Jeff Douglas, who, while hunting in Scotland, get lost in the woods. Out of the mist, the village of Brigadoon appears, celebrating both a fair and the impending wedding of two of the villagers, Charley Dalrymple and Jean MacLaren. Tommy falls in love with Fiona MacClaren, Jean's older sister. Jean's jealous rejected suitor, Harry Beaton, tries to leave town and is hunted down and accidentally killed in a long chase ballet. The two Americans eventually go back home, but Tommy returns, and his love for Fiona makes Brigadoon reappear again long enough for him to join her there. The comic subplot centers on Jeff, the other American, and a naive girl from the village, an Ado Annie–like character in Scotland. (Much of *Brigadoon* feels like Lerner studied Rodgers and Hammerstein's *Oklahoma!* carefully, and, of course, de Mille was around too.)

The long score of *Brigadoon* (which has over thirty minutes of dance music) includes "Waitin' for My Dearie," a song for the heroine that says almost the same thing as Laurey's "Many a New Day" in *Oklahoma!;* "The Love of My Life," the comic subplot heroine's variation on Ado Annie's "I Cain't Say No"; "I'll Go Home with Bonnie Jean," a variation on *Oklahoma!*'s "Kansas City," including a six-minute dance break; "The Heather on the Hill"; "Come to Me, Bend to Me" (Andrew Lloyd Webber's 1988 hit song "The Music of the Night" from *The Phantom of the Opera* begins with exactly the same melody); the big hit tune "Almost Like Being in Love"; and such ballets as a sword dance at the wedding, the big chase after Harry Beaton, and a funeral dance after he's killed. There's an original-cast recording. The 1954 movie, directed by Minnelli, starred Gene Kelly (who also choreographed), Van Johnson, and Cyd Charisse (dubbed by Carol Richards).

Brigadoon

MUSIC: Frederick Loewe

LYRICS/BOOK: Alan Jay Lerner, possibly adapted from a classic German tale

DIRECTOR: Robert Lewis

CHOREOGRAPHER: Agnes de Mille (cowinner of the first Tony for choreography)

ORCHESTRATOR: Ted Royal

DESIGNERS: Oliver Smith (sets), David Ffolkes (costumes), and Peggy Clark (lights)

PRODUCER: Cheryl Crawford

CAST INCLUDES: Marion Bell, Pamela Britton, David Brooks, and Helen Gallagher

PERFORMANCES: 581

Oliver Smith (c. 1918–94, born in Wisconsin) designed for ballet, including de Mille's *Rodeo* and Bernstein and Robbins's *Fancy Free*, and was codirector of the American Ballet Theatre. Among the many musicals, plays, and movies he designed are *Brigadoon, On the Town, High Button Shoes, My Fair Lady, West Side Story, The Sound of Music, Camelot, Hello, Dolly!, Barefoot in the Park,* and *The Odd Couple.*

Suggested Watching and Listening

Annie Get Your Gun
There's a live TV version of the original touring company production of the 1946 show; it has cuts, and the subplot has been dropped. The first scene gives an excellent sense of the whole show. It has six numbers: two for Annie, two for Frank, an opening number, and "There's No Business Like Show Business." It's available on VHS. The MGM movie starring Betty Hutton and Howard Keel and directed by George Sidney is available on Warner Brothers DVD. It cuts Frank's first number, "I'm a Bad, Bad Man," which is no loss.

Brigadoon
The movie version of this 1947 show, directed by Vincente Minnelli and starring Gene Kelly and Cyd Charisse, is available on Warner Brothers DVD.
- "The Heather on the Hill" (performed by Gene Kelly and Cyd Charisse): Although Kelly sings it alone in the movie, it's a singing as well as dancing duet in the original.
- "Almost Like Being in Love" (performed by Gene Kelly with Van Johnson): This is Lerner and Loewe's first big hit song.

Broadway: The American Musical
It's available on PBS Paramount DVD. "Episode 4: Oh, What a Beautiful Mornin' (1943–1960)," would be appropriate viewing at this point.

Finian's Rainbow
The following suggestions are various versions of three songs from this show.
- "How Are Things in Glocca Morra?" (performed by Petula Clark): This version is from the movie directed by Francis Ford Coppola, available on Warner Brothers Home Video DVD.
- "Old Devil Moon" (performed by Ella Logan and Donald Richards): Ella Logan was Scottish, which shows through her attempted Irish accent. The role made her a Broadway star; she also became a very successful nightclub singer. This and the next number are from the original-cast recording and on *Original Cast! The Forties: Part 1* (MET CD).
- "When I'm Not Near the Girl I Love (I Love the Girl I'm Near)" (performed by David Wayne): This is the leprechaun's eleven o'clock number.

St. Louis Woman
The following numbers are from the 1946 original-cast recording of the show, available on Angel Records CD.
- "Any Place I Hang My Hat Is Home" (performed by Ruby Hill)
- "Legalize My Name" (performed by Pearl Bailey)
- "Come Rain or Come Shine" (performed by Ruby Hill and Harold Nicholas): When this song is sung out of context, the lyric "I'm with you, Augie" is changed to "I'm with you always."

Street Scene
There's a video of the 1995 Houston Grand Opera coproduction of this 1947 show. It's directed by Francesca Zambello, conducted by James Holmes, and is available on Image

Entertainment DVD. Act 1 of the show includes the following songs connected by dialogue and underscoring.

- "Wrapped in a Ribbon and Tied in a Bow"
- "Lonely House"
- "Wouldn't You Like to Be on Broadway?"
- "What Good Would the Moon Be?"
- "Moon-Faced, Starry-Eyed"

The scope and variety of Weill's score is evident in this section of the act, encompassing everything from semi-operatic style to a jitterbug.

From *Kiss Me, Kate* to *South Pacific*

Happy talk,
Keep talkin' happy talk,
Talk about things you like to do.
You gotta have a dream;
If you don't have a dream,
How you gonna make a dream come true?

—"HAPPY TALK," *SOUTH PACIFIC,* LYRICS BY OSCAR HAMMERSTEIN II

By the end of the 1940s, the loosely structured star vehicle had been tamed; more often instead of stars selling shows, the shows sold themselves, often making stars out of unknowns. Original-cast recordings—released on long-playing records by the end of the forties—gave listeners a sense of the whole show and helped sell tickets both on Broadway and on the road, as did pop singers' cover recordings of the hit songs. What was soon to become national television frequently featured songs and stars from current Broadway musicals; that too helped sell tickets. Because of all this, musicals were able to have longer runs; they usually needed them, since production costs kept rising. Touring companies, usually with casts of unknowns, were sent out while the shows were still running on Broadway and fresh in people's minds, with songs that were still pop hits.

In 1948, operetta composer Franz Lehar and producer Earl Carroll died. Equity minimum rose to $75 a week, and ticket prices to a maximum of $7.20. By that time, a million U.S. homes had TV sets—up from five thousand in 1945—and 33 ⅓ rpm records, which could play up to an hour of music, began to be marketed and soon replaced 78s. These developments were to have major effects both positive (long-playing records) and negative (TV) on the entertainment world in general and on the musical in particular.

Oklahoma! closed after a five-year run. Again there were only about fifteen new musicals and revues that year. One was *As the Girls Go* (414 performances plus a return engagement of another 141), with a score by Jimmy McHugh and Harold Adamson, about the horny husband of the first female U.S. president. A lavish production by Michael Todd, it starred comic Bobby Clark and a lot of nearly nude women. *Look Ma, I'm Dancing* (188 performances) was a flop with a score by Hugh Martin and book by Jerome Lawrence and Robert E. Lee. It was conceived and choreographed by Jerome Robbins, codirected by George Abbott and Robbins (his first Broadway directing job), produced by Abbott, and starred Nancy Walker. It's a comedy about a woman who finances a ballet company in order to dance in it. There was also a flop operetta by Romberg, *My Romance,* the last of his shows to be produced while he was alive and the Shuberts' last production.

Kiss Me, Kate

MUSIC/LYRICS: Cole Porter

BOOK: Bella and Samuel Spewack, adapted in part from Shakespeare's *The Taming of the Shrew*

DIRECTOR: John C. Wilson

CHOREOGRAPHER: Hanya Holm

ORCHESTRATOR: Robert Russell Bennett

DESIGNER: Lemuel Ayers (sets and costumes)

PRODUCERS: Saint Subber and Lemuel Ayers

CAST INCLUDES: Alfred Drake, Patricia Morison, and Lisa Kirk

PERFORMANCES: 1,077

Kiss Me, Kate, a backstage musical about the out-of-town tryout of a musical version of *The Taming of the Shrew,* incorporates several scenes from the show being tried out. Kate and Petruchio in the musicalized *Shrew* are played by a divorced couple—he's an egomaniac and she's a hellion—bickering but still "so in love." The subplot is about the engaged couple who play Bianca and Lucentio; she has problems with his gambling and he with her only being "true to you, darling, in my fashion." The relationships between the characters in the backstage main plot and subplot cleverly mirror those in Shakespeare's play, and both plots become logically and inextricably connected through a gambling debt and a forged IOU.

> Here was a book with remarkably lifelike, believable protagonists, with every character having a sensible and important bearing on the plot, with every song perfectly related to the action and more often than not advancing it. Here were lyrics and dialogue that never cheapened themselves for effect, that remained literate and witty or touching throughout. (Bordman, 566)

In the hit-filled score (with songs for the musical as well as for the musical within the musical) are "Another Op'nin', Another

Show," Porter's variation on Berlin's "There's No Business Like Show Business"; "Too Darn Hot," a big song-and-dance number to open the second act; "Wunderbar," a parody of bad operetta waltzes that turns into a real love duet for the leads; "Why Can't You Behave?" a ballad for the subplot heroine; "Always True to You in My Fashion," her list song—verse and four choruses—similar in content to Porter's earlier "My Heart Belongs to Daddy"; and "So in Love," the show's hit ballad, sung at different times in the show by both the leads.

> While Kern, Hammerstein, Rodgers, and others had been working toward integrated musical theatre since the mid-twenties, Porter never tried for anything more than the best songs he could write at the time . . . in whatever framework his librettists happened upon. Following a long creative slump, Porter . . . suddenly and unexpectedly came up with one of the very finest musical comedies in Broadway history. . . . *Kiss Me, Kate* was the best, most successful, and most personally gratifying show of Porter's career. (Suskin, *Show Tunes*, 227)

Among the songs for the show within the show are "Where Is the Life That Late I Led?" a list song (verse, three choruses, and patter sections between the choruses) sung by Petruchio on his wedding night as he fondly remembers his many old girlfriends; "Tom, Dick, or Harry," a song-and-dance number for Kate's sister Bianca and her three suitors; and "I Hate Men," a four-chorus list song for Kate, the shrew. "Brush Up Your Shakespeare," a smutty, soft-shoe list song—verse and five choruses—is sung near the end of the show by two gangsters who accidentally end up on the stage of the show within the show, and who suddenly have a surprisingly large classical reference level. It's about how to get a girl by quoting Shakespeare—and would now be considered instructions on how to commit date rape.

> Chorus 1: Brush up your Shakespeare,
> Start quoting him now.
> Brush up your Shakespeare
> And the women you will wow.
> Just declaim a few lines from *Othella*
> And they'll think you're a helluva fella.
> If your blonde won't respond when you flatter 'er
> Tell her what Tony told Cleopaterer.
> If she fights when her clothes you are mussing,
> What are clothes? *Much Ado About Nussing*.
> Brush up your Shakespeare
> And they'll all kowtow.

Where's Charley?

MUSIC/LYRICS: Frank Loesser

BOOK: George Abbott, adapted from Brandon Thomas's 1892 British farce *Charley's Aunt*

DIRECTOR: George Abbott

CHOREOGRAPHERS: George Balanchine and Fred Danielli

ORCHESTRATORS: Philip J. Lang, Ted Royal, and Hans Spialek

PRODUCERS: Gwen Rickard (Ray Bolger's pseudonym), Cy Feuer, and Ernest H. Martin

CAST INCLUDES: Ray Bolger, Allyn Ann McLerie, and Doretta Morrow

PERFORMANCES: 792

Frank Loesser (1910–69, born in New York) at first wrote just lyrics for Tin Pan Alley, radio, and Hollywood, working with such composers as Jule Styne, Hoagy Carmichael, Arthur Schwartz, Burton Lane, and Jimmy McHugh. Eventually, starting with "Praise the Lord and Pass the Ammunition," he wrote both music and lyrics for songs and always wrote both for his Broadway shows. He wrote four more shows after *Where's Charley?* Three of them were *Guys and Dolls*, *The Most Happy Fella*, and *How to Succeed in Business Without Really Trying*. He also coproduced other people's shows through his Frank Productions and published songs by up-and-coming songwriters as well as his own.

Among the couplets in the other choruses are

> When your baby is pleading for pleasure
> Let her sample your *Measure for Measure*.

> Better mention *The Merchant of Venice*
> When her sweet pound o' flesh you would menace.

> If because of your heat she gets huffy
> Simply play on and "Lay on, Macduffy!"

Hanya Holm was the first Broadway choreographer to use the Laban system to notate and copyright her work. The show won the first Tony Award for a musical, has the first original-cast recording on long-playing records, and is frequently revived, including a highly successful 1999 Broadway revival starring Brian Stokes Mitchell and Marin Mazzie. A 1953 three-dimensional movie version directed by George Sidney had Kathryn Grayson, Howard Keel, Ann Miller, and Bob Fosse in the cast. The lyrics of several of the songs were considerably cleaned up to get past the censors.

In *Where's Charley?*, a big hit, Charley disguises himself as his aunt from Brazil, "where the nuts come from," in order to win the hand of Amy and at the same time helps his friend Jack win his beloved Kitty's hand. It was Loesser's first Broadway score; once again George Abbott helped a newcomer learn the ropes.

> Frank Loesser's Hollywood career hardly prepared audiences for the excellence of his Broadway career. His songs, written for a long list of mostly second-rate musicals and comedies, were excellent but they seldom had the depth associated with most of his Broadway scores. He lost none of the spirit of his Hollywood output while gaining emotional impact, a rare feat. . . . [*Where's Charley?*] was a transitional score that contained elements of his Hollywood output and glimpses of his Broadway style. (Bloom, *American Song*, 781)

In the bright and tuneful score for *Where's Charley?* are such numbers as "The New Ashmolean Marching Society and Student Conservatory Band"; "My Darling, My Darling," a pop hit; and "Once in Love with Amy," the biggest hit of the show, which

Bolger sang and danced in 1, even inviting an audience sing-along. (He won a Tony.) Unfortunately, due to a strike by the musicians' union, no original-cast album was made. There's a 1952 movie with the original cast; it hasn't been re-released.

Love Life: A Vaudeville was Lerner's first break from his partnership with Loewe. Another early concept musical, it's an interesting experimental flop that traces a couple as they move through different eras of American history: from colonial days to 1948 and from the happiness of a young couple to disillusionment and divorce. Throughout the changing eras, the couple stay the same age. (As in *Company*, the concept is marriage, though *Love Life* comes from a totally different and far more politicized point of view.) Narration and commentary are provided through a series of satirical, between-scenes vaudeville acts. The very rich score includes "Economics," "Progress," "Green-Up Time," "Here I'll Stay," "Love Song," and "Susan's Dream."

Love Life: A Vaudeville
MUSIC: Kurt Weill
LYRICS/BOOK: Alan Jay Lerner
DIRECTOR: Elia Kazan
CHOREOGRAPHER: Michael Kidd
ORCHESTRATOR: Kurt Weill
DESIGNERS: Boris Aronson (sets), Lucinda Ballard (costumes), and Peggy Clark (lights)
PRODUCER: Cheryl Crawford
CAST INCLUDES: Nanette Fabray and Ray Middleton
PERFORMANCES: 252

With the debuts of Milton Berle's and Ed Sullivan's TV shows, the Broadway revue was soon doomed to near total extinction. However, two successful revues opened in 1948. *Inside USA* (399 performances), songs by Schwartz and Dietz, was one of the last of the big Broadway revues. It used the title of John Gunther's 1947 nonfiction book as its theme: all the songs and sketches (most of them satirical) were about America and Americans. The revue starred Beatrice Lillie, Jack Haley, and Carl Reiner, and there's an original-cast recording.

Lend an Ear (460 performances), music and lyrics by Charles Gaynor, was an intimate revue most acclaimed for Carol Channing's first appearance on Broadway. The show had a parody of twenties musicals called *The Gladiola Girl*, in which Channing played a flapper, a performance that led directly to her being cast (along with costar Yvonne Adair) in *Gentlemen Prefer Blondes*, also set in the twenties. *Lend an Ear* was Gower Champion's first successful Broadway choreography, for which he won a Tony.

Gower Champion (1920–80, born in Geneva, Illinois) and his wife and dancing partner, Marge, left New York for Hollywood soon after *Lend an Ear*. They were in several movies, including *Show Boat*. Champion returned to Broadway and eventually became one of its most successful director/choreographers, with such shows as *Bye Bye Birdie, Carnival!, Hello, Dolly!*, and *42nd Street*. He died on opening day of *42nd Street*.

In 1949, dancer and singer Bill "Bojangles" Robinson died. The League of Off-Broadway Theatres was formed; lead actors were lucky to get $30 a week. Vaudeville was briefly revived at the Palace. Among the fifteen or so new musicals and revues on Broadway was Marc Blitzstein's *Regina* (56 performances), an operatic adaptation of Lillian Hellman's 1939 play *The Little Foxes.*

Miss Liberty (308 performances) had songs by Irving Berlin and a book by Robert E. Sherwood, with help from director Moss Hart. Berlin, Sherwood, and Hart produced it, Oliver Smith and Motley designed it, and it starred Eddie Albert (later in the movie version of *Oklahoma!* and TV's *Green Acres*). It's a lightweight, rather uninspired period musical about France's gift of the Statue of Liberty to the United States and a newspaper photographer's search for the woman who was its model. The second-rate Berlin score includes "Just One Way to Say I Love You" and "Let's Take an Old-Fashioned Walk." There's an original-cast recording.

Lost in the Stars (281 performances) was adapted from Alan Paton's novel *Cry, the Beloved Country* and had music and orchestrations by Kurt Weill, with book and lyrics by Maxwell Anderson. It was directed by Rouben Mamoulian and starred Todd Duncan (the original Porgy). A musical tragedy about apartheid in South Africa, much of the action is narrated and commented on by a chorus, similar to the approach in *Allegro* and *Love Life.* The story is about a black minister's attempts to help his son, who is condemned to death for killing a white man during a bungled robbery. The original-cast recording includes "Cry, the Beloved Country," "Trouble Man," "Stay Well," and the title song. The show was filmed by Daniel Mann in 1974. The very powerful score was Weill's last for Broadway.

Gentlemen Prefer Blondes

MUSIC: Jule Styne

LYRICS: Leo Robin

BOOK: Joseph Fields (brother of Herbert and Dorothy) and Anita Loos, adapted from Loos's 1926 story

DIRECTOR: John C. Wilson

CHOREOGRAPHER: Agnes de Mille

ORCHESTRATOR: Don Walker

DESIGNER: Oliver Smith (sets)

PRODUCERS: Herman Levin and Oliver Smith

CAST INCLUDES: Carol Channing, Yvonne Adair, and Howard Morris

PERFORMANCES: 740

In *Gentlemen Prefer Blondes,* a sex farce set among the flappers and millionaires of the twenties, the central character, gold digger Lorelei Lee, was Channing's first starring role. Most of the action takes place aboard the *Ile de France,* where Lorelei and her friend Dorothy meet many accommodating gentlemen and get involved with a missing diamond tiara and a detective sent by Lorelei's wealthy fiancé to spy on her. Styne's second hit in a row, the show's songs don't attempt to re-create the sounds of the twenties but are tailored by him exactly to the needs of the story and, especially, of the characters—an ability readily apparent in most of his later shows as well. The show was reset to the fifties for the 1953 Howard Hawks movie costarring Marilyn Monroe and Jane Russell. In 1973, it was unnecessarily revised, retitled *Lorelei,* given some new songs by Styne, Comden, and

Green, and had a 320-performance run on Broadway, again starring Channing. The story was told in flashback so Channing could make her first entrance as an older woman, which she definitely was. The original score includes "Bye Bye Baby" and two signature numbers for Channing until *Hello, Dolly!* came along: "A Little Girl from Little Rock" and "Diamonds Are a Girl's Best Friend." There are original-cast recordings of both *Gentlemen Prefer Blondes* and *Lorelei*.

South Pacific, the second musical to win the Pulitzer and the first to win nine Tonys, is set on a South Pacific island where American forces are stationed while waiting to get into the action against the Japanese during World War II, and on the nearby exotic island of Bali Ha'i. The heroine of the romantic main plot, army nurse Nellie Forbush, has to overcome her inbred bigotry before she can marry widower Emile de Becque, the Frenchman she loves; he has two Eurasian children from his relationship with a now deceased Polynesian woman. Lieutenant Cable, the hero of the tragic subplot, is unable to overcome his own bigotry, which prevents him from marrying Liat, the Polynesian girl he loves. He and de Becque volunteer for a dangerous mission; Cable is killed. Liat is the daughter of the saleswoman Bloody Mary, who has comic scenes, serious scenes, and sings the beautiful "Bali Ha'i" and the charming "Happy Talk." There's also a comic subplot about enlisted man Luther Billis's various schemes to keep from getting bored and to make money.

> The villain of *South Pacific* is not the Japanese but man's racism. The idea of the villain of a musical as a part of each character's persona was revolutionary at the time. . . . Hammerstein had been moving in this direction for a long time and continued exploring this idea for the rest of his career. His subsequent shows all contained variations on this theme [i.e., the "villain" lurking within us], which is one reason his characters are so three-dimensional and his shows so full of humanity. Few authors other than Hammerstein explored this concept until Hammerstein's protégé Stephen Sondheim came along. (Bloom, *American Song*, 692)

South Pacific presents us not only with a culture clash between people on the same side during the war but also with a moral

South Pacific

MUSIC: Richard Rodgers

LYRICS: Oscar Hammerstein

BOOK: Oscar Hammerstein and Joshua Logan, based on three of James Michener's *Tales of the South Pacific*: "Our Heroine," "Fo' Dolla," and "A Boar's Tooth"

DIRECTOR/STAGER: Joshua Logan

ORCHESTRATOR: Robert Russell Bennett

DESIGNERS: Jo Mielziner (sets and lights) and Motley (costumes)

PRODUCERS: Richard Rodgers, Oscar Hammerstein, Joshua Logan, and Leland Hayward

CAST INCLUDES: Mary Martin, opera star Ezio Pinza in his Broadway debut at the age of fifty-seven, Myron McCormick, William Tabbert, Barbara Luna, and Juanita Hall

PERFORMANCES: 1,925

dilemma that's a lesson in American racism and bigotry, synthesized in Cable's cry of pain, "You've Got to Be Carefully Taught":

> You've got to be taught to hate and fear,
> You've got to be taught from year to year,
> It's got to be drummed in your dear little ear—
> You've got to be carefully taught!

> You've got to be taught to be afraid
> Of people whose eyes are oddly made,
> And people whose skin is a different shade,
> You've got to be carefully taught.

> You've got to be taught before it's too late,
> Before you are six or seven or eight,
> To hate all the people your relatives hate,
> You've got to be carefully taught!
> You've got to be carefully taught!

Rodgers and Hammerstein refused to cut the song during out-of-town try-outs even though it stirred up controversy with some even wondering if it wasn't too strong for a song in a musical. Oscar Hammerstein firmly maintained that stance when he stated:

> There are few things in life of which I am certain, but I am sure of this one
> thing, that the song is the servant of the play, that it is wrong to write first what
> you think is an attractive song and then try to wedge it into a story. (Oscar
> Hammerstein II, *Lyrics by Oscar Hammerstein II*, 19)

South Pacific had the first original-cast LP to sell over a million copies, and fans bought millions of copies of the sheet music versions of the songs. It was also the first time Rodgers and Hammerstein cast established stars in the leading roles. There are no duets for them: Martin agreed to do the show only if her musical-theater voice wouldn't have to compete with Pinza's operatic one. The hit-filled score includes "A Cockeyed Optimist," "There Is Nothin' Like a Dame," "I'm Gonna Wash That Man Right Outa My Hair" (which Nellie does on stage while washing her hair in a shower stall), "(I'm in Love with) A Wonderful Guy," "Honey Bun," and "Some Enchanted Evening." There's also a great deal of underscoring during the dramatic scenes. The last new song, de Becque's "This Nearly Was Mine," comes a good twenty minutes before the end of the show.

The songs and ensembles develop spontaneously within the action, instead of being thrust upon it. The abandonment of formal choreography in favor of Logan's resourceful and beautifully fluid handling of the group scenes enabled the stage director to control the dramatic values at every point. . . . Rodgers's score . . . was also expertly calculated, for even the set pieces and obvious hit tunes belong to the play and do not disturb its progress. (Smith and Litton, 200)

Mielziner's conceptual design was a major contribution to the further development of Rodgers and Hammerstein's musical form. Sets changed in full view of the audience as the lights cross-faded from one location to another, giving the show a seamless flow without the necessity of playing things in 1 (a practice that soon became fairly standard). Today, with the possibilities allowed by high tech, such fluidity is expected.

The 1958 movie directed by Logan starred Mitzi Gaynor, Rossano Brazzi (dubbed by Georgio Tozzi), John Kerr (dubbed by Bill Lee), Ray Walston, France Nuyen, and Juanita Hall, the original Bloody Mary (but dubbed by Muriel Smith). The movie added "My Girl Back Home," written for the original production but dropped before it opened in New York. For some peculiar reason, Logan chose to shoot each musical number in a different color wash; when he realized he didn't like the way it turned out, it was unfortunately too late to do anything about it. There is also a made-for-TV version that came out in 2000, starring a way-too-mature Glenn Close as Nellie and Harry Connick Jr. as Cable. In 2006, PBS broadcast a concert version starring Reba McEntire, Brian Stokes Mitchell, Alec Baldwin, and Lillias White.

Suggested Watching and Listening

Gentlemen Prefer Blondes
The song "Diamonds Are a Girl's Best Friend," from this 1949 show, is available in two very different interpretations listed below.
- "Diamonds Are a Girl's Best Friend" (performed by Carol Channing): Lorelei's philosophy of life, it's on the original-cast recording and on *Original Cast! The Forties:* Part 2 (MET CD). Channing also does the song on *The Best of Broadway Musicals,* a collection of live sequences taken from Ed Sullivan's old TV show. It's on Good Times Entertainment DVD. Marilyn Monroe's version from the movie, styled specifically to her talents, was directed by Howard Hawks and is available on 20th Century Fox DVD.

Kiss Me, Kate
The following suggestions are various versions of songs from this 1948 show.
- "So in Love" (performed by k.d. lang): Albert Williams refers to it as "Porter's ode to sadomasochistic obsession." The lyrics of the last A are:

So taunt me and hurt me,
Deceive me, desert me.
I'm yours 'til I die,
So in love,
So in love,
So in love with you, my love, am I.

This version is from the AIDS awareness video *Red, Hot + Blue* on Shout! Factory DVD.

- "Tom, Dick, or Harry" (performed by Ann Miller, Bob Fosse, Tommy Rall, and Bobby Van): This version and the following one are from the 1953 movie on Warner Brothers DVD (unfortunately not in 3-D), with choreography by Hermes Pan and Bob Fosse. (The occasionally obsessive repetition of the name *Dick* is not entirely free of double entendre.)
- "I Hate Men" (performed by Kathryn Grayson): Although sung by Kate in the musical within the musical, the lyrics—somewhat cleaned up for Hollywood—are far more appropriate to mid-twentieth-century America than to late sixteenth-century Italy, containing references to such things as secretaries, democracies, and Lassie.

There's also a video of the London company's revival of the show available on Image Entertainment DVD. It's version of "Brush Up Your Shakespeare" is particularly good.

Lost in the Stars
From the 1949 show comes this song at the end of the first act in which the minister questions his own faith.
- "Lost in the Stars" (performed by Todd Duncan): It's on the original-cast recording and on *Original Cast! The Forties: Part 2* (MET CD).

South Pacific
The following songs are from the 1949 Broadway hit.
- "Younger Than Springtime" (performed by Harry Connick Jr.): Lieutenant Cable's hit love song, it's on the 2000 TV movie available on Disney DVD.
- "Some Enchanted Evening" (performed by Ezio Pinza): De Beque's hit love song, it's on the original-cast recording and on *Original Cast! The Forties: Part 2* (MET CD).
- "Carefully Taught" and "This Nearly Was Mine" (performed by Jason Danieley and Brian Stokes Mitchell): The last two songs in the show, they move directly from one to the other with underscored dialogue in between. This version is from the 2006 concert on Rhino DVD. Actually, you can't go wrong with any song from *South Pacific*.

Where's Charley?
This 1948 show includes the hit song "Once in Love with Amy," performed by Ray Bolger. With Bolger including an audience sing-along as part of this number, it grew longer as the run of the show extended. It's on Paul Gruber's *Original Cast! The Forties: Part 2* (MET CD).

From *Guys* *and* *Dolls* to *Peter* *Pan*

Shall I join with other nations in alliance?
If allies are weak, am I not best alone?
If allies are strong with power to protect me,
Might they not protect me out of all I own?
Is a danger to be trusting one another,
One will seldom want to do what other wishes . . .
But unless someday somebody trust somebody,
There'll be nothing left on earth excepting fishes!
—"A PUZZLEMENT," *THE KING AND I*, LYRICS BY OSCAR HAMMERSTEIN II

Starting in the early fifties, the big Broadway revue was killed by TV, almost every successful musical was made into a movie or TV show, and nearly every new musical had an original-cast recording. A lot of this new commercialization of the musical was due to Rodgers and Hammerstein's treatment of it.

> [Rodgers and Hammerstein's] work influenced nearly every musical until the end of the sixties. . . . This influence was commercial as much as artistic. . . . [Their] shows made more money than musicals had ever made before—they sold more tickets and records, and were later turned into hit movies from which best-selling sound-track recordings were marketed. . . . Broadway musicals became big business in the fifties, with major corporations like Twentieth Century–Fox and Columbia Records investing in shows. Ironically, by the time this happened the genre's importance to American cultural life had almost peaked. Prior to the fifties, most American popular music came from the theater and films; by the end of the decade, popular music had shifted . . . to rock, never to return again. (Gruber, *Original Cast! The Fifties: Part 1,* 3)

New York's off-Broadway movement grew and flourished. Since the shows and the theaters were smaller than those on Broadway, production costs were lower, so ticket prices were lower. Off-Broadway shows could therefore afford to take risks that Broadway shows no longer could, especially with more experimental shows.

In 1950, composer Kurt Weill, writer-lyricist-composer B. G. DeSylva, and performers Walter Huston and Al Jolson died. Washington, D.C.'s regional theater Arena Stage opened. The federal government filed an antitrust suit against the Shuberts. Because audiences continued to dwindle and costs to rise, the biggest hit shows were taking more than the lion's share of business, and some pretty good shows (revues in particular) weren't able to run long enough to pay back their investors, a trend that continued throughout the decade.

About twenty-five musicals and revues opened in New York that year, including *Peter Pan* (321 performances)—the 1904 James M. Barrie play to which a few songs by Leonard Bernstein were added—starring Jean Arthur and Boris Karloff. A charming version of Barrie's play, it's been overwhelmed by the 1954 Mary Martin–Jerome Robbins version. Menotti's opera *The Consul*, set in a totalitarian state, ran 269 performances. There was a limited run

Backdrop: 1950–1954

National Dwight David "Ike" Eisenhower becomes the first Republican president in thirty years. The Twenty-second Amendment limits presidential terms to two. Wisconsin senator Joseph McCarthy begins his witch hunt of Communists in America by claiming to have a list of them in the State Department. (It's later revealed to be a lie.) Alger Hiss is found guilty of perjury and jailed for denying he was a Communist spy. Julius and Ethel Rosenberg are executed for selling U.S. atomic secrets to the Soviets. Atomic scientist J. Robert Oppenheimer is charged with having Communist sympathies and with possible treason. McCarthy reveals his true colors to the nation when he conducts his televised hearings about Communists in the Army. Edward R. Murrow, on his TV show *See It Now*, launches an attack against the senator, and Congress votes to condemn him for misconduct. In the twelve years beginning in 1950, 20 percent of U.S. farmers quit the land. The U.S. Consumer Price Index for all goods and services rises 10 percent during the fifties, and suburban land values rise 100 percent. Tennessee senator Estes Kefauver begins a televised congressional investigation of organized crime. The Supreme Court rules that revival of *Brigadoon.* Gwen Verdon made her debut in the Harold Rome revue *Alive and Kicking* (46 performances), and Bob Fosse made his in the revue *Dance Me a Song* (35 performances).

Guys and Dolls, one of the most perfectly balanced musical comedies, is constantly being revived all over the world. One of Broadway's longest-running revivals was the 1992 production (1,143 performances) directed by Jerry Zaks and starring Faith Prince, Nathan Lane, and Peter Gallagher. The story is set in Damon Runyon's unique world of Broadway gamblers, Salvation Army workers, showgirls, crooks, and policemen. The two love stories—between Salvation Army sergeant Sarah Brown and gambler Sky Masterson, and between Hot Box Club singer-stripper Miss Adelaide and gambler Nathan Detroit—are of equal importance to the plot and intersect perfectly, centering around a bet between Sky and Nathan.

Loesser's music and, in particular, his lyrics are always true to Runyon's world. The score produced several hit songs, such as Sky's "Luck Be a Lady Tonight," Sky and Sarah's "I've Never

Guys and Dolls—A Musical Fable of Broadway

MUSIC/LYRICS: Frank Loesser

BOOK: Jo Swerling and Abe Burrows, adapted from three stories by Damon Runyon

DIRECTOR: George S. Kaufman

CHOREOGRAPHER: Michael Kidd

ORCHESTRATORS: George Bassman and Ted Royal

DESIGNERS: Jo Mielziner (sets and lights) and Alvin Colt (costumes)

PRODUCERS: Cy Feuer and Ernest Martin

CAST INCLUDES: Sam Levene, Robert Alda, Vivian Blaine, Isabel Bigley, and Stubby Kaye

PERFORMANCES: 1,194

---

racial segregation in public schools is unconstitutional; all states must begin integrating "with all deliberate speed." Malcolm X joins with Black Muslim leader Elijah Muhammad. Puerto Rico becomes the first U.S. commonwealth. President Eisenhower orders that "one nation, indivisible" be replaced with "one nation, under God" in the Pledge of Allegiance. Armistice Day is renamed Veterans Day.

International   North Korea invades South Korea; Chinese troops fight alongside the North Koreans, financed and equipped by the Soviet Union. Secretary-General Trygve Lie urges UN members to support South Korea. President Truman sends U.S. air and sea forces; it's America's first undeclared war. By the time South and North Korea sign an armistice, both countries lie in ruins. China and the Soviet Union sign an alliance declaring America and Japan their main enemies. The Geneva Conference divides Vietnam in two, with South Vietnam under Bao Dai and North Vietnam under Ho Chi Minh. The United States signs a military assistance pact with France, Cambodia, and Laos and begins supplying arms and military advisers to South Vietnam. Soviet leader Joseph Stalin dies; he's succeeded by Georgy Malenkov. Algeria revolts against France. Guatemala allies itself with the Communists. Gamal Abdel Nasser becomes prime minister of Egypt; he's made president in 1956. Britain's King George VI dies and his daughter becomes Queen Elizabeth II. Dictator Fulgencio Batista resumes

---

Abe Burrows (1910–85, born Abram Solmon Borowitz in New York) totally rewrote the script of *Guys and Dolls* with a lot of uncredited help from director Kaufman, even though Jo Swerling kept his cowriting credit. It was Burrows's first Broadway show; he'd been writing radio comedy shows and making comedy records. He soon began directing as well and was called in to help many shows struggling out of town. (Neil Simon, Mike Nichols, and Jerome Robbins are three other well-respected show doctors.) Among the shows Burrows wrote and/or directed are Porter's *Can-Can* and Loesser's *How to Succeed in Business Without Really Trying*.

Been in Love Before," and Sarah's "If I Were a Bell," which exactly fit the characters who sing them and the situations they're sung in. Also in the score are Sky's "My Time of Day"; "Adelaide's Lament," a great comic monologue for a woman who's been engaged for fourteen years and has developed "a bad, bad cold"; and the title song. There are two eleven o'clock numbers: "Sit Down, You're Rockin' the Boat," a pseudo-gospel number led by gambler Nicely Nicely Johnson at a Salvation Army meeting, and "Marry the Man Today," a comic duet for Sarah and Adelaide sung in 1 while the set's being changed for the last short scene.

The opening is a miracle of musical exposition: "Runyonland Music" (which is wordless) leads into "Fugue for Tinhorns" (a contrapuntal trio for three gamblers), which leads into "Follow the Fold" (a Salvation Army marching song). We learn that we're in midtown Manhattan and that gamblers, pickpockets, and other street people are doing their business while eluding the police and ignoring the sermonizing of Salvation Army recruiter Sarah Brown. Michael Kidd's choreography throughout the sequence helps tell the story.

There's an original-cast recording, one of the 1992 revival, and one of Mankiewicz's 1955 movie starring Marlon Brando, Jean Simmons, and Frank Sinatra, with Vivian Blaine and Stubby

control in Cuba after a military coup. Jomo Kenyatta leads a Mau Mau insurrection against Kenya's white settlers.

New Developments The American Stock Exchange is created. DNA is identified. A hydrogen bomb exploded at Bikini Atoll in the South Pacific is hundreds of times more powerful than the atom bomb. The first nuclear-powered submarine, the *Nautilus,* is launched. Evidence emerges that smoking is hazardous to health and that there's a correlation between heart disease and diets high in animal fats. Harvard physicians perform the world's first successful kidney transplant. Jonas Salk tests a vaccine against polio. Tranquilizer drugs are developed, and LSD is produced. The Mercedes 300 SL is introduced. Chrysler installs the first power-steering mechanisms in autos. The world has 92 million telephones, 52 million of them in the United States. The Diners Club is founded. Otis Elevator installs the first self-service elevators. Smokey the Bear becomes the symbol for forest fire prevention. Wang Laboratories begins making small business calculators. Sony introduces the first pocket-size transistor radios. The first videotape is demonstrated. The Church of Scientology is founded. The first Holiday Inn opens near Memphis. Swanson sells the first frozen TV dinners. Sucaryl, Minute Rice, Sugar Frosted Flakes, and

Kaye repeating their Broadway roles as Miss Adelaide and Nicely Nicely. (Sinatra plays Nathan. He should have played Sky; Brando was no singer.) Kidd re-created his original choreography for the movie, which was designed by Oliver Smith and Irene Sharaff.

Written for Merman, *Call Me Madam* is a lightly satirical look at President Truman's appointment of Perle Mesta to the ambassadorship of Luxembourg, her only qualification being that she was a wealthy party hostess in Washington, D.C. The show is about wealthy D.C. party hostess Sally Adams ("the hostess with the mostes' on the ball" as she sings of herself in her opening number), who's appointed by Truman to the ambassadorship of the small, fictional, Middle European country of Lichtenberg, where she gives away Uncle Sam's money and finds romance. The subplot is between Sally's young male assistant and a Lichtenbergian princess. Berlin's last hit, it shows signs of formula and repetition. The score includes "The Best Thing for You," "It's a Lovely Day Today," and "They Like Ike" (which became Eisenhower's presidential campaign song as "I Like Ike"). The show's biggest hit song and its eleven o'clock number is the contrapuntal duet for Sally and her assistant "You're Just in Love," again with Merman getting the syncopated half; it was encored

Call Me Madam

MUSIC/LYRICS: Irving Berlin
BOOK: Russel Crouse and Howard Lindsay
DIRECTOR: George Abbott
CHOREOGRAPHER: Jerome Robbins
ORCHESTRATOR: Don Walker
PRODUCER: Leland Hayward
CAST INCLUDES: Ethel Merman and Paul Lucas
PERFORMANCES: 644

Sugar Pops are marketed. Stratocaster electric guitars are introduced and used by such rock and roll pioneers as Buddy Holly, Jimi Hendrix, and Eric Clapton.

Sports   Sugar Ray Robinson wins, loses, wins, and relinquishes the world middleweight boxing title. Jersey Joe Walcott beats Ezzard Charles for the world heavyweight title. Rocky Marciano knocks out Walcott to become champion and retires undefeated in 1956. Edmund Hillary reaches the summit of Mount Everest. Ben Hogan wins the U.S. Open and Masters golf tournaments, breaks the Masters record by five strokes, and wins his first British Open. The St. Louis Browns become the Baltimore Orioles, the Boston Braves move to Milwaukee and add Hank Aaron to the team, Willie Mays joins the New York Giants, and Mickey Mantle joins the New York Yankees. The Yankees win the World Series for a fifth consecutive year. Jockey Eddie Arcaro wins his fifth Kentucky Derby.

Art   Raoul Dufy, Henri Matisse, and Frida Kahlo die. There are new paintings by Picasso, Pollock, Hopper, Rivera, Dubuffet, Rauschenberg, Bacon, Rivers, and Braque. Washington's Iwo Jima Memorial Monument is dedicated.

Out of This World

MUSIC/LYRICS: Cole Porter
BOOK: Dwight Taylor and
Reginald Lawrence, based on
the Greek legend of Amphitryon
DIRECTOR: Agnes de Mille (fired
out of town and replaced by
George Abbott)
CHOREOGRAPHER: Hanya Holm
ORCHESTRATOR: Robert Russell
Bennett
DESIGNER: Lemuel Ayers (sets
and costumes)
PRODUCERS: Saint Subber and
Lemuel Ayers
CAST INCLUDES: Charlotte
Greenwood and David Burns
PERFORMANCES: 157

most nights. Since RCA Victor was the sole investor and Merman was exclusive with Decca, she couldn't participate in the original-cast recording and was replaced by Dinah Shore; Merman and Dick Haymes recorded most of the songs for Decca. The 1953 movie stars Merman and Donald O'Connor.

A flop largely because of its awkward book set in the world of Greek gods and goddesses, *Out of This World* takes place both on Mount Olympus and in modern-day Greece. It has one of Porter's most unified scores, although most of the songs give the impression that he was straining. In the score are "What Do You Think About Men?" a trio for three women; "I Am Loved"; "Cherry Pies Ought to Be You," a list song with a verse and six choruses; "Nobody's Chasing Me," a four-chorus list song; and "I Sleep Easier Now," a list song with a verse and four choruses. "From This Moment On" was cut from the score out of town but was incorporated into both the 1953 movie and the 1999 revival of *Kiss Me, Kate*. There's an original-cast recording.

Music/Dance   Vaughan Williams composes his Symphony no. 7 (*Sinfonia Antarctica*) and Robbins choreographs Britten's ballet *Fanfare*. Bernstein's one-act opera *Trouble in Tahiti* and his ballet *The Age of Anxiety* premiere, as do Stravinsky's *The Rake's Progress*, Britten's *Billy Budd*, and Menotti's *Amahl and the Night Visitors* (the first opera written for TV). The Ballet Folklórico de México is founded.

Publications   *TV Guide, Playboy, Sports Illustrated,* and *Mad* magazines begin publication, as do cartoonist Hank Ketcham's *Dennis the Menace* and Charles M. Schulz's *Peanuts*. Essayist/satirist George Orwell dies. New poetry includes Auden's *Nones*, Langston Hughes's "Harlem," and Thomas's "Do Not Go Gentle into That Good Night," as well as collections by Roethke and Shapiro. Among other notable books are Salinger's *The Catcher in the Rye* and *Nine Stories;* Jones's *From Here to Eternity* and Wouk's *The Caine Mutiny* (both about World War II); Styron's *Lie Down in Darkness;* Baldwin's *Go Tell It on the Mountain;* Ellison's *Invisible Man;* Bellow's *The Adventures of Augie March;* Bradbury's take on book burning, *Fahrenheit 451;* Hemingway's *The Old Man and the Sea;* Steinbeck's *East of Eden;* Golding's *Lord of the Flies;* Fleming's first James Bond novel, *Casino Royale;* E. B. White's *Charlotte's Web;* and the first part of Tolkien's *The Lord of the Rings*.

Radio/TV   The first transcontinental TV broadcasting begins. There are eight million TV sets in the United States; 45 million homes have radios. CBS broadcasts color programs though no one owns color sets yet. RCA introduces the first color sets; nineteen-inch, black-and-white ones retail at $187. The highest rated TV shows of the five years are Milton Berle's comedy-variety show *Texaco Star Theater, Arthur Godfrey's Talent Scouts,* and *I Love Lucy*. Max Leibman's *Your Show of Shows*, a weekly hour-and-a-half

In 1951, composer Sigmund Romberg and "funny girl" Fanny Brice died. The House Un-American Activities Committee began its search for Communists on Broadway. There was a limited-run revival of *Oklahoma!* and an unsuccessful revival of the 1932 *Music in the Air.* There were only about fifteen new musical evenings. Barbara Cook made her Broadway debut in Sammy Fain, E. Y. Harburg, Fred Saidy, and Cheryl Crawford's *Flahooley* (40 performances).

One of the last successful, old-style Broadway revues, *Two on the Aisle* (279 performances)—with music by Jule Styne and sketches and lyrics by Comden and Green—wasn't that big a hit that year. It starred Bert Lahr and Dolores Gray; was the first of several collaborations between Styne, Comden, and Green; and was Abe Burrows's first time out as a director. The score includes the comic number "If You Hadn't, But You Did," sung by a woman giving the reasons why she just shot her lover. (Also in 1951, Comden and Green wrote the screenplay for *Singin' in the Rain,* released in 1952.)

Paint Your Wagon (289 performances), music by Frederick Loewe and book and lyrics by Alan Jay Lerner, was directed by Daniel Mann and choreographed by Agnes de Mille. It's set during the California Gold Rush. Although the show had a decent run, it lost money; Lerner's book is often

revue, makes its NBC debut starring Sid Caesar, Imogene Coca, Carl Reiner, and Howard Morris; it's written by some of the best comedy writers ever assembled in one room. The radio version of *Your Hit Parade,* featuring the top ten songs of the week, goes off the air but the TV version continues for several more seasons. Edward R. Murrow's *See It Now,* the soap opera *Search for Tomorrow, The Today Show,* and Dick Clark's *American Bandstand* make their network debuts.

Pop Culture Birdland opens with alto saxophonist Charlie "Bird" Parker. Dave Brubeck and his San Francisco quartet pioneer modern, or progressive, jazz, giving jazz a new complexity of rhythm and counterpoint. The first Newport Jazz Festival is held. The mambo and the cha-cha are introduced to American dance floors. Disc jockey Alan Freed popularizes the term *rock 'n' roll.* Elvis Presley makes his first commercial recording, "That's All Right, Mama" and "Blue Moon of Kentucky." Twenty-nine-year-old, country-western star Hank Williams dies. New pop songs of the half-decade include Williams's "Your Cheatin' Heart"; Conner's "I Saw Mommy Kissing Santa Claus"; Willson's "It's Beginning to Look a Lot Like Christmas"; Livingston and Evans's "Silver Bells"; Gardner's "All I Want for Christmas (Is My Two Front Teeth)"; Garner and Burke's "Misty"; Maxwell and Sigman's "Ebb Tide"; Styne and Cahn's title song for the movie *Three Coins in the Fountain;* Wayne and Morris's "Blue Velvet"; Keyes, the Feasters, McRae, and Edwards's "Sh-boom"; and Calhoun's "Shake, Rattle, and Roll."

Stage George Bernard Shaw and Eugene O'Neill die. Among the new plays are Beckett's *Waiting for Godot;* Miller's *The Crucible;* Williams's *The Rose Tattoo;* Inge's *Come Back, Little Sheba* and *Picnic;* McCullers's adaptation of her *The Member of the Wedding;* French absurdist Ionesco's first plays, *The* awkward, bitter, and heavy-handed. There's an original-cast recording, including "I Talk to the Trees," "They Call the Wind Maria," and "Wand'rin' Star." Avoid Joshua Logan's 1969 movie version, which has a new and even less interesting story. It stars Clint Eastwood and Lee Marvin, both unfortunately doing their own singing.

Top Banana (350 performances), songs by Johnny Mercer, starred Phil Silvers and Rose Marie (later of *The Dick Van Dyke Show*) and was modeled on Milton Berle's huge TV success. It's a frantic musical about a former burlesque and vaudeville star, who is now a TV star. Some of the show is given over to old burlesque and vaudeville routines, as was Berle's TV show. There's an original-cast recording; Mercer's music sounds rather secondhand. *Top Banana* was expensive to produce and had a high weekly operating cost; it didn't break even. It was filmed in 1954.

A Tree Grows in Brooklyn is about a young girl growing up poor and Irish in turn-of-the-century Brooklyn. She has an alcoholic father who dies halfway through the second act and an angry,

A Tree Grows in Brooklyn

MUSIC: Arthur Schwartz

LYRICS: Dorothy Fields

BOOK: Betty Smith and George Abbott, from Smith's novel

DIRECTOR/PRODUCER: George Abbott

CHOREOGRAPHER: Herbert Ross

ORCHESTRATORS: Robert Russell Bennett and Joe Glover

DESIGNERS: Jo Mielziner (sets and lights) and Irene Sharaff (costumes)

CAST INCLUDES: Shirley Booth

PERFORMANCES: 267

Bald Soprano, The Chairs, and The Lesson; Thomas's Under Milk Wood; Christie's The Mousetrap (still playing in London, the longest-running show in history); Anouilh's The Waltz of the Toreadors and Becket; de Hartog's The Fourposter (source of the 1966 musical I Do! I Do!); Loos's adaptation of Colette's Gigi (source of the 1957 movie musical and the 1973 Broadway musical); van Druten's I Am a Camera (adapted from Isherwood's Berlin Stories, source of the 1966 musical Cabaret); Laurents's The Time of the Cuckoo (source of the 1965 musical Do I Hear a Waltz?); and Nash's The Rainmaker (source of the 1963 musical 110 in the Shade).

Screen This Is Cinerama is the first movie in the extremely wide-screen, three-camera process; the biblical epic The Robe is the first movie produced in CinemaScope (wide-screen but not as wide-screen as Cinerama); and Bwana Devil is the first 3-D movie. Notable new movies are All About Eve (adapted from the same story as the 1970 musical Applause), Sunset Boulevard (source of the 1994 musical), The African Queen, Shane, High Noon, From Here to Eternity, The Quiet Man, Strangers on a Train, Rear Window, A Streetcar Named Desire, On the Waterfront, The Lavender Hill Mob, Mr. Hulot's Holiday, Pather Panchali, Miracle in Milan, Rashomon, The Seven Samurai, and La Strada (source of the 1969 musical, which closed on opening night).

About 140 new movie musicals are produced, among them several operettas, including the third adaptation of The Merry Widow; adaptations of Rose-Marie, The Student Prince, and The Desert Song; and Deep in My Heart, a pseudo-biography of Romberg. Other musicals are Three Little Words,

---

undemonstrative mother. (The best-selling novel had already been made into a 1945 nonmusical film.) It's Schwartz's best score for a book show and certainly his best without Dietz, although several of the songs might seem overly sentimental now. Lyricist Fields again shows her ability to adapt to whatever the circumstances of the show, but the book has problems, the biggest being that the star role was written for Shirley Booth, who played the main character of the comic subplot instead, which badly throws off the balance. The show didn't pay back its investment; given the poverty, the alcoholism, the pubescent angst, and the death of the father, a lot of it is downbeat. None of that matters as much now in terms of what audiences expect, and the show is done occasionally in regional theaters. It's worth considering for revival (or revisal). The original-cast recording includes "Make the Man Love Me" and "He Had Refinement." Like *Paint Your Wagon* and *Top Banana*, it ran almost a year without paying off its investors, an early sign of troubles to come.

It was Gertrude Lawrence's idea to musicalize *Anna and the King of Siam*, which had already been made into a nonmusical movie starring Irene Dunne and Rex Harrison. A fictionalized variation on a true story set at the same

a pseudo-biography of songwriters Bert Kalmar and Harry Ruby that stars Fred Astaire and Red Skelton; *Carmen Jones*; *Tea for Two*, a semi-adaptation of *No! No! Nanette!* starring Doris Day; *Where's Charley?* choreographed by Michael Kidd and starring Ray Bolger; *Hans Christian Andersen*, with Danny Kaye and songs by Loesser; *Top Banana*, with Phil Silvers; the revue *New Faces*; *Lovely to Look At*, a remake of *Roberta*; a remake of *Show Boat*; *Kiss Me, Kate* in 3-D; *Annie Get Your Gun*; *Gentlemen Prefer Blondes*, with Marilyn Monroe and Jane Russell; *Call Me Madam*, starring Ethel Merman and Donald O'Connor; *There's No Business Like Show Business*, with Merman, O'Connor, and Monroe and a score of old and new Berlin songs; *White Christmas*, with Bing Crosby and Danny Kaye and another score of old and new Berlin songs; *Call Me Mister*, using the title song and three others from Rome's revue; three directed by Minnelli—an adaptation of *Brigadoon* starring Gene Kelly and Cyd Charisse, *The Band Wagon* with Astaire and Charisse, a script by Comden and Green, and a score of old and new Schwartz and Dietz songs, and *An American in Paris* with Kelly, an all-Gershwin score, and a Lerner script; *Singin' in the Rain* (adapted into a 1985 stage musical), with Kelly and O'Connor, another script by Comden and Green, and a score of old Nacio Herb Brown and Arthur Freed songs; *Royal Wedding*, with Astaire, a Lane and Lerner score, and another Lerner script; *Seven Brides for Seven Brothers*, with choreography by Kidd and a score by Gene Paul and Johnny Mercer (adapted into a 1982 stage musical); *Lili* (source of the 1961 musical *Carnival!*); and Judy Garland and James Mason in *A Star Is Born* (adapted from the 1937 nonmusical, itself a reworking of the 1932 nonmusical *What Price Hollywood?*), with an Arlen and Ira Gershwin score that includes "The Man That Got Away."

The King and I

MUSIC: Richard Rodgers

LYRICS/BOOK: Oscar Hammerstein, based on Margaret Landon's novel *Anna and the King of Siam* and the diaries of Anna Leonowens

DIRECTOR: John van Druten

CHOREOGRAPHER: Jerome Robbins

ORCHESTRATOR: Robert Russell Bennett

DESIGNERS: Jo Mielziner (sets and lights) and Irene Sharaff (costumes)

PRODUCERS: Rodgers and Hammerstein

CAST INCLUDES: Gertrude Lawrence and Yul Brynner

PERFORMANCES: 1,246

time as America's Civil War, *The King and I* is about a Victorian Englishwoman hired by the semi-barbaric King of Siam as a teacher for the many children of his many wives. As in *South Pacific*, the clash of cultures is the main theme, with the King at war with himself about whether or not to move toward the more liberal practices of Western civilization as embodied in Anna. The King dies at the end of the show with Anna mourning at his side, while his son and heir—and Anna's student—begins a liberalization of the country the King felt was right but couldn't do himself. The central characters are deeply drawn, flaws and all. Although there's no acknowledged love between Anna and the King, it's very present subtextually. (Apparently Lawrence and Brynner started playing it during rehearsals, and when Hammerstein saw it, he liked it and augmented it.) The subplot about Tuptim, one of the king's wives, and the man she secretly loved before she was given to the king, ends tragically for both of them.

Anna was Lawrence's last role; she died during the run. The role of the King made Yul Brynner a star; he toured extensively in revivals at various times throughout his career and starred with Deborah Kerr (dubbed by Marni Nixon) in Lang's 1956 movie, for which he won an Academy Award. There was a very successful 1996 Broadway revival (originally produced in Australia) starring Donna Murphy and Lou Diamond Phillips. There are recordings of the original cast, the sound track, and several revivals. The score includes "I Whistle a Happy Tune," for Anna and her young son when they first arrive in Siam; "Hello, Young Lovers," a ballad for Anna; "Getting to Know You," for Anna and the King's children (added out of town); "We Kiss in a Shadow," a duet for the subplot couple; "A Puzzlement," the King's big solo; "Shall We Dance?" the eleven o'clock number, a polka and the only time Anna and the King touch; and "The Small House of Uncle Thomas Ballet," Robbins's "Siamese" ballet interpretation of Stowe's *Uncle Tom's Cabin,* done as an entertainment for the English ambassador. Tuptim uses the occasion to show her unhappiness at having to live a life that's against her will, comparing herself to Eliza escaping over the ice. By then, Robbins was a much sought-after choreographer, having already done such shows as *On the Town, High Button Shoes,* and Berlin's *Miss Liberty* and *Call Me Madam.* He was ready to move on to directing as well.

The King and I is the last innovative Rodgers and Hammerstein show. Their subsequent work gradually seems to be following formulas—their own, granted, but formulas nonetheless. Only one more of their shows, their last one, *The Sound of Music*, was as huge a hit as *Oklahoma!, Carousel, South Pacific,* and *The King and I.*

> In one way or another, all the major Rodgers and Hammerstein shows examine notions of community, civilized behavior, and initiation from a perspective that was considered liberal. . . . The genteel ethos of [their songs] . . . represented everything that rock-and-roll would aim to smash. . . . Certainly rock-and-roll at its rawest represented a spontaneous burst of rebellion by huge segments of American society that found the cultured urbanity of Rodgers and Hammerstein's Broadway songs too sweet, too sophisticated, and too pious to speak for them. (Stephen Holden, "Their Songs Were America's Happy Talk," *New York Times,* 45)

Even so, their shows have remained consistently popular, the five super hits constantly revived all around the world. Hammerstein commented:

> I see plays and read books that emphasize the seamy side of life, and the frenetic side, and the tragic side. I don't deny the existence of the tragic and the frenetic. But I say that somebody has to keep saying that isn't all there is to life. . . . We're very likely to get thrown off our balance if we have such a preponderance of artists expressing the "wasteland" philosophy. (Oscar Hammerstein, quoted in John Lahr's "All the Way to Heaven," *New Yorker,* 105)

About four thousand productions of their shows are presented worldwide every year. In 1995 alone there were 632 productions of *Oklahoma!* in North America and 467 of *South Pacific.* The Australian revival of *The King and I* opened on Broadway in March 1996 and ran for two years, followed by a very successful tour. In March 1996, the stage version of the 1945 movie musical *State Fair* also opened. The team's TV musical *Cinderella,* remade in 1997 with a multiracial cast, received huge ratings and a touring stage version. There was a successful 1998 Broadway revival of *The Sound of Music* starring Rebecca Luker; the movie version is, of course, a TV perennial and now exists in a sing-along version as well; and there was a hit 2006 London revival with the woman playing the lead having been picked by the audience vote on a TV reality show. The very successful 1998 British revival of *Oklahoma!* was moved—not as successfully—to Broadway in 2002. *South Pacific* was made into a 2001 TV movie starring Glenn Close, and a new production went on a national tour the same year. There was an unsuccessful Broadway revisal of *Flower Drum Song* in 2002.

In 1952, Gertrude Lawrence died. The Broadway Equity minimum went up to $85 a week. Only about a dozen musical shows opened on Broadway, most of them flops. A hit revival (542 performances) of *Pal Joey* starred Vivienne Segal (re-creating her original role), Harold Lang, and Elaine Stritch. A revival of *Of Thee I Sing* ran only 72 performances.

New Faces of 1952

MUSIC/LYRICS: various people, including Ronny Graham and June Carroll

SKETCHES: Ronny Graham and Melvin Brooks

DIRECTORS: John Beal and John Murray Anderson

CHOREOGRAPHER: Richard Barstow

ORCHESTRATOR: Ted Royal

DESIGNER: Raoul Pène du Bois (sets and costumes)

PRODUCER: Leonard Sillman

CAST INCLUDES: Eartha Kitt, Paul Lynde, Alice Ghostley, Ronny Graham, and Robert Clary, with Carol Lawrence in the very small chorus

PERFORMANCES: 365

Wish You Were Here

MUSIC/LYRICS: Harold Rome

BOOK: Arthur Kober and Joshua Logan, based on Kober's play *Having Wonderful Time*

DIRECTOR/CHOREOGRAPHER: Joshua Logan

ORCHESTRATOR: Don Walker

DESIGNERS: Jo Mielziner (sets and lights) and Robert Mackintosh (costumes)

PRODUCERS: Leland Hayward and Joshua Logan

CAST INCLUDES: Jack Cassidy, Florence Henderson, and Larry Blyden

PERFORMANCES: 598

New Faces of 1952 was an intimate revue and one of the only new musical evenings that wasn't lavishly produced. Written by many people, it was probably the very best of Sillman's occasional series. It includes such sketches as a still funny parody of *Death of a Salesman* by Mel Brooks. In the score are "Boston Beguine," by Sheldon Harnick; "Love Is a Simple Thing," by Arthur Siegel and June Carroll; and "Lizzie Borden (Or You Can't Chop Your Poppa Up in Massachusetts)," by Michael Brown. The revue was filmed in 1954 with the original cast and extra numbers for Eartha Kitt, who'd become a big recording star by then.

About the search for love at a Catskill Mountains summer camp, *Wish You Were Here* was Rome's first book show. It features a hit title song, an onstage swimming pool, and lots of girls in swimming suits, three of its main selling points. The production was so big it had to preview in town instead of doing out-of-town tryouts, the first important precedent for what eventually became standard practice.

> Devastatingly unfavorable word-of-mouth began to spread as soon as [previews] were inaugurated. The opening was delayed several times, and revisions followed fast and furiously. When the show finally opened, most critics shrugged it off as not worth all the time and effort that had gone into it. (Bordman, 583)

After the opening, Logan did extensive rewrites and Jerome Robbins was brought in to do new choreography, all of which would most probably have happened out of town had the show been able to afford out-of-town tryouts before the New York opening. Even so, word of mouth soon took precedent over the reviews, and business picked up. The title song repeats "wish you were here" twenty times, part of why Eddie Fisher's hit cover recording helped sell the show. RCA Victor, a major investor, released the original-cast recording.

In 1953, Lee Shubert died. The antitrust case against the Shuberts was dropped. Actors' Equity ruled that anyone proven to be a Communist would be expelled from the union. There were about fifteen musical evenings on Broadway during the year, among which were one-person shows by Ethel Waters and Victor Borge; the revue *John Murray Anderson's Almanac* (227 performances), with songs by Richard Adler and Jerry Ross and a cast that included Harry Belafonte, Orson Bean, Polly Bergen, and Tina Louise; and Jule Styne, Bob Hilliard, and Ben Hecht's flop *Hazel Flagg* (190 performances), adapted from Hecht's 1937 movie *Nothing Sacred*. There was also a 305-performance run of *Porgy and Bess*, starring Leontyne Price, William Warfield, and Cab Calloway, which established it once and for all as a true American opera. With the help of the State Department, it toured North America, Europe, the Middle East, South America, and the Soviet Union.

Can-Can tells how that dance scandalized Paris in 1893. It's not top-drawer Porter, but it has several good songs and lots of dancing, and it was a hit. The score includes "Allez-Vous-En (Go Away)," "C'est Magnifique," "I Love Paris," "It's All Right with Me," and, among other big dance numbers, "Quadrille" and "The Garden of Eden Ballet." Walter Lang's 1960 movie with Frank Sinatra, Shirley MacLaine, Maurice Chevalier, Louis Jourdan, and Juliet Prowse added "Let's Do It, Let's Fall in Love" and "Just One of Those Things."

Like *Allegro, Me and Juliet* tells an original story (the only other one Rodgers and Hammerstein did) and wasn't particularly successful, although it did return its investment. It's about the love affairs backstage during the run of a successful musical called *Me and Juliet*, but unlike Porter's *Kiss Me, Kate*, which has a story line that mirrors *The Taming of the Shrew*, this one doesn't mirror *Romeo and Juliet* nor is the show within the show Shakespeare's play. (A contemporary *Romeo and Juliet* musical had to wait until *West Side Story*.) RCA was the show's sole backer. In the score is "No Other Love," a pop hit. For that song, Hammerstein put words to a melody Rodgers had written for the score of *Victory at Sea*, a multipart TV documentary about the U.S. Navy during World War II. When *Me and Juliet* opened, Rodgers and Hammerstein's *South Pacific* and *The King and I* were still running, and

Gwen Verdon (1926–2000, born in Culver City, California), had her first big Broadway role in Porter's *Can-Can*. She stole the show and became a star, even though Lilo did manage to get one of her dance numbers cut. Verdon started as a dancer and was choreographer Jack Cole's assistant. She won a Tony for *Can-Can*. Two years later she won another Tony as the devil's assistant in *Damn Yankees*, choreographed by her soon-to-be husband, Bob Fosse, who either choreographed or directed and choreographed all the rest of her shows, including *Sweet Charity* and *Chicago*. She appeared in several movies both early and late in her career and was the artistic director of the 1999 Broadway hit *Fosse: A Celebration in Song and Dance*.

Can-Can
MUSIC/LYRICS: Cole Porter
BOOK/DIRECTOR: Abe Burrows
CHOREOGRAPHER: Michael Kidd
DESIGNERS: Jo Mielziner (sets and lights) and Motley (costumes)
PRODUCERS: Cy Feuer and Ernest Martin
CAST INCLUDES: Lilo, Gwen Verdon, and Hans Conried
PERFORMANCES: 892

Me and Juliet

MUSIC: Richard Rodgers

LYRICS/BOOK: Oscar Hammerstein

DIRECTOR: George Abbott

CHOREOGRAPHER: Robert Alton

ORCHESTRATOR: Don Walker

DESIGNERS: Jo Mielziner (sets and lights) and Irene Sharaff (costumes)

PRODUCERS: Richard Rodgers and Oscar Hammerstein

CAST INCLUDES: Bill Hayes and Ray Walston, with Shirley MacLaine in the dance ensemble

PERFORMANCES: 358

Wonderful Town

MUSIC: Leonard Bernstein

LYRICS: Betty Comden and Adolph Green

BOOK: Joseph Fields and Jerome Chodorov, adapted from their 1940 play My Sister Eileen, which was itself adapted from short stories by Ruth McKenney

DIRECTOR: George Abbott

CHOREOGRAPHER: Donald Saddler

ORCHESTRATOR: Don Walker

DESIGNERS: Raoul Pène du Bois (sets and costumes), Mainbocher (costumes), and Peggy Clark (lights)

PRODUCER: Robert Fryer

CAST INCLUDES: Rosalind Russell (replaced during the run by Carol Channing, who did the road tour), with Edith (Edie) Adams as Eileen

PERFORMANCES: 559

Oklahoma! was being revived at the New York City Center. Among other Mielziner-designed shows running at the same time as *Me and Juliet* and *Can-Can* were *South Pacific, Guys and Dolls,* and *The King and I.*

Basically a vehicle for movie star Rosalind Russell, *Wonderful Town* is a well-constructed, traditional musical comedy set in New York's Greenwich Village in 1935. The story follows two sisters from Ohio trying to establish lives and careers in the big city—Ruth (Russell) as a writer, Eileen (Edith Adams) as an actress. (Russell had already played Ruth in a 1942 nonmusical movie version of the play.) Under a deadline, Bernstein, Comden, and Green wrote the score in either three, four, or five weeks—depending on who's telling the story—since the producer was going to lose Russell if rehearsals didn't start, and no one liked the songs already written by Leroy Anderson and Arnold B. Horwitt. Robbins was brought in while the show was out of town to rework some of the choreography.

Other than the few songs he wrote for *Peter Pan, Wonderful Town* was Bernstein's first musical since *On the Town;* it was the sixth for Comden and Green. The score helped unify the show by including bits of earlier songs within later songs. Russell had a low and very limited vocal range and could talk very quickly; her songs were written accordingly. The score includes "A Quiet Girl," which—like "The Girl That I Marry" from *Annie Get Your Gun*—is one of a long line of pretty but sexist songs sung by men who end up with very different women from the ones they describe as their ideals; "Ohio," a comic duet for Ruth and Eileen their first night in New York; Eileen's charm song, "A Little Bit in Love"; "Pass That Football," sung by the sisters' stupid upstairs neighbor, who went to college on a scholarship based solely on his ability to play football; "Wrong Note Rag," the eleven o'clock number, another duet for the two sisters; and "One Hundred Easy Ways (To Lose a Man)," Ruth's comic lament about her love life. Here's the first of the four ways she actually gets through in the song:

You've met a charming fellow and you're out for a spin.
The motor fails and he just wears a helpless grin,
Don't bat your eyes and say, "What a romantic spot we're in."

[*Spoken flatly*] Just get out, crawl under the car, tell him
  it's the gasket,
And fix it in two seconds flat with a bobby pin.
That's a good way to lose a man—

A TV version of the musical, also with Russell, was produced in 1958 by CBS, which had backed the show. (The 1955
movie musical *My Sister Eileen* was not a version of *Wonderful
Town* but a new, far less successful musical adaptation of the
original play.) *Wonderful Town* is revived occasionally, including
a 497-performance Broadway revival in 2005 starring Donna
Murphy.

Kismet is a comic desert epic with lyrics set to souped-up operetta versions of melodies by the Russian classical composer
Borodin. Wright and Forrest had done the same thing to Grieg
in the 1944 *Song of Norway* and did it to Rachmaninov in their
1965 *Anya*. Borodin shared the Tony with Wright and Forrest
sixty-seven years after his death. (A similar thing happened
when T. S. Eliot won for the lyrics of *Cats*). The score includes
"And This Is My Beloved," "Baubles, Bangles, and Beads," and
"Stranger in Paradise"; the last two became pop hits. There's a
1955 film version with Howard Keel and Ann Blyth.

In 1954, David Merrick and Harold Prince made their debuts
as producers and Bob Fosse made his as a choreographer.
There were about twenty-five musicals on and off-Broadway,
including a flop revival of *On Your Toes* (revived successfully in
1983); limited-run revivals of *Show Boat* and *Carousel;*
Menotti's opera *The Saint of Bleeker Street* (92 performances);
and Romberg's posthumous *The Girl in Pink Tights* (115 performances), a fictional account of the making of the 1866 *The Black
Crook.*

   The Boy Friend (485 performances) had book, music, and lyrics
by Sandy Wilson and starred nineteen-year-old Julie Andrews in
her Broadway debut. An import from London, where it had
opened in 1953 and ran 2,084 performances, *The Boy Friend* is
both a parody of and an affectionate look back at 1920s musicals.
The charming, period-perfect score includes the title tune, "I
Could Be Happy with You," and "Won't You Charleston with Me?"
The 1971 Ken Russell movie is a backstage story parodying the

**Kismet: A Musical
Arabian Night**

MUSIC/LYRICS: Robert Wright and
George Forrest, adapted from
musical themes by Alexander
Borodin

BOOK: Charles Lederer and Luther
Davis, based on the 1911 play
by Edward Knoblock

DIRECTOR: Albert Marre

CHOREOGRAPHER: Jack Cole

PRODUCERS: Charles Lederer and
Edwin Lester

CAST INCLUDES: Alfred Drake, Joan
Diener, and Richard Kiley

PERFORMANCES: 583

thirties movie musical *42nd Street,* with *The Boy Friend* as the show within the show. The movie's cast included Twiggy, Tommy Tune, and Glenda Jackson. There was a 111-performance Broadway revival in 1970.

The Threepenny Opera

MUSIC: Kurt Weill

LYRICS/BOOK: Bertolt Brecht, translated and adapted by Marc Blitzstein

DIRECTOR: Carmen Capalbo

ORCHESTRATOR: Kurt Weill

PRODUCERS: John Krimsky and Gifford Cochran

CAST INCLUDES: Lotte Lenya (Weill's widow, in the same role she had played in the original 1928 German production), Scott Merrill, and Jo Sullivan

PERFORMANCES: 94 in 1954, then it reopened in 1955 and ran 2,611 performances, all off-Broadway

The Threepenny Opera is about beggars, criminals, and police in London during the time of a coronation; it demands that you "first feed our stomachs, then talk to us about morality." The first run had to close to make room for another show booked into the theater, but *New York Times* critic Brooks Atkinson waged a campaign to bring it back. Blitzstein's translation of the show, using Weill's original orchestrations for a small band, is frequently revived. (An earlier translation failed on Broadway in 1933.) The original-cast recording, along with several Lotte Lenya recordings of Weill's German and American songs, began a widespread revival of interest in the composer and his shows four years after his death. (Kander and Ebb shows like *Cabaret, Chicago,* and *Kiss of the Spider Woman* all carry on the Brecht/Weill tradition, as does Hollmann and Kotis's *Urinetown*). Weill's great score includes "The Ballad of Mack the Knife," which was popularized in a very non-Weill jazz arrangement by Louis Armstrong, and "Pirate Jenny." The production served as a launching pad for many young actors, including Bea Arthur, Charlotte Rae, John Astin, Jerry Orbach, Paul Dooley, and Edward Asner.

The Golden Apple (173 performances), music by Jerome Moross, book and lyrics by John Latouche, is an experimental, through-composed, satiric retelling of *The Iliad* and *The Odyssey* set in turn-of-the-century Washington State after the Spanish-American War. It deals with the probable disadvantages of scientific progress and with the corrupting influence of life in the big city. The music, though mostly not very inspired, is all in forms appropriate to the time and setting, such as barbershop harmony, waltzes, comic vaudeville numbers, and ragtime. The show was so well received when it opened off-Broadway that it immediately transferred to Broadway. Too different to do well there, it closed at a loss, although it probably would have run longer and turned a profit if it had stayed off-Broadway as *The Threepenny Opera* did. On the original-cast recording is the one hit tune, "Lazy Afternoon," sung by the show's version of Helen of Troy.

What Lloyd Webber, Boublil and Schönberg, and other noisy Europeans . . . employ for their through-sung efforts is simply a cruder, less intelligent, and more bombastic version of what Latouche and Moross [accomplished]. . . . A few American writers have dabbled in this form, . . . but it never took commercial root in the Broadway theatre. This is at least in part due to a major pitfall. It becomes much harder for a dramatist to utilize subtext (i.e., the difference between what a character is feeling or thinking and what he or she is saying) when everything is sung. Music, being an abstract medium, is so emotionally persuasive that it usually makes what is being sung sound like it is honestly meant. This reduces the complexity of human character. And Broadway musicals have always been (at least until recently) colloquial and human, unlike opera, where size, grandiosity, and the reduced importance of the text work against nuance and detail. (Erik Haagensen, "Getting to the Core," *Show Music Magazine*, 67)

A generational love story set in the French port of Marseilles, with a soaringly romantic score by Harold Rome, *Fanny* takes place over a twelve-year period.

[It] attempted to cover in one evening much the same ground the three films had covered. With equal shortsightedness in the face of the restricting limitations of a Broadway stage, it attempted to show a fully rigged ship sailing the stage and offer elaborate undersea and circus ballets. (Bordman, 591)

The score includes the title song, "Love Is a Very Light Thing," and "Never Too Late for Love." Logan's 1961 movie has no musical numbers, though some of the show's score is used as background music.

Merrick overcame lackluster reviews [for *Fanny*] with a publicity barrage that has seldom been equaled. He bought time on radio and television to advertise the show. He also was the first to buy full-page ads for Broadway shows in the *New York Times* and the *Tribune*. He stuffed all the fortune cookies in Manhattan with fortunes that happiness lay in store at the Majestic Theatre. Men's rooms throughout the city were plastered with stickers that read "Have You Seen *Fanny?*" Newspapers abroad advertised

David Merrick (1911–2000, born David Margulois in St. Louis, Missouri), often referred to as "The Abominable Showman," made his producing debut with *Fanny*. He went on to produce some of the most successful plays and musicals of all time, including *Carnival!*, *Gypsy*, *Oliver!*, *Hello, Dolly!*, *Promises, Promises*, and *42nd Street*. Many of his shows were British imports or adapted from movies. Merrick conducted notorious publicity stunts throughout his career, often grabbing more headlines than his stars—with whom he frequently feuded publicly.

Fanny

MUSIC/LYRICS: Harold Rome
BOOK: S. N. Behrman and Joshua Logan, adapted from Marcel Pagnol's French film trilogy *Marius*, *Fanny*, and *Cesar*
DIRECTOR: Joshua Logan
CHOREOGRAPHER: Helen Tamiris
DESIGNERS: Jo Mielziner (sets and lights) and Alvin Colt (costumes)
PRODUCERS: David Merrick and Joshua Logan
CAST INCLUDES: Ezio Pinza, Walter Slezak, and Florence Henderson
PERFORMANCES: 888

Bob (Robert Louis) Fosse

(1927–87, born in Chicago) had been a dancer and occasional choreographer in Hollywood. After *The Pajama Game*, he choreographed *Damn Yankees* (where he first worked with Gwen Verdon), *Bells Are Ringing, New Girl in Town*, and *How to Succeed in Business Without Really Trying*. He then both directed and choreographed such shows as *Little Me, Sweet Charity, Pippin, Chicago*, and *Dancin'*. Most of his shows—as well as his choreography for them—were cynical, sensual, and jazz-based. Fosse also directed films, including *Lenny, Sweet Charity, Cabaret*, and *All That Jazz*. In 1972, he won the Academy Award for *Cabaret*, the Tony for *Pippin*, and the Emmy for the Liza Minnelli TV special *Liza with a Z*.

The Pajama Game

MUSIC/LYRICS: Richard Adler and Jerry Ross

BOOK: George Abbott and Richard Bissell, adapted from Bissell's novel *7 ½ Cents*

DIRECTORS: George Abbott (then sixty-seven years old) and Jerome Robbins

CHOREOGRAPHER: Bob Fosse

ORCHESTRATOR: Don Walker

DESIGNER: Lemuel Ayers (sets and costumes)

PRODUCERS: Frederick Brisson, Robert E. Griffith, and Harold Prince

CAST INCLUDES: Janis Paige, John Raitt, Carol Haney, and Eddie Foy Jr.

PERFORMANCES: 1,063

the show as did taxis, ocean liners, and railroad stations. A statue of the belly dancer [in the show] appeared one day in Central Park. The woman herself, in the flesh, was almost bought by a wealthy Arab for $2 million. David Merrick walked his pet ostrich around town and at the marriage of Grace Kelly in Monaco a plane circled overhead urging people to see *Fanny*. Ed Sullivan presented numbers on his show. When receipts fell below the level necessary to keep the show from losing the theatre, Merrick sent runners to the box office to buy tickets. He also called people randomly from the phone book offering free tickets if they would bring a friend. When the show that [had] received . . . lukewarm reviews finally closed, it had made $847,726.74 profit for Merrick and his investors. (Bloom, *American Song*, 194)

Another Arlen flop with a great score, *House of Flowers* (165 performances) had a weak book by Truman Capote about the rivalry between two Caribbean whorehouses. Nineteen-year-old Diahann Carroll, in her first Broadway role, played a novice in one of the houses. The show was notoriously plagued with backstage problems and fights during rehearsals and tryouts (not unusual when Pearl Bailey was in the cast). Both Peter Brook and George Balanchine, the original director and choreographer, were replaced out of town by Herbert Ross. The score includes the title song, "One Man Ain't Quite Enough," "I Never Has Seen Snow," and "A Sleepin' Bee."

A hugely successful, very exuberant show about a strike in a pajama factory for a seven-and-a-half-cent raise, *The Pajama Game* takes the side of labor against management and manages to keep it all lighthearted and fun. The central love story is between Sid, the new superintendent of the factory, and Babe, the head of the union's grievance committee, whose affair comes to grief when a strike is called and they're on opposite sides. (It's a comic Romeo and Juliet relationship.) The subplot centers on Hines, the office efficiency expert, who's overly jealous of his girlfriend, Gladys, the boss's secretary. (Bissell wrote a novel called *Say Darling* about his experiences working on the show, which was itself made into a semi-musical.) Once again George Abbott was working with Broadway novices, having given Robbins his second shot at directing (or codirecting, anyway) a musical and Fosse his first job as choreographer. *The Pajama Game* is the first of two musical comedies by Richard Adler (born 1921) and Jerry Ross (1926–55; both born in New York); they'd had a minor hit with the revue *John Murray Anderson's Almanac* the year before. Their show after *The Pajama Game* was the equally successful *Damn Yankees,* which opened in 1955 shortly before Ross's death at the age of twenty-nine. It was rumored that Frank Loesser, whose company published the score, helped out by writing some of the songs for *The Pajama Game.*

Janis Paige, a movie actress, had never been in a Broadway musical before *The Pajama Game;* John Raitt had been in flops since *Carousel;* Eddie Foy Jr. was a former vaudeville star; and Carol Haney had been Gene Kelly's assistant in Hollywood, preceded Gwen Verdon as Jack Cole's assistant, and had a brief dancing role with Fosse in the movie *Kiss Me, Kate.* Shirley MacLaine, Haney's understudy, had to go on for her at a performance attended by a Hollywood movie scout, and in fairy-tale fashion, he took her off to movieland. Included in the score are "I'm Not at All in Love" and the pop hits "Hey There," "Steam Heat," and "Hernando's Hideaway." There was a well-received, limited-run Broadway revival of *The Pajama Game* in 2006 starring Harry Connick Jr. The 1957 movie version, directed by Abbott and Stanley Donen with Fosse re-creating his choreography, used the Broadway cast but substituted Doris Day for Janis Paige. Fosse's style, built on his own strengths and weaknesses as a dancer (and using hats a lot because of his rapidly thinning hairline), is perhaps the most easily recognizable of any on Broadway and requires his dancers to be able to move almost every part of their bodies separately and at difficult angles.

Peter Pan was Robbins's first time as sole director as well as choreographer. Styne, Comden, and Green were brought in to fix Charlap and Leigh's original work. (The score for the 1953 Disney animated feature differs from the scores for this version and for the 1950 Bernstein version.) The show, after a limited Broadway run, was shown live on NBC. It's been revived several times on Broadway and for tours, with such stars as Sandy Duncan and

Harold Prince (1928–, born in New York) got his first producer credit with *The Pajama Game.* He'd been working in Abbott's office; among other tasks, he was assistant stage manager on *Wonderful Town.* He was twenty-six, Broadway's youngest producer, when *The Pajama Game* opened. He also produced such shows as *Damn Yankees, West Side Story, A Funny Thing Happened on the Way to the Forum,* and *Fiddler on the Roof.* He directed such innovative and/or successful shows as *She Loves Me, Cabaret, Company, Follies, A Little Night Music, Sweeney Todd, Evita, Kiss of the Spiderwoman, Phantom of the Opera,* and the 1995 revival of *Show Boat.* He also directs plays and operas.

Peter Pan

MUSIC: Moose Charlap and Jule Styne

LYRICS: Carolyn Leigh, Betty Comden, and Adolph Green

BOOK: Jerome Robbins, adapted from the 1904 James M. Barrie play

DIRECTOR/CHOREOGRAPHER: Jerome Robbins

PRODUCERS: Richard Halliday and Edwin Lester

CAST INCLUDES: Mary Martin, Cyril Ritchard, and Sondra Lee

PERFORMANCES: 152

Cathy Rigby; pop singer Lulu played Peter in a London revival. The original-cast TV version was taped in 1960.

Hollywood and Broadway were both feeling the effects of the American public's new love affair with national television; by 1954, there were TV sets in twenty-nine million homes. Hollywood responded with three-dimensional movies requiring free special Polaroid glasses, movies shot for wide screens, stereophonic sound, and any other gimmicks they could come up with (including one that literally smelled). Meanwhile, Broadway responded with fewer shows and bigger and more costly production values. Activity off-Broadway increased as Broadway costs continued to rise. Increasing numbers of Americans preferred to stay home, glued to their new TV sets.

Suggested Watching and Listening

Call Me Madam
Available on the 20th Century Fox DVD movie version of this 1950 star vehicle, and directed by Walter Lang, it features this hit double duet.
- "You're Just in Love" (performed by Ethel Merman and Donald O'Connor)

Can-Can
The number "Quadrille" (performed by Gail Benedict and the American Dance Machine) is available on *That's Dancing* (Warner Brothers Home Video VHS). It's a reconstruction of Michael Kidd's original choreography for the 1953 Porter musical.

Guys and Dolls
The recommended version of this musical is from the 1955 MGM movie, available on MGM DVD. It features the following numbers for which Michael Kidd adapted his original stage choreography but with more people added for the wide screen.
- "Runyonland Music," "Fugue for Tinhorns," and "Follow the Fold" (performed by Stubby Kaye, Johnny Silver, Douglas Deane, and Jean Simmons): In the stage show, this entire sequence takes place in one scene and in continuous action. (The three gamblers are introduced betting on horses, but their main concern is finding a place to hold Nathan Detroit's "oldest established permanent floating crap game in New York," as we soon learn.)
- "Crapshooters' Ballet" (performed by the male ensemble).
- "Sit Down, You're Rockin' the Boat" (performed by Stubby Kaye and the ensemble)

Guys and Dolls—Off the Record
It's a 1992 documentary produced by Gail Levin, which was shot during the original-cast recording of director Jerry Zaks's 1992 Broadway revival. It's available on Kultur DVD and features the following numbers.

❖

- "Fugue for Tinhorns" (performed by Walter Bobbie, J. K. Simmons, and Timothy Shew)
- "Adelaide's Lament" (performed by Faith Prince)
- "Sue Me" (performed by Faith Prince and Nathan Lane): A comic duet for Adelaide and Nathan, it's the only singing Nathan did in the original production, since Sam Levene, who created the role, was nearly tone-deaf.
- "The Oldest Established (Permanent Floating Crap Game in New York)" (performed by Nathan Lane, Walter Bobbie, J. K. Simmons, and the male chorus): Nathan, given more to sing in the revival, needs a place to hold his crap game.
- "A Bushel and a Peck" (performed by Faith Prince and the Hot Box Girls): One of the Hot Box numbers for Adelaide and her girls, it was not used in the movie although it was a pop hit. The movie replaced it with "Pet Me, Poppa," with the girls in scanty cat costumes.
- "Luck Be a Lady" (performed by Peter Gallagher and the gamblers): Sky's big second-act number during the crap game, it became a pop hit.
- "Follow the Fold" (performed by Josie de Guzman, John Carpenter, Eleanor Glockner, Leslie Feagan, and Victoria Clark)
- "Marry the Man Today" (performed by Faith Prince and Josie de Guzman): The second of the two eleven o' clock numbers, it was cut from the movie.
- "My Time of Day" (performed by Peter Gallagher): Sky Masterson's philosophy of life, it was not used in the movie. Brando could never have sung it; the intervals between notes frequently are very difficult.
- "I've Never Been in Love Before" (performed by Josie de Guzman and Peter Gallagher): Another pop hit, it was replaced in the movie with "A Woman in Love" because that was easier to sing.
- "If I Were a Bell" (performed by Josie de Guzman): Sarah sings it when Sky gets her drunk.
- "Sit Down, You're Rockin' the Boat" (performed by Walter Bobbie and the ensemble)
- "Guys and Dolls" (performed by the company)

House of Flowers
The following two numbers from this show are on the original-cast recording, a CBS Studios CD.
- "I Never Has Seen Snow" (performed by Diahann Carroll)
- "A Sleepin' Bee" (performed by Diahann Carroll)

The King and I
The movie version, directed by Walter Lang and available on 20th Century Fox DVD, re-creates Jerome Robbins's choreography, including the following story dance performed for the entertainment of the British ambassador.
- "The Small House of Uncle Thomas Ballet" (performed by Rita Moreno and the ensemble): It's Tuptim's version of *Uncle Tom's Cabin*.

Kiss Me, Kate: The Movie
The movie version of the 1948 musical (available on Warner Brothers DVD) is directed by George Sidney and features the following song, cut from the show *Out of This World* and added to both the movie version of *Kiss Me, Kate* and to the 1999 Broadway revival of the show.

- "From This Moment On" (performed by Ann Miller, Tommy Rall, Jeannie Coyne, Bobby Van, Carol Haney, and Bob Fosse): It was choreographed by Hermes Pan but with Fosse choreographing his dance duet with Haney in what is already the "Fosse" style.

The Pajama Game

All of these suggestions are from the movie version of the show, directed by George Abbott and Stanley Donen and available on Warner Brothers Home Video DVD.

- "I'm Not at All in Love" (performed by Doris Day and the women's chorus): It's the equivalent of "Many a New Day" from *Oklahoma!* and "I'm Gonna Wash That Man Right Out of My Hair" from *South Pacific,* but for a tougher heroine.
- "I'll Never Be Jealous Again" (performed by Reta Shaw and Eddie Foy Jr.): It's a funny duet and a charming soft shoe for the jealous Hines and a friend who's a fellow office worker.
- "Hey There" (performed by John Raitt): Sid sings it into a dictaphone, then plays it back so he can sing a duet with himself—only the recording somehow manages to sing the harmony at the end.
- "Once a Year Day" (performed by John Raitt, Carol Haney, and the ensemble): This is Haney's first dance number at a company picnic in the show.
- "There Once Was a Man" (performed by Doris Day and John Raitt): It's a fast, difficult love duet.
- "Steam Heat" (performed by Carol Haney, Buzz Miller, and Kenneth LeRoy): A swing number, it's generally considered to be the first truly "Fosse" number—including the white gloves and derby hats—and Haney the first "Fosse" dancer. The number is barely attached to the plot.
- "Hernando's Hideaway" (performed by Carol Haney and the company): On stage, the dance section was performed in the dark, using matches.

Seven Brides for Seven Brothers

This 1954 movie, directed by Stanley Donen, is available on Warner Brothers DVD. It has some of Michael Kidd's most exhilarating choreography.

- "Barn-Raising Dance" (performed by Jeff Richards, Russ Tamblyn, Tommy Rall, Marc Platt, Matt Mattox, and Jacques d'Amboise; Julie Newmar, Nancy Kilgas, Betty Carr, Virginia Gibson, Rita Kilmonis, and Norma Doggett; Ian Wolfe, Harold Petrie, Dante DiPaolo, Kelly Brown, Matt Moore, and Dick Rich): The dance music is "Bless Your Beautiful Hide," sung earlier in the movie by the oldest of the brothers as he sets out to find a bride.

The Threepenny Opera

This show features the following song, available on the original-cast recording of the off-Broadway revival (Decca CD).

- "Pirate Jenny" (performed by Lotte Lenya): It's a story song about a serving girl in a hotel who hates the customers. She's waiting for a pirate ship to sail in; when it does, the pirates will kill everyone and take her away with them. (In Blitzstein's version, the pirates ask her if they should kill them now or later, and she says now; in the original German she's asked which ones should be killed, and her response is "All of them.")

Wonderful Town

The following numbers are on the original-cast recording of this 1951 show, available on MCA Classics CD.

- "Ohio" (performed by Rosalind Russell and Edith Adams): It's Ruth and Eileen's first night in their less-than-private basement apartment where a new subway line is being blasted underneath them.
- "One Hundred Easy Ways (to Lose a Man)" (performed by Rosalind Russell)

From *Damn Yankees* to *My Fair Lady*

> Wouldn't it be fun not to be famous,
> Wouldn't it be fun not to be rich!
> Wouldn't it be pleasant
> To be a simple peasant
> And spend a happy day digging a ditch!
> Wouldn't it be fun not to be known as an important VIP,
> Wouldn't it be fun to be nearly anyone
> Except me, mighty me!
> —"WOULDN'T IT BE FUN,"
> *ALADDIN,* LYRICS BY COLE PORTER

During the latter half of the 1950s, it became even more difficult and costly to produce new shows on Broadway, and it took longer to pay back a show's original investment. Audience numbers dwindled, partly because of rising ticket prices, partly because of TV, and partly because of the continuing movement to the suburbs. Suburbanites found it increasingly inconvenient and expensive to go into town to see a show or to shop in the downtown areas of the big cities; by 1955, there were eighteen hundred U.S. suburban shopping centers. However, all was not lost for the musical, as Paul Gruber points out:

> If the economic prospect for musicals was beginning to grow bleak, the artistic outlook was much cheerier. The ever-changing American musical was becoming a more mature, more interesting genre, with some of the theater's greatest talents overseeing the development. (Gruber, *Original Cast! The Fifties: Part 2,* 3–5)

At least a dozen new musicals produced between 1955 and 1959 still get revived, including *My Fair Lady, The Sound of Music, The Most Happy Fella, The Music Man, Bells Are Ringing, Gypsy, Candide,* and the pioneering *West Side Story;* about that many hit movies were adapted from musicals as well. Almost every show and movie had an original-cast recording. There were also some important entrances and exits on Broadway during this half-decade: Jerry Bock wrote the music for his first book musical and for his first show with lyricist Sheldon Harnick; Meredith Willson wrote his first show (book, music, and lyrics); Bob Merrill wrote his first music and lyrics; Stephen Sondheim wrote his first lyrics; Cole Porter and Rodgers and Hammerstein wrote original TV musicals; Porter, Harold Arlen, Jerry Ross, and Oscar Hammerstein wrote their last shows; and Elvis Presley made his first four movies.

In 1955, Actors' Equity and Chorus Equity merged. The Princess Theatre, home of the trendsetting Princess musicals, was razed. The Supreme Court ordered the antitrust suit against the Shuberts reinstated. Also during the year, there were limited-run revivals of *Guys and Dolls, South Pacific,* and *Finian's Rainbow,* and the D'Oyly Carte Company returned for a couple of months of Gilbert and Sullivan operettas in repertory. There were about twenty new musical evenings on Broadway.

Backdrop: 1955–1959

National   President Eisenhower is reelected, again beating Adlai Stevenson. Alaska and Hawaii become the forty-ninth and fiftieth states. Richard J. Daley is elected mayor of Chicago, beginning a twenty-one-year reign. Congress passes the first civil rights bill since the Civil War. In Montgomery, Alabama, seamstress Rosa Parks refuses to give up her bus seat to a white man; Reverend Martin Luther King Jr. organizes a boycott of the city's public transportation. Arkansas Governor Orval Faubus stops nine black children from entering Little Rock's Central High School; President Eisenhower sends in federal troops to end the disorder. Japanese Americans put into concentration camps in 1942 regain full citizenship but receive no compensation for their losses until 1989. Congress authorizes construction of a 42,500-mile network of roads linking major U.S. urban centers. The American Federation of Labor and the Congress of Industrial Organizations merge to form the AFL-CIO. The minimum wage rises from seventy-five cents to one dollar. A record 3.1 million Americans are receiving unemployment benefits. In the last ten years, a Chevrolet has gone from $1,255 to $2,081 and a year's tuition at Harvard from $455 to $1,250. Mafia lieutenant Frank "Don Cheech" Scalise, henchman of Murder Inc. boss

Damn Yankees, Adler and Ross's second Broadway collaboration, opened almost exactly a year after *The Pajama Game*, which was still running. It's a fantasy variation on the Faust legend. Joe Boyd, a middle-aged fan of the Washington Senators, sells his soul to the Devil in return for one year of being the young slugger Joe Hardy, who leads the Senators into the World Series and to victory over the hated New York Yankees. The young Joe, played by a different actor, remains in love with his wife (who doesn't recognize him) and even takes a room as a boarder in her home. The Devil—Mr. Applegate—sends his chief temptress, Lola, to make Joe forget his wife, but the plan backfires, and Joe keeps his soul and returns to his middle-aged self. Ross died soon after the opening; Adler never had another Broadway hit, though he did have a very successful TV career. Richard Bissell, who'd cowritten the book of *The Pajama Game*, did some uncredited work on the book of *Damn Yankees* as well.

The score includes "You've Got to Have Heart," a comic number that became a straight pop hit; "A Little Brains, a Little Talent," Lola's self-descriptive first number; "Shoeless Joe from Hannibal, Mo.," a dance number for a reporter and the entire

Damn Yankees

MUSIC/LYRICS: Richard Adler and Jerry Ross

BOOK: George Abbott and Douglass Wallop, adapted from Wallop's novel *The Year the Yankees Lost the Pennant*

DIRECTOR: George Abbott

CHOREOGRAPHER: Bob Fosse

ORCHESTRATOR: Don Walker

PRODUCERS: Frederick Brisson, Harold Prince, and Robert E. Griffith

CAST INCLUDES: Gwen Verdon, Ray Walston, and Jean Stapleton

PERFORMANCES: 1,019

Albert Anastasia, is shot in the head four times while shopping for peaches at a Bronx fruit stand; Anastasia is killed in the Park Sheraton Hotel barbershop by men in the pay of Vito Genovese.

International   Sir Anthony Eden succeeds Sir Winston Churchill as British prime minister. France names General Charles de Gaulle president of the Fifth Republic. The European Common Market is established. The Soviets launch *Sputnik I*, the first man-made Earth satellite. The first U.S. Earth satellite is launched, escalating the space race between the United States and the Soviet Union. Bulganin succeeds Malenkov as Soviet premier, and Krushchev replaces Bulganin as chairman of the Soviet Council of Ministers. Eight European Communist powers sign the Warsaw Pact. Soviet troops occupy Hungary to suppress a revolution. Polish workers riot against the Communists and are also suppressed. By 1960, over 26.3 million Chinese who resist communization will have been killed, the largest massacre in world history. The USSR and the People's Republic of China proclaim their support of the Mideast against Western aggression. United Nations Secretary-General Dag Hammarskjöld arranges a cease-fire between Israel and Jordan, Lebanon, and Syria. Jordan's King Hussein I succeeds King Faisal as head of state. Libya's first oil well goes into production. The United Arab Republic—a union of Egypt, the Sudan, and Syria under the leadership of Egypt's President Nasser—is proclaimed. Nasser seizes control of the Suez Canal from the British. Ghana is the first African state south of the Sahara to attain independence. A military junta in Argentina overthrows dictator Juan Perón. Cuban dictator Batista flees to Miami when his regime falls to the forces of Fidel Castro.

Washington baseball team; and the show's biggest hit, "Whatever Lola Wants," Lola's attempted seduction of the young Joe. After her success in *Can-Can*, Gwen Verdon achieved stardom in *Damn Yankees* as Lola. Of all Fosse's dancers, she most clearly embodied his choreographic style; she seemed able to move every part of her body separately. She was also a charming actress, knew how to sell a song despite her limited vocal capabilities, and could be very funny.

There was a successful 1994 Broadway revival, which later toured with Jerry Lewis as Applegate. The 1958 movie, directed by Abbott and Stanley Donen, with Fosse doing the choreography, used the original Broadway cast but with Tab Hunter instead of Stephen Douglass as the young Joe Hardy.

Pipe Dream didn't pay off its investors—a first for Rodgers and Hammerstein. Both they and director Clurman seemed out of place in Steinbeck's California with characters who are poor, streetwise, and often indigent. Equally out of place for some was the portly, stately, Wagnerian opera star Helen Traubel as the heart-of-gold madam of a friendly neighborhood brothel. Among

Pipe Dream

MUSIC/LYRICS/BOOK: Richard Rodgers and Oscar Hammerstein, adapted from John Steinbeck's novel *Sweet Thursday*

DIRECTOR: Harold Clurman

CHOREOGRAPHER: Boris Runanin

ORCHESTRATOR: Robert Russell Bennett

DESIGNERS: Jo Mielziner(sets and lights) and Alvin Colt (costumes)

PRODUCERS: Richard Rodgers and Oscar Hammerstein

CAST INCLUDES: Helen Traubel

PERFORMANCES: 246

New Developments American scientists begin testing Earth's ozone layer. U.S. sales of small foreign cars, particularly Volkswagens, begin a rapid rise. Yamaha is founded; by 1970, the Japanese will have produced 3.2 million cars, up from 110 cars in 1947. General Motors announces 1955 earnings of more than one billion dollars after taxes and is indicted for anticompetitive actions in its attempt to get an 85 percent monopoly on the U.S. market for new buses. Ford introduces the Edsel, a disaster. Detroit labor leader Jimmy Hoffa gains control of the International Brotherhood of Teamsters. Pan Am and BOAC inaugurate transatlantic jet service. Major John Glenn sets a new transcontinental speed record across the United States. RCA introduces the world's first fully transistorized computer, and Sony the first transistorized TV sets. Ampex demonstrates the first videotape recorder; most TV shows soon switch from live and film broadcasts to tape. Visa and American Express credit cards become available. Kansas City is home to the first Pizza Hut. Tax service H&R Block opens for business, and Crest toothpaste, Cocoa Puffs, Sweet 'N' Low, Colonel Sanders' Kentucky Fried Chicken, Comet cleanser, Salem cigarettes, Frisbees, Barbie dolls, and panty hose are introduced. One hundred million hula hoops are sold in one year. Disneyland opens in California.

Sports The Philadelphia Athletics move to Kansas City, the New York Giants to San Francisco, and the Brooklyn Dodgers to Los Angeles. Brazilian soccer player Pelé signs with the Santos team. Floyd Patterson knocks out Archie Moore, wins the world heavyweight title, then loses it to Swedish boxer Ingemar Johansson. Middleweight champion Sugar Ray Robinson loses the title to Gene Fullmer, regains it, loses it to Carmen Basilio, defeats Basilio, and becomes champion for a record fifth time.

the songs in the score are "All Kinds of People," "Sweet Thursday," "All at Once You Love Her," and "The Man I Used to Be."

Silk Stockings is a mildly successful romantic comedy about some Soviet Communists (in particular, a beautiful young woman named Ninotchka) who find love, freedom, and champagne in Paris. Kaufman and his wife, MacGrath, were replaced out of town by Burrows; Kaufman was also the original director and never again chose to work on Broadway. The score includes "Stereophonic Sound" and "All of You," sung by an agent using "agent-ese" jargon in the lyrics of his love song:

> I'd love to gain complete control of you,
> And handle even the heart and soul of you,
> So love, at least, a small percent of me, do,
> For I love all of you.

The 1957 movie version with Fred Astaire and Cyd Charisse didn't improve on the original. *Silk Stockings* was Mamoulian's last movie and Porter's last Broadway show.

Silk Stockings

MUSIC/LYRICS: Cole Porter
BOOK: Abe Burrows, George S. Kaufman, and Leueen MacGrath, adapted from the 1939 nonmusical Greta Garbo film *Ninotchka*
DIRECTOR: Cy Feuer
CHOREOGRAPHER: Eugene Loring (with some last-minute help from Jerome Robbins)
ORCHESTRATOR: Don Walker
DESIGNERS: Jo Mielziner (sets and lights), and Lucinda Ballard and Robert Mackintosh (costumes)
PRODUCERS: Cy Feuer and Ernest Martin
CAST INCLUDES: Don Ameche and Hildegarde Neff
PERFORMANCES: 478

Art Jackson Pollock is killed in an auto accident; Diego Rivera, Maurice Utrillo, Georges Rouault, and Constantin Brancusi also die. There are new paintings by Rivers, Johns, de Chirico, and Rothko, as well as Picasso's widely reproduced *Peace*, a hand extending a bouquet. Robert Rauschenberg pioneers pop art with a semi-abstract hole containing four Coca-Cola bottles. Frank Lloyd Wright's Guggenheim Museum opens in New York.

Music/Dance Among new operas and ballets are Moore and Latouche's *The Ballad of Baby Doe*, Poulenc's *Dialogues des Carmelites*, Barber and Menotti's *Vanessa*, Britten's *The Prince and the Pagodas*, and Stravinsky's *Agon*. New compositions include Walton's cello concerto and Shostakovich's Concerto no. 2 for Piano and Orchestra and Symphony no. 11. Van Cliburn is the first American to win the Tchaikovsky piano competition in Moscow. Leonard Bernstein becomes the first American-born musical director of the New York Philharmonic. Alvin Ailey founds his American Dance Theater.

Publications The ban on Lawrence's 1928 novel *Lady Chatterley's Lover* is lifted. The *Village Voice* and "Ann Landers Says" begin publication. Senator John F. Kennedy publishes *Profiles in Courage* (ghostwritten by Nevins and Sorenson). The Beat Generation comes to prominence with Ginsberg's *Howl*, Kerouac's *On the Road*, and Burroughs's *Naked Lunch*. Dr. Seuss publishes *The Cat in the Hat*, *How the Grinch Stole Christmas*, *Yertle the Turtle*, and *The Cat in the Hat Comes Back*.

While Porter was as urbane and civilized as the [Paris] he loved, his most identifiable songs were written in a South American beat derived from the African
jungles, often with minor-key melodies he himself termed "Jewish," and his
lyrics were so carefully nuanced and so often knowingly topical they defied
translation or even a sea-crossing. Porter's stylish songs were unique products
of the proverbial but not always successful American melting pot. (Bordman,
594)

In 1956, director/choreographer Hassard Short died, and John Latouche
died while working on the lyrics for Bernstein's *Candide*. The Shuberts
agreed to let go of four of their New York theaters and eight more out of
town, and to end their ties to the United Booking Office. The top ticket price
for a musical was up to $8.05, and it cost about $400,000 to produce a show.
There were limited-run revivals of *The King and I, Kiss Me, Kate,* and *Carmen
Jones.* It was an exciting year for the musical, with over thirty new productions, including some that are now considered classics.

Other new books include Thompson's *Eloise,* the first *Guinness Book of World Records,* Nabokov's
Lolita, Camus' *The Fall,* Pasternak's *Doctor Zhivago,* Grass's *The Tin Drum,* Bellow's *Henderson the
Rain King,* Cheever's *The Wapshot Chronicle,* Metalious's *Peyton Place,* Dennis's *Auntie Mame*
(source of the 1966 musical *Mame*), the last third of White's *The Once and Future King* (source of the
1960 musical *Camelot*), and Capote's *Breakfast at Tiffany's* (source of the 1966 musical that closed
during previews).

Radio/TV   There are 357 U.S. daily newspapers, down from 2,600 in 1909 as Americans rely
more on radio and then TV for the news. By the end of the decade, 90 percent of American homes
have TV sets. The highest-rated TV shows of the five years are *The $64,000 Question, I Love Lucy,*
and *Gunsmoke.* Among the new shows are *Captain Kangaroo, The Mickey Mouse Club,* the much-
acclaimed *Playhouse 90,* and the soap operas *As the World Turns* and *The Edge of Night.* The thirty-
nine half-hour episodes of *The Honeymooners* air. Half of America watches Mary Martin in *Peter
Pan.* Van Heusen and Cahn write the songs, including "Love and Marriage," for a TV musical version of Wilder's *Our Town* starring Frank Sinatra, Eva Marie Saint, and Paul Newman. *Aladdin,*
another original TV musical, has songs by Cole Porter, book by S. J. Perelman, and stars Sal Mineo;
the score includes "Wouldn't It Be Fun," Porter's last lyric. Rodgers and Hammerstein's *Cinderella,*
another original musical for TV, is adapted from the Perrault fairy tale, shot in black and white,
and stars Julie Andrews; in the score are "In My Own Little Corner," "Ten Minutes Ago," and "Do
I Love You Because You're Beautiful?" The show was reshot in color in 1965 with Lesley Ann Warren
in the title role; Disney redid it for TV in 1997, starring Brandy. It was adapted into a stage show
in 2000.

The Most Happy Fella is almost through-composed and a complete change of pace from Loesser's previous show, *Guys and Dolls*. He refused to call it a musical drama or an opera; instead, he called it "a musical with a lot of music."

> The score was an amalgam of recitative, arias, operetta duets, and raucous musical comedy numbers. In spite of, or perhaps because of, its eclecticism, the nearly forty musical numbers provided an uncommonly rich emotionality while remaining completely accessible to typical Broadway audiences. (Bowers, 73–74)

Set in California grape country, the main story is about Tony, an older Italian immigrant, who, instead of sending a photo of himself, sends one of Joe, a younger man, to a waitress he's been courting by mail. When she arrives and discovers the

The Most Happy Fella

MUSIC/LYRICS/BOOK: Frank Loesser, adapted from Sidney Howard's Pulitzer Prize–winning 1924 play *They Knew What They Wanted*

DIRECTOR: Joseph Anthony

CHOREOGRAPHER: Dania Krupska

ORCHESTRATOR: Don Walker

DESIGNERS: Jo Mielziner (sets and lights) and Motley (costumes)

PRODUCERS: Kermit Bloomgarden and Lynn Loesser (Loesser's wife at the time)

CAST INCLUDES: Robert Weede, Jo Sullivan, Art Lund, Shorty Long, and Susan Johnson

PERFORMANCES: 676

Pop Culture   The splintering of listeners into pop versus rock spreads rapidly. Berry Gordy Jr. founds Motown Corporation. Rock-and-roll stars Buddy Holly, Richie Valens, and the Big Bopper die in a plane crash. Pop songs include Ellington, Strayhorn, and Mercer's "Satin Doll"; Cash's "I Walk the Line"; Vance and Pockriss's "Catch a Falling Star"; Bagdasarian's "The Chipmunk Song"; Beal and Boothe's "Jingle Bell Rock"; Berry, Frato, and Freed's "Maybellene"; Presley, Axton, and Durden's "Heartbreak Hotel"; Little Richard's "Tutti Frutti"; Leiber and Stoller's "Hound Dog"; Felice and Boudleaux Bryant's "Bye Bye, Love"; Anka's "Put Your Head on My Shoulder"; Darin and Murray's "Splish Splash"; Cool's "You Send Me"; and Sedaka and Greenfield's "Breaking Up Is Hard to Do."

Stage   Playwrights Maxwell Anderson and Bertolt Brecht die. Arthur Miller marries Marilyn Monroe. Chicago's improvisational cabaret theater The Second City opens. New plays are O'Neill's posthumous *Long Day's Journey into Night, Moon for the Misbegotten,* and *A Touch of the Poet;* Miller's *A View from the Bridge;* Williams's *Cat on a Hot Tin Roof* and *Sweet Bird of Youth;* Inge's *Bus Stop;* Goodrich and Hackett's *The Diary of Anne Frank;* Gibson's *The Miracle Worker;* Anouilh's *The Lark,* adapted by Hellman, with choral passages composed by Bernstein; Osborne's *Look Back in Anger* (beginning a new and vigorous "angry young man" British theater); Pinter's first full-length play, *The Birthday Party;* Behan's *The Hostage;* Beckett's *Endgame* and *Krapp's Last Tape* as well as the Broadway debut of his *Waiting for Godot;* Genet's *The Balcony;* Gibson's *Two for the Seesaw* (source of the 1973 musical *Seesaw*); Wilder's *The Matchmaker* (a rewrite of his play *The Merchant of Yonkers* and source of the 1964 musical *Hello, Dolly!*); and Hansberry's *A Raisin in the Sun* (the first play on Broadway by a black woman and source of the 1973 musical *Raisin*).

truth, there are near-tragic consequences, but it all works out well. The comic subplot, invented by Loesser, enlivens the show considerably, both in terms of the humor and warmth of its love story and in the exuberance of its musical comedy numbers. In the score (over two hours of music) are the title song; "Ooh! My Feet!" the first solo in the show, sung by Cleo, both the heroine of the comic subplot and the heroine's best friend and fellow waitress; "Somebody, Somewhere," a beautiful romantic ballad for Rosabella, the heroine (not really her name, but the name given her by Tony); the pop hit "Standing on the Corner," sung by Herman, the hero of the comic subplot, and his buddies, who all work for Tony; "Joey, Joey, Joey," sung by Joe, the "other man" in the main plot; "Big 'D'," the meeting of Cleo and Herman and a showstopper production number; and "My Heart Is So Full of You," a nearly operatic duet for Tony and Rosabella, played by Jo Sullivan. (Loesser first saw her in *The Threepenny Opera*. His wife divorced him as a result of their affair during rehearsals. Loesser and Sullivan were soon married, and as his widow with total control over his works, Sullivan has played a strong role in overseeing revivals of his shows.)

Screen   Among the new movies are *The 400 Blows, Breathless,* and *Hiroshima, Mon Amour* (the start of the French new wave in cinema); *Mon Oncle; Throne of Blood* (adapted from Shakespeare's *Macbeth*); *Vertigo; North by Northwest; Touch of Evil; Rebel without a Cause* and adaptations of Steinbeck's *East of Eden* and Ferber's *Giant* (the only three James Dean movies); *Paths of Glory; The Searchers; Invasion of the Body Snatchers; The Ten Commandments; The Blackboard Jungle,* with Bill Haley's "Rock Around the Clock" bringing rock into a mainstream American movie; *Godzilla; The Bridge on the River Kwai; Ben Hur;* Logan's adaptations of Inge's *Picnic* and *Bus Stop;* Bergman's *The Seventh Seal, Wild Strawberries,* and *Smiles of a Summer Night* (source of the 1973 musical *A Little Night Music*); Fellini's *La Dolce Vita,* and *Nights of Cabiria* (source of the 1966 musical *Sweet Charity*); *Summertime* (adapted from Laurents's *Time of the Cuckoo,* source of the 1965 musical *Do I Hear a Waltz?*); and *Some Like It Hot* (source of the 1972 musical *Sugar*).

Around ninety new movie musicals are produced during the five years, among them *Oklahoma!, Carousel, South Pacific,* and *The King and I;* Disney's *Sleeping Beauty,* with songs adapted from Tchaikovsky's ballet, and *Lady and the Tramp,* with a Burke and Lee score that has "He's a Tramp" and "Siamese Cat Song"; Doris Day and James Cagney in *Love Me or Leave Me,* the bio of singer Ruth Etting; Gene Kelly, Cyd Charisse, and Michael Kidd in *It's Always Fair Weather,* with music by André Previn, script and lyrics by Comden and Green, and dances choreographed by directors Kelly and

Bells Are Ringing is a solidly constructed, star-vehicle musical comedy about a Manhattan answering-service operator named Ella who gets too involved with the lives of the clients and falls in love with one of them without ever meeting him in person. The subplot is about a bookie operation secretly working through the answering service—Susanswerphone—without the knowledge of the owner, Sue, and her employees. The show has an excellent Styne score, witty Comden and Green lyrics, and a great role that Comden and Green fashioned specifically for their former cabaret-act partner Judy Holliday, already an Academy Award–winning movie star. Sydney Chaplin, son of Charlie, had never done a musical before; his songs were written for a very slight voice. (He later costarred with Barbra Streisand in Styne's *Funny Girl*, where once again the demands on his singing voice were minimal.) Among the show's notable songs are "It's a Perfect Relationship," the heroine's first number about the client she's in love with, who thinks she's an old lady he calls Mom; "It's a Simple Little System," a big comic number during which

Bells Are Ringing

MUSIC: Jule Styne

LYRICS/BOOK: Betty Comden and Adolph Green

DIRECTOR: Jerome Robbins

CHOREOGRAPHERS: Jerome Robbins and Bob Fosse

ORCHESTRATOR: Robert Russell Bennett

DESIGNERS: Raoul Pène du Bois (sets and costumes) and Peggy Clark (lights)

PRODUCER: The Theatre Guild

CAST INCLUDES: Judy Holliday, Sydney Chaplin, and Jean Stapleton

PERFORMANCES: 924

Stanley Donen, done with such props as roller skates, garbage can lids, and prizefighters; Kelly in *Les Girls*, with Cole Porter's last film score; Fred Astaire and Charisse in *Silk Stockings;* Astaire and Audrey Hepburn in *Funny Face*, with some songs and a completely different story from the Gershwin musical, and with new songs by Edens and Gershe; a new adaptation of Fields and Chodorov's play *My Sister Eileen*, choreographed by Bob Fosse (his first full choreography), with a score by Styne and Robin; *The Pajama Game* and *Damn Yankees*, with Fosse re-creating his original choreography; *Guys and Dolls;* a pseudo-adaptation of *Hit the Deck;* a flop adaptation of *The Vagabond King*, its fourth movie version; *Porgy and Bess; Li'l Abner*, with Kidd and Dee Dee Wood re-creating the original choreography; Frank Sinatra in a sort of adaptation of *Pal Joey* that uses some of the show's songs along with several Rodgers and Hart standards; Bing Crosby and Donald O'Connor in *Anything Goes*, with a different story from Porter's musical and only some of his songs; Crosby and Sinatra in *High Society*, a musical version of Barry's *The Philadelphia Story* (source of the unsuccessful 1998 musical), with a Cole Porter score featuring "True Love"; and Minnelli's adaptation of *Kismet* and his *Gigi*, adapted by Lerner and Loewe from Colette's novel and play, with a score that includes "Thank Heaven for Little Girls," "I Remember It Well," and the title song. (Generally considered the finale of the big MGM musicals, *Gigi* won nine Academy Awards. With more Lerner and Loewe songs added, it was adapted into an unsuccessful Broadway musical in 1973.)

the bookie sets up his scam; "I'm Going Back," the heroine's eleven o'clock number; and two songs that became pop standards, "Just in Time" and "The Party's Over." The 1960 Minnelli movie starred Holliday, Dean Martin, Jean Stapleton, and Eddie Foy Jr., with choreography by Charles O'Curran. Styne, Comden, and Green wrote two songs for the movie: "Better Than a Dream" and "Do It Yourself." There was a 68-performance flop Broadway revival in 2001 starring Faith Prince.

Mr. Wonderful

MUSIC: Jerry Bock and George David Weiss

LYRICS: George David Weiss and Larry Holofcener

BOOK: Joseph Stein and Will Glickman

DIRECTOR: Jack Donahue

DESIGNERS: Oliver Smith (sets), Robert Mackintosh (costumes), and Peggy Clark (lights)

PRODUCERS: Jule Styne and George Gilbert

CAST INCLUDES: Olga James, Chita Rivera, and Sammy Davis Jr.

PERFORMANCES: 383

The minimal book for *Mr. Wonderful* was mainly an excuse for featuring the many talents of Sammy Davis Jr., making his Broadway debut. A big chunk of the show was given over to his vaudeville and club act, which he performed with his father and his uncle, known professionally as the Will Mastin Trio. Although the show ran 383 performances, it lost money. It introduced two pop hits: the title song and "Too Close for Comfort." Composer Bock soon teamed with lyricist Sheldon Harnick for a very productive partnership.

Li'l Abner

MUSIC: Gene de Paul

LYRICS: Johnny Mercer

BOOK: Melvin Frank and Norman Panama

DIRECTOR/CHOREOGRAPHER: Michael Kidd

ORCHESTRATOR: Philip J. Lang

PRODUCERS: Michael Kidd, Melvin Frank, and Norman Panama

CAST INCLUDES: Edith Adams, Peter Palmer, Charlotte Rae, Tina Louise, and Stubby Kaye

PERFORMANCES: 693

Li'l Abner was Kidd's first time out as both director and choreographer, working again with de Paul and Mercer, who had written the score for the movie *Seven Brides for Seven Brothers*. *Li'l Abner* is a lightly satiric musical comedy rooted in vaudeville, with highly athletic choreography—typical of Kidd—that drives the story forward. All the characters are out of Al Capp's silly, satiric comic strip about the inhabitants of the mountain village Dogpatch. (It was the most successful show adapted from a comic strip until *Annie* in 1977.) The main plot of the musical (as of the comic strip) revolves around Daisy Mae's love for the dense and resistant Li'l Abner Yokum. The first act ends with Dogpatch's annual Sadie Hawkins Day Race. The runners are the unmarried men and women in town, with the men getting a head start. A man who gets caught has to marry the woman who caught him. Abner gets caught by the wrong woman—Apassionata von Climax—but it all works out. The satiric subplot is about the government's attempt to declare Dogpatch useless so it can be turned into a testing ground for atomic bombs. (Capp became a militant, pro-war hawk during the Vietnam War and lost his sense of humor in the process.) Another subplot has General Bullmoose trying to steal the formula for Mammy Yokum's secret tonic. The 1959 movie version used most of the original cast.

Candide is one of a kind. The show became unquestionably the best-selling album of an unsuccessful show; it still sells well on CD, has had several other recordings, and is frequently produced, often by opera companies. The overture has become a classical concert staple. A parody comic operetta set in eighteenth-century Europe and South America, it has one of the greatest scores ever written for the Broadway stage. However, Hellman's book (her only one for a musical) and Guthrie's production—he was better known for directing Shakespeare and other classics—were considered too heavy-handed, and the show flopped.

The story follows the disastrous adventures of the hero, Candide, who wanders the world searching for his beloved Cunegonde and learning that the philosophy he's been taught by his tutor Pangloss—"All's for the best in this best of all possible worlds"—isn't true. Candide is naive and a slow learner, so the story starts to feel repetitive, especially since his understanding of what the world is really like comes abruptly before the last scene, rather than developing little by little in a more dramatically conventional manner. Bernstein said that the show was a political statement on the aftermath of the government-sponsored hunt for Communists in America. (The show's Spanish Inquisition sequence contains direct quotes from the McCarthy hearings.) There is so little dancing that there's no choreographer credit, only a thank-you in the program to Anna Sokolow.

Several unsuccessful attempts have been made at revising and reviving *Candide* (including one by the author of this book). It became an almost-hit in 1973, fragmented into a circuslike presentation by director Harold Prince and with a new book by Hugh Wheeler—Hellman effectively forbade productions of her original script—and some new lyrics by Stephen Sondheim, but it was too costly to make back its money. Prince revived it again in 1982 at the New York City Opera and unsuccessfully on Broadway in 1997. In 1989, shortly before he died, Bernstein conducted a concert version of what he said was the final version of the much rearranged score, for which he and John Wells wrote the narration. The concert was preserved on video and CD.

My Fair Lady is the story of Eliza Doolittle, a Cockney flower seller in 1912 London, who's transformed into a lady when the misogynistic Henry Higgins, a linguistics professor, agrees to teach her how to speak English correctly, with the help of his fellow linguist

Candide

MUSIC: Leonard Bernstein

LYRICS: John Latouche, Richard Wilbur, Dorothy Parker, Lillian Hellman, and Leonard Bernstein

BOOK: Lillian Hellman, adapted from Voltaire's 1759 satire

DIRECTOR: Tyrone Guthrie

ORCHESTRATORS: Leonard Bernstein and Hershy Kay

DESIGNERS: Oliver Smith (sets), Irene Sharaff (costumes), and Paul Morrison (lights)

PRODUCERS: Lester Osterman and Ethel Linder Reiner

CAST INCLUDES: Barbara Cook, Max Adrian, Robert Rounseville, and Irra Petina

PERFORMANCES: 73

My Fair Lady

MUSIC: Frederick Loewe

LYRICS/BOOK: Alan Jay Lerner, adapted from George Bernard Shaw's 1913 play *Pygmalion*

DIRECTOR: Moss Hart

CHOREOGRAPHER: Hanya Holm

ORCHESTRATORS: Robert Russell Bennett and Philip J. Lang

DESIGNERS: Oliver Smith (sets), Cecil Beaton (costumes), and Feder (lights)

PRODUCER: Herman Levin

CAST INCLUDES: Rex Harrison, Julie Andrews, Stanley Holloway, and Robert Coote

PERFORMANCES: 2,717

Colonel Pickering. The comic subplot is centered around Alfred P. Doolittle, Eliza's father, and how he gets trapped into marriage. Although in *Pygmalion* Eliza goes off at the end to marry Freddy, Shaw himself brought Eliza and Higgins together in the 1938 nonmusical movie version he wrote, and Lerner used the movie ending. *My Fair Lady* beat *Oklahoma!*'s long-run record; it also had more foreign productions than any show before it. Moss Hart had a major role in reshaping the script, always a problem for Lerner. It's one of the most perfect of all musical plays, adapted from Shaw's play with almost no loss of wit, character, or theme. Lerner wisely retained as much of Shaw's dialogue as he could—there is a great deal of it—and his own dialogue and lyrics are seamlessly integrated into the original material. Here are some of the lyrics to Higgins's "A Hymn to Him," after Eliza walks out on him:

Women are irrational, that's all there is to that!
Their heads are full of cotton, hay, and rags!
They're nothing but exasperating, irritating,
Vacillating, calculating, agitating,
Maddening and infuriating hags!

Pickering, why can't a woman be more like a man?
Yes, why can't a woman be more like a man?
Men are so honest, so thoroughly square;
Eternally noble, historically fair;
Who when you win will always give your back a pat.
Why can't a woman be like that?
Why does ev'ry one do what the others do?
Can't a woman learn to use her head?
Why do they do everything their mothers do?
Why can't they grow up like their fathers instead?

My Fair Lady was financed entirely by Columbia Records; at $400,000, it was the most expensive production to date. The original-cast recording sold five million copies, becoming the best-selling record of the year—and the best-selling cast album of all time—and beginning a rush by record companies to finance Broadway shows. Several of the songs became pop standards, including "I've Grown Accustomed to Her Face," "I Could Have Danced All Night," and "On the Street Where You Live," but they also develop character and plot in the show. Rex Harrison made a virtue out of his almost nonexistent singing voice by largely speaking his songs rhythmically, starting a new trend for a lead in a Broadway musical (common practice in Weill and Brecht shows such as *The Threepenny Opera*).

Lerner, in his autobiography, *The Street Where I Live,* says that the role of Eliza was first offered to Mary Martin. She heard five songs and went home upset, saying to her husband, "*How* could it have happened? How *could* it have happened? Richard, those dear boys have *lost their talent.*" Julie Andrews then took the part and became a major star at the age of twenty.

The show was transferred very successfully to the screen by George Cukor in 1964, with Audrey Hepburn as Eliza and Harrison and Holloway repeating their stage roles as Higgins and Doolittle. Harrison refused to prerecord and lip-synch his songs; for one of the only times in movie history since Al Jolson, his songs were done live on the sound stage with the orchestra present. Marni Nixon dubbed Hepburn's singing voice with no great loss to Hepburn's excellent performance in one of musical theater's most difficult acting roles. (Nixon also dubbed Deborah Kerr in *The King and I* and Natalie Wood in *West Side Story.*)

Suggested Watching and Listening

Bells Are Ringing
All the suggested numbers are in the 1960 movie version of this 1956 show, directed by Vincente Minnelli and available on Warner Brothers DVD.

- Ella's first scene (performed by Judy Holliday, Ruth Storey, and Jean Stapleton): The heroine's character and situation are clearly, economically, and humorously defined in the opening scene of the show, re-created accurately in the movie.
- "It's a Perfect Relationship" (performed by Judy Holliday): Ella describes her relationship with the hero she's never met.
- "It's a Simple Little System" (performed by Eddie Foy Jr. and the chorus): The system is about how to place bets through the answering service.
- "Just in Time" (performed by Dean Martin and Judy Holliday): Ella, using the name Melisande, goes to a party with the man she loves.
- "The Party's Over" (performed by Judy Holliday): The verse is show-specific and never used when the song is sung out of context. Holliday, insecure about her singing, was afraid to do a solo ballad and learned what she was told was the harmony—which was, of course, the melody.
- "I'm Going Back" (performed by Judy Holliday): This is Ella's eleven o'clock number.

Candide
These recommendations for the 1956 operetta are from Leonard Bernstein's 1989 concert, available on Deutsche Grammophon DVD. It features the London Symphony Orchestra, a supporting cast, and the London Symphony Chorus.

- "Oh, Happy We" (performed by Jerry Hadley and June Anderson, both American opera stars, with lyrics by Richard Wilbur): A beautiful comic duet for Candide and his Cunegonde.
- "Glitter and Be Gay" (performed by June Anderson with lyrics by Richard Wilbur): Cunegonde bemoans her life as a kept woman, although she likes the jewels that go

with the job. The ultimate parody coloratura aria (most particularly parodying "The Jewel Song" from Gounod's *Faust*), "Glitter and Be Gay" is a staple in the repertory of many opera singers. Barbara Cook's original-cast recording is still the best available. It's on the Sony Broadway Original Cast CD.

- "I Am Easily Assimilated" (performed by Christa Ludwig, June Anderson, and the ensemble, with lyrics by Leonard Bernstein): It's a tango sung by the Old Lady, Cunegonde's companion, who's missing half of her backside.
- "Make Our Garden Grow" (performed by the company with lyrics by Richard Wilbur): The operetta ends with this Mahler-like finale, which also has hints of "Somewhere" from Bernstein's 1957 *West Side Story*.

Damn Yankees

All the listed numbers from this 1955 show are in the 1958 movie directed by George Abbott and Stanley Donen. It's available on Warner Brothers DVD.

- "You've Got to Have Heart" (performed by Russ Brown, Jimmie Komack, Nathaniel Frey, and Eddie Phillips): The coach of the Senators lectures some of his not-overly-bright players.
- "Shoeless Joe from Hannibal, Mo." (performed by Rae Allen and the Washington Senators): A good example of Fosse's developing style for big production numbers.
- "Whatever Lola Wants" (performed by Gwen Verdon and Tab Hunter): Like "Hernando's Hideaway" in *The Pajama Game*, it's a tango.
- "Who's Got the Pain?" (performed by Gwen Verdon and Bob Fosse): It's a mambo performed at a tribute show, not unlike the barely connected occasion for "Steam Heat" in *The Pajama Game*. Fosse performed the number in the film but not on stage.

The Most Happy Fella

All of the following numbers from this 1956 show are available on the original-cast Sony Broadway CD. They show only some of the broad range of styles the score encompasses.

- "Ooh! My Feet!" (performed by Susan Johnson): It's the opening number for the heroine of the comic subplot. The word *bitch* was censored for the fifties original-cast recording but used in the actual show.
- "Somebody, Somewhere" (performed by Jo Sullivan): The heroine dreams about finding love.
- "Standing on the Corner" (performed by Shorty Long, John Hanson, Alan Gilbert, and Roy Lazarus): We meet the hero of the comic subplot.
- "Big 'D'" (performed by Shorty Long and Susan Johnson): The comic subplot characters meet in this number about coming from Dallas.
- "My Heart Is So Full of You" (performed by Jo Sullivan and Robert Weede): It's an operetta love duet for the central characters of the main plot.

My Fair Lady

The following suggestions are various versions of this show's many wonderful numbers.

- "Wouldn't It Be Loverly?" (performed by Julie Andrews): Eliza's first number, showing us her soft side. It's on *The Best of Broadway Musicals*, selections from Ed Sullivan's TV show featuring the original cast, available on Good Times Entertainment DVD.
- "I'm an Ordinary Man" (performed by Rex Harrison and Wilfrid Hyde-White): One of Higgins's numbers showing us he has no soft side. This and the following numbers are from the movie, available on Warner Brothers DVD.

- "The Servants' Chorus" and "The Rain in Spain" (performed by Rex Harrison, Audrey Hepburn dubbed by Marni Nixon, and Wilfrid Hyde-White and the servants): Eliza finally learns to speak English properly, leading to a fandango/tango for her, Higgins, and Higgins's friend Pickering. Servants supply the function of a small chorus for some of the numbers that take place in Higgins's home. A large chorus is required for other scenes.
- "I Could Have Danced All Night" (performed by Audrey Hepburn dubbed by Marni Nixon, and Mona Washbourne and the women servants): It's very much an operetta-style number for Eliza.
- "Get Me to the Church on Time" (performed by Stanley Holloway and the chorus): It's a second-act, British music hall–style song for Doolittle and the full chorus. Doolittle's big number in the first act, "With a Little Bit of Luck" is also in music-hall style. Both numbers are comic.
- "Without You" (performed by Audrey Hepburn dubbed by Marni Nixon, and Rex Harrison): Eliza tells Higgins off.
- "I've Grown Accustomed to Her Face" (performed by Rex Harrison): It became a pop song by pulling out all the sections of the song dealing with plot and character, thereby sentimentalizing it and divesting it of all its sting. In the show, it's the dramatic climax of the show and the eleven o'clock number, when Higgins finally realizes that he needs Eliza.

From West Side Story to The Sound of Music

The air is humming,
And something great is coming!
Who knows?
It's only just out of reach,
Down the block, on a beach . . .
Maybe tonight . . .
—"SOMETHING'S COMING," *WEST SIDE STORY*,
LYRICS BY STEPHEN SONDHEIM

The last half of the 1950s saw the rise of the director/choreographer. In the 1940s, George Balanchine and Agnes de Mille, whose choreographic language was balletic, had both tried their hands at directing without much success. Jerome Robbins, whose choreography incorporated jazz and modern dance into the mix, was the first truly successful director/choreographer of the post-*Oklahoma!* era, and the most important. With *West Side Story* in particular, he revolutionized the use of dance and movement in the musical. Following Robbins's lead, Michael Kidd and Bob Fosse were among those who became directors of their shows, cementing the role of dance as an equal partner in the integration of the musical. Gower Champion directed and choreographed the unsuccessful 1955 revue *Three for Tonight* and starred in it, but his main career in the double role didn't really get started until *Bye Bye Birdie* in 1960.

Many of the new director/choreographers were inexperienced at directing anything but dancing. That was sometimes apparent in their work, particularly in dialogue scenes, which began shrinking in length and number as dance took over more of the storytelling role in their shows. Robbins,

West Side Story

MUSIC: Leonard Bernstein

LYRICS: Stephen Sondheim

BOOK: Arthur Laurents, conceived by Jerome Robbins and freely adapted from Shakespeare's *Romeo and Juliet*

DIRECTOR/CHOREOGRAPHER: Jerome Robbins

ORCHESTRATORS: Leonard Bernstein, Irwin Kostal, and Sid Ramin

DESIGNERS: Oliver Smith (sets), Irene Sharaff (costumes), and Jean Rosenthal (lights)

PRODUCERS: Robert E. Griffith and Harold Prince

CAST INCLUDES: Carol Lawrence, Larry Kert, and Chita Rivera

PERFORMANCES: 732, returning in 1960 for 249 more

however, understood how to direct acting as well as movement; he'd even directed a few straight plays. Furthermore, for him, movement came out of character rather than from a single-visioned dance style. Unlike most of the director/choreographers after him, he changed his dance style to reflect what he felt was right for a specific show and specific characters. Robbins, Kidd, Fosse, and Champion did have at least one thing in common: they all knew how to be funny, which helps.

In 1957, choreographer Robert Alton died. Equity minimum for Broadway rose from $85 to $100; off-Broadway's highest minimum, based on a sliding scale depending on the show's potential weekly gross, was $75. There were limited-run revivals of *Brigadoon, The Merry Widow, South Pacific,* and *Carousel,* and nearly thirty new musical evenings, including *Ziegfeld Follies of 1957* (123 performances) starring Beatrice Lillie. It was the twenty-fourth and final *Follies,* fifty years after the first edition. Fewer movie musicals were being made, and fewer of them were successful. The era of lavish Hollywood musicals was just about over, and Elvis Presley was the biggest movie musical star. Among the new Broadway musicals were two of the best shows of the decade: *The Music Man,* an old-fashioned musical comedy, and *West Side Story,* a groundbreaking contemporary drama with dance used extensively for telling its tragic story.

As in *On the Town,* in *West Side Story* Bernstein and Robbins used contemporary sounds and movement in a contemporary urban setting, but this time to tell a serious, often violent story. *West Side Story*—every bit as much a landmark as *Show Boat* and *Oklahoma!*—is *Romeo and Juliet* set on the streets of New York among rival gangs, one white and one Puerto Rican. (Robbins's original idea had been to make them Jewish and Catholic, but that seemed old hat by the time they got around to writing the show.) The whole story takes place over a period of less than forty-eight hours. Riff and Bernardo (the show's Mercutio and Tybalt) are killed in a rumble at the end of act 1. Tony (Romeo) is shot at the end of the show by Chino (Paris); Maria (Juliet) is left alive. In some ways the show foretold the fragmenting of American society that began in the early sixties. As Bloom points out in *American Song,* "It would have been so easy to make the characters simply caricatures of New York street toughs but Laurents's

Arthur Laurents (1918–, born in New York) first made his name as the author of such plays as *Home of the Brave* and *The Time of the Cuckoo.* Among his books for musicals are *Gypsy* (he directed the 1974 and 1989 revivals) and *La Cage aux Folles.* His movie scripts include Hitchcock's *Rope.*

respect for them comes through, thereby making the show all the more dramatic and moving" (Bloom, 777).

West Side Story is a great musical drama revived frequently all over the world. Robbins shaped his choreography around the everyday movements as well as the contemporary dances of the show's thirty teenage characters. His use of dance for both characterization and story (including a dream ballet to "Somewhere," which isn't in the movie) along with the show's deeply moving and tragic story, eventually influenced the entire development of the musical. Even the principals, in addition to having difficult acting chores, must both sing and dance well—although none of the few adult characters have to do either. The requirement that most of the cast sing *and* dance soon became the norm, especially once economic conditions began making it nearly impossible to afford completely separate singing and dancing choruses. Also, as a result particularly of Robbins's work on *West Side Story* and Michael Kidd's on *Li'l Abner,* one person was hired more frequently both to choreograph and direct shows. Bernstein was going to write the lyrics for *West Side Story* himself but soon realized he had enough to do just writing the music (of which there is a great deal, including a lot of dance music), so he agreed to the hiring of Stephen Sondheim for the job.

After *West Side Story,* Sondheim went on to write the lyrics for *Gypsy* before finally getting the opportunity to write both music and lyrics for *A Funny Thing Happened on the Way to the Forum.* From then on, with the exception of *Do I Hear a Waltz?* with music by Richard Rodgers, Sondheim has always written both music and lyrics for such shows as *Company, Follies, A Little Night Music, Sweeney Todd, Sunday in the Park with George,* and *Into the Woods.* He's the most influential Broadway lyricist/composer of the last thirty years of the twentieth century, though most of his disciples and descendants lack his extraordinary talent. They usually turn out shows that are far less successful than his, whether they're hits or not. For that matter, very few of Sondheim's shows made back their initial investments during their Broadway runs. He's never been concerned with commercial success but rather with being true to his art, to his characters, and to the musical drama as an expression of his view of life and the world.

West Side Story was the first show Harold Prince produced without George Abbott. It made a star of Chita Rivera as Anita (the parallel to Shakespeare's Nurse).

Stephen Sondheim (1930–, born in New York) wrote his first Broadway lyrics for *West Side Story.* Trained as a classical composer, he wanted to write music as well as lyrics, but was talked into taking the job by his friend and mentor Oscar Hammerstein, who'd given him private lessons on how to write musicals. (Hammerstein had semi-adopted the ten-year-old after his parents divorced and his mother moved near the Hammersteins.) Before *West Side Story,* Sondheim had been writing for the TV sitcom *Topper.* He'd written the music and lyrics for the musical *Saturday Night* in 1954, but the producer, Lemuel Ayers, died before the show could go into production, and it was canceled.

Chita Rivera (1933–, born Dolores Conchita del Rivera in Washington, D.C.) made her Broadway debut as a chorus replacement in *Guys and Dolls.* After *West Side Story,* she starred in such shows as *Bye Bye Birdie, Chicago, The Rink,* and *The Kiss of the Spider Woman.*

The Music Man

MUSIC/LYRICS/BOOK: Meredith Willson

DIRECTOR: Morton DaCosta

CHOREOGRAPHER: Onna White

ORCHESTRATOR: Don Walker

PRODUCERS: Frank Productions (Frank Loesser, also the publisher), Kermit Bloomgarden, and Herbert Greene

CAST INCLUDES: Robert Preston, Barbara Cook, Pert Kelton, and the Buffalo Bills

PERFORMANCES: 1,375

Meredith Willson (1902–84, born Robert Meredith Reiniger in Mason City, Iowa) played flute in John Philip Sousa's band and under Arturo Toscanini with the New York Philharmonic Orchestra. He worked as a musical director for ABC radio and then for NBC. He eventually became a radio conductor and performer and wrote a few pop songs. After *The Music Man*, he wrote *The Unsinkable Molly Brown* and *Here's Love*.

Onna White (1922–2005, born in Nova Scotia, Canada) danced in a few shows and choreographed the 1955 revival of *Finian's Rainbow* before *The Music Man*. She went on to choreograph such musicals as *Mame*, *1776*, and *Working*.

Robert Wise and Robbins's 1961 movie version of *West Side Story* won ten Academy Awards, including Best Picture, Best Director, Best Supporting Actress, and Best Supporting Actor, and permanently established the popularity of the show. (Robbins did just the choreography. A very difficult man, no one wanted him around any more than necessary.) It was after the release of the movie that such songs as "Maria" and "Tonight" became pop hits. Among the numbers in the show are "One Hand, One Heart," Tony and Maria's imagined wedding ceremony, and a comic number for the Jets, "Gee, Officer Krupke," both with music originally composed for *Candide*. (In the movie, the placement of "Cool" and "Gee, Officer Krupke" is reversed, leaving no comedy after intermission.) The movie was (and still is) very popular with younger people.

Set in 1912 Iowa, *The Music Man* was Willson's first Broadway show. He worked on it for eight years after Loesser convinced him to do it. It's a big, funny, nostalgic, and tuneful musical comedy about Harold Hill, a con man, and Marian, the small-town librarian he falls in love with. Hill's con is to convince naive citizens of small towns that they need a band to keep their children out of trouble; he collects the money for the uniforms and instruments and disappears. The subplot is about a romance between the mayor's daughter and the town's "wild kid," both played by dancers. Another subplot revolves around Marian's little brother gaining confidence in himself; he has a very pronounced lisp and is embarrassed by it. *The Music Man* is a star vehicle with a strong, solidly constructed book, an excellent role for the leading woman, and good supporting roles. (The show wasn't written for a specific star; Robert Preston was cast after it was written, which had become the more common practice by the late fifties.) The score is period pop—often close to operetta—and has barbershop quartets, marches, Gilbert and Sullivan–like contrapuntal comic choruses, and a wide variety of other forms. White's dance style for the show was a ballet-influenced, highly energized transformation of traditional period steps, with fast movements and many high kicks and jumps.

Robert Preston, who'd never sung or danced before, was one of the chief reasons for the show's success. He repeated his role in the 1962 movie, as did the Buffalo Bills—a barbershop quartet—and Pert Kelton as Marian's mother. (Kelton was Alice in Jackie

Gleason's original *Honeymooners* sketches.) Shirley Jones played Marian in the movie, and little Ron Howard, as her kid brother, lisped his way through the reprise of "Gary, Indiana." Da Costa directed the movie as well, and White choreographed it. Director/choreographer Susan Stroman's successful Broadway revival in 2000 starred Craig Bierko and Rebecca Luker. There was a 2003 TV movie starring a somewhat miscast Matthew Broderick, Kristin Chenoweth, and a somewhat miscast Victor Garber as the mayor. *The Music Man* won all the major Tonys of the year except Best Choreographer, which went to Robbins for *West Side Story*.

Set in early twentieth-century New England, *New Girl in Town* is the story of an embittered woman trying to change her life by going back home to her father, who has sent her away to be raised by relatives on a farm where, unknown to him, she is abused. She eventually runs away and becomes a prostitute. Back home, she falls in love with a sailor who knows nothing about her past; his finding out is the climax of the drama. Unexpectedly for O'Neill, he forgives her.

 New Girl in Town was Merrill's first Broadway show. He originally wrote it as a movie musical for Doris Day that never got made, and for which Day would have been wrong, anyway. Verdon and Ritter were the first tie (Best Actress in a Musical) in Tony Award history.

By the time *Jamaica* (555 performances) opened after lots of trouble out of town, there wasn't much of a book left. It had originally been written for Harry Belafonte to cash in on the calypso craze he'd started, but when he was unable to do it, it was rewritten for Lena Horne and eventually became more of a showcase for her than a good musical. Horne's popularity and David Merrick's publicity campaign turned it into a minor hit. The excellent Arlen and Harburg score, in addition to a dream ballet, includes "Coconut Sweet," "What Good Does It Do?" and "Ain't It the Truth" (written for Horne to perform in the 1943 movie of *Cabin in the Sky* but cut because MGM didn't want a black woman to be seen in a bubble bath).

In 1958, Lew Brown of the songwriting team of Henderson, De-Sylva, and Brown died, as did book writer Herbert Fields. Producer Mike Todd, husband of movie star Elizabeth Taylor, died

New Girl in Town

MUSIC/LYRICS: Bob Merrill
BOOK: George Abbott, adapted from Eugene O'Neill's *Anna Christie*
DIRECTOR: George Abbott
CHOREOGRAPHER: Bob Fosse
ORCHESTRATORS: Robert Russell Bennett and Philip J. Lang
DESIGNER: Rouben Ter-Artunian (sets)
PRODUCERS: Frederick Brisson, Robert E. Griffith, and Harold Prince
CAST INCLUDES: Gwen Verdon and Thelma Ritter
PERFORMANCES: 431, paying back its investors

Jamaica

MUSIC: Harold Arlen
LYRICS: E. Y. Harburg
BOOK: E. Y. Harburg and Fred Saidy
DIRECTOR: Robert Lewis
CHOREOGRAPHER: Jack Cole
ORCHESTRATOR: Philip J. Lang
DESIGNERS: Oliver Smith (sets), Miles White (costumes), and Jean Rosenthal (lights)
PRODUCER: David Merrick
CAST INCLUDES: Lena Horne, Ossie Davis, and Ricardo Montalban
PERFORMANCES: 555

in a plane crash. Cole Porter's right leg had to be amputated. The top ticket price on Broadway was $9.40. David Merrick had four shows running simultaneously on Forty-fifth Street, the only musical among them *Jamaica*. The other three were London imports: *Romanoff and Juliet, Look Back in Anger,* and *The Entertainer.* There were limited-run revivals of *Annie Get Your Gun, Wonderful Town,* and *Oklahoma!* Twenty-odd new musicals premiered in a less-than-stellar year. *The Body Beautiful* (60 performances)—a flop about boxing, with music by Jerry Bock, lyrics by Sheldon Harnick, and book by Joseph Stein and Will Glickman—was the first teaming of Bock and Harnick, neither of whom had yet achieved much recognition.

Set in San Francisco's Chinatown, *Flower Drum Song* is—like *South Pacific* and *The King and I*—about a cultural clash, this one between Chinese immigrants trying to maintain old-world traditions and their less-than-cooperative, very American children. It's lighter than most Rodgers and Hammerstein shows and perhaps a bit bland, though certainly entertaining. And it had real Asians playing most of the roles, a landmark in racial terms for Broadway, whether musical or play. (Henry Koster's 1961 movie version featured an all-Asian cast.)

Flower Drum Song

MUSIC: Richard Rodgers

LYRICS: Oscar Hammerstein

BOOK: Oscar Hammerstein and Joseph Fields (Dorothy and Herbert's brother), based on the novel by C. Y. Lee

DIRECTOR: Gene Kelly

CHOREOGRAPHER: Carol Haney

ORCHESTRATOR: Robert Russell Bennett

DESIGNERS: Oliver Smith (sets), Irene Sharaff (costumes), and Peggy Clark (lights)

PRODUCERS: Richard Rodgers and Oscar Hammerstein in association with Joseph Fields

CAST INCLUDES: Miyoshi Umeki, Keye Luke, Larry Blyden, Pat Suzuki, and Juanita Hall

PERFORMANCES: 600

America was finally dealing with its antiquated attitudes toward Asia, which was becoming more important in the post–World War II, cold war global order. It was the time of such books, movies, and plays as *Sayonara, The Teahouse of the August Moon, The Ugly American,* and *The World of Suzy Wong.* (Albert Williams, personal communication)

Flower Drum Song was Gene Kelly's stage-directing debut and his first time back on Broadway in any capacity since the early forties. The score includes "You Are Beautiful," "A Hundred Million Miracles," "I Enjoy Being a Girl," "Sunday," "Don't Marry Me," and "Love, Look Away." A revival with major book revisions by David Henry Hwang ran unsuccessfully (169 performances) on Broadway in 2002.

In 1959, the 1917 Princess musical *Leave It to Jane* was revived off-Broadway and ran 928 performances. There were around thirty new musical evenings, among them shows by director/choreographers Robbins, Kidd, and Fosse. *Juno* (16 performances), with music and lyrics by Marc Blitzstein and book by Joseph Stein, was an unsuccessful (though highly respected) attempt to musicalize Sean O'Casey's great tragedy *Juno and the Paycock* about the Irish troubles.

Little Mary Sunshine (1,143 performances) had book, music, lyrics, and direction by Rick Besoyan, with Eileen Brennan and John McMartin in the cast. An off-Broadway hit, it's a spoof of operettas, particularly *Rose-Marie* and other such romantic schmaltz. Every song is a silly parody of a real operetta number, which is obvious from such song titles as "Colorado Love Call," "Do You Ever Dream of Vienna?" and "In Izzenschnooken on the Lovely Essenzook Zee." It was the first new off-Broadway musical to get a complete original-cast recording.

Saratoga (80 performances) had music by Harold Arlen, lyrics by Johnny Mercer, and book and direction by Morton DaCosta. DaCosta's stilted and heavy-handed book was adapted from the Edna Ferber novel *Saratoga Trunk*, which had already been made into a less-than-successful 1945 nonmusical movie starring Gary Cooper and Ingrid Bergman. Arlen's last Broadway score is good but not great. He did a little more movie work, then retired. He died in 1986.

> There are those who place Gershwin and Arlen at the top of the lot of American composers, with the slight lead going to Arlen. Gershwin led the way, scattering delightful surprises ("blue notes," catchy rhythms, musical whimsy) throughout his work. The younger composer used these same elements, but not for effect: to Arlen they were *natural*. . . . The music of Harold Arlen has remained ageless; the songs—theatre, screen, and all—are filled with never-ending magic. (Suskin, *Show Tunes*, 269)

A great musical play, *Gypsy: A Musical Fable* is the rather fictionalized story of the early days of stripper Gypsy Rose Lee (whose real name was Louise Hovick), her sister, June (who became the actress June Havoc), and their incredibly driven stage mother, Rose, the central character and a great vehicle for a mature star. *Gypsy* begins when Baby June and Louise are part of a kids' vaudeville act run by Rose, continues through the older Dainty June's running away, and on to Louise's becoming a burlesque star. Usually considered Laurents's best work as a book writer, it

Joseph Stein (1912–, born in New York) debuted on Broadway in 1948 with sketches he'd written for the revue *Lend an Ear* and the book for *Mr. Wonderful*, with music by Bock. He went on to write the books for such shows as *Take Me Along*, with Bob Merrill, and *Fiddler on the Roof*, with Bock and Harnick.

Gypsy: A Musical Fable

MUSIC: Jule Styne

LYRICS: Stephen Sondheim

BOOK: Arthur Laurents, adapted (freely) from the memoirs of Gypsy Rose Lee

DIRECTOR/CHOREOGRAPHER: Jerome Robbins

ORCHESTRATORS: Robert Ginzler and Sid Ramin

DESIGNERS: Jo Mielziner (sets) and Raoul Pène du Bois (costumes)

PRODUCERS: David Merrick and Leland Hayward

CAST INCLUDES: Ethel Merman, Jack Klugman, and Sandra Church

PERFORMANCES: 702

Bob Merrill (1920–98, born Henry Robert Merrill Levan in Atlantic City, New Jersey) worked in Hollywood as a TV casting director and production consultant, and wrote such pop hits as "If I Knew You Were Comin' I'd've Baked a Cake" and "(How Much Is) That Doggie in the Window?" He started composing by picking out tunes on a toy xylophone, which he continued doing later. His Broadway work was of much higher quality and included either music and lyrics or just lyrics for such shows as *Take Me Along, Carnival!,* and *Funny Girl.*

tells a universal and ultimately not very pleasant story about what parents and children can do to each other in the pursuit of the American dream of "making it," echoed in a conceptual tracing of the decline of vaudeville in America. (The set included vaudeville cards on each side of the stage identifying the location and city of each scene.) The show also deals with the career choices then available to women. Rose lives her life through her children and expects them to live it her way; "I had a dream," a phrase that appears in the lyrics of several of the numbers, becomes a catchphrase for Rose's next pushy plan. Her dream is that her daughters will be vaudeville stars (as she would have liked to have been) just at the time when vaudeville is dying.

It's a big show, with a chorus of children, later teenagers, two actors each for Louise and June (though not in the 1962 movie), many supporting roles, and a live dog and lamb. It was another triumph for director/choreographer Robbins, even more as a director than as a choreographer this time, since *Gypsy* has considerably less dancing than usual in his shows. Sondheim, still waiting for his chance to write music too, had his second hit in a row as a lyricist. Merrick had originally hired the *West Side Story* team of Sondheim, Laurents, and Robbins, with Sondheim to write both music and lyrics. However, when Merman signed on, she insisted on Styne for the music, because he knew how to write for her voice and because she didn't want a novice. Fortunately, Sondheim was persuaded to stay on as lyricist.

Rose was probably Merman's greatest performance, the first time she was called on to really act, not just be Merman. The role climaxes in the difficult and demanding eleven o'clock soliloquy, "Rose's Turn," built around snatches of songs from earlier in the show, during which she has a kind of nervous breakdown. (Merman, nearly in tears when she first heard it, called it "a goddamned aria.") Also in the score are two songs that show Rose's softer side: "Small World" and "You'll Never Get Away from Me," the latter a duet for Rose and her suitor, Herbie. As the kids' act gets bookings, Herbie becomes the act's manager and Rose's perpetual fiancé; married three times, she's frightened of trying again. Furthermore, she's afraid marriage might interfere with the act. Other songs are "Some People," Rose's song of determination; "Little Lamb," Louise's little ballad on her birthday; "If Momma Was Married," a bitter duet for Louise and June; "All I Need Is the Girl," a song-and-dance number for the young man June runs away with; "You've Gotta Have a Gimmick," for three strippers teaching Louise the ropes; and the biggest hit tune, "Everything's Coming Up Roses," which, in context, isn't the "There's No Business Like Show Business" anthem most people think but rather a demonstration of Rose's obsessive need to follow her dream. At the end of the first act when the song is sung, June has run off, all the others have quit the act, Herbie and Louise want to quit too, and Herbie wants Rose to marry him and settle down somewhere with Louise. The song is Rose's response to it all, another of her dreams ignoring the wants and needs of Herbie and Louise.

> You can do it,
> All you need is a hand.
> We can do it,
> Momma is gonna see to it!
> Curtain up, light the lights,
> We got nothing to hit but the heights!
> I can tell,
> Wait and see!
> There's the bell,
> Follow me,
> And nothing's gonna stop us till we're through!
> Honey, everything's coming up roses and daffodils,
> Everything's coming up sunshine and Santa Claus,
> Everything's gonna be bright lights and lollipops,
> Everything's coming up roses for me and for you!

Albert Williams observed:

> Note the pun on *roses* and *Rose's*—signaling her selfishness: "Everything's coming up Rose's." The brilliance of this show lies in the way the authors, with Robbins's guidance, use repeated motifs and images to express its themes in the context of a gripping dramatic story about flawed but compelling characters. (Williams, personal communication)

Gypsy is frequently revived, most recently on Broadway in 2003 with Bernadette Peters as Rose. Angela Lansbury was very successful in the role on Broadway in 1974 (after playing it in London), as was Tyne Daly in 1989, both directed by Laurents and both winning Tony Awards. In the 1962 movie, the role of Rose was played by Rosalind Russell, with Lisa Kirk partially dubbing her songs; Louise was played by Natalie Wood. Bette Midler played Rose in a 1993 TV movie for which Bonnie Walker re-created the original Robbins choreography; Cynthia Gibb played the older Louise. Neither film does the show full justice, though both women playing Louise are excellent, and this time Natalie Wood did her own singing.

Destry Rides Again

MUSIC/LYRICS: Harold Rome

BOOK: Leonard Gershe, adapted from the Max Brand short story and the 1939 James Stewart and Marlene Dietrich movie

DIRECTOR/CHOREOGRAPHER: Michael Kidd

ORCHESTRATOR: Philip J. Lang

DESIGNERS: Oliver Smith (sets), Alvin Colt (costumes), and Jean Rosenthal (lights)

PRODUCERS: David Merrick and Max Brown

CAST INCLUDES: Andy Griffith, Dolores Gray, and Scott Brady

PERFORMANCES: 472

A Western musical, *Destry Rides Again* is about a sheriff who tries to clean up the town without toting a gun; he eventually has to start shooting. Kidd's first show since *Li'l Abner*, it's not as dance-oriented but does include a bullwhip dance. The show didn't pay back its investors despite its long run and Merrick's raucous promotional tactics. It has a good score and a lot of humor as well as several deaths; it's occasionally considered for revival.

Take Me Along (448 performances) is a nostalgic musical comedy set in small-town Connecticut at the turn of the century. It's adapted from Eugene O'Neill's *Ah, Wilderness!* One of the love stories is between a middle-aged woman and the alcoholic she loves, the other is about overly romantic (and a bit overly cute) teenagers discovering puppy love. Because Jackie Gleason was playing the male teenager's alcoholic uncle, his story became the main plot; in O'Neill's play, the teenager's story is the main plot. As a result of this switch, the balance of the show is slightly off. *Take Me Along* is Bob Merrill's second musical and, like *New Girl in Town*, an adaptation of an O'Neill play. (There'd been a 1948 movie musical of the play called *Summer Holiday* starring Mickey Rooney.) The score of *Take Me Along* includes the title song, "Promise Me a Rose," "I Get Embarrassed," "Nine O'Clock," and a second-act dream ballet when the teenager (played by Robert Morse) gets drunk and passes out. Even with 448 performances, the show didn't make a profit.

Redhead

MUSIC: Albert Hague

LYRICS: Dorothy Fields

BOOK: Herbert and Dorothy Fields (Herbert died while working on the show), Sidney Sheldon, and David Shaw

DIRECTOR/CHOREOGRAPHER: Bob Fosse

ORCHESTRATORS: Robert Russell Bennett and Philip J. Lang

DESIGNERS: Rouben Ter-Arturian (sets) and Jean Rosenthal (lights)

PRODUCERS: Robert Fryer and Lawrence Carr

CAST INCLUDES: Gwen Verdon and Richard Kiley

PERFORMANCES: 452

A mystery set in London in 1907, with a Jack-the-Ripper-like serial killer on the loose, much of *Redhead* takes place in a wax museum. Fosse's first time out as director as well as choreographer, it ran largely on the strength of his and Verdon's talents. (Fosse didn't have a really big hit as a director/choreographer until *Sweet Charity* in 1966; it also starred Verdon and had lyrics by Dorothy Fields.) The book of *Redhead* is very thin and the music rather ordinary. Much of the show is danced, including a second-act dream ballet. Fosse and Verdon married during the run. Sidney Sheldon went on to write TV shows (such as *I Dream of Jeannie*) and best-selling, potboiling novels that made him rich and famous.

Once upon a Mattress is a fairly intimate musical farce about a queen setting a test for any princess who wishes to marry her son: only a true princess will feel a pea under the mattresses in her bed. Though set in a proper fairy-tale time and place, the show is written from a contemporary point of view, spoofing the story at the same time that it tells it. Burnett's role is that of a klutzy princess who ends up unable to sleep on the mattresses because they've had much more than a pea placed under them by various people who want to be sure she'll feel something. Among them are the subplot juvenile and ingenue, whose love for each other has made it necessary for them to marry—quickly. The queen, however, has decreed that no one in the kingdom can marry until the prince does; and she's set such an impossible test for any would-be bride because she doesn't want him to get married. Along with having this reverse Oedipal complex, she's also a shrew and a tyrant. Her husband the king, under a spell, is mute until the very end of the show, when the spell is broken. He talks, and the queen is turned mute, which makes for a very happy ending for him and everyone else in the kingdom. Burnett performed the show on TV in 1964; there was a not particularly successful 1996 Broadway revival starring Sarah Jessica Parker, and there was a 2005 TV movie version with Burnett playing the queen this time.

Jerry Bock and Sheldon Harnick's first hit, *Fiorello!* is a musical biography of New York mayor Fiorello La Guardia and how he fought the corrupt New York political machine known as Tammany Hall; it follows his life and his career from 1915 to 1945. The third musical to win the Pulitzer, it tied with *The Sound of Music* for the Best Musical Tony. The score is so well integrated into the fabric of the show that it doesn't include any really extractable hit songs. In it are "Till Tomorrow," "When Did I Fall in Love?" and three very funny songs for the corrupt politicians: "Politics and Poker," "The Bum Won," and "Little Tin Box."

The Sound of Music marked the end of an era, the last Rodgers and Hammerstein collaboration. (For the first time, Hammerstein didn't write or cowrite the book; Mary Martin had commissioned

---

Once upon a Mattress

MUSIC: Mary Rodgers (Richard Rodgers's daughter)

LYRICS: Marshall Barer

BOOK: Marshall Barer, Dean Fuller, and Jay Thompson, adapted from the fairy tale "The Princess and the Pea"

DIRECTOR: George Abbott

CHOREOGRAPHER: Joe Layton

ORCHESTRATORS: Arthur Beck and Hershy Kay

DESIGNERS: Jean and William Eckart (sets and costumes) and Tharon Musser (lights)

PRODUCERS: Jean and William Eckart, T. Edward Hambleton, and Norris Houghton

CAST INCLUDES: Carol Burnett (in her first starring role) and Jack Gilford

PERFORMANCES: 216 off-Broadway before moving to Broadway for another 244

Fiorello!

MUSIC: Jerry Bock

LYRICS: Sheldon Harnick

BOOK: George Abbott and Jerome Weidman

DIRECTOR: George Abbott

CHOREOGRAPHER: Peter Gennaro

ORCHESTRATOR: Irving Kostal

PRODUCERS: Robert E. Griffith and Harold Prince

CAST INCLUDES: Tom Bosley and Howard da Silva

PERFORMANCES: 795

Jerry Bock (1928–, born in New Haven, Connecticut) wrote his first Broadway music for the 1955 revue *Catch a Star,* with lyrics by Larry Holofcener. *Mr. Wonderful* was their second show. Lyricist **Sheldon Harnick** (1924–, born in Chicago) had been writing revue songs. Together he and Bock wrote the songs for such shows as *Fiorello!, She Loves Me, Fiddler on the Roof,* and *The Rothschilds.*

Crouse and Lindsay to write it before Rodgers and Hammerstein joined the project.) Based on a true story, it's a sweet-and-sour musical about an unharmonious Austrian family learning to harmonize literally and figuratively just before they flee from the Nazis to Switzerland in the late thirties. The central character is Maria, a former novice in a convent who's sent to take care of the children of Captain von Trapp, a rich, bitter widower engaged to a rich, bitchy woman. Maria, the Captain's seven children, and true love win out. (Martin won the Tony for Best Actress in a Musical, beating Merman in *Gypsy*). The subplot love story between the Captain's oldest daughter, who's "sixteen going on seventeen," and her young man turns sour when he becomes a Nazi. Much of the show is given over to Maria's teaching the children how to sing together; they're amazingly quick learners.

> The overflowing sentiment in this Rodgers and Hammerstein operetta is chiefly blamed as the primary flaw. In fact, although sometimes Hammerstein's metaphors can be too poetic for their own good, and although the show pits nuns against Nazis and contains another typical Rodgers and Hammerstein overly inspirational number ("Climb Every Mountain"), the criticism is largely unjustified. This show was simply a little too old-fashioned. . . . It seemed to appeal mainly to children and the elderly while teenagers, who increasingly controlled the direction of American mass entertainment, stuck to their side of the generation gap. The times they were a-changin' but not Rodgers and Hammerstein. . . . Regrettably, this supposed cloying sentimentality became symbolic of all of Rodgers and Hammerstein's shows. . . . It soon became hip to slam this show . . . and all other Rodgers and Hammerstein shows were found guilty by association. (Bloom, *American Song,* 691)

The Sound of Music

MUSIC: Richard Rodgers

LYRICS: Oscar Hammerstein

BOOK: Russel Crouse and Howard Lindsay, based on Maria Augusta von Trapp's *The Story of the Trapp Family Singers*

DIRECTOR: Vincent J. Donehue

CHOREOGRAPHER: Joe Layton

ORCHESTRATOR: Robert Russell Bennett

DESIGNERS: Oliver Smith (sets), Lucinda Ballard and Mainbocher (costumes), and Jean Rosenthal (lights)

PRODUCERS: Richard Rodgers and Oscar Hammerstein, Leland Hayward, and Richard Halliday (Mary Martin's husband)

CAST INCLUDES: Mary Martin and Theodore Bikel

PERFORMANCES: 1,443

There isn't much dance in the show. The score has the title song for Maria, "Do-Re-Mi" and "Favorite Things" for Maria and the children, and "Edelweiss" for the Captain. It was Hammerstein's last lyric:

> Edelweiss,
> Edelweiss,
> Every morning you greet me.
> Small and white,

Clean and bright,
You look happy to meet me.
Blossom of snow,
May you bloom and grow,
Bloom and grow forever—
Edelweiss,
Edelweiss,
Bless my homeland forever.

Tharon Musser (1925–) began designing lights for musicals and straight plays in the fifties. Among the many other musicals she's designed are the original productions of *Mame*, *A Little Night Music*, *The Wiz*, *A Chorus Line*, *Follies*, *42nd Street*, *Dreamgirls*, and *The Secret Garden*.

There was a 1998 Broadway revival of *The Sound of Music* starring Rebecca Luker. In the 2006 London production, Maria was cast in a contest held on TV and voted in by the viewers. Robert Wise's 1965 movie version, starring Julie Andrews, is one of the highest-grossing films of all time, is shown annually on TV, and was re-released in 2000 in a sing-along version. Rodgers wrote both music and lyrics for two songs added to the movie: "I Have Confidence in Me" and "Something Good." The movie inspired a lot of big movie musicals that flopped, bankrupted movie studios, and pretty much ended the day of the big Hollywood musical.

Oscar Hammerstein—from his American operettas with Friml and Romberg, to *Show Boat* and his other shows with Kern, to his musical plays with Rodgers—was the single most important influence on the development of the musical form from the 1920s until his death in 1960. He understood that the book was the structural imperative of the show and how to use dance to help tell its story. He knew that a musical could take on serious themes and could treat them seriously. His shows were as seamless as possible, with scene flowing into scene and dialogue flowing into and out of song and dance. He helped contemporize both the language and the characters in musicals.

It was soon after his death that Hammerstein came to represent the "old." He was, however, both the teacher and the mentor of Stephen Sondheim, whose 1970 concept musical *Company* (directed by Harold Prince) is, if not *the* most significant step in the transition to the "new," certainly *among* the most significant. Hammerstein had, therefore, a major influence on the continuing development of the form even after his own work seemed out-of-date.

It was during the sixties that the "new" began to develop out of such forerunners as *West Side Story* and *Gypsy,* both directed and choreographed by Robbins, both with books by Laurents and lyrics by Sondheim, both serious in intention and complex in characterization and musicalization, both as concerned with art as with entertainment. And it was in the sixties that Harold Prince began directing as well as producing.

Suggested Watching and Listening

Broadway: The American Musical
This PBS series is available on DVD from PBS Paramount. The section "Part 5: Tradition (1957–1979)" covers a long transitional period in the development of the musical's form, structure, and sound.

Fiorello!
The song "Little Tin Box" (performed by Howard da Silva and the politicians) is available on the 1959 original-cast recording of this show (on Angel Records CD) and on Paul Gruber's *Original Cast! The Fifties: Part 2* (MET CD). This comic number is sung by the corrupt politicians as they deal with a trial for graft.

Gypsy
The following numbers from this 1959 show are from the TV version, directed by Emile Ardolino. It's available on Lions Gate DVD.
- The opening and "May We Entertain You" (performed by Bette Midler and Tony Shalhoub): In the opening of the show, Rose comes through the theater audience. This scene establishes time, place, and environment, and sets up Rose's character (although Midler frequently seems to be headed toward a nervous breakdown far before the end of the show), Louise's lack of talent, and June's being by far the favorite child. It also makes us part of the show; whenever anything in *Gypsy* takes place on a stage—as the opening scene does—we're clearly the audience at the show within the show. (Along with being a great dramatic musical play, *Gypsy* foreshadows the concept musicals to come, most particularly *Cabaret* and *Chorus Line*). "May We Entertain You" is a number in the kids' act. (At the top of the show, Louise and June are played by children, replaced by older actors during a time-transition, strobe-lit dance sequence partway through the first act.)
- "Some People" (performed by Bette Midler and Ed Asner): Rose's first song, it gives psychological depth to her obsessiveness; it also establishes the melody to which her catchphrase, "I had a dream," is set. Rose sings it to her father, trying to get "eighty-eight bucks" out of him for the act. When he refuses, she steals his gold plaque.
- "Baby June and Her Newsboys" (performed by the kids): This is the act that Rose puts together for June, Louise, and a chorus of boys. (Later in the act, it's redone on a farm, with Louise playing the front half of a cow.) The lyrics of Baby June's song "Let Us Entertain You" have been changed to "Let Me Entertain You" since June is now a vaudeville star. The strobe-lit transition from younger to older actors is done near the end of this number.

The following numbers are from the actual movie of *Gypsy*, directed by Mervyn LeRoy and available on Warner Home Video DVD.

- "If Momma Was Married" (performed by Natalie Wood and Ann Jillian): It's a duet for the two daughters.
- "All I Need Is the Girl" (performed by Paul Wallace and Natalie Wood): Tulsa is one of the boys in the act. His only solo in the show, it's Louise's dance too, without doing a step till the end. (She's wearing the bottom half of her cow costume.) Although it's clear in the number that Louise wants to be the girl he needs as partner and as girlfriend, Tulsa runs off with June.
- "Everything's Coming Up Roses" (performed by Rosalind Russell partially dubbed by Lisa Kirk, and Natalie Wood and Karl Malden): Rose will go on with the act with no regard for what Louise and Herbie want.
- "Let Me Entertain You" (performed by Natalie Wood): The song is now transformed into Louise/Gypsy's strip song without changing a word. Another time-transition occurs during this number as Gypsy gets famous, sophisticated, and rich.
- "Rose's Turn" (performed by Ethel Merman): It's a dramatic soliloquy in which Rose, during a near crack-up, finally admits the truth about herself to herself, allowing her to begin a new and better relationship with her daughter Gypsy (which didn't happen in real life). Merman's version is available on the original-cast recording.

The Music Man

All of the following selections are from the movie directed by Morton DaCosta, which is available on Warner Home Video DVD.

- "Rock Island" (performed by the traveling salesmen): The opening is rhythmic speech rather than singing, a device also used in much of "Ya Got Trouble." It tells us all we need to know about con man Harold Hill.
- "Ya Got Trouble" (performed by Robert Preston and the citizens of River City, Iowa): Harold Hill's first solo, and the first solo in the show, the song needs its context and staging for full effect; it's how the music man/con man introduces himself to the townspeople of River City and learns how gullible they are. The number helps define character and further the plot.
- "Piano Lesson" and "Goodnight My Someone" (performed by Shirley Jones, Pert Kelton, and Monique Vermont): "Goodnight My Someone" is Marian's first solo, a melodious, sentimental waltz.
- "Seventy-six Trombones" (performed by Robert Preston, Timmy Everett, Susan Luckey, and the ensemble): The same tune as "Goodnight My Someone," it's now a rousing march while Hill continues his scam on the people of River City; it became a pop hit. The subplot's young couple lead the big dance sequence.
- "Sincere" (performed by the Buffalo Bills): Hill forms a barbershop quartet out of four feuding councilmen. The Buffalo Bills were a genuine barbershop quartet.
- "Marian, the Librarian" (performed by Robert Preston, Shirley Jones, Timmy Everett, Susan Luckey, and the chorus): A dance number for the leads of both plots and the younger members of the chorus.
- "Shipoopi" (performed by Buddy Hackett, Timmy Everett, Susan Luckey, and the ensemble): Another big dance number, it's a solo for Hill's comic accomplice. Again the dance is led by the subplot's young couple.
- "Till There Was You" (performed by Shirley Jones and Robert Preston): It became a pop hit. The Beatles made a recording of it early in their career when they were still occasionally doing songs by other people. It's the eleven o'clock number.

New Girl in Town

This show features the song "On the Farm" (performed by Gwen Verdon), in which the heroine tells how she was abused by her relatives. It's on the original-cast recording and on Paul Gruber's *Original Cast! The Fifties: Part 2* (MET CD).

Once upon a Mattress

Both of the following numbers from this 1959 Broadway show are available on the original-cast recording (Decca U.S. CD). (The 1964 black-and-white TV version, with Burnett re-creating her role, is available in some online markets.)

- "Shy" (performed by Carol Burnett): In the Princess's first number, she's so excited to meet the prince that she's swum the moat instead of waiting for the very slow drawbridge to open. Now she wants to know which man is the prince.
- "The Swamps of Home" (performed by Carol Burnett): Another comic number for the princess, this time about her homeland.

The Sound of Music

Just watch the movie again starring Julie Andrews and Christopher Plummer. It's available on video and DVD from 20th Century Fox, and once a year on TV. Or listen to the 1959 original-cast recording, available on Sony CD.

Take Me Along

The following song is from the 1959 original-Broadway-cast recording of this show, available as a CD from RCA Records.

- "Nine O'clock" (performed by Robert Morse): It's sung by the teenager, waiting for his date.

West Side Story

This 1957 musical is available on DVD and VHS from MGM. Jerome Robbins re-created his original choreography for the movie. The opening—there was no overture in the stage musical—tells us through dance that we're in New York in the late fifties, and two gangs, the white Jets and the Puerto Rican Sharks, are in competition for the turf. (It was shot among tenements that were going to be demolished in order to make way for the construction of Lincoln Center.)

- "Prologue" and "The Jet Ballet" (performed by Russ Tamblyn, George Chakiris, the Jets, and the Sharks): In the stage show, this entire sequence takes place in one street scene and in continuous action, which, as Albert Williams points out, makes the effect of "the fight for territorial primacy all the more explosive."
- "The Dance at the Gym" (performed by the Sharks, the Jets, and their girlfriends): Several different contemporary dance forms are used as the two gangs bring their differences onto the dance floor. It's during this extended sequence that Tony and Maria first meet, just as Romeo and Juliet do at the Capulets' ball.
- "Tonight" (performed by Carol Lawrence and Larry Kert): This version of Maria and Tony's duet can be seen on *The Best of Broadway Musicals—Original Cast Performances from The Ed Sullivan Show* (available on Sofa studio DVD). This duet, which became a pop hit, is the parallel to Shakespeare's balcony scene, only it takes place on a fire escape.
- "America" (performed by Rita Moreno, George Chakiris, the Sharks, and their girlfriends): In the show, this number is done by Anita and the other Shark girlfriends

alone. The original choreography (reproduced in the 1980 Broadway revival starring Debbie Allen) is available on the Acorn Media DVD *Broadway's Lost Treasures III—The Best of the Tony Awards,* a collection of numbers from televised Tony Awards shows.

- "Quintet" (performed by Rita Moreno, Natalie Wood dubbed by Marni Nixon, Richard Beymer dubbed by Jim Bryant, and the two gangs): On stage, each section of this complex and nearly operatic quintet is in a separate area.
- "The Rumble" (performed by Richard Beymer, Russ Tamblyn, George Chakiris, and the two gangs): This extended fight ballet is the end of the first act.
- "Cool" (performed by Tucker Smith, the Jets, and their girlfriends): In the movie, they're trying to stay cool after the rumble; in the show, it's before the rumble.
- "A Boy Like That" and "I Have a Love" (performed by Rita Moreno dubbed by Betty Wand and Natalie Wood dubbed by Marni Nixon): It's an extended sequence for Maria and Anita, made up of two solos and a duet. Like the "Quintet" and several other numbers in the show, this duet is nearly operatic in its difficulty and complexity, and, as Albert Williams points out, "emphasizes the grandeur of Bernstein's aspiration and achievement." It's the eleven o'clock number.

From *Bye Bye Birdie* to *A Funny Thing Happened on the Way to the Forum*

Kids!
You can talk and talk till your face is blue.
Kids!
But they still do just what they want to do.
Why can't they be like we were—
Perfect in every way?
What's the matter with kids today?
—"KIDS," *BYE BYE BIRDIE*, LYRICS BY LEE ADAMS

Although few were aware of it at the time, the years between 1960 and 1964 marked the end of the golden age of musical theater and the beginning of a transition in the history of the musical as well as in the history of America. There were many lasts: Irving Berlin's and Moss Hart's last shows; Loewe's and Robbins's last new shows; Abbott's last new hit and Willson's and Loesser's last two shows. But these years saw many firsts as well: Rodgers's first show after Hammerstein's death, for which he wrote lyrics as well as music for the first time; the first two shows for which Sondheim wrote music as well as lyrics; Jerry Herman's first two shows; Cy Coleman and Carolyn Leigh's first shows; Charles Strouse and Lee Adams's first collaboration; Harold Prince's first time out as a director; and the first Broadway musical to run five hundred performances without paying off its investors. By the early sixties, rock and roll songs were the top-selling singles and the affordable market for younger buyers—the kids that something was the matter with, according to the parents in *Bye Bye Birdie*, the first show to incorporate rock into its score. It was older people who were the most frequent purchasers of LPs, including original-cast recordings, of which there were many during the sixties.

> Theater's boundaries were growing, in terms of both subject matter and style; even the literal boundaries were expanding, with more of the action taking place in off-Broadway theaters. . . . Productions seemed to be getting bigger. . . . The competition for a shrinking audience became more intense . . . [and] several good shows . . . got fine reviews, but could not stay open long enough to reach profitability on Broadway. (Gruber, *Original Cast! The Sixties: Part 1,* 3–5)

In 1960, Oscar Hammerstein II died; to honor him, the entire Broadway theater district was blacked out for one minute, and traffic in Times Square stopped. Comic performer Bobby Clark also died. Equity minimum on Broadway went up to $115 a week. There were about thirty new musical evenings on and off-Broadway, including the return of *West Side Story* and revivals of *Finian's Rainbow* and *The King and I,* as well as flops by several significant contributors to musical theater.

Backdrop: 1960–1964

National African Americans begin sit-ins at lunch counters in Greensboro, North Carolina. The Freedom Riders begin a civil rights demonstration in Birmingham, Alabama, and are attacked by a white mob in Montgomery; U.S. marshals are sent in by Attorney General Robert F. Kennedy. Rioting breaks out as black student James Meredith tries to enter the University of Mississippi. More than one hundred thousand Americans, both black and white, march on Washington in support of civil rights. Martin Luther King Jr. delivers his "I Have a Dream" speech at the Lincoln Memorial. Three civil rights workers are killed by white supremacists in Philadelphia, Mississippi. The Twenty-fourth Amendment, making poll taxes unconstitutional, takes effect. Congress votes to guarantee women equal pay for equal work. The Supreme Court rules that reading the Lord's Prayer or verses from the Bible in schools is unconstitutional. John F. Kennedy defeats Vice President Nixon to become the first Roman Catholic president. He creates the Peace Corps. President Kennedy is assassinated, Vice President Lyndon Johnson is sworn in as president, suspected JFK assassin Lee Harvey Oswald is shot by Jack Ruby, and NAACP leader Medgar Evers is murdered. President Johnson signs the Medicare Act and is reelected in

One of the few successful shows of the fifties and early sixties about contemporary life, *Bye Bye Birdie* was the first to deal with contemporary pop music. Because it's a fictional lampoon of the furor caused by Elvis Presley's having been drafted into the army—Conrad Birdie is a very funny parody of Presley—the score has an occasional easy rock flavor, though mellowed down for Broadway audience consumption. The central character is Albert Peterson, Birdie's agent, who turns his star's being drafted into national news with the help of Rose, his girlfriend and secretary. Their love story is complicated by Albert's overbearing mother, who doesn't want him to marry Rose. The subplot deals with Kim McAfee, the teenage girl from Sweet Apple, Ohio, who's chosen at random to give Birdie a farewell kiss on *The Ed Sullivan Show,* and with Kim's parents and her jealous boyfriend. Many of the characters are a step away from being cartoon figures, and the audience is never asked to take anything seriously.

Strouse and Adams's first complete score together, they wrote about fifty-five songs for it till they got the ones that worked best. Among those are "An English Teacher," the opening number and

Bye Bye Birdie

MUSIC: Charles Strouse

LYRICS: Lee Adams

BOOK: Michael Stewart

DIRECTOR/CHOREOGRAPHER: Gower Champion

PRODUCERS: J. Slade Brown and Edward Padula

CAST INCLUDES: Dick Van Dyke, Chita Rivera, Kay Medford, and Paul Lynde

PERFORMANCES: 607

a landslide victory over conservative Republican candidate Barry Goldwater. Jimmy Hoffa brings all U.S. truckers under a single Teamsters Union contract. The U.S. federal budget is nearly one hundred billion dollars, up from nine billion in 1939, almost half going for military appropriations. A free speech movement at the University of California, Berkeley, starts a long period of national campus unrest that develops into the antiwar movement.

International   American money, arms, and field observers help the South Vietnamese against the Vietcong. The South Vietnamese government of Ngo Dinh Diem falls in a coup. The Tonkin Gulf Resolution, approved by Congress, authorizes Johnson to take all necessary measures to repel any armed attack against U.S. forces and to prevent further aggression in Southeast Asia. The Vietnamese Communists (the Vietcong) organize the National Front for the Liberation of South Vietnam. Washington, D.C., severs relations with Cuba. The United States admits having sent aerial reconnaissance flights over Soviet territory. Premier Khrushchev threatens to use Soviet rockets to protect Cuba from U.S. military intervention. The Bay of Pigs invasion ends in disaster and embarrassment for the United States. The Cuban missile crisis, a nuclear confrontation between Washington and Moscow, ends with Khrushchev dismantling the Cuban missile sites and the United States doing the same in Turkey. East German authorities erect the Berlin Wall between East Berlin and West Berlin. West Germany's industrial production reaches 176 percent of its

Charles Strouse (1928–, born in New York) and **Lee Adams** (1924–, born in Mansfield, Ohio) had written songs for summer-resort and off-Broadway revues. Before that, Strouse had been a rehearsal pianist, Adams a journalist. *Birdie* was their biggest hit show. Among their others were *It's a Bird, It's a Plane, It's Superman* and *Applause*. Strouse also wrote the music for *Annie* and several flops.

a solo for Rose about what she thinks Albert should really be; "The Telephone Hour," introducing the kids of Sweet Apple; "How Lovely to Be a Woman," Kim's first number; "One Boy," a duet for Kim and her boyfriend; "Kids," for Kim's parents; "One Last Kiss," Birdie's song on *The Ed Sullivan Show*, written by Albert; "A Lot of Livin' to Do," another of Birdie's rock songs; and the pop hit "Put on a Happy Face," sung by Albert. The show brought more young people into the theater than had been the case in a while.

Birdie was Gower Champion's first time out as director; it established him as a major director/choreographer. The show won the Tony for Best Musical. An altered 1963 movie with Van Dyke and Lynde in their original roles (and with Janet Leigh, Ann-Margret, Bobby Rydell, and Maureen Stapleton) was directed by George Sidney and choreographed by Onna White.

With ultrasexy, voluptuous movie star Ann-Margret as the teenager picked to receive the kiss, the role took on vastly different dimensions than on stage, where the teenager was played by a still-immature, average-looking "girl next door" type. Bobby Rydell, who played Ann-Margret's boyfriend, was a real teen pop

1936 level. Leonid Brezhnev succeeds Khrushchev as Soviet party leader. Israeli authorities hang Nazi war criminal Adolf Eichmann. Jawaharlal Nehru, prime minister of India, dies. The Organization of Petroleum Exporting Countries (OPEC) meets for the first time in Baghdad. Uganda and Algeria become independent states, Rwanda and Tanganyika become republics, Kenya gains independence from Britain, and Zambia is created out of Northern Rhodesia and Barotseland. South Africa expands apartheid racial segregation laws. The world population has gone from two billion to three billion in the last thirty years.

New Developments   Soviet astronaut Yuri Gagarin orbits the Earth in the first manned spaceship. Alan B. Shepard Jr. makes the first American manned space expedition. Methadone is used to help rehabilitate heroin addicts. The tranquilizers Librium and Valium receive FDA approval, and Enovid 10 is the first commercially available oral contraceptive. The laser is perfected at the Hughes Laboratory in Malibu, California. The first communications satellite, *Echo I*, is launched. The Xerox 914 copier is the first production-line copier, and the Bulova Accutron is the first electronic wristwatch. New Hampshire has the first state lottery. Two-thirds of the world's automobiles are in the United States. Studebaker-Packard becomes the first U.S. automaker to offer seat belts as standard equipment. The Stationery Company of Tokyo introduces Pentel, the first felt-tip pen. Aluminum cans are used commercially for the first time.

star of the sixties. Casting him and Ann-Margret made their roles much more glamorous than the Broadway show intended. Rydell was "immortalized" when Jim Jacobs and Warren Casey named the high school in *Grease* after him. (Albert Williams, personal communication)

The 1991 Broadway revival, directed by Gene Saks, starred and was choreographed by Tommy Tune. There was also a 1995 TV version with Jason Alexander, Vanessa Williams, Tyne Daly, and George Wendt, directed by Saks and choreographed by Ann Reinking, a Fosse protégé. Strouse and Adams added songs for this version: "Settle Down" for Rose, "A Mother Doesn't Matter Anymore" for Albert's mother, "One Giant Step" for Albert (from the 1991 revival), and "Bye Bye Birdie" (from the 1963 movie). They make the show feel too long.

A frequently beautiful score couldn't save the odd *Greenwillow*, Loesser's only failure and another change of pace for him, different in sound and mood from *Where's Charley?*, *Guys and Dolls*, or *The Most Happy Fella*. It's about a young man in the mythical town of Greenwillow who refuses to marry the girl he

Michael Stewart (1929–87, born Michael Stewart Rubin in New York) had written for Sid Caesar's TV show and went on to write the books for such hits as *Carnival!*, *Hello, Dolly!*, and *42nd Street*.

Greenwillow

MUSIC/LYRICS: Frank Loesser
BOOK: Frank Loesser and Lesser Samuels, adapted from the novel by B. J. Chute
DIRECTOR: George Roy Hill
CHOREOGRAPHER: Joe Layton
PRODUCERS: Frank Productions (Frank Loesser) and Robert A. Willey
CAST INCLUDES: Anthony Perkins
PERFORMANCES: 95

Domino's Pizza opens in Detroit. The GI Joe doll is marketed, as are Sprite, Tylenol, Coffee-Mate, Total and Lucky Charms breakfast cereals, Pop Tarts, Touch-Tone phones, and Instamatic cameras. Polaroid begins selling color film that develops in one minute. The first Wal-Mart and the first Kmart open. Weight Watchers is founded. The topless bathing suit is introduced, as are topless dancers (in San Francisco).

Sports   Floyd Patterson regains the world heavyweight boxing championship from Ingemar Johansson; he loses it to Sonny Liston, who knocks him out in the first round. Liston is defeated by Cassius Clay (later Muhammad Ali), who holds the title until 1967. The Minnesota Twins, the Los Angeles Angels, the New York Mets, and the Houston Colt .45s (later the Astros) play their first seasons. Roger Maris breaks Babe Ruth's home run record. Golfer Jack Nicklaus beats Arnold Palmer in the U.S. Open.

Art   Georges Braque dies, as does Grandma Moses at the age of 101. There are new paintings by de Kooning, Johns, Magritte, Warhol, Picasso, Miró, Lichtenstein, Rauschenberg, Hockney, and Bacon, among others.

Music/Dance   Britten's *War Requiem* and Shostakovich's Symphony no. 13 premiere. New York's Philharmonic Hall (now Avery Fisher Hall) opens at Lincoln Center.

Tenderloin

MUSIC: Jerry Bock

LYRICS: Sheldon Harnick

BOOK: Jerome Weidman and George Abbott, adapted from the novel by Samuel Hopkins Adams

DIRECTOR: George Abbott

CHOREOGRAPHER: Joe Layton

PRODUCERS: Robert E. Griffith and Harold Prince

CAST INCLUDES: Shakespearean actor Maurice Evans

PERFORMANCES: 216

Do Re Mi

MUSIC: Jule Styne

LYRICS: Betty Comden and Adolph Green

BOOK/DIRECTOR: Garson Kanin, adapted from his short novel

PRODUCER: David Merrick

CAST INCLUDES: Phil Silvers, Nancy Walker, and David Burns

PERFORMANCES: 400

loves because he believes he's got the family curse, which is to marry and then spend his life wandering, returning home only occasionally and only for long enough to impregnate his wife again. The subplot involves two preachers with different points of view. The score includes "Never Will I Marry" and "Faraway Boy."

An unsuccessful musical set in late nineteenth-century New York, *Tenderloin* is about the fight between Victorian morality and the gambling, fighting, and whoring life of the district known as the Tenderloin. Unfortunately, the leading role, a preacher trying to clean up the area, and the other central characters, who are the "good" people in the show, aren't very interesting. (Two shows in a row with preachers as major characters, both flops; perhaps there's a lesson there.) The sermonizing takes itself too seriously, just as the whimsy does in *Greenwillow*, and the show is a disappointing follow-up to Bock and Harnick's *Fiorello!* (also a historical musical about cleaning up corruption in New York).

A satirical look at jukebox racketeering in the contemporary pop music scene, *Do Re Mi* was a financial flop, even with 400 performances. Again the book is weak. Kanin's story had already been made into the 1957 movie *The Girl Can't Help It*,

Publications *The New York Review of Books* begins publication. William Faulkner dies. Sylvia Plath publishes *The Bell Jar* and commits suicide. There are new books of poems by Lowell, Shapiro, and Larkin. Other new books include Baldwin's *Nobody Knows My Name* and *The Fire Next Time*, Friedan's *The Feminine Mystique*, McLuhan's *Understanding Media*, Bellow's *Herzog*, Updike's *Rabbit, Run*, Knowles's *A Separate Peace*, Heller's *Catch-22*, Salinger's *Franny and Zooey*, Kesey's *One Flew over the Cuckoo's Nest*, Vonnegut's *Cat's Cradle*, Solzhenitsyn's *One Day in the Life of Ivan Denisovich*, Le Carré's *The Spy Who Came in from the Cold*, Pynchon's *V.* Burgess's *A Clockwork Orange*, Sendak's *Where the Wild Things Are*, and Dahl's *James and the Giant Peach* and *Charlie and the Chocolate Factory*.

Radio/TV FM radio begins broadcasting in stereo. ABC begins color telecasts. Kennedy and Nixon hold the first televised presidential debates. Kennedy holds the first live presidential press conference on TV. Johnny Carson takes over as host of *The Tonight Show*. Among the top-rated TV shows are which he hadn't liked. In the score are "Adventure" and "Make Someone Happy," the show's hit tune.

Wildcat has a fairly weak book about a woman conning her way into owning an oil well in a 1912 Southwestern town. Ball (whose TV series *I Love Lucy* had recently completed its original run) left the show early because she was either ill or tired of it; it closed. Both Coleman and Ball's first musical, it was also Ball's last. (Ricky, Ethel, and Fred were right: Lucy couldn't sing. Unfortunately, she later starred in the movie version of *Mame* anyway.) The score includes "Hey, Look Me Over," which became a pop hit tune.

The Unsinkable Molly Brown was a successful but not particularly good new musical by Meredith Willson, set in more or less the same period as *The Music Man*. It's based on the true story of a Denver woman whose husband got rich on a gold strike. Unable to be accepted by Denver society, she buys herself into English society. Then, on her way back to America on the *Titanic*, she becomes a heroine (played by Kathy Bates in the 1997 movie *Titanic*) when she helps save people aboard the sinking boat. This finally gets her accepted into Denver society. Debbie Reynolds and Presnell were in Walters's 1964 movie version. The fairly mundane score includes "Belly Up to the Bar, Boys," "I Ain't Down Yet," "I'll Never Say No," and "My Own Brass Bed."

Wildcat

MUSIC: Cy Coleman
LYRICS: Carolyn Leigh
BOOK: N. Richard Nash
DIRECTOR/CHOREOGRAPHER: Michael Kidd
DESIGNERS: Peter Larkin (sets) and Alvin Colt (costumes)
PRODUCERS: N. Richard Nash and Michael Kidd
CAST INCLUDES: Lucille Ball
PERFORMANCES: 171

The Unsinkable Molly Brown

MUSIC/LYRICS: Meredith Willson
BOOK: Richard Morris
DIRECTOR: Dore Schary
CHOREOGRAPHER: Peter Gennaro
PRODUCERS: The Theatre Guild and Dore Schary
CAST INCLUDES: Tammy Grimes and Harve Presnell
PERFORMANCES: 532

Gunsmoke, Wagon Train, Have Gun Will Travel, Bonanza, The Beverly Hillbillies, Candid Camera, The Red Skelton Show, and The Dick Van Dyke Show. New shows include The Flintstones, The Fugitive, Bewitched, The Munsters, and Gilligan's Island. The Fantasticks is broadcast on NBC.

Pop Culture   Robert A. Moog invents the Moog, the first practical electronic musical synthesizer. Audiocassette tapes are introduced. Guy Carawan copyrights "We Shall Overcome." Ray Charles wins his first Grammy. The Brazilian bossa nova becomes popular. Ballard's "The Twist," recorded by Ernest "Chubby Checker" Evans, launches an international dance craze. Go-go dancing becomes popular. Bob Dylan begins singing in New York coffeehouses and is discovered by Columbia Records, which releases his first album. The Supremes (Diana Ross, Mary Wilson, and Florence Ballard) sign a contract with Berry Gordy's Motown Corporation. Sam Cooke is shot during an attempted rape. Jazz saxophonist John Coltrane gains his first wide acclaim. Barbra Streisand records her first album. *Billboard* begins listing rhythm and blues records separately. New pop songs include Drake's "It Was a

Cy Coleman (1929–2005, born Seymour Kaufman in New York) went from playing classical piano to fronting a jazz trio, then started writing music for revues and Tin Pan Alley. He eventually teamed with lyricist **Carolyn Leigh** (1926–83, born Carolyn Rosenthal in New York) to write pop tunes, including the very successful "Witchcraft." Leigh had been an advertising copywriter and, with Mark ("Moose") Charlap, had written some songs for the Mary Martin version of *Peter Pan*. After writing the songs for *Little Me*, Coleman and Leigh went their separate ways. Leigh's career slowed down considerably. Coleman went on to write several film scores and such shows as *Sweet Charity*, *Barnum*, *City of Angels*, and *The Will Rogers Follies*.

Camelot tells the ultimately tragic tale of King Arthur, Queen Guenevere, Sir Lancelot, and the Knights of the Round Table. The book gets very heavy-handed in the second act. When the show opened for tryouts in Toronto, it ran four and a half hours and was in deep trouble. Lerner developed a bleeding ulcer, and a week later Hart had a heart attack and was unable to complete shaping and directing the show. Lerner took over against Loewe's wishes. (Loewe had had a heart attack the year before, and he retired after this show.) *Camelot* opened in New York to mixed reviews. Hart came back after the opening and, with Lerner, improved it considerably. Then Ed Sullivan featured it on his very powerful, Sunday-night TV variety hour, and overnight the show was a hit. Hart died the next year, as did his former writing partner, George S. Kaufman.

> *Camelot* was a perhaps too self-conscious effort to duplicate the success of *My Fair Lady*—another Lerner/Loewe/Hart show based on a British classic, pairing soprano Julie Andrews with a classically trained actor who spoke-sang his songs, with Robert Coote, Pickering in *My Fair Lady*, on hand again for comic support, a lavish Oliver Smith set, etc. (Albert Williams, personal communication)

After the assassination of John F. Kennedy, his widow revealed that the final reprise of the song "Camelot" had been his favorite; it includes the lyrics:

Very Good Year"; Jobim, de Moraes, and Gimbel's "The Girl from Ipanema"; Gibson's "I Can't Stop Loving You"; Miller's "King of the Road"; Seeger's "Where Have All the Flowers Gone?"; Dylan's "Blowin' in the Wind," "It Ain't Me, Babe," and "Mr. Tambourine Man"; Lipton and Yarrow's "Puff, the Magic Dragon"; Russell and Medley's "Twist and Shout"; Lee's "Let the Good Times Roll"; Orbison and Melson's "Only the Lonely"; Orbison and Dees's "Oh, Pretty Woman"; Mann and Goffin's "Who Put the Bomp (in the Bomp Ba Bomp Ba Bomp?)"; Little Stevie Wonder's first hit, "Fingertips," by Cosby and Paul; Mack's "He's So Fine"; Gold, Gluck, and Weiner's "It's My Party"; Madara and White's "You Don't Own Me"; Crewe and Gaudio's "Walk Like a Man"; Weil, Leiber, and Stoller's "On Broadway"; Clark and Smith's "Glad All Over"; Barry, Greenwich, and Spector's "Chapel of Love"; Barry, Greenwich, and Morton's "Leader of the Pack"; Pitney's "He's a Rebel"; Hatch's "Downtown"; Wilson and Jan Berry's "Surf City"; the Beach Boys' "Surfin' Safari"; Chuck Berry's "Surfin' USA"; and Richard

Don't let it be forgot
That once there was a spot
For one brief shining moment
That was known as Camelot.

The phrase "one brief shining moment" came to represent people's memory of the Kennedy administration. Also in the score are "Then You May Take Me to the Fair," "I Loved You Once in Silence," "How to Handle a Woman," "What Do the Simple Folk Do?" and the show's hit tune, "If Ever I Would Leave You." The 1967 movie, lavishly but ponderously directed by Joshua Logan, starred Richard Harris and Vanessa Redgrave. Burton and Harris both starred in touring revivals of the show in the seventies and eighties.

Playing in the same 153-seat, off-Broadway theater where it opened on May 3, 1960, *The Fantasticks* (which started as a one-act) had the longest consecutive run in the history of American theater, topped worldwide only by Agatha Christie's mystery *The Mousetrap*, which has run even longer in London in a larger theater. A sweet, simple show (although it does include an abduction), *The Fantasticks* has a cast of eight (originally nine). It's about two fathers bringing two young lovers together by pretending to keep them apart, hiring a bandit to help them in their plot. The score has two hit songs: "Try to Remember" and "Soon It's Gonna Rain." There was a 1964 TV version starring

Camelot

MUSIC: Frederick Loewe

LYRICS/BOOK: Alan Jay Lerner, adapted from T. H. White's novel *The Once and Future King*

DIRECTOR: Moss Hart

CHOREOGRAPHER: Hanya Holm

ORCHESTRATORS: Robert Russell Bennett and Philip J. Lang

DESIGNERS: Oliver Smith (sets), Adrian and Tony Duquette (costumes), and Feder (lights)

PRODUCERS: Alan Jay Lerner, Frederick Loewe, and Moss Hart

CAST INCLUDES: Richard Burton, Julie Andrews, Roddy McDowall, John Cullum, Robert Coote, and Robert Goulet in his Broadway debut as Lancelot

PERFORMANCES: 873

The Fantasticks

MUSIC: Harvey Schmidt

LYRICS/BOOK: Tom Jones, adapted from Edmond Rostand's play *Les Romanesques*

DIRECTOR: Word Baker

PRODUCER: Lore Noto

CAST INCLUDES: Jerry Orbach, Rita Gardner, and Kenneth Nelson

PERFORMANCES: 17,162

Berry's "Louie Louie." In 1964, The Beatles' first top-of-the-charts hit, Lennon and McCartney's "I Want to Hold Your Hand," is released in the United States. Three weeks later the group sings on Ed Sullivan's TV show; eight of their songs are top sellers during the year. The Rolling Stones release their first album.

Stage Playwrights Clifford Odets, Brendan Behan, Sean O'Casey, and Ben Hecht die. Joseph Papp's New York Shakespeare Festival moves to its new summer headquarters, the Delacorte, in Central Park. Among the new plays are Pinter's *The Dumb Waiter* and *The Caretaker;* Orton's *Entertaining Mr. Sloan;* Albee's *The Zoo Story, The American Dream, The Death of Bessie Smith,* and *Who's Afraid of Virginia Woolf?;* Miller's *After the Fall;* Williams's *The Night of the Iguana;* Simon's *Come Blow Your Horn* and *Barefoot in the Park;* Kopit's *Oh, Dad, Poor Dad, Mama's Hung You in the Closet and I'm Feelin' So Sad*

Harvey Schmidt (1929–, born in Dallas, Texas) and **Tom Jones** (1928–, born in Littlefield, Texas) wrote their first show, *The Fantasticks*, together—not counting several college efforts and songs for cabaret revues—and it's still their most successful. (Jones, using the name Thomas Bruce, played the Old Actor in the original cast.) Among their Broadway musicals are *110 in the Shade* and *I Do! I Do!*

Milk and Honey

MUSIC/LYRICS: Jerry Herman
BOOK: Don Appell
DIRECTOR: Albert Marre
CHOREOGRAPHER: Donald Saddler
PRODUCER: Gerard Oestreicher
CAST INCLUDES: Molly Picon (for many years a star of the Yiddish theater)
PERFORMANCES: 543

Ricardo Montalban, Bert Lahr, John Davidson, and Stanley Holloway, and a movie starring Joel Grey, which was released in 2000 after sitting on the shelf for several years.

In 1961, writer-directors George S. Kaufman and Moss Hart died, as did performer Chico Marx.

> Almost all the [1961–62] season's musicals were steadfastly set in the present day. Sentimentality took several severe knockings and even romance was often either relegated to a subservient role or given an unhappy denouement. Although dancing remained generally excellent, there were fewer of the kind of ballets that had become commonplace since *Oklahoma!* especially "dream ballets." (Bordman, 621–22)

There were limited-run revivals of *Show Boat, South Pacific, Porgy and Bess,* and *Pal Joey* in 1961, as well as around fifty new musical evenings on and off-Broadway, few of them successful. One of the flops was *From the Second City,* a satirical revue from Chicago with Alan Arkin and Barbara Harris in the cast; it moved to an off-Broadway cabaret theater at the beginning of 1962, where it ran in several different editions for four years.

Set in a still very young Israel, *Milk and Honey* is about a group of American tourists looking for love. With neither an inspired

(directed by Jerome Robbins, his first nonmusical); *An Evening with Mike Nichols and Elaine May;* Beckett's *Happy Days;* Ionesco's *Rhinoceros* and *Exit the King;* Fugard's *Blood Knot;* Baldwin's *Blues for Mr. Charlie;* and Davis's *Purlie Victorious* (source of the 1970 musical *Purlie*). Sam Shepard's first plays, *Cowboys* and *The Rock Garden,* premiere off-off-Broadway.

Screen Marilyn Monroe dies. New movies are *Jules and Jim; Shoot the Piano Player; L'Avventura; Viridiana; Psycho; The Birds; Dr. Strangelove, or How I Learned to Stop Worrying and Love the Bomb;* adaptations of Hansberry's *A Raisin in the Sun* and Lee's *To Kill a Mockingbird; The Hustler; The Great Escape; A Fistful of Dollars,* the first spaghetti Western; the first version of *The Manchurian Candidate; The Pink Panther,* the first Inspector Clouseau movie; *Lawrence of Arabia;* the first three James Bond movies; *Never on Sunday* (source of the 1967 musical *Illya Darling*), including the pop-hit title song, score nor a particularly good script, it was the first musical to run over 500 performances without making back its investment.

A sentimental flop about homeless people, *Subways Are for Sleeping* had one of David Merrick's funniest and most notorious advertising tricks. Knowing the reviews would be bad, he found seven people with the same names as the seven most powerful critics, gave them tickets, and published favorable quotes from them in a full-page newspaper ad, using their names and photographs. The real critics were outraged, and the ad was pulled from the papers.

> That neither Jule Styne nor Comden and Green achieved their greatest successes with each other is odd. Comden and Green wrote better scores with Leonard Bernstein and Cy Coleman while Styne's best scores were written with Stephen Sondheim and Bob Merrill. Maybe the three of them never really challenged each other. Certainly the shows take no chances, simply content to amuse in classic style. Some of the songs in the shows are exceptional but no one score is quite equal to those written with other collaborators. (Bloom, *American Song*, 708)

A charming show set in a European circus, *Carnival!* is about a very lonely young woman named Lili who forms a relationship with a moody, lame carnival puppeteer by improvising for the public with his puppets. (The idea came from the children's TV

Subways Are for Sleeping
MUSIC: Jule Styne
LYRICS/BOOK: Betty Comden and Adolph Green, based on Edmund G. Love's stories
DIRECTOR/CHOREOGRAPHER: Michael Kidd
PRODUCER: David Merrick
CAST INCLUDES: Carol Lawrence, Sydney Chaplin, Valerie Harper, and Phyllis Newman
PERFORMANCES: 205

also used in the musical; *The Apartment* (source of the 1968 musical *Promises, Promises*); and *8½* (source of the 1982 musical *Nine*).

Only about forty new movie musicals are made during the first half of the sixties, among them Wise and Robbins's enormously successful adaptation of *West Side Story* and Cukor's equally successful adaptation of *My Fair Lady*. Also released are adaptations of *Bells Are Ringing*; *Can-Can*, with Frank Sinatra; *Gypsy*; *Flower Drum Song*; *State Fair*, which has five new songs with words and music by Rodgers; *The Music Man*; *The Unsinkable Molly Brown*; *Billy Rose's Jumbo*, with Doris Day; *Bye Bye Birdie*; and *Babes in Toyland*. Among the new original movie musicals are *Mary Poppins*, starring Julie Andrews, with songs by Richard M. and Robert B. Sherman; nine Elvis Presley movies; and The Beatles in *A Hard Day's Night*, with musical numbers that are the forerunners of music videos.

MUSIC/LYRICS: Bob Merrill

BOOK: Michael Stewart, adapted from the 1953 movie *Lili* and the short story "The Man Who Hated People," by Paul Gallico

DIRECTOR/CHOREOGRAPHER: Gower Champion

ORCHESTRATOR: Philip J. Lang

DESIGNERS: Will Steven Armstrong (sets and lights) and Freddy Wittop (costumes)

PRODUCER: David Merrick

CAST INCLUDES: Jerry Orbach, Kaye Ballard, and Anna Maria Alberghetti as Lili

PERFORMANCES: 719

show *Kukla, Fran, and Ollie*.) During the show's overture, the carnival tent is set up. The score includes "Love Makes the World Go Round" (written to replace the only song in the movie *Lili*, the hit tune "Hi Lili, Hi Lo") and "Mira." *Carnival!* was the third show for which Merrill wrote both music and lyrics, and it was his biggest hit so far. Champion and Stewart had just done *Bye Bye Birdie*. Merrick, who often favored producing musicals based on nonmusical movies, misbehaved a lot to get publicity, including demanding publicly that Alberghetti take a lie detector test when she was hospitalized during the run of the show.

A wickedly funny, cartoon-like satire on big business, *How to Succeed in Business Without Really Trying* was the fourth musical to win the Pulitzer. The hero is J. Pierpont Finch, a seemingly innocent but actually very clever, young schemer who, by following the instructions in Mead's satirical self-help book, rises from a window washer at World Wide Wicket Company to chairman of the company's board in about a week, finding true love along the way. (No one in the show seems to know what a "wicket" is.) As with Loesser's *Guys and Dolls*, Burrows was brought in to completely rewrite the book (originally written as a straight play); this time he also directed. Fosse was brought in to replace Lambert, the original choreographer, who kept the credit although Fosse reworked most of the numbers. The show was Loesser's biggest hit and turned out to be his last produced on Broadway. Morse and Vallee repeated their roles in the 1967 movie directed by David Swift, with Fosse's original choreography re-created by Dale Moreda. (Unfortunately his truly funny "Coffee Break" number wasn't used in the film.) The show had a successful 1995 Broadway revival starring Matthew Broderick. Finch sings the show's hit tune, "I Believe in You," to himself in a mirror.

MUSIC/LYRICS: Frank Loesser

BOOK: Abe Burrows, Willie Gilbert, and Jack Weinstock, adapted from Shepherd Mead's book, subtitled *A Dastard's Guide to Fame and Fortune*

DIRECTOR: Abe Burrows

CHOREOGRAPHERS: Bob Fosse and Hugh Lambert

ORCHESTRATOR: Robert Ginzler

DESIGNERS: Robert Randolph (sets and lights) and Robert Fletcher (costumes)

PRODUCERS: Cy Feuer and Ernest Martin

CAST INCLUDES: Robert Morse, Rudy Vallee, Virginia Martin, and Charles Nelson Reilly

PERFORMANCES: 1,417

In 1962, comic actor Victor Moore died. Actors' Equity ruled that no member of the union could perform at a theater where the audience was segregated. The Ford Foundation began giving grants to regional theaters. A nearly four-month New York newspaper strike began, which cut off the prime source of advertising—and of good reviews. *My Fair Lady* closed after six and a half years with a record 2,717 performances. The D'Oyly Carte returned for a four-week season of Gilbert and Sullivan operettas. There were limited-run revivals of *Can-Can, Brigadoon,* and *Fiorello!* Nearly forty new musical evenings opened on and off-Broadway—few of them successful. One exception was *This Was Burlesque* (634 performances), a revue of old burlesque material developed by and starring stripper Ann Corio.

Mr. President had music and lyrics by Irving Berlin, book by Howard Lindsay and Russel Crouse, direction by Joshua Logan, choreography by Peter Gennaro, and Robert Ryan and Nanette Fabray as its stars. It was seventy-four-year-old Berlin's last score, a gentle poke at the lifestyles (if not the lives) of President Kennedy and his wife; uninspiring, it flopped at only 256 performances.

A Family Affair (65 performances) had book, music, and lyrics by James Goldman, John Kander, and William Goldman. A flop about a Jewish wedding, it was the first show for John Kander (more will be said about him later, when he teams up with Fred Ebb). Robbins, Abbott, and Champion were all asked to help while the show was out of town; all three refused, so Harold Prince took over for Ward Baker, making it Prince's first time out as director, though uncredited. Choreographer John Butler was replaced out of town by Bob Herget. Nothing helped.

I Can Get It for You Wholesale is a tough, rather unpleasant show with a good score about a brash and unprincipled, young Jewish man fighting his way to the top in the Depression-era New York garment district. Its central character is as big a louse as Pal Joey, and not as charming. (The novel, with its central character changed to a woman, had been made into a 1951 movie starring Susan Hayward.) The show ran nine months without making a profit. It introduced the nineteen-year-old Streisand (in a supporting role) to Broadway, to stardom, and to Gould, her future first husband.

Merrick liked imports as much as he liked adaptations of non-musical movies; *Stop the World—I Want to Get Off* first played in London in 1961 for a 485-performance run. It's a sentimental allegory about Mr. Littlechap and the women in his life. For reasons now difficult to understand, Newley made a big hit with his corny, throaty, vibrato-ridden singing of "What Kind of Fool Am I?" (a pop hit when recorded by Sammy Davis Jr.). When the *New York Times* slammed the show, Merrick said the review was so

Jerry Herman (1933–, born in New York) had done some revue work off-Broadway; *Milk and Honey* was his first Broadway musical. *Hello, Dolly!, Mame, Mack and Mabel,* and *La Cage aux Folles* are among his other shows. Throughout his career, his music has always sounded as if it belongs in the golden age of the musical, even after rock and the more complex sounds of Stephen Sondheim made it seem old-fashioned to devotees of the newer sounds. He's always wanted the audience to leave the theater humming his tunes.

I Can Get It for You Wholesale

MUSIC/LYRICS: Harold Rome
BOOK: Jerome Weidman, adapted from his 1937 novel
DIRECTOR: Arthur Laurents
CHOREOGRAPHER: Herbert Ross
PRODUCER: David Merrick
CAST INCLUDES: Elliott Gould, Lillian Roth, Harold Lang, and Barbra Streisand
PERFORMANCES: 300

Stop the World—I Want to Get Off

MUSIC/LYRICS/BOOK: Anthony Newley and Leslie Bricusse
DIRECTOR: Anthony Newley
DESIGNERS: Sean Kenny (sets and lights) and Kiki Byrne (costumes)
PRODUCER: David Merrick
CAST INCLUDES: Anthony Newley and Anna Quayle
PERFORMANCES: 556

impossible to understand that it might as well have been written in Greek. He then had a Greek translation made that he printed in a newspaper ad. A production with Tony Tanner was filmed in 1966, and another with Sammy Davis Jr. in 1978. Newley directed a major London revival in 1995. The score also includes "Gonna Build a Mountain" and "Once in a Lifetime." Newley and Bricusse went on to write *The Roar of the Greasepaint—The Smell of the Crowd*. In addition, Bricusse wrote lyrics for *Victor/Victoria* and *Jekyll and Hyde,* and music and lyrics for such films as *Dr. Doolittle* (the Rex Harrison version) and *Willy Wonka and the Chocolate Factory.*

No Strings

MUSIC/LYRICS: Richard Rodgers

BOOK: Samuel Taylor

DIRECTOR/CHOREOGRAPHER: Joe Layton

ORCHESTRATOR: Ralph Burns

DESIGNERS: David Hays (sets and lights) and Donald Brooks (costumes)

PRODUCER: Richard Rodgers

CAST INCLUDES: Richard Kiley and Diahann Carroll

PERFORMANCES: 580

Rodgers's first show after Hammerstein's death, *No Strings* is the only full score for which he wrote the lyrics as well as the music. (He wrote lyrics for a few songs added to revivals and filmings of his shows with Hammerstein.) *No Strings* is about a romance between two Americans, a fashion model and a writer, both living in Paris and both looking for a relationship with no strings attached. That they are a racially mixed couple is a true rarity in a musical; the lovers part at the end rather than deal with their relationship back in the United States. The onstage band had no strings except a harp, and dancers moved the scenery. The score includes the title song, the ballad "Nobody Told Me," the heroine's comic "An Orthodox Fool," and the lyrical duet "The Sweetest Sounds."

Little Me

MUSIC: Cy Coleman

LYRICS: Carolyn Leigh

BOOK: Neil Simon, adapted from the Patrick Dennis novel, subtitled *The Intimate Memoirs of the Great Star of Stage, Screen, and Television, Belle Poitrine*

DIRECTORS: Bob Fosse and Cy Feuer

CHOREOGRAPHER: Bob Fosse

ORCHESTRATOR: Ralph Burns

DESIGNERS: Robert Randolph (sets and lights) and Robert Fletcher (costumes)

PRODUCERS: Cy Feuer and Ernest Martin

CAST INCLUDES: Sid Caesar, Nancy Andrews, Virginia Martin, and Swen Swenson

PERFORMANCES: 257

Told in the form of the memoirs of untalented but great-looking semi-star Belle Poitrine, *Little Me* is the story of how lowborn Belle (born Schlumpfert) pursued "wealth, culture, and social position" so she'd be acceptable enough to marry highborn and snobbish Noble Eggleston, the love of her life. The older Belle dictates her life story to a fictional Patrick Dennis, glossing over the sordid truth, while in flashbacks the younger Belle acts out what the older Belle avoids. The two Belles have a second-act duet, the title song. A funny show with a good score (more a series of connected revue sketches than a fully developed book show), it never quite built an audience, perhaps because the novel focuses on Belle, while the show was really written as a vehicle for Sid Caesar to display his gift for caricatures. Caesar played Noble, who attends both Harvard and Yale simultaneously, becoming both a doctor and a lawyer before becoming a World War I flying ace and then governor of both North and South Dakota. Caesar also played six other men in Belle's life: a miserly old banker, a French entertainer, a hick soldier, a German movie director, and the ruler of the duchy of Rosenzweig. Each dies, leaving Belle progressively better off financially, culturally, and socially. (Patrick Dennis also wrote the novel from which *Mame* was adapted.)

Coleman and Leigh's score for *Little Me* is a huge improvement over their score for *Wildcat*. Its score includes "The Other Side of the Tracks," the older Belle's introductory song; "I Love You," a duet for the young Belle and Noble; "I've Got Your Number," a big, seductive dance number for a secondary character; "Real Live Girl," a sweet ballad for the hick soldier; and "Goodbye," a very funny eleven o'clock number for the dying ruler of Rosenzweig and the chorus. Years after the original production, Simon rewrote the book, lessening its impact by dividing Caesar's roles between two actors. In a 1998 revival, Martin Short played all seven roles and even added an eighth. Faith Prince played both Belles (and sang the duet for the two Belles with the chorus), which didn't work as well as two actresses splitting the role.

A Funny Thing Happened on the Way to the Forum is a wildly funny and flagrantly sexist farce based on the ancient Roman comedies of Plautus and performed in American burlesque style. (All of Sondheim's later shows are considerably less frivolous.) The story revolves around the schemes of the slave Pseudolus, who's trying to gain his freedom by getting his young master married to the woman he loves. The script is so fast and frantic that Sondheim has said, only half-jokingly, that he wrote the songs as rest periods. Besides being Sondheim's first chance to write music as well as lyrics, *Forum* was Prince's first solo effort as a producer and Abbott's last new hit. (His last hit—twenty years later—was a revival of Rodgers and Hart's *On Your Toes*, which he directed at the age of ninety-two.) Robbins was brought in as play doctor while *Forum* was in trouble out of town. He saved it, mainly by getting Sondheim to write a new opening number, "Comedy Tonight," in order to set the proper tone, and then by staging the number himself. (Sondheim says

Neil Simon (1927–, born in New York) had been one of Sid Caesar's TV writers. *Little Me,* his first book for a musical, was written after his first Broadway hit comedy, *Come Blow Your Horn,* and was followed the next year by his first megahit, *Barefoot in the Park.* Although mostly known for his many successful plays, Simon also wrote books for such musicals as *Sweet Charity, Promises, Promises, They're Playing Our Song,* and *The Goodbye Girl.*

A Funny Thing Happened on the Way to the Forum
MUSIC/LYRICS: Stephen Sondheim
BOOK: Burt Shevelove and Larry Gelbart
DIRECTOR: George Abbott
CHOREOGRAPHER: Jack Cole
ORCHESTRATORS: Irwin Kostal and Sid Ramin
DESIGNERS: Tony Walton (sets and costumes) and Jean Rosenthal (lights)
PRODUCER: Harold Prince
CAST INCLUDES: Zero Mostel, David Burns, John Carradine, and Jack Gilford
PERFORMANCES: 964

Tony Walton (c. 1935–, born in Walton-on-Thames, England) has designed sets for musicals, straight plays, and movies since the sixties. Among the many musicals he's designed are the original productions of *Golden Boy* (for which he also designed the costumes), *The Apple Tree, Chicago, Pippin, Sophisticated Ladies, Grand Hotel,* and *The Will Rogers Follies;* the 1992 revival of *Guys and Dolls;* and the completely redesigned 1995 revival of *Forum.* He also designed the 1964 Disney movie *Mary Poppins* and Fosse's 1979 *All That Jazz.* He was, for a while, married to Julie Andrews.

he learned from this how important it is to make sure the audience knows early on what a show is about.) The score also includes "Love, I Hear," "Lovely," and "Everybody Ought to Have a Maid."

The 1966 Richard Lester movie of *Forum,* which used about half the score, starred Mostel and Gilford in their stage roles, Phil Silvers (for whom the Mostel role had been originally intended and who played it in a 1972 revival), Buster Keaton, and Michael Crawford. Unfortunately, Lester fragmented the musical numbers by using the same kind of quick cuts he'd used for the pop songs in his Beatles movies, and the lyrics tended to get somewhat lost in the process. Since the lyrics of a show song are important to what's going on—none more so than Sondheim's, which are also extremely funny in *Forum*—Lester's work hurt the show and made the movie less successful than it might have been. *Forum* is often revived; a 1996 Broadway production directed by Jerry Zaks ran for two years. Its original star, Nathan Lane, was replaced during the run by Whoopi Goldberg, the first time Pseudolus has been played by anyone but a white male.

Suggested Watching and Listening

Bye Bye Birdie

The following numbers from this 1960 show are in the movie, directed by George Sidney and available on video and on Sony DVD.

- "The Telephone Hour" (performed by the teenagers): In the stage show, it was performed in a stage full of boxes and panels, like a Sunday, color-comics cartoon strip.
- "Honestly Sincere" (performed by Jesse Pearson and the ensemble): It's Birdie's first number, sung when he arrives in Sweet Apple. In the movie, it ends with a parody of the famous hospital-scene crane shot in *Gone with the Wind.*
- "A Lot of Livin' to Do" (performed by Jesse Pearson, Ann-Margret, and Bobby Rydell): Ann-Margret's costume for this number certainly calls attention to itself.
- "The Shriners' Ballet" (performed by Chita Rivera and the American Dance Company): Rose decides to leave Albert and be wild and free. This is the original Gower Champion choreography re-created in 1982; it's on *That's Singing: The Best of Broadway,* available on OnStage video.

The Fantasticks

This 1960 show features the song "Soon It's Gonna Rain" (performed by Rita Gardner and Kenneth Nelson), which is available on the original-cast recording (Decca Broadway CD) and on Paul Gruber's *Original Cast! The Sixties: Part 1.*

A Funny Thing Happened on the Way to the Forum

The movie of this musical is available on video and on MGM DVD.

- "Comedy Tonight" (performed by Zero Mostel and the company): This is the comic opening from the movie.
- "Love, I Hear" (performed by Brian Davies): The young hero isn't very bright. Cut from the movie, it's on the original-cast recording.
- "Lovely" (performed by Annette Andre and Michael Crawford): The young heroine isn't very bright either. This is from the movie.
- "Lovely (Reprise)" (performed by Zero Mostel and Jack Gilford): In one of Pseudolus's many schemes, he convinces Hysterium, a fellow slave and the show's second banana, that he can play a dead woman believably. This is from the movie.

How to Succeed in Business Without Really Trying

The following numbers from this 1961 hit show are from the movie version available on video and DVD from MGM.

- "How To" (performed by Robert Morse and the ensemble): It's the opening of the show as Finch moves from window washer to employee of the World Wide Wicket Company.
- "A Secretary Is Not a Toy" (performed by the executives and the ensemble): It's sexism pretending not to be.
- "It's Been a Long Day" (performed by Robert Morse, Michele Lee, and Kay Reynolds): The hero and heroine hesitantly make their first date, while her best friend comments and interprets for the audience.
- "I Believe in You" (performed by Robert Morse and the executives): Finch, the hero, sings it to himself in the mirror of the executive men's room to give himself courage for his big presentation, while his rivals sing a countermelody. (The sound of electric razors is made by kazoos.)
- "The Brotherhood of Man" (performed by Robert Morse, Sammy Smith, and the executives): The eleven o'clock number—a pseudo-revivalist number similar to "Sit Down, You're Rockin' the Boat," the eleven o'clock number in *Guys and Dolls*—it's a satiric comment on the mediocrity of the employees of World Wide Wicket (and any other big business). It's also laughing at the idea of community, so beloved of Hammerstein.

Little Me

The listed numbers from this 1962 show are available on the original-cast CD recording from RCA Records.

- "I Love You" (performed by Sid Caesar and Virginia Martin): It's a comic duet for the young Belle and Noble.
- "Real Live Girl" (performed by Sid Caesar): Sung by Fred Poitrine, the shy and extremely nearsighted, young World War I soldier, he then marries Belle just before going off to be killed.
- "Goodbye (The Prince's Farewell)" (performed by Sid Caesar and the company): On his deathbed, Prince Cherney of Rosenzweig bids his subjects farewell in an eleven o'clock number tailored to Caesar's comic talents.

From *She Loves Me* to *Fiddler on the Roof*

Ask ev'ry person if he's heard the story;
And tell it strong and clear if he has not;
That once there was a fleeting wisp of glory
Called Camelot.

—"CAMELOT (REPRISE)," *CAMELOT,* LYRICS BY ALAN JAY LERNER

By 1964—the end of Broadway's golden age—the whole country had begun splitting into "culture" and "counterculture," and Broadway didn't know which it was or which to be. Furthermore, the country was beginning to splinter, not only in terms of what kinds of music people listened to but, more importantly, because of such issues as the war in Vietnam and the burgeoning movements asserting the rights of women, minorities, and gays. In November 1963, when President Kennedy was assassinated, the mood of the country began to change. In the confusion, musical comedies and musical plays moved further and further apart. Abe Burrows, Comden and Green, and Michael Stewart were among those who continued George Abbott's musical comedy tradition of books that were light, fast, and funny. Arthur Laurents, Alan Jay Lerner, and Joseph Stein were among those whose books continued Oscar Hammerstein's tradition of dramatic musical plays. However, the plays seemed to be getting more serious and heavy-handed, the comedies more trivial. (Who can blame the makers of musicals for beginning to lose their sense of humor when the same thing was happening to the entire country?)

In 1963, writer/lyricist Otto Harbach, performer William Gaxton, and J. J. Shubert (the last of the Shubert brothers) died. There were about thirty musical evenings on Broadway, including limited-run revivals of *Wonderful*

She Loves Me: The Happiest Musical

MUSIC: Jerry Bock

LYRICS: Sheldon Harnick

BOOK: Joe Masteroff, adapted from Miklós László's 1937 play *Parfumerie*

DIRECTOR: Harold Prince

CHOREOGRAPHER: Carol Haney

ORCHESTRATOR: Don Walker

DESIGNERS: Jean and William Eckart (sets and lights) and Patricia Zipprodt (costumes)

PRODUCERS: Harold Prince, Lawrence Kasha, and Philip C. McKenna

CAST INCLUDES: Barbara Cook, Daniel Massey, Barbara Baxley, and Jack Cassidy

PERFORMANCES: 302

Town, Brigadoon, Pal Joey, Oklahoma! and *The King and I.* There were off-Broadway revivals of *The Boys from Syracuse* (500 performances) and of *Best Foot Forward* (224 performances), which introduced Liza Minnelli and Christopher Walken. Schwartz and Dietz's flop *Jennie* (82 performances) starred Mary Martin.

Although its original production closed at a loss, *She Loves Me: The Happiest Musical* is occasionally and even successfully revived. Intimate and small-scale (seven principals and a small chorus who play a variety of roles), with a score that alternates between operetta and Broadway pop, it's about coworkers in a 1930s perfume shop, Amalia Balash and Georg Nowack, who hate each other without knowing they're each other's secret pen pals. The other workers in the shop supply the subplots. The show was Prince's first solo directing effort. The original play had already been adapted into the 1940 movie *The Shop Around the Corner* and into the 1949 movie musical *In the Good Old Summertime*, which had a score of golden oldies. It was also the source of the 1998 movie *You've Got Mail.* There was a well-received but financially unsuccessful Broadway revival in 1995. The score includes the title song and "Tonight at Eight," both sung by Georg, and "Will He Like Me?", "Dear Friend," and "Ice Cream," sung by Amalia.

110 in the Shade

MUSIC: Harvey Schmidt

LYRICS: Tom Jones

BOOK: N. Richard Nash, adapted from his TV and Broadway play *The Rainmaker*

DIRECTOR: Joseph Anthony

CHOREOGRAPHER: Agnes de Mille

ORCHESTRATOR: Hershy Kay

DESIGNERS: Oliver Smith (sets), Motley (costumes), and John Harvey (lights)

PRODUCER: David Merrick

CAST INCLUDES: Inga Swenson, Robert Horton, Lesley Ann Warren, and Will Geer

PERFORMANCES: 330

110 in the Shade was Schmidt and Jones's first Broadway show, following the success of their off-Broadway musical *The Fantasticks.* The original play, *The Rainmaker,* had been made into a 1956 movie with Katharine Hepburn and Burt Lancaster. A good though not terribly successful show, *110 in the Shade* is about Starbuck, a con man claiming to be a rainmaker, and Lizzie, the repressed farm woman who learns to believe in herself through him. It was overwhelmed by its competition during the 1963–64 Broadway season, as was *She Loves Me.* In addition, according to Albert Williams, "the original Broadway show suffered because its intimate story was padded into a big-scale show with a full chorus (which of course also made it expensive). Jones and Schmidt later reworked it into a chamber piece, cutting the chorus." There are rumors that over a hundred songs were written for the sixteen-song score, which includes "Raunchy," "Old Maid," "Is It Really Me?", "Melisande," and "Simple Little Things." It's one of eight shows Merrick produced that season.

Here's Love is a mediocre show about the real Santa Claus working at Macy's department store and the little girl who doesn't believe in him. Occasionally revived by local theater companies at Christmastime, it was Willson's last Broadway show. Stick with the 1947 nonmusical, black-and-white movie with Edmund Gwenn as Kris Kringle and little Natalie Wood.

Merrick imported *Oliver!* from London, where it opened in 1960 and ran 2,618 performances. Dickens's story about an orphan boy named Oliver Twist who runs away to London and falls in with a gang of thieves is too big and sprawling to be contained within a normal-length musical; the book of the show is often choppy and poorly written. But Lionel Bart wrote an infectious, hummable score; the show appeals to the whole family; and it makes a virtue of having a lot of children onstage. In the score are "Food, Glorious Food," the opening number for a group of orphans (*Annie* wasn't first); "Oom-Pah-Pah," the heroine Nancy's eleven o'clock number, right before the melodrama takes over, ending in her murder, the death of the villain, Bill Sykes, and the return of Oliver to his kind and wealthy grandfather; "Where Is Love?" sung by the sad and lonely orphan boy but, out of context, a perfectly good ballad; "Consider Yourself," Oliver's introduction to the young gang of thieves by a character known as the Artful Dodger; "You've Got to Pick a Pocket or Two," in which Fagin, the adult head of the gang, demonstrates their profession; "I'd Do Anything," an ensemble number for Oliver, Nancy, the Dodger, and the gang; and Nancy's big hit ballad "As Long as He Needs Me." Sean Kenny designed an influential unit set that revolved and had platforms, stairs, ramps, arches, and bridges, with only suggestions of specific locations. It allowed the action to happen in several places at once or to move immediately from scene to scene. It helped change the nature of set design on Broadway, inspiring the sets of such shows as *Company, Dreamgirls, Sweeney Todd,* and *Les Misérables.* The 1968 David Lean movie, choreographed by Onna White, won the Academy Award for Best Motion Picture.

In 1964, Cole Porter, Marc Blitzstein, and performers Carol Haney, Gracie Allen, Harpo Marx, and Eddie Cantor died. The top Broadway ticket price was now $9.90. The D'Oyly Carte returned for a five-week run of Gilbert and Sullivan operettas. There were limited-run City Center revivals of *West Side Story, Porgy*

Here's Love

MUSIC/LYRICS/BOOK: Meredith Willson, adapted from the movie *Miracle on 34th Street*
DIRECTOR/PRODUCER: Stuart Ostrow
CHOREOGRAPHER: Michael Kidd
CAST INCLUDES: Janis Paige, with Michael Bennett in the chorus
PERFORMANCES: 334

Oliver!

MUSIC/LYRICS/BOOK: Lionel Bart, adapted from Dickens's *Oliver Twist*
DIRECTOR: Peter Coe
ORCHESTRATOR: Eric Rogers
DESIGNERS: Sean Kenny (sets and costumes) and John Wyckham (lights)
PRODUCERS: David Merrick and Donald Albery
CAST INCLUDES: Clive Revill, Georgia Brown, and David Jones (later one of the Monkees)
PERFORMANCES: 774

Golden Boy

MUSIC: Charles Strouse
LYRICS: Lee Adams
BOOK: William Gibson and Clifford Odets, adapted from the 1937 play by Odets
DIRECTOR: Arthur Penn
CHOREOGRAPHER: Donald McKayle
ORCHESTRATOR: Ralph Burns
DESIGNERS: Tony Walton (sets and costumes) and Tharon Musser (lights)
PRODUCER: Hillard Elkins
CAST INCLUDES: Sammy Davis (he dropped the "Jr."), Billy Daniels, and Paula Wayne
PERFORMANCES: 569

Anyone Can Whistle: A Musical Fable

MUSIC/LYRICS: Stephen Sondheim
BOOK/DIRECTOR: Arthur Laurents
CHOREOGRAPHER: Herbert Ross
ORCHESTRATOR: Don Walker
DESIGNERS: Jean and William Eckart (sets), Theoni V. Aldredge (costumes), and Jules Fisher (lights)
PRODUCERS: Kermit Bloomgarden and Diana Krasny
CAST INCLUDES: Lee Remick and Angela Lansbury (making their musical debuts) and Harry Guardino
PERFORMANCES: 9

Patricia Zipprodt (1925–99, born in Chicago) started designing costumes for Broadway in 1957. Along with many plays, she designed such musicals as *Fiddler on the Roof, Cabaret, 1776, Pippin, Chicago, Sunday in the Park with George,* and *Into the Woods.*

Jules Fisher (1937–, born in Norristown, Pennsylvania) has designed lights for many plays and such musicals as *Hair, Jesus Christ Superstar, Pippin, Chicago, Dancin', Grand Hotel, Jelly's Last Jam, Bring in 'Da Noise, Bring in 'Da Funk,* and *Ragtime.* He also has his own firm as a creative consultant.

and Bess, My Fair Lady, and *Brigadoon.* The New York State Theatre began a series of low-priced, limited-run revivals with *The King and I* and *The Merry Widow.* There were over forty new musical evenings on and off-Broadway, including *High Spirits* (376 performances) by Timothy Gray and Hugh Martin; an unsuccessful musical adaptation of Noël Coward's 1941 *Blithe Spirit,* starring Beatrice Lillie (her last Broadway show) and Tammy Grimes.

A pretty good score by the *Birdie* team and a good performance by Sammy Davis made *Golden Boy* at least moderately successful. It's about an African American (Italian in the original play) who becomes a boxer to get out of the ghetto; he's eventually corrupted by money and fame and dies in a car crash. Odets died while working on the book; Gibson was brought in to finish it. The play by Odets had been filmed in 1939 with Barbara Stanwyck, William Holden, and a happy ending.

A heavy-handed allegory about some inmates of a lunatic asylum saving a town from a mean mayor, *Anyone Can Whistle* has an excellent Sondheim score. However, because the show was such a resounding flop, he didn't get to write the music for another show until *Company* in 1970. The show does have its admirers though, and, as usual, Sondheim wrote some extraordinary lyrics. The score, a favorite of cabaret singers, includes the title song, "With So Little to Be Sure Of," "There Won't Be Trumpets," and "Everybody Says Don't." A 1995 concert version of the show starred Scott Bakula, Bernadette Peters, and Madeline Kahn.

Three blockbusters opened in 1964 with either Champion or Robbins involved; all three have become standard repertory.

Thornton Wilder had based *The Matchmaker* (from which *Hello, Dolly!* was adapted) on an earlier flop of his, *The Merchant of Yonkers,* which was based on an earlier German play that was based on an earlier British play. (Tom Stoppard also did an adaptation called *On the Razzle.*) *The Matchmaker* was made into a 1958 movie starring Shirley Booth, Paul Ford, Shirley MacLaine, Anthony Perkins, and Robert Morse. *Hello, Dolly!* is a star vehicle—but with several other good roles—with nothing more on its mind than to provide purely escapist entertainment. It even has a burlesque-style runway around the orchestra pit, used to great effect in the spectacular title number. The show, set in turn-of-the-century New York, is about matchmaker Dolly Gallagher Levi's plot to capture "half-millionaire" Horace Vandergelder for herself. The main subplot follows Vandergelder's two shop assistants on their big night on the town with two hatmakers. There's another subplot dealing with Vandergelder's daughter's elopement. Dolly has a hand in both subplots, all as part of her plan to get Horace, who's courting one of the hatmakers.

Hello, Dolly! is Herman's second Broadway show and one of the biggest hits of all time, certainly the biggest for Herman and Stewart. (Bob Merrill was brought in while the show was out of town to write some songs, including "Elegance" and "Motherhood.") Also in the score are "It Only Takes a Moment" for the hero of the main subplot, "Ribbons Down My Back" for the hatmaker courted by Vandergelder, "Before the Parade Passes By" for Dolly and the ensemble to close the first act, and Dolly's eleven o'clock number, "So Long, Dearie." The show won several Tonys, including Best Musical, and established a new long-run record it kept for ten months. After Channing left the Broadway production to do the show on tour, Merrick's huge promotional campaign to keep the show running included bringing in new stars of a certain age to play the title role. Among those who played Dolly on Broadway or on the road were Ethel Merman (for whom the role had been conceived but who decided not to do it initially) in her last Broadway appearance, Phyllis Diller, Ginger Rogers, Betty Grable, and Pearl Bailey with Cab Calloway and an all-black cast. (There was even talk at one point of Jack Benny playing Dolly in drag.) Barbra Streisand, far too young for the role and playing Dolly as if she were Barbra, did the 1969 movie directed by Gene Kelly, choreographed by Michael Kidd, and costarring Walter Matthau and Michael Crawford, with Tommy Tune in a supporting role and Louis Armstrong making a cameo appearance during the title song. (He'd made a hit recording of it.) In 1995, Channing toured the show again to great success and even brought it back to Broadway.

Funny Girl is another star vehicle but without supporting roles as rewarding as those in *Hello, Dolly!* Robbins was brought in while the show was out of town to save it, and he did. It tells of Fanny Brice's rise to stardom in the *Ziegfeld Follies* and of her unhappy first marriage to gambler Nick Arnstein. There's no subplot; the show gives equal time to Brice's career (complete with

Hello, Dolly!

MUSIC/LYRICS: Jerry Herman

BOOK: Michael Stewart, adapted from Thornton Wilder's play *The Matchmaker*

DIRECTOR/CHOREOGRAPHER: Gower Champion

ORCHESTRATOR: Philip J. Lang

DESIGNERS: Oliver Smith (sets), Freddy Wittop (costumes), and Jean Rosenthal (lights)

PRODUCER: David Merrick (who had produced *The Matchmaker*)

CAST INCLUDES: Carol Channing (Mary Martin in London), David Burns, Eileen Brennan, Sondra Lee, and Charles Nelson Reilly

PERFORMANCES: 2,844

Angela Lansbury (1925–, born in London, England) escaped the London blitz by coming to the United States in 1940. She was a movie actress before *Anyone Can Whistle*, mostly in dramatic roles in such films as *Gaslight, The Picture of Dorian Gray, Samson and Delilah,* and *The Manchurian Candidate.* Her only lead in a movie musical was in Disney's *Bedknobs and Broomsticks.* Her other Broadway musicals include *Mame,* the 1974 revival of *Gypsy,* and *Sweeney Todd.* She starred for many years on TV in *Murder, She Wrote* and played the title role in the 1996 Jerry Herman TV musical *Mrs. Santa Claus.*

Funny Girl

MUSIC: Jule Styne

LYRICS: Bob Merrill

BOOK: Isobel Lennart, based on the early life of Fanny Brice

DIRECTORS: Garson Kanin and Jerome Robbins

CHOREOGRAPHER: Carol Haney

ORCHESTRATOR: Ralph Burns

DESIGNERS: Robert Randolph (sets and lights) and Irene Sharaff (costumes)

PRODUCER: Ray Stark (Brice's son-in-law)

CAST INCLUDES: Barbra Streisand, Sydney Chaplin, Kay Medford, and Jean Stapleton

PERFORMANCES: 1,348

Fiddler on the Roof

MUSIC: Jerry Bock

LYRICS: Sheldon Harnick

BOOK: Joseph Stein, adapted from stories by Sholom Aleichem

DIRECTOR/CHOREOGRAPHER: Jerome Robbins

ORCHESTRATOR: Don Walker

DESIGNERS: Boris Aronson (sets), Patricia Zipprodt (costumes), and Jean Rosenthal (lights)

PRODUCER: Harold Prince

CAST INCLUDES: Zero Mostel, Maria Karnilova, Bert Convy, Austin Pendleton, and Beatrice Arthur

PERFORMANCES: 3,242

Ziegfeld-like production numbers) and to her relationship with Arnstein, most of which is highly fictionalized. For the first time, Merrill wrote lyrics but not music. Among the songs are "His Love Makes Me Beautiful" (a pseudo-Ziegfeld number with Fanny as a pregnant bride); "I'm the Greatest Star," her first number; "People," which became a big pop hit; "Don't Rain on My Parade," her closing number for act 1; and "The Music That Makes Me Dance," her eleven o'clock number and a ballad similar in tone to Brice's signature torch song "My Man." Brice was Streisand's first starring role and her last Broadway show; she was twenty-one years old when it opened. Her character sings almost all the songs. (Styne apparently wrote around fifty while working on the show.) Streisand won an Academy Award for the 1968 movie, directed by William Wyler and choreographed by Herbert Ross; it was her first film role.

Fiddler on the Roof is another star vehicle, this time for a man, but with several other excellent roles. As Ken Bloom notes:

> Some argue this is the best musical yet . . . the epitome of the Rodgers and Hammerstein school of musical theatre. . . . It's interesting to note what a truly integrated score and book this musical had. None of the songs stand on their own divorced from the book (Bloom, *American Song*, 199).

Fiddler on the Roof is a great musical drama set beginning in 1905 among Russian Jews trying to hold on to their traditions while dealing with their children's more modern ideas and with the extreme anti-Semitism and pogroms that eventually drive them out of the country. The central characters are the poor milkman Tevye, his wife, the three oldest of their five daughters, and the men they marry. As Gerald Bordman points out in *American Musical Theatre*, "By emphasizing ongoing problems of family bonds and religious interaction against a backdrop of disintegrating social order, the authors gave the work a universality that allowed the evening to transcend what might have otherwise been an appeal limited largely to the sizable Jewish segment of playgoers" (p. 637).

With this show Robbins brought dance and drama together even more seamlessly than in *On the Town* and *West Side Story.* (It was his last new show; after it, he concentrated on ballet.) The show even has a dream ballet, "Tevye's Dream," in which the dancers act out a lie being told by Tevye, who makes it up in order to convince his wife, Golde, that their daughter should marry the man she loves instead of the older butcher to whom she's been betrothed. Also in the score are "Tradition," the opening number for Tevye and the entire cast, which introduces the town, its traditions, and its problems; "If I Were a Rich Man," Tevye's famous plea to God, with whom he has frequent one-sided conversations; "Matchmaker, Matchmaker," for the three oldest daughters hoping for husbands; "Miracle of Miracles," sung by the young tailor in love with Tevye's oldest daughter; "Do You Love Me?", a charming second-act duet for Tevye and Golde added during out-of-town tryouts; "To Life," a spectacular number celebrating the betrothal of Tevye's oldest daughter to the older butcher; and "Sunrise, Sunset," when she marries the young tailor she really loves.

Fiddler established a new Broadway long-run record, beating not only *Hello, Dolly!* but also the straight play *Life with Father*, which had till then been the longest-running Broadway show of any kind. It's frequently revived and was filmed by Norman Jewison in 1971, with Robbins's choreography adapted by Tom Abbott, and with Israeli actor Topol as Tevye the Milkman (the role he had played in the London production).

And so ended the so-called golden age of the Broadway musical. Economics played a large role in determining what happened next as did, of course, the increasing splintering of the country. By 1964, the costs of producing a Broadway musical had risen so high that shows needed long runs just to pay off their investors. Producers had to keep raising ticket prices, which made it more and more difficult for less affluent people to attend. Young people who did have money weren't interested. Ticket sales kept dwindling while the audience's average age kept rising throughout the rest of the sixties and seventies, as did the cost of putting on a show, until by the eighties it seemed that only spectacularly and expensively produced megahits could survive even though fewer and fewer people could afford the tickets to see them.

Also by 1964, most of the great composers and lyricists of the twenties, thirties, and forties were dead, dying, or giving up; fewer pop hit singles were coming from Broadway; and New York was no longer the only or even the main center for pop composers: Los Angeles had achieved that status. With vaudeville, burlesque, and revue either dead or dying, new writers and performers had few opportunities to hone their skills and establish their reputations except on TV, and most network TV had also moved to the West Coast. Performers, directors, and writers were therefore as willing as composers to desert New York and the stage for the more national and lucrative exposure provided by movies and television—if they could get it. And when they could, they seldom came back to the stage. (In most other countries, the principal theater, film, and TV centers are located in one city—London, Paris, Rome, Toronto, etc.—and artists therefore find it easier to go back and forth between the three media.) Furthermore, stars whose names could sell tickets to shows were aging, and few younger performers were able to establish big enough names before they were whisked off to Hollywood.

By 1964, director/choreographers like Robbins, Kidd, Champion, and Fosse were taking over the reins from the more traditional teams of director and choreographer. These double-threat men often told big chunks of their shows through dance. Unfortunately, not all of them were as expert at storytelling as Robbins in particular, or as able to change styles depending on the needs of the show. The director/choreographers who followed were usually even less skillful at it. In fact, many of Robbins's successors concentrated so much on movement—and on advancing technology—that they minimized the importance of the book, lyrics, and ideas, something Robbins never did.

As we will soon see, in all of this change, Broadway musicals had begun to lose their way, but hardly anyone was noticing yet.

Suggested Watching and Listening

Anyone Can Whistle
The 1995 concert held at Carnegie Hall was initially intended as a benefit performance of this 1964 Stephen Sondheim flop. However, it featured many famous people, some from the original Broadway cast (including Angela Lansbury as the narrator and host, who played the Mayoress in the 1964 production), and the performances were so well done that it was recorded live and released as a CD from Sony.
- "There Won't Be Trumpets" (performed by Bernadette Peters)
- "Anyone Can Whistle" (performed by Bernadette Peters)
- "Everybody Says Don't" (performed by Scott Bakula)

Fiddler on the Roof
All the following song selections are from the movie of this musical, directed by Norman Jewison and available on MGM DVD and VHS.
- "Tradition" (performed by Topol and the ensemble): The opening introduces us to the whole town of Anatevka. It also explains the title of the show.
- "Matchmaker, Matchmaker" (performed by Rosalind Harris, Michele Marsh, and Neva Small): Tevye's three oldest daughters dream about their future husbands.
- "To Life" (performed by Topol, Paul Mann, and the men): Tevye has arranged a match for his oldest daughter with the butcher Lazar Wolf, an older man, and they celebrate at the local tavern. It becomes a big dance number based on traditional Jewish and Russian dance steps, the only time in the show when it looks like the Russians and the Jews could get along together.

- "Sunrise, Sunset" (performed by Topol, Norma Crane, Leonard Frey, Rosalind Harris, Michael Glaser, and Michele Marsh): At the wedding of the eldest daughter to the tailor, tradition is broken by the young radical in love with the second daughter. Men and women never touched in public, and if they danced together, held a handkerchief between them. The wedding celebration is disrupted by an anti-Semitic pogrom, which ends the first act with Tevye silently asking God, "Why?"

Funny Girl

The first three numbers listed below are from the movie version of this show, available on video and on Sony Pictures DVD.
- "I'm the Greatest Star" (performed by Barbra Streisand)
- "People" (performed by Barbra Streisand): It's the big hit ballad of the show.
- "Don't Rain on My Parade" (performed by Barbra Streisand): At the end of act 1, Brice decides, against advice, to quit the *Follies* and marry Arnstein.
- "The Music That Makes Me Dance" (performed by Barbra Streisand): An excellent ballad and the last new song in the show, it's on the original-cast recording. In the movie version, Streisand sings Brice's "My Man" instead.

Hello, Dolly!

The following song from this show is featured on the Sofa Studio DVD *The Best of Broadway Musicals: Original Cast Performances from The Ed Sullivan Show.*
- "Before the Parade Passes By" (performed by Pearl Bailey and the chorus): Dolly's determined first-act closer, it leads into a big production number.

She Loves Me

The following versions of these numbers from this 1963 show are from the original-cast recording available on Decca Broadway CD.
- "Tonight at Eight" (performed by Daniel Massey): Georg is excited about finally meeting his unknown pen pal; they've arranged to meet at a restaurant.
- "Dear Friend" (performed by Barbara Cook): It's the end of the first act. Amalia is saddened because her pen pal hasn't shown up at the restaurant. The reason is that Georg has seen her waiting and realized Amalia must be his pen pal. Instead of telling her, he invents an apology from the man she thinks she's waiting for, describing him in quite unflattering terms, and buys her an ice cream.
- "Ice Cream" (performed by Barbara Cook): Amalia is writing to her pen pal, but remembering how nice Georg was.
- "She Loves Me" (performed by Daniel Massey)

PART SIX

Fade Out—Fade In, 1965–1969

Overleaf: (*left*) Joel Grey and the Kit Kat Klub performers in *Cabaret* (1966); (*right*) *Hair* (1968)

From Kelly to Cabaret

Those smug little men with their smug little schemes,
They forgot one thing:
The play isn't over by a long shot yet!
There are heroes in the world,
And one of them will save us.
Wait and see!
Wait and see!
—"THERE WON'T BE TRUMPETS," *ANYONE CAN WHISTLE,*
LYRICS BY STEPHEN SONDHEIM

As anger and paranoia increased in America and the country began fragmenting, it became difficult to know who the audiences for musicals were and what they wanted to see. Paul Gruber observes:

> More and more, Broadway musicals were hit or miss propositions, either
> blockbusters or flops. Productions routinely ran for longer than a year without returning their investments, and eventually became much more difficult
> to finance. (Gruber, *Original Cast! The Sixties: Part 2,* 3)

By 1965 the Rodgers and Hammerstein musical-play form had been as nearly perfected as it was going to be, both as musical drama and as musical comedy. Almost all musicals integrated the music, lyrics, dance, and design into the needs of the plot and characters—some better than others, of course. It's true of any art form that, once it reaches "perfection," it tends to grow rigid and stale unless new ideas start to stretch and eventually break it open. (Haydn and Mozart, for example, "perfected" the major classical music forms, so Beethoven had to stretch and break them in order to move on; Mozart had even done some stretching himself.) However, the economics of producing—rising union costs, rising theater rentals, rising material costs, rising advertising costs, and so forth—was making it less and less likely that producers could take chances with new forms and new ideas about what a musical could be.

One way producers began to cut back on expenses was by having more electronic instruments used in orchestrations and fewer traditional instruments. Electrified instruments make it nearly impossible for unmiked voices to be heard, so by the end of the decade all voices were miked. This eventually led to the overamplification that's now the norm for most shows, often making it impossible to tell where the sound's coming from onstage except by seeing whose lips are moving. (The 1997 musical *Titanic,* for example, had several numbers with many people in them, each with solo lines; in the Broadway production the overamplification made it impossible to tell who was singing by where the sound was coming from, and by the time you figured out whose lips were moving, another character was already singing and the search had to be resumed. This took away a lot from whatever appreciation there might have been for what was being sung.)

Along with becoming predictable, unimaginative, derivative, and increasingly costly, most shows by the mid-sixties were stubbornly out of touch with younger audiences and their rock-and-roll music taste: musicals were starting to fall way behind the times. It was, however, between 1965 and 1969 that producer/director Harold Prince began his ascendance into the top ranks of influential musical theater creators (without ever taking a writing credit). Then, in 1970, he linked up with Stephen Sondheim and, with *Company,* began a new era in the musical. Also during these five years, John Kander and Fred Ebb wrote their first four shows together, including the very influential *Cabaret* (directed by Prince), the only one of the four that was a hit.

Meanwhile, more-established writers continued to work into the seventies, but with very mixed results. Cy Coleman and Dorothy Fields had a hit; Jerry Herman had his last hit until 1983; Richard Rodgers wrote shows with Stephen Sondheim and with Martin Charnin, neither a major work; Alan Jay Lerner wrote shows with Burton Lane and André Previn, both unsuccessful; Jule Styne had three flops; Bock and Harnick had two; and Strouse and Adams wrote two shows, a pretty good one that flopped and a mediocre one that was a hit. Off-Broadway, where the financial stakes were less extreme, had several successful revues and musicals.

In 1965, composer Harry Tierney and performer Judy Holliday died. There was a nearly monthlong New York newspaper strike, and when the *Herald Tribune* was forced to shut down as a result, only three daily newspapers remained in New York City. The top ticket price on Broadway rose to $11.20.

Producers were starting to cut back on chorus sizes and production values. The Broadway area was becoming a favored hangout for pushers, prostitutes, and hustlers, and was beginning to get a reputation for possibly being dangerous.

Over thirty new musical evenings were produced on and off-Broadway, very few of them memorable or revivable and most of them financial flops. None of them seemed aware of the revolution in younger people's listening habits that began with the invasion of the Beatles, or of the changing tenor of the times. Lincoln Center did short runs of *Kismet* and *Carousel,* and City Center did limited-run revivals of *Guys and Dolls, Kiss Me, Kate, South Pacific, The Music Man,* and *Oklahoma!*

Kelly—music by Moose Charlap, book and lyrics by Eddie Lawrence, directed and choreographed by Herbert Ross—is the show that has gone down in the annals of history as the first (but not the last) Broadway musical to close after its opening night performance. It's about a real person who claimed to have jumped off the Brooklyn Bridge. It lost $650,000 and, given the reviews, would have lost more if it had stayed open.

Do I Hear a Waltz? is the story of an unmarried, middle-aged American schoolteacher on summer holiday in Venice who falls in love with a married man; she returns home alone at the end.

Do I Hear a Waltz?

MUSIC: Richard Rodgers

LYRICS: Stephen Sondheim

BOOK: Arthur Laurents, adapted from his play *The Time of the Cuckoo*

DIRECTOR: John Dexter

CHOREOGRAPHER: Herbert Ross

DESIGNERS: Beni Montresor (sets and costumes) and Jules Fisher (lights)

PRODUCER: Richard Rodgers

CAST INCLUDES: Elizabeth Allen and Sergio Franchi

PERFORMANCES: 220

Backdrop: 1965–1969

National The number of antiwar protests and race riots is growing and getting angrier on both sides. Thurgood Marshall is the first black Supreme Court justice. Edward W. Brooke of Massachusetts is the first black senator since Reconstruction. The U.S. Department of Housing and Urban Development (HUD) is inaugurated. The National Endowment for the Arts is created. Betty Friedan founds the National Organization for Women (NOW). The U.S. population passes two hundred million, double what it was fifty years earlier. In 1968, President Johnson signs the Civil Rights bill stressing open housing. Otherwise, it's one of the worst years in American history: Reverend Martin Luther King and Senator Robert Kennedy are assassinated within two months of each other; the My Lai massacre occurs as the war in Vietnam continues to escalate, costing the United States millions of dollars a day; the Democratic Party's convention in Chicago is more notable for anti-Vietnam protests and bloody riots than for sensible politics; there's a Poor People's Campaign march on Washington; and FBI director J. Edgar Hoover

The subplot is about an American couple staying at the same villa as the teacher; the husband has an affair with the Italian woman who owns the villa. (Laurents's play *The Time of the Cuckoo* had already been made into the non-musical Katharine Hepburn movie *Summertime*). *Do I Hear a Waltz?* is the third and last show for which Sondheim only wrote lyrics. (Laurents wrote the book for all three, as well as for *Anyone Can Whistle*. This was the last time he and Sondheim worked together.) After *A Funny Thing Happened on the Way to the Forum* and *Anyone Can Whistle*, Sondheim didn't want to go back to just lyric writing, but he agreed to do this show because he wanted to work with Rodgers (which turned out to be a less-than-happy experience for both of them) and because he was having trouble getting work after the enormous flop of *Anyone Can Whistle*. In the score of *Do I Hear a Waltz?* are the title song; the comic quintet "What Do We Do? We Fly!"; the ballads "Someone Like You" and "Take the Moment"; "Bargaining," a comic patter song for the male lead; and "Moon in My Window," sung by three women in their separate rooms at the villa.

launches a "Counter-Intelligence Program" against "Black Nationalist Hate Groups." Increasing gas consumption begins to eat into the nation's natural gas reserves. Enzyme detergents create problems in U.S. water and sewage systems; the Department of the Interior estimates that fifteen million fish are killed by pollution each year. The U.S. Coast Guard reports 714 major oil spills during the year. Richard Nixon is elected president.

International International days of protest in many world cities criticize U.S. policy in Vietnam. North Vietnamese leader Ho Chi Minh dies. Nicolae Ceausescu becomes president of the state council of Romania, beginning his reign of terror and despotism. Indonesia is the first nation to withdraw from the United Nations. Indira Nehru Gandhi is elected India's prime minister. Botswana and Guyana become independent nations. In the Arab-Israeli Six-Days War, Israel gains Arab Jerusalem, the Golan Heights in Syria, and the West Bank of the Jordan. Golda Meir becomes Israel's prime minister. Che Guevara is killed by Bolivian troops. Czech Communist Party secretary Alexander Dubcek resists Soviet authority; "Prague Spring" ends with an invasion by Soviet and satellite troops. Japan passes West Germany to become the second strongest economic power after the United States. Britain legalizes abortion.

New Developments In 1969, Neil A. Armstrong is the first man to walk on the moon. The Stonewall Inn riot in New York begins a movement for gay rights. Nixon begins trying to intimidate the press and the electronic media. Chicago police kill Black Panther leader Fred Hampton and fellow Panther Mark Clark. Charles Manson and his cult brutally murder seven people, including actress Sharon Tate. The cost of medical care escalates. South African surgeon Christiaan Barnard performs the world's first heart transplant. The Concorde supersonic jet makes its first flight. Early Bird is the first commercial satellite put into orbit. Diet Pepsi and Pampers, the first disposable diapers, are introduced, as are the

On a Clear Day You Can See Forever was Lerner's first show after Loewe's retirement. Lane took over as composer when Richard Rodgers bowed out of the project; Lerner and Lane had worked together in Hollywood on the 1951 Fred Astaire movie *Royal Wedding*. With the exception of *My Fair Lady*, Lerner's shows usually evidenced book problems; *On a Clear Day* is no exception. It's about a girl named Daisy—the show was originally to be called *I Picked a Daisy*—who has extrasensory perception: she can hear phones ring before they ring and make flowers grow by singing to them. She goes to a psychoanalyst to help her quit smoking and, under hypnosis, recalls a past life in the eighteenth century as a woman named Melinda. Daisy falls in love with her psychiatrist, who unfortunately falls in love with Melinda; he finally realizes he really loves Daisy. The score includes the title song, which became a minor pop hit; "Hurry! It's Lovely up Here!" which Daisy sings to some flowers in the psychiatrist's office to

On a Clear Day You Can See Forever

MUSIC: Burton Lane

LYRICS/BOOK: Alan Jay Lerner

DIRECTOR: Robert Lewis

CHOREOGRAPHER: Herbert Ross

DESIGNERS: Oliver Smith (sets), Donald Brooks and Freddy Wittop (costumes), and Feder (lights)

PRODUCER: Alan Jay Lerner

CAST INCLUDES: Barbara Harris and John Cullum

PERFORMANCES: 273

first compact microwave ovens, automatic teller machines, and the Jacuzzi Whirlpool bath. The National Association of Broadcasters phases out cigarette advertising on radio and TV. MasterCard begins operations. New York installs the first 911 emergency phone number in America. Fashion designer Ralph Lauren opens for business in New York. The miniskirt debuts in London. Panty hose production reaches 624 million pairs as miniskirted American women switch to them from nylon stockings.

Sports   Heavyweight champion Muhammad Ali, denied conscientious objector status, refuses induction into the army, is arrested, and is stripped of his title. Joe Frazier wins the championship. The Houston Astrodome opens. The Green Bay Packers beat the Kansas City Chiefs in the first Super Bowl. The New York Yankees' Mickey Mantle hits his 500th homer. Baseball's major leagues split into eastern and western divisions and add the Montreal Expos, the San Diego Padres, the Kansas City Royals, and the Seattle Pilots.

Art   The John Hancock Center opens in Chicago. St. Louis's Gateway Arch is completed. Painters Edward Hopper, Marcel Duchamp, and Ben Shahn die. There are new paintings by, among others, Lichtenstein, Warhol, Rothko, de Kooning, and Chagall. Op art becomes fashionable.

Music/Dance   The Metropolitan Opera Company moves to Lincoln Center, opening with Barber and Menotti's new opera *Antony and Cleopatra*, a flop. Arthur Mitchell founds the Dance Theatre of Harlem.

Publications   The comic strip *Doonesbury* and *Penthouse* magazine make their debuts. *The Saturday Evening Post* folds after 148 years. Among the new books are Malcolm X and Haley's *The Autobiography of Malcolm X*, Nader's *Unsafe at Any Speed*, Brown's *Manchild in the Promised Land*, Black prove her ability to make them grow; "What Did I Have That I Don't Have?" in which Daisy bemoans the fact that the psychiatrist loves her former self instead of her present one; and "Come Back to Me," which the psychiatrist sings when he realizes he loves Daisy. Both the musical and Vincente Minnelli's 1970 movie with Barbra Streisand, Yves Montand, and Jack Nicholson (whose only song ended up on the cutting-room floor) were financial flops.

Flora, the Red Menace

MUSIC: John Kander
LYRICS: Fred Ebb
BOOK: George Abbott and Robert Russell, adapted from Lester Atwell's novel *Love Is Just Around the Corner*
DIRECTOR: George Abbott
CHOREOGRAPHER: Lee Theodore
PRODUCER: Harold Prince
CAST INCLUDES: Liza Minnelli and Bob Dishy
PERFORMANCES: 87

Flora, the Red Menace is a romance set against the breadlines and young Communist intellectuals of the Depression. Flora's a naive young art student from Brooklyn who falls in love with a Communist but is eventually disenchanted with him and with the Party. Kander and Ebb's first stage partnership, it was a flop with good songs for the nineteen-year-old Minnelli, making her Broadway debut; she won the Tony for Best Actress in a Musical, the youngest person ever to win it. The last show Abbott and Prince worked on together, *Flora, the Red Menace* was seventy-eight-year-old Abbott's 105th Broadway show. In its score is "A Quiet Thing," "Not Every Day of the Week," and "All I Need (Is One Good Break)," a song reminiscent of "I'm the Greatest Star," Streisand's first number in *Funny Girl.*

The Roar of the Greasepaint—The Smell of the Crowd, with book and score by Anthony Newley and Leslie Bricusse, was directed by

Panther Eldridge Cleaver's *Soul on Ice* (written in prison), *Quotations of Chairman Mao,* Brand's *The Whole Earth Catalog,* Capote's *In Cold Blood,* Styron's *The Confessions of Nat Turner,* Márquez's *One Hundred Years of Solitude,* Roth's *Portnoy's Complaint,* Herbert's *Dune,* Susann's *The Valley of the Dolls,* Levin's *Rosemary's Baby,* and Puzo's *The Godfather.*

Radio/TV By 1968, TV sets are in 98 percent of American homes. President Johnson creates the Corporation for Public Broadcasting, which will, within three years, produce National Public Radio (NPR) and the Public Broadcasting Service (PBS). The TV show *Amos 'n' Andy,* with its stereotyped black characters, is withdrawn from syndication. The highest-rated TV shows during the five years include *Bonanza, Bewitched, Batman, The Lucy Show, Green Acres, The Andy Griffith Show, Gomer Pyle, USMC, Rowan and Martin's Laugh-In,* and *Gunsmoke.* Among the new TV shows are *Hogan's Heroes, I Dream of Jeannie, Star Trek, Mission: Impossible, The Carol Burnett Show, The Smothers Brothers*

Newley (who costarred with Cyril Ritchard). It was produced by David Merrick, who again imported a Newley/Bricusse musical; it had opened in London in 1964. The show, an even more cloying, pretentious, and arch follow-up to *Stop the World*, was less successful than its predecessor (232 performances) and has a far worse book.

> [It] was about "The Game" [of Life] being played between the Establishment (embodied by "Sir") and Everyman (called "Cocky"). Sir continually keeps Cocky from winning until the latter makes demands, at which time Sir backs down, and they decide they must work together. (Gruber, *Original Cast! Visitors from Abroad*, 48)

Another vehicle for Newley's rather smarmy performing talents, the score includes "Feeling Good," "(On) A Wonderful Day Like Today," "The Joker," and "Who Can I Turn To (When Nobody Needs Me)?" the show's hit tune.

Man of La Mancha is a musical drama within a musical drama. Cervantes, in jail during the Spanish Inquisition, saves the manuscript of his novel *Don Quixote* from destruction by the other prisoners by telling them some of the episodes from the book, which are acted, sung, and danced out. The actor playing Cervantes plays Quixote, and other prisoners take roles as well. Al-

John Kander (1927–, born in Kansas City, Missouri) had been a rehearsal pianist, musical director, and dance music arranger (including for *Gypsy*). He wrote the music for *A Family Affair* before teaming up with **Fred Ebb** (1932–2004, born in New York), who'd been writing lyrics for revues. Their first song together, "My Coloring Book," became a pop hit. After *Flora, the Red Menace*, they went on to write such shows as *Cabaret, Chicago, Woman of the Year*, and *Kiss of the Spider Woman*. They've also had successes separately. Kander, for example, has written music for movies, including *Kramer vs. Kramer*, and Ebb produced TV shows, including Liza Minnelli's *Liza with a Z*.

Comedy Hour, *60 Minutes, Sesame Street, Hee Haw, The Brady Bunch,* and *Monty Python's Flying Circus* (on England's BBC). Groundbreaking nightclub comedian Lenny Bruce dies of a drug overdose.

Pop Culture Mick Jagger's Rolling Stones gain wide recognition with their recording of "(I Can't Get No) Satisfaction." The popularity of British bands spurs on the formation of such American rock groups as Jerry Garcia's The Grateful Dead and Big Brother and the Holding Company, soon joined by Janis Joplin. Jimi Hendrix popularizes the use of the electric guitar. The Byrds help create folk rock by experimenting with electronically amplified folk songs like "Turn! Turn! Turn!" and Dylan's "Mister Tambourine Man." Dylan further blurs the lines between folk and rock when he switches from acoustic to electric guitar at the Newport Folk Festival. The Monterey Pop Festival is the first large rock gathering. Otis Redding dies in a plane crash. Diana Ross and the Supremes have several hits, including "Stop! In the Name of Love." Aretha Franklin establishes herself as the "Queen of

Man of La Mancha

MUSIC: Mitch Leigh

LYRICS: Joe Darion

BOOK: Dale Wasserman, adapted from Miguel de Cervantes's novel *Don Quixote de la Mancha* and Wasserman's TV drama *I, Don Quixote*

DIRECTOR: Albert Marre

CHOREOGRAPHER: Jack Cole

PRODUCERS: Hal James and Albert W. Selden

CAST INCLUDES: Richard Kiley and Joan Diener

PERFORMANCES: 2,328

donza, a bar girl, plays Quixote's beloved Dulcinea. The show, which is frequently pretentious and plodding, was made into a terrible 1972 Arthur Hiller movie with Peter O'Toole, Sophia Loren, and James Coco. (By 1972, what was left of Hollywood's love affair with the musical was practically dead; *Man of La Mancha* was one of the last nails in the coffin.)

> At the time many people thought this was one of the great musicals. But time has not been so kind, and the show is revealed as a series of well-done theatre tricks strung together. "The Impossible Dream" is the sort of mock inspirational ballad that is sure to push the right buttons for the audience. . . . This is one of those shows that are marvelous to watch and surefire as a theatrical event, but don't hold up when removed from their theatricality. (Bloom, *American Song*, 447)

Along with "The Impossible Dream," the score—which has a frequent flamenco feel to it and needs operetta-sized voices for several of the principal roles—includes "Man of La Mancha (I, Don Quixote)" and "Dulcinea."

The Decline and Fall of the Entire World as Seen Through the Eyes

Soul" with such recordings as "Respect" and "(You Make Me Feel Like) A Natural Woman." The group Cream is formed and breaks up in two years; guitarist Eric Clapton becomes a solo superstar. Frank Sinatra has a hit recording of Kaempfert and Snyder's "Strangers in the Night," his return to the pop charts after an absence of several years. His daughter, Nancy, has a hit with Hazlewood's "These Boots Are Made for Walkin'." Barbra Streisand's concert in New York's Central Park draws about 135,000 people. Guitar sales in the United States rise from $35 million in 1960 to $130 million by 1968. The Beatles have many hit songs and albums, mostly written by Lennon and McCartney, play their last public concert, and make their last record together. Among other pop songs are Hatch's "Downtown," Stoller and Leiber's "Love Potion No. 9," Sonny and Cher's recording of his "I Got You Babe," The Temptations' "My Girl," Legrand and the Bergman's "The Windmills of Your Mind," and Mandel and Webster's "The Shadow of Your Smile." Middle-of-the-road, soft-rock hit recordings include Simon and Garfunkel's "Sounds of Silence" and "The 59th Streeet Bridge Song (Feelin' Groovy)," The Lovin' Spoonful's "Summer in the City," The Mamas and the Papas' "Monday Monday" and "California Dreamin'," Donovan (Leitch)'s "Mellow Yellow," and The Association's "Cherish." New albums and additional hit songs include *Jefferson Airplane Takes Off*, The Who's *Happy Jack*, Led Zeppelin's *No. 1*, The Beach Boys' "Good Vibrations," The Monkees' "Last Train to *of Cole Porter* (273 performances) was produced and directed by Ben Bagley and had a cast of five: Kaye Ballard, Carmen Alvarez, Harold Lang, William Hickey, and Elmarie Wendel. A sophisticated and successful, off-Broadway collection of Cole Porter songs, with his biography told between numbers, it was the first significant revue to do a retrospective of a single composer's work. It revived interest in Porter and in the intimate musical revue; in effect, it started a trend. There continued to be hit off-Broadway revues (both originals and anthologies), such as *The Mad Show,* based on the magazine; *You're a Good Man, Charlie Brown,* based on the comic strip; *Ain't Misbehavin',* an anthology of songs associated with Fats Waller that eventually moved to Broadway; *Jacques Brel Is Alive and Well and Living in Paris,* an anthology of Brel's songs; *Harry Chapin: Lies and Legends,* a Chapin anthology; *Side by Side by Sondheim,* a Sondheim anthology; *And the World Goes 'Round,* a Kander and Ebb anthology; and *Forbidden Broadway,* a frequently annual series of revues satirizing Broadway shows and stars through new lyrics set to already existing songs. Some more recent revues on Broadway have been *Sophisticated Ladies,* an Ellington anthology; *Bring in 'Da Noise, Bring in 'Da Funk: A Rap/Tap Discourse on the Staying Power of the Beat,* a history of African Americans told through tap and original songs; and *Smokey Joe's Café,* a Jerry Leiber and Mike Stoller anthology. The originality in most cases, both on and off-Broadway, has been in how the material is presented, not in the material itself. The revues have now

Clarksville," Seeger's "Guantanamera," The Doors' "Light My Fire," Gentry's "Ode to Billy Joe," Webb's "Up, Up, and Away" and "By the Time I Get to Phoenix," Whitfield and Strong's "I Heard It Through the Grapevine," Diamond's "I'm a Believer," Hartford's "Gentle on My Mind," Mitchell's "Both Sides Now," The Bee Gees' "Gotta Get a Message to You," Wynette and Sherrill's "Stand by Your Man," Blood, Sweat and Tears' "Spinning Wheel" and "And When I Die" (written by Laura Nyro), Peter, Paul, and Mary's recording of Denver's "Leaving on a Jet Plane," The Hollies' recording of Russell and Scott's "He Ain't Heavy . . . He's My Brother," Creedence Clearwater Revival's "Proud Mary," Cash's recordings of "Folsom Prison (Blues)" and of Silverstein's "A Boy Named Sue," and The Fifth Dimension's recording of "Aquarius" and "Let the Sunshine In" from *Hair,* one of the only pop hits to come from a Broadway show.

In 1969, the Woodstock (New York) Music and Art Fair, a festival of "peace, love, and rock," draws more than three hundred thousand people to hear dozens of rock stars over a three-day period. The Altamont Music Festival outside San Francisco draws over three hundred thousand to a Rolling Stones concert, where members of the Hell's Angels motorcycle gang, hired as security guards, beat up several people and kill one. John Lennon marries Yoko Ono.

largely been supplanted in audience popularity by musicals with books constructed around a catalogue of songs by a person or group. These shows, such as *Mamma Mia!*, have been labeled "jukebox musicals."

In 1966, producer Billy Rose, comedian Ed Wynn, singer Sophie Tucker, and book writers Russel Crouse and Joseph Fields died. (Of all four show-business members of the Fields family, only Dorothy was still alive.) Urban's Ziegfeld Theatre met the wrecking ball. The top ticket price went up to $12. *The Fantasticks* became the longest-running show in New York history. A musical version of Capote's *Breakfast at Tiffany's*, starring Mary Tyler Moore and Richard Chamberlain and produced by David Merrick, closed during previews; Edward Albee (of all people) was brought in to replace Abe Burrows as book writer while the show was out of town. There was a limited-run Lincoln Center revival of Berlin and the Fieldses' *Annie Get Your Gun*, with Ethel Merman back as Annie Oakley. For this production, Berlin wrote his last song for a show: the double duet "An Old-Fashioned Wedding." Lincoln Center also presented a revival of *Show Boat*. City Center produced short-run revivals of *How to Succeed in Business Without Really Trying*, *The Most Happy Fella*, *Where's Charley?*, *Guys and Dolls*, and *Carousel*. It was a good year for musicals

Stage Lorraine Hansberry dies. The Negro Ensemble Company, organized by Douglas Turner Ward, Robert Hooks, and Gerald S. Krone, is funded by the Ford Foundation; their first production is Weiss's *Song of the Lusitania Bogey*. Jerzy Grotowski publishes *Towards a Poor Theatre*. Government censorship of theater in England is abolished. Chicago's Off-Loop movement begins with the founding of the Body Politic Theater. Among the new plays are Baldwin's *The Amen Corner*, Elder's *Ceremonies in Dark Old Men*, and Gordone's *No Place to Be Somebody* (the first play by a black author to win a Pulitzer). Also new are Miller's *The Price*, Albee's *A Delicate Balance*, Simon's *The Odd Couple*, van Itallie's *America Hurrah*, Pinter's *The Homecoming*, Stoppard's *Rosencrantz and Guildenstern Are Dead*, Orton's *Loot* and his posthumous *What the Butler Saw*, Crowley's *The Boys in the Band* (a breakthrough in gay theater), and Sackler's *The Great White Hope* (beginning a trend for trying out Broadway-bound shows at a not-for-profit regional theater, Washington's Arena Stage in this case).

Screen As attendance decreases, many movie theaters around the country close down. New movies of the five years include *Blowup*, *Juliet of the Spirits*, *Satyricon*, *Persona*, *Belle de Jour*, *Weekend*, *Z*, *2001: A Space Odyssey*, *Bonnie and Clyde*, and *The Graduate*, with a sound track of old and new Simon and Garfunkel songs (including "Mrs. Robinson"). There are adaptations of Albee's *Who's Afraid of Virginia Woolf?*, Simon's *The Odd Couple*, and Levin's *Rosemary's Baby*. Also new are *Alfie*, with Bacharach and David's pop-hit title song; *Butch Cassidy and the Sundance Kid*, with their "Raindrops Keep Falling on My Head"; *Planet of the Apes*; *The Wild Bunch*; *Bullitt*, which included the first great car with about thirty new shows opening, several of them still frequently revived.

Sweet Charity is about hostesses in a sleazy New York dance hall who are employed by the management to provide partners for men looking for someone to dance with. (Fellini's movie was about Roman streetwalkers.) The musical—which is heavy on dance—focuses on the optimistic, rather naive Charity Hope Valentine, who, unlike Candide and Pippin, survives a series of personal disasters without losing her faith that things will get better. *Sweet Charity* was the first musical to play the old king of the vaudeville houses, the Palace, which had been a movie theater since 1932. The show also was Fosse's first big hit as director/choreographer. (He directed the unsuccessful 1969 movie version with Shirley MacLaine, John McMartin, Ricardo Montalban, Sammy Davis Jr., Chita Rivera, Paula Kelly, and Stubby Kaye.) The score includes "Big Spender," "Rich Man's Frug," "If My Friends Could See Me Now," "There's Gotta Be Something Better Than This," and "I'm a Brass Band." As usual, Dorothy

Sweet Charity

MUSIC: Cy Coleman

LYRICS: Dorothy Fields

BOOK: Neil Simon (from a first draft by Bob Fosse), adapted from Fellini's movie *Nights of Cabiria*

DIRECTOR/CHOREOGRAPHER: Bob Fosse

ORCHESTRATOR: Ralph Burns

DESIGNERS: Robert Randolph (sets and lights) and Irene Sharaff (costumes)

PRODUCERS: Lawrence Carr, Robert Fryer, and Joseph P. Harris

CAST INCLUDES: Gwen Verdon, Helen Gallagher, and John McMartin

PERFORMANCES: 608

chase; *Night of the Living Dead,* the first "midnight" movie; *Midnight Cowboy; Easy Rider;* and *The Producers,* source of the 2001 musical.

There are about thirty new movie musicals during the five years, including the Beatles' *Help!;* about a dozen Elvis Presley movies; the extremely popular adaptation of *The Sound of Music,* staring Julie Andrews; *When the Boys Meet the Girls,* a total rewrite of *Girl Crazy* set in Florida during spring break; the animated *Yellow Submarine* (made originally for British TV), with the Beatles supplying songs and singing voices; and adaptations of *Funny Girl* and the Oscar-winning *Oliver!* The following were box-office flops: *The Night They Raided Minsky's,* with songs by Strouse and Adams; Julie Andrews as Gertrude Lawrence in *Star!;* Rex Harrison in a musicalized adaptation of Lofting's *Doctor Dolittle,* with a Leslie Bricusse score that introduces the hit "Talk to the Animals;" and a musical adaptation of the Hilton novel and 1939 movie *Goodbye, Mr. Chips,* with a dull Bricusse score. Among the adaptations of Broadway musicals that flopped were *How to Succeed in Business Without Really Trying; Camelot; Paint Your Wagon,* with additional songs by André Previn and Alan Jay Lerner; Fred Astaire in *Finian's Rainbow; Hello, Dolly!* with choreography by Kidd and two new songs for Barbra Streisand by Jerry Herman: "Just Leave Everything to Me" (replacing "I Put My Hand In") and "Love Is Only Love" (rejected from *Mame*); and Fosse's *Sweet Charity.* It's close to the end of the old-style movie musicals; in 1969, the two most successful movie musicals are *Alice's Restaurant,* made from Arlo Guthrie's hit song "The Alice's Restaurant Massacre," and *Monterey Pop,* a documentary about the 1967 rock festival.

Mame

MUSIC/LYRICS: Jerry Herman

BOOK: Jerome Lawrence and Robert E. Lee, adapted from their play *Auntie Mame*, itself adapted from Patrick Dennis's novel

DIRECTOR: Gene Saks

CHOREOGRAPHER: Onna White

ORCHESTRATOR: Philip J. Lang

DESIGNERS: Jean and William Eckart (sets), Robert Mackintosh (costumes), and Tharon Musser (lights)

PRODUCERS: Lawrence Carr, Robert Fryer, and Joseph P. Harris

CAST INCLUDES: Angela Lansbury, Beatrice Arthur, and Jane Connell

PERFORMANCES: 1,508

I Do! I Do!

MUSIC: Harvey Schmidt

LYRICS/BOOK: Tom Jones, adapted from Jan de Hartog's play *The Fourposter*

DIRECTOR/CHOREOGRAPHER: Gower Champion

DESIGNERS: Oliver Smith (sets), Freddy Wittop (costumes), and Jean Rosenthal (lights)

PRODUCER: David Merrick

CAST INCLUDES: Mary Martin and Robert Preston

PERFORMANCES: 584

The Mad Show

MUSIC: Mary Rodgers

LYRICS: Marshall Barer, Larry Siegel, and Steven Vinaver

BOOK: Stan Hart and Larry Siegel, licensed by *Mad* magazine

DIRECTOR: Steven Vinaver

PRODUCERS: Ivor David Balding and Establishment Theatre Co. Inc.

CAST OF FIVE INCLUDES: MacIntyre Dixon, Linda Lavin, Richard Libertini, Paul Sand, and a pre-*Laugh-In* Jo Anne Worley

PERFORMANCES: 871 off-Broadway

Fields's lyrics were up-to-date and well matched to the music. There was an unsuccessful 2005 Broadway revival starring Christina Applegate.

Mame is about a madcap New York society woman and her orphaned nephew, Patrick, whom she raises. (Mary Martin turned down the title role before it was offered to Lansbury.) Mame's philosophy on life is: "Life is a banquet, and most poor sonsabitches are starving to death." The show, clearly derivative of Herman's *Hello, Dolly!* which was still running, was almost as successful and is almost as frequently revived. (Herman has rarely stretched himself from show to show, but he's an expert within his limited range.) "It's Today" is Mame's first number, sung at a party she's giving for no special reason. It's really the big opening number of the show, preceded, however, by a short duet for young Patrick and Gooch, his nanny, who are waiting to meet Mame, with whom they're now going to live. (Patrick is played by two actors, one as a child, the other as a young man.) Also in the score are the title song (the "Hello, Dolly!" number of the show); "Bosom Buddies," a comic duet for Mame and her on-again, off-again actress friend Vera Charles; "Gooch's Song," a comic showstopper for the pregnant, unmarried Gooch; and "If He Walked into My Life," a ballad (and a minor pop hit) for Mame when she's unhappy with the grown-up Patrick. The straight play was adapted into a 1958 movie; both starred Rosalind Russell. Avoid the 1974 Gene Saks movie of the musical with Lucille Ball and Beatrice Arthur repeating her stage role; it was a deserved financial disaster.

A two-character musical set in a bedroom, *I Do! I Do!* follows the ups and downs of a fifty-year marriage. The show, frequently revived by small theaters, is Schmidt and Jones's most successful musical after *The Fantasticks*. In the original production, the characters aged by applying makeup in front of the audience between scenes. "Flaming Agnes" and "Nobody's Perfect" are in the score.

The Mad Show is a series of well-written, silly, and lightly satirical sketches and songs. "The Boy from . . . ," with lyrics by Esteban Ria Nido, is a parody of the pop hit "The Girl from Ipanema";

the boy comes from Tacarembo la Tumbe del Fuego Santa Mali-pas Zacatecas la Junta del Sol y Cruz. Esteban Ria Nido is a pseu-donym for Stephen Sondeim.

A big change from Bock and Harnick's *Fiddler on the Roof*, all three mini-musical comedies in *The Apple Tree* use the same three principal performers; the second and third also use a small chorus, whose members play supporting roles. Though not connected in plot, characters, or setting, each is about the temptations of love—hence the title *The Apple Tree*. The first one, "The Diary of Adam and Eve," with only three characters (the third is the snake) and, of course, an actual apple tree as part of the plot, is occasionally performed on its own. The second is set in a barbaric country with a prince forced to chose between two doors: if he opens one, out comes a princess to marry him; if he opens the other, out comes a tiger to eat him. As in the frustrating original story, we never find out which door he opens. The third is a satiric, contemporary retelling of the story of Cinderella based on Jules Feiffer's illustrated story. The heroine, a cleaning woman, is turned into a movie star. The lyrics for all three are very show-specific and difficult to perform out of context. There was a limited-run Broadway revival in 2007, starring Kristen Chenoweth, Brian d'Arcy James, and Marc Kudisch.

A frequently funny musical comedy, many believe that *It's a Bird! It's a Plane! It's Superman!* was an undeserved flop, caused possibly by the equally silly and campy TV series *Batman*, which stole its thunder. The newspaper strike was also blamed. The score is mostly mid-sixties soft rock in tone and sound, and the show is big and very expensive to produce (another possible reason for its financial failure), with several huge sets, flying people and props, Chinese acrobats, a quick-change phone booth, and a large chorus. Some think the show is almost as good as Strouse and Adams's *Bye Bye Birdie;* some think it's better. In the score are "The Woman for the Man" and "You've Got Possibilities." Newman and Benton cowrote *Superman—The Movie* and *Bonnie and Clyde.*

Kander and Ebb's first and biggest hit, *Cabaret* is a bitter and powerful musical drama about the rise of Nazism in Germany

The Apple Tree *(an evening of three one-act musicals)*

MUSIC: Jerry Bock

LYRICS: Sheldon Harnick

BOOK: Jerry Bock, Sheldon Harnick, and Jerome Coopersmith, adapted from Twain's "The Diary of Adam and Eve," Stockton's "The Lady or the Tiger," and Feiffer's "Passionella"

DIRECTOR: Mike Nichols

CHOREOGRAPHERS: Herbert Ross and Lee Theodore

DESIGNERS: Tony Walton (sets and costumes) and Jean Rosenthal (lights)

PRODUCER: Stuart Ostrow

CAST INCLUDES: Barbara Harris, Alan Alda, and Larry Blyden, with Robert Klein in the small chorus

PERFORMANCES: 463, without paying back its investors

It's a Bird! It's a Plane! It's Superman!

MUSIC: Charles Strouse

LYRICS: Lee Adams

BOOK: David Newman and Robert Benton, based on the DC comic strip

DIRECTOR/PRODUCER: Harold Prince

CHOREOGRAPHER: Ernest Flatt

ORCHESTRATOR: Eddie Sauter

DESIGNERS: Robert Randolph (sets and lights) and Florence Klotz (costumes)

CAST INCLUDES: Jack Cassidy, Patricia Marand, Bob Holiday, and Linda Lavin

PERFORMANCES: 129

Florence Klotz (1920–2006, born in Brooklyn) began designing costumes for Broadway in 1951. Along with many plays, she designed such musicals as *Follies, A Little Night Music, On the Twentieth Century, City of Angels, Kiss of the Spider Woman,* and Prince's 1997 revival of *Show Boat.*

Cabaret

MUSIC: John Kander
LYRICS: Fred Ebb
BOOK: Joe Masteroff, adapted from John van Druten's play *I Am a Camera* (based on Christopher Isherwood's *Berlin Stories*)
DIRECTOR/PRODUCER: Harold Prince
CHOREOGRAPHER: Ron Field
DESIGNERS: Boris Aronson (sets), Patricia Zipprodt (costumes), and Jean Rosenthal (lights)
CAST INCLUDES: Jill Haworth, Bert Convy, Lotte Lenya, Jack Gilford, and Joel Grey
PERFORMANCES: 1,165

through the metaphor of "life is a cabaret." In the original production, the first set, Berlin's Kit Kat Klub (which included a stage for its own small, onstage band), could be seen by the audience as they entered the auditorium. On the back wall was a mirror in which they could also see themselves. The Emcee of the Klub's show welcomed the audience at the top of the show, addressing them as if they were in the Berlin cabaret in 1931. (For the hit 1998 Broadway revival, the theater was converted into an actual cabaret. That production ran 2,377 performances.) Sally Bowles, the central character who performs at the Klub, refers to the place as "divine decadence." It eventually becomes clear that the Kit Kat Klub is a symbol of the German decadence that, along with the country's desperate economic situation, allowed and encouraged the rise of Nazism. According to Albert Williams, "This decay is reflected in the Emcee's increasingly ugly songs: he starts out with the benignly escapist 'Willkommen,' but soon begins to celebrate anti-Semitism, sexual decadence, etc."

All the cabaret numbers are performed for the audience here and now who are simultaneously the audience there and then—a device similar to the one used in the vaudeville and burlesque sequences in *Gypsy*, though in this case for a more intentionally telling effect. It's all part of the show's brilliant way of saying, among other things, that it could happen again. The cabaret is a concept, and the cabaret sequences are Prince's landmark first move toward the concept musical. The Emcee and the Kit Kat Klub performers have no role in the show's plot, and their songs further neither plot nor character but rather serve as metaphors for what's happening outside the cabaret. They *are* 1930s German decadence and incipient Nazism; therefore, we are the passive audience letting it all happen while we're being entertained by it.

The rest of the story is told as a traditional musical play with dialogue leading to songs that develop plot and character, while the cabaret sequences form perfect parallels. The main story line follows cabaret performer and extravagant personality Sally Bowles, a British expatriate (American in the movie). The show is seen from the point of view of Cliff, an American expatriate (a British man called Brian in the movie), who is based on the camera of van Druten's play *I Am a Camera,* the young Christopher

Isherwood himself of the *Berlin Stories*. The subplot of the show is about a Jewish grocer engaged to Sally and Cliff's gentile landlady. At the end, Cliff leaves Germany before it gets worse, Sally stays, and the landlady breaks off her engagement. The landlady was played by Lotte Lenya, star of both the original German production and the hit off-Broadway revival of Weill and Brecht's *The Threepenny Opera*. Particularly in the handling of her songs, which are in the Weill/Brecht tradition, she helped make *Cabaret* even more intensely real to audiences.

Cabaret made a star of Joel Grey as the Emcee. He won an Academy Award for his re-creation of the role in the 1972 movie adaptation starring Liza Minnelli (who also won an Oscar) and Michael York. The movie, directed and choreographed by Oscar-winning Bob Fosse, focuses more than the musical on the Sally Bowles character and uses a different subplot involving a poor young man who falls in love with a rich Jewish woman. (Both subplots are in van Druten's play and Isherwood's stories.) As Albert Williams points out, "The movie also explores Brian's emerging homosexuality, which the original version of the stage musical does not; however, the show has been revised to incorporate this and other elements from the movie."

The movie, to which "Maybe This Time" was added, uses only songs that are sung in the cabaret or, in one case, in a beer hall; unlike the stage show, the characters never break into song during the dramatic scenes. The show's score includes the title song, which became a hit; "Don't Tell Mama," Sally's first cabaret song, replaced in the movie by "Mein Herr"; "It Couldn't Please Me More," a duet for the landlady and her suitor, the Jewish grocer, who has brought her a pineapple as a present; "What Would You Do?" the landlady's practical and political explanation of why, with the rise to power of the Nazis, she can't marry the Jewish grocer after all; "The Money Song," another of the Emcee's songs, replaced in the movie by "Money, Money," sung by the Emcee and Sally; and "Tomorrow Belongs to Me," a lovely folk-like song that the Emcee and the Klub workers sing while cleaning up the cabaret and that is gradually and horrifyingly revealed to be a Nazi anthem. In the movie, it's sung in an outdoor beer hall, led by a blonde youth who's rather quickly and less effectively revealed to be wearing a swastika. Because he isn't someone we've already gotten to know, the movie scene is

Ron Field (1934–88, born in New York) began his Broadway career as a dancer; he started choreographing shows in the early sixties, had his first big hit as a choreographer with *Cabaret*, and had a hit as director/choreographer with *Applause* in 1970.

less chilling than its counterpart on stage. Prince, Kander, Ebb, and Masteroff set a new standard for the dramatic musical play at the same time they were halfway toward a different form altogether.

Suggested Watching and Listening

The Apple Tree

This number is available on *Broadway's Lost Treasures* (Acorn Media DVD). The *Broadway's Lost Treasures* DVDs are selections from live Tony Awards TV shows.

- "Movie Star Gorgeous" (performed by Barbara Harris): It's the number in the third story when the cleaning woman is transformed into a movie star.

Cabaret

The following numbers are from various versions of this hit musical.

- "Willkommen" (performed by Joel Grey and the Kit Kat Klub Girls): This is the opening of the show welcoming the audience to the decadent 1931 German cabaret. In the film, the song is crosscut with Brian's arrival in Berlin, immediately setting up the parallel between the cabaret and Germany, both of which are saying welcome. This number is available live on *Broadway's Lost Treasures* (Acorn Media DVD) with Grey and the staging of the original production.
- "It Couldn't Please Me More" (performed by Jack Gilford and Lotte Lenya): The Jewish grocer brings the landlady a present from his store. This is from the original-cast recording, available on Sony CD.
- "Maybe This Time" (performed by Liza Minnelli): Added to the movie, which was directed by Bob Fosse and is available on Warner Home Video DVD, this song is now used in productions of the show.
- "The Money Song" (performed by Joel Grey): Sung by the Emcee, with the Kit Kat Klub Girls dressed in the currencies of various countries and little else, it's on the original-cast recording (Sony CD).
- "Money, Money" (performed by Joel Grey and Liza Minnelli): The substitute for "The Money Song" used in the movie. (In the movie, Sally isn't fired from the Kit Kat Klub.)
- "If You Could See Her (With My Eyes)" (performed by Joel Grey and one of the Kit Kat Klub Girls in an ape costume): A cabaret song with a real punch of a punch line. This version is from the movie.
- "I Don't Care Much" (performed by Alan Cumming): Cut from the original production, it's on the original-cast recording of the 1998 Broadway revival (RCA Victor Broadway CD).
- "Cabaret" (performed by Liza Minnelli): Along with being an entertainment at the cabaret, it's Sally's near-breakdown eleven o'clock number, her conscious refusal to change or to recognize the growing danger inherent in the rise of Nazism (not unlike the mid-thirties appeasement of Hitler). After the number, she decides to get an abortion and stay in Berlin rather than keep the baby and leave with Cliff. In the movie, Sally has already had the abortion, and the song is followed immediately by the Emcee's reprise of "Willkommen." He looks straight into the camera at the end; in the show, the audience is left seeing itself in the mirror on the back wall of the cabaret set.

Do I Hear a Waltz?

The following number from this 1965 show is from the original-cast recording, available on Sony CD.

- "What Do We Do? We Fly!" (performed by Madeleine Sherwood, Jack Manning, Elizabeth Allen, Julienne Marie, and Stuart Damon): Five tourists staying at the same villa in Venice get acquainted. The lyrics make it necessary for a revival to keep the show in the mid-sixties, since they don't show Doris Day movies on airplanes anymore.

Mame

The following two numbers are from the original-cast recording, available on Sony CD.

- "Bosom Buddies" (performed by Angela Lansbury and Beatrice Arthur): Mame and her actress friend Vera sing about their relationship.
- "Gooch's Song" (performed by Jane Connell): Gooch, who's been very repressed, has taken Mame Burnside's advice to "live life to the hilt," gone out for a night on the town, and is now very pregnant.

Man of La Mancha

The song "The Impossible Dream (The Quest)" (performed by Richard Kiley) from this show is available both on the original-cast recording (Decca U.S. CD, which includes bonus tracks) and on *The Best of Broadway Musicals: Original Cast Performances from The Ed Sullivan Show* (Sofa Studio DVD). It's very easy to get very tired of this song.

On a Clear Day You Can See Forever

The following number from this 1968 show is from the original-cast recording, available on RCA Victor Broadway CD.

- "What Did I Have That I Don't Have?" (performed by Barbara Harris): Sung by Daisy when she realizes her analyst is in love with the woman she was in a past life; out of context, it's a good torch song.

The Roar of the Greasepaint—The Smell of the Crowd

The following number is available on the original-cast recording and on *The Best of Broadway Musicals: Original Cast Performances from The Ed Sullivan Show* (Sofa Studio DVD).

- "Who Can I Turn to (When Nobody Needs Me)?" (performed by Anthony Newley): Similar in many ways to the equally big hit "What Kind of Fool Am I?" from *Stop the World . . .* , in the show it's asked of God, but it becomes a love ballad when sung out of context. Newley has to be seen to be believed.

Sweet Charity

The first three numbers are from the movie version of this 1966 show, directed by Bob Fosse and available on Universal Studios DVD.

- "Big Spender" (performed by Chita Rivera, Paula Kelly, and the dance hall girls): It's the come-on song for the dance-hall hostesses.
- "Rich Man's Frug" (performed by the ensemble, including Ben Vereen and Ann Reinking): This is performed when a famous movie star takes Charity to a snobbish nightclub.
- "There's Gotta Be Something Better Than This" (performed by Shirley MacLaine, Chita Rivera, and Paula Kelly): The three principal women are sick of their work at the dance hall.

- "I'm a Brass Band" (performed by Gwen Verdon and the dancers): It's sung by Charity when she thinks she's getting married. In the show, her boyfriend chickens out at the last minute; the movie version was filmed with that ending, then had an alternate ending tacked on in which he returns. (In the Fellini movie, he not only leaves her, he steals all her money and tries to drown her.) This version is available on *The Best of Broadway Musicals: Original Cast Performances from The Ed Sullivan Show* (Sofa Studio DVD).

From *Hair* to *1776*

When the moon is in the seventh house
And Jupiter aligns with Mars,
Then peace will guide the planet,
And love will steer the stars.
This is the dawning of the Age of Aquarius,
The Age of Aquarius,
Aquarius,
Aquarius.

—"AQUARIUS," *HAIR,* LYRICS BY GEROME RAGNI AND JAMES RADO

Rock had almost totally captured the pop-music scene by the end of the sixties. Unfortunately, few rock performers thought of themselves as actors—justifiably—and didn't give Broadway a second thought. Moreover, rock composers and performers (often the same person or persons) found records, concerts, TV, and movies far more likely than Broadway to make them very rich and very famous very quickly.

In 1967, performer Bert Lahr died. The off-Broadway Equity minimum rose to $70 a week. Joseph Papp opened his off-Broadway Public Theater with a limited run of the first draft of *Hair.* The Tony Awards were televised for the first time. Pearl Bailey, Cab Calloway, and an all-black cast took over in *Hello, Dolly!* Newcomer Bette Midler took over the role of Tzeitel, one of Tevye's daughters, in *Fiddler on the Roof.* There was an unsuccessful off-Broadway revival of Rodgers and Hart's *By Jupiter* with a revised book by Fred Ebb. Among City Center's short-run revivals were *Finian's Rainbow, The Sound of Music, Wonderful Town,* and *Brigadoon.* Lincoln Center revived *South Pacific,* some Gilbert and Sullivan operettas, and *The King and I.* There were fewer than twenty new musical evenings, and only one of them, an off-Broadway revue, is still revived occasionally.

❖

A gentle and successful revue, *You're a Good Man, Charlie Brown* has dialogue straight out of Schulz's comic strips and songs based on ideas and even lines from them. It follows a day in the lives of Charlie Brown, Lucy, Linus, Schroeder, Patty, and Snoopy, all played by adults. It was a record album before it was a show. An unsuccessful and far less intimate "revisal" opened on Broadway in 1999, with the character of Patty replaced by Charlie Brown's sister, Sally, and played by Kristen Chenoweth.

Hallelujah, Baby! has a pretty good score but a heavy-handed Laurents book about race relations in the United States as seen through yet another show-business metaphor. The show follows a black woman's singing career from the beginning of the century to the sixties; as in Weill and Lerner's *Love Life*, the characters don't age. It was Leslie Uggams's Broadway debut.

In 1968, George White, producer of the nearly annual *Scandals* from 1919 to 1939, died, as did playwright and book-writer Howard Lindsay (whose many successes included coauthorship of the book for *The Sound of Music*) and novelist Edna Ferber, author of *Show Boat*. The top off-Broadway ticket price was $10. There was an unsuccessful off-Broadway revival of the previously unsuccessful *House of Flowers*. City Center did short-run revivals of *My Fair Lady* and *Carnival!* and Lincoln Center did one of *West Side Story*. There were about thirty-five new musical evenings, most of them unsuccessful. Among the flops were shows by such major figures as Jule Styne (who never had a hit after *Funny Girl* in 1964), E. Y. Harburg (who died in 1981 without writing another show), Gower Champion, and two by Kander and Ebb. There was also an unsuccessful edition of Leonard Sillman's *New Faces*, with Madeline Kahn and Robert Klein in the cast. It was the year that counterculture and dimly lit, full-frontal nudity (both sexes) arrived on Broadway.

After *Hair: The American Tribal Love-Rock Musical* opened off-Broadway at the Public Theater—where it was directed by Gerald Freedman and designed by Ming Cho Lee, Theoni Aldredge, and Martin Aronstein—it transferred to Cheetah, a discotheque. Finally, with a lot of revisions (including the removal of clothing and most of whatever plot there had been), it moved to Broadway. It's a concept musical describing a rebellious and disenchanted young counterculture: the hippies of the late sixties. The thin plot is about whether Claude, who has received his draft notice, should fight it or go to Vietnam.

> Claude and his tribe of hippies wrestle with this dilemma, which is the hook on which the show hangs a series of songs and vignettes examining pressing issues that were dividing the United States in the late 1960s: race relations, alternative sexuality, women's equality, new (i.e., non-Western) religious forms, the generation gap, and above all the Vietnam War, which *Hair* depicts as just the latest in America's long history of genocidal violence dating back to the seizure of the land from the Indians and the importation of African slaves. The songs are mostly litanies, lists that state a position or examine an issue, often in a formal, almost prayerful way. "Aquarius," the opening number, is a hymn to the new age, establishing the show's ritualistic, quasi-religious nature. (Albert Williams, personal communication)

Along with the full frontal nudity, the show used language never before heard in a musical, "desecrated" the American flag, and incorporated audience participation. It created a scandal and was a gigantic commercial success, bringing new audiences of young people (and dirty old men) to the theater for the first time in a long time. (At one point fourteen road companies were playing simultaneously, both nationally and internationally.) Soon there were a great many shows with nudity, particularly off-Broadway, and a rash of really bad and costly derivatives of *Hair* that pretty much killed rock on Broadway for a long time. A considerably rewritten 1979 movie, directed by Miloš Forman and choreographed by Twyla Tharp, put the songs into more plot- and character-driven situations than the show does.

> "Aquarius" became the anthem of a generation, and the show itself marked the first steps toward an acceptance of the sixties mentality. *Hair* was the closest Broadway would come to an authentic rock sound. . . . Ultimately its promise for a refurbishment of the stale Broadway sound was not fulfilled. (Ken Bloom, *American Song*, 281)

The antihero of *Promises, Promises*, who frequently stops the action to talk to the audience, gets ahead in business by lending

Theoni V. (Vachlioti) Aldredge (1932–, born in Athens, Greece) has designed costumes for musicals and straight plays. Among the many other new musicals she's designed are *Mr. President, A Chorus Line* (and its 2006 revival), *42nd Street, Dreamgirls, La Cage aux Folles, Annie, Chess,* and *The Secret Garden.*

Robin Wagner (1933–, born in San Francisco, California) has designed sets for musicals and straight plays. He's been nominated for the Tony Award for Best Scenic Designer nine times and has won it three times. Among the many other new musicals he's designed are *Jesus Christ Superstar, A Chorus Line, 42nd Street, On the Twentieth Century, Dreamgirls, City of Angels, Crazy for You,* and *The Producers.*

Promises, Promises

MUSIC: Burt Bacharach
LYRICS: Hal David
BOOK: Neil Simon, adapted from Billy Wilder's 1960 movie *The Apartment*
DIRECTOR: Robert Moore
CHOREOGRAPHER: Michael Bennett
ORCHESTRATOR: Jonathan Tunick
DESIGNERS: Robin Wagner (sets), Donald Brooks (costumes), and Martin Aronstein (lights)
PRODUCER: David Merrick
CAST INCLUDES: Jerry Orbach, Jill O'Hara, and Donna McKechnie
PERFORMANCES: 1,281

Michael Bennett (1943–87, born Michael Bennett Di Figlia in Buffalo, New York) started as a dancer, first as Baby John in a 1960 tour of *West Side Story,* and had choreographed two Broadway flops. *Promises, Promises* was his first hit. His work on it received a great deal of notice; even the set changes were choreographed, including dancing scenery. Bennett went on to choreograph such shows as *Coco* and both *Company* and *Follies,* the latter of which he also codirected with Harold Prince. He's best known as the director/choreographer of *A Chorus Line* and *Dreamgirls.*

out his apartment key to his married bosses so they can have secret assignations with their girlfriends. He falls in love with one of the girls—an elevator operator who attempts suicide after her married boyfriend leaves her in the apartment—and eventually develops a moral center. The show, though entertaining and a hit, seemed sexist even in 1968, let alone now; it also had some new sound requirements.

> There were four back-up singers in the orchestra pit, and *Promises* was the first show to use a sound technician to balance the electronic sounds of the orchestra with the onstage performers (a practice that unfortunately has led to the over-amplification of Broadway shows). (Gruber, *Original Cast! The Sixties: Part 2,* 82)

Burt Bacharach and Hal David were already famous for such pop hits as "What the World Needs Now," "Alfie," "What's New, Pussycat?" and "Do You Know the Way to San Jose?" Bacharach brought his personal sound with him, using extensive technology, including some prerecording. *Promises, Promises* was his only musical. Many of the songs are rhythmically similar.

The Happy Time

MUSIC: John Kander

LYRICS: Fred Ebb

BOOK: N. Richard Nash, adapted from the play by Samuel Taylor and the novel by Robert L. Fontaine

DIRECTOR/CHOREOGRAPHER: Gower Champion

DESIGNERS: Peter Wexler (sets), Freddy Wittop (costumes), and Jean Rosenthal (lights)

PRODUCER: David Merrick

CAST INCLUDES: Robert Goulet and David Wayne

PERFORMANCES: 286

The Happy Time is about three generations of a French Canadian family. Despite all the talent involved, it was a flop. Champion's huge and complicated multimedia design concept—the central character is a photographer—overwhelmed the show, which got further bent out of shape by out-of-town rewrites.

In *Zorba,* Kander, Ebb, Prince, and Field continued their partnership from *Cabaret,* but the material was too dark and the book too heavy for Broadway. (The show is a sort of gloomy, Greek variation on *Fiddler.*) Its message is "Enjoy life to the fullest, as if each time were the first time," yet it's a very difficult show to enjoy. It includes a serious and often unpleasant commenting chorus (as in Greek tragedies), the death of the central female character, a suicide, a knifing, and other depressing events. It didn't return its investment and was Kander and Ebb's second flop of the year. Anthony Quinn, who'd starred in the 1964 movie version of the novel, also starred in a 1984 Broadway revival of the musical.

Three small-cast, off-Broadway hits couldn't be more different in sound.

Dames at Sea is a silly, charming parody of 1930s Busby Berkeley–Ruby Keeler musicals with miniature, pseudo-Berkeley production numbers that both mock and admire his geometric patterns, a tap routine as the eleven o'clock number, a song with rain and umbrellas, and an understudy who goes on for the lead on opening night. The songs are all parodies of thirties hits, including a Porter-like beguine and a torch song. The show, which began as a forty-five-minute cabaret act, works as a full-length, small-cast musical comedy. It's often revived nationally.

Your Own Thing is a multimedia soft-rock, soft-centered musical update of Shakespeare's comedy *Twelfth Night*—about twins, love, and sexual confusion. An onstage rock band is part of the cast. Michael Bennett did some uncredited work on the staging. Unknowns Sandy Duncan and Raul Julia took over two of the leads during the run of the show. (It closed in six weeks in London.)

Jacques Brel Is Alive and Well and Living in Paris is a revue of songs by the Belgian-born, Paris-based singer/songwriter who died in 1978. The twenty-two songs, many of them excellent minidramas (such as "Carousel," "Marieke," "Fannette," and "Sons of . . ."), need to be acted as well as they're sung—in a Weill/Brecht manner, though more lyrically. They tend toward sameness over an entire evening. The show is revived occasionally, including a 2006 off-Broadway revival long after Brel died.

In 1969, composer/lyricist Frank Loesser, composers Vernon Duke and Jimmy McHugh, producer Vinton Freedley, and dancer Irene Castle died. Noël Coward was knighted. Lincoln Center revived *Oklahoma!*, the last of the yearly revivals by either Lincoln Center or City Center. There were under thirty new musical evenings, very few of them successful. Among the flops were Katharine Hepburn in *Coco* (332 performances) by André Previn and Alan Jay Lerner, based on the life of fashion designer Coco Chanel; Angela Lansbury in *Dear World* (132 performances) by Jerry Herman, Jerome Lawrence, and Robert E. Lee, adapted from Giraudoux's *The Madwoman of Chaillot;* and Bernadette Peters and Larry Kert in Lionel Bart's *La Strada* (1 performance), adapted from the Fellini movie.

Zorba

MUSIC: John Kander

LYRICS: Fred Ebb

BOOK: Joseph Stein, adapted from Nikos Kazantzakis's novel and the 1964 movie *Zorba the Greek*

DIRECTOR/PRODUCER: Harold Prince

CHOREOGRAPHER: Ron Field

DESIGNERS: Boris Aronson (sets), Patricia Zipprodt (costumes), and Richard Pilbrow (lights)

CAST INCLUDES: Herschel Bernardi, Maria Karnilova, and Carmen Alvarez

PERFORMANCES: 305

Dames at Sea

MUSIC: Jim Wise

LYRICS: Robin Miller

BOOK: Robin Miller and George Haimsohn

DIRECTOR/CHOREOGRAPHER: Neal Kenyon

PRODUCERS: Jordan Hott and Jack Milstein

CAST OF SIX INCLUDES: David Christmas, Steve Elmore, Tamara Long, Bernadette Peters, Joseph R. Sicari, and Sally Stark

PERFORMANCES: 575 off-Broadway

Your Own Thing

MUSIC/LYRICS: Hal Hester and Danny Apolinar

BOOK/DIRECTOR: Donald Driver, adapted from Shakespeare's *Twelfth Night*

PRODUCERS: Zev Bufman and Dorothy Love

CAST INCLUDES: Leland Palmer, Danny Apolinar, and Marion Mercer

PERFORMANCES: 933 off-Broadway

Jacques Brel Is Alive and Well and Living in Paris

MUSIC/LYRICS: Jacques Brel (English lyrics: Eric Blau and Mort Shuman)

DIRECTOR: Moni Yakim

PRODUCERS: 3W Productions Inc. and Lily Turner

CAST OF FOUR INCLUDES: Mort Shuman, Shawn Elliott, Elly Stone, and Alice Whitefield

PERFORMANCES: 1,847 off-Broadway

George M!

MUSIC/LYRICS: selected from the works of George M. Cohan and revised by Mary Cohan

BOOK: Fran and John Pascal and Michael Stewart

DIRECTOR/CHOREOGRAPHER: Joe Layton

PRODUCERS: David Black, Konrad Matthaei, and Lorin E. Price

CAST INCLUDES: Joel Grey and Bernadette Peters

PERFORMANCES: 435

Oh! Calcutta!

MUSIC/LYRICS/BOOK: organized by Kenneth Tynan and written by a lot of people, including Peter Schickele, John Lennon, Samuel Beckett, Sam Shepard, and Jules Feiffer

DIRECTOR: Jacques Levy

CHOREOGRAPHER: Margo Sappington.

PRODUCER: Hillard Elkins

CAST INCLUDES: Bill Macy, Alan Rachins, and Margo Sappington

PERFORMANCES: 704 off-Broadway, then 610 on Broadway

The very loosely structured book of *George M!* takes quite a kindly view of the life and personality of George M. Cohan as filtered through the very different personality of Joel Grey. Bernadette Peters made her Broadway debut in the show.

A largely witless revue about sex, *Oh! Calcutta!* had a lot of male and female nudity, including a nude ballet *pas de deux* and several scenes of simulated sex. A 1976 revival ran 5,959 performances as a tourist attraction in the Broadway area; no one except the producers count it as the longest-running Broadway show.

A hit about the writing of the Declaration of Independence, *1776* is Sherman Edwards's only musical. The show humanizes historical characters—tinkering some with history in the process—and shows the roots of many contemporary problems, including the most important one: the results of allowing the ownership of slaves. The show ends with each delegate signing the Declaration of Independence as the Liberty Bell tolls. (The signing actually happened over several months, not all at the same time as in the famous painting, which is also the final stage picture of the show.) *1776* is almost more a play with songs, including one forty-minute section without any music at all. The songs are show-specific and not easily taken out of context. The cast is all men except for John Adams's and Thomas Jefferson's wives. In 1970, it became the first full-length musical to play the White House. (It doesn't have an intermission.) Of all the year's musicals, only *1776* was made into a movie (which flopped), in 1972, directed by Hunt and choreographed by White. It used several members of the original cast, including Daniels as John Adams, da Silva as Ben Franklin, and Howard as Thomas Jefferson. There was a 1997 Broadway revival.

Broadway was clearly in trouble. Prices were zooming. Both the newly successful composers, writers, and directors, and the old ones (those few still alive) were floundering, and too many of them were too interested in duplicating the success of earlier hits. Trying to reflect the darkening mood of the times, shows were often uninspired and ponderous. Even established stars no longer guaranteed success, and since the concept show *Hair* produced few successful theatrical descendants, the young audiences it drew to Broadway lost interest again. Something had to happen; the musical was dying. Again.

Suggested Watching and Listening

Hair

All of the following numbers from this 1968 show are from the movie on an MGM DVD.

- "Aquarius" (performed by Ren Woods and the ensemble): It's the opening of the show.
- "Sodomy" (performed by Don Dacus): A list of sexual taboos sung by a young man wrestling with his homosexuality.
- "I Got Life" (performed by Treat Williams and Charlotte Rae)
- "Where Do I Go?" (performed by John Savage): It's a character song written as a list.
- "Easy to Be Hard" (performed by Cheryl Barnes): Albert Williams points out that this is a "good AABA rock ballad that defines a crucial theme in the show: the tension between virtuous social attitudes and personal selfishness."
- "Good Morning Starshine" (performed by Beverly D'Angelo, Treat Williams, Dorsey Wright, Don Dacus, Annie Golden, and Cheryl Barnes)

Promises, Promises

The following are two contrasting songs from the 1968 show.

- "She Likes Basketball" (performed by Jerry Orbach): It's available live on *Broadway's Lost Treasures III* (Acorn Media DVD).
- "I'll Never Fall in Love Again" (performed by Jill O'Hara and Jerry Orbach): Available on the original-cast recording (Varese Sarabande CD) and on Paul Gruber's *Original Cast! The Sixties: Part 2* (MET CD), it's usually considered the best song in the show. It was a pop hit for Dionne Warwick.

You're a Good Man, Charlie Brown

The song "My New Philosophy" (performed by Kristin Chenoweth), from the 1997 revival of this 1967 show, was written for Sally, the new character in the revival. It's available live on *Broadway's Lost Treasures III* (Acorn Media DVD).

1776

MUSIC/LYRICS: Sherman Edwards

BOOK: Peter Stone

DIRECTOR: Peter Hunt

CHOREOGRAPHER: Onna White

DESIGNERS: Jo Mielziner (sets and lights) and Patricia Zipprodt (costumes)

PRODUCER: Stuart Ostrow

CAST INCLUDES: William Daniels, Howard da Silva, Betty Buckley, and Ken Howard

PERFORMANCES: 1,217

Bernadette Peters (1948–, born Bernadette Lazarro in Ozone Park, New York) became a star in late 1968 in the off-Broadway musical *Dames at Sea* and went on to star in such Broadway musicals as *Mack and Mabel*, *Song and Dance*, *Sunday in the Park with George*, *Into the Woods*, the 1999 revival of *Annie Get Your Gun*, and the 2003 revival of *Gypsy*. She's also been in several movies.

Peter Stone (1930–2003, born in Los Angeles), after two flops in the sixties, had his first hit with *1776*. He also wrote the books for such shows as *Two by Two*, *My One and Only*, *The Will Rogers Follies*, and *Titanic*.

PART SEVEN

Overleaf: (*left*) The finale from *A Chorus Line* (1975); (*right*) Bobby (Larry Kert) in the finale from *Company* (1970)

From *Company* to *Jesus Christ Superstar*

It's the little things you share together,
Swear together,
Wear together,
That make perfect relationships.
The concerts you enjoy together,
Neighbors you annoy together,
Children you destroy together,
That keep marriage intact.
—"THE LITTLE THINGS YOU DO TOGETHER," *COMPANY,*
LYRICS BY STEPHEN SONDHEIM

As we've seen, the development of the musical from a loosely structured entertainment to an art form has in part been an exploration of ways of using the book as the spine on which to attach the other elements of the show in order to achieve a more tightly integrated whole. (Failures these days are most often—though not always accurately—blamed on the book.) This exploration moved from haphazardly structured musical comedies to the carefully structured musical plays of Rodgers and Hammerstein and their contemporaries of the golden age. Now we'll see that, as the form began to rigidify, it splintered.

The splitting apart of the musical comedy and the musical play began in earnest with the revolutionary 1957 musical drama *West Side Story,* which had Stephen Sondheim's first Broadway lyrics. For Sondheim—as for his teacher, mentor, and friend Oscar Hammerstein—the book is always the source of inspiration for all the other elements of his shows and their production concepts. However, Sondheim's shows deal with subject matter that is a distinct change from the usual Broadway musical fare, including such virgin territory as urban angst, fear of commitment, serial murderers, cannibalism, American imperialism, the lie of "happily ever after," U.S. presidential assassins, and the destructive power of obsessive love. His shows, which frequently reflect the mood of the times (not always in ways audiences want to deal with), are often angry and bitter, the events often bleak, the emotions often painful or inaccessible. Few of the characters are admirable, although they're examined in greater psychological depth than in any previous musicals.

Sondheim has, in fact, rejected the fundamentally optimistic philosophy of almost all his predecessors in musical theater. He rarely even suggests that "there's a place for us somewhere" in his shows, as he had to in *West Side Story* and as he was convinced to do for the final song in *Company*. (He wanted to have the hero continue fearing marriage and commitment at the end of the show.) Sondheim also seems to have little belief in the possibility of community in today's world that was so prominent in all the shows of Oscar Hammerstein, though he clearly regrets this loss.

> His is the most systematic and unsentimental mind that has ever addressed itself to the American musical. . . . At the very moment when playwrights like Pinter and Albee were demonstrating that theatrical dialogue could be used to demonstrate what words hide instead of what they express, Sondheim recognized that songs could function in the same way. And therein lies his greatest advance beyond Hammerstein. What Sondheim brought to the American musical for the first time was subtext. . . . [He said,] "It's important that a score be not just a series of songs—that it should in some way be developed, just the way the book is. There's a great confusion these days, you know, because, with a lot of those British shows, people say they're through-composed. No, they're not through-composed, they're through-sung. They just repeat, over and over. Composition is about development, not about repetition."
> (Stephen Schiff, "Deconstructing Sondheim," *New Yorker,* March 8, 1993)

Starting with *Company* in 1970, Sondheim, who's written both music and lyrics for all his shows since then, has continuously explored and stretched the possibilities of the musical drama's form as well as its content. *Company,* in fact, was the beginning of his exploration of the concept musical.

> The usual Broadway musical has a plot with the characters traveling a time line on the road to some change. In the [concept show] the characters usually reach a conclusion, but the path is not always chronological and does not always tell a story. . . . This was a pretty radical idea at the time. (Bloom, *American Song,* 134)

Two of the longest-running shows in Broadway history were also concept musicals: *A Chorus Line*, about Broadway "gypsies" at an audition, and *Cats*, about cats. (A sign of the poverty of the 1982 Broadway musical season is that *Cats* won a Tony for Best Lyrics, which were adapted from *Old Possum's Book of Practical Cats*, by Nobel Prize–winning poet T. S. Eliot, who had died seventeen years earlier and who probably would have hated the show if he'd lived to see it. In fact, he probably wouldn't have granted the rights to Lloyd Webber in the first place; his widow did the granting, received the royalties, and collected the Tony.)

Although Sondheim began his Broadway work with Robbins and Bernstein, his shows have rarely used Robbins's *West Side Story* methods of telling story through dance and movement. He has, however, continued Bernstein's more complex and classical approach to music for the Broadway stage. (Although classically trained, his interest has always been in musical theater.) He rarely writes anything that could be construed as pop music except when he's purposely writing in old song forms, as he did with about half the score of *Follies*. Many of his songs are used by cabaret singers. As Schiff points out in his article "Deconstructing Sondheim," his "songs make a fetish of surprise, especially in their melodies, which squirm and double back on themselves, and even end seemingly in midphrase—anything to avoid predictability."

Just as Rodgers and Hammerstein's musical plays were American operettas in disguise, so Sondheim's musical plays and concept musicals are often close to contemporary operas not only in their seriousness but also in the complexity of their scores and in their overthrow of the traditional musical theater balance between dialogue and score. Straight dialogue sections in many of Sondheim's musicals are usually shorter and fewer in number than in the musicals of his predecessors. It's the lyrics and music of most of his shows that develop plot and, particularly, character most fully.

I suppose it's important to point out that, brilliant as Sondheim's scores usually are, only three of the shows for which he wrote both music and lyrics paid back their investors during their Broadway runs: *A Funny Thing Happened on the Way to the Forum*—not typical of the rest of his work, *Company*, and *A Little Night Music*, though tours, revivals, and regional productions have made a financial difference to most of them. Even though five of his shows have won Tonys for Best Musical (the three listed above, *Sweeney Todd*, and *Passion*), and one was awarded the Pulitzer Prize (*Sunday in the Park with George*), given the subject matter and musical complexity of most of his shows, it's easy to understand why they rarely made back their investments on Broadway, why some of them get revived in concert form and even by opera companies (though they don't really work as well with opera voices), and why most of those who've followed Sondheim's lead, lacking his genius, fail miserably and badly depress audiences in the process. Yet Sondheim is unquestionably *the* genius of American musical theater in the last quarter of the twentieth century, and the most influential.

> The trouble is he has no heirs. The British and French composers whose work has proved so successful on Broadway—principally Andrew Lloyd Webber and Alain Boublil and Claude-Michel Schoenberg—are still essentially laboring with the Rodgers-and-Hammerstein model, using a musical language that has advanced very little since Puccini. And in a Broadway environment, where mounting a musical is almost prohibitively expensive and perilously dependent on the approbation of a single newspaper [the *New York Times*], it's hard to imagine investors taking a flyer on anyone as daring as Sondheim—anyone, that is, except Sondheim himself. He has changed the musical forever, it appears, but he has left a lot of scorched earth behind him. (Schiff, "Deconstructing Sondheim")

In 1970, burlesque star Gypsy Rose Lee, composer Ray Henderson (of Henderson, DeSylva, and Brown), and Billie Burke (actress and Ziegfeld's widow) died. The top Broadway ticket price went up to $15. There were fewer than thirty new musical evenings, most of them mediocre, including

Backdrop: 1970–1971

National The Kent State University antiwar demonstrations lead to the deaths of four students and the wounding of eight more by National Guardsmen. American troops are now in Laos as well as Cambodia and Vietnam. Lieutenant William Calley is convicted of having killed twenty Vietnamese civilians at My Lai; President Nixon frees him pending further review. Daniel Ellsberg releases the Pentagon Papers, revealing facts about U.S. involvement in Vietnam kept secret from the public. Unemployment is at its highest since 1965; 25.5 million Americans live below the poverty level. U.S. imports exceed exports for the first trade deficit since 1888. The Environmental Protection Agency is created. The Twenty-sixth Amendment is ratified, lowering the voting age to eighteen. An L.A. earthquake kills 51 people and injures 880.

International The Palestine Liberation Organization (PLO) moves to Lebanon. The Organization of Petroleum Exporting Countries (OPEC) raises the price of Persian Gulf oil and increases taxes. Plane several that closed within a week. Two longer-running flops were Jule Styne, Sammy Cahn, Leonard Spigelgass, and Joshua Logan's twenty-five-performance *Look to the Lilies*, starring Shirley Booth, an adaptation of the novel and movie *Lilies of the Field;* and Larry Grossman, Hal Hakady, Arthur Marx, and Robert Marx's seventy-six-performance musical biography *Minnie's Boys*, starring Shelley Winters as the mother of the Marx Brothers, which closed at a loss of $750,000. There was an unsuccessful revival of *The Boy Friend*, and Ethel Merman, in her last Broadway appearance, took over the title role in *Hello, Dolly!*, which beat *My Fair Lady* as the longest running musical on Broadway and closed at the end of the year.

The Me Nobody Knows (587 performances, first off-Broadway, then on) is a rock-based revue with lyrics and dialogue adapted from poems written by poor New York children and teenagers. It was Irene Cara's Broadway debut among a cast of seven- to eighteen-year-old unknowns.

For better or worse, beginning with *Company*, Prince and Sondheim had a profound influence on the very nature of the American musical (ultimately and unintentionally driving many

Company

MUSIC/LYRICS: Stephen Sondheim
BOOK: George Furth
DIRECTOR/PRODUCER: Harold Prince
CHOREOGRAPHER: Michael Bennett
ORCHESTRATOR: Jonathan Tunick
DESIGNERS: Boris Aronson (sets), D. D. Ryan (costumes), and Robert Ornbo (lights)
CAST INCLUDES: Dean Jones (replaced soon after opening by Larry Kert), Barbara Barrie, Beth Howland, Charles Kimbrough, Donna McKechnie, and Elaine Stritch
PERFORMANCES: 706

---

hijacking occurs more and more frequently. The People's Republic of China is seated as a member of the United Nations.

New Developments Soft contact lenses win FDA approval. Amtrak takes over nearly all U.S. passenger railroad traffic. Joe Frazier regains the world heavyweight boxing title by knocking out Jimmy Ellis. The Seattle Pilots become the Milwaukee Brewers.

Publications The weekly magazine *Look* ceases publication after thirty-four years. New books include Reich's *The Greening of America*, Millett's *Sexual Politics*, and Brown's *Bury My Heart at Wounded Knee: An Indian History of the American West.*

TV *Masterpiece Theatre, The Electric Company, Columbo, The Mary Tyler Moore Show,* and *The Partridge Family* make their TV debuts. The top TV shows of the two years are *All in the Family, The Flip Wilson Show, Marcus Welby, M.D.,* and *Here's Lucy.*

Pop Culture The Who's rock opera *Tommy* is performed at New York's Metropolitan Opera House; Ken Russell films it in 1975, and it becomes a high-tech Broadway musical in 1993. Jimi Hendrix, Jim Morrison, and Janis Joplin die of alcohol and drug abuse. The Beatles, as well as Diana Ross and the audience members away from new American musicals and, by the 1980s, toward extravagant European pop operas and revivals of old hits). Nonetheless, *Company* is as much a landmark as *Show Boat, Oklahoma!, West Side Story,* and *Cabaret.*

Company began as eleven short plays about married couples written by George Furth. He showed them to Sondheim, who wanted to musicalize some of them into a show about the difficulties and perplexities of marriage and personal commitment in the angry and disaffected age of Vietnam. Sondheim suggested creating the central character of Bobby, who ties together the various couples in the short plays by being a best friend to all of them. Bobby is thirty-five years old and unable to make a commitment to a permanent relationship. During the show we meet three of his frustrated girlfriends. We also meet couples from three of Furth's plays and two more he wrote for the show, all well-to-do Manhattanites who use Bobby as an escape from their mundane and alienated existences in the urban jungle. The show, which is quite brittle in tone, takes place in Bobby's mind and memory in the minute before he's going to walk into a surprise birthday party being held for him by the five couples. There is no chorus; it's an ensemble show with the principals also acting as the chorus commentators. (The show was relatively inexpensive to run.) Each couple and each girlfriend gets a scene or song or dance, making the show almost revue-like in structure. The songs,

Supremes, make their last group recordings. Groups like Jethro Tull, Pink Floyd, Genesis, and Emerson, Lake, and Palmer popularize progressive rock. The Eagles debut at Disneyland. Soul music's Philly sound comes from such groups as the Stylistics and the Spinners. Among the new records are Hayes's title song for the movie *Shaft*; Denver's "Take Me Home, Country Roads"; Newton-John's "If Not for You"; Simon and Garfunkel's "Bridge over Troubled Water"; the Jackson Five's "The Love You Save"; the Carpenters' "We've Only Just Begun"; Stevens's "Everything Is Beautiful"; King's *Tapestry,* including "You've Got a Friend"; *Blood, Sweat and Tears III*; *Black Sabbath*; Mitchell's *Blue*; the Rolling Stones' *Sticky Fingers*; Lennon's *Imagine*; Led Zeppelin's *Runes*; John's *Tumbleweed Connection*; Pink Floyd's *Dark of the Moon*; Dylan's *Self Portrait*; Crosby, Stills, Nash, and Young's *Deja Vu*; Santana's *Abraxas*; and Burris and Haggard's "Okie from Muskogee."

Stage The Pilobolus Dance Theatre is founded. Guare's *The House of Blue Leaves,* Rabe's Vietnam plays *The Basic Training of Pavlo Hummel* and *Sticks and Bones,* and Fugard's *Boesman and Lena* are among the new plays.

according to Sondheim, are used "in a Brechtian way as comment and counterpoint."

> While . . . [the] score was filled with contemporary rhythms, it
> was anything but "pop." Words and music revealed character in
> a highly personal, self-analytical way. . . . [They] told more about
> the characters—and the times—than any monologue or book
> scene could hope to do. . . . The age of Sondheim . . . has been
> distinguished by scores full of analytical, personalized musical
> portraits. (Suskin, *Show Tunes*, 449)

There's not much dance in the show; more often Bennett's work was in movement patterns, much of it as the set also moved. Aronson's structural Plexiglas and chrome set (with elevators that moved as the scenes changed) contributed mightily and brilliantly to the sense of urban disengagement, often putting people into what seemed like separate cages. And Prince made sure that all the elements blended into a perfect whole. (Prince, Aronson, and orchestrator Jonathan Tunick remained part of the team on Sondheim's shows until 1981, the year of the major flop *Merrily We Roll Along*.)

Jonathan Tunick (1938–, born in New York City) has also orchestrated such shows as *Promises, Promises, Follies, A Little Night Music, A Chorus Line, Sweeney Todd, Into the Woods, Titanic,* and *The Color Purple.* He won the very first Tony for orchestration for *Titanic* in 1997. He's one of the few artists to have won an Oscar, a Tony, a Grammy, and an Emmy.

Screen New movies include Harold Prince's flop *Something for Everyone, The French Connection, Bananas, Dirty Harry, McCabe and Mrs. Miller, Five Easy Pieces, M*A*S*H, Patton,* an adaptation of Burgess's *A Clockwork Orange,* and Ophul's documentary *The Sorrow and the Pity.*

Among the new movie musicals are an adaptation of Dahl's *Charlie and the Chocolate Factory,* retitled *Willie Wonka and the Chocolate Factory* (remade under Dahl's title in 2006), and the documentaries *Woodstock* and *Gimme Shelter* (about the Rolling Stones concert tour that ended at Altamont). Also new are the adaptation of *Fiddler on the Roof* and the semi-adaptation of *The Boy Friend.* Three flops are important to Hollywood's decision that big, old-style movie musicals are box-office poison: Minnelli's weak adaptation of the unsuccessful *On a Clear Day You Can See Forever;* the hopeless *Song of Norway* (an attempt at duplicating the success of the movie of *The Sound of Music* and a huge loss at the box office); and Julie Andrews in the original, large-scale, expensive *Darling Lili,* with a score by Mancini and Mercer. Hollywood's decision doesn't take into account that they simply aren't very good movies.

Company ends with Bobby's song "Being Alive" as he's encouraged by the rest of the characters to come to self-realization. Sondheim originally intended to have Bobby end the show with "Marry Me a Little" (which some revivals add for Bobby to sing at the end of the first act):

> Marry me a little,
> Love me just enough,
> Cry but not too often,
> Play but not too rough.
> Keep a tender distance
> So we'll both be free.
> That's the way it ought to be.
> I'm ready!

It was soon replaced by "Happily Ever After":

> Someone to hold you too close,
> Someone to hurt you too deep.
> Someone to love you too hard,
> Happily ever after.
>
> Someone to need you too much,
> Someone to read you too well,
> Someone to bleed you of all
> The things you don't want to tell—
> That's happily ever after,
> Ever, ever, ever after
> In hell.

Prince felt that "Happily Ever After" was too downbeat for the end of the show. It was replaced by "Being Alive," which begins with the same first three lines and says much the same thing but in a more positive tone. (Both dropped songs are in Craig Lucas and Norman René's 1980 two-character, off-Broadway revue *Marry Me a Little,* an evening of unused Sondheim songs.) There's an original-cast recording of *Company* and of nearly all Sondheim's shows. The successful 2006 Broadway revival of *Company,* directed by John Doyle, dispensed with the pit orchestra, as did his 2005 revival of Sondheim's *Sweeney Todd.* All the actors played instruments as well as their roles in both productions, and the score was reorchestrated accordingly.

A not particularly good musical and very different from Strouse and Adams's *Bye Bye Birdie, Applause* had a successful run largely thanks to Bacall's star power in her musical theater debut. She was excellent even though she couldn't really sing or dance very well. This was Field's first time out as director. It was also the first time Comden and Green did the book of a stage musical without doing the lyrics. The show is about Eve Harrington, a conniving actress who lies, cheats, and seduces her way to the top, stepping over anyone in her way (including Bacall's character, Margo Channing, a Broadway star). Joseph Mankiewicz's Academy Award–winning 1950 movie *All About Eve,* starring Bette Davis as Margo and Anne Baxter as Eve, was also adapted from Orr's short story. (Baxter replaced Bacall as Margo during the run of the musical; she couldn't sing or dance very well either.) The musical could get rights to only the story and couldn't use anything added to the screenplay, including any of Mankiewicz's great dialogue or the important character of critic Addison De-Witt; the show is far less effective without him. Bonnie Franklin got a lot of notice in a supporting role as a chorus gypsy who sings the title song; she soon moved on to TV sitcom land.

An entertaining musical comedy, *Purlie* is about a fast-talking African American preacher who overcomes bigotry in a small Georgia town; he gets his church, and he gets the girl. It drew large numbers of black audience members to Broadway musicals for the first time in many years. The score includes the title song; "Walk Him up the Stairs," the opening number, which is a full-company gospel number sung at a funeral; "Down Home"; "Skinnin' a Cat"; and the hit tune "I Got Love."

A musical about Noah, the flood, and the love problems of Noah's three sons, *Two by Two* ran as long as it did and made a small profit thanks almost entirely to the drawing power of Danny Kaye, who hadn't been seen on Broadway since Porter's *Let's Face It!* in 1941. The less-than-first-class Rodgers score includes the title song, "Something Doesn't Happen," and "I Do Not Know a Day I Did Not Love You."

This show wasn't so hot to begin with, but Danny Kaye brought it down to a new low. He tried his best to make it the "Danny

Applause

MUSIC: Charles Strouse

LYRICS: Lee Adams

BOOK: Betty Comden and Adolph Green, adapted from Mary Orr's "The Wisdom of Eve"

DIRECTOR/CHOREOGRAPHER: Ron Field

PRODUCERS: Joseph Kipness and Lawrence Kasha

CAST INCLUDES: Lauren Bacall, Len Cariou, and Bonnie Franklin

PERFORMANCES: 896

Purlie

MUSIC: Gary Geld

LYRICS: Peter Udell

BOOK: Peter Udell, Ossie Davis, and Philip Rose, adapted from Davis's play *Purlie Victorious*

DIRECTOR: Philip Rose

CHOREOGRAPHER: Louis Johnson

PRODUCER: Philip Rose

CAST INCLUDES: Cleavon Little, Melba Moore, Sherman Hemsley, and Novella Nelson

PERFORMANCES: 688

Two by Two

MUSIC: Richard Rodgers

LYRICS: Martin Charnin

BOOK: Peter Stone, adapted from Clifford Odets's *The Flowering Peach*

DIRECTOR/CHOREOGRAPHER: Joe Layton

PRODUCERS: Joe Layton and Richard Rodgers

CAST INCLUDES: Danny Kaye, Joan Copeland, and Madeline Kahn

PERFORMANCES: 343

Kaye Show" by stepping out of character, trying to make fellow cast members crack up on stage, etc., etc. He even went so far as to unzip Joan Copeland's dress during her big ballad. (Bloom, *American Song*, 752)

The Rothschilds

MUSIC: Jerry Bock

LYRICS: Sheldon Harnick

BOOK: Sherman Yellen, adapted from Frederic Morton's biography

DIRECTOR/CHOREOGRAPHER: Michael Kidd

PRODUCERS: Lester Osterman and Hillard Elkins

CAST INCLUDES: Hal Linden, Jill Clayburgh, and Chris Sarandon

PERFORMANCES: 505

A rather dark and moody show, *The Rothschilds* covers a fifty-year period as it tells how the famous Jewish family got their European banking business going. Although different in tone and technique, it's judged a second-rate follow-up to Bock and Harnick's *Fiddler on the Roof*. It also marked the end of their partnership, caused in part by some huge disagreements they had while the show was trying out. (Bock retired from the business.) One of the show's biggest problems is that, in trying to cover a fifty-year period, it moves in fits and starts. Also, as part of the same problem, it switches focus from the father in the first act to one of his five sons, a far less interesting character, in the second act. (The five sons are played by children at the beginning of the show, by adults when they grow up.) Along with book problems, the show wasn't right for Kidd's bouncy and super-energetic style, and although it ran for over a year, it closed at a loss.

In 1971, writer Sam Spewack, producer Leland Hayward, and funny girl Fanny Brice died. The Broadway Equity minimum rose to $185 a week. It was a big year for rock musicals and nostalgia, though with few box-office successes. Ron Field directed and choreographed an unsuccessful seventy-three-performance revival of *On the Town*, with Bernadette Peters, Donna McKechnie, and Phyllis Newman in the cast. There was also an unsuccessful revival of *You're a Good Man, Charlie Brown* and a one-performance revival of *Johnny Johnson*, which also had failed in 1936, though not as badly.

The nostalgia hit of the year was a revival of the 1925 musical comedy, *No! No! Nanette* (861 performances), adapted and directed by Burt Shevelove and choreographed by Donald Saddler. Busby Berkeley was listed as the production supervisor, and it starred Ruby Keeler, Jack Gilford, Susan Watson, Bobby Van, and Helen Gallagher. Berkeley was nearly senile and no help on the show, but he did get a lot of publicity for it, as did Keeler, who came out of a long retirement. Shevelove revised the book extensively, but the score remained basically intact. This production is often considered the beginning of the many Broadway revivals produced over the following thirty years.

Follies, a bitter, anti-nostalgic look at the past, takes place on the night before the wrecking ball is to descend on a Broadway theater that once housed the *Weismann Follies,* a fictional version of the *Ziegfeld Follies.* Prince got the idea from a *Life* magazine photo of silent-screen star Gloria Swanson standing in the ruins of the Roxy Theatre while it was being demolished.

In the show, former *Follies* performers have been invited to a party onstage in the crumbling old theater. The four central characters are two of the former *Follies* girls, Sally and Phyllis, and their husbands, Buddy and Ben, who courted them when they were showgirls. Ben and Phyllis have gotten very rich and jaded. Buddy and Sally are a middle-class, suburban couple. Sally thinks she should have married Ben. Buddy has had to struggle to make a decent living; he's also a philanderer. During the long night's journey into dawn, memories are invoked, both painful and happy, but mostly painful. The ghosts of their happy, confident younger selves (in white makeup and dressed in black and white) haunt all the characters, reminding them that they haven't become what they'd dreamed or that if they have, it hasn't made them happy.

The show climaxes in a lavish fantasy *Follies* sequence set in Loveland, with Aronson's huge set of the decayed theater's stage transformed into a Ziegfeld-like set with lots of red hearts. During this sequence, each of the four central characters has a solo number dealing with the folly of his or her life. Here's part of "Buddy's Blues":

> I've got those
> "God-why-don't-you-love-me-oh-you-do-I'll-see-you-later"
> Blues,
> That
> "Long-as-you-ignore-me-you're-the-only-thing-that-
>   matters"
> Feeling,
> That
> "If-I'm-good-enough-for-you-you're-not-good-enough"
> And "Thank-you-for-the-present-but-what's-wrong-with-
>   it" stuff.

Follies

MUSIC/LYRICS: Stephen Sondheim

BOOK: James Goldman

DIRECTORS: Harold Prince and Michael Bennett

CHOREOGRAPHER: Michael Bennett

ORCHESTRATOR: Jonathan Tunick

DESIGNERS: Boris Aronson (sets), Florence Klotz (costumes), and Tharon Musser (lights)

PRODUCER: Harold Prince in association with Ruth Mitchell

CAST INCLUDES: Alexis Smith, Dorothy Collins, Gene Nelson, John McMartin, and Yvonne De Carlo

PERFORMANCES: 522

Those

"Don't-come-any-closer-'cause-you-know-how-much-I-love-you"

Feelings,

Those

"Tell-me-that-you-love-me-oh-you-did-I-gotta-run-now"

Blues.

The central characters' remaining illusions are destroyed since, in to-day's world, romance and dreams are no longer possible. They walk out into the early morning sunlight hoping for a better future (or at least a more honest one), while the echoes of their younger selves can be heard as the wrecking ball begins its work.

> *Follies* was a landmark in the American musical theater—a big Broadway show that attempted no less than to seriously examine the unfulfilled prom-ise of the United States. . . . The disappointments in the lives of the four middle-aged principals became the disappointments of America following the Second World War. An entire form of entertainment [the lavish Broad-way revue] that had embodied the fantasies and hopes of several generations had collapsed, and what was there to replace it? (Gruber, *Original Cast! The Seventies,* 23–25)

Sondheim says the show is about the loss of innocence not only in the characters but in the country. (Prince had a great deal to do with this con-cept as well as with the staging concept.) In fact, the show is in part a musical about the death of the musical. Performed on Broadway without an inter-mission, it was hardly the thing for the tired businesspeople in the Broadway audiences, and the original production, which was very expensive, lost $650,000 of its $800,000 initial investment despite its long run. This was Prince and Bennett's last collaboration; Bennett soon became a director/choreographer on his own. Book writer James Goldman is probably best known as the author of the play *The Lion in Winter.*

The score of twenty-two songs includes pastiche numbers sung by for-mer *Follies* women (played in the original production by elderly, formerly well-known performers). Those numbers imitate old songs but, in context, also take on a haunting life of their own. They include songs meant to sound like Romberg operettas, Berlin *Follies* numbers, Kern ballads, Arlen blues, and Porter list songs. They're very different in tone and sound from the songs sung as part of the present-day story. Along with the original-cast recording, there's a recording and DVD of a 1985 concert with Barbara

Cook, Lee Remick, George Hearn, Mandy Patinkin, Elaine Stritch, and Carol Burnett, among others. A 1987 London production had rewrites, cuts, and some different numbers. Other revivals have gone back to the original, including a successful 1998 revival at the Paper Mill Playhouse in New Jersey, which included eight songs cut from the show at various stages in its life; it was recorded. The Roundabout Theatre Company revived it in 2001 (117 performances). Directed by Matthew Warchus and choreographed by Kathleen Marshall, the show's cast included Blythe Danner, Gregory Harrison, Judith Ivey, Treat Williams, Polly Bergen, Marge Champion, Betty Garrett, and Joan Roberts (who was Laurey in the original production of *Oklahoma!*).

Two Gentlemen of Verona is a joyous, multiethnic, Latin-flavored, rock and jazz adaptation of Shakespeare's comedy; it transferred to Broadway from Joseph Papp's summer, outdoor Shakespeare Festival in Central Park, amplification intact. It is MacDermot's only hit other than *Hair* and is worth exploring for revival.

A ten-person show, *Godspell* is basically a concept musical in which sixties flower children (in most productions, Jesus wears a Superman shirt and they all wear partial clown makeup) reenact their versions of scenes, sermons, and parables from the Gospel. The original billing said: "Original author: St. Matthew." By the time the show reached Broadway, Tebelak had a credit for having conceived it as well as having directed it. The show began as a series of improvisations and theater games by Tebelak and some fellow students at Carnegie Mellon University. It has an easy-rock score and is frequently revived by both amateur and professional groups. The original-cast album sold over a million copies. The 1973 movie version, directed by David Greene and choreographed by Sammy Bayes, had Victor Garber as Jesus (he played it in the first Toronto production) and several members of the original cast. In the score are "Day by Day" (the show's hit song), "All Good Gifts," "By My Side," "We Beseech Thee," "Save the People," "Turn Back, O Man," "Bless the Lord," and "All for the Best."

Two Gentlemen of Verona

MUSIC: Galt MacDermot

LYRICS: John Guare

BOOK: John Guare and Mel Shapiro, adapted from Shakespeare's play

DIRECTOR: Mel Shapiro

CHOREOGRAPHERS: Jean Erdman and Dennis Nahat

DESIGNERS: Ming Cho Lee (sets), Theoni V. Aldredge (costumes), and Lawrence Metzler (lights)

PRODUCER: Joseph Papp and his New York Shakespeare Festival

CAST INCLUDES: Raul Julia and Clifton Davis

PERFORMANCES: 613 on Broadway after running 14 performances off-Broadway

Godspell

MUSIC/LYRICS: Stephen Schwartz

DIRECTOR: John-Michael Tebelak, who adapted it from the Gospel according to St. Matthew

ORCHESTRATOR: Steve Reinhardt

DESIGNERS: Spencer Mosse (lights) and Susan Tsu (costumes)

PRODUCERS: Joseph Beruh, Stuart Duncan, and Edgar Lansbury (and The Shubert Organization on Broadway)

CAST INCLUDES: Stephen Nathan and David Haskell

PERFORMANCES: 2,124 off-Broadway and another 527 on Broadway after a 1976 move

Jesus Christ Superstar

MUSIC: Andrew Lloyd Webber

LYRICS: Tim Rice

BOOK: Tom O'Horgan, based on the New Testament

DIRECTOR: Tom O'Horgan

DESIGNERS: Robin Wagner (sets), Randy Barcelo (costumes), and Jules Fisher (lights)

PRODUCERS: Robert Stigwood and MCA

CAST INCLUDES: Jeff Fenholt, Yvonne Elliman, and Ben Vereen

PERFORMANCES: 711

Andrew Lloyd Webber

(1948–, born in London) has written the music for several incredibly successful shows, including *Joseph and the Amazing Technicolor Dreamcoat, Evita, Cats,* and *The Phantom of the Opera.* He's also done such shows as *Starlight Express* and *Sunset Boulevard.* His Really Useful Theatre Group has been a producer of his shows starting with *Cats.*

A large-cast retelling of the last seven days in the life of Christ set to a "wall-to-wall" rock score, *Jesus Christ Superstar* originated as a record album that sold two million copies in a year. Christ is treated as a pop music idol who's loved and then crucified by the public. (It would be difficult to follow the story if one didn't already know it.) The costly, flashy, overamplified, and controversial production was a huge hit (Lloyd Webber's first), particularly with younger audiences, and a simpler, less controversial (though equally overamplified) production soon opened in London and ran 3,358 performances. The show is frequently revived. There's a 1973 movie version directed by Norman Jewison and choreographed by Rob Iscove, with Ted Neeley as Christ, Carl Anderson as Judas, and Yvonne Elliman re-creating the role of Mary Magdalene. (In the mid-nineties, Neeley and Anderson were in a very successful touring revival.) The songs include the hit "I Don't Know How to Love Him," "King Herod's Song," and "Superstar." The show made Ben Vereen, who played Judas, a star.

Lloyd Webber and Rice had already written *Joseph and the Amazing Technicolor Dreamcoat* and would soon write *Evita,* their last show together. Once they stopped working together, Lloyd Webber and Rice followed two divergent paths taken by the musical as the form continued to splinter: pop operas and Disney.

Suggested Watching and Listening

Applause
The number "Applause" (performed by Bonnie Franklin and the ensemble) is on *Broadway's Lost Treasures* (Acorn Media DVD).

Company
Director D. A. Pennebaker's film *Original Cast Album: Company* (New Video Group DVD) is a chronicle of the eighteen-and-a-half-hour recording session of the original-cast album. The songs are listed in the order in which they are sung in the show; the documentary does not include the entire score.
- "Company" (performed by the company)
- "The Little Things You Do Together" (performed by Elaine Stritch, Barbara Barrie, and Charles Kimbrough): A vivid description of the joys of marriage.
- "Sorry-Grateful" (performed by Charles Kimbrough, George Coe, Charles Braswell, and Dean Jones): Three of the married men try to tell Bobby that marriage is OK.

- "You Could Drive a Person Crazy" (performed by Pamela Myers, Donna McKechnie, and Susan Browning): It's sung by Bobby's three girlfriends.
- "Another Hundred People" (performed by Pamela Myers): One of Bobby's girlfriends talks about what it's like in the big city.
- "Getting Married Today" (performed by Beth Howland, Steve Elmore, and Teri Ralston): In the act 1 finale, Amy, one of Bobby's friends, tries to get out of getting married because she's too neurotic to handle it.
- "Side by Side by Side" (performed by the company): It's a full-company dance number to open act 2.
- "Barcelona" (performed by Dean Jones and Susan Browning): One of Bobby's girlfriends, an airline hostess, tries to leave Bobby's bed for work.
- "The Ladies Who Lunch" (performed by Elaine Stritch): A showstopper sung by the oldest and most jaded of the married women.
- "Being Alive" (performed by Dean Jones): In the eleven o'clock number, Bobby, encouraged by the rest of the cast, comes to some sort of positive conclusions about commitment.

Follies

All these numbers are taken from the live recording of a 1985 concert of the show, available as a two-disc CD set from RCA Victor Broadway or on Image Entertainment DVD.

- "Broadway Baby" (performed by Elaine Stritch): A pastiche sung by one of the oldest ex-*Follies* girls.
- "I'm Still Here" (performed by Carol Burnett): Sung by a former *Follies* girl who became a star, it was a replacement during out-of-town tryouts and is a strong favorite of older cabaret singers. As Albert Williams points out, "The numerous experiences and incarnations this veteran describes encapsulate the history of American entertainment as represented by its female icons, touching on such issues as age, the Depression, the McCarthy witch hunts, the rebirth of onetime ingenues as camp cult figures, etc. The song is a tribute to survival—at any cost."
- "Losing My Mind" (performed by Barbara Cook): It's Sally's *Follies* number and a great torch song.

Godspell

The following numbers are from the movie version of this show, directed by David Greene and available on DVD from Sony Pictures.

- "Save the People" (performed by Victor Garber and the company): It's Jesus' first song.
- "Turn Back, O Man" (performed by Joanne Jonas, Victor Garber, and the company)
- "Bless the Lord" (performed by Lynne Thigpen and the company)

Jesus Christ Superstar

The following numbers are from the movie version of this show, which was directed by Norman Jewison and is available on Universal Studios DVD.

- "I Don't Know How to Love Him" (performed by Yvonne Elliman): It's Mary Magdalene's first solo and became a pop hit.
- "Gethsemane" (performed by Ted Neeley as Jesus)

- "King Herod's Song" (performed by Joshua Mostel)
- "Superstar" (performed by Carl Anderson as Judas)

Purlie

The original-cast recording of this show is available on CD from RCA Victor Broadway. It features the following two numbers.
- "Purlie" (performed by Melba Moore)
- "I Got Love" (performed by Melba Moore): It was a big hit for the show and for Moore.

Sondheim: A Celebration at Carnegie Hall

This is a 1993 concert directed by Scott Ellis and choreographed by Susan Stroman, available on Kultur DVD.
- "Loveland" (from *Follies*) and "Getting Married Today" (from *Company*, performed by Mark Jacoby, Madeline Kahn, Jeanne Lehman, and the Ensemble)
- "Not a Day Goes By" (from *Merrily We Roll Along*, performed by Bernadette Peters)
- "A Weekend in the Country" (from *A Little Night Music*, performed by Kevin Anderson, George Lee Andrews, Mark Jacoby, Beverly Lambert, Maureen Moore, Susan Terry, Ron Baker, Peter Blanchet, Carol Meyer, Bronwyn Thomas, and Blythe Walker)

From *Grease* to *A Chorus Line*

Give me somebody to dance for,

Give me somebody to show.

Let me wake up in the morning to find

I have somewhere exciting to go,

To have something that I can believe in,

To have someone to be.

Use me.

Choose me.

—"THE MUSIC AND THE MIRROR," *A CHORUS LINE,*

LYRICS BY EDWARD KLEBAN

Most people who created successful musicals in the golden age believed that a musical needed a hit pop song or two that people wanted to dance and romance to. One of the wonders of *West Side Story* was that it found a way to be true to itself moment to moment and still created such out-of-context pop hits as "Tonight" and "Maria." There were also hit songs in most Rodgers and Hammerstein shows, of course, and in such other fully integrated shows as *My Fair Lady* and *Gypsy.* However, the number of hit songs from musicals diminished during the seventies, as did the number of hit shows.

The more tightly unified a show is, the less likely that any of its music will work well enough out of context to become a pop hit that young people will want to dance to. Sondheim, for instance, seldom concerns himself with the danceability of the music of his shows, and, aside from "Send in the Clowns" from *A Little Night Music,* his songs hardly ever have a life outside their shows except in cabaret acts—nor does he intend them to.

In much of the pop music from the seventies on, the lyrics are purposely kept simple, unsubtle, and repetitive so that the rhythm can be the most pervasive aspect of the song. Listeners, therefore, don't develop the habit of listening to lyrics as carefully as show lyrics need. Also, the song forms used in rock are usually too simple to be structured into the kind of dramatic action needed in the songs for musicals. (Hammerstein taught Sondheim to think of each song as a one-act play with a beginning, a middle, and an end. Rock songs aren't written that way; in fact, they rarely have a middle and often fade away rather than end.)

On top of that, contemporary songs are usually tailored to the singers and bands who perform them and who are often their own songwriters. Before rock took over, covers of Broadway songs by pop performers often greatly contributed to the success of those songs and of their shows. Now, few pop performers make cover recordings of other people's songs.

There were some successful early rock musicals, including *Hair, Godspell,* and *Jesus Christ Superstar.* These shows don't have strong books or lyrics, to say the least. The latter two are both basically concept musicals with stories familiar enough not to need real dramatic coherence; audiences can fill in the gaps themselves. *Hair* is practically plotless, and most of its song lyrics are illustrative lists rather than dramatic constructions. With the weaknesses in their books and lyrics and with their rather soft rock scores, all three shows were very much of their moment, appealing as they did to the baby boomer generation's disaffection with society, government, religion, and the old pop music. All three—particularly *Hair*—often feel like nostalgia pieces when revived today. (The same might be true of *Rent* in thirty years.) All drew large crowds of younger audiences at a time when young people were looking for

Backdrop: 1972–1975

National   Nixon is reelected. The Watergate break-in and cover-up occur, beginning the downfall of his administration. He opens trade with China and is the first president to visit the Soviet Union. A cease-fire in Vietnam ends direct involvement of U.S. ground troops in the Indochinese war, but bombing continues. Vice President Spiro Agnew resigns during the Watergate investigation when he is charged with income tax evasion. Gerald Ford is appointed to replace him. Nixon is the first American president to resign and Ford the first president not to have been elected to either the presidency or vice presidency. He pardons Nixon. The Supreme Court rules the death penalty unconstitutional and, with *Roe v. Wade,* legalizes abortion. Congress passes the Age Discrimination in Employment Act. School new ways to lead their lives. However, this new audience was interested only in those particular shows and not in musicals in general. (They are still popular with many of today's younger people, especially in their movie versions.)

In 1972, operetta composer Rudolf Friml and gossip columnist Walter Winchell died. For the first time, the touring companies of Broadway shows earned a larger total gross than the shows on Broadway did. Fifties rock nostalgia and Bob Fosse's staging and choreography produced the two hits of the Broadway year. Otherwise, nothing much happened despite nearly fifty musical evenings opening during the year. *Dude (The Highway Life)* and *Via Galactica*, concept shows with music by Galt MacDermot, tried to cash in on his success with *Hair* but ran a total of 23 performances between them. Revivals included *A Funny Thing Happened on the Way to the Forum* (136 performances), with Pseudolus played by Phil Silvers (for whom the role had originally been written), and *Lost in the Stars* (39 performances). There were three successful revues: *Don't Bother Me, I Can't Cope* (1,065 performances), a twelve-person African American Broadway revue with music and lyrics by, and starring, Micki Grant; *Oh Coward!* (294 performances), a small-cast, off-Broadway revue of Noël Coward songs; and *Berlin to Broadway with Kurt Weill* (152 performances), a small-cast, off-Broadway revue of Weill's songs. The Coward and Weill revues—neither of which had any new songs—were the first real stirrings of what eventually has been referred to as jukebox musicals, although they're really jukebox revues.

desegregation causes violence in South Boston. Teamster boss Jimmy Hoffa disappears, never to reappear. The Vietnam War ends.

International Britain imposes direct rule over Northern Ireland. The Yom Kippur War is the fiercest Arab-Israeli conflict since 1948, with the United States and Russia on opposite sides. Israel and Egypt sign a disengagement agreement. Yasser Arafat's Palestine Liberation Organization helps create a civil war in Lebanon. Oil shortages, an Arab embargo, and rising grain prices begin a world monetary crisis and the worst recession since the thirties. Grenada gains independence after more than two hundred years of British rule. Argentine dictator Juan Perón dies. India announces that it has the atomic bomb. Hundreds of thousands die of famine in Bangladesh. Nationalist China's Chiang Kai-shek and Spain's Generalissimo Francisco Franco die. Saudi Arabia's King Faisal is assassinated. Political unrest, revolution, and terrorism break out all over the world till the end of the decade and on into the present.

Grease

MUSIC/LYRICS/BOOK: Jim Jacobs and Warren Casey

DIRECTOR: Tom Moore

CHOREOGRAPHER: Patricia Birch

PRODUCERS: Kenneth Waissman and Maxine Fox

CAST INCLUDES: Barry Bostwick, Marilu Henner, and Adrienne Barbeau

PERFORMANCES: 3,388 on Broadway after 128 performances off-Broadway

An affectionate spoof of 1950s high school greasers, their girls, and their rock-and-roll music, *Grease* was created by two unemployed actors and initially produced at a small, storefront, non-Equity theater in Chicago. It ran there for eight months, then was expanded and produced off-Broadway before transferring to Broadway. It succeeded *Fiddler on the Roof* as the longest-running show on Broadway; both parents and their children were able to laugh at the older generation when they were young. (It had the same effect on audiences as the 2002 musical comedy *Hairspray*, although the latter, being set in the sixties, has a much stronger sociopolitical agenda than the creators of *Grease* had in mind, as well as a leading female character played by a man in drag and a fat suit.) Cast replacements and road companies included such up-and-coming young performers as Treat Williams, Richard Gere, Patrick Swayze, and John Travolta. The glitzy 1994 revival (called *Grease!*) ran for nearly four years on Broadway and on the road. The score includes "Those Magic Changes," "Freddy, My Love," "Alone at a Drive-in Movie,"

New Developments Federal Express, Nike, and Microsoft are founded. Word processors begin to replace typewriters. The Heimlich maneuver is published. Sony introduces the Betamax, the first home videocassette recorder. Miller Lite beer is marketed.

Sports Bobby Fischer is the first American to win the world chess title; he gives up the title and is succeeded by Anatoly Karpov. George Foreman beats Joe Frazier for the world heavyweight boxing title; Muhammad Ali knocks Foreman out and regains the title, which he holds for four years. Secretariat wins U.S. horse racing's Triple Crown. With Jimmy Connors, Arthur Ashe, and Chris Evert winning at Wimbledon and Forest Hills, tennis racquet sales are the highest ever. Hank Aaron hits his 715th home run, breaking Babe Ruth's career record.

Art New York's World Trade Center and Chicago's Sears Tower open. Pablo Picasso dies. There are new paintings by, among others, de Kooning, Johns, Hockney, and Lichtenstein.

Music/Dance Benjamin Britten's opera adapted from Mann's *Death in Venice* has its premiere. *Mass*, by Leonard Bernstein and Stephen Schwartz, is the opening event of the John F. Kennedy Center for the Performing Arts in Washington, D.C. Russian ballet dancer Mikhail Baryshnikov defects to the West.

Publications *Life* magazine ends weekly publication after thirty-six years; it's eventually restored as a monthly. *Ms., People,* and *High Times* magazines begin publication. Among the new books

"Summer Nights," "Look at Me, I'm Sandra Dee," "Greased Lightnin'," and "Beauty School Dropout." The hit 1978 movie version, directed by Randal Kleiser and choreographed by Patricia Birch, starred Travolta, Olivia Newton-John, and Stockard Channing. The two leads in the 2007 Broadway revival were cast *American Idol*–style in a TV contest voted on by home viewers.

After the success of *Godspell* off-Broadway, Stephen Schwartz made his Broadway debut with *Pippin,* which he wrote while still in college. The show was rewritten to Fosse's concept, after which he had the writers locked out of rehearsals. A musical fable done without an intermission and set in the ninth century, it tells the story of Pippin, the Candide-like son of the emperor Charlemagne. With the help of a group of commedia dell'arte–like players, he spends the show searching for his "corner of the sky" and therefore for the meaning of life. He gets himself and us rather depressed in the process and learns at the end that the best way to lead your life is more or less to keep it simple and

Pippin

MUSIC/LYRICS: Stephen Schwartz
BOOK: Roger O. Hirson
DIRECTOR/CHOREOGRAPHER: Bob Fosse
DESIGNERS: Tony Walton (sets), Patricia Zipprodt (costumes), and Jules Fisher (lights)
PRODUCER: Stuart Ostrow
CAST INCLUDES: John Rubinstein, Ben Vereen, Irene Ryan, and Jill Clayburgh
PERFORMANCES: 1,944

are Halberstam's *The Best and the Brightest;* Pynchon's *Gravity's Rainbow;* Jong's *Fear of Flying;* Woodward and Bernstein's *All the President's Men;* Pirsig's *Zen and the Art of Motorcycle Maintenance;* Solzhenitsyn's *The Gulag Archipelago;* Comfort's *The Joy of Sex;* Stephen King's first novel, *Carrie;* Terkel's *Working* (source of the 1978 musical); and Doctorow's *Ragtime* (source of the 1998 musical).

TV   The TV shows M*A*S*H, The Waltons, Happy Days, The Rockford Files, Wheel of Fortune, and Saturday Night Live are introduced. Among the highest-rated shows of the four years are *All in the Family, Sanford and Son, Hawaii Five-O, The Waltons, Chico and the Man, The Six Million Dollar Man,* and *Rhoda.*

Pop Culture   Discotheques come back in style; disco recordings by such performers as Donna Summer and the Bee Gees dominate pop music until the end of the decade. McCoy's "The Hustle" sets off the most popular dance craze since the twist. Rock influenced by country-western music is popularized by groups like the Allman Brothers Band and ZZ Top. New pop recordings include McLean's "American Pie," Reddy's "I Am Woman," MacColl's "The First Time Ever I Saw Your Face," Albert's "Feelings," Sedaka and Greenfield's "Love Will Keep Us Together," Levine and Brown's "Tie a Yellow Ribbon Round the Ole Oak Tree," Fox and Gimbel's "Killing Me Softly with His Song," Weiss's "Rhinestone Cowboy," Croce's "Bad, Bad Leroy Brown," Wonder's "You Are the Sunshine of My Life," Frampton, Dylan's *Blood on the Tracks,* Springsteen's *Born to Run,* John's *Goodbye Yellow Brick Road,* the Rolling Stones' *Goat's Head Soup,* and McCartney and Wings' *Band on the Run.*

to tend your own garden, just as Candide learned before him. The often heavy-handed book and lyrics were saved by truly exciting work from director/choreographer Fosse (his first show since *Sweet Charity* six years earlier), by his designers, and by an excellent cast, particularly Vereen in the pseudo-*Cabaret* Emcee role of the Leading Player. In the score are "Magic to Do" (the opening of the show, introducing the Leading Player and his Players with black light, disconnected hands, and magic tricks), "Corner of the Sky" (Pippin's first song setting up his search), and "No Time at All" (advice sung to Pippin by his grandmother, who turns the number into an audience sing-along). *Pippin* was the first to use clips from the show in a TV commercial, which revolutionized Broadway advertising. *Pippin* was taped live at a Los Angeles performance starring Vereen, William Katt, Chita Rivera, and Martha Raye; David Sheehan directed and Kathryn Doby re-created Fosse's staging.

Sugar was an unsuccessful, unnecessary adaptation of the great 1959 Billy Wilder and I. A. L. Diamond movie comedy *Some Like It Hot*. Set in the twenties, it's about two musicians who, after witnessing the St. Valentine's Day massacre, flee by disguising themselves as women and joining an all-girl band on its way to Florida, where the girls in the band hope to find husbands among the wealthy and retired. Sugar is the name of the character played in the movie by Marilyn Monroe; she's the singer in the band. Champion locked the writers out of rehearsals, but to

Sugar

MUSIC: Jule Styne

LYRICS: Bob Merrill

BOOK: Peter Stone

DIRECTOR/CHOREOGRAPHER: Gower Champion

DESIGNERS: Robin Wagner (sets), Alvin Colt (costumes), and Martin Aronstein (lights)

PRODUCER: David Merrick

CAST INCLUDES: Robert Morse, Tony Roberts, Elaine Joyce, and Cyril Ritchard

PERFORMANCES: 505

Stage Among the new plays are Stoppard's *The Real Inspector Hound, Jumpers,* and *Travesties;* Shepard's *The Tooth of Crime;* Walker's *The River Niger;* Wilson's *The Hot l Baltimore;* Ayckbourn's *Absurd Person Singular, Absent Friends,* and *The Norman Conquests;* Shaffer's *Equus;* Piñero's *Short Eyes;* Fugard's *Sizwe Banzi Is Dead* and *The Island;* Mamet's *Sexual Perversity in Chicago;* and Pinter's *No Man's Land.*

Screen New movies include adaptations of Puzo's *The Godfather* (and *The Godfather, Part 2*); Dickey's *Deliverance;* Allen's *Play It Again, Sam;* Kesey's *One Flew over the Cuckoo's Nest;* Blatty's *The Exorcist;* and Benchley's *Jaws,* which begins the era of the movie blockbuster. Some other movies are *The Conversation; Superfly; Sounder; Mean Streets; American Graffiti; The Way We Were,* with a hit title song by Hamlisch and the Bergmans recorded by Barbra Streisand; *The Sting,* with a sound track adapted by Hamlisch that stirred a revival of interest in ragtime and particularly in the music of Scott less effect than when Fosse did the same thing with *Pippin*. The show was renamed *Some Like It Hot* in 2001 and had a long tour starring Tony Curtis (who'd played one of the young leads in the original movie) playing one of the supporting roles and singing and dancing for the first time in his long career.

In 1973, playwright/composer/lyricist/performer Sir Noël Coward died. The discount ticket office opened in Times Square, charging half price plus a small fee, with tickets available only on the day of performance. Other than Sondheim and Hugh Wheeler's *A Little Night Music*, again there was nothing much to report from on or off-Broadway. Cashing in on the nostalgia craze was a 604-performance revisal of Tierney, McCarthy, and Montgomery's 1919 *Irene*, starring Debbie Reynolds. The book was almost completely rewritten by Wheeler and Joseph Stein, and little of the original score was used. Gower Champion replaced director Sir John Gielgud during tryouts, undoubtedly a wise choice. The off-Broadway parody revue *El Grande de Coca-Cola* ran 1,114 performances. There were failed revivals of *The Desert Song* and *The Pajama Game*. A flop stage version of Lerner and Loewe's 1958 movie *Gigi* (103 performances), starring Alfred Drake, had some additional but not very effective songs.

The story of *A Little Night Music* is more conventional than those of most Sondheim shows, recounting the flirtations and affairs of a group of mostly cynical people gathered together for a

A Little Night Music

MUSIC/LYRICS: Stephen Sondheim
BOOK: Hugh Wheeler, based on Ingmar Bergman's 1955 film *Smiles of a Summer Night*
DIRECTOR: Harold Prince
CHOREOGRAPHER: Patricia Birch
DESIGNERS: Boris Aronson (sets), Florence Klotz (costumes), and Tharon Musser (lights)
PRODUCER: Harold Prince in association with Ruth Mitchell
CAST INCLUDES: Glynis Johns, Len Cariou, Laurence Guittard, and Hermione Gingold
PERFORMANCES: 601

Joplin; *Chinatown; Blazing Saddles; Young Frankenstein; Dog Day Afternoon; Monty Python and the Holy Grail; Amarcord; Day for Night;* and Fosse's *Lenny.* Stephen Sondheim and Anthony Perkins write the script of *The Last of Sheila.*

The few new movie musicals include Liza Minnelli and Joel Grey in Fosse's film version of *Cabaret,* as well as adaptations of *The Magic Flute, 1776, Jesus Christ Superstar, Godspell, Lost in the Stars,* and the truly awful versions of *Mame* and *Man of La Mancha.* Other movie musicals are Saint-Exupéry's fantasy *The Little Prince,* with a mediocre score by Lerner and Loewe; the Who's rock opera *Tommy,* with an all-star cast; *Lady Sings the Blues,* with Diana Ross as Billie Holiday; the animated *Charlotte's Web,* with a score by the Sherman brothers; *That's Entertainment,* a compilation of excerpts from MGM musicals; *Nashville;* the costly flop *At Long Last Love,* with a score of old Cole Porter songs; and *Funny Lady,* an unsuccessful sequel to *Funny Girl,* with Streisand, some old songs, and some new ones by Kander and Ebb.

weekend in the country in turn-of-the-century Sweden. The main characters are an actress, her former lover (a lawyer whom she still loves but he doesn't know it, although he still loves her), the lawyer's very young wife (who isn't ready to sleep with him yet), his son (who plays the cello and loves his father's young wife), the actress's current lover (an egotistic and rigid count), his cynical wife, and the lawyer's young maid looking for a good time—including with the lawyer's son—before she settles down to the humdrum prospect of marriage. The actress's mother, an elderly former courtesan, perhaps sums up the show best in "Liaisons," about the differences between then and now:

> Too many people muddle sex
> With mere desire,
> And when emotion intervenes,
> The nets descend.
> It should on no account perplex,
> Or worse, inspire.
> It's but a pleasurable means
> To a measurable end.
> Why does no one comprehend?
> Let us hope this lunacy is just a trend.

The show ends with almost all the characters getting what they want, an actual happy ending. Instead of a chorus, there's a quintet that comments on the action and supplies transitions between scenes. Almost all the music is in permutations of 3/4 time, so that the score is very nineteenth-century waltz-like. It's Sondheim's most accessible and financially successful show after *A Funny Thing Happened on the Way to the Forum*. Along with "Liaisons" and "Send in the Clowns" (sung by the actress when she thinks she's lost the lawyer for good), the score has "You Must Meet My Wife" (a duet for the actress and the lawyer), "Every Day a Little Death" (the virgin and the cynical wives compare notes), "A Weekend in the Country" (as the entire cast gets ready to go), and "The Miller's Son" (the maid's song about her decision to have fun while she can, and the eleven o'clock number). Harold Prince directed a disastrous film version in 1977 starring Elizabeth Taylor, Len Cariou, Diana Rigg, and Hermione Gingold.

Seesaw

MUSIC: Cy Coleman
LYRICS: Dorothy Fields
BOOK: Michael Bennett, adapted from William Gibson's 1958 play *Two for the Seesaw*
DIRECTOR: Michael Bennett
CHOREOGRAPHERS: Michael Bennett, Grover Dale, Bob Avian, and Tommy Tune
DESIGNERS: Robin Wagner (sets), Ann Roth (costumes), and Jules Fisher (lights)
PRODUCERS: 5 listed
CAST INCLUDES: Ken Howard, Michele Lee, and Tommy Tune
PERFORMANCES: 296

Based on a two-character play, *Seesaw* is about the brief affair between a rather staid, Midwestern attorney and a free-spirited, young New Yorker. It didn't pay back its investment. Michael Bennett took credit for the book because no one else would after it was almost completely rewritten out of town. He also took over as director out of town; it was his first time out as director/choreographer. In the score of *Seesaw* are "It's Not Where You Start, It's Where You Finish" and "Nobody Does It Like Me." The show is probably best remembered for having first focused attention on Tommy Tune.

Seesaw was Dorothy Fields's final show. The last of the three show-business Fields siblings to survive, she'd written books and/or lyrics for shows going all the way back to the early days of the Cotton Club.

> Of all lyricists [Dorothy Fields] was most able to keep abreast of the times. She utilized slang and idiomatic phrases without sounding forced or trendy, a skill which almost all other lyricists lacked. Her poetic lyricism never becomes cloying and her imagery remains sharp, fresh, and hip. . . . It's to her credit that she could successfully collaborate with as widely divergent stylists as Arthur Schwartz, Jerome Kern, and Cy Coleman. (Bloom, *American Song*, 647–48)

Raisin is a successful but not particularly memorable musical version of Hansberry's great drama about a black family struggling to get out of the ghetto in 1950s Chicago. The play didn't need musicalizing. The score includes "Whose Little Angry Man," "Runnin' to Meet the Man," "A Whole Lotta Sunlight," and "Measure the Valleys." It won the Tony for Best Musical.

National Lampoon's Lemmings was an off-Broadway revue; the first act was a series of sketches and songs, the second a parody of rock festivals. Most of the creative team and cast had been connected with *National Lampoon* magazine and/or Chicago's satiric improvisational theater the Second City and were soon involved with the groundbreaking TV series *Saturday Night Live*. Touring versions of *Lampoon* shows included such future stars as Gilda Radner, Harold Ramis, and Joe Flaherty, all of whom also started at the Second City and went on to *Saturday Night Live* or *SCTV*.

Raisin

MUSIC: Judd Woldin
LYRICS: Robert Brittan
BOOK: Robert Nemiroff and Charlotte Zaltzberg, adapted from Lorraine Hansberry's 1959 play *A Raisin in the Sun*
DIRECTOR/CHOREOGRAPHER: Donald McKayle
PRODUCER: Nemiroff (who'd been married to Hansberry)
CAST INCLUDES: Virginia Capers, Deborah Allen, and Ernestine Jackson
PERFORMANCES: 847

National Lampoon's Lemmings

MUSIC: Paul Jacobs
LYRICS: John Boni, Sean Kelly, Doug Kenney, and P. J. O'Rourke
SKETCHES: David Axelrod, Tony Hendra, Sean Kelly, and the cast
DIRECTOR/PRODUCER: Tony Hendra
CAST OF SEVEN INCLUDES: John Belushi, Chevy Chase, Gary Goodrow, Christopher Guest, Paul Jacobs, Mary-Jennifer Mitchell, and Alice Playten
PERFORMANCES: 350

Tommy Tune (1939–, born in Wichita Falls, Texas), six feet six inches tall, choreographed his own numbers for *Seesaw*. A singer/dancer, he also became a director/choreographer. He won Tony Awards in all four categories, nine in all. Among his shows as director/choreographer are *The Best Little Whorehouse in Texas*, *Grand Hotel*, *Nine*, and *The Will Rogers Follies*.

In 1974, writer/lyricist Dorothy Fields, performer Josephine Baker, Broadway columnist and TV host Ed Sullivan, comedian Jack Benny, and composer/performer/bandleader Duke Ellington died. The Broadway Equity minimum went up to $245 a week. There was an off-Broadway, circus-like, environmental revisal of *Candide*, with some new lyrics by Sondheim and a new book by Hugh Wheeler, directed by Prince, and choreographed by Patricia Birch. It moved to Broadway for 740 performances but was so expensive to produce (they had to tear apart the interior of the theater to reproduce the environmental feeling) that it didn't make its money back. (Prince and Birch also did a 1997 Broadway revival of this version—this time on a proscenium stage—starring Jim Dale and Andrea Martin, which also flopped.)

There was a 320-performance revisal of 1949's *Gentlemen Prefer Blondes* called *Lorelei*, with Carol Channing again playing the lead and some new songs by Styne, Comden, and Green. There were also a 120-performance revival of *Gypsy* starring Angela Lansbury, a 76-performance revival of *Where's Charley?* starring Raul Julia, and a nostalgic, 16-performance rewrite of the 1927 college football musical *Good News* starring former movie star Alice Faye in what had been a supporting role in the original show—and still was.

Again there was nothing much in the way of new musicals: there were now fewer shows per year and an even larger percentage of flops. *Words and Music,* a revue of songs with lyrics by, and starring, Sammy Cahn, ran 127 performances on Broadway, and *Sgt. Pepper's Lonely Hearts Club Band on the Road,* a revue of Beatles songs with a very thin plot, was directed by Tom O'Horgan and ran 66 performances off-Broadway.

The Frogs (8 scheduled performances) has music and lyrics by Stephen Sondheim; a book, based on the play by Aristophanes, by Burt Shevelove, who also directed it; and choreography by Carmen de Lavallade. It was produced by the Yale Repertory Theatre with a cast that included Larry Blyden, Alvin Epstein, de Lavallade, Christopher Durang, Meryl Streep, and Sigourney Weaver. Since most of its characters are frogs, it was produced in the pool at Yale and has rarely been done since. There was a flop Broadway revisal in 2004.

Mack and Mabel

MUSIC/LYRICS: Jerry Herman
BOOK: Michael Stewart
DIRECTOR/CHOREOGRAPHER: Gower Champion
DESIGNERS: Robin Wagner (sets), Patricia Zipprodt (costumes), and Tharon Musser (lights)
PRODUCER: David Merrick
CAST INCLUDES: Robert Preston, Bernadette Peters, and Lisa Kirk
PERFORMANCES: 66

A mixed-media failure about a doomed romance between self-absorbed silent filmmaker Mack Sennett and drug-addicted silent film star Mabel Normand, *Mack and Mabel* lost its entire investment. The combination of slapstick silent movie routines and a rather tragic love story doesn't jell. The score has many devotees, and several of the songs have become staples of the cabaret circuit, but each attempted revival of the show flops again. The score includes "Time Heals Everything," "Wherever He Ain't," and "I Won't Send Roses."

An excuse for Doug Henning's magic act, *The Magic Show* has almost no plot, a small cast and band, and a totally mediocre score by Schwartz, his third hit after *Godspell* and *Pippin*. It was a family show, meaning parents took their children.

Over Here! is a World War II comedy starring the two living Andrews Sisters, who, with their late sister, were a successful pop recording trio during the thirties and forties. In the show, they're searching for someone to be a new third in the trio while on a tour to entertain the troops. The woman they pick turns out to be a spy. The producers, director, choreographer, and designers of *Over Here!* had done the fifties nostalgia show *Grease* and were trying for the same kind of success with the forties.

> The songs were adept in their recreation of the forties-style big band sound but they never really had a life beyond parody. Also, the untheatricality of their style made this show practically a revue, since most of the songs were not sung as expressions of emotion by the characters. (Ken Bloom, *American Song,* 551)

True, but the show was a lot of fun, with lots of wonderful period dancing. The score includes "Since You're Not Around," "The Good-Time Girl (The VD Polka)," "Where Did the Good Times Go?", "The Big Beat," and "Charlie's Place." The Sherman brothers wrote the songs for Disney's 1964 film adaptation of Travers's 1934 children's novel *Mary Poppins* and for the Disney–Cameron Mackintosh stage adaptation, which opened in London in 2005 and on Broadway in 2006. They also wrote the songs for Disney's *Bedknobs and Broomsticks,* for Hanna-Barbera's 1973 animated adaptation of White's children's novel *Charlotte's Web,* and for the 1968 film adaptation of Fleming's 1964 children's novel *Chitty Chitty Bang Bang,* adapted into a stage musical that opened in London in 2002 and on Broadway in 2005, where it ran 285 performances.

The Magic Show

MUSIC/LYRICS: Stephen Schwartz

BOOK: Bob Randall, based on magic by Doug Henning

DIRECTOR/CHOREOGRAPHER: Grover Dale

DESIGNERS: David Chapman (sets), Randy Barcelo (costumes), and Richard Nelson (lights)

PRODUCERS: Joseph Beruh, Edgar Lansbury, and Ivan Reitman

CAST INCLUDES: Doug Henning and David Ogden Stiers

PERFORMANCES: 1,920

Over Here!

MUSIC/LYRICS: Richard M. and Robert B. Sherman

BOOK: Will Holt

DIRECTOR: Tom Moore

CHOREOGRAPHER: Patricia Birch

PRODUCERS: Maxine Fox and Kenneth Waissman

CAST INCLUDES: Patty and Maxine Andrews, Marilu Henner, Ann Reinking, John Travolta, and Treat Williams

PERFORMANCES: 341

In 1975, lyricist Noble Sissle and writer/lyricist P. G. Wodehouse, one of the creators of the Jerome Kern Princess musicals, died. There was a 304-performance revival of the Princess musical *Very Good Eddie*. After a three-week strike that stopped all performances of musicals on Broadway, the musicians' minimum rose to $350 a week.

Though 1975 was a much better year for the musical, it was still filled with far more short-run flops than hits, including a 9-performance run of *Lieutenant*, a fictionalized, rock-opera version of the trial of Lieutenant Calley for his role in the My Lai massacre. *The Rocky Horror Show* by Richard O'Brien, a campy, gender-bending, rock-based spoof of horror movies with Tim Curry and Meat Loaf in the cast, was a 32-performance flop. It had had successful runs in London and in Los Angeles but flopped again in a 2001 Broadway revival. (*The Rocky Horror Picture Show*, Sharman's 1975 movie version with Curry, Loaf, Susan Sarandon, and Barry Bostwick, was also a flop; however, it had some success as a late-night, cult movie.) *Rodgers and Hart*, a revue of their songs, ran 111 performances, and a revival of *Hello, Dolly!* with Pearl Bailey ran 51 performances.

Shenandoah

MUSIC: Gary Geld

LYRICS: Peter Udell

BOOK: James Lee Barrett, Peter Udell, and Philip Rose, adapted from Barrett's screenplay for the 1965 James Stewart movie

DIRECTOR: Philip Rose

CHOREOGRAPHER: Robert Tucker

PRODUCERS: Philip Rose and Gloria and Louis K. Shee

CAST INCLUDES: John Cullum

PERFORMANCES: 1,050

Shenandoah is a not particularly memorable show about a Virginia family trying to stay out of the Civil War. Written by the people who did *Purlie*, it was received poorly by the press and had a rocky start. Eventually—through publicity, word of mouth, and half-price tickets—it caught on as a family show and turned into a hit.

The Wiz

MUSIC/LYRICS: Charlie Smalls

BOOK: William F. Brown, adapted from L. Frank Baum's novel and the MGM movie *The Wizard of Oz*

DIRECTOR: Geoffrey Holder

CHOREOGRAPHER: George Faison

DESIGNERS: Tom H. John (sets), Geoffrey Holder (costumes), and Tharon Musser (lights)

PRODUCER: Ken Harper

CAST INCLUDES: Stephanie Mills, Tiger Haynes, Andre De Shields, and Hinton Battle

PERFORMANCES: 1,672

The Wiz is a funny, high-energy, African American reimagining of the classic *Wizard of Oz* book and movie. Financed by 20th Century Fox, it has the only score written by Smalls, who based his music on rhythm and blues, rock, and soul, with an occasional Caribbean flavor. The musical was revived unsuccessfully on Broadway in 1984. (In the 1978 movie version, Diana Ross played Dorothy as an adult New York school teacher—definitely not in Kansas anymore. It didn't work.) Although it was created for an all-black cast, *The Wiz* has also been done in multiracial "rainbow" productions. The score includes "Home," "I Was Born on the Day Before Yesterday," "Ease on Down the Road," and "Don't Nobody Bring Me No Bad News." It won seven Tony Awards, including Best Musical of the 1974–75 season.

A cynical, racy, bitterly funny, pseudo-Brechtian satire set in the Roaring Twenties, *Chicago* is about Roxie Hart, who becomes a celebrity when she goes on trial for murder. After she's found not guilty (even though she is), she and Velma Kelly—a fellow murderer also found not guilty through the manipulations of the same lawyer who got Roxie off—become vaudeville headliners. The world depicted in the show is totally lacking in morality. Written to Fosse's concept, it was done as if it were a vaudeville show, and many of the numbers are in the style of old vaudeville and revue performers such as Marilyn Miller, Rudy Vallee, Bing Crosby, Eddie Cantor, and Helen Morgan. "Mr. Cellophane," for example, is like Bert Williams's *Ziegfeld Follies* song "Nobody," and "When You're Good to Mama" is reminiscent of Sophie Tucker's "Some of These Days." Also in the score are "All That Jazz," "I Can't Do It Alone," "My Own Best Friend," "Me and My Baby," "Razzle Dazzle," and "Nowadays." Although the songs are pastiches of old vaudeville numbers, they're not there for entertainment alone: they define character, establish atmosphere, and carry a lot of the plot.

Chicago was Verdon's last Broadway show. She was ill for a while during the run and was replaced by Liza Minnelli. Ginger Rogers starred in *Roxie Hart*, the 1942 movie version of Watkins's play. The hit 1997 revival of *Chicago* (still running ten years later), directed by Walter Bobbie and choreographed by Ann Reinking (based on the Fosse original), had Reinking, Bebe Neuwirth, James Naughton, and Joel Grey in the cast. It started as a semi-concert staging—one costume per person and the band onstage—then got transferred to Broadway in the same form, where it's been running for longer than the original production (4,442 performances as of July 15, 2007). The Oscar-winning 2002 movie version (directed by Rob Marshall and starring Renée Zellweger, Catherine Zeta-Jones, Richard Gere, Queen Latifah, and John C. Reilly), along with Baz Luhrmann's 2001 movie *Moulin Rouge*, produced hope for a rebirth of the movie musical, albeit with MTV-style quick cutting during the musical numbers, which more often showcased directorial flash rather than the songs or the singing and dancing talents of the performers (rather justifiably, unfortunately, in *Chicago*). Movies such as *Ray* and *Dreamgirls* have continued the gradual rebirth of the big-budget movie musical, although flops like the movie adaptations of *Rent* and *The Producers* could hurt the cause.

Chicago

MUSIC: John Kander

LYRICS: Fred Ebb

BOOK: Fred Ebb and Bob Fosse, adapted from the 1926 play by Maurine Dallas Watkins

DIRECTOR/CHOREOGRAPHER: Bob Fosse

DESIGNERS: Tony Walton (sets), Patricia Zipprodt (costumes), and Jules Fisher (lights)

PRODUCERS: Robert Fryer and James Cresson

CAST INCLUDES: Gwen Verdon, Chita Rivera, Jerry Orbach, and Mary McCarty

PERFORMANCES: 923

A Chorus Line

MUSIC: Marvin Hamlisch

LYRICS: Edward Kleban

BOOK: James Kirkwood and Nicholas Dante, from Michael Bennett's concept (with Neil Simon contributing a few funny lines)

DIRECTOR/CHOREOGRAPHER: Michael Bennett

DESIGNERS: Robin Wagner (sets), Theoni V. Aldredge (costumes), and Tharon Musser (lights)

PRODUCER: The New York Shakespeare Festival and Joseph Papp

CAST INCLUDES: Donna McKechnie, Wayne Cilento, Priscilla Lopez, and Robert LuPone

PERFORMANCES: 6,137

Marvin Hamlisch (1944–, born in New York) made his Broadway debut with the music for *A Chorus Line*. He'd already had a pop hit with Leslie Gore's 1965 recording of "Sunshine, Lollipops, and Rainbows." His other shows include *They're Playing Our Song* and *The Goodbye Girl*. He's also written music for many movies, including Woody Allen's *Take the Money and Run* and *Bananas*. He won three Academy Awards in 1974: Best Dramatic Score and Best Song for *The Way We Were*, and Best Adapted or Original Score for his adaptation of Scott Joplin's music for *The Sting*.

Another huge triumph in the history of the American musical and a truly great work of theater, *A Chorus Line* made director/choreographer/conceiver Bennett a Broadway superstar. Based on taped recollections of some Broadway gypsies (chorus dancers), it was workshopped at Papp's off-Broadway Public Theater. (Workshopping was unheard of at the time, but partly because of *A Chorus Line*, it has now become a common practice before a show is given a full production.) The show ran briefly at the Public before opening on Broadway. It won the Pulitzer and nine Tony Awards, including Best Musical of the 1975–76 season, and ran for fifteen years, beating *Grease* and holding the long-run record until June 1997, when it was beaten—unfortunately—by *Cats*.

A Chorus Line is an intermissionless concept musical about a group of seventeen gypsies auditioning for eight spots in the chorus of a new Broadway musical, many of whom tell their individual life stories in the process. Zach, the director who is auditioning them, is a voice at the back of the house asking them questions about their lives and experience as he judges their work. Because he's in the audience—behind the audience, really—the audience members become witnesses, even fellow judges, of the process, since everything that happens onstage is directed at them as well as at Zach (who isn't a nice guy). The original production even used a *Cabaret*-like mirrored back wall at the end of the show, so the audience saw itself as part of the final chorus line. In this way, the show transcends its show business subject matter and becomes universal—another take on the American dream, this one about looking for fulfilling, rewarding work. The score includes "I Can Do That," "At the Ballet," "Nothing," "The Music and the Mirror," "Dance: Ten; Looks: Three," "One," and "What I Did for Love." (The last two became hit songs.) The show was made into a terrible movie in 1985, directed by Richard Attenborough. Since it's a true stage piece in which a live audience and a live director are part of what the show is about, any movie version was doomed to fail. The 2006 Broadway revival (325 performances as of July 15, 2007), like the 1997 revival of *Chicago*, is a faithful re-creation of the original production.

Suggested Watching and Listening

Chicago

The following number is on *Broadway's Lost Treasures III* (Acorn Media DVD).

- ■ "All I Care About" (performed by Jerry Orbach and the girls): Lawyer Billy Flynn is a perfect hypocrite and, therefore, a very successful lawyer.

All of the following suggestions are available on the original-cast recording (Arista CD) and on the 2002 movie version (Miramax Home Entertainment DVD), respectively.

- ■ "All That Jazz" (performed by Chita Rivera and the company, and by Catherine Zeta-Jones and the company): The opening number is led by Velma.
- ■ "Mr. Cellophane" (performed by Barney Martin, and by John C. Reilly): Roxie's husband, Amos, sings his woes.
- ■ "Razzle Dazzle" (performed by Jerry Orbach and the company, and by Richard Gere and the company): Billy Flynn explains his strategy for getting Roxie off on the murder charges.
- ■ "Nowadays" (performed by Gwen Verdon and Chita Rivera, and by Renée Zellweger and Catherine Zeta-Jones): Roxie and Velma's vaudeville act, and the end of the show.

A Chorus Line

All of the following suggestions for numbers from this 1975 musical are available on the original-cast recording (Sony CD).

- ■ "I Can Do That" (performed by Wayne Cilento)
- ■ "At the Ballet" (performed by Carole Bishop, Nancy Lane, and Kay Cole)
- ■ "Nothing" (performed by Priscilla Lopez)
- ■ "Dance: Ten; Looks: Three" (performed by Pamela Blair)
- ■ "One" (performed by the company)
- ■ "What I Did for Love" (performed by Priscilla Lopez and the company)

Grease

The following number from this 1972 show is available on the video *That's Dancing!* (MGM VHS).

- ■ "Summer Nights" (performed by Barry Bostwick, Carole Demas, and the American Dance Machine): The young leads tell their separate groups of friends about their summer romances.

The following numbers are from the 1978 movie, available on Paramount DVD.

- ■ "Look at Me, I'm Sandra Dee" (performed by Stockard Channing and the girls): Making fun of a popular teen movie actress.
- ■ "Greased Lightnin'" (performed by John Travolta, Jeff Conaway, and the boys): The boys sing about a car.
- ■ "Beauty School Dropout" (performed by Frankie Avalon, Didi Conn, and the girls): A dream sequence with Avalon as Teen Angel.

A Little Night Music

All the following numbers from this 1973 musical are on the original-cast recording (Sony CD).

- "You Must Meet My Wife" (performed by Glynis Johns and Len Cariou): It's a duet for the actress and her former lover.
- "Every Day a Little Death" (performed by Patricia Elliott and Victoria Mallory): This duet is for two unhappy wives.
- "The Miller's Son" (performed by D. Jamin-Bartlett): The maid is very honest about how she'll live her life till she marries the miller's son.

Mack and Mabel

The following numbers from this 1974 show are available on the original-cast recording (Decca U.S. CD).

- "I Won't Send Roses" (performed by Robert Preston)
- "Wherever He Ain't" (performed by Bernadette Peters)
- "Time Heals Everything" (performed by Bernadette Peters)

Over Here

The number "Charlie's Place" (performed by Donna McKechnie, Wayne Cilento, and the American Dance Machine) is available on the video *That's Dancing!* (MGM VHS).

Pippin

The following numbers from this show are available on VCI video and DVD.

- The opening sequence: "Magic to Do" (performed by Ben Vereen, Chita Rivera, and the players)
- "Corner of the Sky" (performed by William Katt): Pippin, in his opening number, sets up his quest.
- The war sequence: "War Is a Science" (performed by Benjamin Rayson, William Katt, Christopher Chadman, and the players): It's done as a parody minstrel number with interlocutor and end men.
- "Glory" (performed by Ben Vereen and the players): Pippin rejects war.
- The sex sequence: "With You" (performed by William Katt and the players): Pippin gets exhausted by too much sex.

The Wiz

All the suggestions are available on the 1975 original-cast recording (Atlantic CD).

- "Soon As I Get Home" (performed by Stephanie Mills): This is Dorothy in Oz.
- "Ease on Down the Road" (performed by Stephanie Mills and Hinton Battle): It's the show's version of "Follow the Yellow Brick Road."
- "Don't Nobody Bring Me No Bad News" (performed by Mabel King): The wicked witch makes her attitude toward life crystal clear.

From Pacific Overtures to Evita

The party's over
It's time to call it a day.
They've burst your pretty balloon
And taken the moon away.
It's time to wind up
The masquerade.
Just make your mind up,
The piper must be paid.
—"THE PARTY'S OVER," *BELLS ARE RINGING,*
LYRICS BY BETTY COMDEN AND ADOLPH GREEN

How did Broadway producers try to get audiences into the theater, especially as ticket prices kept rising? Enter the super-production, which brought with it the super-director/choreographer. Harold Prince is the primary exception: a super-director who isn't a choreographer as well. Also with the exception of Prince, who was a producer first, the super-director/choreographers all started as dancers and, unlike the earlier directors of musicals, had little or no experience with straight plays or with the difficulties of structuring a show dramatically. Along with their designers, they gradually took control of the musical and became its *auteurs.* Even when they did shows that were little more than well-constructed star vehicles like *Hello, Dolly!,* only the stars were usually able to maintain their individuality; almost everything else tended to be overpowered by the star turns of the super-director/choreographers and their designers.

The trend began innocently and well with Agnes de Mille's groundbreaking conceptual ballets for *Oklahoma!* and *Carousel.* By using dance to help tell the story and define the characters, she took on some of the jobs usually done by the writers of lyrics and dialogue and by the director. Jerome Robbins (with shows like *On the Town*) and Michael Kidd (with shows like *Guys and Dolls*) continued the exploration of de Mille's use of dance, which reached its first full flowering with director/choreographer Robbins's *West Side Story* and *Fiddler on the Roof*. It progressed through the work of Prince—who worked with several choreographers and whose production concepts got more elaborate with the passing years—and of director/choreographers like Gower Champion and Bob Fosse, followed by Michael Bennett and Tommy Tune. Unlike Robbins and Bennett, whose styles changed depending on the differing needs of each show, most of these men have an identifiable style; each has his own way of reaching out for the audience's approval, just as the old-time stars used to do.

As the seventies progressed, super-productions frequently stopped needing stars altogether as the shows got more chilly and faceless, technologically expensive, and dance- and/or spectacle-heavy—glittering shells with little or

Backdrop: 1976–1979

National Jimmy Carter is elected president, defeating President Ford. He pardons almost all Vietnam-era draft dodgers. Capital punishment is reinstated. Chicago's first Mayor Daley dies. Data show that 451 U.S. companies control 70 percent of U.S. manufacturing assets, up from 50 percent in 1960. The leveraged buyout is pioneered and junk bonds are soon being used for financing. America officially recognizes the People's Republic of China. Jonestown, Guyana, is the scene of the mass suicide of almost nine hundred people by drinking cyanide-laced Kool-Aid; they are followers of cult leader Jim Jones, a former San Francisco clergyman. Dan White shoots San Francisco mayor George Moscone and gay supervisor Harvey Milk. Many residents whose houses were built over an abandoned toxic waste dump are evacuated from Love Canal, New York. Some 144,000 people are evacuated after an accident at the Three Mile Island nuclear generating station near Harrisburg, Pennsylvania. Jerry Falwell founds the Moral Majority.

International Unemployment rises throughout the world. China's chairman Mao Zedong and premier Jou En-lai die. Pope Paul VI dies, is succeeded by John Paul I, who soon dies and is succeeded by John Paul II. China and the Soviet Union end their treaty of friendship. Rioting in South Africa is violently suppressed. A white South African magistrate rules that security police were blameless in the death of black leader Steve Biko. OPEC raises oil prices, creating a major oil crisis. The Shiite Muslim Ayatollah Ruhollah Khomeini takes over Iran. President Carter engineers a peace accord between Egypt and Israel. Margaret Thatcher becomes the United Kingdom's first woman prime minister. An Irish terrorist no good writing in their books and music that was often forgettable or worse. ("You cannot walk out of a show humming the set" is an old but true cliché; it's not too easy to hum the directing or choreography either.) A show that must have spectacle to survive is a second-rate show. (Revivals that have stripped the extraneous spectacle from Prince's original production of Sondheim's *Sweeney Todd* have made the show itself seem better, for instance. The same is true of revivals of *Pacific Overtures*.) The notion that directors, choreographers, and designers need to save a show rather than serve it eventually made it seem as though they also needed to start with second-rate (or worse) material in order to *have* to save it. (Tommy Tune seems particularly guilty of doing that.) Maybe they just don't know the difference.

In 1976, songwriter Johnny Mercer, singer/actor Paul Robeson, and designer Jo Mielziner died. It wasn't a good year for musical theater, with flops by

bomb kills Queen Elizabeth's cousin Lord Mountbatten. Nicaraguan dictator Anastasio Somoza flees the country, which is taken over by Sandinista rebels.

New Developments Apple Computer is founded. Word processors begin revolutionizing offices with workstations that share central computers. Fax machines become popular. The Orient Express, in service since 1883, makes its last trip from Paris to Istanbul. The first MRI scanner is tested. The world's last known case of smallpox is reported. Blue jeans sales in the United States top five hundred million pairs, up from two hundred million in 1967. Perrier water is introduced in the United States. Congress moves to ban U.S. manufacture of nearly all aerosol products containing fluorocarbons in order to protect the Earth's ozone layer. The world's first test-tube baby is born. The first recombinant DNA product—human insulin—is produced in California. Sony's Walkman cassette player is introduced.

Sports Chris Evert, Jimmy Connors, Björn Borg, Martina Navratilova, John McEnroe, and Tracy Austin win important tennis tournaments. Ali loses his heavyweight boxing title to Leon Spinks, then regains it. Affirmed wins horse racing's Triple Crown. The first legal gambling casino outside Nevada opens in Atlantic City, New Jersey.

Art Painters Norman Rockwell and Giorgio de Chirico die, as do Josef Albers, Max Ernst, and Man Ray. There are new paintings by Warhol, Hockney, Johns, and Wyeth, among others. Neo-expressionist art is introduced. Christo covers three miles of footpaths with nylon in Kansas City's Loose Park.

Music/Dance Sarah Caldwell is the first woman to conduct at the Metropolitan Opera House. Glass and Wilson's opera *Einstein on the Beach* premieres.

Sondheim, Rodgers, Harnick, Bernstein, Lerner, Merrick, and Prince. The new top Broadway ticket price for a musical was $17.50.

Among the revivals were *Oh, Calcutta!* (5,959 performances) at a small theater in the Broadway area; *The Threepenny Opera* (307 performances), starring Raul Julia; *Fiddler on the Roof* (167 performances), starring Zero Mostel; the Houston Grand Opera's production of *Porgy and Bess* (122 performances), with almost all the cuts restored; a failed revival of *Guys and Dolls* with an all-black cast; and a nearly yearlong run of *My Fair Lady.*

Gower Champion was the director/choreographer of a 7-performance attempt at retelling Shakespeare as a rock musical called *Rockabye Hamlet,* written by Cliff Jones, with Beverly D'Angelo, Judy Gibson, and Meat Loaf in the cast. George Abbott (nearly ninety years old) directed and Patricia Birch choreographed *Music Is,* an 8-performance attempt at updating Shakespeare's *Twelfth Night,* with a score by Richard Adler, lyrics by Will Holt, and book by Abbott.

Rex (48 performances), by Richard Rodgers, Sheldon Harnick, and Sherman Yellen, was based on the life of Henry VIII of England (and his six wives). Harold Prince was brought in to try to save it, but nothing helped; it was impossible to make the king into a sympathetic musical theater hero.

Publications The cartoon strip *Garfield* begins syndication. New books include *The Hite Report: A Nationwide Study of Female Sexuality,* Morrison's *Song of Solomon,* Irving's *The World According to Garp,* Mailer's *The Executioner's Song,* Wolfe's *The Right Stuff,* Styron's *Sophie's Choice,* and Puig's *The Kiss of the Spider Woman* (source of the 1990 musical).

Radio/TV TVs are in 98 percent of American households. Among the new shows during the four years are *The Muppet Show, Charlie's Angels, The MacNeil/Lehrer Report, The Love Boat, Fantasy Island, Taxi, Dallas, Diff'rent Strokes,* and a miniseries adapted from Haley's *Roots,* which runs for eight consecutive nights. Top-rated shows are *Happy Days, Baretta, M*A*S*H, Laverne and Shirley, 60 Minutes, Three's Company, Mork and Mindy,* and *That's Incredible.* Garrison Keillor begins broadcasting *A Prairie Home Companion* on National Public Radio.

Pop Culture Punk rock, a reaction against the mainstreaming of rock and roll and of disco, gets popularized by bands like the Sex Pistols, Blondie, and the Ramones. New pop recordings include Johnston's "I Write the Songs," Brooks's "You Light Up My Life," Miller's "Fly Like an Eagle," Chicago's "If You Leave Me Now," Joel's "Just the Way You Are," Jagger and Richards's "Miss You," Jabara's "Last Dance," Mangione's "Feels So Good," Steely Dan's "Peg," Loggins and McDonald's "What a Fool Believes," Stewart's "Do Ya Think I'm Sexy?" and "Tonight's the Night (Gonna Be Alright)," and *Frampton Comes Alive,* Fleetwood Mac, Queen's *A Night at the Opera,* Costello's *My Aim Is True,* The Eagles' *Hotel California,* and Wonder's *Songs in the Key of Life.* Eleven concertgoers are crushed in a stampede for seats at a Cincinnati concert by the Who.

1600 Pennsylvania Avenue, a 7-performance flop for Leonard Bernstein and Alan Jay Lerner, was a preachy and lugubrious concept musical that wore its liberal heart on its sleeve. Mostly paid for by the Coca-Cola Company—which hoped to use it as part of its bicentennial promotional plan—the show presented an upstairs-downstairs look at U.S. presidents and their wives from George Washington to Teddy Roosevelt (played by the same two actors throughout), and at their African American house staff over the years (played by another pair of actors throughout). Bernstein's last Broadway show, the score is mostly excellent. There's no original-cast recording, but the score has been reworked as a concert piece called *A White House Cantata.*

Home Sweet Homer—a musical by Mitch Leigh, Charles Barr, Forman Brown, Roland Kibbee, and Albert Marre, based on *The Odyssey* and starring Yul Brynner—closed after its opening-night performance. *The Baker's Wife,* by Stephen Schwartz (composer of *Godspell* and *Pippin*) and Joseph Stein (author of the book of *Fiddler on the Roof*), was adapted from the 1940 French film. Producer David Merrick closed it out of town. There've been a couple of attempts at redoing it, but they too have failed. It's occasionally revived in smaller, regional productions.

Stage   New plays include Rabe's *Streamers,* Shange's *For Colored Girls Who Have Considered Suicide/When the Rainbow Is Enuf,* Mamet's *American Buffalo,* Shepard's *The Curse of the Starving Class,* Leonard's *Da* and *A Life,* Wilson's *The 5th of July* and *Talley's Folly,* Pinter's *Betrayal,* Churchill's *Cloud Nine,* Cristofer's *The Shadow Box,* and Shaffer's *Amadeus.* Steppenwolf Theatre begins life in a Chicago suburb. Shepard's *Buried Child* wins the Pulitzer Prize after it closes off-Broadway. (None of his plays made it to Broadway until the unsuccessful Steppenwolf revival of *Buried Child* in 1996.)

Screen   New movies include an adaptation of Woodward and Bernstein's *All the President's Men, Network, National Lampoon's Animal House, Rocky, Taxi Driver, Annie Hall, Manhattan, Close Encounters of the Third Kind, Star Wars, Halloween, Superman, Kramer vs. Kramer, Apocalypse Now,* and—the beginning of international recognition of the Australian film industry—*Breaker Morant, Mad Max,* and *My Brilliant Career.*

Among the movie musicals are the disco movie *Saturday Night Fever,* with songs by the Bee Gees, including the title song, "Stayin' Alive," and "How Deep Is Your Love?"; *That's Entertainment, Part 2;* the remake of *A Star Is Born,* with Williams and Streisand's hit song "Evergreen"; Liza Minnelli in *New York, New York,* with old standards and some new songs by Kander and Ebb, most notably the title song; *The Last Waltz,* a documentary about The Band's farewell concert; *American Hot Wax,* about rock-and-roll disc jockey Alan Freed; *The Buddy Holly Story; Elvis,* a biography of Presley; and Fosse's *All That Jazz.* Movies based on Broadway musicals are *Grease,* with additional songs by Gibb, Farrar, St. Louis, and Simon; *The Wiz; Hair;* and Prince's adaptation of *A Little Night Music.*

Pacific Overtures

MUSIC/LYRICS: Stephen Sondheim
BOOK: John Weidman, with additional material by Hugh Wheeler
DIRECTOR: Harold Prince
CHOREOGRAPHER: Patricia Birch
DESIGNERS: Boris Aronson (sets), Florence Klotz (costumes), and Tharon Musser (lights)
PRODUCER: Harold Prince, in association with Ruth Mitchell
CAST INCLUDES: Mako and Sab Shimono
PERFORMANCES: 193

The Robber Bridegroom

MUSIC: Robert Waldman
LYRICS/BOOK: Alfred Uhry, adapted from Eudora Welty's novella
DIRECTOR: Gerald Freedman
CHOREOGRAPHER: Donald Saddler
PRODUCERS: John Houseman, Margot Harley, and Michael B. Kapon
CAST INCLUDES: Barry Bostwick
PERFORMANCES: 145

Bubbling Brown Sugar

MUSIC: Danny Holgate
LYRICS: Loften Mitchell and Emme Kemp, plus songs from the 1920s and 1930s by Duke Ellington, Sissle and Blake, Andy Razaf, Fats Waller, and others
BOOK: Loften Mitchell
DIRECTOR: Robert M. Cooper
CHOREOGRAPHER: Billy Wilson
PRODUCERS: J. Lloyd Grant, Richard Bell, Robert M. Cooper, and Ashton Springer
CAST INCLUDES: Avon Long and Josephine Premice
PERFORMANCES: 766

Eve Merriam's *The Club* (667 performances), a small-cast, off-Broadway, satiric, feminist concept musical, is set in an all-male club at the turn of the century. The men are played by seven women in drag. The songs all date from the period and show how sexist the times were. It was Tommy Tune's first show as director/choreographer.

Pacific Overtures is about the arrival of American imperialism to the shores of Japan when Admiral Perry opened trade there in the 1850s and about how much Japanese culture was lost in the name of progress. The show lost its entire investment, and because Prince was having too much trouble raising money for his projects, it was the last one he produced on his own.

> Prince employed some of the conventions of Kabuki and Noh theater; Boris Aronson's deceptively simple and very beautiful sets used screens and a *hanamichi* (runway), and were changed by stagehands wearing black. There was a "reciter" . . . who narrated, sometimes commenting on the action, sometimes playing a role. And until the final scene, by which time Japan was completely Westernized, all the roles were played by men. (Gruber, *Original Cast! The Seventies*, 67–69)

Pacific Overtures has had several successful revivals in smaller, simpler productions.

The Robber Bridegroom follows the adventures of the title character as he searches for his bride-to-be abducted by her wicked stepmother. The year before its Broadway production, it played 15 performances off-Broadway with a cast that included Kevin Kline and Patti LuPone. It's now usually considered an underserved flop and is frequently and successfully revived by smaller theater companies. The score has a country-western flavor.

Bubbling Brown Sugar, featuring a predominantly black cast, is a revue of the history of Harlem's songs and dances, tied together as a tour of Harlem in the twenties and thirties.

In 1977, performers Charlie Chaplin, Zero Mostel, Groucho Marx, Cyril Ritchard, Ethel Waters, Bing Crosby, and Elvis Presley died. It was a mediocre year for the musical, with one big hit. A new version of the 1938 Olsen and Johnson revue *Hellza-poppin'*, starring an apparently very difficult Jerry Lewis, closed out of town at a loss of well over a million dollars. Beatles impersonators performed in the multimedia revue *Beatlemania* (929 performances). Yul Brynner and Constance Towers in *The King and I* (696 performances), Richard Kiley in *Man of La Mancha* (124 performances), *Hair* (108 performances), and *Jesus Christ Superstar* (96 performances) were among the revivals.

Annie is a Tony Award–winning family show about how the little orphan Annie—with her orphan friends and her dog, Sandy—successfully escapes the wiles of evil Miss Hannigan, who runs the orphanage, and ends up being adopted by the impossibly wealthy and suitably named Daddy Warbucks. It's Strouse's biggest hit, bigger even than *Bye Bye Birdie*. Since it involved children and a dog, Jule Styne called it "*Oliver!* in drag." He had a point, but the show unquestionably works (as does *Oliver!*). It was one of the most financially successful shows of the decade, was filmed by John Huston in 1982, spawned an unsuccessful 1993 off-Broadway sequel called *Annie Warbucks,* had a badly received 1997 Broadway revival starring Nell Carter, and was broadcast in 2000 in a successful TV version starring Kathy Bates, Alan Cumming, Audra McDonald, and Victor Garber. The score includes "Easy Street," "It's the Hard-Knock Life," and, of course, "Tomorrow."

A four-character, four-chorus show with a small onstage orchestra, *I Love My Wife* was a moderately successful comedy about wife-swapping (called swinging in the seventies). It now seems dated in its attitude toward women, but it seemed that way even then.

The Act is about the creating of a Las Vegas nightclub act for a star making a comeback and is interspersed with her biographical memories. It's basically a one-woman show tailored for Minnelli; the rest of the cast consists of Nelson in the nonsinging role of her ex-husband and a six-person backup group. Scorsese had directed her in the movie *New York, New York* (with new songs by Kander and Ebb), and Minnelli insisted he be hired to direct *The Act,* although he'd never directed for the stage and apparently wasn't very good at it. Gower Champion was brought in out of town to help. The show ran strictly on the strength of Minnelli's drawing power. There was a slight scandal when it was

Annie

MUSIC: Charles Strouse
LYRICS: Martin Charnin
BOOK: Thomas Meehan, based on the comic strip *Little Orphan Annie*
DIRECTOR: Martin Charnin
CHOREOGRAPHER: Peter Gennaro
DESIGNERS: David Mitchell (sets), Theoni V. Aldredge (costumes), and Judy Rasmuson (lights)
PRODUCERS: Mike Nichols, Irwin Meyer, Stephen R. Friedman, and Lewis Allen
CAST INCLUDES: Andrea McArdle, Reid Shelton, and Dorothy Loudon
PERFORMANCES: 2,377, after trying out at the Goodspeed Opera House

I Love My Wife

MUSIC: Cy Coleman
LYRICS/BOOK: Michael Stewart
DIRECTOR: Gene Saks
CHOREOGRAPHER: Onna White
PRODUCERS: Terry Allen Kramer and Harry Rigby
CAST INCLUDES: Lenny Baker, Joanna Gleason, Ilene Graff, and James Naughton
PERFORMANCES: 857

The Act

MUSIC: John Kander
LYRICS: Fred Ebb
BOOK: George Furth
DIRECTOR: Martin Scorsese
CHOREOGRAPHER: Ron Lewis
DESIGNERS: Tony Walton (sets), Halston (costumes), and Tharon Musser (lights)
PRODUCERS: the Shubert Organization, Cy Feuer, and Ernest H. Martin
CAST INCLUDES: Liza Minnelli and Barry Nelson
PERFORMANCES: 233

revealed during the run of the show that she was lip-synching at a couple of spots during heavy dance numbers; since the whole show was highly amplified, it was difficult to tell the difference. *The Act* was the first show to raise ticket prices to $25. The score includes "City Lights" and "It's the Strangest Thing."

Side by Side by Sondheim

MUSIC/LYRICS: Stephen Sondheim

BOOK/DIRECTOR: Ned Sherrin

CHOREOGRAPHER: Bob Howe

DESIGNERS: Peter Docherty (sets), Florenz Klotz (costumes), and Ken Billington (lights)

PRODUCER: Harold Prince in association with Ruth Mitchell and the Income Company, Ltd.

CAST OF FOUR INCLUDES: Millicent Martin, Julia McKenzie, David Kernan, and Ned Sherrin

PERFORMANCES: 390

Side by Side by Sondheim is an informal, frequently revived, four-person revue (including a narrator) of pre-1977 Sondheim songs from various sources, including some for which he wrote only the lyrics. It was first produced with the same cast in London, where it ran for three years. The British producers were H. M. Tennent, Ltd. and Cameron Mackintosh at the beginning of his incredibly successful career.

In 1978, singer Ruth Etting and producer Max Gordon died. Production values were getting more elaborate and expensive. It was a year of interesting musical failures and not-always-interesting successes; the general quality of the writing and the music was getting noticeably worse. The British were coming: Andrew Lloyd Webber and Tim Rice's *Evita* opened in London.

Carol Channing starred in a 145-performance revival of *Hello, Dolly!* and Sammy Davis Jr. in a short-lived revival of *Stop the World—I Want to Get Off*, which was filmed. *Timbuktu!* (243 performances) was a reworking of *Kismet* for an African American cast starring Eartha Kitt, Melba Moore, and Gilbert Price. Choreographer Lee Theodore formed the American Dance Machine to re-create and preserve dance numbers from as many old musicals as possible. The top ticket price for a straight play went up to $20. Probably the best show of the year was a revue of old Fats Waller songs.

Cameron Mackintosh

(1946–, born in Enfield, England) after a few tries had his first big hit with *Side by Side by Sondheim* in London in 1976 before bringing it to Broadway. He then produced some successful West End revivals before linking up with Andrew Lloyd Webber. Since then he's produced such gigantic hits as *Cats*, *Les Misérables*, *The Phantom of the Opera*, and *Miss Saigon*. He's one of the only producers now working on Broadway whose name helps advance sales and whose mark is on his shows.

Ain't Misbehavin', which presented an African American cast in a revue of songs written and/or performed by Fats Waller, is often revived. It won the Tony for Best Musical even though it's a jukebox revue with basically no dialogue. A 1988 revival with the same cast was taped in performance.

There were several other new revues as well. *Eubie!* (439 performances) was a revue of Eubie Blake and Noble Sissle songs that had Gregory and Maurice Hines in the cast. *Dancin'* (1,774 performances), conceived and set by director/choreographer Bob Fosse to various already-existing pieces of music, was an all-dance revue with a cast of sixteen that included Ann Reinking and Wayne Cilento. *Runaways* (267 Broadway performances after 80 off-Broadway), written and directed by Elizabeth Swados and produced by Joseph Papp and his New York Shakespeare Festival, was a revue about runaway kids performed by a cast of young unknowns, including Diane Lane, Trini Alvarado, Josie de Guzman, and some real runaways.

Studs Terkel's book *Working* is an oral history based on interviews with hundreds of Americans about their jobs. The show tried out at the Goodman Theatre in Chicago—appropriately, since Terkel is a Chicagoan. It's a cross between a revue and a concept musical, and, although it flopped on Broadway, it's often revived by community theaters and colleges. The original production lost over a million dollars. There was a mediocre TV version produced by PBS.

As is clear from the seven producers for *Ain't Misbehavin'*, money for shows was getting more and more difficult to find; six producers and a producing company are listed in the credits for *On the Twentieth Century*. It's a farce about a 1930s Broadway producer trying to convince a glamorous movie actress (and former lover), whom he'd discovered, to star in his new play so that he won't go bankrupt. Almost the entire show takes place on the title train on its way from Chicago to New York. (The play had been turned into a very successful 1934 movie starring John Barrymore and Carole Lombard.) It was the first unalloyed comedy Prince had directed in years.

> Comden and Green's book and lyrics recalled the youthful enthusiasm and playfulness of their best shows. Coleman's score, his most ambitious, employed a variety of musical styles while still remaining a unified whole with a single voice (Bloom, *American Song*, 542).

The score is mostly parody operetta and not particularly memorable at first hearing (not necessarily a flaw). In it are the title song, "Veronique," "Our Private World," "I've Got It All," "Babette," and "The Legacy." A sign of the growing emphasis on spectacle, the show had a gorgeous, multidimensional, frequently changing, art deco set, including the engine of the train

---

Ain't Misbehavin'

SCORE: Thomas "Fats" Waller, Luther Henderson (arranger)

DIRECTOR: Richard Maltby Jr., from an idea by Maltby and Murray Horwitz

MUSICAL STAGING: Arthur Faria

DESIGNERS: John Lee Beatty (sets), Randy Barcelo (costumes), and Pat Collins (lights)

PRODUCERS: seven listed, including the Shubert Organization

CAST INCLUDES: Nell Carter, André De Shields, Amelia McQueen, Ken Page, and Charlaine Woodard

PERFORMANCES: 1,565 on Broadway after first opening at the Manhattan Theatre Club

---

Working

SCORE: Craig Carnelia, Micki Grant, Mary Rodgers, Susan Birkenhead, Stephen Schwartz, and James Taylor

BOOK: Stephen Schwartz, adapted from Studs Terkel's book

DIRECTOR: Stephen Schwartz

CHOREOGRAPHER: Onna White

PRODUCERS: Stephen R. Friedman and Irwin Meyer

CAST INCLUDES: Patti LuPone and Bob Gunton (soon to be Evita and Juan Perón in Lloyd Webber's *Evita*), Joe Mantegna, and Lynne Thigpen

PERFORMANCES: 25

On the Twentieth Century

MUSIC: Cy Coleman

LYRICS/BOOK: Betty Comden and Adolph Green, adapted from Hecht and MacArthur's 1932 play *Twentieth Century*, itself adapted from Bruce Millholland's *The Napoleon of Broadway*

DIRECTOR: Harold Prince

CHOREOGRAPHER: Larry Fuller

DESIGNERS: Robin Wagner (sets), Florence Klotz (costumes), and Ken Billington (lights)

PRODUCERS: The Producers Circle II, Inc., Robert Fryer, Mary Lea Johnson, James Cresson, and Martin Richards

CAST INCLUDES: John Cullum, Madeline Kahn (replaced soon after opening by Judy Kaye), Imogene Coca, and Kevin Kline

PERFORMANCES: 449

in motion with Imogene Coca tied to the front. The show closed at a loss, having cost $1.2 million to produce. It made a star of Kevin Kline in a very funny, very physical performance.

After being workshopped at the Actors Studio, *The Best Little Whorehouse in Texas* opened off-Broadway and then moved to Broadway. It's based on the closing of a real Texas bordello known as the Chicken Ranch. (Hall, King, Masterson, and Tune are all Texans.) It has a pseudo-country-western sound and is a pleasant, harmless, frequently mediocre show—with excellent choreography by Tune. It made no demands whatsoever on its audience, many of whom attended simply because of the title and the TV ad. The unsuccessful 1982 movie starred Burt Reynolds and Dolly Parton, and there was an equally unsuccessful 2001 attempt at a revival starring Ann-Margret. The musical had a 1994 sequel, *The Best Little Whorehouse Goes Public,* a notoriously inept rip-off that closed quickly after deservedly humiliating reviews and with some openly admitted embarrassment on the part of its creators, including Tune.

Ballroom, Michael Bennett's first show after *A Chorus Line,* was intensively workshopped (with help from Larry Gelbart, Tommy Tune, and Ron Field, among others) and still never found itself. Set mostly in a Bronx ballroom patronized largely by middle-aged people, it focuses on a new widow who falls in love and has an affair with a married man she meets there. The show lost over $2 million.

The Best Little Whorehouse in Texas

MUSIC/LYRICS: Carol Hall

BOOK: Larry L. King and Peter Masterson, based on an article by King

DIRECTORS: Peter Masterson and Tommy Tune

MUSICAL STAGING: Tommy Tune

DESIGNERS: Marjorie Kellogg (sets), Ann Roth (costumes), and Dennis Parichy (lights)

PRODUCER: Universal Pictures

CAST INCLUDES: Henderson Forsythe and Carlin Glynn

PERFORMANCES: 1,584 after 96 performances in two locations off-Broadway

In 1979, Richard Rodgers, Guy Bolton, a creator of the Princess musicals, and "Tin Man" Jack Haley died. It cost an average of $1 million to produce a musical on Broadway. The year was an important one for the musical, for both negative and positive reasons: it brought Rodgers's last musical, a flop; Sondheim's next musical, an undeserved flop; and the beginning of the ascendancy of Lloyd Webber in his first pairing with Prince. *Grease* passed *Fiddler on the Roof* as the longest-running show in Broadway history. Revivals included *Peter Pan* starring Sandy Duncan (551 performances), *The Most Happy Fella* (52 performances), the 1928 *Whoopee!* which ran six months, and a nine-month run of *Oklahoma!*

One Mo' Time (1,372 performances) was an off-Broadway

revue consisting of black vaudeville material from the 1920s. *Sugar Babies* (1,208 performances) was a hit revue made up mostly of old vaudeville and revue songs, a script of old burlesque routines assembled by Ralph G. Allen, a dog act, and a fan dancer. Mickey Rooney and Ann Miller toured with it off and on for years. Burton Lane, Alan Jay Lerner, and Joseph Stein's *Carmelina,* adapted from the 1968 nonmusical movie *Buona Sera, Mrs. Campbell,* was a 17-performance flop. *The Grand Tour* (61 performances), starring Joel Grey, was adapted by Jerry Herman, Mark Bramble, and Michael Stewart from Franz Werfel and S. N. Behrman's 1944 nonmusical play *Jacobowsky and the Colonel.*

A sad finale to Rodgers's career, *I Remember Mama* is about an indomitable Norwegian immigrant holding her family together and encouraging her oldest daughter to be a writer. The subplot is about who will inherit mean Uncle Chris's money, if only he'd die already. A middling show, the intimacy of its story and relationships was further harmed by its staging in a large theater and the resulting, apparently necessary overamplification. The property had already been made into a nonmusical movie starring Irene Dunne and a nonmusical TV series starring Peggy Wood.

They're Playing Our Song, Hamlisch's first score since *A Chorus Line,* is a two-character musical with a chorus of six whose members function as the couple's alter egos. It has a soft rock score and some good Neil Simon jokes. It's about a songwriting team who have a rocky personal relationship—he's nerdy, she's an eccentric free spirit. The story is based partly on the relationships that Hamlisch and Simon were in at the time: Hamlisch with Bayer Sager and Simon with his then-wife Marsha Mason. The score includes the title song, "Fallin'," "Workin' It Out," "Fill in the Words," and "I Still Believe in Love."

Adapted originally from a Victorian melodrama, *Sweeney Todd: The Demon Barber of Fleet Street* has a straightforward plot about the title character, a London barber who slashes people's throats and sends them down a chute to his landlady, Mrs. Lovett, who sells delicious meat pies made from the corpses. She considers this "a nice respectable business," and Sweeney agrees:

Ballroom

MUSIC: Billy Goldenberg

LYRICS: Alan and Marilyn Bergman

BOOK: Jerome Kass, adapted from his 1975 TV movie *Queen of the Stardust Ballroom*

DIRECTOR/PRODUCER: Michael Bennett

CHOREOGRAPHERS: Michael Bennett and Bob Avian

DESIGNERS: Robin Wagner (sets), Theoni V. Aldredge (costumes), and Tharon Musser (lights)

CAST INCLUDES: Dorothy Loudon, Vincent Gardenia, and Marilyn Cooper

PERFORMANCES: 116

I Remember Mama

MUSIC: Richard Rodgers

LYRICS: mostly Martin Charnin

BOOK: Thomas Meehan, based on the play by John van Druten that was adapted from the stories by Kathryn Forbes

DIRECTOR: Cy Feuer (who replaced Martin Charnin)

CHOREOGRAPHER: Danny Daniels

PRODUCERS: Alexander H. Cohen and Hildy Parks

CAST INCLUDES: Liv Ullmann and George Hearn

PERFORMANCES: 108

They're Playing Our Song

MUSIC: Marvin Hamlisch

LYRICS: Carole Bayer Sager

BOOK: Neil Simon

DIRECTOR: Robert Moore

CHOREOGRAPHER: Patricia Birch

DESIGNERS: Douglas W. Schmidt (sets), Ann Roth (costumes), and Tharon Musser (lights)

PRODUCER: Emanuel Azenberg

CAST INCLUDES: Lucie Arnaz and Robert Klein

PERFORMANCES: 1,082

For what's the sound of the world out there? . . .
Those crunching noises pervading the air? . . .
It's man devouring man, my dear,
And who are we
To deny it in here? . . .
The history of the world, my love . . .
Is those below serving those up above. . . .
How gratifying for once to know
That those above will serve those down below! . . .
We'll not discriminate great from small.
No, we'll serve anyone—
Meaning anyone—
And to anyone
At all!

Sweeney Todd: The Demon Barber of Fleet Street

MUSIC/LYRICS: Stephen Sondheim

BOOK: Hugh Wheeler, based on the 1973 play by Christopher Bond

DIRECTOR: Harold Prince

CHOREOGRAPHER: Larry Fuller

DESIGNERS: Eugene and Franne Lee (sets and costumes) and Ken Billington (lights)

PRODUCERS: seven listed, including Charles Woodward and Richard Barr

CAST INCLUDES: Angela Lansbury, Len Cariou, and Victor Garber

PERFORMANCES: 557

Sweeney had been falsely imprisoned by a judge who wanted Sweeney's wife and daughter. After his release, he seeks vengeance not only against the judge but also against the whole world. The subplot is a love story between Sweeney's daughter, Johanna, and a young sailor, which does not end happily. Nearly every main character dies violently. Prince's huge physical production somewhat overwhelmed the melodramatic story by focusing too much on the social problems inherent in the class struggles of the Industrial Revolution. The production was too expensive to pay back its investors, but the show has had many revivals, even by opera companies. Much of the show is musicalized, including a great deal of underscored dialogue; there are very few extended, unaccompanied dialogue sequences.

> The music is pervasive because Mr. Sondheim is trying to evoke Victorian English melodrama, where the eerie goings on were almost continually accompanied by musical murmurings in the orchestra pit, or background refrains in the chorus. (Tommasini, "Woe to Shows That Put on Operatic Airs," *New York Times*, 5)

Despite Sondheim's protests, *Sweeney Todd* is almost an opera, though, like Weill's *Street Scene*, it works better with musical theater performers than with most opera singers. A live performance was taped while it was on tour after its Broadway run; by then, George Hearn had replaced Cariou. The 2006 revival with the cast and the onstage orchestra ran 349 performances. It was made into a movie in 2007.

Evita examines the facts and myths surrounding Argentine icon Eva Perón, from her beginnings as a prostitute to her end as dictator Juan Perón's wife and something close to a saint to the people of Argentina. A political, pageantlike potboiler with wall-to-wall music, it had a brilliant and cinematic staging by Prince and his choreographer, Larry Fuller. *Evita* made both Lupone and Patinkin stars. It was Patinkin's first musical; he played revolutionary-to-be Che Guevara, an angry and cynical narrator/commentator rather than an active participant in the plot. Like Lloyd Webber and Rice's *Jesus Christ Superstar*, the show began life as a best-selling record album. In the score are such numbers as "Another Suitcase in Another Hall," "Don't Cry For Me, Argentina" (the hit tune of the show), and "I'd Be Surprisingly Good for You." It won the Tony for Best Musical of the 1979–80 season. The original-cast recording sold 3.5 million copies. The London production—where the stage version first premiered—starred Elaine Paige, Joss Ackland, and David Essex, and ran 2,913 performances. Madonna, Antonio Banderas, and Jonathan Pryce starred in Parker's 1996 movie version. The show's structure and flow, when adapted to film, feel choppy and undramatic; Madonna's performance doesn't help.

And so begins the reign of the imported, through-composed, romantic musical spectacular, from Sondheim to Lloyd Webber, from antiromanticism to romantic pop operas (really pop operettas), from content to spectacle, from complexity to its opposite, whatever you might want to call it.

Evita

MUSIC AND ORCHESTRATION: Andrew Lloyd Webber

LYRICS: Tim Rice, based on the life of Evita Perón

DIRECTOR: Harold Prince

CHOREOGRAPHER: Larry Fuller

DESIGNERS: Timothy O'Brien and Tazeena Firth (sets and costumes) and David Hersey (lights)

PRODUCER: Robert Stigwood

CAST INCLUDES: Patti LuPone, Bob Gunton, and Mandy Patinkin

PERFORMANCES: 1,567

Tim Rice (1944–, born in Buckinghamshire, England) has written lyrics for such shows as *Joseph and the Amazing Technicolor Dreamcoat*, *Evita*, *Chess*, the new songs for the stage version of *Beauty and the Beast*, and all the songs for *The Lion King* and *Aida*.

Suggested Watching and Listening

The Act
This 1977 Broadway show features the song "City Lights" (performed by Liza Minnelli), available on the original-cast recording (DRG CD).

Annie
Sung by the trio of villains, the following song from this 1977 show is in the 1999 TV version of *Annie*, available on video and DVD from Walt Disney Video.
- "Easy Street" (performed by Kathy Bates, Alan Cumming, and Kristin Chenoweth)

Evita

The following number is on *Broadway's Lost Treasures* (Acorn Media DVD).

- "A New Argentina" (performed by Patti LuPone, Bob Gunton, Mandy Patinkin, and the cast)

All of the following numbers are from the movie version of this 1979 Andrew Lloyd Webber show, directed by Alan Parker and available on Miramax DVD.

- "Another Suitcase in Another Hall" (performed by Madonna): Evita wants to improve her life. In the show, it's sung by Perón's ex-mistress as she's on her way out, not by Evita.
- "I'd Be Surprisingly Good for You" (performed by Madonna and Jonathan Pryce): Evita comes on to Perón.
- "Don't Cry for Me, Argentina" (performed by Madonna): Evita sings to the populace.

Sweeney Todd

All of the suggestions below are from the 1982 taping, available on Turner Home Entertainment DVD.

- "Prelude: The Ballad of Sweeney Todd" (performed by the company): It begins the story and sets the dark and angry tone of the show.
- "The Worst Pies in London" (performed by Angela Lansbury): Mrs. Lovett sings about her pre-Sweeney pies.
- "Johanna" (performed by Chris Groenendaal): It's sung by Anthony, the young sailor in love with Sweeney's daughter.
- "Pretty Women" (performed by George Hearn and Edmund Lyndeck): It's a duet as Sweeney shaves Judge Turpin, who ruined his life.
- "Epiphany" (performed by George Hearn): Sweeney realizes what he must do.
- "A Little Priest" (performed by Angela Lansbury and George Hearn): Mrs. Lovett has a plan for what to do with the dead bodies.
- "Not While I'm Around" (performed by Angela Lansbury and Ken Jennings): Mrs. Lovett and the half-wit Tobias vow to protect each other while she's trying to figure out how to kill him.

From <u>42nd Street</u> to <u>Cats</u>

> Hear the beat
> Of dancing feet,
> It's the song I love
> The melody of,
> Forty-second Street.
>
> —"42ND STREET," *42ND STREET,* LYRICS BY AL DUBIN

By the end of the seventies, business began to dictate aesthetics more than ever. To be safe investments, new shows had to be like ones that had already succeeded, with the rules determined by whether it was a comedy or a drama. Creativity and imagination were often squandered on making similarities seem different; after a while, the differences got substantially harder to see. (This is, of course, even more the situation in contemporary TV and movie production.) At the same time, as ticket prices continued to increase, most members of the seventies' Me Generation and the eighties' Greed Generation—who could well afford theater tickets—were going to their exercise clubs and dinner afterwards instead of to the theater. The Times Square area was getting a reputation for being dangerous, yet Broadway was increasingly dependent on the tourist trade: people out for a good time in the big city, often with their families. Revues and romantic operettas were becoming popular again—only the revues usually had no comedy sketches or new songs and little or no dialogue, and the operettas were through-sung, were called rock or pop operas, and were generally British imports.

Creativity was waning just when the marketing of Broadway was becoming more sophisticated, bringing in a wider but less demanding audience. Blockbusters were now created by television advertising, and the result was longer runs for shows, some of which were mediocre at best. . . . The top ticket prices doubled. . . . The high cost of pre-Broadway tryout tours forced many shows to play lengthy previews in New York instead (usually a dangerous practice, as the early word on a show is almost always bad, and in New York word gets out very fast). (Gruber, *Original Cast! The Seventies*, 3–4)

In 1980, performers Jimmy Durante and Mae West and director/choreographer Gower Champion died. The top ticket price went to a new high of $30. Equity minimum rose to $475 a week on Broadway. *Grease* closed with the long-run record of 3,388 performances. The New York City Opera revived *The Student Prince*. Other revivals included *West Side Story* (333 performances), *Brigadoon* (133 performances), and limited-run revivals of *The Music Man* with Dick Van Dyke and *Camelot* with Richard Burton. There were few new musical evenings either off-Broadway or on.

The season's biggest hit—billed as a "musical extravaganza"—the success of *42nd Street* was an exception to the usual fate of movie musicals adapted to

Backdrop: 1980–1989

National Acquired immunodeficiency syndrome (AIDS) spreads throughout the world. President Carter ends diplomatic relations with Iran when that country holds fifty-two U.S. citizens hostage; they're finally released in 1981. In 1980, Ronald Reagan beats Carter in a landslide and is elected the fortieth president of the United States; George H. W. Bush is his vice president. They're reelected in 1984 in an even greater landslide. Reagan's first budget includes huge tax and spending cuts. Reagan backs Nicaragua's Contra rebels against the Sandinista government and later admits that despite an arms embargo against Iran, there'd been secret arms deals with that country; the Iran-Contra scandal is dubbed Irangate. Would-be assassin John Hinckley wounds Reagan, press secretary Jim Brady, and two others. American troops invade Grenada, end a military coup, and institute civil rule. Shiite Muslims bomb the U.S. embassy in Beirut, Lebanon, killing eighty-seven people. Unemployment rises to over twelve million, the highest since the Depression, and more banks fail than at any time since 1937. The U.S. space shuttle *Challenger* explodes, killing all seven aboard. Congress passes a bill that prohibits the National Endowment for the Arts from funding artworks deemed obscene. The *Exxon Valdez* runs aground in Alaska, causing the world's largest oil spill. The Equal Rights Amendment is defeated. The stock market crashes in 1987. In 1988, George H. W. Bush becomes the forty-first president, with Dan Quayle his vice president. Bush authorizes spending $300 billion to prevent the total collapse of the savings and loan industry. The use of crack cocaine spreads throughout the United States. Martin Luther the stage. A nostalgic trip back in time to the dance-heavy, tap-heavy, free-and-easy style of the pre–Rodgers and Hammerstein musical plays, its book is so slight that Stewart and Bramble's credit actually reads "Lead-ins and Crossovers." The show has songs mostly by Warren and Dubin from several thirties films, including the original movie. The story's the one about the lead breaking her ankle on opening night and being replaced by the understudy, who becomes a star overnight. Champion, who did some of his most exciting and inventive work on *42nd Street*, died on the morning of opening night. Merrick announced it from the stage during the curtain calls, having kept it from the cast and the press until then. It was Merrick's last hit, his first show since the 1974 flop *Mack and Mabel* and his first hit since the 1968 *Promises, Promises*. There's an original-cast recording. The score includes the title song, "We're in the Money," "Lullaby of Broadway," and "Shuffle Off to Buffalo." The show won the Tony

42nd Street

MUSIC: Harry Warren

LYRICS: Al Dubin, with additional lyrics by Johnny Mercer and Mort Dixon

BOOK: Michael Stewart and Mark Bramble, based on the novel by Bradford Ropes and the 1933 movie

DIRECTOR/CHOREOGRAPHER: Gower Champion

ORCHESTRATOR: Philip J. Lang

DESIGNERS: Robin Wagner (sets), Theoni V. Aldredge (costumes), and Tharon Musser (lights)

PRODUCER: David Merrick

CAST INCLUDES: Jerry Orbach and Tammy Grimes

PERFORMANCES: 3,486

King's birthday becomes a national holiday. Harold Washington, Wilson Goode, Harvey Grant, and David Dinkins become the first black mayors of Chicago, Philadelphia, Charlotte, and New York, respectively. At the end of the decade, Richard M. Daley, son of the late mayor Richard J. Daley, is elected mayor of Chicago. General Colin Powell is the first African American to become chairman of the Joint Chiefs of Staff. Sandra Day O'Connor is the first woman to become a justice of the Supreme Court.

International Soviet troops retreat from Afghanistan after a nine-year occupation. In Poland, Lech Walesa leads his Solidarity trade union in a strike against the Communist regime; during the decade, the union's power increases. In the USSR, Leonid Brezhnev dies and Yuri Andropov succeeds him as leader of the Soviet Union; when he dies, he's succeeded by Konstantin Chernenko; and when he dies, he's succeeded by Mikhail Gorbachev. Gorbachev stops the deployment of mid-range missiles in Europe, cuts down on the number of Soviet troops, and begins his campaign for openness (glasnost) and economic and government reform (perestroika). McDonald's opens restaurants in Moscow. A nuclear reactor blows up at the Chernobyl power station in the Soviet Union—the world's worst nuclear accident. In 1989, the Berlin Wall is demolished, allowing the eventual reunification of East Germany and West Germany for the first time since 1945. International terrorism increases. Zimbabwe and Belize gain their independence. The French Socialist Party's François Mitterand is elected president. Yugoslavian leader Marshal Tito dies. Egyptian president Anwar Sadat and Indian prime minister Indira Gandhi are assassinated. Benazir Bhutto becomes the first woman prime minister of Pakistan. Iraq invades Iran, beginning a war that lasts through much of the decade. Israel annexes the Golan Heights and returns the Sinai to Egypt. Palestinians begin an intifada, an armed uprising against Israeli rule of for Best Musical of the 1980–81 season. There was a successful 2001 Broadway revival (1,524 performances) also with an original-cast recording. It's more fun to watch the numbers in the old Busby Berkeley movies.

Barnum

MUSIC: Cy Coleman
LYRICS: Michael Stewart
BOOK: Mark Bramble
DIRECTOR/CHOREOGRAPHER: Joe Layton
ORCHESTRATOR: Hershy Kay
DESIGNERS: David Mitchell (sets), Theoni V. Aldredge (costumes), and Craig Miller (lights)
PRODUCERS: six listed, including Cy Coleman
CAST INCLUDES: Jim Dale and Glenn Close
PERFORMANCES: 854

Barnum, a semiconcept musical with the theater transformed into a circus, is about P. T. Barnum, the nineteenth-century showman and promoter whose motto was "There's a sucker born every minute." He toured freak shows and opera singers and eventually joined with Bailey to form the circus billed as "the greatest show on earth." (They, of course, later merged with Ringling Brothers.) The show covers the years from 1830 to 1880.

This was the closest thing to a real theatrical pageant Broadway had seen in a long time. . . . [It] overcame a sprawling, unfocused book and an average score to create a sometimes

---

the West Bank and Gaza Strip. Yasser Arafat and four thousand members of the PLO move to Tunisia. Argentine troops invade the Falkland Islands and are driven out by British troops. Britain's Margaret Thatcher is elected for a third term as prime minister. Prince Charles of England marries Lady Diana Spencer. Romanian president Nicolae Ceausescu is overthrown and executed. Ethiopia seeks money for millions of drought victims. Playwright Vaclav Havel and a largely non-Communist government take power in Czechoslovakia. Thousands of students take over Tiananmen Square in Beijing; the Chinese government uses tanks to disperse them, killing many.

New Developments   The first space shuttles are launched. The wreck of the *Titanic* is found. When AT&T loses an antitrust suit, it must sell off two-thirds of its assets. Standard Oil of California buys Gulf Oil in the world's largest corporate merger so far. Time, Inc., buys Warner Communications and becomes the world's largest entertainment combine. General Motors becomes the biggest company in the United States. Disney opens EPCOT, the Experimental Community of Tomorrow, in Florida. Chinese scientists clone a fish. Test-tube triplets and quadruplets are born in Britain. Scientists become certain there's a black hole in the center of our galaxy. The personal computer is introduced by IBM. Apple's Macintosh computer is marketed.

Sports   Boxing champs of the decade include Sugar Ray Leonard and Mike Tyson. Former champs Joe Lewis, Jack Dempsey, and Sugar Ray Robinson die, and Muhammad Ali retires. Tennis champs include Björn Borg, Boris Becker, Martina Navratilova, and Steffi Graf. Baseball's Pete Rose beats Ty Cobb's 1928 record for the most career hits; he's later banned from the sport for betting on the games. Twenty-two-year-old Gary Kasparov beats Anatoly Karpov to become the world's youngest chess champion.

thrilling, eye-catching theatrical event. (Bloom, *American Song*, 51)

With *Barnum* and *42nd Street*, Stewart and Bramble had two hits in a year. During the run Jim Dale, who was magnetic in the title role, was replaced by Tony Orlando and then by Mike Burstyn. There's an original-cast recording.

A Day in Hollywood/A Night in the Ukraine consists of two mediocre one-act musicals well staged by Tommy Tune. The first is a revue made of parodies of old movies, including a section with the audience only able to see dancing feet. The second is a Russian play (loosely based on Chekhov's "The Bear") done as a parody of Marx Brothers movies. There's an original-cast recording. Along with original numbers, the show has songs by Jerry Herman, Cole Porter, Harold Arlen, and Hoagy Carmichael, among others.

A Day in Hollywood/A Night in the Ukraine

MUSIC: Frank Lazarus, mostly

LYRICS/BOOK: Dick Vosburgh, mostly

DIRECTOR/CHOREOGRAPHER: Tommy Tune, with co-choreographer Thommie Walsh

DESIGNERS: Tony Walton (sets), Michel Stuart (costumes), and Beverly Emmons (lights)

PRODUCERS: Alexander H. Cohen and Hildy Parks

CAST INCLUDES: Priscilla Lopez of *A Chorus Line*

PERFORMANCES: 588

Art   Architect R. Buckminster Fuller and painters Oscar Kokoschka, Georgia O'Keeffe, Salvador Dalí, and Andy Warhol die. Paris's Museé d'Orsay opens. Van Gogh's *Irises* sells for $49 million. Maya Lin's Vietnam Veteran's Memorial is completed on the mall in Washington, D.C.

Music/Dance   New operas include Glass's *Satyagraha*, Messiaen's *Saint Francis of Assisi*, Adams's *Nixon in China*, and Davis's *X (The Life and Times of Malcolm X)*.

Publications   *USA Today* begins publication. New books in a range of styles and examining a variety of social, political, and/or personal concerns include: Hawking's *A Brief History of Time*, Morrison's *Tar Baby* and *Beloved*, Tyler's *Dinner at the Homesick Restaurant* and *The Accidental Tourist*, Walker's *The Color Purple* (source of the 2005 musical), García Márquez's *Chronicle of a Death Foretold* and *Love in the Time of Cholera*, Kundera's *The Unbearable Lightness of Being*, McInerney's *Bright Lights, Big City*, McMurtry's *Lonesome Dove*, Spiegelman's *Maus: A Survivor's Tale*, Atwood's *The Handmaid's Tale*, Bloom's *The Closing of the American Mind*, Rushdie's *The Satanic Verses*, DeLillo's *Libra*, Tan's *The Joy Luck Club*, and Van Allsburg's *The Polar Express*.

TV   By 1983, 20 million homes have cable TV. CNN (Cable News Network), TNN (The Nashville Network), the Fox TV Network, and MTV begin broadcasting. *Late Night with Dave Letterman*, *L.A. Law*, *The Oprah Winfrey Show*, *Baywatch*, and *The Simpsons* make their debuts. Among the top-rated TV shows of the decade are *60 Minutes*; *Three's Company*; *That's Incredible*; *Dallas*; *The Dukes of Hazard*; *The Jeffersons*; *M*A*S*H*; *Magnum, P.I.*; *Dynasty*; *The Cosby Show*; *Murder, She Wrote*; *Cheers*; *A Different World*; and *Roseanne*. Jackie Gleason and Lucille Ball die.

In 1981, lyricist and writer E. Y. "Yip" Harburg, composer Harry Warren, orchestrator Robert Russell Bennett, producer Leonard Sillman, and performers Lotte Lenya and Adele Astaire died. It was an active year for the musical, though few of the new shows were particularly memorable. The Ziegfelds and the Merricks gave way to groups of producers with no discernable identity of their own and no particular mark on their shows.

> Most of the biggest hits turned to old shows, old songs, or simply the general appeal of bygone days for inspiration. At the same time, the public and often the critics turned increasingly cold shoulders to revivals of gems from the post-*Oklahoma!* era. . . . It meant staggering losses when a show failed, and it precipitated the closing of doubtful entries. . . . A disheartening number of shows . . . threw in the towel after a single performance. (Bordman, 703)

There was a clever revival of Gilbert and Sullivan's *The Pirates of Penzance* (787 performances) produced on Broadway by Joseph Papp's New York Shakespeare Festival after the show's run at Papp's outdoor theater in Central Park. It starred Rex Smith, Linda Ronstadt, George Rose, Estelle Parsons, and Kevin Kline as an extremely clumsy Pirate King. (It was later

Pop Culture Mark Chapman shoots John Lennon. Marvin Gaye is shot by his father. Bill Haley, Benny Goodman, Hoagy Carmichael, Harry Chapin, Karen Carpenter, Dennis Wilson, and Roy Orbison die. Compact discs (CDs) are marketed and soon replace LPs. Break dancing and rap music become popular; rap's Grandmaster Flash and the Furious Five's "The Message" sweeps the country. Live Aid, a multistar rock concert, raises money for charities. By the end of the decade, heavy metal groups like Guns 'n' Roses, Def Leppard, Van Halen, and Metallica make the charts. Bowie's "Let's Dance"; Tina Turner's "What's Love Got to Do with It?" by Lyle and Britten; and Live Crew's "As Nasty as You Want to Be" are among the pop singles. Notable albums include Steely Dan's *Gaucho*; Elvis Costello and the Attractions' *Get Happy*; Michael Jackson's *Thriller*, with "Beat It" and "Billie Jean," and *Bad*; Talking Heads' *Remain in Light*; Cougar's *American Fool*; Joel's *The Nylon Curtain*; Sting and the Police's *Synchronicity*; Springsteen's *Born in the USA*; Madonna's *Like a Virgin*; Richie's *Dancing on the Ceiling*; Collins's *No Jacket Required*; Dylan's *Biography*; Franklin's *Who's Zoomin' Who?*; Wonder's *In Square Circle*; Simon's *Graceland*; Pink Floyd's *A Momentary Lapse of Reason*; Fleetwood Mac's *Tango in the Night*; U2's *The Joshua Tree*; Michael's *Faith*; New Kids on the Block's *Hangin' Tough*; Abdul's *Forever Your Love*; Christopher Cross; and Whitney Houston.

Stage Minority voices are heard in such new plays as August Wilson's *Ma Rainey's Black Bottom*, *Joe Turner's Come and Gone*, *Fences*, and *The Piano Lesson*; Fuller's *A Soldier's Play*; Simon's *Brighton Beach Memoirs*, *Biloxi Blues*, and *Broadway Bound*; Wasserstein's *The Heidi Chronicles*; Fierstein's *Torch Song Trilogy*; and Hwang's *M. Butterfly*. Also new are Mamet's *Glengarry Glen Ross*; Uhry's *Driving* filmed.) There were also a 5-performance flop revival of *Can-Can*, a limited-run revival of Herschel Bernardi in *Fiddler on the Roof,* a 120-performance revival of Rex Harrison in *My Fair Lady,* and a failed revival of Richard Harris in *Camelot.* The New York City Opera revived *Song of Norway.* The one-woman show *Lena Horne: The Lady and Her Music* ran 333 performances; Horne still looked great and sang wonderfully forty-seven years after her debut at the Cotton Club. *Bring Back Birdie* was a disastrous 4-performance attempt by Charles Strouse, Lee Adams, and Michael Stewart to create a sequel to *Bye Bye Birdie;* it starred Donald O'Connor, Chita Rivera, and Maurice Hines.

Dreamgirls is about a trio of black women from Chicago called the Dreamettes, later changed to the Dreams; it bears some resemblance to the rise of Berry Gordy, producer of Motown Records, and of Diana Ross and the Supremes. Bennett's last hit—and an exciting, moving, beautifully put-together musical play—it goes behind the scenes over a ten-year period (1962–72) to trace the efforts of the Dreams to break into the white mainstream under

Dreamgirls

MUSIC: Henry Krieger

LYRICS/BOOK: Tom Eyen

DIRECTOR/CHOREOGRAPHER: Michael Bennett, with co-choreographer Michael Peters

ORCHESTRATOR: Harold Wheeler

DESIGNERS: Robin Wagner (sets), Theoni V. Aldredge (costumes), and Tharon Musser (lights)

PRODUCERS: Michael Bennett, Bob Avian, Geffen Records, and the Shubert Organization

CAST INCLUDES: Jennifer Holliday, Ben Harney, and Obba Babatundé

PERFORMANCES: 1,521

Miss Daisy; Henley's *Crimes of the Heart;* Shepard's *True West* and *Fool for Love;* Durang's *Beyond Therapy;* Norman's *'Night, Mother;* and McNally's *Frankie and Johnny in the Clair de Lune.* Among the shows from foreign shores are Fugard's *Master Harold . . . and the Boys* and *The Road to Mecca,* Hare's *Plenty,* Hampton's *Les Liaisons Dangereuses,* Stoppard's *The Real Thing,* Churchill's *Top Girls,* Frayn's *Noises Off* and *Benefactors,* and Wertenbaker's *Our Country's Good.*

Screen Alfred Hitchcock, François Truffaut, Bette Davis, and John Belushi die. New movies include: *The Empire Strikes Back* and *Return of the Jedi, Raging Bull,* adaptations of King's *The Shining* and Shaffer's *Amadeus, E.T.: The Extra-Terrestrial, Raiders of the Lost Ark* and *Indiana Jones and the Temple of Doom, Tootsie, Aliens, Ghost Busters, Splash, Back to the Future, Brazil, Who Framed Roger Rabbit, The Terminator, Do the Right Thing, Batman, Hannah and Her Sisters, Platoon, Das Boot, Fanny and Alexander, Ran, The Last Emperor, Kiss of the Spider Woman* (source of the 1993 musical), and *Big* (source of the 1996 musical).

New movie musicals include an adaptation of *Little Shop of Horrors; The Blues Brothers; Fame;* Sissy Spacek as country singer Loretta Lynn in *Coal Miner's Daughter; Flashdance; Purple Rain,* with a score by Prince, who also stars; *Yentl,* with songs by Michel Legrand and Alan and Marilyn Bergman, all sung by Barbra Streisand, who also directs; Julie Andrews and Robert Preston in *Victor/Victoria,* with songs by Henry Mancini and Leslie Bricusse (source of the 1995 musical); and the mockumentary *This Is Spinal Tap.*

the guidance of their manager, Curtis Taylor Jr. It shows how the pursuit of success causes people to sell out. The Dreams get their first break as backup singers for another of the manager's clients, James Thunder Early. As the trio starts toward the top of the pop field as a separate act, the manager fires one of the women, Effie White, possibly the most talented—and his former mistress—basically because she's too fat and raunchy for the new look and more mainstream sound needed to achieve total success. Effie then pursues a career on her own. The manager also eventually drops Jimmy Early when his career starts taking a dive and his drug habit worsens.

> At a time when the Broadway musical has been described as static or, worse, terminal, at a time when Broadway's sources have wormed in on themselves with borrowed scores and hand-me-down reprises, *Dreamgirls* has rediscovered a bypassed origin: the mainstream music of America. (Kevin Kelly's liner notes for the original-cast recording)

The occasionally Motown-like score includes the title song, "And I Am Telling You I'm Not Going," and "Steppin' to the Bad Side." Conceptual in design, *Dreamgirls* has little spoken dialogue and lots of recitative. Much of the scenery consisted of large, moving towers and draperies that allowed for cinematically seamless transitions without stopping the action or, sometimes, without having the actors move as the set changed around them. Bennett workshopped *Dreamgirls* four times at his own rehearsal space after Papp had workshopped it and lost interest. The show tried out in Boston. There's an original-cast recording. There was a 177-performance revival in 1987 and a highly successful movie version released in 2006 with Jamie Foxx, Beyoncé Knowles, Eddie Murphy, and Jennifer Hudson. It's available on DVD.

Merrily We Roll Along

MUSIC/LYRICS: Stephen Sondheim

BOOK: George Furth, based on the 1934 play by George S. Kaufman and Moss Hart

DIRECTOR: Harold Prince

CHOREOGRAPHER: Larry Fuller

ORCHESTRATOR: Jonathan Tunick

DESIGNERS: Eugene Lee (sets), Judith Dolan (costumes), and David Hersey (lights)

PRODUCERS: four listed, including Harold Prince

CAST INCLUDES: Jim Walton, Ann Morrison, Lonny Price, and Jason Alexander

PERFORMANCES: 16 after 56 previews

It was Prince's idea to adapt the Kaufman and Hart play *Merrily We Roll Along*, which hadn't been very successful, into a musical. As in the play, the story is told backwards chronologically, covering a twenty-five-year period from 1980 to 1955. It's about teenage idealism gone sour, but it begins with the breakup of the friendship of the three central characters, a lyricist, a writer, and a composer. They've become jaded and have let success compromise their ideals. By the time the story goes back far enough in time to make the characters likeable, it's too late for the audience to care. With no workshop or out-of-town tryouts, the show had a rough preview period with many changes; the word of mouth was very bad by the time it finally opened, and the critics agreed. (Along with cast changes, the original costumes were thrown out, and Fuller replaced Ron Field as choreographer during previews.)

The production had an unfortunate jungle-gym design concept and a cast of young, unseasoned unknowns, who ended up needing their characters' relationships written on their costumes in order to be distinguished one from the other. Furthermore, they were all too young for their roles in the first half of the show. It was the sixth and last collaboration between Sondheim and Prince until *Bounce* in 2003. Sondheim and Furth have rewritten the show, but they still haven't been able to get it to work despite the excellence of the score, which is very accessible and very close to traditional show tunes. It includes the title song, "Not a Day Goes By," "Good Thing Going," and "Old Friends." There's an original-cast recording.

In *Joseph and the Amazing Technicolor Dreamcoat*, Joseph's eleven brothers, jealous of his multicolor coat and because he's their father's favorite, sell him into slavery in Egypt, where he rises to power second only to the Pharaoh. He eventually forgives his family and saves them from famine by bringing them to Egypt (where, within generations, they became slaves, though that wasn't part of Joseph's plan or of the musical). The show is a comedy and a family entertainment, including a chorus of children being told the story by a *Cabaret*-like, *Pippin*-like narrator— only this time played by a cheerful woman. Although it's the first show Lloyd Webber and Rice wrote together, *Jesus Christ Superstar* had already played Broadway and *Evita* was still running. A short, pop-rock opera, it began as a twenty-minute oratorio written for schoolchildren, was then turned into a long-playing record, and was finally staged in London in 1972 and in Brooklyn in 1976. It had its belated off-Broadway debut in 1981; the production was moved to Broadway in 1982. There was a 231-performance revival in 1993 and an extremely successful

Joseph and the Amazing Technicolor Dreamcoat

MUSIC: Andrew Lloyd Webber

LYRICS: Tim Rice, adapted from the story in Genesis

DIRECTOR/CHOREOGRAPHER: Tony Tanner

DESIGNERS: Karl Eigsti (sets), Judith Dolan (costumes), and Barry Arnold (lights)

PRODUCERS: Zev Bufman, Melvin J. Estrin, and Susan R. Rose

CAST INCLUDES: Bill Hutton and Laurie Beechman

PERFORMANCES: 747

production starring Donny Osmond, which toured North America. There are several recordings of the show and a video and DVD of the Osmond production.

Woman of the Year

MUSIC: John Kander

LYRICS: Fred Ebb

BOOK: Peter Stone, based on Ring Lardner Jr. and Michael Kanin's 1942 screenplay

DIRECTOR: Robert Moore

MUSICAL STAGING (an increasingly popular choreographer's credit): Tony Charmoli

ORCHESTRATOR: Michael Gibson

DESIGNERS: Tony Walton (sets), Theoni V. Aldredge (costumes), and Marilyn Rennagel (lights)

PRODUCERS: seven listed, including David Landay and Stewart Lane

CAST INCLUDES: Lauren Bacall, Harry Guardino, and Marilyn Cooper

PERFORMANCES: 770

Woman of the Year is a clunky adaptation of the Spencer Tracy–Katharine Hepburn nonmusical movie about a sophisticated, world-traveling columnist and her marriage to a streetwise sportswriter. Lauren Bacall costarred with Gregory Peck in a 1957 nonmusical, wide-screen remake called *Designing Woman* in which she was a clothing designer and he was still a sportswriter. To update it, the musical turns the characters into a Barbara Walters–like TV personality and a political cartoonist. Bacall's voice hadn't improved since *Applause*. Nonetheless, she could still draw audiences, though not enough for the show to make back its investment, especially since she didn't stay with the production for the whole run. Among her replacements were Raquel Welch and Debbie Reynolds. There's an original-cast recording. In the score are "Sometimes a Day Goes By" and "The Grass Is Always Greener."

Sophisticated Ladies

MUSIC: Duke Ellington mostly

LYRICS: many listed

DIRECTOR: Michael Smuin

CHOREOGRAPHERS: Michael Smuin, Donald McKayle, and Henry LeTang, from a concept by McKayle

DESIGNERS: Tony Walton (sets), Willa Kim (costumes), and Jennifer Tipton (lights)

PRODUCERS: seven listed, including Roger S. Berlind

CAST INCLUDES: Hinton Battle, Gregg Burge, Gregory Hines, Judith Jamison, Terri Klausner, and Phyllis Hyman

PERFORMANCES: 767

Set at the Cotton Club at the height of its popularity, with the band onstage, *Sophisticated Ladies* is a large-cast, dialogue-free, song-and-dance revue of Ellington's songs—a jukebox revue. The idea for the show came from Ellington's son, Mercer. Lavishly produced and dance-heavy—with lots of tap dancing especially—it's frequently revived around the country. It was the first Broadway show to be broadcast live on pay-per-view TV; a video of the broadcast, which has most of the original cast, is available on DVD. There's also an original-cast recording. Although it ran for two years, the show didn't pay off its investors.

March of the Falsettos (310 performances) opened off-off-Broadway in a workshop at Playwrights Horizons, then moved to off-Broadway. A through-composed one-act with book, music, and lyrics by William Finn, it is the second of Finn's Marvin trilogy. (The first one-act, *In Trousers*, was produced unsuccessfully in 1985.) A fresh and funny five-character show, it's about a man who leaves his wife and young son for a male lover; the fifth character is the man's psychiatrist, who ends up with the wife. There's an original-cast recording. The score includes "Four

Jews in a Room Bitching," "The Thrill of First Love" (sung by two men), and "My Father's a Homo." Director James Lapine went on to write the books for and direct such shows as Sondheim's *Sunday in the Park with George* and *Into the Woods.*

In 1982, performer Victor Moore and conductor/teacher/pop-music authority Lehman Engle died. In London, Gilbert, Sullivan, and D'Oyly Carte's opera company folded. The top Broadway ticket price went up to $40 for *Cats. The Best Little Whorehouse in Texas* returned for 63 more performances. About sixty crates of scores by Herbert, Kern, Gershwin, Rodgers, and Porter, some of which were thought to be lost forever, were found in a Warner Brothers warehouse in New Jersey.

> At the beginning of June, *Variety* noted that the closing of Katharine Hepburn's tour in *West Side Waltz* meant that for the first time in memory not a single straight play was on the road. The trade sheet called this "the culmination of a trend that has been developing for several years as Broadway musicals have come to dominate the road almost exclusively." (Bordman, 710)

A revival of Cohan's 1904 *Little Johnny Jones,* starring Donny Osmond, ran one night. A failed revival of *Little Me* had Sid Caesar's multiple roles divided between James Coco and Victor Garber, thus lessening the fun considerably. Among the twenty or so new musical evenings was *Forbidden Broadway* (2,332 performances), written and directed by Gerald Alessandrini and the first in a series of off-Broadway revues that parodied shows and stars by setting new lyrics to existing tunes. It had several changes of material during the run to keep it current. There's an original-cast recording. *Pump Boys and Dinettes* (573 performances) was a small-cast, country-and-western, audience-participation semi-revue–semi-musical set in a combination gas station and dinette. It, too, has a recording.

Seven Brides for Seven Brothers (5 performances), adapted from the 1954 movie, was another pointless and failed attempt at making a stage show out of a movie musical. Although the movie had some of Michael Kidd's best film choreography, he didn't do the stage show, nor would his choreography—designed for the camera—have worked on stage. The show is occasionally done by community theater groups. *A Doll's Life* (also 5 performances), directed by Harold Prince, was Larry Grossman, Comden, and Green's attempt to write a musical about what happened to Ibsen's Nora after she walked out on her husband at the end of *A Doll's House.* It doesn't work and partially subverts Ibsen's feminist message. There's an original-cast recording.

Nine

MUSIC/LYRICS: Maury Yeston

BOOK: Arthur Kopit, adapted by Mario Fratti from Fellini's 1963 film 8½

DIRECTOR/CHOREOGRAPHER: Tommy Tune

ORCHESTRATOR: Jonathan Tunick

DESIGNERS: Lawrence Miller (sets), William Ivey Long (costumes), and Marcia Madeira (lights)

PRODUCERS: eleven listed, including Roger Berlind

CAST INCLUDES: Raul Julia, Karen Akers, Taina Elg, Liliane Montevecchi, and Anita Morris

PERFORMANCES: 729

Nine is a semiconcept musical about an Italian movie director trying to regain his creativity by examining his relationships with the many women in his life. Except for the director, the director as a boy, and a few other little boys, the cast is entirely female. There's an original-cast recording. In the score are "In a Very Unusual Way," "Only with You," "Be Italian," and "Be on Your Own." The more traditional sounding *Nine* won the 1981–82 Tony over *Dreamgirls*. Maury Yeston also wrote songs for *Grand Hotel* and *Titanic,* among other shows. There was a 2003 Broadway revival (283 performances) with Antonio Banderas, Jane Krakowski, Mary Stuart Masterson, and Chita Rivera.

Little Shop of Horrors

MUSIC: Alan Menken

LYRICS/BOOK: Howard Ashman, adapted from Roger Corman's 1960 parody horror movie

DIRECTOR: Howard Ashman

DESIGNERS: Scott Pask (sets), William Ivey Long (costumes), and Donald Holder (lights)

PRODUCERS: WPA Theatre (where it was first performed), David Geffen, Cameron Mackintosh, and the Shubert Organization

CAST INCLUDES: Lee Wilkof, Ellen Greene, and Hy Anzell

PERFORMANCES: 2,209 off-Broadway

Little Shop of Horrors is about a plant that talks and eats people and about Seymour, the nerdy young man who tends it and loves Audrey, the rather simpleminded, young woman who loves him back. Seymour names the plant Audrey II. With a parody fifties rock score (which is when the show is set) and a plant that survives on human blood, it was a hugely successful off-Broadway hit and an even more successful 1986 movie, available on DVD. In the movie, the plant is destroyed and the hero and heroine have a happy ending, although baby plants are seen growing in their front yard. In the musical, everyone is eaten by the plant, which then starts dropping down onto the audience as the lights go out. The show closed as the third-longest-running, off-Broadway musical (after *The Fantasticks* and *The Threepenny Opera*). There's an original-cast recording and a sound-track recording. The score includes "Somewhere That's Green" and "Suddenly Seymour." Alan Menken (1949–, born in New Rochelle, New York) and Howard Ashman (1950–91, born Howard Elliott Gershman in Baltimore, Maryland) went on to write the scores for Disney's animated *The Little Mermaid* and *Beauty and the Beast.* There was a 2003 Broadway production of *Little Shop* (372 performances) with Hunter Foster as Seymour.

With fewer American works being produced, the Broadway musical stage was soon taken over by imports from Great Britain. . . . Ironically, most of these were either written by

Andrew Lloyd Webber and/or produced by Cameron Mackintosh, both of whom cheerfully acknowledge the American musicals of the forties and fifties as their inspiration. These productions also started the trend for the spectacular in Broadway musicals (coinciding with a dearth of musical star performers). (Gruber, *Original Cast! Completing the Century,* 3–4)

Cats is a completely danced, sung, and overamplified concept revue. All the characters are cats, who occasionally spend time in the audience; they tell us about themselves in song after song and dance after dance. The show is set in a junkyard built to scale, and there's basically no plot. It began life as a song cycle, the first time Lloyd Webber had written music to existing lyrics—poems, actually. It's also the first time he worked with producer Cameron Mackintosh. Betty Buckley played Grizabella, the cat who sings "Memory" several times and is chosen at the end of the show to go up to cat heaven to be reborn, which is as much of a plot as there is. The role was created by Elaine Paige in the original London production. In 1997, *Cats* became the longest-running show in Broadway history, overtaking *A Chorus Line;* for a while its advertising slogan, "Now and forever," seemed likely. It won the 1982–83 Tony with hardly any competition for it that's worth mentioning. The show attracted a largely family and tourist audience. Singing the complex Eliot poems makes them difficult to understand even for English-speaking audiences; non-English-speaking tourists therefore enjoyed the show just as much as speakers of English did, thanks to the production values and the hardworking dancers. *Cats* was videotaped in London in 1998 and is available on DVD. There are several cast recordings.

Cats

MUSIC: Andrew Lloyd Webber

LYRICS: T. S. Eliot, adapted from his 1939 book of poems *Old Possum's Book of Practical Cats,* with additional lyrics by Trevor Nunn and Richard Stilgoe

DIRECTOR: Trevor Nunn

ASSOCIATE DIRECTOR/CHOREOGRAPHER: Gillian Lynne

ORCHESTRATORS: David Cullen and Andrew Lloyd Webber

DESIGNERS: John Napier (sets and costumes) and David Hersey (lights)

PRODUCERS: Cameron Mackintosh, Lloyd Webber's Really Useful Theatre Group, David Geffen, and the Shubert Organization

CAST INCLUDES: Betty Buckley, Harry Groener, and Terrence V. Mann

PERFORMANCES: 7,485

Suggested Watching and Listening

Broadway: The American Musical
The final chapter of the series, "Episode 6: Putting It Together (1980–2004)," is available on DVD from PBS Paramount and would be worth watching at this point.

Cats
The following is available on *Broadway's Lost Treasures* (Acorn Media DVD).
- "Jellicle Songs" and "Memory" (performed by Betty Buckley and the cast)

Dreamgirls

The following numbers from this 1981 show are available on the original-cast recording (Decca U.S. CD) or on the Dreamworks Home Entertainment DVD.

- "Fake Your Way to the Top" (performed by Cleavant Derricks, Loretta Devine, Jennifer Holliday, and Sheryl Lee Ralph or by Eddie Murphy, Anika Noni Rose, Jennifer Hudson, and Beyoncé Knowles): Jimmy Early, backed by the Dreams, sings what could be their manager Curtis's theme song.
- "Dreamgirls" (performed by Sheryl Lee Ralph, Loretta Devine, and Jennifer Holliday or by Beyoncé Knowles, Anika Noni Rose, and Jennifer Hudson): It's the trio's theme song.
- "And I Am Telling You I'm Not Going" (performed by Jennifer Holliday or by Jennifer Hudson): Effie's cry of rage and hurt when she's fired, it's the sensational close of act 1. Holliday can be seen singing it in a live concert on *My Favorite Broadway: The Leading Ladies* (Image Entertainment DVD).
- "When I First Saw You" (performed by Ben Harney and Sheryl Lee Ralph or by Jamie Foxx and Beyoncé Knowles): The lead singer of the Dreams wants to pursue a Hollywood career on her own, but Curtis doesn't want her to break up the act or their personal relationship.
- "I Meant You No Harm," "The Rap," and "Firing of Jimmy" (performed by Cleavant Derricks, Ben Harney, and Loretta Devine or by Eddie Murphy, Jamie Foxx, and Anika Noni Rose): Jimmy can't handle the new image Curtis wants, so he's fired.
- "I Miss You, Friend" and "One Night Only" (performed by Obba Babatundé, Jennifer Holliday, Sheryl Lee Ralph, Loretta Devine, and Deborah Burrell or by Keith Robinson, Jennifer Hudson, Beyoncé Knowles, Anika Noni Rose, and Sharon Leal): Effie's on her way to establishing a solo career, helped by a song written by her brother, who also writes the Dreams' songs. Curtis tries to ruin Effie's chances by having the Dreams record the song in their more homogenized and more popular style.

42nd Street

The following number from this 1980 show is on *Broadway's Lost Treasures* (Acorn Media DVD).

- "Lullaby of Broadway" (performed by Jerry Orbach and the ensemble): It's how the director convinces the understudy to stay.

The following numbers are from the original-cast recording of the 2001 revival (Atlantic/Wea CD), unless you'd rather watch the old Busby Berkeley movies (*The Busby Berkeley Collection*, a six-disc Warner Home Video DVD box set).

- "You're Getting to Be a Habit with Me" (performed by Christine Ebersole, it's from the 1933 movie *42nd Street*): It's sung by the star before she breaks her ankle.
- "I Only Have Eyes for You" (performed by Christine Ebersole and David Elder, it's from the 1934 movie *Dames*): The star is in love with her leading man, who's in love with the understudy.
- "42nd Street" (performed by Kate Levering and David Elder, it's from the 1933 movie *42nd Street*): The understudy and the leading man are a hit.

Little Shop of Horrors

The following numbers in this 1982 show are from the movie, directed by Frank Oz and available on Warner Home Video DVD and VHS.

- "Somewhere That's Green" (performed by Ellen Greene): Audrey dreams of life in the suburbs as it was lived on 1950s sitcoms.
- "Suddenly Seymour" (performed by Rick Moranis and Ellen Greene): Seymour declares his love to Audrey after her sadistic dentist boyfriend has disappeared. She doesn't know he's been eaten by the plant.

Merrily We Roll Along

The following numbers from this show are available on the original-cast recording (RCA CD).

- "Old Friends" (performed by Ann Morrison, Jim Walton, and Lonny Price)
- "Good Thing Going" (performed by Lonny Price, Jim Walton, and the company)

From *La Cage aux Folles* to *City of Angels*

Art isn't easy.
Every minor detail
Is a major decision.
Have to keep things in scale,
Have to hold to your vision.
—"PUTTING IT TOGETHER," *SUNDAY IN THE PARK WITH GEORGE,*
LYRICS BY STEPHEN SONDHEIM

By the end of the seventies, the musical play and the concept musical were taking themselves very seriously. Many new American shows left far behind the musical's origins in vaudeville, revue, and musical comedy. Artistic integrity left less and less room for stopping to amuse the audience, one reason attendance went down. Most new shows just weren't much fun anymore, opening the door for many successful revivals of old shows.

In the eighties, only Sondheim, the chief American exponent of the musical as an art form, was still allowed to succeed or fail almost entirely on his own terms. Since his shows usually failed commercially, it got harder even for him to get them produced. His 1990 show *Assassins* didn't get to Broadway until 2004 and ran only 101 performances, and his 1994 show *Passion* also flopped. His newest show, *Bounce,* had its world premiere at the Goodman Theatre in Chicago in 2003 and still hasn't been seen in New York.

In 1985, a producer of the needless and unsuccessful attempt to turn the movie musical *Singin' in the Rain* into a Broadway show said in the *New York Times,* in response to the deservedly unfavorable reviews, "Highbrowism is ruining musical theater. Critics want the musical to be fine art. It isn't, and I'm not sure it ever was. It's popular entertainment, and that requires a different eye than serious drama." The quote is saying that popular entertainment can't be fine art or serious drama—demonstrably untrue of such shows as *West Side Story, Cabaret, Company, A Little Night Music, A Chorus Line,* and *Ragtime,* to name only a few. Also, critics have liked such purely "popular entertainments" as *Annie, 42nd Street,* and *Crazy for You.* It's not either *Passion* or *Singin' in the Rain,* as if one had more right to exist than the other; it's that neither show happened to be good enough to make it on Broadway, although both have their supporters.

Musicals concerned with being works of art need to entertain—which doesn't necessarily mean amuse, although it helps. (More dance would help too.) If a serious musical doesn't entertain while saying what it's trying to say, most audiences don't listen, and the writers find themselves preaching to the few already converted. Popular entertainment, on the other hand, should have a fresh or at least a clever approach—and it doesn't hurt if it has something to say. Disney's *The Lion King* delighted both critics and audiences largely because of Julie Taymor's inventive and frequently exhilarating stagecraft as well as the chance to see familiar animated characters played by living, breathing, overamplified people. Though this obviously doesn't suggest that trying to duplicate movie musicals on stage is advisable (*Singin' in the Rain, Gigi,* and *Seven Brides for Seven Brothers,* for example), movies have been the source of some very successful entertainments. The highly praised and hugely successful *The Full Monty, The Producers,* and *Hairspray* are entertaining musical comedies adapted from movies that weren't musicals, though there was music in all of them (and they all dealt with aspects of show business, as a matter of fact). However, until the arrival of those shows on Broadway in 2000, 2001, and 2002, respectively, the musical comedy in particular seemed destined to become a forgotten art. The producer of *Singin' in the Rain* wasn't totally wrong: a certain amount of snobbery had set in. General audiences, however, were clearly interested in something more mindless. It was the time of more blockbuster movies, more multiplex movie theaters, more choices on TV with the advent of cable, more ways to turn off the world, and that's what Broadway audiences wanted as well.

In 1983, composer Eubie Blake, choreographer George Balanchine, playwright Tennessee Williams, and lyricists Howard Dietz and Ira Gershwin died. The top ticket price went up to $45, still behind the rise in the cost of production. A revival of Rodgers, Hart, and Abbott's 1936 *On Your Toes* (505 performances) had ninety-six-year-old George Abbott (who married a fifty-two-year-old woman during the year) directing and Hans Spialek re-creating his original orchestrations; there's an original-cast recording. There were short-run revivals of *Porgy and Bess, Show Boat* (with Lonette McKee, the first black woman to play Julie), and *Mame* with Angela Lansbury, and a 362-performance revival of *Zorba* with Anthony Quinn.

Annie closed after 2,377 performances, and *A Chorus Line* became the longest-running show and remained so for fourteen years. There were few successful new musical evenings. *Dance a Little Closer,* by Charles Strouse and Alan Jay Lerner (1 performance), was adapted from Robert E. Sherwood's play *Idiot's Delight;* the cast included Lerner's eighth wife, Liz Robertson. They were his last show and his last wife. *The Tap Dance Kid* (669 performances), by Henry Krieger, Robert Lorick, and Charles Blackwell, starred Hinton Battle. It's about a young black man who wants to be a tap dancer despite the disapproval of his father, a doctor. The seriousness of what the show has to say doesn't blend all that well with its lively tap numbers.

La Cage aux Folles is a comedy largely set in a gay nightclub, with cross-dressing and a happily married gay couple—a first for Broadway musicals. (There's no physical intimacy in the show.) They are Georges, the owner of the gay club that gives the show its title, and Albin, the star female impersonator of the club's show. The central plot revolves around problems involving Georges' son, engaged to a woman whose father is a homophobe. The chorus has both the men and the women dressed as women in the nightclub numbers. During the curtain calls, the men took off their wigs; only then could audiences be sure who was which sex. *La Cage aux Folles* was Herman's first hit since *Mame.* Unlike most shows by 1983, it got an out-of-town tryout to work out the problems, and RCA recorded it before it opened. The show follows the formulas of the golden age without pretending to be anything but the entertainment it is, given its semi-controversial subject matter.

La Cage aux Folles

MUSIC/LYRICS: Jerry Herman

BOOK: Harvey Fierstein, adapted from the French play by Jean Poiret and the 1979 French film

DIRECTOR: Arthur Laurents

CHOREOGRAPHER: Scott Salmon

ORCHESTRATOR: Jim Tyler

DESIGNERS: David Mitchell (sets), Theoni V. Aldredge (costumes), and Jules Fisher (lights)

PRODUCERS: eight listed, including Allan Carr

CAST INCLUDES: George Hearn and Gene Barry

PERFORMANCES: 1,761

> Although the show and score lacked depth or really strong emotions, [Herman] is the most accessible of all Broadway songwriters. However, his lyrics, never his strong suit, hit new lows here. . . . This show represented, as do all Herman shows, the height of Broadway glamour and professionalism. (Bloom, *American Song,* 385)

The score includes "The Best of Times" and "I Am What I Am." In 1996, the original French film was remade into the American film *The Birdcage.*

My One and Only

MUSIC: George Gershwin

LYRICS: Ira Gershwin

BOOK: Peter Stone and Timothy S. Mayer

DIRECTORS/CHOREOGRAPHERS: Tommy Tune and Thommie Walsh

PRODUCERS: seven listed, including Paramount Theatre Productions

CAST INCLUDES: Tommy Tune, Twiggy, Roscoe Lee Brown, and Charles "Honi" Coles

PERFORMANCES: 767

Baby

MUSIC: David Shire

LYRICS: Richard Maltby Jr.

BOOK: Sybille Pearson, based on a story by Susan Yankowitz

DIRECTOR: Richard Maltby Jr.

MUSICAL STAGING: Wayne Cilento

DESIGNERS: John Lee Beatty (sets), Jennifer von Mayrhauser (costumes), and Pat Collins (lights)

PRODUCERS: five listed, including Ivan Bloch

CAST INCLUDES: Liz Callaway, Beth Fowler, and Kim Criswell

PERFORMANCES: 241

A hit with lots of dancing, *My One and Only* is based on the Gershwins' 1927 *Funny Face,* considerably changed though and with only five songs from the original show and many other Gershwin songs added. All the chorus men were African Americans, and all the chorus women were white. The new script, still set in the twenties and still silly, is about the love affair between an American pilot and a British swimmer. There's an original-cast recording. It was *Cats'* chief competition for Best Musical.

Baby was a nice show that never quite made it with Broadway audiences. A small-cast musical about three couples on the verge of or trying to have a baby, it was too sentimental and unspectacular for the times. Maltby and Shire's first show to reach Broadway, it's occasionally revived by small theaters and schools. There's an original-cast recording.

In 1984, composer Arthur Schwartz, composer/lyricist/writer Meredith Willson, and performer Ethel Merman died. The off-Broadway Equity minimum went up to $225 a week, and the Broadway musicians' minimum rose to $650. It cost about $3 million to produce a musical on Broadway. It was a very lean year for the musical, with only Sondheim adding to the permanent repertory. *Evita* closed after 1,567 performances. There were revivals of *Oliver!* (17 performances) and *The Wiz* (13 performances), still with Stephanie Mills.

The Rink (204 performances), with music by John Kander, lyrics by Fred Ebb, and book by Terrence McNally, was a bleak, coldhearted show. It starred Liza Minnelli (replaced during the run by Stockard Channing) and Chita Rivera as daughter and mother, respectively (the mother owns a roller rink). These two characters mostly bicker through two acts but ultimately resolve their conflicts. There's an all-male chorus whose members play women as well as men. The original-cast recording includes "Colored Lights," "The Apple Doesn't Fall Very Far from the Tree," and "We Can Make It."

Sunday in the Park with George, Sondheim's first show without Prince since *Company* in 1970 and Lapine's first book for a musical, was workshopped by Playwrights Horizons. The first act is about Georges Seurat as he paints his famous pointillist work

A Sunday Afternoon on the Island of La Grande Jatte, now hanging in Chicago's Art Institute. The music and lyrics are frequently built out of little dots of sound, just as the painting is built out of little dots of paint. The second act is about Seurat's present-day great-grandson, who's into laser-light art. The show is about being an artist, regardless of the pull of the commercial world. Patinkin played Seurat in the first act and his great-grandson in the second; Peters played Seurat's mistress, Dot, in the first act and their daughter, Marie (the younger Seurat's grandmother), in the second. The rest of the cast also played different characters in each act. Most audiences have trouble with one of the acts, usually the second, which can feel rather overloaded with message about art versus commerce.

> What's a little cocktail conversation
> If it's going to get you your foundation,
> Leading to a prominent commission
> And an exhibition in addition? . . .
> Be new, George,
> They tell you till they're blue, George:
> You're new or else you're through, George,
> And even if it's true, George—
> You do what you can do. . . .
> The art of making art
> Is putting it together—
> Bit by bit—
> Link by link—
> Drink by drink—
> Mink by mink—
> And that
> Is the state
> Of the
> Art!

A certain kind of Broadway show inspires polarized responses by audience and critics. The audience on opening night of this show seemed to be divided into four camps: the people who genuinely loved it in spite of its flaws; those who loved it because it was a Sondheim musical and equated their positive response with their own worth as members of the intelligentsia; those who honestly hated the show; those who hated the show because it

Terrence McNally (1939–, born in St. Petersburg, Florida) was raised in Corpus Christi, Texas, and eventually moved to New York. His writing impressed Edward Albee, who helped him at the beginning of his career. *The Rink* was his first credited book for a musical. He also wrote the books for such musicals as *Kiss of the Spider Woman, Ragtime,* and *The Full Monty.* He's also written such plays as *Frankie and Johnny in the Claire de Lune, Love! Valour! Compassion!* and *Master Class.* He's won four Tony Awards.

Sunday in the Park with George

MUSIC/LYRICS: Stephen Sondheim

BOOK/DIRECTOR: James Lapine

ORCHESTRATOR: Michael Starobin

DESIGNERS: Tony Straiges (sets), Patricia Zipprodt and Ann Hould-Ward (costumes), and Richard Nelson (lights)

PRODUCERS: The Shubert Organization and Emanuel Azenberg in association with Playwrights Horizons

CAST INCLUDES: Mandy Patinkin, Bernadette Peters, Dana Ivey, and Charles Kimbrough

PERFORMANCES: 604

was the thing to do but will love the album. . . . The nomination of this show and *La Cage aux Folles* for the [1983–84] Best Musical Tony Award led to a not so cold war between lovers of Broadway pizzazz and those who aspired to advancement of the art form. Those that could accept both styles of show sat on the sidelines and scratched their heads. (Bloom, *American Song*, 712–13)

La Cage won the Tony; *Sunday in the Park* won the Pulitzer Prize for drama. In its score are "Finishing the Hat," "Putting It Together," and "Move On." Besides the original-cast recording, there's a live performance on videotape and DVD. The show lost half a million dollars in its original run.

In 1985, writer Morrie Ryskind, writer/director Abe Burrows, lyricist Carolyn Leigh, and performer Phil Silvers died. Boublil and Schönberg's *Les Misérables* opened in London. Yul Brynner starred in a 191-performance revival of *The King and I;* when it closed he'd played the role of the King 4,625 times, not counting the movie. He died soon after. There was a 1-performance revival of *Take Me Along*. The New York City Opera had a limited run of *Kismet. Singin' in the Rain*, with Twyla Tharp's first Broadway choreography, ran 367 performances at a loss. Although there were more productions in 1985 than in the previous couple of years, the 1984–85 Broadway season was so bad that there were no Tony nominations for Leading Actor, Leading Actress, or Choreographer of a Musical.

An August article in *Variety* noted another major reason for problems Broadway had been confronting and would continue to confront. In the ten years since 1975, prices on goods in general had gone up 60 percent. But the [*New York*] *Times*'s advertising rates had jumped 300 percent and union benefits 600 percent. The trade sheet estimated that tickets could have cost a third less if increases had merely doubled that of the national inflation average. (Bordman, 719)

There were jukebox revues both off-Broadway and on: *Leader of the Pack* (120 performances) was a Broadway revue of sixties rock songs by Ellie Greenwich, Jeff Barry, and Phil Spector. Among the cast were Greenwich, Patrick Cassidy, Jasmine Guy, and Dinah Manoff. There's an original-cast recording. *Jerry's Girls* (141 performances) was a revue of Jerry Herman songs, with Dorothy Loudon, Chita Rivera, and Leslie Uggams; it has an original-cast recording of the road company with Carol Channing, Andrea McArdle, and Uggams. *Lies and Legends: The Musical Stories of Harry Chapin* (79 performances) was an off-Broadway revue of Chapin's songs; it began life in Chicago. The off-Broadway spoof musical *Nunsense* (3,672 performances) opened; it's about a group of untalented nuns putting on a show to raise funds.

Big River couldn't possibly encompass enough of Twain's novel to do it justice. The country-western score by pop artist Miller was the biggest attraction of the show; unfortunately, it's his only Broadway score. The show tried out at the American Repertory Theatre and at La Jolla Playhouse, both not-for-profit regional theaters. It was the first Broadway show produced by Rocco Landesman, soon the head of Jujamcyn Theaters. It won the 1984–85 Tony pretty much by default and six other Tonys as well. There's an original-cast recording. In the score are "Muddy Water," "Leavin's Not the Only Way to Go," and "Free at Last." A 2003 revival directed by Jeff Calhoun had seven deaf and eleven hearing actors performing in spoken English and American Sign Language.

The Mystery of Edwin Drood moved to Broadway after being produced by Joseph Papp at his outdoor Central Park summer theater. Although Rupert Holmes usually wrote rock music, it doesn't have a rock score. The show is presented in the style of a Victorian-English music-hall evening and is done as a show within the music hall show. It requires the audience to choose who the murderer is, since Dickens died before revealing it; Holmes wrote slightly different endings depending on who was picked. There's an original-cast recording. The score includes "Don't Quit While You're Ahead" and "Moonfall." The show won the 1985–86 Tony, again with little competition. During the run, the title was changed to *Drood!*

Song and Dance has two nearly unconnected acts. The first act, originally a 1980 TV musical called *Tell Me on a Sunday*, is a one-woman song cycle. The second act is a ballet based on Lloyd Webber's Variations on Paganini's Caprice in A Minor. The principal male dancer of act 2 ends up with the woman of act 1, and that's the only connection between the two halves. It was the first Lloyd Webber show on Broadway that didn't make back its investment. During the run Betty Buckley replaced Bernadette Peters. There's an original-cast recording.

Big River

MUSIC/LYRICS: Roger Miller

BOOK: William Hauptman, adapted from Mark Twain's novel *The Adventures of Huckleberry Finn*

DIRECTOR: Des McAnuff

CHOREOGRAPHER: Janet Watson

DESIGNERS: Heidi Landesman (sets), Patricia McGourty (costumes), and Richard Riddell (lights)

PRODUCERS: five listed, including Heidi Landesman and Rick Steiner

CAST INCLUDES: René Auberjonois, John Goodman, and Bob Gunton

PERFORMANCES: 1,005

The Mystery of Edwin Drood

MUSIC/LYRICS/BOOK: Rupert Holmes, adapted from the unfinished Charles Dickens novel

DIRECTOR: Wilford Leach

CHOREOGRAPHER: Graciela Daniele

ORCHESTRATOR: Rupert Holmes

PRODUCER: New York Shakespeare Festival

CAST INCLUDES: George Rose, Betty Buckley, Cleo Laine, Donna Murphy, and Judy Kuhn

PERFORMANCES: 608

Song and Dance

MUSIC: Andrew Lloyd Webber

LYRICS: Don Black (American adaptation and additional lyrics: Richard Maltby Jr.)

DIRECTOR: Richard Maltby Jr.

CHOREOGRAPHER: Peter Martins, with Gregg Burge for the tap dancing

ORCHESTRATORS: Andrew Lloyd Webber and David Cullen

PRODUCERS: Cameron Mackintosh, the Shubert Organization, and FMW Productions Group by arrangement with Lloyd Webber's Really Useful Theatre Group

CAST INCLUDES: Bernadette Peters and Christopher D'Amboise, with Charlotte D'Amboise and Gregg Burge

PERFORMANCES: 474 (781 in London)

Grind (71 performances) has music by Larry Grossman, lyrics by Ellen Fitzhugh, and book by Fay Kanin. It was directed by Harold Prince, was produced by Prince and six others, and had a cast that included Stubby Kaye and Ben Vereen. It was set in and around a 1933 Chicago burlesque house that has a racially mixed cast but keeps blacks and whites segregated. Racial tensions are far more prominent than entertainment values; the show ends with a race riot outside the theater. Preachy and bleak, *Grind* was a quick flop.

> The musical prompted an interesting attack by John Podhoretz in the *Washington Times,* even if the attack, coming when the musical theatre was at a nadir, was something like hitting a man when he's down. The attack was leveled as much at one man— Hal Prince—as it was at the whole modern school of musicals in which Prince and his erstwhile associate, Stephen Sondheim, loom so large. Opening by accusing Prince of "art-slaughter," Podhoretz reached back to suggest that "the musical took a crucial, and in retrospect suicidal, step into the realm of social commentary" with *West Side Story,* and continued that Prince and Sondheim, with the "concept musical," actually created "an antimusical, a self-destructive form in which characters were taken to task and made fun of for doing things like bursting into song." He concluded that a grating ugliness had replaced the sweet, memorable melodies, the care-chasing fun, and the winning attractiveness of the musicals of old. . . . He might also have attacked the ubiquitous amplification and the resigned acceptance of it by responsibility-shirking critics. (Bordman, 717–18)

Again, there's an either-or attitude at play that refuses to see that both kinds of shows are equally valid. Just because *Grind* was a flop doesn't make everything that came before it culpable. A flop is a flop, regardless of its ancestry.

In 1986, composer Harold Arlen and writer/lyricist Alan Jay Lerner died. *The Phantom of the Opera* opened in London. Business on Broadway was down for the fifth year in a row. The New York City Opera revived *Brigadoon* and *The New Moon* in limited runs. Fosse directed a 365-performance revival of *Sweet Charity* starring Debbie Allen. His last new show, a 70-performance flop, was *Big Deal,* set in the thirties. Based on the Italian film comedy

Big Deal on Madonna Street, it's about a robbery gone comically wrong, and it uses real songs of the period. Marvin Hamlisch and Howard Ashman's *Smile* (48 performances) was adapted from the 1975 nonmusical movie about a teenage beauty contest. *Beehive* (600 performances), a jukebox revue paying tribute to sixties women singers, opened off-Broadway. There were two failed revues of Jerome Kern songs, one on and one off-Broadway.

Rags—music by Charles Strouse, lyrics by Stephen Schwartz, book by Joseph Stein—was directed by Gene Saks, choreographed by Ron Field and starred opera singer Teresa Stratas, Larry Kert, Lonny Price, and Terrence Mann. A 4-performance flop by an all-star team of writers, director, and choreographer, it's about a Jewish immigrant from the time she lands at Ellis Island in the early twentieth century through her first years of struggle and poverty on Manhattan's Lower East Side. Most people blame the extreme heavy-handedness of the book for the show's failure. There have been attempts at revising and reviving it that have been more successful than the Broadway production.

The only hit of the meager musical year was the old British show *Me and My Girl* (1,420 performances), which has music by Noel Gay, book and lyrics by Arthur Rose and Douglas Furber, and a book revised by Stephen Fry and Mike Ockrent. It was directed by Ockrent, choreographed by Gillian Gregory, and starred Robert Lindsay, Maryann Plunkett, Jane Connell, and George S. Irving. A 1937 British musical comedy, it was successfully revived in London in 1985 starring Lindsay and Emma Thompson and then produced in the United States for the first time ever. Silly, charming, and old-fashioned, it's about a Cockney who inherits a title and has to learn to deal with the snobbish aristocracy. Lindsay was brilliant in the leading role, calling into play his vast resources of charm, timing, and physical dexterity. The U.S. production tried out in Los Angeles. The original-cast recording includes the big hit of 1937 in Britain, "The Lambeth Walk."

In 1987, director/choreographers Michael Bennett and Bob Fosse, writer Michael Stewart, director Rouben Mamoulian, and performers Fred Astaire, Ray Bolger, and Danny Kaye died. With the Broadway opening of *Les Misérables* (with a top ticket price of $47.50), the European pop opera rose considerably in popularity, and the American musical—and, in particular, the musical comedy—was clearly in jeopardy. There was a 177-performance revival of *Dreamgirls*, and Joel Grey returned in a 261-performance revival of *Cabaret.* The New York City Opera revived *South Pacific, The Student Prince,* and *The Desert Song* for limited runs. Harvey Schmidt and Tom Jones wrote a musical version of Thornton Wilder's *Our Town* called *Grovers Corners,* which tried out at a dinner theater outside Chicago and never got to New York.

Jerry Zaks (1946–, born in Stuttgart, Germany, educated in the United States), the son of Holocaust survivors, began his Broadway career as a replacement in *Grease* and was soon directing plays. The revival of *Anything Goes* was his first Broadway musical. He's won four Tony Awards and has been responsible for such hits as *Smokey Joe's Café* and the revivals of *Guys and Dolls* in 1995 and of *A Funny Thing Happened on the Way to the Forum* in 1996. Zaks is a founding member of the Ensemble Studio Theatre.

The most successful American musical of the year was Lincoln Center Theater's revival of Cole Porter's *Anything Goes* (804 performances), with a new book by Timothy Crouse (son of Russel Crouse, one of the original writers) and John Weidman. It was directed by Jerry Zaks, choreographed by Michael Smuin, and starred Patti LuPone (making mush of Porter's lyrics, as you can hear on the cast recording). Songs from other Porter shows were interpolated.

Despite the popularity of European pop operas, there was at least one expensive failure: *Starlight Express,* with music by Andrew Lloyd Webber, lyrics by Richard Stilgoe, direction by Trevor Nunn, and with Andrea McArdle (who'd played the title role in the original production of *Annie*) in the cast. Like all of Lloyd Webber's later shows, it opened first in London. At $8 million, it was the most expensive show to be mounted on Broadway to date, and although it was a huge hit in London, the Broadway version was the second Lloyd Webber show to close at a loss, despite its 761 performances. The faceless cast, playing train cars this time instead of cats, are on roller skates and in gaudy futuristic costumes. (It's sort of *The Little Engine That Could Skate.*) Some of the skating was done around the audience. There's an original-cast recording of the score, badly missing the skating.

Les Misérables

MUSIC: Claude-Michel Schönberg

LYRICS: Herbert Kretzmer, with additional material by James Fenton

BOOK: Alain Boublil and Jean-Marc Natel, adapted from Victor Hugo's 1862 novel

DIRECTORS: Trevor Nunn and John Caird (adapters of the French musical drama)

ORCHESTRATOR: John Cameron

DESIGNERS: John Napier (sets), Andreane Neofitou (costumes), and David Hersey (lights)

PRODUCER: Cameron Mackintosh

CAST INCLUDES: Colm Wilkinson, Randy Graff, Terrence Mann, Judy Kuhn, and Frances Ruffelle

PERFORMANCES: 6,680

Les Misérables is a through-composed, dramatic pop opera with lots of spectacle and lushly romantic music, adapted from Hugo's epic novel about poverty, love, obsession, redemption, revolution, and sewers in nineteenth-century France. Jean Valjean, imprisoned for twenty years for stealing a loaf of bread, is at last released. When he's caught for a second, similar crime, he escapes with the help of a priest, after which he's pursued remorselessly by the obsessed inspector Javert. In the end, he saves Javert's life by carrying him through the sewers of Paris, and the humiliated Javert commits suicide. The main subplot is a love triangle: Marius, a young revolutionary, is in love with Cosette, Valjean's adopted daughter, and is himself loved by Eponine, a young waif. Although there's no way to compress Hugo's sprawling novel into three hours, the story isn't told as choppily as it might have been—the show certainly does a better job than *Oliver!* did, for example.

Les Misérables was originally a French record album, which was followed by a full production in Paris. The show was considerably rewritten by the directors and lyricists for its English version and was first produced in London in 1985 starring Wilkinson, Ruffelle, and Patti LuPone. It has since been done all over the world. (After ten years on Broadway, producer Mackintosh decided it was not in good shape and demanded that, except for the lead, the entire cast—almost all replacements and replacements of replacements—re-audition for codirector Caird. Not all of them were recast.) Like *Cats,* the show's Broadway audience was largely made up of tourists, who could enjoy the spectacle, the performances, and the music even if they didn't necessarily know what was going on every minute. Along with several recordings, there's a video of a live concert performance celebrating the London production's tenth anniversary. The score includes "I Dreamed a Dream," "Empty Chairs at Empty Tables," "Bring Him Home," and "On My Own." The show won the 1986–87 Tony. It closed in 2003 but was revived on Broadway by producer Mackintosh in 2006 (285 performances as of July 15, 2007).

The first act of *Into the Woods* takes four fairy tales to their happily-ever-after conclusions: "Cinderella," "Rapunzel," "Jack and the Beanstalk," and "Little Red Riding Hood." There's also an invented story that ends happily and that ties all the other stories together. It's about a childless couple—a baker and his wife—and a witch (the one who keeps Rapunzel in her tower) who sends them on a quest that will allow them to break her curse on them and thus conceive a child. The quest involves Cinderella's glass slipper, Rapunzel's hair, Jack's cow, and Little Red Riding Hood's hooded cape. The second act shows how untrue happily-ever-after is: Cinderella's and Rapunzel's princes are unfaithful, the wife of the giant killed by Jack in the first act comes seeking revenge, and several characters are killed, including Jack's mother and the baker's wife.

Many people prefer the first act as if it were a separate entity, which it is not. The show is about family and about the need for cooperation within a community in order to battle the "giants" in our midst (which is really what Hammerstein's shows were about). The woods come to represent the battles of life one must go through—win or lose. The show tried out at San Diego's Old Globe Theatre. It didn't pay back its entire investment during its long Broadway run, although it has done so

Into the Woods

MUSIC/LYRICS: Stephen Sondheim

BOOK/DIRECTOR: James Lapine

CHOREOGRAPHER: Lar Lubovitch

ORCHESTRATOR: Jonathan Tunick

DESIGNERS: Tony Straiges (sets), Ann Hould-Ward (costumes), and Richard Nelson (lights)

PRODUCERS: six listed, including Jujamcyn Theaters

CAST INCLUDES: Bernadette Peters, Joanna Gleason, and Chip Zien

PERFORMANCES: 765

since; it's revived a lot all over the world. Among the songs are the funny duet "Agony" for the two princes and its equally funny reprise, "Giants in the Sky," "No One Is Alone," and "Children Will Listen." There was a 2002 revival starring Vanessa Williams. There's a video and a DVD of a live performance with the original cast.

In 1988, writer/director Joshua Logan, director/choreographer Ron Field, and composer Frederick Loewe died. (Field was the third important director/choreographer to die within a year.) The top ticket price rose to $50. The New York City Opera had limited-run revivals of *The Merry Widow* and *The New Moon.* There was a 176-performance revival of *Ain't Misbehavin'.* Michael Gore, Dean Pitchford, and Lawrence D. Cohen's adaptation of Stephen King's *Carrie*—Betty Buckley, blood bucket, and all—closed after 5 performances. *Chess,* with music by Benny Andersson and Björn Ulvaeus of the Swedish rock group ABBA and lyrics by Tim Rice, was a big success in London but ran only 68 performances on Broadway; it was directed by Trevor Nunn and includes the hit song "One Night in Bangkok." The only successful new musical was another British import: *The Phantom of the Opera.*

Another tourist attraction, *The Phantom of the Opera* is a romantic operetta (with a score that frequently wishes it sounded like Puccini) about a masked man who haunts the Paris Opera House and saws down a chandelier in order to make his favorite soprano a star. It doesn't tell its story as clearly as one might wish. In fact, besides its brooding, romantic, masked antihero, it's most famous for its production values, such as a boat that glides along the stage floor, lit candelabras that rise from below the stage floor, lots of fog, a second-act opener with costumes and a staircase that together could pay for an entire season's budget for any regional theater, and a chandelier that falls from above the audience's head directly onto the stage to end the first act. The show broke the record for the greatest advance ticket sales in Broadway history: $16.5 million. (When it opened, Brightman was married to Lloyd Webber—the show has far outlasted the marriage.) In the score are "All I Ask of You" and the endlessly repeated "The Music of the Night" (which starts out ex-

The Phantom of the Opera

MUSIC: Andrew Lloyd Webber
LYRICS: Charles Hart, with additions by Richard Stilgoe
BOOK: Richard Stilgoe and Andrew Lloyd Webber, based on the 1916 novel by Gaston Leroux
DIRECTOR: Harold Prince
CHOREOGRAPHER: Gillian Lynne
ORCHESTRATORS: David Cullen and Andrew Lloyd Webber
DESIGNERS: Maria Björnson (sets and costumes) and Andrew Bridge (lights)
PRODUCERS: Cameron Mackintosh and Lloyd Webber's Really Useful Theatre Group
CAST INCLUDES: Michael Crawford and Sarah Brightman (both also starred in the original London production)
PERFORMANCES: 8,117 as of July 15, 2007, and the longest-running show in Broadway history till that date

actly like the tune of Lerner and Loewe's "Come to Me, Bend to Me" from their 1947 *Brigadoon*). *Phantom* won seven 1987–88 Tony Awards, including Best Musical, beating *Into the Woods*, which won for Best Book and Best Score. Several recordings are available. There've been numerous movie versions of the novel, going all the way back to the silent film starring Lon Chaney. A movie version of Lloyd Webber's pop opera starring Gerald Butler, Emmy Rossum, Patrick Wilson, and Minnie Driver (released in 2004) was a flop. There's another musical theater version of the story called *Phantom* by Maury Yeston and Arthur Kopit, which has had many productions outside of New York City.

Romance/Romance (297 performances) has music by Keith Herrmann and book and lyrics by Barry Harman, who also directed it. It was choreographed by Pamela Sousa and orchestrated by Michael Starobin. The show is two one-act musicals, each using the same four performers—Scott Bakula, Alison Fraser, Deborah Graham, and Robert Hoshour. The first, "The Little Comedy," is based on a Schnitzler short story about two rich people pretending to be poor for romantic reasons. The second, "Summer Share," about two couples who almost switch partners, is based on Jules Renard's 1899 play *Le Pain de Ménage* reset to contemporary times. The show was workshopped at the Actor's Outlet in 1987. There's an original-cast recording.

In 1989, Irving Berlin, 101 years old, and performer Beatrice Lillie died. *Miss Saigon* opened in London. The weekly Equity minimum for Broadway rose to $813.75. It was only a slightly better year for the American musical, including a revival of *Gypsy* (476 performances) starring Tyne Daly, that returned in 1991 for 105 more performances. The New York City Opera did limited runs of *The Pajama Game*, *The Merry Widow*, *The Desert Song*, and *Candide*. There was also a 188-performance, well-received, off-Broadway revival of *Sweeney Todd* in a far more intimate production than the original. Rock star Sting starred in a flop revival of *The Threepenny Opera*. *Black and Blue* (829 performances) was an African American jukebox revue of songs and dances from the thirties and forties; young dancer Savion Glover was in the cast. There were no nominees for Best Book or Best Score of a Musical at the 1988–89 Tony Awards; the best shows of the year opened in the 1989–90 season and weren't considered till 1990.

Meet Me in St. Louis (252 performances) had music and lyrics by Ralph Blane and Hugh Martin and book by Hugh Wheeler, adapted from Sally Benson's "The Kensington Stories" and the 1944 Vincente Minnelli movie musical starring Judy Garland. The cast included Betty Garrett, George

Hearn, and Milo O'Shea. Another failed attempt at bringing a movie musical to the stage, the score incorporated the movie score and several other songs by Blane and Martin.

Jerome Robbins' Broadway, a revue of musical numbers from shows Robbins had choreographed, was his first Broadway show since *Fiddler on the Roof* twenty-five years earlier, and his last. It had a cast of sixty-two dancers in numbers by twenty-two composers and writers, and the sets and costumes of twelve designers. It rehearsed for twenty-two weeks.

> The important thing about this show was to affirm the power of a great choreographer's personal touch—dances that had become taken for granted over years of movie versions and routine revivals took on bold new life because Robbins oversaw this production. (Albert Williams, personal communication)

The cast included Jason Alexander as both narrator and performer, Faith Prince, Charlotte D'Amboise, Debbie Shapiro, and Scott Wise. The most expensive musical evening of the decade, it cost over $8 million and lost half of it despite a 634-performance run. It took eight months to reconstruct all the numbers selected for the show, and the result was too big and expensive ever to make back its money even though the top ticket price was raised to $60 during the run. It won the Tony without any real competition. There's an original-cast recording.

Even with its long run, *Grand Hotel* didn't pay back its investment. (*At the Grand*, an earlier version by Wright and Forrest, had flopped in Los Angeles in 1958.) *Grand Hotel*, about the many occupants of a Berlin hotel between the two world wars, is a hollow shell of a musical that barely allows us to know any of its characters well enough to care what happens to them. Every move was choreographed to a largely uninteresting script and score. Tune workshopped the show in New York and was, perhaps, so concerned with how to stage and design it that he accepted second-rate material from the writers. There's an original-cast recording. Watch the old all-star MGM movie instead.

A satire on Hollywood in the late 1940s, *City of Angels* alternates between two stories. The main one is about the personal and professional problems of a writer of detective novels brought

Grand Hotel

MUSIC/LYRICS: Robert Wright and George Forrest, with additional material by Maury Yeston and Wally Harper

BOOK: Luther Davis (with an uncredited assist from Peter Stone), adapted from Vicki Baum's novel and play and from the 1932 movie

DIRECTOR/CHOREOGRAPHER: Tommy Tune (who also conceived it)

ORCHESTRATOR: Peter Matz

DESIGNERS: Tony Walton (sets), Santo Loquasto (costumes), and Jules Fisher (lights)

PRODUCERS: seven listed, including Jujamcyn Theaters and Paramount Pictures

CAST INCLUDES: Liliane Montevecchi, Karen Akers, Michael Jeter, and Jane Krakowski

PERFORMANCES: 1,017

out to Hollywood to adapt one of his novels into a movie; the second story is that of the movie he's writing. The writer's scenes were in color, the movie scenes in black, white, and gray. (The sets and costumes were among the highlights of the show.) Except for the writer and his fictional detective, everyone is double-cast, playing roles in both the writer's life and in the movie, making for clever parallels between the two. Because of the technical complexities of the huge set, the show had no workshop or out-of-town tryouts. Gelbart's script is excellent. (He also cowrote *A Funny Thing Happened on the Way to the Forum*, the TV series *M*A*S*H*, and the movie *Tootsie*, among his many accomplishments.) There's an original-cast recording of the *City of Angels* jazz-based score, including "You're Nothing Without Me" and "You Can Always Count on Me." The show won the 1989–90 Tony.

City of Angels
MUSIC: Cy Coleman
LYRICS: David Zippel
BOOK: Larry Gelbart
DIRECTOR: Michael Blakemore
CHOREOGRAPHER: Walter Painter
ORCHESTRATOR: Billy Byers
DESIGNERS: Robin Wagner (sets), Florence Klotz (costumes), and Paul Gallo (lights)
PRODUCERS: five listed, including the Shubert Organization and Jujamcyn Theaters
CAST INCLUDES: James Naughton, Gregg Edelman, Randy Graff, Dee Hoty, and René Auberjonois
PERFORMANCES: 879

By the end of the eighties, the standard top price for a musical on Broadway was $75. Going into the nineties, the musical—whether art, entertainment, or both—therefore faced the impossible task of being a populist entertainment at an elitist price. Who were the audiences paying those prices? Mostly people out to have a good time, often with their families, and with the money to afford it. As part of their good time, they wanted to see the price of the ticket up there on the stage, they wanted to know what they were buying before they bought it, and they didn't come to the theater to be made to think. So both producers and audiences were making artistic demands with economic justifications. One of the many resulting problems was that both groups had conservative standards that kept the musical from growing and changing with the times. No wonder so many younger potential audience members in particular, even those who could afford the tickets, thought of musicals as old-fashioned and avoided them.

Suggested Watching and Listening

Big River: The Adventures of Huckleberry Finn
The following song from this 1985 musical is on the original-cast recording (Decca U.S. CD) and on Paul Gruber's *Original Cast! Completing the Century: 1980–1994* (MET CD).
- "Muddy Water" (performed by Daniel Jenkins and Ron Richardson): Huck and Jim are on the raft.

Black and Blue
This 1989 show includes the number "T'Ain't Nobody's Business If I Do" (performed by the cast), available on *Broadway's Lost Treasures III* (Acorn Media DVD).

La Cage aux Folles
This 1983 show features the song "I Am What I Am" (performed by George Hearn), available on the DVD *Broadway's Lost Treasures II* (Acorn Media DVD) and on the original-cast recording (RCA Victor Broadway CD).

City of Angels
The original-cast recording of this 1989 show is available as a Sony CD. It features the following numbers.
- "Double Talk" (performed by Gregg Edelman): Stine, the detective story writer, is excited about going to Hollywood.
- "You Gotta Look Out for Yourself" (performed by Scott Waara, Peter Davis, Amy Jane London, Gary Kahn, and Jackie Presti): Radio star Jimmy Powers and the Angel City 4 are radio performers in Stine's mystery who also act as commentators on the story.
- "With Every Breath I Take" (performed by Kay McClelland): It's sung by a lounge singer in the mystery. She also plays the writer's wife.
- "You're Nothing Without Me" (performed by Gregg Edelman and James Naughton): Stine, the writer, and Stone, his fictional detective, close the first act with this challenge duet.
- "You Can Always Count on Me" (performed by Randy Graff): It's sung by the detective's secretary in the mystery. She also plays the Hollywood studio head's secretary.

Grand Hotel
This 1989 show includes the number "Take a Glass Together" (performed by Michael Jeter, Brent Barrett, and the chorus), which is on *Broadway's Lost Treasures II* (Acorn Media DVD).

Into the Woods
This version of the 1987 show is from the 1990 taping of a live performance with the original cast, available on Image Entertainment DVD.
- "Prologue: Once Upon a Time . . .", "Into the Woods," "Fly Birds, Back to the Sky!" and "Jack, Jack, Head in a Sack . . .": This is the opening sequence. We learn that we're in a fairy-tale land in a fantasy time and that characters from several stories are on their way into the woods for various personal reasons. The tone is a mixture of musical comedy and operetta, with a through-composed score that accompanies much of the occasional dialogue passages. There isn't much at all in the way of dance here or anywhere else in the show.
- "Hello, Little Girl" (performed by Robert Westenberg as the Wolf and Danielle Ferland as Little Red Riding Hood)
- "Giants in the Sky" (performed by Ben Wright as Jack)
- "Agony" (performed by Robert Westenberg and Chuck Wagner): The princes sing about the women they have fallen in love with, Cinderella and Rapunzel.
- "It Takes Two" (performed by Chip Zien and Joanna Gleason): The message of the show, understood by the Baker's wife and realized by the Baker.
- "Stay with Me" (Bernadette Peters as the Witch and Pamela Winslow as Rapunzel)

- "Agony Reprise" (performed by Robert Westenberg and Chuck Wagner): Now that they're married to Cinderella and Rapunzel, the princes have fallen in love with Sleeping Beauty and Snow White (who never appear).
- "Children Will Listen" and "The Finale" (performed by Bernadette Peters and the company)

Les Misérables: The Dream Cast in Concert

The following numbers are from the 1995 tenth-anniversary concert of the original London production, available on DVD from Sony Pictures.

- "I Dreamed a Dream" (performed by Ruthie Henshall): Fantine is a prostitute taken under Jean Valjean's wing. When she dies, he takes charge of her daughter, Cosette.
- "Master of the House" (performed by Alun Armstrong, Jenny Galloway, and the company): The innkeeper Thénardier and his wife are the comic relief in this very sober show. They're also scoundrels who bilk a lot of money out of Valjean for looking after Cosette until he realizes how mistreated she's been and takes her out of their keeping.
- "Stars" (performed by Philip Quast): Inspector Javert is obsessed with needing to capture Valjean.
- "A Heart Full of Love" (performed by Michael Ball, Judy Kuhn, and Lea Salonga): Cosette has grown up and fallen in love with the student revolutionary Marius, who is, in turn, loved by the waif Eponine.
- "On My Own" (performed by Lea Salonga): Eponine knows her love is hopeless.
- "Bring Him Home" (performed by Colm Wilkinson): Valjean prays for Marius, wounded in the failed revolution.
- "Empty Chairs at Empty Tables" (performed by Michael Ball): Marius, recovered, mourns his friends killed in the revolution. It's what we would call survivor guilt.

The first-act finale can be seen on *Broadway's Lost Treasures II* (Acorn Media DVD).

My One and Only

The 1983 show closes with "Chasing the Clouds Away" (performed by Tommy Tune, Twiggy, and the chorus), which is on *Broadway's Lost Treasures* (Acorn Media DVD).

The Rink

This 1984 show features the song "Colored Lights" (performed by Liza Minnelli), which is available on the original-cast recording (Jay Records CD) and on Paul Gruber's *Original Cast! Completing the Century: 1980–1994* (MET CD).

Sunday in the Park with George

The selections listed below are from the taping of the original production, directed by Terry Hughes and available on Image Entertainment DVD.

- Act 1: Paris, A Series of Sundays, 1884–1886 (performed by the company): Act 1 is worth watching in its entirety to see how the painting comes into being. It includes the title song, "No Life," "Color and Light," "Gossip," "The Day Off," "Everybody Loves Louis," "Finishing the Hat," "We Do Not Belong Together," "Beautiful," and "Sunday."
- "Putting It Together" (performed by Mandy Patinkin and the company): The contemporary George has to deal with people at a cocktail party.

From *Assassins* to *Ragtime*

You're living in America
At the end of the millennium
You're living in America
Where it's like the twilight zone

And when you're living in America
At the end of the millennium
You're what you own

So I own not a notion
I escape and ape content
I don't own emotion—I rent
—"WHAT YOU OWN," *RENT,* LYRICS BY JONATHAN LARSON

During the eighties, America was ready to get over angst and move on to greed. The American musical was not. In the nineties, risks of any kind were avoided; even Stephen Sondheim's name on *Assassins* in 1990 couldn't get the show moved to Broadway from its off-Broadway workshop, most likely because of its subject matter. Here's an example of why risk aversion was so widespread (and still is): the original 1951 *The King and I* cost $360,000 to produce; the 1996 Broadway revival cost $5.5 million. Today, producing a new musical can easily cost $10 million on Broadway and $3 million or more off-Broadway. And that's without budgeting in the now usually cost-prohibitive but badly missed tradition of taking a show out on the road to test it before bringing it to New York. Even the deeply flawed *The Goodbye Girl, Victor/Victoria,* and *Sweet Smell of Success* got noticeably better—not good, but better—with help from the negative reviews they got during their Chicago tryouts. *Movin' Out* also had a tryout in Chicago, where it got mostly very negative reviews (particularly for the first act), which helped prompt a rewrite that saved the show and turned it into a hit. Chicago is a good, albeit picky, tryout town, but at least the critics there wait till the producers say it's OK to come. Even *The Producers* did a little fine-tuning during its tryout there. Out-of-town try-outs almost always prove their worth, regardless of the cost.

> While as late as the 1980–81 season *Variety* counted twenty new musicals on Broadway, the count in 1994–95 was down to two. . . . There's little if any argu-ment about what the killer was: economics. Inflation on Broadway has been rampant. . . . Ticket prices doubled [between 1980 and 1994], . . . deterring many from attending the theater regularly, and yet not even keeping up with the cost of production. (Gruber, *Original Cast! Completing the Century,* 3–4)

If costs continue escalating, the $100 ticket will soon be the norm. It was al-ready the top price for *The Producers* in 2002, not counting the producers' at-tempt to circumvent the scalpers by setting aside tickets at each performance for $480, still less than what the scalpers were charging.

In 1990, composer/conductor Leonard Bernstein, performers Mary Martin, Rex Harrison, and Jack Gilford, writer Bella Spewack, and designer Erté died. There was an all-black, 77-performance revisal of the 1926 *Oh, Kay!* Re-vivals included *Fiddler on the Roof* with Topol (241 performances) and *Peter Pan* with Cathy Rigby (45 performances). The New York City Opera revived

Backdrop: 1990–1999

National   The U.S. national debt is over $3 trillion. Saddam Hussein's Iraq invades Kuwait, which is liberated by U.S. and allied troops in 1991 in Operation Desert Storm. Bill Clinton is elected presi-dent in 1992, defeating the first President Bush, and reelected in 1996, defeating Senator Bob Dole. He's impeached for perjury before a grand jury about his affair with an intern and for obstruction of justice, but he gets off. Clinton signs the North American Free Trade Agreement (NAFTA), strategic arms reduction treaties between the United States and Russia, and the Brady Bill, which requires a five-day waiting period for buyers of handguns. The Senate bans the sale of most assault rifles. A bomb destroys the Federal Building in Oklahoma City, and a terrorist's bomb explodes at the New York World Trade Center. Ted Kaczynski, the Unabomber, is caught and convicted. Los Angeles police are acquitted of the beating of Rodney King, which causes a major outbreak of violence and looting. In

The Sound of Music with Debby Boone. *A Chorus Line* closed after 6,137 performances.

Stuart Rose's cabaret revue of fifties songs and attitudes, *Forever Plaid,* ran 1,811 performances off-Broadway. Among the musicals of the year were such disasters as the hugely expensive, 72-performance flop *Shogun: The Musical,* which lost about $7 million. There was an attempt by Strouse, Charnin, and Meehan to write a sequel to their *Annie.* Called *Annie 2: Miss Hannigan's Revenge,* it closed out of town, was rewritten, and opened off-Broadway in 1993 as *Annie Warbucks* (200 performances). There were also three attempts at making a musical out of Stevenson's *Dr. Jekyll and Mr. Hyde,* all called *Jekyll and Hyde;* the one by Wildhorn and Bricusse finally opened on Broadway in 1997. Both Sondheim and Lloyd Webber had flops.

Assassins was never moved to a commercial run in New York from its workshop production at Playwrights Horizons (which also workshopped *Sunday in the Park with George*). The show had rather successful productions in small theaters in London and elsewhere, and finally made it to Broadway in 2004 for 101 performances. (An earlier production was planned for the 2001–2 season, but it was canceled after the 9/11 destruction of the

Assassins

MUSIC/LYRICS: Stephen Sondheim

BOOK: John Weidman

DIRECTOR: Jerry Zaks

CHOREOGRAPHER: D. J. Giagni

PRODUCER: Playwrights Horizons

CAST INCLUDES: Patrick Cassidy, Victor Garber, Terrence Mann, Debra Monk, and Jonathan Hadary

PERFORMANCES: 25 off-Broadway

criminal court, a jury acquits O. J. Simpson of murdering his wife and her friend, but he's found guilty in a civil suit filed by the victims' families. When the Branch Davidian fundamentalist religious cult, led by David Koresh, holes up in their compound near Waco, Texas, the FBI moves in with tear gas; cult members set fire to the compound and more than eighty people are killed, including twenty-four children. Panamanian Manuel Noriega is convicted of helping the Colombian drug cartel. Mafia boss John Gotti is convicted of murder. Junk bond tycoon Michael Milliken is fined $600 million for fraud. Flooding of the Mississippi and Missouri rivers causes about $12 billion in damages and at least fifty deaths. A workman's mistake causes the Chicago River to flood the city's downtown. More than 10 percent of Americans rely on food stamps. Between 1972 and 1997, the number of billionaires in the United States goes from 13 to 170.

International Boris Yeltsin resigns from the Soviet Communist Party. The Soviet Union collapses. Lech Walesa is elected president of Poland. Czechoslovakia splits into two independent republics. Nelson Mandela is freed after twenty-eight years in a South African prison. White minority rule ends in

World Trade Center.) *Assassins* is a concept musical built around a series of revue sketches performed by people who have assassinated or tried to assassinate presidents of the United States. Like many concept musicals, it's an ensemble show rather than a star vehicle.

Aspects of Love

MUSIC/BOOK: Andrew Lloyd Webber

LYRICS: Don Black and Charles Hart

DIRECTOR: Trevor Nunn

CHOREOGRAPHER: Gillian Lynne

DESIGNERS: Maria Björnson (sets and costumes) and Andrew Bridge (lights)

PRODUCER: Lloyd Webber's Really Useful Theatre Group

CAST INCLUDES: Michael Ball and Kevin Colson

PERFORMANCES: 377

All of these men and women were misfits filled with disappointments, but to Sondheim and Weidman their biggest disappointment was with the American dream itself. *Assassins* says that the reason why assassinations (or attempts) happen frequently in America is because we're led to believe that any dream can come true here. When that proves false someone has to be blamed, and who better to blame than the President? (Gruber, *Original Cast! Completing the Century,* 66)

The musical numbers reflect the periods of the various characters portrayed, such as John Wilkes Booth, Lee Harvey Oswald, Squeaky Fromme, and John Hinckley. There's an original-cast

South Africa, and Mandela is elected president. Egyptian Boutros Boutros-Ghali becomes secretary-general of the United Nations. Yitzhak Rabin becomes prime minister of Israel. Margaret Thatcher resigns and John Major becomes prime minister of England. Prince Charles and Princess Diana of England separate. Bosnia-Herzegovina declares its independence from Yugoslavia, causing new hostilities in the Balkans. Serbs in Bosnia begin a campaign of ethnic cleansing against Muslims.

New Developments   The first mammal, a sheep named Dolly, is cloned. Sears Roebuck discontinues its ninety-seven-year-old merchandise catalogue. The Chunnel, a tunnel beneath the English Channel connecting England and France, is completed.

Sports   The heavyweight boxing champions of the decade include James "Buster" Douglas, Mike Tyson, Riddick Bowe, and Evander Holyfield (twice). Tennis champs include Andre Agassi, Steffi Graf, Stefan Edberg, Monica Seles, and Pete Sampras. The Florida Marlins and Colorado Rockies play their first National League baseball seasons. The Chicago Bulls win their sixth NBA title. With his sixty-second home run Mark McGwire beats Roger Maris's previous one-season record; McGwire ends the season with seventy home runs.

Art   Painter Francis Bacon dies. After ten years of work, Michelangelo's Sistine Chapel paintings are cleaned and restored. Ellis Island in New York opens as an immigration museum. The U.S. Holocaust Memorial Museum opens in Washington. Architect Frank Gehry's Guggenheim Museum in Bilbao, Spain, opens, as does Richard Meier's Getty Center in Los Angeles. The National Endowment for the recording. The score includes "The Ballad of Booth" and "Gun Song."

Aspects of Love is a small-cast, quite intimate, through-composed show about shifting love affairs, which flopped on Broadway but did better in London. As with nearly all Lloyd Webber shows, there are several recordings. The most frequently played song, both onstage and off, is "Love Changes Everything."

A romantic calypso musical, *Once on This Island* is a Caribbean version of Hans Christian Andersen's "The Little Mermaid" that focuses on class distinctions between light- and dark-skinned blacks rather than distinctions between humans and sea creatures. The show is unassuming, colorful, and often quite funny. It was workshopped first at Playwrights Horizons. There's an original-cast recording. In the score are "Forever Yours," "We Dance," and "Waiting for Life." It was the Broadway debut of Stephen Flaherty (1960–, born in Pittsburgh) and Lynn Ahrens

Once on This Island
MUSIC: Stephen Flaherty
LYRICS/BOOK: Lynn Ahrens, adapted from Rosa Guy's 1985 novel *My Love, My Love*
DIRECTOR/CHOREOGRAPHER: Graciela Daniele
DESIGNERS: Loy Arcenas (sets), Judy Dearing (costumes), and Allen Lee Hughes (lights)
PRODUCERS: five listed, including the Shubert Organization
CAST INCLUDES: La Chanze
PERFORMANCES: 469

Arts (NEA) revokes grants to performance artists Karen Finley, John Fleck, Holly Hughes, and Tim Miller for controversial sexual content, and to Pennsylvania's Institute of Contemporary Art for exhibiting Robert Mapplethorpe's photos. Actress Jane Alexander is named head of the NEA, which grants the four artists money rather than face a lawsuit. Van Gogh's *Portrait of Dr. Gachet* sells for $82.5 million, and Monet's *At the Moulin de la Galette* for $78.1 million. A two-year tour begins in Los Angeles of the exhibition Degenerate Art: The Fate of the Avant-Garde in Nazi Germany, which contains art repressed by Hitler.

Music/Dance New operas include Adams and Goodman's *The Death of Klinghoffer* and Philip Glass's *The Voyage*. The Joffrey Ballet premieres *Billboards*, set to music by the artist known as Prince.

Publications Toni Morrison wins the Nobel Prize in Literature. *Entertainment Weekly* begins publication. Maya Angelou reads her poem "On the Pulse of Morning" at President Clinton's first inauguration. Among the new books are Tan's *The Kitchen God's Wife*, Coupland's *Generation X: Tales for an Accelerated Culture*, Smiley's *A Thousand Acres*, McMillan's *Waiting to Exhale*, McCarthy's *All the Pretty Horses*, Proulx's *The Shipping News*, Sheehan's *A Bright Shining Lie*, McCourt's *Angela's Ashes*, Frazier's *Cold Mountain*, and the first three Harry Potter books.

TV By 1991, 93.1 million homes have TV sets, 98 percent have color TV, and 60.3 percent have cable. The WB and UPN networks begin operations. Johnny Carson retires and Jay Leno becomes the new host of *The Tonight Show;* David Letterman, who wanted the job, becomes host of *The Late Show*

(1948–, born in New York); they've gone on to write such shows as *Ragtime* and *Seussical*.

Falsettoland

MUSIC/LYRICS: William Finn
BOOK: William Finn and James Lapine
DIRECTOR: James Lapine
PRODUCERS: four listed, including Playwrights Horizons
CAST OF SEVEN INCLUDES: Michael Rupert, Stephen Bogardus, Faith Prince, Lonny Price (who replaced Chip Zien when the show moved), Danny Gerard, Janet Metz, and Heather MacRae
PERFORMANCES: 253 off-off- and then off-Broadway

Falsettoland is the third of Finn's Marvin trilogy of one-acts. (Marvin is the central character in all three, but some of the other characters are also in all of them.) The main plot threads of the show deal with Marvin's son's bar mitzvah and with Marvin's lover Whizzer dying of AIDS. Like *In Trousers* and *March of the Falsettos*, it was workshopped at Playwrights Horizons and has an original-cast recording.

In 1991, lyricist Howard Ashman, author/performer Gerome Ragni, and producer Joseph Papp died. The Shubert Organization sold the last of its seven Chicago theaters to the Nederlanders, who sold Broadway's Mark Hellinger Theatre to the Times Square Church. During the nineties, the Nederlanders and in direct competition. Ellen DeGeneres comes out on her sitcom. Top TV shows are *The Cosby Show, Cheers, Roseanne, 60 Minutes, Murphy Brown, Home Improvement, Seinfeld, ER, Friends,* and *Frasier.* New shows include *Everybody Loves Raymond, The Sopranos, Oz, Sex and the City, The Real World, The Larry Sanders Show, NYPD Blue, Mad About You, The X-Files, The Practice,* and *Law and Order.*

Pop Culture   Polygram and Universal merge, creating the largest record company in the world; five multinational conglomerates now control by far the majority of the recording industry. Freddie Mercury of Queen dies, Kurt Cobain and Del Shannon commit suicide, and Tupac Shakur and Selena are shot. Milli Vanilli is exposed as lip-synching, not singing. The Lollapalooza Festival, a cross-country tour of alternative rock bands, begins in 1992; Lilith Fair, a traveling music festival featuring women musicians, begins touring in 1997. Chicago alternative music bands include Urge Overkill, Smashing Pumpkins, and Liz Phair. Garth Brooks, Reba McEntire, Vince Gill, Clint Black, and Wynonna and Naomi Judd are stars of the country music scene. Nirvana, Stone Temple Pilots, and Pearl Jam are the leading alternative rock grunge groups. Popular boy groups include 'N Sync and the Backstreet Boys. Snoop Doggy Dogg and Ice-T are leading gangsta rappers. Among the new recordings are Stevie B's "Because I Love You (The Postman Song)," Adams's "(Everything I Do) I Do for You," Houston's "I Will Always Love You," Carey's "Dreamlover," Los Del Rio's "Macarena," Clapton and Jennings's "Tears in Heaven," Morisette's "Jagged Little Pill," Boyz II Men's "End of the Road" and "I'll Make Love to You," Sonic Youth's *Goo,* Natalie Cole's *Unforgettable* with twenty-two of her father Nat King Cole's old hits, Guns 'n' Roses' *Use Your Illusions,* Clapton's *Unplugged,* Brooks's *Ropin' the Wind,* Jackson's *Dangerous,* Nirvana's *In Utero,* Billy Joel's *River of Dreams,* Moby's *Everything Is Wrong,* and Pearl Jam's *Vs.*

Jujamcyn secured their positions alongside the Shuberts as major theater owners and producers. Cathy Rigby returned for another 48 performances of *Peter Pan*. The most publicized musical flop of the year (71 previews and 9 performances) was Charles Strouse, Richard Maltby Jr., and Arthur Laurents's *Nick and Nora*, a new murder mystery based on the characters created in Dashiell Hammett's novel *The Thin Man*. The cast included Barry Bostwick, Joanna Gleason, Christine Baranski, Faith Prince, Debra Monk, and Chris Sarandon. In trouble from the beginning, the show couldn't afford to go out of town; it previewed on Broadway to disastrous word of mouth and two postponements of its opening. Apparently writer/director Laurents was nearly intractable about making changes; at least that was the word on the street. There's an original-cast recording.

The pop opera *Miss Saigon* is a Vietnam War version of Puccini's tragic opera *Madama Butterfly*. Set in Saigon in 1975, during the last days of the American presence there, it's about Chris, an American marine (sailor in the opera),

Stage   Playwrights Eugene Ionesco and John Osborne and actress Helen Hayes die. Trevor Nunn becomes the artistic director of London's National Theatre. For the first time a Neil Simon play—*London Suite*—opens off-Broadway instead of on, where it would have cost almost a million dollars more to produce. Among the other new plays are Simon's *Lost in Yonkers;* Albee's *Three Tall Women;* Guare's *Six Degrees of Separation;* Baitz's *The Substance of Fire;* McNally's *Love! Valor! Compassion!* and *Master Class;* Wilson's *The Piano Lesson, Two Trains Running,* and *Seven Guitars;* Galati's adaptation of Steinbeck's *Grapes of Wrath;* both parts of Kushner's *Angels in America;* Vogel's *How I Learned to Drive;* Matura's *Playboy of the West Indies;* Friel's *Dancing at Lughnasa;* and Stoppard's *Arcadia.*

Screen   Italian film director Federico Fellini dies. DVDs of movies and concerts become popular; by 2003, they overtake videos in sales. New movies include *Dick Tracy,* with songs by Stephen Sondheim sung by Madonna, *Schindler's List, Glengarry Glen Ross, The Joy Luck Club, Goodfellas, Silence of the Lambs, Pretty Woman, Boyz N Da Hood, Thelma and Louise, Unforgiven, Malcolm X, Philadelphia, Jurassic Park, Fargo, Pulp Fiction, The Usual Suspects, The Sixth Sense, Howards End, The Crying Game,* and *Forrest Gump.*

What's Love Got to Do with It? is a new movie musical about Tina and Ike Turner. Disney produces four new animated musicals: *Beauty and the Beast,* with songs by Howard Ashman and Alan Menken (source of the hit 1994 stage musical); *Aladdin,* with songs by Menken and Tim Rice; *The Lion King,* with songs by Elton John and Rice (source of the hit 1997 stage musical); and *Pocahontas,* with songs by Menken and Stephen Schwartz.

Miss Saigon

MUSIC: Claude-Michel Schönberg

ENGLISH LYRICS: Richard Maltby Jr. and Alain Boublil, from the original lyrics by Boublil and with additional material by Maltby

BOOK: Alain Boublil and Claude-Michel Schönberg

DIRECTOR: Nicholas Hytner

MUSICAL STAGING: Bob Avian

ORCHESTRATOR: William D. Brohn

DESIGNERS: John Napier (sets), Andreane Neofitou and Suzy Benzinger (costumes), and David Hersey (lights)

PRODUCER: Cameron Mackintosh

CAST INCLUDES: Jonathan Pryce, Lea Salonga, Hinton Battle, and Liz Callaway

PERFORMANCES: 4,092, the sixth longest run on Broadway when it closed

and Kim, an Asian geisha girl, who fall in love. He's evacuated back home; she has a baby and waits and waits for his promised return. When he does come back, he brings his American wife with him, and Kim kills herself. The leading role is a deeply cynical, *Cabaret*-like emcee (based on a secondary character in Puccini's opera) called the Engineer, who ties things together. Jonathan Pryce and Lea Salonga had played the Engineer and Kim in the original London production. The show is most famous for the helicopter that seems to land onstage at the end of the first act (the point in the show when the chandelier falls in *Phantom of the Opera*). Like Schönberg and Boublil's *Les Misérables*, *Miss Saigon* began life in Paris; it was translated and produced in London in 1989, then brought to Broadway. It cost almost $11 million to produce—*Phantom* cost $8 million—and opened in New York to a $37 million box-office advance, beating *Phantom*'s record.

> The opening was hyped by a heated controversy over the appropriateness of casting Jonathan Pryce, a Welshman, in the role of a Eurasian pimp. . . . Despite protests from some in the Asian American arts community, Mackintosh insisted on casting him—and reaped a bumper crop of publicity. (Albert Williams, personal communication)

There are several recordings of *Miss Saigon*. The score includes "The American Dream," "I'd Give My Life for You," "The Last Night of the World," "The Movie in My Mind," and "Sun and Moon." Like *Cats, Phantom,* and *Les Misérables,* the show was a tourist and expense-account attraction.

> I don't remember ever hearing anyone complain about the hypocrisy quotient in *Les Misérables.* . . . Mostly what seemed laughable . . . was the dramaturgy: a character appeared, sang a generic song, then died, and we were supposed to care. . . . *Miss Saigon* has the same paint-by-number approach to narrative: we know nothing about any of the characters except their names. In a quiet but incisive piece in the Sunday *Times* the novelist Robert Stone used the term "moral kitsch" to describe *Miss Saigon*. It's a curiously apt phrase, and one that's useful in distinguishing Boublil and Schönberg from Andrew Lloyd Webber. People tend to lump them together, because Cameron

Mackintosh, who produced *Les Misérables* and *Miss Saigon,* is also Lloyd Webber's producer. But Boublil and Schönberg, though Lloyd Webber's equals in shrewdness, are angling for a more so-phisticated audience—one that prefers its entertainment laced with self-loathing. For Lloyd Webber's audiences the mere pres-ence of an expensive or movable gimmick—the roller skates, the falling chandelier—is enough to hang a show on. In *Les Mis-érables* and *Miss Saigon,* the gimmick is a kind of piety. . . . If you listen to the French recording, one of the things you can hear is the badness of the music, its vulgarity—specifically, its roots in Parisian bubble-rock. (Mimi Kramer, from her review of *Miss Saigon* in the *New Yorker*)

The first Broadway musical to be produced, written, directed, and designed by women, *The Secret Garden* is about an orphaned girl adjusting to life in her moody uncle's home while helping his neurotically ill son get better. It cost over $6 million to pro-duce and didn't break even. Neither pop singer/songwriter Lucy Simon (sister of pop singer Carly) nor serious dramatist Marsha Norman had ever written a musical before. The show in-cludes actors playing the ghosts that haunt the characters, which is not always a helpful addition to the story. The ghosts were considerably pared down after the show opened and received mixed reviews. (An example of how badly missed is the practice of taking a show out on the road: in an article in the *New York Times* of May 3, 1991, shortly after the show opened, one of the producers is quoted as saying, "We always thought the show could be shorter and crisper. But we ran out of time in pre-views." According to an anonymous company member, "The re-views the show got in New York would have been the perfect reviews to get out of town, if the show had gone out of town, to jolt everyone into an awareness of the problems.") The revised version is done quite often by regional theaters. There's an original-cast recording, including "If I Had a Fine White Horse," "Winter's on the Wing," "Hold On," "Race You to the Top of the Morning," and "How Could I Ever Know?"

Based on the life and career of rope-twirling cowboy satirist Will Rogers, the *Ziegfeld Follies* star, *The Will Rogers Follies* is a flashy and sexist (though correct for the period in which the show is set) concept musical told as if it were itself an old *Follies* starring Will

The Secret Garden
MUSIC: Lucy Simon
LYRICS/BOOK: Marsha Norman, adapted from Burnett's 1911 children's novel
DIRECTOR: Susan H. Schulman
CHOREOGRAPHER: Michael Lichtefeld
DESIGNERS: Heidi Landesman (sets), Theoni V. Aldredge (costumes), and Tharon Musser (lights)
PRODUCERS/ASSOCIATE PRODUCERS: fourteen listed, including Jujamcyn Theaters
CAST INCLUDES: Daisy Eagen, Mandy Patinkin, John Cameron Mitchell, and Rebecca Luker
PERFORMANCES: 709

The Will Rogers Follies
MUSIC: Cy Coleman
LYRICS: Betty Comden and Adolph Green
BOOK: Peter Stone
DIRECTOR/CHOREOGRAPHER: Tommy Tune
ORCHESTRATOR: Billy Byers
DESIGNERS: Tony Walton (sets), Willa Kim (costumes), and Jules Fisher (lights)
PRODUCERS: seven listed, including Pierre Cossette and Martin Richards
CAST INCLUDES: Keith Carradine, Dee Hoty, and Cady Huffman, with Gregory Peck as the (recorded) voice of Ziegfeld
PERFORMANCES: 963

Rogers. It includes dog acts, lots of scantily clad girls, lavish production numbers, and frequent fantasy appearances by aviator Wiley Post to invite Rogers on a flight, thereby reminding us from time to time that he and Rogers are going to die in a crash. Again, Tune was working with inferior material; Coleman's music and Comden and Green's lyrics aren't much better than Stone's book, whose best material comes from Rogers's vintage comic commentaries. (Steven Suskin points out in *Show Tunes, 1905–1991* that within two days of the opening, Comden and Green turned 151 years old between them.) The show, which workshopped in New York, cost $7.5 million to produce and didn't break even despite the long run. There's an original-cast recording.

And the World Goes 'Round

MUSIC: John Kander
LYRICS: Fred Ebb
CONCEPT: Scott Ellis, Susan Stroman, and David Thompson
DIRECTOR: Scott Ellis
CHOREOGRAPHER: Susan Stroman
PRODUCERS: five listed
CAST INCLUDES: Bob Cuccioli, Karen Mason, Brenda Pressley, Jim Walton, and Karen Ziemba
PERFORMANCES: 408 off-Broadway

An off-Broadway, small-cast jukebox revue of Kander and Ebb songs mostly from their flops, *And the World Goes 'Round* was first done at a theater in New Jersey. There's an original-cast recording. The inventive choreography of Susan Stroman (c. 1954–, born in Wilmington, Delaware) is one of the chief reasons for the show's success. She went on to choreograph such shows as *Crazy for You*, the 1997 revisal of *Show Boat*, and the 2002 revival of *Oklahoma!* and was director/choreographer of such shows as *Contact*, the 2001 revival of *The Music Man*, and *The Producers*.

In 1992, performers Vivienne Segal and Alfred Drake died. The Broadway theater district had become so seedy and even dangerous that private security guards were hired in addition to police patrolling the area. The 42nd Street Development Project was under way, and the State of New York bought Ziegfeld's old New Amsterdam Theatre and began renovation plans. The Supreme Court OK'd giving landmark status to Broadway theaters.

One of the biggest hits of the year (1,143 performances) was a revival of *Guys and Dolls* directed by Jerry Zaks; choreographed by Christopher Chadman; designed by Tony Walton, William Ivey Long, and Paul Gallo; and starring Peter Gallagher, Nathan Lane, Faith Prince, Josie de Guzman, and Walter Bobbie. There was also a 229-performance revival of *The Most Happy Fella*—making it a big Loesser year—and a 108-performance revival of *Man of La Mancha*, starring Raul Julia.

Falsettos (497 performances), with music and lyrics by William Finn, book by Finn and James Lapine, is a two-act combination of *March of the Falsettos* and *Falsettoland* about "Life, Love, Sex, and other unscheduled events." It was directed by Lapine and had Michael Rupert, Stephen Bogardus, Chip Zien, Carolee Carmello, Jonathan Kaplan, Barbara Walsh, and Heather MacRae as the cast. It tells the story of Marvin from when he leaves his wife and son for his male lover, Whizzer, through the first awareness of the spread of AIDS, to the son's bar mitzvah and Whizzer's AIDS-related death. The other characters are Marvin's psychiatrist, who becomes Marvin's wife's lover, and a pair of lesbian lovers who live next door to Marvin and his lover. There's an original-cast recording.

Five Guys Named Moe (445 performances), a revue with an African American cast, was centered on the rhythm-and-blues songs of Louis Jordan. It was produced by Cameron Mackintosh.

Jelly's Last Jam is a concept biography of Jelly Roll Morton, the "grandfather of jazz."

> *Jelly's Last Jam* was far more ambitious than the usual biographical show. Morton was born into Black Creole society in New Orleans, and as a result spent much of his life denying that he was black, all the while using black music as his inspiration. Wolfe saw this unique life story as an opportunity to explore a number of themes, including the connection between culture and racism, and the denial of heritage. (Gruber, *Original Cast! Completing the Century*, 84)

The show was workshopped several times and first produced in Los Angeles; it cost over $5 million. There's an original-cast recording that includes "That's How You Jazz," "Play the Music for Me," "The Last Chance Blues," and "Creole Boy."

Crazy For You, set in the 1930s, is Ken Ludwig's rewrite of the Gershwins, Bolton, and McGowan's *Girl Crazy,* which was about a rich playboy sent to Arizona to work on a dude ranch; in the rewrite he's sent to close down a theater. The show uses six songs from *Girl Crazy*—"Bidin' My Time," "But Not for Me," "Embraceable You," and "I Got Rhythm" among them—and fills in with many other Gershwin songs, such as "They Can't Take That Away from Me" and "Slap That Bass" from 1930s Astaire-Rogers movies and "Someone to Watch Over Me." The plot and characters are

Jelly's Last Jam

MUSIC: Jelly Roll Morton, with additional music by Luther Henderson

LYRICS: Susan Birkenhead

BOOK/DIRECTOR: George C. Wolfe

CHOREOGRAPHER: Hope Clarke (tap choreography: Gregory Hines and Ted L. Levy)

DESIGNERS: Robin Wagner (sets), Toni-Leslie James (costumes), and Jules Fisher (lights)

PRODUCERS/ASSOCIATE PRODUCERS: twelve listed, including Jujamcyn Theaters

CAST INCLUDES: Gregory Hines, Tonya Pinkins, and Savion Glover as the young Jelly

PERFORMANCES: 569

Crazy for You

MUSIC: George Gershwin

LYRICS: Ira Gershwin

BOOK: Ken Ludwig, conceived by Ludwig and Mike Ockrent

DIRECTOR: Mike Ockrent

CHOREOGRAPHER: Susan Stroman

ORCHESTRATOR: William D. Brohn

DESIGNERS: Robin Wagner (sets), William Ivey Long (costumes), and Paul Gallo (lights)

PRODUCERS: Roger Horchow and Elizabeth Williams

CAST INCLUDES: Harry Groener, Jodi Benson, and Jane Connell

PERFORMANCES: 1,622

thin, the jokes are corny, and the songs often seem shoehorned in, but the show is charming and tuneful. The production had an enormous amount of funny, prop-heavy parody choreography and was wonderfully designed and steadily entertaining. It was Susan Stroman's first Broadway hit. *Crazy for You* cost over $8 million to produce and made everyone a lot of money. (Only two producers for a change, and neither of them Cameron Mackintosh or Lloyd Webber.) The show is done frequently by professional, amateur, and school theaters throughout the country. There's a noisy, original-cast recording and a PBS video of the 1999 Paper Mill Playhouse revival that re-created the original direction, choreography, and designs, and even had some of the original cast.

My Favorite Year

MUSIC: Stephen Flaherty
LYRICS: Lynn Ahrens
BOOK: Joseph Dougherty, adapted from the 1982 movie
DIRECTOR: Ron Lagomarsino
MUSICAL STAGING: Thommie Walsh
ORCHESTRATOR: Michael Starobin
DESIGNERS: Thomas Lynch (sets), Patricia Zipprodt (costumes), and Jules Fisher (lights)
PRODUCER: Lincoln Center Theater
CAST INCLUDES: Tim Curry, Lainie Kazan, Andrea Martin, Josh Mostel, and Evan Pappas
PERFORMANCES: 36 after 45 previews

My Favorite Year, set in New York City in 1954, was Flaherty and Ahrens's unsuccessful follow-up to *Once on This Island.* About the making of a live TV show not unlike the old Sid Caesar *Your Show of Shows,* it centers around problems with an alcoholic guest star and the young man assigned to be his caretaker. There's an original-cast recording.

In 1993, director and choreographer Agnes de Mille, songwriter Harold Rome, and performer Ruby Keeler died. Andrew Lloyd Webber, Christopher Hampton, and Don Black's *Sunset Boulevard* opened in London with Patti LuPone and Kevin Anderson. Sondheim and Weidman's *Assassins* also got a London production. Broadway revivals included *She Loves Me* (354 performances), starring Boyd Gaines and Judy Kuhn, directed by Scott Ellis, and choreographed by Rob Marshall; *Joseph and the Amazing Technicolor Dreamcoat* (231 performances); and (making it a big Lerner and Loewe year) *Camelot* (56 performances), with Robert Goulet (the original Lancelot) as King Arthur, and *My Fair Lady* (165 performances), with Richard Chamberlain and Melissa Errico.

Set at a cocktail party, *Sondheim—Putting It Together* was a limited-run (59 performances), off-Broadway revue of Sondheim songs from shows written after the 1977 revue *Side by Side by Sondheim.* Julie Andrews, Stephen Collins, Christopher Durang, Michael Rupert, and Rachel York made up the five-person cast. There's an original-cast recording. The show was partially rewritten in 1999 without Sondheim's name in the title and had a short Broadway run starring Carol Burnett.

A Grand Night for Singing was a five-person, 52-performance flop revue of the songs of Rodgers and Hammerstein. Jule Styne, Marsha Norman, and Paul Stryker's *The Red Shoes*, based on the 1948 ballet movie, closed after 51 previews and 5 performances. It was Styne's last show.

The Who's *Tommy* (899 performances) had music and lyrics by Peter Townshend with John Entwistle and Keith Moon and a book by Townshend and Des McAnuff. It was directed by McAnuff and choreographed by Wayne Cilento. It was a sight-and-sound, high-tech staging of Townshend and the Who's old rock-opera concept album about a pinball champion, who had been struck deaf, dumb, and blind as a child when his father accidentally murdered his mother's lover. It had already been made into a 1975 Ken Russell movie. There's an original-cast recording.

Blood Brothers (840 performances) has book, music, and lyrics by Willy Russell and was directed by Bill Kenwright and Bob Tomson. It's an imported British musical about twin brothers and their birth mother. The twins are separated at birth and raised in different class and economic environments. They end up killing each other. The show didn't do well at first, but business improved enormously when British pop star Petula Clark and American pop stars David and Shaun Cassidy took over the leading roles. There are several recordings.

In *The Goodbye Girl*, Bernadete Peters and Martin Short play unwilling roommates who eventually fall in love. By 1993, the 1977 movie script felt dated, and Neil Simon did nothing to dispel that feeling. It didn't help that the score is fairly ordinary and the central female character is too sour too much of the time.

Kiss of the Spider Woman is about a homosexual window dresser and a Marxist political prisoner who are cell mates in a Latin American prison.

Molina, the homosexual, acts out old movies starring his favorite film goddess Aurora (a sort of cross between Garbo, Dietrich, and Maria Montez)—her roles include the "Spider Woman," who becomes the story's symbol of death (which there is plenty of in the fascist prison the two men are incarcerated in). Aurora is Molina's fantasy alter ego—but as he develops a sense of self-worth through his friendship with his revolutionary cell mate Valentin, he comes to see himself not as a pseudo-woman but as

The Goodbye Girl

MUSIC: Marvin Hamlisch

LYRICS: David Zippel

BOOK: Neil Simon, adapted from his screenplay

DIRECTOR: Michael Kidd (who replaced Gene Saks while the show was trying out in Chicago)

MUSICAL STAGING: Graciela Daniele

DESIGNERS: Santo Loquasto (sets and costumes) and Tharon Musser (lights)

PRODUCERS: six listed, including Stewart F. Lane

CAST INCLUDES: Bernadette Peters and Martin Short

PERFORMANCES: 188

Kiss of the Spider Woman

MUSIC: John Kander

LYRICS: Fred Ebb

BOOK: Terrence McNally, adapted from the novel by Manuel Puig and the 1985 movie

DIRECTOR: Harold Prince

CHOREOGRAPHER: Vincent Paterson, with additional choreography by Rob Marshall

ORCHESTRATOR: Michael Gibson

DESIGNERS: Jerome Sirlin (sets and projections), Florence Klotz (costumes), and Howell Binkley (lights)

PRODUCER: Livent (USA) Inc.

CAST INCLUDES: Chita Rivera, Brent Carver, and Anthony Crivello

PERFORMANCES: 904

a proud gay man; this emotional change is reflected in the choreography, which begins with the homosexual imitating Aurora and ends with him partnering her as her equal. (Albert Williams, personal communication)

The show was workshopped disastrously in 1991 in Purchase, New York, where it was received negatively by the New York critics, who'd been asked to stay away. After extensive rewrites (which included beefing up the Aurora role to make the show more of a star vehicle for Rivera), it tried out again in 1992 in Toronto, where the producing company, Livent, was based. It opened in London, then came to New York. There's an original-cast recording as well as a recording of the second Broadway cast, which starred Vanessa Williams as Aurora. The score includes the title song, "Her Name Is Aurora," "Dressing Them Up," "Marta," and "She's a Woman."

In 1994, composer Jule Styne, director/choreographer Joe Layton, and designer Oliver Smith died. Over nine million tickets were sold on Broadway for the first time since 1981. Disney bought the New Amsterdam Theatre from the state of New York. Encores! began its series of concert versions of old musicals with *Fiorello!*

There were seventeen revivals of plays and musicals on Broadway during the 1993–94 season. Several important and successful ones opened in 1994, all with original-cast recordings. The revival of *Show Boat* (947 performances) was directed by Harold Prince, choreographed by Susan Stroman, and produced by Livent (USA) Inc.; in the cast were Mark Jacoby, Rebecca Luker, Lonette McKee, John McMartin, Elaine Stritch, Michel Bell, and Gretha Boston. It had a top ticket price of $75.

Britain's National Theatre's revival of *Carousel* (337 performances) was directed by Nicholas Hytner and choreographed by Kenneth MacMillan; among the cast were Michael Hayden, Sally Murphy, and opera star Shirley Verrett. With a very sexy, main-plot couple, an interracial subplot couple with a veritable rainbow of children, and absolutely naturalistic acting, the show seemed as relevant to the nineties as it did to the forties, and without noticeable rewrites. It was the Broadway debut of Audra McDonald (1970–, born in Germany), who has a great voice and real acting talent. She later went on to star in such shows as *Ragtime* and *Marie Christine,* as well as the TV version of *Annie.* She champions the newer musical theater composers in her concerts and on her recordings.

Damn Yankees (718 performances) was directed and revised by Jack O'Brien, choreographed by Rob Marshall, and starred Victor Garber, Bebe Neuwirth, and Jarrod Emick; the national tour of the revival starred Jerry Lewis as the Devil.

The hugely successful revival of Jacobs and Casey's *Grease!* (1,505 performances) was directed and choreographed by Jeff Calhoun; it was a production by Tommy Tune, produced by Barry and Fran Weissler and Jujamcyn Theaters (whatever that language means). To keep business healthy, stars mostly from TV were brought in one or two at a time for short runs.

The year also included *The Best Little Whorehouse Goes Public*, an embarrassing, 16-performance flop sequel with music and lyrics by Carol Hall, book by Larry L. King and Peter Masterson, direction by Masterson and Tommy Tune, and choreography by Jeff Calhoun and Tune.

A Christmas Carol has music by Alan Menken, lyrics by Lynn Ahrens, and book by Ahrens and Mike Ockrent; it was directed by Ockrent and choreographed by Susan Stroman. The show became a seasonal, limited-engagement spectacle repeated yearly. Its top ticket price was only $67.50. Merry Christmas.

Beauty and the Beast was the beginning of what's been called the "Disneyfication" of Broadway and, in particular, of Times Square. It cost around $14 million to produce and tried out in Houston. Since Ashman died in 1991, Rice was brought on to write lyrics for some new songs. The score includes the title song, "Gaston," "Belle," "Be Our Guest," "There's Something There," and "If I Can't Love Her" (one of the new songs). There is, of course, a beautifully packaged original-cast recording. Although the show got rather negative reviews, it set a one-day record of $603,494 in ticket sales the day after opening.

Passion tells, partly through letters, the story of an ugly woman's obsessive love for a handsome young army captain. It ends tragically for nearly everyone concerned. (*Obsession* would be a more accurate title.) The show has a lot of underscored dialogue and song fragments, and it runs two hours without an intermission. It won the Tony for Best Musical; its main competition was *Beauty and the Beast*. Along with the original-cast recording, it was videotaped for PBS shortly before it closed at a loss. Critic Harry Stein had the following to say just as the video was about to be broadcast:

> [Sondheim] is as gifted as any of his predecessors; not only an
> inspired lyricist but as capable of an achingly beautiful melody

Beauty and the Beast

MUSIC: Alan Menken

LYRICS: Howard Ashman and Tim Rice

BOOK: Linda Woolverton, based on the 1991 Disney animated feature and the fairy tale

DIRECTOR: Robert Jess Roth

CHOREOGRAPHER: Matt West

DESIGNERS: Stan Meyer (sets), Ann Hould-Ward (costumes), and Natasha Katz (lights)

PRODUCER: Walt Disney Theatrical Productions

CAST INCLUDES: Terrence Mann, Susan Egan, Tom Bosley, Gary Beach, and Beth Fowler

PERFORMANCES: 5,464

Passion

MUSIC/LYRICS: Stephen Sondheim

BOOK/DIRECTOR: James Lapine, based on Iginio Tarchetti's 1869 novel *Fosca* and on Ettore Scola's Italian film *Passione d'Amore*

ORCHESTRATOR: Jonathan Tunick

DESIGNERS: Adrianne Lobel (sets), Jane Greenwood (costumes), and Beverly Emmons (lights)

PRODUCERS: four listed, including Roger Berlind

CAST INCLUDES: Donna Murphy, Jere Shea, Marin Mazzie, Tom Aldredge, Linda Balgord, George Dvorsky, Gregg Edelman, and Cris Groenendaal

PERFORMANCES: 280

as Gershwin or Fritz Loewe—when he chooses to be. Yet what Sondheim and his collaborators have most often done is give us shows impossible to love. The music can be so complex and jarring that to hum it is to put on airs. . . . It is a measure of the man's gift that any Sondheim piece can turn out to be fascinating, even deeply moving. No one has ever dealt more stirringly with the longing for human connection. . . . Yet for all his genius—and all his many imitators—Sondheim's appeal will always be limited by his worldview. (Stein, "Our Times," *TV Guide*)

Sunset Boulevard

MUSIC: Andrew Lloyd Webber
LYRICS/BOOK: Christopher Hampton and Don Black, adapted from the 1950 movie
DIRECTOR: Trevor Nunn
MUSICAL STAGING: Bob Avian
ORCHESTRATORS: David Cullen and Andrew Lloyd Webber
DESIGNERS: John Napier (sets), Anthony Powell (costumes), and Andrew Bridge (lights)
PRODUCERS: Lloyd Webber's Really Useful Theatre Group and Paramount Pictures (producer of the original movie)
CAST INCLUDES: Glenn Close, Alan Campbell, George Hearn, and Alice Ripley
PERFORMANCES: 977, at a loss of $1.3 million

Sunset Boulevard is a very dark show—with an amazing set—about Norma Desmond, a silent film star, slowly going mad twenty years after sound killed her career, and about her eventually murderous relationship with her screenwriter gigolo, who's secretly carrying on an affair with his best friend's girlfriend. The script follows the movie very closely and even uses much of its dialogue set to music. (Billy Wilder, who directed and cowrote the movie, received no money for the stage production.) The show is very much a star vehicle for the actress playing Norma, and she has to be charismatic as well as able to sing and act well.

Sunset Boulevard premiered in London in 1993 to very mixed reviews for the show itself and mixed reactions to its star, Patti LuPone, as Norma. It was rewritten before opening in Los Angeles to better reviews for the show and raves for its replacement star, Glenn Close. The rewrites were then put into the London production, and Close went to Broadway with the show. To achieve this, Lloyd Webber paid LuPone $1 million to buy her out of her contract, which had guaranteed her the New York production; she was also replaced in London by Betty Buckley. When Close left for Broadway, her replacement in Los Angeles was to be Faye Dunaway, but Lloyd Webber closed the show and took the cast to New York rather than letting Dunaway go on in front of an audience; he felt her singing wasn't good enough.

Sunset Boulevard had a $37 million advance sale on Broadway and broke *Beauty and the Beast*'s one-day sales record by taking in $1,491,110 on the day after its opening. Nevertheless, the show lost money on its New York, London, and aborted Los Angeles runs and on its road company tour. It's almost wall-to-wall music, including the title song, "With One Look," and "As If We Never Said Goodbye." There are several recordings, although none with Dunaway. It was one of only two new musical evenings on Broadway in the 1994–95 Broadway season.

In 1995, director/writer George Abbott (nearly 108 years old), composer/lyricist Ralph Blane, and performer Ginger Rogers died. By then, the Shubert Organization had sold off all but three of its theaters outside of New York. The New Victory Theatre across from the New Amsterdam on Forty-second Street was renovated.

Smokey Joe's Cafe (2,037 performances) was a jukebox revue of the rock songs of Jerry Leiber and Mike Stoller and their many collaborators, such as Phil Spector and Barry Mann. The show was conceived by Stephen Helper and Jack Viertel. When it tried out in Chicago, it was called *Baby, That's Rock and Roll.* Besides a new title by the time it reached New York, it also had direction by Jerry Zaks, musical staging by Joey McNeely with Otis Sallid, and seven producers, among which was Jujamcyn Theaters. The show had a cast of seven and thirty-nine songs, including "Young Blood," "On Broadway," "Yakety Yak," "Hound Dog," "Love Potion #9," "Jailhouse Rock," "Spanish Harlem," and "Stand by Me." The closing night on Broadway was taped and is available on video and DVD. *Sunset Boulevard* and *Smokey Joe's Café* were the only Tony nominees for Best Musical of the 1994–95 season; *Sunset Boulevard* won. (The category should be renamed Best Musical or Revue.)

Among the Broadway revivals were *Gentlemen Prefer Blondes* (24 performances) and *Company* (60 performances), directed by Scott Ellis and choreographed by Rob Marshall, which had a limited run because it couldn't raise the money to move to a regular Broadway house. *How to Succeed in Business Without Really Trying* (548 performances) was directed by Des McAnuff and choreographed by Wayne Cilento. It starred Matthew Broderick and Megan Mullally (replaced late in the run by Sarah Jessica Parker) and had a road company starring Ralph Macchio. *Hello, Dolly!* (116 performances), again starring Carol Channing, toured the country successfully for a year, then opened on Broadway to excellent reviews but not enough business.

Victor/Victoria is a romantic farce about a woman (Victoria) who becomes a successful drag nightclub performer by pretending to be a man (Victor) impersonating a woman. She falls in love

Victor/Victoria

MUSIC: Henry Mancini, with additional songs by Frank Wildhorn and Leslie Bricusse after Mancini died

LYRICS: Leslie Bricusse

BOOK/DIRECTOR: Blake Edwards, adapted from his 1982 movie musical

CHOREOGRAPHER: Rob Marshall

DESIGNERS: Robin Wagner (sets), Willa Kim (costumes), and Jules Fisher (lights)

PRODUCERS: eight listed, including Blake Edwards

CAST INCLUDES: Julie Andrews (Edwards's wife) re-creating her movie role, Michael Nouri, Tony Roberts, and Rachel York

PERFORMANCES: 734

with a straight man who doesn't know she's a woman. In the score are "Le Jazz Hot," "Crazy World," and "Chicago, Illinois," where it tried out. There's an original-cast recording as well as a DVD of the show, videotaped for Japanese TV. (Rent the original movie with Andrews, Robert Preston, James Garner, and Lesley Ann Warren; it's better.) Raquel Welch replaced Andrews during the run; the show closed soon after.

Among those who died in 1996 were performers Gene Kelly, George Burns, and Ella Fitzgerald; composer/lyricist Jonathan Larson; and 101-year-old lyricist Irving Caesar, whose first hit, with George Gershwin, was "Swanee" in 1919.

There were several revivals, all with original-cast recordings. *A Funny Thing Happened on the Way to the Forum* (715 performances) was directed by Jerry Zaks, choreographed by Rob Marshall, and starred Nathan Lane (replaced during the run by Whoopi Goldberg), Mark Linn-Baker, and Lewis J. Stadlen. *The King and I* (780 performances), which was originally produced in Australia, was directed by Christopher Renshaw and reproduced some of Jerome Robbins's original choreography with new musical staging by Lar Lubovitch. It starred Donna Murphy (replaced during the run by Faith Prince) and Lou Diamond Phillips. *Once upon a Mattress,* starring Sarah Jessica Parker, got pretty good reviews and a cast recording but closed after 187 performances.

The revival of *Chicago* (4,442 performances as of July 15, 2007—far longer than the original production's run) began as one of the semi-staged (though in this case, almost fully staged) concerts of the Encores! series and was then transferred to Broadway nearly intact. It was directed by Walter Bobbie, choreographed in the style of Fosse by Reinking, produced by Barry and Fran Weissler, and designed by John Lee Beatty, William Ivey Long, and Ken Billington. It used Ralph Burns's original orchestrations, with the band onstage, and starred Ann Reinking, Bebe Neuwirth, James Naughton, Joel Grey, and Marcia Lewis. The 2002 Academy Award–winning movie was directed and choreographed by Rob Marshall, who edited most of the musical numbers as if they were MTV videos.

Floyd Collins, with music and lyrics by Adam Guettel (1965–, born in New York City, son of Mary Rodgers and grandson of Richard Rodgers) and book and direction by Tina Landau, was produced off-Broadway by Playwrights Horizons. In the cast were Christopher Innvar, Brian d'Arcy James, and Jason Danieley. The show is based on the true story of Floyd Collins, trapped in a Kentucky cave in 1925, whose failed rescue created a media blitz. John Guare, in his liner notes to the original-cast recording, says:

Floyd Collins is a work unto itself that trusts its dreams, trusts its music, trusts its audience, trusts you to follow it deeper and deeper into its dark territory there below the earth. As Stephen Sondheim musicalized the unexplored territory of modern neuroses to let us see ourselves, Guettel and Landau have dramatized the paradox of what it's like to live in the most bountiful country in the world and at the same time be on the edge of an abyss that separates you from ever getting there. . . . But the music celebrates the unquenchable spirit of man to go on. This musical sings about the hope that is never a solution.

State Fair (110 performances) was adapted by Tom Briggs and Louis Mattioli from the 1945 Rodgers and Hammerstein movie; was directed by James Hammerstein (son of Oscar) and Randy Skinner and choreographed by Skinner; had seven producers, including David Merrick (his last Broadway credit); and starred John Davidson, Donna McKechnie, Kathryn Crosby, Scott Wise, and Andrea McArdle. Like its two earlier movie versions, it's about a couple of romances, a cooking contest, and a pig contest. Added to the original movie score were "More Than Just a Friend," from the movie remake; "Boys and Girls Like You and Me" and "When I Go Out Walking with My Baby," both cut from *Oklahoma!* before it opened; and "You Never Had It So Good," cut from *Me and Juliet.* Also added were "That's the Way It Happens," from *Me and Juliet;* "The Man I Used to Be" and "The Next Time It Happens," from *Pipe Dream;* and "So Far," from *Allegro.* The show tried out with an extensive tour, which did well, but it got decidedly mixed reviews when it opened on Broadway, including a rather negative one from the *New York Times* deriding the show's lack of sophistication. Although it closed at a loss, it continues to do well in regional productions.

Big (193 performances) was an overblown adaptation of the 1988 Tom Hanks movie about a boy who is mysteriously granted his wish to be a grown-up and works for a toy company until he becomes a boy again. It has music by David Shire, lyrics by Richard Maltby Jr., and book by John Weidman, adapted from Gary Ross and Anne Spielberg's screenplay; it was directed by Mike Ockrent and choreographed by Susan Stroman (husband and wife). An expensive flop, it's been scaled down and rewritten in an attempt to make a comeback.

In a sense, watching performers in musicals is like watching athletes: there's a heady pleasure in the physical charge they give off. . . . Not every show in recent years has capitalized on this. . . . The English-bred megamusicals of Andrew Lloyd Webber and Cameron Mackintosh took center stage away from the performers. It was the theme (as in theme park), the spectacularly realized mise-en-scène, that became the star. The actors, more often than not, were additions to the scenery, which usually seemed to dance more than they did. The experience for the audience is more passive, closer to that of watching a movie. The level of visceral, vicarious engagement with the people on stage is automatically diminished (something encouraged by the dislocating use of microphones). . . . But while devotees of the American musical may have had little new to feast on in the 1980's, the genre is hardier than most people suspect. There are definite sparks of hope being struck by *Rent* and *Bring In da Noise*, shows that differ radically in form from their classic predecessors but that grab their audiences by the hearts and guts in the same way. (Ben Brantley, "That Singable Psychodrama, the Musical," *New York Times*, Arts and Leisure, March 23, 1997, 11)

Rent

MUSIC/LYRICS: Jonathan Larson, with additional lyrics by Billy Aronson

BOOK/CONCEPT: Billy Aronson and Jonathan Larson

DIRECTOR: Michael Greif

CHOREOGRAPHER: Marlies Yearby

DESIGNERS: Paul Clay (sets), Angel Wendt (costumes), and Blake Burba (lights)

PRODUCERS: four listed, including the New York Theatre Workshop

CAST INCLUDES: Adam Pascal, Anthony Rapp, Taye Diggs, Daphne Rubin-Vega, and Idina Menzel

PERFORMANCES: 4,885 as of July 15, 2007, after playing off-Broadway

Rent is a rock opera based on Puccini's opera *La Bohème;* it's set in Manhattan's East Village in the present time of AIDS, and not everyone is heterosexual. It's very much an ensemble show. Jonathan Larson, who wrote the show, died just before it began previewing off-Broadway, where it had been workshopped several times. The show won the Pulitzer Prize. There's a bestselling, original-cast recording that has the title song, "Light My Candle," "Another Day," "We're Okay," "I Should Tell You," the hit song "Seasons of Love," "Take Me or Leave Me," "What You Own" and "Goodbye Love." The 2005 movie version, directed by Chris Columbus, used many of the original cast and most of the original score.

Bring in 'Da Noise, Bring in 'Da Funk: A Rap/Tap Discourse on the Staying Power of the Beat (1,135 performances) was conceived and cocreated by George C. Wolfe, Savion Glover, and Reg E. Gaines; composed by Ann Duquesnay, Zane Mark, and Daryl Waters; directed by Wolfe; and starred Glover and Duquesnay. It traces three centuries of African American history through tap dancing. There's no dialogue, just songs sung at the side of the stage and wall-to-wall dancing. Like *Rent*, it was so successful in its off-Broadway production that it moved to Broadway. There's an original-cast recording that could definitely use the visuals.

There had been other rock and pop shows since *Hair, Godspell,* and *Jesus Christ Superstar* that brought younger audiences into the theater, including *Grease* and *Little Shop of Horrors* (which were period parodies when they opened and thus feel as fresh today as they did then), *Purlie, The Wiz, Dreamgirls,* and the high-tech stage version of The Who's *Tommy.* However, none of them helped those audiences develop the habit of going to the theater. (The same is true of the occasional shows that brought in black audiences, many of them the same ones that brought in younger audiences.) It's still too soon to know whether any of the newer shows will be more successful at audience-building than the older ones were. But by halfway through the first decade of the twenty-first century, the signs were fairly positive.

In 1997, composer Burton Lane died. In June, Lloyd Webber's *Cats* overtook the 6,137-performance record set by *A Chorus Line* and went on to 7,485 performances. (*Cats* had achieved the London long-run record seven years earlier, overtaking the 3,358-performance record of Lloyd Webber's *Jesus Christ Superstar. Cats* ran in London for 8,949 performances. Lloyd Webber's *Starlight Express,* a flop on Broadway, ran 7,406 performances there. Until *Sunset Boulevard* closed in 1997, Lloyd Webber had six shows running in London at the same time.)

The year brought several revivals including *Annie* (239 performances), starring Nell Carter; it was poorly received and closed at a loss. Harold Prince's revised version of his revisal of *Candide* (104 performances), starring Jim Dale, Andrea Martin, Jason Danieley, Harolyn Blackwell, and Arte Johnson, got mixed reviews and closed at a loss. A revival of *1776* (333 performances), directed by Scott Ellis and choreographed by Kathleen Marshall, starred Tom Aldredge, Michael Cumpsty, Gregg Edelman, Linda Emond, Pat Hingle, and Brent Spiner.

There were two shows with music by Frank Wildhorn. *Jekyll and Hyde* (1,543 performances), with book and lyrics by Leslie Bricusse, was conceived by Wildhorn and Steve Cuden and adapted from Stevenson's *The Strange Case of Dr. Jekyll and Mr. Hyde.* Directed by Robin Phillips and choreographed by Joey Pizzi, it starred Robert Cuccioli, Linda Eder, and Christiane Noll. A flagrantly romantic adaptation of the 1886 story, it went through several revisions over several years and a successful recording before it got to Broadway, where it opened to mostly scalding reviews and lost money despite its long run. The transformations from Jekyll to Hyde (and back) were mainly accomplished by a change of hairdo. There's a DVD of a live performance.

Wildhorn's other show, *The Scarlet Pimpernel* (772 performances)—book and lyrics by Nan Knighton, adapted from Baroness Orczy's 1905 novel—was directed by Peter Hunt, choreographed by Adam Pelty, and starred Douglas Sills, Christine Andreas, and Terrence Mann. Set in England and France during the French Revolution, it's a tale of derring-do about an English aristocrat who pretends to be vague and silly but who, in disguise as the Scarlet Pimpernel, rescues French aristocrats from the guillotine. It got only slightly better reviews than *Jekyll and Hyde,* and after running at a loss for almost a year, was revised by new director Robert Longbottom, with Rachel York and Rex Smith replacing Andreas and Mann. A year later, it was scaled down to prepare for a tour, and Sills was replaced by Ron Bohmer, York by Carolee Carmello, and Smith by Marc Kudisch. After all that, it still closed at a loss, and it lost even more money on the tour. Lloyd Webber and Wildhorn are the Friml and Romberg of the last two decades of the twentieth century.

Forever Tango (332 performances) was a revue of Argentine music and dance. *Dream* (109 performances) was a jukebox revue of songs by lyricist Johnny Mercer, with music by Mercer, Harold Arlen, Duke Ellington, Billy Strayhorn, Hoagy Carmichael, Henry Mancini, and Harry Warren, among others; it was directed and choreographed by Wayne Cilento, and Lesley Ann Warren, John Pizzarelli, and Margaret Whiting were in the cast. *Play On!* (61 performances), a jukebox musical with a score of Ellington songs arranged by Luther Henderson, was a retelling of Shakespeare's *Twelfth Night* set in Harlem in the 1940s; it was conceived by Sheldon Epps, had a book by Cheryl L. West, and starred André DeShields and Tonya Pinkins. It told a story with old songs and new dialogue—a true jukebox musical.

Titanic

MUSIC/LYRICS: Maury Yeston
BOOK/STORY: Peter Stone
DIRECTOR: Richard Jones
CHOREOGRAPHER: Lynne Taylor-Corbett
ORCHESTRATOR: Jonathan Tunick
DESIGNERS: Stewart Laing (sets and costumes) and Paul Gallo (lights)
PRODUCERS: Dodger Endemol Theatricals, Richard S. Pechter, and the John F. Kennedy Center for the Performing Arts
CAST INCLUDES: Michael Cerveris and Brian d'Arcy James
PERFORMANCES: 804

Titanic, a semi-operetta, was so amplified that the only way to tell who was singing during group numbers was to look for whose mouth was moving. It's about the boat that hit the iceberg in 1912, with a large cast representing the passengers and crew on all levels of the boat; no one character's story takes prominence over the others. The huge, costly, multileveled set tilted impressively as the boat sank. The first act ended with a sailor in a crow's nest swinging out into the audience in approximately the same place as the chandelier in *Phantom of the Opera.* The sailor turns stage left, looks startled, and yells out, "Iceberg!" The lights go down and across the back of the stage we see a miniature *Titanic,* with steam rising from its stacks, crossing from stage right to stage left (an effect going back to George M. Cohan's 1904 *Little Johnny Jones*); as the boat exits left, we hear a terrible crash.

Blackout. Intermission. It won the Tony, which helped make it a box-office hit in the same year as the nonmusical movie with the same title.

The Lion King is about a young lion prince who learns to be king after his father is killed. Its brilliant staging and unique design elements don't quite succeed in masking the fact that it's a kids' show. And the amplification creates what feels to some like a wall of sound between the stage and the audience, which contributes to the feeling that it's a living movie.

Three shows opened during 1997 that deserved far better runs but didn't have rave reviews, big stars, or the Disney name to help sell them to audiences. All three were written and staged by Broadway veterans still at or near the top of their craft, and all three had truly talented casts; yet all three appeared to be too serious, unpleasant, and/or unglamorous to attract most Broadway ticket buyers.

Set at Steel Pier in Atlantic City in 1933, *Steel Pier* is about the hard lot of Depression-era marathon dancers. In marathons, couples danced continuously, often for days with only short breaks, until only one couple remained standing. The prize was cash. The show was a very expensive flop.

Set around Manhattan's Forty-second Street before the area got cleaned up and Disneyfied, *The Life* is about that area's whores, pimps, pushers, and other denizens of the night. The score includes rhythm and blues, funk, and blues. The show closed at a loss but has continued to have a life in theaters around the country.

Mostly through-sung, *Side Show* is about real-life American conjoined twins Violet and Daisy Hilton, who worked in the circus, vaudeville, and movies, trying to live in a world of "normals." Though mostly praised by the critics, it closed at a loss, apparently because audiences thought they would be turned off by the subject matter. It's an excellent show—not at all depressing. It's occasionally revived when two women can be found to play the extremely difficult central roles.

The Lion King

MUSIC: Elton John

LYRICS: Tim Rice, with additional music and lyrics by Lebo M, Mark Mancina, Jay Rifkin, Julie Taymor, and Hans Zimmer

BOOK: Roger Allers and Irene Mecchi, adapted from the 1994 Disney animated feature by Mecchi, Jonathan Roberts, and Linda Woolverton

DIRECTOR: Julie Taymor

CHOREOGRAPHER: Garth Fagan

DESIGNERS: Richard Hudson (sets), Julie Taymor (costumes, with masks and puppets by Taymor and Michael Curry), and Donald Holder (lights)

PRODUCER: Walt Disney Theatrical Productions

CAST INCLUDES: Samuel E. Wright, Max Casella, Tracy Nicole Chapman, and Heather Headley

PERFORMANCES: 4,027 as of July 15, 2007

Steel Pier

MUSIC: John Kander

LYRICS: Fred Ebb

BOOK: David Thompson, and conceived by Scott Ellis, Susan Stroman, and Thompson

DIRECTOR: Scott Ellis

CHOREOGRAPHER: Susan Stroman

DESIGNERS: Tony Walton (sets), William Ivey Long (costumes), and Peter Kaczorowski (lights)

PRODUCER: Roger Berlind

CAST INCLUDES: Karen Ziemba, Debra Monk, Gregory Harrison, and Kristen Chenoweth

PERFORMANCES: 76

MUSIC: Cy Coleman

LYRICS: Ira Gasman

BOOK: David Newman, Ira Gasman, and Cy Coleman

DIRECTOR: Michael Blakemore

CHOREOGRAPHER: Joey McKneely

ORCHESTRATORS: Don Sobesky and Harold Wheeler

DESIGNERS: Robin Wagner (sets), Martin Pakledinaz (costumes), and Richard Pilbrow (lights)

PRODUCERS: Roger Berlind, Martin Richards, Cy Coleman, and Sam Crother

CAST INCLUDES: Vernel Bagneris and Lillias White

PERFORMANCES: 466

Side Show

MUSIC: Henry Krieger

LYRICS/BOOK: Bill Russell

DIRECTOR/CHOREOGRAPHER: Robert Longbottom

ORCHESTRATOR: Harold Wheeler

DESIGNERS: Robin Wagner (sets), Gregg Barnes (costumes), and Brian MacDevitt (lights)

PRODUCERS: five listed, including Emanuel Azenburg and Joseph and Scott Nederlander

CAST INCLUDES: Alice Ripley and Emily Skinner

PERFORMANCES: 91

In 1998, director/choreographer Jerome Robbins, songwriter Bob Merrill, and performer Frank Sinatra died. There was a hugely successful, sexually charged production of the British revival of *Cabaret* (2,377 performances—longer than the original), with the old Studio 54 converted into the show's Kit Kat Klub. The show was directed by Sam Mendes, codirected and choreographed by Rob Marshall, produced by the Roundabout Theatre Company, and starred Natasha Richardson, Alan Cumming, Ron Rifkin, and Mary Louise Wilson. There was also a hit revival of *The Sound of Music* (533 performances), directed by Susan H. Schulman, choreographed by Michael Lichtefeld, and starring Rebecca Luker. A scaled-down—miniaturized, really—version of Irving Berlin and Moss Hart's 1933 revue *As Thousands Cheer* played off-Broadway. It had six actors accompanied by piano and bass and used seven of the original twelve songs (not including "Easter Parade"), interpolating other Berlin songs as well.

There were flop revivals of *Little Me* (99 performances), directed and choreographed by Rob Marshall and starring Faith Prince and Martin Short, and of *On the Town* (69 performances), directed by George C. Wolfe and choreographed by Keith Young. *Peter Pan*, starring Cathy Rigby, did another limited run of 43 performances and returned later for another 166.

New shows included Paul Simon and Derek Walcott's controversial $11 million failed rock opera *Capeman* (68 performances after 59 previews). It's about a real New York murder committed by the seemingly unfeeling teenager Salvador Agrón (played at different ages by Ruben Blades and Marc Anthony, with Ednita Nazario as his mother), and it covers his life from 1959 to 1977. It went through three directors and a lot of protests from the families of Agrón's victims.

The 85-performance *Parade* (music and lyrics by Jason Robert Brown, book by Alfred Uhry, based on a real event) was directed by Harold Prince, choreographed by Patricia Birch, and produced by Lincoln Center Theater. It starred Brent Carver as Leo Frank, a Jew in the South in the early part of the century who was falsely arrested for murder and lynched. Carolee Carmello played his wife. The show had many fans but, like *Side Show*, didn't suit the temper of the times, at least not on Broadway. It gets occasional regional productions.

There were 23 performances of the revue *An Evening*

with Jerry Herman and 124 performances of Matthew Bourne's modernized production of Tchaikovsky's ballet *Swan Lake,* imported from London with all swan roles danced by males. (Part of it is shown at the end of the film *Billy Elliot.*) A flop stage version (144 performances) of the Cole Porter movie musical *High Society* (itself an adaptation of Barry's play *The Philadelphia Story*), it had additional Porter songs with lyrics added by Susan Birkenhead, and book by Arthur Kopit. Directed by Christopher Renshaw and choreographed by Lars Lubovitch, it starred Melissa Errico, Randy Graff, and John McMartin. It couldn't find enough Porter songs relevant to character and situation.

Among the musical evenings off-Broadway were *I Love You, You're Perfect, Now Change,* a hit revue with music by Jimmy Roberts, book and lyrics by Joe DiPietro, and direction by Joel Bishoff, that was still running in July 2007; *Dinah Was,* a biographical jukebox musical about singer Dinah Washington that included many songs she'd recorded; *Forbidden Broadway Strikes Back!* another in the series of revues satirizing contemporary Broadway; and *Hedwig and the Angry Inch,* a musical about a transvestite would-be hard-rock diva from formerly Communist East Berlin—written by and starring John Cameron Mitchell, with music and lyrics by Stephen Trask—which was filmed in 2001. *The Fantasticks* was in its thirty-first year.

Footloose is about a young man (played by Jeremy Kushnier) who moves with his family to a small town where dancing has been forbidden by an uptight minister. The youth gets everyone dancing again, including the minister and his wife.

Ragtime is about America at the beginning of the twentieth century. Ragtime music is used as a sign of the changing times, which included the crushing rise of big business and the devastating effects of bigotry. The plot focuses mainly on three fictional stories—those of a white family, a black family, and an immigrant father and daughter—that intersect and intertwine as the characters come into contact and conflict with the changing world. Several historical personages also appear in the show, including Emma Goldman, Henry Ford, Harry Houdini, and Evelyn Nesbitt. There's an original-cast recording; among its

Footloose

MUSIC: Tom Snow

LYRICS: Dean Pitchford, with additional songs by Kenny Loggins, Sammy Hagar, Jim Steinman, and Eric Carmen

BOOK: Dean Pitchford and Walter Bobbie, from Pitchford's 1984 screenplay

DIRECTOR: Walter Bobbie

CHOREOGRAPHER: A. C. Ciulla

PRODUCER: Dodger Endemol Theatricals

CAST INCLUDES: Jeremy Kushnier and Dee Hoty

PERFORMANCES: 709

Ragtime

MUSIC: Stephen Flaherty

LYRICS: Lynn Ahrens

BOOK: Terrence McNally, adapted from Doctorow's 1975 novel

DIRECTOR: Frank Galati

MUSICAL STAGING: Graciela Daniele

ORCHESTRATOR: William David Brohn

DESIGNERS: Eugene Lee (sets), Santo Loquasto (costumes), and Jules Fisher and Peggy Eisenhauer (lights)

PRODUCER: Livent (U.S.) Inc.

CAST INCLUDES: Brian Stokes Mitchell, Peter Friedman, Marin Mazzie, Mark Jacoby, Audra McDonald, and Judy Kaye

PERFORMANCES: 834

songs are "The Crime of the Century," "Your Daddy's Son," "New Music," "Make Them Hear You," and "Wheels of a Dream."

In 1999, George Forrest of the team of Wright and Forrest, writer/director Mike Ockrent, writer/composer/performer Anthony Newley, and writer/composer Lionel Bart died. There was a hugely successful revisal (1,045 performances) of *Annie Get Your Gun,* with the book redone by Peter Stone. Directed by Graciela Daniele, choreographed by Daniele and Jeff Calhoun, and produced by Barry and Fran Weissler, it starred Bernadette Peters (replaced during the run by Cheryl Ladd, Crystal Bernard, Susan Lucci, and, most successfully, Reba McEntire) and Tom Wopat (replaced during the run by Brent Barrett and Patrick Cassidy). In the revisal, the show was restructured to be a show within the show put on by Buffalo Bill's troupe.

There was an almost equally successful revival (881 performances) of *Kiss Me, Kate* (the first since the original production in 1952), directed by Michael Blakemore, choreographed by Kathleen Marshall, produced by Roger Berlind and Roger Horchow, and starring Marin Mazzie and Brian Stokes Mitchell.

There was a 149-performance flop revisal of *You're a Good Man, Charlie Brown* that was directed by Michael Mayer, choreographed by Jerry Mitchell, and had Roger Bart, Kristin Chenoweth, Anthony Rapp, and B. D. Wong in the cast.

Among the new revues—none of which had original songs—were *Fosse: A Celebration in Song and Dance* (1,043 performances), which re-created Fosse's dances from various musicals, movies, and TV shows. It was conceived by Richard Maltby Jr., Chet Walker, and Ann Reinking; directed by Maltby; and codirected by Reinking, with Gwen Verdon as artistic advisor. *Putting It Together* (101 performances) was a revised version of the 1993 off-Broadway revue of Sondheim songs; it was produced by Cameron MacKintosh, directed by Eric D. Schaeffer, with musical staging by Bob Avian, orchestrated by Jonathan Tunick (who received the first Tony for Orchestration), and starred Carol Burnett (with Kathie Lee Gifford doing a couple of performances each week), Bronson Pinchot, George Hearn, Ruthie Henshall, and John Barrowman. It used the songs to show the interconnecting relationships between five people at a cocktail party. There are DVDs of live performances of both *Fosse* and *Putting It Together.*

Swing! (461 performances) was a revue of period swing music starring Ann Hampton Callaway. *It Ain't Nothin' but the Blues* (284 performances) was a revue of blues songs starring Gretha Boston.

Among the flops was Frank Wildhorn, Gregory Bond, and Jack Murphy's semi-cantata *The Civil War* (61 performances), starring Michel Bell. Another was Michael John LaChiusa's *Marie Christine* (42 performances), which transfers the story of Medea to New Orleans and Chicago at the end of the nineteenth century. Directed and choreographed by Graciela Daniele, it was produced by Lincoln Center Theater, orchestrated by Jonathan Tunick, and starred Audra McDonald and Anthony Crivello.

Also arriving on Broadway in 1999 was the London hit adaptation of the 1977 movie *Saturday Night Fever* (501 performances), set in "1976 (or whenever you were 19)." With music by the Bee Gees and many others, it was adapted by Nan Knighton from Norman Wexler's screenplay, directed and choreographed by Arlene Phillips, produced by Robert Stigwood, and designed by Robin Wagner, Andy Edwards, and Andrew Bridge. James Carpinello starred as Tony Manero, who dances and romances his way from Brooklyn to Manhattan, most famously in a white suit. The show never figured out how to make the movie stage-worthy, especially since the music in the movie was on the sound track rather than sung by the characters, just as in the movie *Footloose*. However, the songs added to the stage version of *Footloose* fit the dramatic progress of the show (not true of the songs added to *Saturday Night Fever*).

During the nineties, Andrew Lloyd Webber's name on a show still guaranteed advance sales; he could get anything he wanted produced and could, in fact, produce it himself. His pseudo-pop, pseudo-Rodgers, pseudo-Puccini scores sold amazing numbers of tickets and records—usually with one or two hit songs per score repeated over and over again. The full-scale London productions of some of his shows have themselves served as tryouts; he's used the response there to fix them before opening in the United States. (Only Lloyd Webber could think of London as a tryout town.) However, *Sunset Boulevard* didn't pay back its investment in New York or London, and *Whistle Down the Wind*, more intimate than his usual work, did so poorly at its American tryout in 1997 in Washington, D.C., that the production was canceled until it could be rewritten. The rewrite flopped when it opened in England, and the rewrite of his and Alan Ayckbourn's 1975 *Jeeves*, later called *By Jeeves*, flopped in London and New York in 2001.

Also extremely successful were two shows by Claude-Michel Schönberg and Alain Boublil, *Les Misérables* and *Miss Saigon*. Their shows were produced in French, translated into English, and then produced in England. Their third one, *Martin Guerre*, opened in London to mixed reviews and closed at a loss without ever crossing the Atlantic. It would appear that the British invasion was in retreat by the end of the nineties.

Suggested Watching and Listening

Almost every new, revived, or revised nineties show discussed in this chapter has an original-cast recording. (The British imports have at least two—the London cast and the Broadway cast.) There are also more videos and DVDs than there used to be of live performances, though not necessarily of the original cast, and these are usually preferable to the recordings. Among them are *Crazy for You, Passion, Victor/Victoria* (before Raquel Welch replaced Julie Andrews), *Smokey Joe's Café, Jekyll and Hyde,* the British cast (mostly overplaying) of the 1999 revival of *Kiss Me, Kate, Fosse,* and *Putting It Together.* There's also an excellent documentary of the making of the original-cast recording of the 1992 revival of *Guys and Dolls* and movie versions of *Hedwig and the Angry Inch* and *Rent.* (The movie version of *Chicago* is not by any means a filming of the stage production.) The original animated movies of *Beauty and the Beast* and *The Lion King* are available; they have the best of the scores of those two shows. And the yearly televised Tony Awards show has a number from each of the nominated new shows and from each of the revivals. (We can hope the show will continue to be televised, despite the ratings.)

Broadway's Lost Treasures (Full Series)

This series (available on Acorn Media DVD) includes live performances of numbers from 1990s shows nominated for Tony Awards.

- "The American Dream" (performed by Jonathan Pryce and the ensemble): This number from *Miss Saigon* is on volume 3.
- "That's How You Jazz" (performed by Hinton Battle and the ensemble): This number from *Jelly's Last Jam* is on volume 2.
- "I Can't Be Bothered Now" (performed by Harry Groener and the women's chorus): This number from *Crazy for You* is on volume 3.
- "Where You Are" (performed by Chita Rivera, Brent Carver, and the ensemble): This number from *Kiss of the Spider Woman* is on volume 3.
- "Swing" (performed by the cast): This number from *Fosse* is on volume 3.

You might also try to get in a couple of numbers from *Floyd Collins, Side Show,* and *Ragtime.*

Exit Music

Ven you got it, flaunt it,
Step right up and strut your stuff.
People tell you modesty's a wirtue,
But in the theater modesty can hurt you.

Ven you got it, flaunt it;
Show your assets, let 'em know you're proud.

Your goodness you must push,
Stick your chest out, shake your tush,
Ven you got it, shout it out loud!
—"WHEN YOU GOT IT, FLAUNT IT," *THE PRODUCERS,*
LYRICS BY MEL BROOKS

At first the musicals of the twentieth century were meant to be pure entertainment and were not conceived of as art. In the struggle that ensued while the
form was trying to become legitimate art as well as popular entertainment, the
musical has moved back and forth from being star-driven to composer-driven
to librettist-driven to producer-driven to director-choreographer-designer-
driven and so forth. Of course, the making of a truly successful musical is
a collaboration of all the talents involved. Stars, composers, writers, directors,
choreographers, designers, producers, and art and entertainment have
to blend, or the show feels heavy-handed, empty, derivative, incomplete—
unsatisfactory in some way or other.

As part of the development of the form, most successful shows over the
years, comic or serious, have tried to keep up with theatrical and technolog-
ical fashions; some have even been relevant to the political and social pre-
occupations of the times. However, with the advent of rock, few shows
produced before the end of the century seemed interested in keeping up

with pop music trends. Most of the older Broadway composers were inactive during the last thirty years of the twentieth century, or should have been, and there was a distinct paucity of younger American composers who could write the kind of sustained and varied scores required for musicals. Instead, the most successful scores were coming from across the Atlantic.

According to the *New York Times,* in 1965 a musical could recoup its investment in twenty weeks at 95 percent capacity or thirty weeks at 90 percent. By 1995, it took three times as long to break even. And because the cost of producing musicals was escalating even faster than ticket prices, producers tended to fear the unknown, be it new composers, writers, or ideas, all of which were soon found mostly in regional theaters and off-Broadway, if at all. Broadway producers preferred shows that had first been hits elsewhere, were revivals with stars, or that repeated old formulas; if there were deficiencies, they covered them up with production values and directorial concepts. Even the larger regional and off-Broadway theaters couldn't afford to take many chances; they were more likely to do the kinds of shows they hoped would transfer to Broadway.

On March 12, 2000, Frank Rich wrote in his *New York Times Magazine* article "Conversations with Sondheim":

> [Sondheim] is now the greatest and perhaps best-known artist in the American musical theater. But that is a somewhat empty distinction. Sondheim may be the last major creator of Broadway musicals, period, still actively devoted to the trade. He may have even outlived the genre itself, which was long ago exiled by rock music from center stage to niche status in American culture and is now barely a going concern. . . . "You have two kinds of shows on Broadway— revivals and the same kind of musicals over and over again, all spectacles," says Sondheim. "You get your tickets for *The Lion King* a year in advance, and essentially a family comes as if to a picnic, and they pass on to their children the idea that that's what the theater is—a spectacular musical you see once a year, a stage version of a movie. It has nothing to do with theater at all. It has to do with seeing what is familiar. We live in a recycled culture." (38–40)

So it seemed at the beginning of the twenty-first century. The Rodgers and Hammerstein musical play—be it comic, romantic, or dramatic—was having a rough time. It had become apparent that there wasn't going to be another golden age soon—a time when at least half a dozen new shows a season premiered that are still being revived years later and whose songs are still being sung. Shows that try to follow in the Rodgers and Hammerstein tradition without creating a new approach or a contemporary sound usually feel old-fashioned and can't find an audience. *La Cage aux Folles* (1983) had a fresh approach to subject matter—even though neither the score nor the structure broke any new ground—while *Victor/Victoria* (1995), set in more or less the same milieu, had neither a fresh approach nor a particularly good score (especially the new songs added for the stage production) and consequently felt dated and empty. Both shows were set in the world of show business, which usually offers good opportunities for musicalization. And both shows were adapted from popular movies, a frequent practice that gives producers the advantage of presold titles. However, transforming old hit movies like *La Cage* into new musicals seldom succeeds; among recent examples are the stage versions of *Sunset Boulevard, Big, The Goodbye Girl,* and *Sweet Smell of Success.* Turning movie musicals like *Victor/Victoria* into stage musicals also rarely works, as illustrated by such examples as *Singin' in the Rain, Seven Brides for Seven Brothers, Gigi, State Fair, High Society,* and the two dance movies turned into singing shows: *Footloose* and *Saturday Night Fever.* None of these shows intended to break new ground, but they also didn't seem to know how to even if they'd wanted to. At best they did only decent business, which is not sufficient to keep a big show running long enough to pay off its initial investment. None of them managed to do so.

Throughout the eighties and nineties there were occasional hit songs from shows by Lloyd Webber and by Schönberg and Boublil that helped sell tickets and original-cast recordings, though rarely more than one or two songs a season, if that. "Memory" from Lloyd Webber's *Cats* is a particularly overplayed example. So is "The Music of the Night," from his *The Phantom of the Opera.* (Lloyd Webber's visually spectacular pop operas were usually successful despite their many book flaws, clumsy lyrics, and repetitive scores. It's been suggested that they'd be better shows if they'd had better lyricists. Maybe. He picks them. At least equally spectacular visually, the pop operas of Schönberg and Boublil tell their stories more coherently than *Phantom.*) Despite these hit songs, until *Rent* most new American musicals—particularly musical comedies—didn't sell many records; there was even a period when few original-cast recordings were being made. However, beginning in the 1990s, small record companies such as Ghostlight and Rhino cropped up that have assiduously produced original-cast recordings of most new musicals and revivals.

Starting in the seventies, very few musicals from any country were filmed, not that there were that many to film or record. Some of the more successful or important shows were taped before live audiences and released on DVD, including *Pippin* and several later Sondheim shows. In 1996, Lloyd Webber's *Evita* was made into an unsuccessful film starring Madonna; his *Cats* is supposed to be made into an animated feature, which is probably where it belongs; and his *Phantom of the Opera* was filmed unsuccessfully in 2004. (The satirical newspaper *The Onion* ran a front-page article in the December 23–29, 2004, issue with the headline "Psychiatrists Treating *Phantom of the Opera* Viewers for Post-Melodramatic Stress Disorder.") With the success of its 1997 revival, *Chicago* was filmed in 2002 and won the Academy Award for Best Picture. Then came the flop film versions of *Rent* (2005) and *The Producers* (2006), followed—also in 2006—by the highly successful movie version of *Dreamgirls*. It's hard to predict how many more chances Hollywood will be willing to take on Broadway shows.

The 1995–96 season offered more hope than there'd been in a long time for the rejuvenation of the American musical theater. New shows with pop scores, like *Rent* and *Bring in 'Da Noise, Bring in 'Da Funk*, as well as the revivals of the sexist musical farce *A Funny Thing Happened on the Way to the Forum* and the romantic musical drama *The King and I*, led the way to the most financially successful season in years. All of these are American musicals, and most of them brought in both younger and more racially integrated audiences. Unfortunately the 1996–97 season was disappointing. (When *The Life, Jekyll and Hyde*, and *Titanic* are, according to the Tony nominations, the best—and almost the only—new musicals of the year, you know you've got problems. *Titanic* won even though *The Life* probably deserved it.) The 1997–98 season was better again, given such shows as *Ragtime* and the revival of *Cabaret*, and such excellent—though financially unsuccessful—shows as *Sideshow*.

And then there's the Disney organization. Howard Ashman and Alan Menken, authors of *Little Shop of Horrors*, wrote the scores for the animated musicals *The Little Mermaid* and *Beauty and the Beast*, both structured exactly like golden-age musicals. When Ashman died before completing his collaboration with Menken for Disney's animated *Aladdin*, Tim Rice finished the lyrics and wrote the additional ones for the stage production of *Beauty and the Beast*. And, of course, the stage version of *The Lion King* could easily end up as the longest-running show of all time. Excluding *Aida*, the first Disney shows of the twenty-first century were also stage adaptations of animated movies—*Tarzan* and *The Little Mermaid*—as well as of the partially animated *Mary Poppins*. It would be sad to think that the last bastion of the golden-age Broadway musical play is in animated children's films and Disney's live-action productions of them. However, the Disney corporation deserves a great deal of credit for revitalizing Times Square, especially with the sensational refurbishing of Ziegfeld's old Forty-second Street New Amsterdam Theatre, even though it does include a Disney store. At least the store sells many original-cast recordings of the Disney shows.

When revivals do well at the box office, they also sell original-cast recordings and even help sell re-releases of the original original-cast recordings. Furthermore, when pop artists like Krall, Ronstadt, Streisand, and Bennett have recorded show tunes, the CDs have sold well. *Rent* was the first best-selling original-cast recording of a new American musical in a long time. The cast recording of *Ragtime* also sold well, as have the original-cast recordings of the early twenty-first-century shows *The Full Monty, The Producers, Hairspray,* and *Wicked,* and at least two very popular jukebox musicals: *Jersey Boys* and *Mamma Mia!* There have always been audiences out there; it's just that too many of the musicals of the eighties and nineties didn't sing to them, no matter what their tastes in shows or pop music.

Of course, another problem was that there was no homogeneous audience to attract. Long before the 1990s, musical tastes had so splintered that where there used to be one list of the top-ten songs of the week, several lists were needed in order to accommodate everyone's tastes. By the end of the twentieth century, none of these styles had found their way to Broadway on a regular basis except in African American musicals.

There were, however, other encouraging signs by the end of the nineties. *Rent* and *Bring in 'Da Noise, Bring in 'Da Funk* paved the way for smaller off-Broadway shows to transfer successfully to Broadway without troubling to add expensive new production values. Limited-run concert stagings of old musicals became sell-out attractions. Several of them were recorded, and one of them—*Chicago*—was so successful it transferred to a long Broadway run, longer, in fact, than the run of the original production.

At the end of the twentieth century, it also seemed that the light-hearted, tuneful, romantic, and sophisticated musical comedy was dead. Pseudo-operas and other through-composed works, plotless and substanceless shows, and heavy dramas were what constituted most new Broadway musicals. Hardly anything was funny—the unintentional legacy of Oscar Hammerstein (with Kern and with Rodgers) and of his protégé Stephen Sondheim—although things have begun to look up in the first years of the twenty-first century, both for the rebound of the musical comedy and for a real understanding of how to use contemporary sounds in a Broadway musical.

Unfortunately, during those years, Broadway lost composer Cy Coleman, lyricist Fred Ebb, writer/lyricist/performers Adolph Green and Betty Comden, writer Peter Stone, choreographer Onna White, producers David Merrick and Alexander Cohen, and performers Gwen Verdon, Jerry Orbach, and John Raitt.

Cats closed after 7,485 performances; *Les Misérables* after 6,680 (and re-opened just three and a half years later); *Miss Saigon* after 4,092; the revival

Mamma Mia!

MUSIC/LYRICS: ABBA (Björn Ulvaeus and Benny Andersson)

BOOK: Catherine Johnson

DIRECTOR: Phyllida Lloyd

CHOREOGRAPHER: Anthony Van Laast

DESIGNERS: Mark Thompson (sets and production) and Howard Harrison (lighting)

PRODUCERS: five listed, including Björn Ulvaeus, in association with Universal Music Group

CAST INCLUDES: Louise Pitre, Judy Kaye, and Karen Mason as a former girl group, and Tina Maddigan as the former lead singer's daughter

PERFORMANCES: 2,390 as of July 15, 2007

Movin' Out

MUSIC/LYRICS: Billy Joel

DIRECTOR/CHOREOGRAPHER: Twyla Tharp, assisted by Scott Wise

DESIGNERS: Santo Loquasto (sets), Suzy Benzinger (costumes), and Donald Holder (lights)

PRODUCERS: six listed, including Clear Channel Entertainment

CAST INCLUDES: Benjamin Bowman, Michael Cavanaugh (lead vocals), Keith Roberts, Scott Wise, John Selya, Elizabeth Parkinson, and Ashley Tuttle

PERFORMANCES: 1,303

of *Cabaret* after 2,377; and *The Fantasticks* after 17,162. Among the many Broadway revivals and revisals in the first years of the century—not all of them successful—were *The Rocky Horror Show* and *Little Shop of Horrors;* golden age and beyond musicals including *Bells Are Ringing, Wonderful Town, The Music Man, Gypsy, Man of La Mancha, Big River, Nine, The Pajama Game, Fiddler on the Roof, The Apple Tree, La Cage aux Folles, Sweet Charity, 42nd Street,* and *A Chorus Line;* Rodgers's *The Boys from Syracuse, Oklahoma!* and *Flower Drum Song;* and Sondheim's *Company, Follies, Pacific Overtures, Sweeney Todd, Into the Woods,* and *Assassins* (for the first time on Broadway).

Because of the success of his show *Rent,* Jonathan Larson's posthumous *tick, tick . . . BOOM!* was produced off-Broadway. Larson originally wrote it as a monologue about his desperation at turning thirty and still waiting tables. David Auburn, author of the play *Proof,* turned it into a three-character musical: Larson, his best friend, and his girlfriend.

There were some huge flop jukebox shows during the first years of the twenty-first century, including *Good Vibrations* (94 performances) with Brian Wilson and the Beach Boys songs; *All Shook Up* (213 performances) with Elvis Presley songs; *Lennon* (49 performances) with John Lennon songs, and several actors playing him; *Ring of Fire* (57 performances) with Johnny Cash songs; and *The Times They Are A-Changin'* (28 performances) with Bob Dylan songs and Twyla Tharp choreography. The Dylan show was so bad that Ben Sisario, on the first page of the *New York Times* Weekend Arts section on October 27, 2006, referred to it as "the latest heart-rending episode in Broadway's reality soap opera, 'When Bad Shows Happen to Great Songwriters,'" and described jukebox musicals as shows "in which pop hits are beaten up by singing robots." Fortunately, there were also some successful ones and even a couple of good ones.

Mamma Mia! uses songs by the Swedish group ABBA to cobble together a simple story about the former lead singer in a girl group and the question of which of three men is the father of her daughter. It was first produced in London in 1999 and toured North America before opening to great success on Broadway in 2001. It had audiences literally dancing in the aisles and cemented the commercial viability of jukebox musicals.

Another hit jukebox show, *Movin' Out* was really a full-length jazz ballet set to songs by Billy Joel; the songs were performed live by a singer situated with the band on a bandstand elevated behind the dancers. The very dramatic story is about a group of friends and lovers before, during, and after the Vietnam War. *Movin' Out* had the budget to afford out-of-town tryouts and was able to work out its problems before coming to Broadway in 2002.

A biographical musical about Frankie Valli and the Four Seasons, *Jersey Boys* opened on Broadway in 2005 after trying out at the La Jolla Playhouse in California. The story traces the lives and careers of the four Italian kids from Belleville, New Jersey, who made up the original group, starting from the time they sang together on street corners in the 1950s to a career that lasted (with replacements) into the new century, winning the group many gold records along the way. The show also includes scenes and songs about the effect their careers had on their lives together and with their families. Each of the Four Seasons gets to narrate parts of the show, giving us different perspectives on the good times and the bad. Although *Jersey Boys* is both a concert and a jukebox musical, it has a strong book, and the old songs are often used successfully to further plot and character development. It won four Tony Awards, including Best Musical.

There were a couple of flop musicals by major players in the early years of the new century. Andrew Lloyd Webber and Alan Ayckbourn's *By Jeeves*, adapted from some Wodehouse stories about the English twit and his very smart man's man, closed after 73 performances. Susan Stroman directed and choreographed Harry Connick Jr. and David Thompson's *Thou Shalt Not* (85 performances), adapted from *Thérèse Raquin*, Emile Zola's 1867 novel of sexual compulsion leading to adultery, murder, and retribution. Reset to the New Orleans of 1946, the show was conceived by Stroman, Connick, and Thompson, with Craig Bierko, Norbert Leo Butz, Kate Levering, and Debra Monk leading the cast. The songs are mostly jazz, without much ability to further character or plot.

There were also quite a few new hit musicals during the early years of the twenty-first century.

Contact, which opened in 2000, consists of three original, unconnected, and almost entirely danced one-acts with prerecorded

Jersey Boys

MUSIC: Bob Gaudio

LYRICS: Bob Crewe

BOOK: Marshall Brickman and Rick Elise

DIRECTOR: Des McAnuff

CHOREOGRAPHER: Sergio Trujillo

DESIGNERS: Klara Zieglerova (sets), Jess Goldstein (costumes), and Howell Binkley (lights)

PRODUCERS: ten producers and associate producers listed, including Dodger Theatricals

CAST OF THIRTEEN INCLUDES: John Lloyd Young as Frankie Valli and Daniel Reichard as Bob Gaudio

PERFORMANCES: 705 as of July 15, 2007

Contact

MUSIC/LYRICS: various artists

BOOK: John Weidman and Susan Stroman

DIRECTOR/CHOREOGRAPHER: Susan Stroman

DESIGNERS: Thomas Lynch (sets), William Ivey Long (costumes), and Peter Kaczorowski (lights)

PRODUCER: Lincoln Center Theater

CAST INCLUDES: Boyd Gaines, Deborah Yates, and Karen Ziemba

PERFORMANCES: 1,010

music ranging from classical to rock. The three one-acts are "Swinging," a curtain-raiser based on Fragonard's painting *The Swing* and set to Rodgers and Hart's "My Heart Stood Still"; "Did You Move?" set in an Italian restaurant, where an abused wife imagines herself dancing with everyone there except her husband, with music by Grieg and Tchaikovsky; and "Contact," set mostly in a lonely man's apartment and in a bar and dance hall, where he's attracted to a woman in a yellow dress, with music by the Beach Boys and Van Morrison, among others. To qualify for the Tonys, the show went from off- to on Broadway by moving from the Mitzi E. Newhouse downstairs at Lincoln Center Theater to the Vivian Beaumont upstairs. Although there's no original music, no singing by the cast, and hardly any dialogue, it won the Tony Award for Best Musical in a very meager year for musicals. There's a video.

Also opening in 2000 was Disney's *Aida* (1,852 performances). A loose adaptation by Linda Woolverton, Robert Falls, and David Henry Hwang of the story of the Verdi opera, the songs are by Elton John and Tim Rice. Set in ancient Egypt, *Aida* was directed by Falls, choreographed by Wayne Cilento, designed by Bob Crowley and Natasha Katz, and featured Heather Headley, Adam Pascal, and Sherie René Scott as the leads in a romantic triangle that ends sadly for all three. It had a very expensive series of out-of-town tryouts.

The original movie of *The Full Monty* is about a group of unemployed men in the north of England who become strippers in order to make a living. The musical transplants the story to Buffalo, New York. *The Full Monty* began life at the Old Globe Theatre in San Diego, California, before opening on Broadway in 2000.

The pseudo-Brechtian, satiric *Urinetown* is a self-referential musical comedy about a police state with such a severe water shortage that citizens have to pay to use the washroom. The price keeps rising, which eventually leads to a revolution. Things work out badly. The show includes a couple of characters who comment on the show itself (and its title) as the action progresses, keeping audience members at the proper Brechtian distance and helping them understand not to take things too seriously.

The Full Monty

MUSIC/LYRICS: David Yazbek

BOOK: Terrence McNally, adapted from the 1997 British movie

DIRECTOR: Jack O'Brien

CHOREOGRAPHER: Jerry Mitchell

DESIGNERS: John Arnone (sets), Robert Morgan (costumes), and Howell Binkley (lights)

PRODUCERS: Fox Searchlight Pictures, Lindsay Law, and Thomas Hall

CAST INCLUDES: Patrick Wilson, Jason Danieley, Emily Skinner, Kathleen Freeman, and André DeShields

PERFORMANCES: 770

Urinetown

MUSIC: Mark Hollmann

LYRICS: Mark Hollmann and Greg Kotis

BOOK: Greg Kotis

DIRECTOR: John Rando

MUSICAL STAGING: John Carrafa

DESIGNERS: Scott Pask (sets), Gregory Gale and Jonathan Bixby (costumes), and Brian MacDevitt (lights)

PRODUCERS: four producers and associate producers listed, including The Araca Group and Dodger Theatricals

CAST INCLUDES: John Cullum and Hunter Foster

PERFORMANCES: 965

Several of the musical numbers were clearly staged as parodies of such musicals as *West Side Story, Les Misérables,* and *Fiddler on the Roof.* John Cullum played the businessman villain and Hunter Foster was the poor but plucky hero who's pushed off a roof to his death. (Foster's sister Sutton was starring in *Thoroughly Modern Millie* at the same time. Maybe they ought to revive an old Fred and Adele Astaire musical for them.) *Urinetown* opened off-Broadway before moving to Broadway in 2001.

Also opening in 2001 was *The Producers,* with funny lyrics and easy to hum music by Mel Brooks in old pop styles. The musical is about Max Bialystock and Leopold Bloom searching for and finding a show to produce that's so bad it's sure to close in one night, so that they won't have to pay off its investors. They collect far more cash than they'll need, planning to keep all the extra money for themselves. Unfortunately, *Springtime for Hitler,* the show they find, is an accidental hit, and the two men end up in jail. *The Producers* was every bit as big a hit as *Springtime for Hitler;* it was also the funniest musical comedy in years. Like *Urinetown,* it's self-referential and often laughs at itself for being a musical, with asides to the audience, a character asking why another character just moved downstage right, and Bialystock (in jail in the second act) recounting the entire show up to that point—including the intermission. It's also deliberately politically incorrect and indiscriminately offensive in pretty much every area you can think of. The flop 2006 movie adaptation was directed by Stroman, with Lane and Broderick re-creating their original roles.

Set in New York in 1922, *Thoroughly Modern Millie* has new music by Jeanine Tesori that sounds proper for the period and fits in well with the movie's score. The show was originally produced at the La Jolla Playhouse in California before opening on Broadway in 2002. It's a musical comedy about the romantic adventures of two young couples and their encounter with the white slave trade. It was a hit, but not groundbreaking or even very good (neither was the movie), though it certainly tried hard—too hard, actually. It's harmless, though, and has lots of singing and dancing and show business pizzazz. It's a family show and did very well on the road.

The Producers

MUSIC/LYRICS: Mel Brooks

BOOK: Mel Brooks and Thomas Meehan, adapted from Brooks's 1968 movie

DIRECTOR/CHOREOGRAPHER: Susan Stroman

DESIGNERS: Robin Wagner (sets), William Ivey Long (costumes), and Peter Kaczorowski (lights)

PRODUCERS: thirteen producers and associate producers listed, including Bob and Harvey Weinstein

CAST INCLUDES: Nathan Lane and Matthew Broderick, with Brad Oscar, Gary Beach, Roger Bart, and Cady Huffman

PERFORMANCES: 2,502

Thoroughly Modern Millie

NEW MUSIC: Jeanine Tesori

NEW LYRICS: Dick Scanlon

BOOK: Richard Morris and Dick Scanlon, adapted from Morris's 1967 movie musical

DIRECTOR: Michael Mayer

CHOREOGRAPHER: Rob Ashford

DESIGNERS: David Gallo (sets), Martin Pakledinaz (costumes), and Donald Holder (lights)

PRODUCERS: sixteen producers and associate producers listed, including Michael Leavitt and Fox Theatricals

CAST INCLUDES: Sutton Foster, Harriet Harris, and Marc Kudisch

PERFORMANCES: 903

Hairspray

MUSIC: Marc Shaiman

LYRICS: Scott Wittman and Marc Shaiman

BOOK: Mark O'Donnell and Thomas Meehan, adapted from John Waters's 1988 movie

DIRECTOR: Jack O'Brien

CHOREOGRAPHER: Jerry Mitchell

DESIGNERS: David Rockwell (sets), William Ivey Long (costumes), and Kenneth Posner (lights)

PRODUCERS: twenty producers and associate producers listed, including New Line Cinema and Clear Channel Entertainment

CAST INCLUDES: Harvey Fierstein and Marissa Jaret Winokur

PERFORMANCES: 2,048 as of July 15, 2007

Hairspray, which tried out at Seattle's Fifth Avenue Theatre before opening on Broadway in 2002, starred Harvey Fierstein in drag and a fat suit (Divine in the original movie didn't need one) as Edna Turnblad, mother of Tracy Turnblad, played by Marissa Jaret Winokur. It's a comedy with a social conscience set in Baltimore in 1962. The story is about Tracy, an overweight teenage girl with big hair and a big mother, who manages to integrate a local TV show not unlike Dick Clark's "American Bandstand." It's funny, filled with good songs that sound like they're authentically from the period, and lots of dancing. A shortened version of the show ran only a few months in Las Vegas, which doesn't seem to be particularly hospitable to Broadway shows. The movie of *Hairspray,* starring John Travolta in drag and a fat suit, was released in 2007.

With such shows as *Thoroughly Modern Millie, The Full Monty, Mamma Mia!, Urinetown, The Producers,* and *Hairspray,* by the end of 2002 there was hope again for the musical comedy—with dance.

Avenue Q

MUSIC/LYRICS: Robert Lopez and Jeff Marx

BOOK: Jeff Witty

DIRECTOR: Jason Moore

CHOREOGRAPHER: Ken Roberson

DESIGNERS: Anna Louizos (sets), Mirena Rada (costumes), and Howell Binkley (lights)

PRODUCERS: seven listed, including the Vineyard Theatre

CAST INCLUDES: John Tartaglia and Stephanie D'Abruzzo

PERFORMANCES: 1,652 as of July 15, 2007

Originally opening off-Broadway, *Avenue Q* moved to Broadway in 2003. It's an adult *Sesame Street,* with most of the nine characters also playing the characters of the large hand puppets they're holding. Set on a run-down city street, the show is about its twenty-something-year-old residents, all of them trying to work out their unsatisfying lives. Despite the puppets, some of them clearly modeled on *Sesame Street* characters, the show is definitely not for children; among the subjects dealt with in song and dialogue are racism, pornography, and sexual orientation. Shortly after winning the Tony for Best Musical, the producers of *Avenue Q* announced that instead of taking the show on the road, they were going to open a shortened version of it in Las Vegas. It wasn't what Las Vegas audiences wanted to see, and, like *Hairspray,* it closed there rather quickly.

Wicked also opened on Broadway in 2003; it had gone through extensive rewrites after its San Francisco tryout. The show, a prequel to Frank Baum's *The Wizard of Oz,* is set in a much darker world than Baum's original creation. It's about green-skinned Elphaba (Idina Menzel), a caring idealist with an obsessive need to free all the caged animals in Oz, and how she became known as the Wicked Witch of the West even though it was Glinda (Kristen Chenoweth), determined to be the most popular girl at school, who was the spiteful and ruthless one of the pair. A huge hit with a number of power ballads that appealed in particular to the many preteen and teenage girls in the audience, the show earned back its $14 million investment in a little over a year. It was able to sustain open-end runs (known as sit-down runs) simultaneously in Chicago, Los Angeles, and London, as well as a touring company. Christmas week 2005, *Wicked* broke the record for the highest weekly box-office gross in Broadway history. The original-cast recording went platinum and won the Grammy Award for Best Musical Show Album. It lost the Tony Awards for Best Score and Best Book as well as for Best Musical to *Avenue Q. Wicked* is as likely as *The Lion King* to beat the record for the longest-running show on Broadway.

The Tony Award–winning musical comedy *Spamalot* is a satiric, off-kilter telling of various episodes purporting to be part of the story of King Arthur and his Knights of the Round Table and their quest for the Holy Grail. Like *Urinetown*, it's self-referential and has several numbers that parody specific musicals. The show tried out in Chicago and, with the help of reviews and audience reaction, was able to fix up most of its problems before opening on Broadway in 2005.

Adapted from the movie starring Michael Caine and Steve Martin, *Dirty Rotten Scoundrels* tried out at the Old Globe Theatre in San Diego, California, before opening on Broadway in 2005. It's about two con artists of very different natures and temperaments; they have a contest to see who can con a wealthy woman out of her money. She turns out to be an even better con artist and cons them instead.

The score of *The Light in the Piazza*, orchestrated by Ted Sperlin, Adam Guettel, and Bruce Coughlin for a very small orchestra, is highly romantic and nearly operatic in its scope and complexity. It's also quite beautiful. The show is about an overly protective American mother touring Florence with her daughter in 1953. The daughter and a young Italian man fall in love, but the mother is opposed to the match. It's gradually revealed that because of an accident, the daughter, though seemingly

Wicked

MUSIC/LYRICS: Stephen Schwartz
BOOK: Winnie Holzman, adapted from Gregory Maguire's novel *Wicked: The Life and Times of the Wicked Witch of the West*
DIRECTOR: Joe Mantello
CHOREOGRAPHER: Wayne Cilento
DESIGNERS: Eugene Lee (sets), Susan Hilferty (costumes), and Kenneth Posner (lights)
PRODUCERS: five listed, including Universal Pictures
CAST INCLUDES: Kristen Chenoweth, Idina Menzel, Norbert Leo Butz, Joel Grey, and Carol Shelley
PERFORMANCES: 1,548 as of July 15, 2007

Spamalot

MUSIC: John Du Prez and Eric Idle
LYRICS/BOOK: Eric Idle, adapted from the 1975 movie *Monty Python and the Holy Grail*
DIRECTOR: Mike Nichols
CHOREOGRAPHER: Casey Nicholaw
DESIGNERS: Tim Hatley (sets and costumes) and Hugh Vanstone (lights)
PRODUCERS: fifteen listed, including the Shubert Organization
CAST INCLUDES: Hank Azaria, Tim Curry, David Hyde Pierce, and Sarah Ramirez, with John Cleese as the recorded voice of God
PERFORMANCES: 972 as of July 15, 2007

Dirty Rotten Scoundrels

MUSIC/LYRICS: David Yazbek

BOOK: Jeffrey Lane, adapted from the 1988 movie

DIRECTOR: Jack O'Brien

CHOREOGRAPHER: Jerry Mitchell

DESIGNERS: David Rockwell (sets), Gregg Barnes (costumes), and Kenneth Posner (lights)

PRODUCERS: twenty-three producers and producing companies listed, including Harvey Weinstein and Clear Channel Entertainment

CAST INCLUDES: John Lithgow, Norbert Leo Butz, Sherie René Scott, Joanna Gleason, and Gregory Jbara

PERFORMANCES: 627

The Light in the Piazza

MUSIC/LYRICS: Adam Guettel

BOOK: Craig Lucas, adapted from Elizabeth Spencer's 1960 short novel

DIRECTOR: Bartlett Sher

MUSICAL STAGING: Jonathan Butterell

DESIGNERS: Michael Yeargan (sets), Catherine Zuber (costumes), and Christopher Akerlind (lights)

PRODUCER: Lincoln Center Theater

CAST OF SIXTEEN INCLUDES: Victoria Clark, Mark Harelik, Kelli O'Hara, and Matthew Morrison

PERFORMANCES: 504

normal, has had some brain damage. The mother learns to be honest and to let go, and the love affair moves forward to marriage. The show tried out at the Intiman Playhouse in Seattle and at the Goodman Theatre in Chicago before moving to Broadway in 2005. It was taped in performance and broadcast on PBS.

The 25th Annual Putnam County Spelling Bee (920 performances as of July 15, 2007) has very funny music and lyrics by William Finn and a book by Rachel Sheinkin from a concept by Rebecca Feldman with additional material by Jay Reiss. It listed six producers, was designed by Beowulf Borit, Jennifer Caprio, and Natasha Katz, and had a cast of nine. The show transferred from off-Broadway in 2005. Members of the audience are chosen shortly before curtain time each night to become contestants in the spelling bee and sit onstage among the misfit teenage contestants who are the central characters. The characters and all the chosen audience members are gradually eliminated as the spelling bee and the show proceed. Although the characters are larger-than-life, audiences really learn to care about who's going to win.

Originally produced by the Alliance Theatre Company of Atlanta, Georgia, *The Color Purple* reached Broadway in 2005. The show traces the life of a Southern black woman named Celie from 1909 to 1949. It deals with her struggles and ultimate victory over oppression of various kinds, including abuse by her unwanted and cruel husband, Mister. She finally leaves him and in time learns to be independent and to love herself. There are several subplots in the novel that are also tracked over the book's forty-year period, and the show tries to cover a little too much of everything in too short a time. It is, however, fast-moving and filled with solid pop-soul music that changes with the changing sounds of Southern blues and gospel music heard during the first half of the twentieth century. *The Color Purple* lost the Tony Award for Best Musical to *The Drowsy Chaperone*.

Developed in Toronto and Los Angeles before opening in New York in 2006, *The Drowsy Chaperone: A Musical Within a Comedy* features coauthor Martin as the narrator, Man in a Chair. Sitting in his apartment in contemporary New York, he tells the audience he's going to play them the LP of his favorite 1920s musical, *The Drowsy Chaperone,* by the fictional team of Gable and Stein. As he starts the record, everyone in the cast of the old musical appears in his living room. They perform the corny, two-act romantic farce live for him—and for the audience. There are occasional interruptions, explanations, and comments from Man in a Chair. Stephen Holden, on the front page of the *New York Times* Weekend Arts section on June 16, 2006, wrote that Man in a Chair "gleefully extols the quaint Broadway values embodied in this imaginary 1928 show. 'It does what a musical is supposed to do,' he declares. 'It takes you to another world, and it gives you a little tune to carry in your head when you're feeling blue.'" The songs are all in the style of 1920s musical comedies.

Grey Gardens (307 performances), with music by Scott Frankel, lyrics by Michael Korie, and book by Doug Wright, was adapted from the 1976 documentary film about Edith and "Little" Edie Bouvier Beale, the eccentric aunt and cousin of Jackie Kennedy Onassis. The show listed seven producers, was designed by Allen Moyer, William Ivey Long, and Peter Kaczorowski, and starred Christine Ebersole and Mary Louise Wilson. At the end of the first act, set in 1941, the daughter, "Little" Edie, is jilted by John F. Kennedy's older brother, Joseph Jr., who is later killed in World War II. In the second act, set in 1973, mother and daughter have withdrawn into their rotting twenty-eight room mansion in East Hampton, New York, where they live in total squalor. Christine Ebersole played the mother in the first act and the totally wrecked daughter in the second act. Her performance had a lot to do with the success of the show. It was moved to Broadway in 2006 from its original off-Broadway production.

Also having moved from off-Broadway to Broadway in 2006 was *Spring Awakening.* The musical is set in a German town at the time of Wedekind's play, which was written in 1891 but wasn't produced until 1906. It's about the pains and confusions of teenage love and lust exacerbated by a strict, small-minded society's unwillingness or inability to talk with their children about sex. The musical is quite faithful to the original play; the story includes teenage rebellion, suicide, abortion, and death. The biggest difference between the play and the musical is that the inner thoughts of the teenagers in the musical are expressed in rock

The Color Purple

MUSIC/LYRICS: Brenda Russell, Allee Willis, and Stephen Bray

BOOK: Marsha Norman, adapted from Alice Walker's novel

DIRECTOR: Gary Griffin

CHOREOGRAPHER: Donald Byrd

DESIGNERS: John Lee Beatty (sets), Paul Tazewell (costumes), and Brian MacDevitt (lights)

PRODUCERS: eighteen listed, including Oprah Winfrey, Quincy Jones, and Bob and Harvey Weinstein

CAST INCLUDES: La Chanze and Felicia P. Fields

PERFORMANCES: 676 as of July 15, 2007

The Drowsy Chaperone: A Musical Within a Comedy

MUSIC/LYRICS: Lisa Lambert and Greg Morrison

BOOK: Bob Martin and Don McKellar

DIRECTOR/CHOREOGRAPHER: Casey Nicholaw

DESIGNERS: David Gallo (sets), Gregg Barnes (costumes), and Ken Billington and Brian Monahan (lights)

PRODUCERS: six listed

CAST INCLUDES: Sutton Foster, Georgia Engel, and Bob Martin

PERFORMANCES: 504 as of July 15, 2007

Spring Awakening

MUSIC: Duncan Sheik

LYRICS/BOOK: Steven Sater, adapted from Frank Wedekind's play

DIRECTOR: Michael Mayer

CHOREOGRAPHER: Bill T. Jones

DESIGNERS: Christine Jones (sets), Susan Hilferty (costumes), and Kevin Adams (lights)

PRODUCERS: twenty-nine producers, producing companies, and associate producers listed, including the Atlantic Theater Company

CAST INCLUDES: Jonathan Groff, Lea Michele, and John Gallagher Jr.

PERFORMANCES: 249 as of July 15, 2007

songs sung into suddenly appearing handheld microphones. The songs make all the parallels necessary to the problems of teenagers anywhere and at any time, and the show quickly developed a young audience. Along with the seats in the auditorium, there were seats on both sides of the stage that helped give the show a visual metaphor for the hemmed-in feeling of the young characters, as did the band placed behind the actors. Cast members would even occasionally sing from among the audience members seated on the stage as if they were singing for the audience as well as for themselves. The show also had an interesting casting idea in that one man and one woman (Stephen Spinella and Christine Estabrook) played all the adult characters. It won the 2006–7 Tony Award for Best Musical.

In mid-July 2007, five out of the ten all-time, longest-running shows in Broadway history were still running in their original productions. All of them were musicals: _Rent, The Lion King,_ the 1996 revival of _Chicago, The Phantom of the Opera,_ and _Beauty and the Beast. A Chorus Line_ and _Les Misérables,_ two of the other five longest-running shows, were playing in revivals that were fairly exact replicas of the original productions. Of the twenty-seven shows on Broadway at the time, twenty-three were musicals. Musicals were keeping Broadway alive and reasonably healthy.

Eventually an art form decays and has to die in order to be reborn; art is like a phoenix, always rising out of its ashes. A synthesis of old forms eventually produces a new form, once the rough edges and disjunctions are smoothed out. The new form then expands until it grows stale or bursts. Beethoven expanded on Mozart, the romantics on Beethoven, Wagner and Mahler on the romantics, until the forms were ready to burst and there seemed nowhere new to go. Debussy, Ravel, and Stravinsky let out a lot of the hot air while pushing out the boundaries of tonality, and Schoenberg's twelve-tone system burst the balloon into what turned out to be a dead end that went on for too many years, preaching only to the converted. Rodgers and Hammerstein synthesized musical comedy with operetta to create their musical plays. Sondheim and Prince synthesized musical plays with revues to create their concept musicals. (Hammerstein, with _Show Boat_ and _Allegro,_ was at the root of both forms.) By the end of the century, both forms had expanded as far as they seemed able to go. (It's always been a bad sign in the history of the musical when spectacle sells the most tickets.) It was time, like Stravinsky had done, to apply what was new to the classical forms. After all, Disney was doing musicals in the golden-age Rodgers and Hammerstein form, and Lloyd Webber and Boublil and Schönberg had gone all the way back to the operetta, and even further, with their hits.

Great musicals both entertain and provide a deeper, richer understanding of the human experience. Good ones usually do one or the other better. Most musical comedies of the last decades of the century presented us with stereotypes rather than characters, who sang songs we thought we'd heard before while they dealt with situations and dialogue that might give TV sitcom writers pause. Most musical plays and concept musicals tended toward anger, coldness, fatalism, depression, and difficult music—the theatrical heritage of Brecht, Beckett, Peter Brook, Sondheim, Prince, and the 1960s. Their authors usually had no solutions and saw little promise of things getting better. These serious and occasionally difficult shows may present an accurate reflection of the world, and some of them are good, or even great, works of art; it's just that their authors apparently lack the desire to create the kinds of entertainments that are commercially viable. In fact, most of these shows tend to turn off those members of the Broadway audience who venture into them; they then become even more wary of going to the theater at all, especially at the current high ticket prices. And since these shows usually lose money, their producers become that much more averse to anything new or different.

Any art form, to remain vital, must be submitted to frequent questioning, stretching, pulling, battering, even ripping to pieces. Most art forms are fortunate in that they don't require collaboration to the extent that musicals do. An unusually complex and difficult medium of expression, a musical requires its many collaborators to continue working on it for as long as it takes to blend their diverse efforts into a cohesive whole. And, before anyone can risk a Broadway production, a new show has to be tested. Many shows that didn't have the budget to afford out-of-town tryouts—or at least staged workshops without production values—have suffered accordingly. It's only in workshops or out-of-town that writers and composers have the time and lack of pressure to make adjustments to the material. A lot can be learned quickly under those conditions without risking the integrity of the piece.

One of the less obvious benefits to writers and composers of workshops is that the shows have to be smaller than the *Saigon*s, *Phantom*s, and *Titanic*s of the world—and, therefore, closer to the intimacy of those old Princess musicals. This need for relative intimacy can have the same salutary effect on the contemporary musical it had on the earliest ones, making it dependent on story, character, words, and music for success. *Rent, Urinetown,* and *Spring Awakening* did little to improve their production values or the size of their casts when they moved from small, off-Broadway stages to Broadway. The revival of *Chicago* retained the production values of its original concert staging: minimal set, one costume per performer, orchestra on stage. They're all hits, and because the shows themselves are good, no one seems to mind the lack of major production values.

Another important benefit of workshops and out-of-town tryouts is that time can be spent adjusting the script and score to the talents of the cast. (Actors' Equity requires that the performers who workshop a show have to be offered their roles in the first full production or be bought out—which can get expensive.) Until the twentieth century, playwrights knew, while writing, which actor would be playing which character, and what each actor's talents were. The Greeks, Shakespeare, Molière, and Chekhov (and Gilbert and Sullivan) all wrote for companies of actors. The same principle was used in the early musicals—those loosely structured star turns that first caught the audience's attention to the form—and was used to even greater effect in the tailoring that was done for stars and supporting players alike when most musicals could afford to go out on the road and stay there till they were ready or never were going to be ready.

The necessary elements of a great, or at least really good, modern musical are strong performers playing fully realized characters; songs—and dances, please—that further the plot or concept and help define character; a style that will be pleasing to contemporary ears and contemporary minds; and, if possible, a theme that's either timely or timeless. And it helps if the show is funny; if it isn't, it should at least have room for comedy and lots of dance. (Shows such as *The Lion King*, the revival of *Chicago*, *The Full Monty*, *The Producers*, *Thoroughly Modern Millie*, *Hairspray*, *Wicked*, and *The Color Purple* have clearly restored dance to its proper place in the integrated musical.)

In addition to having talent and the ability to craft a dramatic event, the book writers of the new American musicals must know how to create stories that make us want to know what happens next, with events that entertain us and characters who involve us and can believably sing their feelings as well as speak them. And they must know how to write scripts that leave room for appropriate musical numbers but still use dialogue to carry at least a decent amount of the plot and comedy. We can hope that they also have ideas that provoke us.

And the songwriters? Audiences want expressions of feeling in the music as well as good tunes in contemporary rhythms and styles. (Sometimes nostalgic sounds work too, as in the pastiche scores for *Hairspray* and *The Drowsy Chaperone*.) There should be wit, dexterity, and ideas in the lyrics, and of course the songs and dances must be plot- and character-appropriate.

The director/choreographer and the designers? Their job is to be at the service of the show rather than its main sources of creativity. That's the job of the writers of the book, the lyrics, and the music; they are the creators, and it's their vision that must be the show's vision. If how a show looks and moves is its primary artistic thrust, there's no art left, only artistry, which can't do more than preserve the hollow shell of the show.

We live in a time when, more and more, the response to trouble is violence; when too many individual communities have become too insular for the good of the larger community; when too much beyond one's immediate world seems to exist either to be feared or taken advantage of; when too many people try not to feel deeply or try to disguise their feelings with catch phrases, crudeness, inarticulateness, and sentimentality. It is one of the most important functions of both art and entertainment to help us transcend such times, sometimes by helping us to think things through, sometimes by helping us not to think at all. Musicals—serious or comic—have done both of those things in the past, mainly by keeping up with the country's changing moods and changing times, whether the need is to laugh or to feel deeply or both. Of course, it was a lot easier when it didn't take years and a small fortune to get a show produced, but it can still be done. Musicals of the twenty-first century as different as *The Producers* and *Spring Awakening* prove it.

ACKNOWLEDGMENTS

All possible care has been taken to trace ownership and secure permission for the song lyrics quoted in this book. The author and publisher would like to thank the following organizations and individuals for permission to reprint copyrighted material:

"Alexander's Ragtime Band" by Irving Berlin. Copyright © 1911 by Ted Snyder Co. Copyright renewed and assigned to Irving Berlin; international copyright secured. Reprinted by permission. All rights reserved.

Allegro libretto excerpt ("Dearly Beloved") used by permission of the Rodgers and Hammerstein Organization. Copyright © 1947 by Richard Rodgers and Oscar Hammerstein II. Copyright renewed. International copyright secured. All rights reserved.

"All of You," words and music by Cole Porter. Copyright © 1954 by Cole Porter. Copyright renewed, assigned to Robert H. Montgomery, trustee of the Cole Porter Musical and Literary Property Trusts. Publication and allied rights assigned to Chappell & Co. Reprinted by permission of Alfred Publishing Co., Inc. All rights reserved.

"Any Old Place with You" (from *A Lonely Romeo*), words by Lorenz Hart and music by Richard Rodgers. Copyright © 1919 by Warner Bros., Inc. Reprinted by permission of Alfred Publishing Co., Inc. All rights reserved.

"Aquarius" (from *Hair*), lyrics by James Rado and Gerome Ragni, music by Galt MacDermot. Copyright © 1966, 1967, 1968, 1970 (copyrights renewed) James Rado, Gerome Ragni, Galt MacDermot, Nat Shapiro, and EMI U Catalog, Inc. All rights administered by EMI U Catalog, Inc. (publishing) and Alfred Publishing Co., Inc. (print). Reprinted by permission of Alfred Publishing Co., Inc. All rights reserved.

"Bewitched" by Richard Rodgers and Lorenz Hart. Copyright © 1941 (renewed) Chappell & Co. Rights for extended renewal term in the United States controlled by the Estate of Lorenz Hart (administered by WB Music Corp.) and the Family Trust under the will of Richard Rodgers and the Family Trust under the will of Dorothy F. Rodgers (administered by Williamson Music). Reprinted by permission. All rights reserved.

"Brother, Can You Spare a Dime?" (from *Americana*), lyrics by E. Y. "Yip" Harburg and music by Jay Gorney. Published by Glocca Morra Music (ASCAP) and Gorney Music (ASCAP); rights administered by Next Decade Entertainment, Inc. All rights reserved.

"Brush Up Your Shakespeare" (from *Kiss Me, Kate*), words and music by Cole Porter. Copyright © 1949 (renewed) Chappell & Co. Reprinted by permission of Alfred Publishing Co., Inc. All rights reserved.

"Buddy's Blues" (from *Follies*), words and music by Stephen Sondheim. Used by permission of Herald Square Music, Inc., on behalf of Range Road Music, Inc., Jerry Leiber Music, Mike Stoller Music, and Rilting Music, Inc.

"Camelot" (from *Camelot*), words by Alan Jay Lerner and music by Frederick Loewe. Copyright © 1960 (renewed) by Alan Jay Lerner and Frederick Loewe. Publication and allied rights assigned to Chappell & Co., Inc. Reprinted by permission of Alfred Publishing Co., Inc. All rights reserved.

"Dance Little Lady" (from *This Year of Grace*), words and music by Noël Coward. Copyright © 1928 (renewed) Chappell Music Ltd. Reprinted by permission of Alfred Publishing Co., Inc. All rights reserved.

"Edelweiss" by Richard Rodgers and Oscar Hammerstein II. Copyright © 1959 by Richard Rodgers and Oscar Hammerstein II. Copyright renewed. Williamson Music owner of publication and allied rights throughout the world. International copyright secured. Reprinted by permission. All rights reserved.

"Ev'rything I've Got" (from *All's Fair* [*By Jupiter*]), lyrics by Lorenz Hart and music by Richard Rodgers. Copyright © 1942 by Chappell & Co., Inc. Copyright renewed. Copyright assigned to Williamson Music and WB Music Corp. for the extended renewal period of copyright in the United States. Reprinted by permission of Alfred Publishing Co., Inc. International copyright secured. All rights reserved.

"Everything's Coming Up Roses" (from *Gypsy*), lyrics by Stephen Sondheim and music by Julie Styne. Copyright © 1959 (renewed) by Norbeth Productions Inc. and Stephen Sondheim. Publication and allied rights assigned to Williamson Music Co. and Stratford Music Corporation, administered by Chappell & Co. Reprinted by permission of Alfred Publishing Co., Inc. All rights reserved.

"Falling in Love with Love" (from *The Boys from Syracuse*), lyrics by Lorenz Hart and music by Richard Rodgers. Copyright © 1938 (renewed) Chappell & Co., Inc. All rights for the extended renewal term in the United States controlled by WB Music Corp. and Williamson Music. Reprinted by permission of Alfred Publishing Co., Inc. International copyright secured. All rights reserved.

"Follow the Minstrel Band" (from *Show Girl*), music by George Gershwin and lyrics by Ira Gershwin and Gus Kahn. Copyright © 1929 (renewed) WB Music Corp. Reprinted by permission of Alfred Publishing Co., Inc. All rights reserved.

"Forty-second Street" (from *42nd Street*), words by Al Dubin and music by Harry Warren. Copyright © 1932 (renewed) WB Music Corp. Reprinted by permission of Alfred Publishing Co., Inc. All rights reserved.

"The Half of It, Dearie, Blues" (from *Lady, Be Good!*), music and lyrics by George Gershwin and Ira Gershwin. Copyright © 1924 (renewed) WB Music Corp. Reprinted by permission of Alfred Publishing Co., Inc. All rights reserved.

"Heat Wave" by Irving Berlin. Copyright ©1933 by Irving Berlin, Inc. Copyright renewed; international copyright secured. Reprinted by permission. All rights reserved.

"Howdy to Broadway" (from *Peggy Anne*), words and music by Lorenz Hart and Richard Rodgers. Copyright © 1927 (renewed) Chappell & Co. and Williamson Music, Inc. Reprinted by permission of Alfred Publishing Co., Inc. All rights reserved.

"A Hymn to Him" (from *My Fair Lady*), words by Frederick Loewe and music by Alan Lerner. Copyright © 1956 (renewed) Chappell & Co. Reprinted by permission of Alfred Publishing Co., Inc. All rights reserved.

"I've Told Ev'ry Little Star" (from *Music in the Air*), music by Jerome Kern and lyrics by Oscar Hammerstein II. Copyright © 1932 by Universal–Polygram Int. Publ., Inc. Copyright renewed. All rights administered by Universal–Polygram Int. Publ., Inc./ASCAP. Reprinted by permission. All rights reserved.

"Just One of Those Things" (from *High Society*), words and music by Cole Porter. Copyright © 1935 (renewed) Warner Bros., Inc. Reprinted by permission of Alfred Publishing Co., Inc. All rights reserved.

"Kansas City" and "Oklahoma" by Richard Rodgers and Oscar Hammerstein II. Copyright © 1943 by Williamson Music. Copyright renewed; international copyright secured. Reprinted by permission. All rights reserved.

"Kids!" (from *Bye Bye Birdie*), lyric by Lee Adams and music by Charles Strouse. Copyright © 1960 (renewed) Strada Music. Rights administered by Williamson Music. Reprinted by permission. All rights reserved.

"The Lady Is a Tramp" by Richard Rodgers and Lorenz Hart. Copyright © 1937 (renewed) Chappell & Co. Rights for extended renewal term in the United States controlled by the Estate of Lorenz Hart (administered by WB Music Corp.) and the Family Trust under the will of Richard Rodgers and the Family Trust under the will of Dorothy F. Rodgers (administered by Williamson Music). Reprinted by permission of Alfred Publishing Co., Inc. All rights reserved.

"Let's Do It (Let's Fall in Love)" (from *Paris*), words and music by Cole Porter. Copyright © 1928 (renewed) WB Music Corp. Reprinted by permission of Alfred Publishing Co., Inc. All rights reserved.

"Let's Face the Music and Dance" by Irving Berlin. Copyright © 1935 by Irving Berlin. Copyright renewed; international copyright secured. Reprinted by permission. All rights reserved.

"Let's Have Another Cup of Coffee" by Irving Berlin. Copyright © 1931 by Irving Berlin, Inc. Copyright renewed; international copyright secured. Reprinted by permission. All rights reserved.

"Let's Not Talk About Love" (from *Let's Face It*), words and music by Cole Porter. Copyright © 1941 (renewed) Chappell & Co. Reprinted by permission of Alfred Publishing Co., Inc. All rights reserved.

"Liasons" (from *A Little Night Music*), words and music by Stephen Sondheim. Copyright © 1973 (renewed) Ritling Music, Inc. All rights administered by WB Music Corp. Reprinted by permission of Alfred Publishing Co., Inc. All rights reserved.

"Life Upon the Wicked Stage" and "Why Do I Love You" (from *Show Boat*), music by Jerome Kern and lyrics by Oscar Hammerstein II. Copyright © 1927 by Universal–Polygram Int. Publ., Inc. Copyright renewed. All rights administered by Universal–Polygram Int. Publ., Inc./ASCAP. Reprinted by permission. All rights reserved.

"Little Priest" (from *Sweeney Todd*), words and music by Stephen Sondheim. Copyright © 1978 Ritling Music, Inc. All rights administered by WB Music Corp. Reprinted by permission of Alfred Publishing Co., Inc. All rights reserved.

"Little Jazz Bird" (from *Lady, Be Good!*), music and lyrics by George Gershwin and Ira Gershwin. Copyright © 1924 (renewed) WB Music Corp. Reprinted by permission of Alfred Publishing Co., Inc. All rights reserved.

"The Little Things You Do Together," "Marry Me a Little," and "Happily Ever After" (from *Company*), words and music by Stephen Sondheim. Used by permission of Herald Square Music, Inc., on behalf of Range Road Music, Inc., Jerry Leiber Music, Mike Stoller Music, and Rilting Music, Inc.

"Manhattan" (from *The Garrick Gaieties*), by Lorenz Hart and Richard Rodgers. Used by permission of Piedmont Music Company.

"The Music and the Mirror" (from *A Chorus Line*), music by Marvin Hamlisch and lyrics by Edward Kleban. Copyright © 1975 (renewed) Edward Kleban and Famous Music LLC. All rights for Edward Kleban controlled by Wren Music Co. Reprinted by permission. All rights reserved.

"My Funny Valentine," words by Lorenz Hart and music by Richard Rodgers. Copyright © 1937 (renewed) Chappell & Co., Inc. All rights for the extended renewal term in the United

States controlled by WB Music Corp. and Williamson Music. Reprinted by permission of Alfred Publishing Co., Inc. All rights reserved.

"Night and Day," words and music by Cole Porter. Copyright © 1932 (renewed) WB Music Corp. Reprinted by permission of Alfred Publishing Co., Inc. All rights reserved.

"Oh Me! Oh My!" (from *Two Little Girls in Blue*), words and music by Arthur Francis (pseudonym for Ira Gershwin) and Vincent Youmans. Copyright © 1921 (renewed) Warner Bros. Inc. Reprinted by permission of Alfred Publishing Co., Inc. All rights reserved.

"One Hundred Easy Ways to Lose a Man" (from *Wonderful Town*), lyrics by Betty Comden and Adolph Green and music by Leonard Bernstein. Copyright © 1953 by Amberson Holdings LLC, Betty Comden and Adolph Green. Copyright renewed. Chappell & Co. and Leonard Bernstein Music Publishing Company LLC, Publishers. Boosey & Hawkes, Inc., agent. Copyright for all countries. Reprinted by permission. All rights reserved.

"On the Sunny Side of the Street," lyrics by Dorothy Fields and music by Jimmy McHugh. Copyright © 1930 Shapiro, Bernstein & Co., Inc., New York, and Cotton Club Publishing for the U.S.A. Copyright renewed. All rights for Cotton Club Publishing controlled and administered by EMI April Music Inc. International copyright secured. Reprinted by permission. All rights reserved.

"The Party's Over" (from *Bells Are Ringing*), lyrics by Betty Comden and Adolph Green and music by Jule Styne. Copyright © 1956 (renewed) Stratford Music Corporation. All rights administered by Chappell & Co. Reprinted by permission of Alfred Publishing Co., Inc. All rights reserved.

"People Will Say We're in Love" by Richard Rodgers and Oscar Hammerstein II. Copyright © 1943 by Williamson Music. Copyright renewed; international copyright secured. Reprinted by permission. All rights reserved.

"Please Don't Monkey with Broadway" (from the movie *Broadway Melody of 1940*), words and music by Cole Porter. Copyright © 1940 (renewed) Chappell & Co., Inc. Reprinted by permission of Alfred Publishing Co., Inc. All rights reserved.

"A Pretty Girl Is Like a Melody" by Irving Berlin, copyright © 1919 by Irving Berlin, Inc. Copyright renewed; international copyright secured. Reprinted by permission. All rights reserved.

"Putting It Together" (from *Sunday in the Park with George*), words and music by Stephen Sondheim. Copyright © 1984 Revelation Music Publishing Corp. and Rilting Music, Inc. Reprinted by permission of Alfred Publishing Co., Inc. All rights reserved.

"A Puzzlement" by Richard Rodgers and Oscar Hammerstein II. Copyright © 1951 by Richard Rodgers and Oscar Hammerstein II. Copyright renewed. Williamson Music owner of publication and allied rights throughout the world. International copyright secured. Reprinted by permission. All rights reserved.

"The Real American Folk Song (Is a Rag)" (from *Show Girl*), music and lyrics by George Gershwin and Ira Gershwin. Copyright © 1959 (renewed) Chappell & Co., Inc. Reprinted by permission of Alfred Publishing Co., Inc. All rights reserved.

"So in Love," words and music by Cole Porter. Copyright © 1948 (renewed) Chappell & Co., Inc. Reprinted by permission of Alfred Publishing Co., Inc. All rights reserved.

"Something's Coming" (from *West Side Story*), lyrics by Stephen Sondheim. Copyright © 1956, 1957, 1958, 1959 by Amberson Holdings, Inc., and Stephen Sondheim. Copyright renewed. Leonard Bernstein Music Publishing Company, LLC, publisher; Boosey & Hawkes, Inc., agent. International copyright secured. Reprinted by permission.

"Speak Low," words by Ogden Nash and music by Kurt Weill. Copyright © 1943 (renewed) Ogden Nash Music Publishing and Tro-Hampshire House Publishing Corp. All rights on behalf of Ogden Nash Music Publishing administered by WB Music Corp. Reprinted by permission of Alfred Publishing Co., Inc. All rights reserved.

"Strike Up the Band," music and lyrics by George Gershwin and Ira Gershwin. Copyright © 1927 (renewed) WB Music Corp. Gershwin ® and George Gershwin ® are registered trademarks of Gershwin Enterprises. Reprinted by permission of Alfred Publishing Co., Inc. All rights reserved.

"Supper Time" by Irving Berlin. Copyright © 1933 by Irving Berlin. Copyright renewed; international copyright secured. Reprinted by permission. All rights reserved.

"Swingin' the Jinx Away" (from *Born to Dance*), words and music by Cole Porter. Copyright © 1936 (renewed) Chappell & Co. Reprinted by permission of Alfred Publishing Co., Inc. All rights reserved.

"Tea for Two" (from *No, No, Nanette!*), words by Irving Caesar and music by Vincent Youmans. Copyright © 1924 (renewed) Warner Bros., Inc. All rights on behalf of Irving Caesar Music Corp. administered by WB Music Corp. Canadian rights controlled by Warner Bros., Inc. Reprinted by permission of Alfred Publishing Co., Inc. All rights reserved.

"There Won't Be Trumpets" (from *Anyone Can Whistle*), words and music by Stephen Sondheim. Copyright © 1964 (renewed) Burthen Music Co., Inc. All rights administered by Chappell & Co. Reprinted by permission of Alfred Publishing Co., Inc. All rights reserved.

"This Funny World" (from *Betsy*), lyrics by Lorenz Hart and music by Richard Rodgers. Copyright © 1926 (renewed) Warner Bros., Inc. and Williamson Music, Inc. Reprinted by permission of Alfred Publishing Co., Inc. All rights reserved.

"This Is the Army, Mister Jones" by Irving Berlin. Copyright © 1942 by Irving Berlin, Inc. Copyright renewed by Irving Berlin. International copyright secured. Reprinted by permission. All rights reserved.

"To Keep My Love Alive" (from *A Connecticut Yankee*), words by Lorenz Hart and music by Richard Rodgers. Copyright © 1944 (renewed) Warner Bros., Inc., and Williamson Music, Inc. Reprinted by permission of Alfred Publishing Co., Inc. All rights reserved.

"What'll I Do" by Irving Berlin, copyright © 1924 by Irving Berlin, Inc. Copyright renewed; international copyright secured. Reprinted by permission. All rights reserved.

"What You Own" (from *Rent*), lyrics by Jonathan D. Larson. Copyright © 1996 by Universal Music Corp., Finster & Lucy Music Ltd. Co. All rights administered by Universal Music Corp./ASCAP. Reprinted by permission. All rights reserved.

"When You Got It, Flaunt It" (from *The Producers*), music and lyrics by Mel Brooks. Reprinted by permission of Mel Brooks.

"Wouldn't It Be Fun" (from *Aladdin*), words and music by Cole Porter. Copyright © 1958 (renewed) Chappell & Co. Reprinted by permission of Alfred Publishing Co., Inc. All rights reserved.

"You Gotta Have a Gimmick" (from *Gypsy*), words by Julie Styne and music by Stephen Sondheim. Copyright © 1959 (renewed) Stratford Music Corporation and Williamson Music, Inc. All rights administered by Chappell & Co., Inc. Reprinted by permission of Alfred Publishing Co., Inc. All rights reserved.

"You've Got To Be Carefully Taught" and "Happy Talk" by Richard Rodgers and Oscar Hammerstein II. Copyright © 1949 by Richard Rodgers and Oscar Hammerstein II. Copyright renewed. Williamson Music owner of publication and allied rights throughout the world. International copyright secured. Reprinted by permission. All rights reserved.

BIBLIOGRAPHY

Bloom, Ken. *American Song: The Complete Musical Theatre Companion.* Vol. 1. New York: Facts on File, 1985.

———. *Broadway: An Encyclopedic Guide to the History, People, and Places of Times Square.* New York: Facts on File, 1991.

Bordman, Gerald. *American Musical Theatre: A Chronicle.* 2nd ed. New York: Oxford University Press, 1992.

Bowers, Dwight Blocker. *American Musical Theater: Shows, Songs, and Stars.* Washington, D.C.: Smithsonian Collection of Recordings, 1989.

Brantley, Ben. "That Singable Psychodrama, the Musical." *New York Times,* March 23, 1997, Arts & Leisure section, p. 11.

Crook, Richard. "Crooners and Torchsingers." *Gramophone Magazine,* August 1997, p. 102.

Engle, Lehman. *The American Musical Theater: A Consideration.* New York: CBS (distributed by the Macmillan Co.), 1967.

Ewen, David. *New Complete Book of the American Musical Theater.* Austin, Texas: Holt, Rinehart, and Winston, 1970.

Fields, Armond, and L. Marc Fields. *From the Bowery to Broadway.* New York: Oxford University Press, 1993.

Flinn, Denny Martin. *Musical! A Grand Tour.* New York: Schirmer Books, 1997.

Goodfriend, James. The booklet included with *American Musicals: Jerome Kern—Show Boat/Very Good Eddie/Roberta.* Time-Life Records, 1981. Audiocassette.

Gruber, Paul. The booklet with *Original Cast! The Early Years.* Metropolitan Opera Guild, 1995.

———. The booklet with *Original Cast! The Thirties.* Metropolitan Opera Guild, 1995.

———. The booklet with *Original Cast! The Forties: Part 1.* Metropolitan Opera Guild, 1994.

———. The booklet with *Original Cast! The Forties: Part 2.* Metropolitan Opera Guild, 1994.

———. The booklet with *Original Cast! The Fifties: Part 1.* Metropolitan Opera Guild, 1993.

———. The booklet with *Original Cast! The Fifties: Part 2.* Metropolitan Opera Guild, 1993.

———. The booklet with *Original Cast! The Sixties: Part 1.* Metropolitan Opera Guild, 1994.

———. The booklet with *Original Cast! The Sixties: Part 2.* Metropolitan Opera Guild, 1994.

———. The booklet with *Original Cast! The Seventies,* Metropolitan Opera Guild, 1995.

————. The booklet with *Original Cast! Completing the Century: 1980–1994*. Metropolitan Opera Guild, 1996.

————. The booklet with *Original Cast! Visitors from Abroad: 1900–1994*. Metropolitan Opera Guild, 1996.

Haagensen, Erik. "Getting to the Core." *Show Music Magazine,* Fall 1995, p. 67.

Hammerstein II, Oscar. *Lyrics by Oscar Hammerstein II*. Milwaukee: Hal Leonard Books, 1985.

Holden, Stephen. "A Contrarian Who Raised Musicals' 'I.Q.' " *New York Times,* May 5, 2002, Arts & Leisure section, p. 45.

————. "Their Songs Were America's Happy Talk." *New York Times,* January 24, 1993, Arts & Leisure section, p. 1.

Kimball, Robert. "The Road to *Oklahoma!*" *Opera News Magazine,* July 1993, p. 24.

Kramer, Mimi. Review of *Miss Saigon. The New Yorker,* April 29, 1991.

Kreuger, Miles. The liner notes for *Show Boat* (1936). Directed by George Sidney. The Criterion Collection. Laserdisc, 1989.

Lahr, John. "All the Way to Heaven." *The New Yorker,* January 18, 1993, p. 105.

Lax, Roger, and Frederick Smith. *The Great Song Thesaurus*. 2nd ed. New York: Oxford University Press, 1989.

Mordden, Ethan. *Broadway Babies: The People Who Made the American Musical*. New York: Oxford University Press, 1983.

————. "A Proud Flagship Keeps On Rollin' in Deeper Currents." *New York Times,* September 25, 1994, Arts & Leisure section, p. 22.

Morris, Joan. From the essay with *After the Ball plus Highlights from Vaudeville*. Cast Recording, copyright 1990. Elektra/Nonesuch CD.

Nachman, Gerald. "Lorenz Hart: Little Boy Blue." *Theatre Week,* May 8, 1995, pp. 35–36.

Schiff, Stephen. "Deconstructing Sondheim," *The New Yorker,* March 8, 1993, pp. 76–87.

Smith, Cecil, and Glenn Litton. *Musical Comedy in America*. New York: Theater Arts Books, 1981.

Stein, Harry. "Our Times: A Column About Values and TV." *TV Guide,* February 28, 1993.

Suskin, Steven. *Berlin, Kern, Rodgers, Hart, and Hammerstein: A Complete Song Catalogue*. Jefferson, N.C.: McFarland & Company, Inc., 1990.

————. *Show Tunes, 1905–1991*. New York: Limelight Editions, 1992.

Tommasini, Anthony. "A Crowd of Old Musicals Squeezes the New." *New York Times,* August 16, 1998, Arts & Leisure section, p. 1.

————. "Woe to Shows That Put On Operatic Airs." *New York Times,* July 20, 1997, Arts & Leisure section, p. 5.

Wilder, Alec. *American Popular Song: The Great Innovators, 1900–1950*. New York: Oxford University Press, 1972.

INDEX

Edwards, Cliff ("Ukulele Ike"), 116, 135, 140, 154

Edwards, Gus, 93

Edwards, Sherman, 402–3

Egan, Susan, 501

Eigsti, Karl, 461

Eileen (Herbert and Blossom), 111

Eisenhauer, Peggy, 511

Eisenhower, Dwight, 295

Elder, David, 466

eleven o'clock number, 166, 171, 278, 294

Elg, Taina, 464

Eliot, T. S., 305, 409, 465

Elise, Rick, 521

Elkins, Hillard, 402, 416

Ella Fitzgerald Sings the Irving Berlin Songbook (CD), 159

Elliman, Yvonne, 420, 422

Ellington, Duke, 78, 129, 223, 239, 432; biography of, 131; music by, 45, 129, 273, 444, 508, (criticism of) 140

Ellington, Mercer, 462

Elliott, Patricia, 438

Elliott, Shawn, 402

Ellis, Herb, 184

Ellis, Mary, 138

Ellis, Scott, 422, 496, 498, 503, 507, 509

Elmore, Steve, 401, 421

Emick, Jarrod, 500

Emmett, Daniel Decatur, 36

Emmons, Beverly, 457, 501

Emond, Linda, 507

Encores! series, 273, 500, 504

Engel, Georgia, 527

Englander, Ludwig, 64

Engle, Lehman, 228, 234, 463

English, Ellia, 169

Entertainer, The (London import), 336

Entwhistle, John, 499

Epps, Sheldon, 508

Epstein, Alvin, 432

Erdman, Jean, 418

Errico, Melissa, 498, 511

Errol, Leon, 94, 105, 106, 108, 110, 122

Erté (designer), 79, 126, 135, 136

Essex, David, 451

Estabrook, Christine, 528

Estrin, Melvin J., 461

Etting, Ruth, 78, 79, 157, 161, 179, 203, 213, 218, 220, 446

Eubie! (revue), 446

Evangeline (Rice and Goodwin), 56, 120

Evans, Damon, 200

Evans, Maurice, 354

Evening with Jerry Herman, An, 510–11

Everett, Timmy, 345

Ever Green (Rodgers and Hart), 203

Evita (Lloyd Weber and Rice), 420, 446, 451, 452, 461, 472; movie version, 517

Ewen, David, 201

extravaganza, 41–42, 86; burlesque-extravaganza, 65–66, 71, 72, 105

Eyen, Tom, 459

Fabray, Nanette, 198, 242, 275, 285, 361

Face the Music (Berlin and Hart), 187, 194

Fade Out–Fade In (Styne, Comden, and Green), 370

Fagan, Garth, 509

Fain, Sammy, 193, 297

Faison, George, 434

Falls, Robert, 522

Falsettoland (Finn), 492, 497; and *Falsettos*, 496–97

Family Affair, A (Goldman, Kander, and Goldman), 361, 385

Fancy Free (ballet), 254, 255

Fanny (Rome), 227, 307

Fantasticks, The (Schmidt and Jones), 357–58, 364, 388, 511; closes, 520

farce-comedy, 58–60, 65, 71, 72

Faria, Arthur, 447

Farrell, Eileen, 198

Faye, Alice, 197, 220, 432

Feagan, Leslie, 311

Feder (lighting by), 325, 357, 383

Federal Theatre Project, 224, 228

Feiffer, Jules, 391, 402

Feigay, Paul, 254

Feldman, Rebecca, 526

Feliz, Seymour, 179

Fenholt, Jeff, 420

Fenton, James, 478

Ferber, Edna, 154, 164, 337, 398

Ferland, Danielle, 484

Fetter, Ted, 243

Feuer, Cy, 293, 303, 319, 360, 362, 445, 449

Ffolkes, David, 277

Fiddle-Dee-Dee (burlesque-extravaganza), 66

Fiddler on the Roof (Bock and Harnick), 265 (illus.), 372–73, 391, 397, 440; long run of, 426, (surpassed) 448; movie, 374–75; revivals, 442, 459, 488, 520

Field, Ron, 392, 393, 401, 415, 416, 448, 461, 477, 480

Fields, Armond and L. Marc, 37, 40, 65

Fields, Dorothy, 64, 183, 298, 340, 380, 388, 432; adaptability of, 257, 299, 389–90, 431; and brother Herbert, 129, 148, 242, 253, 256, 257, 269, and Kern, 196, 203; lyrics quoted, 218; and McHugh, 58, 128, 129, 130, 180, 181, 202, 218

Fields, Felicia P., 527

Fields, Herbert, 64, 157, 335; collaborates with sister, *see* Fields, Dorothy; and Gershwins, 191, 223; and Porter, 182, 209, 212, 217; and Rodgers and Hart, 120, 147–49, 151, 155, 158, 178, 203

Fields, Joseph, 64, 148, 286, 304, 336, 388

Fields, Lew, 64, 91, 92, 120, 147, 216, 240; as director, 136, 157; as producer, 122, 148, 155, 178. *See also* Weber and Fields

Fields, W. C., 40, 125, 126, 204, 268; in *Scandals*, 180; in *Ziegfeld Follies*, 79, 110, 112, 122, 123, 135

Fierstein, Harvey, 471, 524

Fifty Miles from Boston (Cohan), 92

Fifty Million Frenchmen (Porter and Fields), 182

Fine, Sylvia, 243

Finian's Rainbow (Lane and Harburg), 192, 236, 268, 276, 334; movie, 276, 278; revivals, 316, 397

Finn, William, 462, 492, 496, 526

Fiorello! (Bock and Harnick), 341, 344, 354, 361, 500

Firebrand of Florence, The (Weill and Gershwin), 257

Firefly, The (Friml and Harbach), 104, 105; movie version, 105–6

Firth, Tazeena, 451

Fisher, Eddie, 303

Fisher, Jules, 370, 381, 398, 420, 427–35 passim, 471, 482, 497–503 passim, 511

Fitzgerald, Ella, 159, 160, 192, 212, 504

Fitzgerald, F. Scott, 127

Fitzhugh, Ellen, 476

Five Guys Named Moe (revue), 497

Flaherty, Joe, 431

Flaherty, Stephen, 8, 491, 498, 511

Flahooley (Fain and Harburg), 297

Flatt, Ernest, 391

Fledermaus, Die (Strauss), 29, 32, 56, 181, 246

Fleming, Ian, 433

Fletcher, Robert, 360, 362

Flinn, Denny Martin, 104

Flora, the Red Menace (Kander and Ebb), 384, 385

Florodora (Stuart et al.), 63

Flower Drum Song (Rodgers and Hammerstein), 301, 336, 520

Floyd Collins (Guettel), 504–5, 514

Flying Colors (Schwartz and Dietz), 17, 183, 222

Flying Down to Rio (movie), 116, 212

Flying High (Henderson, DeSylva, and Brown), 217

Fly With Me (Rodgers and Hart), 148

Fokine, Michel, 79, 126

Folies Bergère, 79, 130

Follies (Sondheim), 333, 409, 417–19, 421, 422; revival of, 520. See also *Ziegfeld Follies*

Follow the Fleet (movie), 196, 199

Follow Thru (Henderson, DeSylva, and Brown), 181

Fonda, Henry, 224

Fontaine, Robert L., 400

Footloose (Snow and Pitchford), 511, 513, 517

Forbes, Kathryn, 449

Forbidden Broadway (revue), 387, 463

Forbidden Broadway Strikes Back! (revue), 511

Ford, Paul, 371

Forever Plaid (revue), 489

Forever Tango (revue), 508

Forman, Miloš, 399

For Me and My Gal (movie), 43

Forrest, George, 257, 305, 482, 512

Forsythe, Henderson, 448

Fortune Teller, The (Herbert and Smith), 66

Forty-five Minutes from Broadway (Cohan), 92

40 Thieves, The (Thompson burlesque), 42

42nd Street (Warren and Dubin), 285, 306, 453, 454–56, 466, 470; movie, 179, 229, 456, 466; revival, 520

Fosse, Bob, 305, 308, 353, 477; as choreographer, 301, 305, 308, 309, 317, 318, 323, 335, 360, 362; as director/ choreographer, 331–32, 337, 340, 374, 389, 425, 427–28, 435, 440, 446,

(flop), 476; as performer, 272, 284, 290, 293, 312, 328; wins Oscar, 393

Fosse: A Celebration in Song and Dance, 301, 403, 512, 514

Foster, Hunter, 464, 522, 523

Foster, Stephen, 33–34, 44, 61, 95

Foster, Sutton, 523, 527

Fowler, Beth, 472, 501

Fox, Maxine, 426, 433

Foxx, Jamie, 460, 466

Foy, Eddie Jr., 181, 217, 308, 309, 312, 324, 327

Franchi, Sergio, 381

Francis, Arthur. *See* Gershwin, Ira

Frank, Melvin, 324

Frankel, Scott, 527

Franklin, Bonnie, 415, 420

Fraser, Alison, 481

Freed, Arthur, 198, 204

Freedley, Vinton, 135, 154–58 passim, 180, 191–92, 210, 239, 242, 401

Freedman, David, 155, 193

Freedman, Gerald, 398, 444

Freeland, Thornton, 185

Freeman, Kathleen, 522

Freischütz, Der (Weber), 26, 41

Frey, Leonard, 375

Frey, Nathaniel, 328

Friedman, Charles, 250, 274

Friedman, Peter, 511

Friedman, Stephen R., 445, 447

Friend, Cliff, 183

Friml, Rudolf, 30, 78, 104, 138, 146, 178, 216, 425; and collaborations, 105, 106, 139, 155, 218; last Broadway show, 223; writes for *Ziegfeld Follies*, 104, 123, 127

Frogs, The (Sondheim), 432

From the Bowery to Broadway (Fields and Fields), 37, 40

From the Second City (revue), 358

From This Moment On: The Songs of Cole Porter (CD), 244

Fry, Stephen, 477

Klotz, Florence, 391, 392, 417, 429, 444, 446, 448, 483, 499

Klugman, Jack, 337

Knickerbocker Holiday (Weill), 226, 228, 229

Knighton, Nan, 507, 513

Knoblock, Edward, 305

Knowles, Beyoncé, 460, 466

Kober, Arthur, 302

Koehler, Ted, 130, 218, 220, 222–23

Komack, Jimmie, 328

Kopit, Arthur, 464, 481, 511

Korie, Michael, 527

Kostal, Irwin, 332, 341, 363

Koster, Henry, 336

Kotis, Greg, 8, 306, 522

Krakowski, Jane, 464, 482

Krall, Diana, 519

Kramer, Mimi, 495

Kramer, Terry Allen, 445

Kramer vs. Kramer (movie), 385

Krasny, Diana, 370

Kretzmer, Herbert, 27, 478

Kreuger, Miles, 163

Krieger, Henry, 459, 471, 510

Krimsky, John, 306

Krupa, Gene, 191

Krupska, Dania, 321

Kubelik, Jan, 104

Kudisch, Marc, 391, 508, 523

Kuhn, Judy, 475, 478, 485, 498

Kukla, Fran, and Ollie (TV show), 360

Kuller, Sid, 240

Kushnier, Jeremy, 511

LaBelle, Patti, 21

LaChiusa, Michael John, 513

Ladd, Cheryl, 512

Ladies First (Gershwin and Gershwin), 85, 112, 134

Lady, Be Good! (Gershwin and Gershwin), 8, 116, 133, 134–35, 136, 138, 139; movie version, 135, 203; recording of show (CD), 140–41

Lady Comes Across, The (Duke), 246

Lady in the Dark (Weill, Gershwin, and Hart), 134, 156, 195, 227, 233, 241–42, 244, 267; movie version, 242

Lady Teazle (burlesque-extravaganza), 88

La Guardia, Fiorello, 341

Lahr, Bert, 138, 174, 182, 358, 397; as Broadway star, 180, 188, 193, 212, 217, 256, 297

Lahr, John, 302

Laine, Cleo, 192, 475

Laing, Stewart, 508

Lake, Harriet, 203

La! La! Lucille (Gershwin, Jackson, and DeSylva), 122, 133

Lamas, Fernando, 30, 138

Lambert, Beverly, 422

Lambert, Hugh, 360

Lambert, Lisa, 527

Lampoon shows, 431

Lancaster, Burt, 368

Landau, Tina, 504

Landay, David, 462

Landesman, Heidi, 475, 495

Landesman, Rocco, 475

Landon, Margaret, 300

Lane, Burton, 165, 192, 219, 236, 274, 284, 380, 383, 449, 507

Lane, Diane, 447

Lane, Jeffrey, 526

Lane, Nancy, 437

Lane, Nathan, 188, 293, 311, 364, 496, 504, 523

Lane, Stewart F., 462, 499

Lang, Harold, 302, 361, 387

lang, k. d., 289

Lang, Philip J., 269, 275, 284, 324, 325, 335, 340, 357, 360, 371, 390, 455

Lang, Walter, 300, 303, 311

Lannin, Paul, 125

Lansbury, Angela, 51, 339, 370, 390, 401, 432, 450, 471; recorded performances, 114, 375, 395, 452

Lansbury, Edgar, 419, 433

Lanza, Mario, 138, 141

Lapine, James, 463, 472, 479, 492, 496–97

Lardner, Ring Jr., 462

Larkin, Peter, 355

Larson, Jonathan, 8, 27, 504, 520; lyrics by, 487

Laska, Edward, 114

László, Miklós, 368

Latham, Fred G., 105

Latifah, Queen, 435

LaTouche, John, 45, 239, 246, 273, 306–7, 320, 325

Laurel and Hardy, 65, 204

Laurents, Arthur, 58, 254, 332, 337, 338, 367, 382, 398, 471; as director, 339, 361, 370; show flops, 493

Lavin, Linda, 390, 391

Law, Lindsay, 522

Lawford, Peter, 158

Lawrence, Carol, 224, 302, 332, 346, 359

Lawrence, Eddie, 381

Lawrence, Gertrude, 136, 149, 156, 218, 241, 242, 299–300, 302

Lawrence, Jerome, 282, 390, 401

Lawrence, Reginald, 296

Lax, Roger, 112

Layton, Joe, 74, 341, 342, 353, 354, 362, 402, 415, 456, 500

Lazarus, Frank, 457

Lazarus, Milton, 257

Lazarus, Roy, 328

Leach, Wilford, 51, 475

Leader of the Pack (revue), 474

Leal, Sharon, 466

Lean, David, 369

Leathernecking (movie), 178

Leave It to Jane (Princess musical), 103, 111, 158; revival of, 103, 336

Leave It to Me (Porter), 210, 211, 228, 251

Leavitt, Michael B., 57, 523

Lebo M, 509

Lederer, Charles, 305

Lederer, George, 64

Lee, Bill, 289

Lee, C. Y., 336

Lee, Eugene, 450, 460, 511, 525

Lee, Franne, 450

Zeta-Jones, Catherine, 435, 437

Ziegfeld, Florenz, 60, 77–80, 82, 85, 89, 122, 155, 178–81 passim, 203; competition with, 90, 94, 157; first show produced by, 64; and Marilyn Miller as star, 78, 108, 159, 217; produces *Show Boat*, 164; revues produced by, 116, 127 (see also *Ziegfeld Follies*); ruined in stock market crash, 181, (dies in debt) 79, 221; Urban as designer for, *see* Urban, Joseph

Ziegfeld Follies, 65, 68 (illus.), 77–80, 86, 116–17, 197; first black star of, 89; movie revue of (DVD), 161; popularity of, 137; *of 1907–1911,* 77, 92, 93, 94, 97; *of 1912–1918,* 105, 106, 108, 110, 112; *of 1919–1925,* 78, 83, 118, 122, 123, 126, 127, 130, 135; *of 1927–1934,* 157, 161, 164, 220, 224; *of 1936,* 134, 193, 200, 227; of *1943,* 254; of *1957,* 332

Ziegfeld Theatre, 110, 157, 222; reopened, 256, (demolished) 388

Zieglerova, Klara, 521
Ziemba, Karen, 496, 509, 521
Zien, Chip, 479, 484, 492, 497
Zimmer, Hans, 509
Zinnemann, Fred, 19
Zip Goes a Million (Kern et al.), 112, 131
Zippel, David, 483, 499
Zipprodt, Patricia, 368–73 passim, 392, 401, 403, 427–35 passim, 473, 498
Zola, Emile, 521
Zorba (Kander and Ebb), 400–401, 471
Zorina, Vera, 207, 239
Zuber, Catherine, 526

About the Author

Sheldon Patinkin is chair of the theater department at Columbia College Chicago, artistic director of the Getz Theater, a member of the Gift Theatre ensemble, and artistic consultant for The Second City and Steppenwolf Theatre. He was one of the first directors of The Second City and has directed more than two hundred plays, musicals, operas, and revues throughout the United States and around the world. In 2002, Patinkin was the recipient of a lifetime achievement award from both the Chicago Improv Festival and the Israeli Film Festival. His translation of Brecht's *The Good Person of Setzuan* was directed by Frank Galati at the Goodman Theatre of Chicago and starred Cherry Jones. He is the author of *The Second City: Backstage at the World's Greatest Comedy Theater.*